The Mexican American Experience

The Mexican American Experience:
An Interdisciplinary Anthology

Edited by
Rodolfo O. DE LA GARZA
Frank D. BEAN
Charles M. BONJEAN
Ricardo ROMO
Rodolfo ALVAREZ

University of Texas Press, Austin

Cover art: "Ante Pasados" by Amado M. PEÑA, Jr.

Copyright © 1985 by the University of Texas Press
All rights reserved
Printed in the United States of America

First Edition, 1985

Requests for permission to reproduce material from this
work should be sent to Permissions, University of Texas
Press, Box 7819, Austin, Texas 78713.

LIBRARY OF CONGRESS CATALOGING IN PUBLICATION DATA
Main entry under title:
The Mexican American experience.
   Bibliography: p.
   1. Mexican Americans—Addresses, essays, lectures.
2. Mexicans—United States—Addresses, essays, lectures.
I. De la Garza, Rodolfo O.
E184.M5M5   1985   305.8′6872′073   85-5317
ISBN 0-292-75088-9
ISBN 0-292-75083-8 (pbk.)

Contents

III. Political Participation, Organizational Development, and
Institutional Responsiveness

IV. The Social and Cultural Context of the Mexican American
Experience in the United States

Contents

PREFACE

The Mexican origin population in the United States has almost doubled since 1970 and has played an increasingly important role in our nation's economic, social, and political life. Yet with few exceptions, social science research on our nation's second largest minority has either found its way to the pages of our major social science journals on rare occasions or has been published in journals and books oriented primarily to the Chicano community of scholars. Only one major journal, *Social Science Quarterly*, has had a consistent policy of publishing research on the Mexican origin population and since 1973 has offered two double-length special issues on this topic.

SSQ's 1973 topical issue on *The Chicano Experience in the United States* included 22 articles by 35 authors and represented a thorough treatment of a previously neglected topic. Issue contents were widely cited and stimulated considerable subsequent research. Yet, for the most part, the contents of that volume are now outdated both substantively and methodologically. That research on this topic has come a long way since 1973 was reflected by the tremendous response in terms of the number of manuscripts submitted for possible inclusion in *SSQ*'s 1984 special issue on *The Mexican Origin Experience in the United States*, as well as their quality. More solid papers were received for this issue than could be included in the 400-page issue. The 35 articles selected for publication dealt with social justice and the legal system, political access and participation, labor force experience, the "cost" of being Mexican American, undocumented migrants, language, fertility and mortality, socialization and the family, and changing world views and cultural perspectives. Their methodology ranged from in-depth case studies to the sophisticated analysis of national survey data and census materials.

The purpose of this volume is to bring the best of that material together in a form and format appropriate for classroom use or for individual students. Thus, while about two-thirds of the selections in this anthology are reprinted from the June 1984 *Social Science Quarterly*, the remainder includes chapters written especially for this volume, an article from the 1973 special issue of *SSQ*, introductions by the editors and their colleagues, and several articles from the 1984 *SSQ* special issue which were rewritten by their authors for a student, rather than a collegial, audience. In short, the editors have endeavored to present a well-organized sampler of current social science research on significant aspects of the Mexican origin experience in the United States and its relationship to the larger society. Major issues which are not treated by reprinted articles are covered in the three essays comprising an introductory overview, as well as in the introductions to the substantive sections of this volume. Some omissions are inevitable because of the constraints of space and the quality or level of research available. Concerning the latter, several excellent articles on demographic characteristics of the Mexican origin population appearing in the 1984 SSQ special issue were not included in the present volume because their methodology was deemed too complicated for undergraduate comprehension. This is not to underestimate the abilities of our intended readers, as they will soon learn from the materials we did include.

We acknowledge with gratitude the support of the Center for Mexican American Studies at The University of Texas, the Hogg Foundation for Mental Health, and the Southwestern Social Science Association for making possible the issue on which this anthology is in great part based. We have also appreciated the professional assistance of Janet Fisher, Marilyn Kuehlem, and Howard Simms of the University of Texas Press, and Barbara Ann Lynch, Pat Boerner, and Sherry Brown of the Social Science Quarterly staff. Amado M. Peña, Jr., generously allowed us to use his "Ante Pasados" for the cover of the special issue and this anthology. Numerous Social Science Quarterly reviewers contributed time and expertise in helping us select the papers for the special issue and this volume and, in most cases, were instrumental in improving them. Finally, we are grateful to the 52 authors who decided to undertake the significant research included in this volume and who granted us permission to reprint it. Unless otherwise noted, contributions are reprinted from Social Science Quarterly, Volume 65, June 1984.

We hope our readers will find more questions raised than answered by the contents of this volume and that some of them will be among the future generations of scholars interested in the Mexican origin population, its problems, its contributions, and its future in the United States.

I. INTRODUCTION AND OVERVIEW

1. THE ORIGINS AND DEVELOPMENT OF THE MEXICAN AMERICAN PEOPLE[1]

S. Dale McLEMORE, *The University of Texas at Austin*

Ricardo ROMO, *The University of Texas at Austin*

The rise of the Mexican American ethnic group is traced from its beginnings to the present. Since the settlements within the "Spanish borderlands" developed along independent lines, distinctive patterns of interethnic relations emerged as the "Anglos" occupied the Southwest during the nineteenth century. During the twentieth century, a large immigration from Mexico has contributed to a rapid increase in the size of the Mexican American group. The conquest of the nineteenth century and the immigration of the twentieth underlie two competing interpretations of the Mexican American experience. The two views are presented and evaluated.

Nearly five centuries have passed since Europeans first began to settle in parts of what is now the United States of America. In the intervening years the original inhabitants of this land, the "Indians," have been joined by successive waves of immigrants from all over the world to create a new society. Out of this intermingling of millions of human beings has emerged "a nation of nations" whose residents generally are referred to as "Americans" and who usually think of themselves as Americans; however, many, perhaps most, Americans also think of themselves as having additional national and cultural (or ethnic) identities. The additional identities are rooted in the diverse cultures they have inherited from their parents, grandparents, and earlier ancestors.

While the members of every American ethnic group have possessed multiple ethnic identities, probably no other group has given this fact

[1] This chapter is based in part on material previously published in S. Dale McLemore, *Racial and Ethnic Relations in America*, 2d ed., Boston: Allyn & Bacon, Inc., 1983. We gratefully acknowledge the permission of Allyn & Bacon, Inc., to rely on these materials. This chapter also is based in part on Ricardo Romo, "Mexican Americans in the Southwest: Patterns of Immigration and Integration," presented at the International Conference on Regionalism in American Society and Culture, Amerika Haus, Berlin, 9 June 1982.

greater attention than have the Mexican Americans; consequently, a number of terms of identification have been adopted by various segments of this group. In addition to the term Mexican American, the terms Chicano, Mexicano, Latin American, Hispano, Spanish surname, and La Raza are among the identifiers that have been prominently used to designate this group. Each of these terms is preferred by certain group members and is considered inaccurate or offensive by others. Each of them also has a fairly specific connotation that sets it apart from the others. The term Chicano, for instance, frequently is preferred by the younger or more politically active members of the group. The term Mexicano is popular in South Texas and along other portions of the Mexican border, while Hispano and Spanish American designate those in northern New Mexico and southern Colorado who trace their ancestry directly to the Spanish explorers (see, e.g., J. Garcia, 1981; Nostrand, 1973).

The special importance of the issues of group identity and group reference among the Mexican Americans grows out of the unique historical circumstances that have surrounded the creation and development of this group. Unlike the Irish, Germans, Jews, Italians, Japanese, Norwegians, Poles, and all of the other groups who first entered American society by leaving an "old country" and crossing oceans, the Mexican Americans did not originally become a part of American society through voluntary immigration. Rather, like the American Indians, the Mexican Americans became an American ethnic minority through the direct conquest of their homelands. Since the southwestern "borderlands" were settled by people of Spanish-Mexican-Indian ancestry long before they were settled by Anglo Americans, the Mexican Americans "are not," in Sanchez's (1961–62) words, "truly an immigrant group, for they are in their traditional home" (p. 123). Some analysts believe that this fact is of overriding importance in our effort to understand the contemporary status of the Mexican Americans within American society.

The "conquered minority" perspective conflicts with the most common approach to an analysis of the adjustments of American ethnic groups to the larger society—the three-generation approach. The latter view assumes that most members of a minority group will wish to enter fully into various aspects of the life and activities of the host society, but that the "penetration" of an immigrant group into the new society will be slowed by differences in language, job skills, and so on. The immigrants may master a substantial portion of the Anglo American culture but may, at the same time, maintain many of the customs of the old country, live in a neighborhood that the Americans call "Little Italy" or "Little Tokyo," and spend most of their leisure hours with others of the same ethnic group.

The children of the immigrants—the second generation—will, according to this perspective, penetrate still more deeply into the host society. The second generation's members, typically, have been born in the United States and are, therefore, U.S. citizens. These individuals learn American

English early, attend the public schools, and adopt "American" ways of thinking and acting. As adults, many of their close friends will be members of their ethnic group, and they probably will select a spouse from within the group. They will be largely "Americanized" in their culture and general participation in the activities of the society, but they will still be "ethnics" in their closest human relationships.

The third generation—the grandchildren of the immigrants—will, from the perspective we are discussing, be completely indistinguishable from other native U.S. citizens. They may still know a few words or phrases of their grandparent's native tongue; they may still celebrate certain special holidays in distinctive ways; and they may take pride in a few family heirlooms or recipes; but none of these remnants of the past detracts from the third generation's basic identity as Americans.

In this account of the adaptation or assimilation process, the grandchildren of the immigrants are presumed to have *substituted* Anglo American culture for the culture carried by their grandparents. There can be little doubt that millions of American families have gone through a sequence of adaptation similar to that described above.

A number of factors may act to accelerate or retard the rate at which the members of different ethnic groups adapt to conditions within the receiving society. Differences in religion and race, for example, frequently lead to intergroup conflict and a slowing of the adaptation process. In general, the more similar are the cultures of the host society and a specific ethnic group, the more rapidly and easily does the assimilation occur. American history, for example, has shown that white Protestant groups from Western Europe are most likely to be accepted by the members of the dominant group and, therefore, to approximate the three-generation pattern within the United States.

One result of the contact between a majority group and a minority group is of special significance. Each group may decide how far it wishes the process of adaptation to go, and for a minority group this decision is powerfully affected by the extent to which its members have entered the host society *voluntarily*. A moment's reflection may assist us to see why this is so. Groups that enter a new society in the hope they will, thereby, gain certain advantages or reach certain goals are likely to wish to embrace the new ways and to discard the old. In contrast, those who are having a new way of life thrust upon them are likely to resist strongly the unwanted demands of the new society and to cling tenaciously to their old, established ways. Under these circumstances, the new culture is likely to be seen as a threat to a cherished way of life rather than as a beacon of hope. Hence, one's expectations concerning the probable pattern of mutual adjustment that will occur when a majority group and a minority group come together may depend noticeably on whether the minority group is viewed primarily as an immigrant group (the immigrant analogy) or as a conquered group (the colonial analogy).

To assess the value of these competing views, we first consider the way in which the Mexican American group came into being.

Spain and Mexico

In the second decade of the sixteenth century, approximately one hundred years before the English began to settle on the Atlantic coast of North America, explorers from Spain entered Mexico. Here, for the first time, a conquering European group established itself on lands previously occupied by native American groups.

As in the case of the landings of the English approximately one hundred years later, an invading immigrant group gradually expanded its frontiers to create an increasingly large colonial territory. In what is now the United States, the Spanish colonization effort began in Florida with the founding of St. Augustine (the oldest European town in the United States) and spread westward toward Georgia and Alabama. Later, in the seventeenth and eighteenth centuries, Spain concentrated on northward expansion from New Spain (Mexico) rather than from her Caribbean base. After 1821, when Mexico achieved independence from Spain, the westward thrust of the United States brought these two massive enterprises into competition within the "Spanish borderlands" of northern Mexico (Bannon, 1970:28–48).

The course of colonial development in the Spanish and English territories shared certain similarities. In both cases the newcomers were interested in acquiring lands and precious metals. In both cases the Europeans were interested in converting the Indians to Christianity, and in both cases the relations between the groups were marked by hostility and conflict.

One difference between the Spanish and English policies toward the Indians, however, is of particular interest. The efforts of the Spanish to Christianize the Indians were much more successful than were those of the English. Even though the Spanish took an enormous toll in human lives, they followed a policy of bringing Christianized Indians into the colonial society that they were building. The "place" of the Indians in this society was at the very bottom; nevertheless, they were counted "in" rather than "out." This policy of the Spanish led to a much higher degree of intermarriage with the dominant Europeans than was true in the English colonies. As a result, by the time Mexico achieved independence in 1821, the culture and population of Mexico was much more "Indianized" than was the culture and population of the United States (see, e.g., Johansen and Maestas, 1983:48).

The Hispano-Indian society of Mexico and the Anglo American society of the United States came into direct and continuous contact after the Louisiana Purchase in 1803. The treaty through which the United States secured Louisiana from France did not give a detailed description of the boundaries of the territory; therefore, a struggle for control of the borderlands was set into motion. When Mexico won its independence from Spain, she too was faced by the Americans' ambition to expand.

Conflict in the Borderlands

Texas. The first main arena of competition between the Mexicans and groups from the United States occurred in the province of Texas. Although U.S. claims to Texas had been given up in a treaty with Spain in 1819, many U.S. citizens still coveted Texas. The Mexican government realized full well that holding the territory against both the Indians and the U.S. groups would present formidable problems. In an effort to help bring into the area frontiersmen who would be loyal to Mexico, the Mexican government agreed in 1823 to allow U.S. immigrants to settle in Texas. At this time Mexicans also were establishing trade relations with U.S. citizens in other parts of the borderlands, particularly in places like Santa Fe and San Francisco. The U.S. immigrants to Texas were expected to become Mexican citizens and members of the Roman Catholic Church. Mexican officials hoped that naturalized American Mexicans would serve as a buffer between Mexico and the United States, thereby improving relations between the two countries and decreasing the possibility of a military invasion. For a while it seemed that this strategy might work; but less than fifteen years after Mexico achieved independence from Spain, Texas broke away from Mexico to establish yet another new nation.

Some observers have argued that the revolt of the Texans was an inevitable result of differences and conflicts between two rival cultures; however, the main cleavage in Texas during the prerevolutionary period was not between the native Mexicans and the "Anglos."[2] It was, rather, between those who favored a strong central government and those who favored provincial autonomy. It is true that those favoring autonomy were mainly Anglos; but it is also true that a large proportion of the native Mexicans opposed the central government.

The conflict between Texas and Mexico continued during the period of Texas's independence (1836–45), and as it did, the relations between the native Texans (*Tejanos*) and the Anglos deteriorated. Although the ethnic distinctions had been there from the first contacts, they had not always served as badges of superior or inferior social status, and the numerically smaller *Tejano* population was not yet cast in the role of a subordinated ethnic minority. The Anglos, however, increasingly failed to distinguish the *Tejanos* from the Mexican nationals with whom they were struggling; and,

[2]This is not to say that the majority of the natives and newcomers accepted one another as individuals. For excellent discussions of the mutual antipathies of the members of the two groups see De Leon, (1983) and Paredes (1978). The term "Anglo" refers to all Caucasian residents of the United States, even though, as Barrera (1979:4) observed, that may seem illogical to some.

in the process, the ethnic boundary between the groups gradually was sharply drawn.

The conflict in Texas was destined to spread. Many Anglos in Texas and in the United States had longed for Texas to become a state in the Union; so there was little surprise when the annexation actually occurred. The Mexican government, though, considered the annexation to be an act of war and prepared to defend the northern frontier. When U.S. troops approached the Rio Grande in April 1846, a battle ensued; and soon thereafter, a war between Mexico and the United States was underway (Meyer and Zoraida Vazquez, 1982:25–52; Price, 1967:153–68). U.S. forces invaded not only the border area but also the central valley of Mexico. In 1848, Mexico surrendered under the terms of the Treaty of Guadalupe Hidalgo. The Treaty provided that Mexico would give up all claims to Texas and would sell "the rest of the Southwest, including Arizona, California, New Mexico, Utah, Nevada, and part of Colorado for $15,000,000 to the United States" (Moquin and Van Doren, 1971:252).

Colonial Isolation. The role of Texas as the first theater of combat between Mexicans and U.S. groups was strongly influenced (1) by its place in the plan of settlement adopted by the Spanish and (2) by geography.[3] The Spanish were forced to build their settlements in small, isolated areas because of the arid and mountainous conditions in the borderlands, the refusal of large groups of Indians to capitulate, and the difficulty of luring settlers to the frontier (see, e.g., Hinojosa, 1983). The result was that New Mexico, Arizona, and California were practically isolated not only from the United States but from the rest of Mexico as well. The pattern of Spanish settlement on the frontier has been described by McWilliams (1973) as:

> a fan thrust north from Mexico with its tip resting on Santa Fe. Gradually the fan unfolds—eastward to Texas, westward to California—with the ribs . . . of the fan extending northward from the base in Mexico. (P. 54)

This pattern of settlement also meant that the colonies were practically isolated from one another. The "fan" had north-south "ribs"; but there were almost no east-west connections. As a consequence, each of the colonial provinces developed along noticeably different lines. New Mexico was at the center of the Spanish effort, and at the time of the Treaty of Guadalupe Hidalgo it contained the largest Mexican population in the borderlands (between 60,000 and 70,000 people).[4] At this time, the Mexican populations of California, Texas, and Arizona were approximately

---

[3]The original plan had been to settle the entire region from Florida to California, but in 1819 Florida became a part of the United States.

[4]See e.g. Cortes (1980:705). This was not the largest human population in the borderlands, however. McWilliams (1973:52) estimated that there were concurrently around 250,000 Indians in the American Southwest.

13,000, 5,000, and 1,000 people, respectively.[5] Another indication of the extent to which New Mexico, Arizona, and California were isolated may be found in the numbers of Anglos who had settled in these areas before 1848. In Texas, the Anglos outnumbered the native Mexicans by about six to one.[6] In New Mexico and California, by contrast, Anglos probably numbered only in the hundreds, while in Arizona almost no Anglos settled until after the war with Mexico had ended.

The "Creation Generation."[7] We have seen that by 1846 the *Tejanos* had been placed in a subordinate position by the Anglos of Texas. One may argue, therefore, that when Texas was brought into the United States, thus transforming all Texans into U.S. citizens, the first segment of the Mexican American ethnic group was created. With the signing of the Treaty of Guadalupe Hidalgo, all of the remaining Mexican nationals in the conquered borderlands came under the political control of the United States and, consequently, were then subject to the laws and government of the United States.[8] In a sense, this "transfer" of people completed the process that had been started in Texas. At this point, a new ethnic group existed within the vast expanse of the American Southwest. But the main elements of this newly formed group were still isolated from one another, and the processes leading to the actual dominance of the Anglos varied in the different territories (see, e.g., M. Garcia, 1981; Weber, 1982).

New Mexico. The central rib in the fan of Spanish settlement was New Mexico. As noted previously, by far the largest concentration of Mexican nationals (*Hispanos*) was here—most of them in the vicinity of Santa Fe and Albuquerque. The penetration of the Anglos into *Hispano* society was slowed by geography and the continued presence of "wild" Indians, especially the Apaches. Moreover, the *Hispano* leaders of the prewar ruling group were able to remain in power after the war ended. Through alliances with Anglos in ranching, railroading, and banking, their power continued throughout the remainder of the nineteenth century (Swadesh, 1974:67–96).

The completion of the railroad in 1881 and the subjugation of the Apaches in 1886, however, permitted the Anglos to enter the territory in

[5] Some estimates of the size of California's population at this time are as low as 7,500 (McWilliams, 1973:52). The figure of 13,000 is presented by Cortes (1980:704).

[6] The imbalance was greater in some parts of Texas than in others. For example, in Bexar County (San Antonio) among males of voting age (21 and over) Anglos outnumbered *Tejanos* by two to one (De Leon, 1982:26).

[7] This term has been suggested by Alvarez, 1973, to designate the Mexicans who remained in the United States after the war with Mexico.

[8] The treaty specified that those living in the conquered territories could remain citizens of Mexico; however, if they did not declare this intention within one year, they automatically became citizens of the United States, with all of the rights and privileges of other American citizens (Moquin and Van Doren, 1971:246).

larger numbers than previously. Gradually, large tracts of land were trans-
ferred to Anglo individuals and business interests, and the traditional economic mainstay—sheepherding—declined in importance (Lamar, 1970:
169). By the first decade of the twentieth century, outside business interests and large numbers of new settlers had forced "a considerable portion of Mexicans into the status of a dependent minority" (Moore, 1976:16).

California. Balancing Texas on the east was California on the west. Both
territories had small Mexican populations when compared to New Mexico, and both had established ties with the United States before the out-
break of the war with Mexico. By the time Texas was annexed, most of the
native Mexicans of California (*Californios*) were themselves ready to join
the United States. As in New Mexico, there was a small, wealthy ruling
elite who considered themselves to be Spanish (Nava and Barger, 1976:
265–66). Most of the rest, however, were poor and thought of themselves
as Mexicans or as Indians. There was additionally a tiny, but influential,
group from the United States and Europe. These outsiders had generally
been accepted into the ruling group provided they joined the Catholic
Church and became citizens of Mexico (McWilliams, 1973:90). After Mexico became a republic, the ruling group took control of most of the usable
land in California and established a flourishing cattle business.

As the Mexican war neared, the U.S. population of California began to
increase; and when the war broke out, the Anglo settlers instigated the
"Bear Flag Revolt" against the Mexican government. When the U.S. forces
that had captured Santa Fe reached California, they found the conquest
practically complete.

The discovery of gold in California in 1848 brought an enormous influx
of people from the United States into the northern part of the territory. This
population grew rapidly, and by 1850 the original *Californios* comprised
only 15 percent of the total population (Cortes, 1980:705). The Anglos'
majority, of course, assured their success at the ballot box, while droughts,
floods, the new legal system, and squatters all assisted to remove the
Californios from their lands. This process of subordination involved overt
conflict too, including lynchings and physical expulsion (Moore, 1976:18).

We must not assume that the only important line of social division in
California at this time was between *Californios* and Anglos. As was true in
Texas, the relations between the two peoples were more complicated
than that (del Castillo, 1979). For example, some of the owners of prewar
land grants were Anglos, and most of the new landowners were not ordinary Anglo settlers. Moreover, most of the *Californios* were not landowners to begin with. Consequently, as Barrera (1979) noted:

> while it is true that Californios were being displaced from the land, many Cali-
> fornios owned no land from which to be displaced. While it is true that Anglos
> were taking over the land, . . . the new masters . . . were . . . likely to be men
> of means. (p. 20)

The major result was that by 1880 the Anglos had gained control of the machinery of politics and of the economy. The traditional society of the *Californios* crumbled in the face of the industrial and agricultural developments that were ushering in the twentieth century (Camarillo, 1979: 51–52).

Our review of events in the borderlands has shown that the Mexican American ethnic group arose with the annexation of Texas and the conquest of the remaining territory of the present Southwest by the United States. The time at which we may say the Mexican Americans existed as a subordinate group varies with the region of the country that is under discussion. In Texas, this condition had been reached by the beginning of the war with Mexico. In California, particularly in the north, the process was well advanced by 1880, and in New Mexico the change was not effected until the first decade of the twentieth century. We may say, then, that the process of subordination that was set into motion in Texas was substantially complete throughout the American Southwest by the end of the nineteenth century.

One final point should be stressed before we leave the events of the last half of the nineteenth century. Interethnic violence and bloodshed was very common within the border region during this period, especially in Texas. Although there exists no accurate tabulation of the violent encounters that took place between individuals and groups, it has been reported that the number of Mexican Americans killed in the Southwest during the years 1850–1930 was greater than the number of lynchings of black Americans during that same period (Moquin and Van Doren, 1971:253). In Moore's (1976) opinion, "No other part of the United States saw such prolonged intergroup violence as did the Border States from 1848 to 1925" (p. 36).

The strip of land between the Nueces River and the Rio Grande in Texas was the scene or staging area for many of the most spectacular conflicts. Numerous so-called filibustering expeditions were launched by U.S. groups into Mexico while some Mexicans—the most flamboyant of whom was General Juan N. Cortina—initiated deadly raids into Texas (Rosenbaum, 1981:41– 45).

These activities fanned the flames of ethnic hatred. The Anglos became increasingly suspicious of all "Mexicans," which led to numerous shootings, lynchings, and beatings. The Mexican raiders also frequently suspected the *Tejanos* as informers and dealt with them accordingly. Each incident usually led to some form of retaliation from the injured side, which, in turn, aggravated matters still further. The mutual hatred of many of the Anglos and Tejanos became so intense that many on both sides of the ethnic line began to consider killing a representative of the other to be a source of pride rather than a crime. Since the Texas Rangers frequently were used during these decades to maintain the control of Anglos over *Tejanos*, the latter increasingly viewed the Rangers as an official expression of the dominant group's hatred (Paredes, 1958:23–32; Samora, Bernal, and Pena, 1974).

We now are in a position to see why many students of the Mexican Americans emphasize the fact that initially the members of this group did not immigrate to the United States but, rather, were brought into it against their will. Under these circumstances, it has been argued, there is little reason to believe that the experience of the Mexican Americans should have conformed to the three-generation pattern;[9] and, in fact, there is little evidence that by the beginning of the twentieth century the members of this group were rushing to embrace the "American Way." Given that fact, what basis is there for assuming that any valid comparison may be made between Mexican Americans and the many European groups that have immigrated to the United States?

Population Shifts and Economic Change

The principal reason for believing the Mexican American ethnic group may undergo the changes described by the three-generation theory—despite the group's "historical primacy" in the Southwest and its birth in conquest—is that comparatively few people of Mexican ancestry lived on the U.S. side of the border prior to 1900.[10] As we have noted, the entire Mexican population of the Southwest in 1848 may have been no more than 80,000;[11] and even though there was a substantial movement of people back-and-forth across the border during the last half of the nineteenth century, there was not a very large increase in the permanent Mexican American population. Indeed, the movement of people across the border during this period was considered a matter of such little consequence that during the period 1886–1893, no official records were kept of immigration from Mexico into the United States. Altogether, during the last half of the nineteenth century, the total official number of immigrants from Mexico was less than 17,000 people. One may well see why some have argued that those who "immigrated" from Mexico during this period may not really be regarded as immigrants in the same sense as those who were immigrating from Europe during this same period.

Not until 1904 did the number of legal or documented immigrants from Mexico in a single year exceed 1,000 (U.S. Bureau of the Census, 1960: 58–59). Beginning with that year, however, the number of documented entrants began to rise substantially. The official count for the decade 1900–1909 was over 31,000; but one official report estimated that at least 50,000 "nonstatistical" Mexicans were arriving each year (Gomez-

[9]This is the argument of the colonial analogy referred to earlier.

[10]Jordan (1982:276) estimated the Mexican population of Texas in 1887 at 83,433 or 4.14 percent of the Texas population.

[11]This was approximately 1 percent of Mexico's population at that time.

Quinones, 1974:84), and another estimate suggested that the figure may have reached 100,000 annually (Bryan, 1971:334).

The years immediately following 1904, however, witnessed a sudden, sizable flow of people from Mexico into the United States. For instance, the decade 1910–19 produced an official count of over 185,000, while in the following decade almost one-half million Mexican immigrants were counted (Cardoso, 1980:53, 94); thus, altogether, more then 700,000 documented immigrants entered from Mexico during the entire thirty-year period. Thus we may see that the Mexican origin population increased dramatically during the first three decades of the twentieth century. As noted below, the number of Mexican Americans has increased still more dramatically since the end of World War II to at least eight million people. It may be argued, therefore, that if one starts the analysis of the adaptation process with the "Migrant Generation" (Alvarez, 1973:926), then the three-generation process may be found to be operating in a fairly "normal" way.[12]

Why have all of these people come to the United States? And what sort of welcome has awaited them? The reasons for immigration are always complex, but two general factors lay behind the population shift that commenced early in this century. First, there were economic "pulls" in the United States; and, second, there were political and economic "pushes" in Mexico.

The first quarter of the century held great promise for those who were willing to work in the Southwest (Acuna, 1981). For example, the Federal Reclamation Act of 1902 poured millions of dollars into the development of agriculture in the region. Numerous water reservoirs, dams, and irrigation projects were undertaken. These activities were paralleled by the efforts of large mining interests in the East to develop the rich mineral deposits of southern Arizona and New Mexico. The expansion of agriculture and mining, in turn, were made possible by, and added impetus to, the construction of railroads and communications networks. These economic developments sharply increased the demand for unskilled laborers. As the news spread throughout Mexico that the developing industries of the Southwest offered wages that were two to five times as high as those offered in Mexico, the idea of a northward trek became more attractive to thousands of workers.

The new demand for unskilled laborers in the Southwest coincided with unstable political conditions in Mexico. The dictatorial regime of Porfirio Díaz, who remained in power for 36 years, was a triumph for foreign investors and the economic and political elites of Mexican society (Ruiz, 1980:43, 101). These groups obtained special favors from Díaz such as tax reductions, control over large tracts of Indian lands, and the power to force people to work at slave wages (Coatsworth, 1982:260–73). Under

---

[12] This is the argument of the immigrant analogy referred to earlier.

these conditions, the new work opportunities north of the border became still more attractive.

Matters came to a head in 1910 when insurgent forces in Mexico mounted an offensive against Díaz. In the prolonged civil strife that followed, the majority of the peasant population was uprooted, and more than a million people lost their lives. Revolution and counterrevolution kept Mexico in a state of agitation for the next several years. Throughout this period, workers seeking better opportunities and safety from the fighting moved into the borderlands.

We should emphasize, however, that the "better opportunities" awaiting the Mexican workers were mainly in the hard, dirty, and poorly paid jobs in railroading, agriculture, and mining. The conditions of work in these three industries at this time have had a lasting effect on the Mexican American ethnic group. Railroad work, for example, assisted to spread Mexican workers to areas outside of the Southwest, where they sometimes remained to start new communities (Gomez-Quinones, 1974:88; Kerr, 1977:294). Also, railroad work was performed in work gangs, which might include most or all of the members of a single family. This circumstance meant that entire families might be engaged in unsafe, backbreaking labor. It also meant that the children of such families might be living in temporary, frequently unsanitary, housing and might be denied adequate schooling and health care.

Mexican labor moved even more strongly into agricultural work after war broke out in Europe in 1914. The war not only interrupted the flow of unskilled labor from Europe, but it diverted to the North many black American workers who might otherwise have been attracted to the Southwest. The alterations in migration patterns restricted the labor supply in the American border region and increased the desire of U.S. employers to hire Mexican workers. These workers were needed in California to tend the citrus, melon, tomato, and other crops. They were needed in Texas to work and harvest the cotton, spinach, and onions, and in Arizona, Colorado, and New Mexico, they were needed to raise vegetables, forage crops, and sugar beets (Reisler, 1976:77–100). The work done in these settings helped create a stereotype of the Mexican worker as one who lives in a rural area and does seasonal, "stoop" labor.

We see, therefore, that although the Mexican immigrant workers found "better opportunities" for employment in the United States, they were still in an economically disadvantaged position. Along with the Mexican Americans, the newcomers were fitted into a developing labor system in which workers of Mexican origin were expected to perform jobs that the Anglos would not accept or to do the same work at a lower wage.[13]

[13] The type of labor system we are describing has been called a colonial labor system by some scholars (e.g. Barrera, 1979:39) and a labor-repressive system by others (e.g. Montejano, 1979:132).

Despite the lowly position accorded them, the Mexican workers were highly desired by the employers, and they were very successful in completing the tasks for which they were hired. Indeed, when the United States government was preparing the immigration quota law that was enacted in 1924, southwestern employers argued vigorously against immigration quotas for Mexicans, and Mexico was kept off the quota list. When the law went into effect, immigration from overseas was restricted still further while Mexican immigration continued at a high level.

The desire of the U.S. employers for Mexican labor began to decline, however, soon after the immigration quota system had gone into effect. The agricultural sector of the U.S. economy went into a downturn, and various interest groups, including organized labor, began to demand that Mexico be placed on the quota list (Levenstein, 1968:206–19). As matters developed, an extension of the restrictions to Mexico became unnecessary, because after the financial crash of 1929 job opportunities in the United States were drastically reduced.

The labor system we have discussed drew the Mexican immigrants at first mainly to rural settings. The Southwest was still a sparsely populated region, and its cities were small and scattered. In 1900, only Los Angeles and San Francisco had populations of over 100,000; however, during and following World War I, the increased use of petroleum products, the development of port facilities, and the continued expansion of the railway system spurred industrial development and population growth throughout the region. The population of Los Angeles, for instance, grew tenfold between 1900 and 1930 (Romo, 1983:61). San Antonio doubled its population in the 1920s. These and other southwestern cities attracted a growing number of Mexicans and Mexican Americans. For example, the Mexican origin population of Los Angeles in 1920 was 29,757; but in 1930 this population had more than tripled to 97,116. The comparable figures for San Antonio were 41,469 and 82,373, respectively.

The urbanization process brought drastic changes in the lives of the Mexican seasonal workers. As opportunities improved in the cities, these workers moved into them and sought urban occupations. The jobs available to "Mexicans" still were mainly of a menial type. The low wages paid for this type of work forced the newcomers to accept inexpensive housing, and the inexpensive housing available to them was, for the most part, segregated. Although this residential segregation was to some unknown degree a matter of the people's choice, it also was to some degree a matter of social, as well as financial, necessity. Sales agreements and restrictive covenants frequently limited their options to housing in "Mexican districts" (Bogardus, 1930:74–80). Under these conditions, Mexican American and Mexican workers were unable to achieve rapid upward social mobility. Nonetheless, the urban conditions were sufficiently positive so that by the onset of the Great Depression—and in contrast to the stereotype—the majority of the Mexican origin population in the Southwest lived in urban communities.

The Great Depression

The Great Depression increased the concentration of Mexican origin workers in the manual occupations of the urban areas. It also intensified the hostility of Anglo workers toward those who looked "foreign" and who might be blamed for the catastrophic loss of jobs that was taking place. At the same time, various government agencies were searching for ways to reduce their costs by reducing services. Public officials discovered that it was much less expensive to pay for the transportation and other costs of sending people to Mexico than it was to maintain them on welfare rolls. The desires of Anglo workers and government officials were combined by President Hoover in a proposal to "send the Mexicans home" (Hoffman, 1974:39). With such a purpose in mind, thousands of people in various cities who looked "Mexican" were rounded up and deported. These immigration raids were especially prevalent in large cities such as Los Angeles, Detroit, and San Antonio. Naturalized Mexican Americans frequently were "repatriated" along with the Mexican nationals. Many native U.S. citizens of Mexican ancestry were scrutinized closely and intimidated by immigration officials, and they, too, sometimes were deported. In some cases families were broken apart when those who were Mexican were sent "home" while their American relatives remained behind. The entire repatriation program emphasized to the Mexicans and Mexican Americans just how vulnerable they were to the actions of government officials (Balderrama, 1982:15). It is likely that many U.S. citizens in the barrios failed to apply for benefits to which they were entitled because they feared they might be deported. The total effect of the repatriation program on the Mexican Americans was enormous. Not only were hundreds of thousands of people forced out of the United States, but the U.S. citizens of Mexican ancestry were shown that they were second-class citizens. They were welcomed when there was a shortage of cheap labor, but when economic times were bad they were told to go "home."

The repatriation program, of course, did little to solve the crisis of unemployment; so, with the coming of President Franklin Roosevelt's New Deal, government programs such as the WPA and AAA put thousands of people back to work. Even under these improved conditions, the Mexican origin population encountered some special problems. For instance, the government's program to pay farmers to take acreage out of cultivation also reduced the number of farm workers who were needed. Given the repatriation program and the economic hardships, it is little wonder that by the end of the decade the Mexican origin population had fallen from a high of 639,000 to around 377,000 (Grebler, Moore, and Guzman, 1970:526).

The *Bracero* Program

The problem of unemployment did not disappear until World War II created a manpower emergency. As large numbers of men went into military service or into jobs in defense industries, labor shortages were created in many other sectors of the economy. Although this void was partially filled by a massive influx of women into occupations outside of the home, many of the lowest-paying jobs were still not taken, especially on the railroads and in agriculture. To make matters worse for those who needed workers, the usual reservoir of additional laborers—the Mexican immigrants—was being held back by improved economic conditions in Mexico and by the Mexican government. At the urging of U.S. employers, the governments of the United States and Mexico started an informal program to allow manual laborers (*braceros*) to enter the United States to work in railroad construction and maintenance and in agriculture. The conditions under which the *braceros* were to work and live were specifically outlined in the agreement: the *braceros* were to receive free transportation and food, guaranteed wages, safe working conditions, and sanitary living quarters. With these guarantees and protections, Mexican workers flocked to the program. Between 1942 and 1945, over 167,000 workers were recruited under the plan (Dinnerstein and Reimers, 1982:93).[14]

Although the *bracero* program was initiated as a wartime measure and, presumably, would be discontinued at the end of the war, the program was so popular among farmers, particularly those who owned large businesses, that it was extended in various stages until 1964.[15] Moreover, the program was popular with the *braceros* themselves. As Cornelius (1978) has observed:

> rural unemployment in Mexico was at a high level when the *bracero* program was terminated; those who had gone to the U.S. initially as *braceros* continued to go, but now illegally. In this sense, the *bracero* program never really ended, it simply went underground. (P. 18)

Some of the advantages for the growers are obvious: they could depend on a steady, reliable, labor supply; the government was helping to pay for the program; the workers were obligated to remain in their jobs until their contract expired; and when the contract expired, the workers were required to return to Mexico. But for U.S. workers, the program had various negative effects. Although the law required that if domestic workers were available *braceros* could not be hired, the employers "used every pos-

[14] Mexico initially excluded the state of Texas from the *bracero* program charging that Mexican nationals were subjected there to overt discrimination.

[15] The informal arrangement started during the war was formalized in 1951 by the passage of Public Law 78 (Dunne, 1967:48). Another factor operating to maintain the program was that Mexico had become dependent on it. Cross and Sandos (1981) have argued that "during the Bracero Era (1942–1964), migration to the United States became ... Mexico's 'way out' of its development crisis" (p. 35).

sible ruse to get around this provision" (Dunne, 1967:48). The presence of a cheap, dependable pool of reserve laborers made it easier for the employers to keep wages low and to resist the efforts of U.S. citizens to organize strong labor unions or even to keep their jobs in the fields (American G.I. Forum, 1953; Barrera, 1979: 118). By the late 1950s, hundreds of thousands of *braceros* were being used in the harvests (Dinnerstein and Reimers, 1982: 93).

The *bracero* program raised many issues concerning the relationship of Mexican American workers to Mexican workers, of each of these categories of workers to U.S. employers, and of the United States government to all workers and employers. The employers, as we've noted, found it inexpensive and convenient to have workers from Mexico who could be sent back home when they were no longer needed. The federal government was faced with the task of guaranteeing food production and rail transportation during wartime and also of guaranteeing fair treatment to workers, while the Mexican American community was torn between a desire, on the one hand, to see their culture replenished and strengthened and a desire, on the other hand, to decrease the competition for jobs and the discrimination that the presence of the *braceros* frequently generated. Not to be ignored either is the fact that the program had negative effects on the *braceros* themselves. In many cases, the promises made to the workers in their contracts were not kept.

The problem of discrimination against Mexican Americans and Mexican nationals during these war years was by no means restricted to jobs. Despite their high rates of enlistment in the military services and their many other contributions to the war effort, Mexican Americans were denied admission to many public places and were segregated in many others. Even distinguished military service to the country did not exempt Mexican Americans from overt and covert humiliations. For example, when Sgt. Macario Garcia, a winner of the Congressional Medal of Honor, ordered a cup of coffee in a cafe in Sugarland, Texas, he was refused service and then, when he protested, was arrested on a charge of aggravated assault (McWilliams, 1973:261).

The Pachucos

The most widely noted incidents of discrimination against Mexican Americans during the war, however, occurred in California. Many Mexican American youths in the east side barrio of Los Angeles, like the young people of many other groups in the city, spent much of their time in one another's company—in what the newspapers referred to as "gangs." The main thing that caused these youthful groups to become a subject of public discussion is that their members—who called themselves pachucos—were openly, defiantly, proud of their Mexican heritage (Sanchez, 1943). They flaunted their distinctiveness by dressing in a manner that most Anglos considered "outlandish." They wore tight-cuffed trousers that bloused at the knee and were belted high on the body. Their costumes also included wide-brimmed hats, long-tailed coats, high boots, ducktail haircuts, and ankle-length watch chains. Anglos called these costumes "zoot suits" and tended to identify those who wore them as "hoodlums." The newspapers exacerbated this tendency by referring to the pachucos as "gangsters" and by giving their activities sensational coverage.

The summers of 1942 and 1943 produced two widely noted events involving the pachucos. The first event concerned the death of a young Mexican American named Jose Diaz near an East Los Angeles swimming hole. Twenty-four pachucos were arrested on the suspicion that they had killed Diaz, but an autopsy showed that he might have died in an automobile accident. After a trial that lasted several months, nine of the defendants were convicted of second-degree murder, and eight others were convicted of lesser offenses. Throughout the trial the press coverage was highly sensationalized. The swimming hole was referred to as "The Sleepy Lagoon," and the fact that the defendants were of Mexican heritage and wore "zoot suits" was emphasized. The convictions were appealed on the grounds that the trial had been conducted in a biased and improper way, and, after the defendants had suffered nearly two years of imprisonment, the convictions were overturned "for lack of evidence" (McWilliams, 1973:231).

The publicity surrounding the Sleepy Lagoon Trial strengthened a widely held impression among Anglos that there was some sort of innate connection between Mexicanness and criminality. A report by the Los Angeles sheriff's office to the grand jury contained the revelation that those of Mexican ancestry are more likely than those of Anglo-Saxon ancestry to engage in violent crimes because such behavior is an "inborn characteristic" (McWilliams, 1973:234), while the press headlined cases in which Mexicans had been involved in crimes and harassed the police for failing to curtail the "crime wave." The trial, the sheriff's report, and the continued press coverage of problems between the police and pachuco "gangs" prepared the way for a major confrontation between Anglos and Mexican Americans.

The U.S. Navy had located a training facility in the east side barrio of Los Angeles. In time, various misunderstandings arose between some of the sailors and some of the Mexican American residents of the area, and on 3 June 1943 the accumulated tensions erupted into a number of disorders that became known as the "Zoot-Suit Race Riots." The "riots" may be more accurately described as a series of mob attacks by U.S. servicemen and off-duty policemen directed at Mexican Americans who wore zoot suits.[16]

After a group of sailors allegedly were beaten by a gang of pachucos, a

[16] Mazon (forthcoming) has suggested that the "riots" also may be described as a form of mutiny by the servicemen.

large group of servicemen "invaded" the east side barrio and severely beat at least four Mexican American youths wearing zoot suits. By 7 June the number of people engaged in the disorders had swelled into the thousands. The Los Angeles police department took few steps during this period to protect the Mexican Americans or restrain the servicemen. In some cases, the police merely followed the servicemen and arrested the Mexican Americans who were the victims of an attack! Miraculously, no one was killed in these disorders.

The "Zoot Suit Race Riots" in Los Angeles ended in about ten days, but bitter feelings lingered for many years among the Mexican Americans. There can be little doubt that many members of the Anglo "establishment" approved of the efforts of the servicemen to "clean out" the "zooters" and that the zoot suit itself was considered a symbol of an ethnic defiance and solidarity that could not be tolerated.[17]

When similar disorders broke out in other cities, the repercussions were felt throughout the United States and abroad. The ambassador from Mexico protested this evidence of prejudice and discrimination against people of Mexican ancestry, and America's allies in the war against fascist tyranny were given ample reason to wonder about the commitment of the United States to the ideals of equality and freedom for which they were fighting.

Alternate Identities

Throughout this period, many Mexican American youths (as well as some Mexican nationals) were serving in the armed forces of the United States. Ironically, the members of groups that have been subjected to discrimination generally are exceptionally eager to demonstrate their loyalty to the country by fighting for it; and such was the case for the Mexican Americans. Not only did Mexican Americans enlist at a disproportionately high level, but also they contributed a disproportionately high share to the casualty lists and were frequently cited for their outstanding military performance (Scott, 1974:140).

Their wartime experiences profoundly altered the perspectives and expectations of many Mexican Americans. They had received training in the service that had raised their aspirations and taught them new skills. The G.I. Bill of Rights gave thousands of veterans the opportunity to improve their economic status through home loans and stipends for college training. Moreover, these returning warriors believed that their contributions to winning the war entitled them to new respect and a generally improved status within American society. They had worked and fought side by side with Americans from all over the country and, in the process, had come to expect that as equals in battle they were entitled to equal opportunities in

[17] For a contemporary analysis of the pachucos see Horowitz (1983).

civilian life. To a much higher degree than did their parents, these men were likely to feel that they were "Americans," not "Mexicans." They were more likely to stress that "like descendants of people from so many other lands, I was born here" (Alvarez, 1973:932). In short, participation in the war had caused many Mexican Americans to emphasize their identity as Americans and attempt to reduce or discard their identity as Mexicans. Such an emphasis is consistent with the operation of the three-generation process.

The hopes of the returning veterans were frequently dashed. They found that the prejudices and the various forms of discrimination that had existed before the war still remained. Public accommodations, schools, and housing were still segregated, and jobs outside the traditional pattern were still hard to get.

Organizing against Discrimination

The trend toward urbanization among Mexican Americans and Mexicans that had started before the Great Depression intensified following World War II; consequently, increasing numbers of Mexican Americans with raised expectations concerning their lives in the postwar world were placed in situations that served to highlight the fact that opportunities were limited for "Mexicans."

The continuation of discrimination against Mexican Americans, when combined with their increased desire to participate fully in the "mainstream" of American life, suggested that they should organize to achieve their goals. This idea was not new, of course, *La Alianza Hispano-Americana*, for instance, had been founded in the nineteenth century (Servin, 1974:35), and the famous and successful League of United Latin-American Citizens (LULAC) had been active since 1929. But until after World War II, Mexican American organizations tended to play down the "political" side of their activities and to adopt programs that concentrated on objectives that did not arouse the suspicions of the Anglo leaders (Cuellar, 1970:143; Foley et al., 1977:101−2).

Such prewar submissiveness no longer suited the mood of many Mexican Americans, so the new organizations were intended to pursue more aggressively the ideal of equal participation for minority group members in American society. The Community Service Organization (CSO), for example, was founded in California to combat discrimination in schooling, police-community relations, housing, and employment. The CSO focused attention on getting Mexican Americans to vote in order to force the Anglos to respond to their needs (Cuellar, 1970:146; Stoddard, 1973:189). Another new organization, the American G.I. Forum, was founded in Texas to promote civic and political action among Mexican Americans. Like CSO, the G.I. Forum emphasized registering people to vote and getting them to exercise their political rights (Allsup, 1982:128−31).

The efforts of these and other organizations produced results that encouraged many of their members to believe equal treatment for Mexican Americans would soon become a reality; but as the 1950s drew to a close and the civil rights movement among black Americans began to capture the nation's attention, many Mexican Americans came to feel that the existing organizations were not pressing hard enough for the civil rights of their ethnic group; consequently, some newer organizations were founded to attempt to get Mexican Americans into political office by gaining the support of the existing political parties. This changed emphasis led to the creation of the Mexican American Political Association (MAPA) and the Political Association of Spanish-speaking Organizations (PASO). A widely noted example of the success of the approach of these organizations was the election in 1963 of a slate of Mexican American candidates to replace the Anglo incumbents of the city council of Crystal City, Texas (Tirado, 1970:64–66).

By this time many of the participants in the black protest movement had adopted the strategy of direct confrontation, and many Mexican Americans began to favor such an approach for themselves. Hence, a number of still newer organizations representing more militant Mexican Americans were formed. The Mexican American Youth Organization (MAYO), the United Mexican-American Students (UMAS), and the National Farm Workers Association (NFWA) were examples of this further shift. The NFWA (which later became the United Farm Workers) and its leader, Cesar Chavez, won national recognition and widespread support of a lengthy, conflict-filled strike against the owners and operators of the grape vineyards of California (see, e.g., Taylor, 1975). The grape strike was seen by insiders and outsiders alike as a part of a broad social movement, *La Causa* or *El Movimiento* (Valdez, 1982:271). To succeed in the strike and boycott, the UFWA recognized the importance of soliciting the support of people in the cities; so when their representatives spoke on college campuses, at churches, or at other public gatherings, they presented their case through *corridos* (folk ballads) sung in the traditional style. They also established a bilingual newspaper, *El Malcriado*, and encouraged the development of *El Teatro Campesino*. This farm workers' theater, founded by Luis Valdez, grew from simple one-act plays that poked fun at the grape growers to more sophisticated presentations about oppression and social change.

The members of the new organizations referred to themselves as Chicanos and increasingly questioned the idea that people of Mexican ancestry are destined to be transformed by the three-generation process. Instead, they championed an interpretation of the experience of those of Mexican origin that has been called *chicanismo*. This perspective emphasizes the relationship of Chicanos not only to the broad streams of civilization flowing from the Spanish-Indian cultures of Mexico and Central. and South America but also to the ancient heritages stemming from the

Aztecs, Incas, Mayas, Toltecs, and other pre-Columbian people. Such a view reminds Chicanos of the antiquity and grandeur of their heritage and increases their consciousness of themselves as members of an oppressed group (see, e.g., Castro, 1974). Such a view rejects the three-generation process as a suitable avenue for the achievement of the full benefits of American citizenship. It offers, in contrast, the idea that one may be a full-fledged "American" while retaining to a significant degree one's ethnic heritage.[18]

Cultural Development and Assimilation

We have seen that during the first three decades of the twentieth century the Mexican American ethnic group grew very rapidly. Following a decline in size during the Great Depression, this group began to grow again in response to the expanded job opportunities created by World War II. The *braceros* were moving in and out, of course, but they were not the only Mexican workers coming into the country at this time. Many more workers were entering without proper papers but with the intention to work and, possibly, to stay. This stream of undocumented workers has continued to grow and has become a source of acrimonious debate (see, e.g., Cornelius, 1978). The Immigration and Naturalization Service annually deports hundreds of thousands of these workers, but all observers agree that only a fraction of those who cross the border illegally are arrested and that the present Mexican origin population of the United States contains a very large proportion of people who have entered in this way.[19]

Among the several important consequences of these events, one is of special interest to us here. Although a large majority of Mexican Americans in 1900 had been born in the United States, most of those comprising the Mexican origin population during the twentieth century have been of foreign or foreign-native parentage; hence, the cultural heritage of the Mexican Americans has continuously been reinforced by newcomers. This reinforcement, in turn, has made it easier for Mexican Americans to exercise a choice concerning whether to accept Anglo values and modes of behavior or to strengthen their ties to Mexican American culture.

A clear understanding of the extent to which the Mexican Americans are moving toward the American mainstream or are building and maintaining a distinctive ethnic identity would require a much longer treatment than may be attempted here. We, nevertheless, may gain some apprecia-

[18]The idea that one may have "the best of both" heritages is not unique to the Chicanos. Some version of this idea, called cultural pluralism, has been advocated by many different groups in American history.

[19]Bean, King, and Passel (1983:105) have estimated the number of illegal immigrants from Mexico living in the United States in 1980 to have been between 1.5 and 3.8 million people.

tion of the changes taking place by referring to several important areas of social life.

Consider first the matter of language. Although practically all ethnic groups in America have attempted to maintain their native languages, the general pattern—despite some variations—has been for the use of the ancestral tongue to decline noticeably as the generations pass and for English to become the principal language among the third and subsequent generations. The Mexican Americans afford a marked contrast to this usual pattern (Hernandez-Chavez, Cohen, and Beltramo, 1975; Penalosa, 1980; Sanchez, 1983). While the number of speakers of other non-English languages in America has been declining, the number of Spanish speakers has been growing. The Mexican American group is not, of course, the only Spanish-speaking group on the scene; but it is definitely the largest and surely has been the primary contributor to the survival of Spanish in the United States.

One may well wonder, though, whether the spread of the Spanish language is not just a reflection of the fact that the number of immigrants from Mexico and other Spanish-speaking countries is so great. What about the status of Spanish among those who were born in the United States? Grebler, Moore, and Guzman (1970:424) studied samples of Mexican Americans living in different residential areas within Los Angeles and San Antonio to gather information on this question. The researchers found, first, that a majority of the people interviewed in both cities were bilingual. They found, second, that those with higher incomes were more fluent in English than those with lower incomes; and they found, third, that while Spanish was more frequently used in the homes of the lower-income group, sizable numbers in all income groups prefer to use Spanish when speaking to their children.

The high degree of bilingualism among Mexican Americans strongly suggests that they have not followed the usual three-generation pattern of *substituting* English for their native language. Although many *individual* Mexican Americans have, no doubt, followed the three-generation route, the more common pattern has been for the members of the group to *add* English to their language repertoire.

We should not assume that the reinforcing effect afforded Mexican American culture by the recent arrivals from Mexico means that the cultures of the two peoples are identical. They are continuous, highly related, human creations; but they are, nevertheless, distinguishable. Mexican American culture—including art, folklore, literature, music, and poetry— is enjoying its own distinctive mode of development; and this development enriches and strengthens the ethnic group members' sense of pride and unity (see, e.g., Huerta, 1982).

These trends in the cultural sphere are related to what has been called the Mexican Americans' "strategic penetration" in the political sphere (Stoddard, 1973:219). Although the mood of America changed during the 1970s and the confrontation approach lost support, the development of *chicanismo* has continued, and many Mexican American political organizations—of both the left and the right—have adopted pragmatic approaches to the acquisition of political power. For example, a much more determined effort has been made to win the election of Mexican Americans to local, state, and national offices (Garcia and de la Garza, 1977; de la Garza and Brischetto, 1983). One result of this effort may be seen in the following statistics: in 1950 there were 20 Mexican American legislators in the five states of the Southwest; in 1979 there were 82 (Pachon and Moore, 1981:123). Since then, Mexican Americans have been elected as mayors of two of the largest cities in the United States (Denver and San Antonio), and the influence of Mexican Americans in the presidential campaigns has been growing steadily.

Let us consider now, in this brief review of Mexican American assimilation, the extent of upward occupational mobility among Mexican American workers. As noted previously, during the first third of the twentieth century Mexican American and Mexican workers were concentrated in low-paying jobs, primarily in farming, mining, and railroading. Since then, though, the Mexican origin population has become highly urbanized (over 80 percent by 1980) and has moved toward an occupational distribution that more nearly resembles the occupational distribution for all other workers in the country. For example, Mexican Americans are fairly well represented in clerical, craft, service, and transport occupations; and although they are still more likely than other Americans to be engaged in farm work, only 6 percent of them are so employed (Pachon and Moore, 1981:117). Mexican Americans also are much more prominent now than formerly in professional, technical, managerial, and administrative occupations. For instance, the proportion of Mexican Americans engaged in professional occupations rose between 1950 and 1978 from 2.1 percent to 5.6 percent. Even so, they are definitely underrepresented in these high-prestige, high-paying jobs. That underrepresentation, in turn, is partly responsible for the median income difference that still exists between Mexican Americans and Anglos. In 1979, for example, the median income of all white families in the United States was $20,500 dollars. For Mexican Americans the comparable figure was $15,171. Stated differently, in that year, the median income for Mexican American families was about 74 percent of the median for all white families (Fogel, 1983:37).

Why are Mexican Americans still underrepresented in the higher-paying occupations? This question is by no means easy to answer; but given the history of discrimination toward people of Mexican origin that we have reviewed in this chapter, it would be simply amazing to discover that discrimination is not a part of the answer. But there is more to it than that. It is known, for instance, that Mexican Americans, on the average, have completed fewer years of schooling than Anglos (9.8 versus 12.1 in 1979) and that, in general, the more schooling people complete the more likely they are to qualify for the higher-paying jobs. Hence, some of the difference in the average earnings of the two groups may be attributed to the difference in their levels of education. But, how much? It is extremely difficult to assess the general effects of discrimination on incomes, and it is especially difficult to specify how much of the apparent discrimination in hiring and firing is a result of earlier discrimination in, say, education.

Several important studies of these complex issues have attempted to calculate what it actually costs, in dollars, to be a Mexican American worker. Consider, for instance, the following question: "How much does one additional year of schooling increase the annual earnings of a Mexican American or an Anglo worker?" The answer to this question appears to be that one additional year of schooling leads to an annual increase in the earnings of Mexican American men of about 4 or 5 percent compared to an increase of from 5 to 7 percent for Anglo males (Fogel, 1983:38). We see, therefore, that although it "pays" a Mexican American worker to gain additional schooling it does not pay as much as the same increase does for an Anglo worker. While this difference may be a reflection of discrimination, it may also reflect some other average differences that exist between Mexican American and Anglo workers. For example, Mexican American workers, as noted above, are still somewhat more likely to be located in rural areas; they are more likely to be located in the Southwest; and they are more likely to be newcomers to the United States. Each of these factors may lower an individual's earnings even in the absence of discrimination. For this reason it is Fogel's (1983:40) opinion that the earnings differences between Mexican Americans and Anglos "result chiefly from group differences in these earnings traits." But not all students of this subject would agree. When Mexican American and Anglo workers are "matched" for similar social characteristics, the Anglo workers still receive higher average incomes (Poston, Alvirez, and Tienda, 1976:629; Stephens, Oser, and Blau, 1980:252).

The final social area to be considered is that of intermarriage between Mexican Americans and "outsiders." The extent to which intermarriages are occurring between the members of any minority ethnic group and the members of the dominant group in the society is generally regarded as a key indication of the extent to which the minority is assimilating or maintaining its separate identity. Not nearly enough is known about this vital subject; but, fortunately, some very good studies are available. These studies call attention to three major points. First, we are reminded by them that the regional variations stemming from the fan pattern of colonial settlement remain with us and that the contemporary Mexican Americans are still a very diverse group. For instance, the Mexican Americans are marrying "out" more frequently in Los Angeles and in the area around Albuquerque than they are in South Texas. The rate of exogamous marriage in Los Angeles in 1963 was 40 percent (Grebler, Moore, and Guzman, 1970:406); in Albuquerque in 1971 the rate was 39 percent (Murguia and

Frisbie, 1977:384); but in Edinburg, Texas, the rate in 1971 was 9 percent (Alvirez and Bean, 1976:383).[20]

A second important point in this regard is that there has been a gradual long-term increase in the exogamy rate among Mexican Americans. Bradshaw and Bean (1970:393), for instance, have shown that the rate of exogamy for San Antonio in 1850 was about 10 percent, but one hundred years later the rate had approximately doubled. Similarly, Murguia (1982: 49) reported that the exogamy rate in Albuquerque rose from 14 percent in 1915 to 39 percent in 1971, and in Los Angeles the rate rose from 17 percent during the period 1924–33 to 40 percent in 1963. We should note that the upward exogamous trend is much more gentle in some places than in others and, also, that there have been some recent declines. In Corpus Christi, Texas, the rate rose only from 15 to 16 percent between 1961 and 1971, while in California as a whole the rate declined from 55 percent in 1962 to 51 percent in 1974 (Schoen, Nelson, and Collins, 1978).

The third main finding of interest here concerns the generational differences in exogamy among Mexican Americans. Those who have been born in the United States of parents who also were born in the United States (and who, therefore, are at least third-generation Americans) are more likely to marry out than are those who have only one parent who has been born in the United States. The latter, in turn, are more likely to marry out than those who were born in Mexico (Grebler, Moore, and Guzman, 1970:409). This pattern suggests that the three-generation process is at work among Mexican Americans.

Taken altogether, the information presented concerning language use, political success, occupational mobility, and intermarriage may be interpreted as offering general support for the immigrant analogy. To be sure, the continued bilingualism of the Mexican Americans, the probable presence of discrimination against them in employment, the comparative slowness of their political penetration, and the regional variations in their intermarriage rates each depart to some extent from the expected "normal" pattern of assimilation. It seems clear, moreover, that Mexican Americans have chosen not to discard their ethnic heritage. Most of them appear determined to find a middle way wherein American culture may be added to, rather than substituted for, their own heritage. Consequently, the evidence we have reviewed also may be interpreted to lend partial support to the colonial analogy. Neither of the interpretations we have considered appears to encompass all of the facts.

In several very significant spheres of social life, nevertheless, there is a clear movement by the members of this ethnic group toward the American mainstream. This observation has led some scholars to suggest that the Mexican Americans of today resemble "a European immigrant group

---

[20] These figures present rates for *marriages*. Rates for individuals would be lower.

of a generation ago" (Penalosa, 1970:50). Despite the many inequities that have yet to be overcome, and the difficulties of maintaining a separate ethnic identity within American society, there is optimism in the barrios. Many who live there believe the future holds a bright promise for the Mexican American people.

REFERENCES

Acuna, Rodolfo. 1981. *Occupied America*. 2d ed. (New York: Harper & Row).

Allsup, Carl. 1982. *The American G.I. Forum: Origins and Evolution*. Center for Mexican American Studies Monograph no. 6 (Austin: University of Texas Press).

Alvarez, Rodolfo. 1973. "The Psycho-Historical and Socioeconomic Development of the Chicano Community in the United States," *Social Science Quarterly*, 53 (March): 920–42.

Alvirez, David, and Frank D. Bean. 1976. "The Mexican American Family," in C. H. Mindel and R. W. Habenstein, eds., *Ethnic Families in America: Patterns and Variations* (New York: Elsevier): pp. 271–92.

American G.I. Forum and the Texas State Federation of Labor. 1953. *What Price Wetbacks?* (Austin: Texas American Federation of Labor).

Balderrama, Francisco E. 1982. *In Defense of La Raza: The Los Angeles Mexican Consulate and the Mexican Community, 1929 to 1936* (Tucson: University of Arizona Press).

Bannon, John Francis. 1970. *The Spanish Borderlands Frontier, 1513–1821* (New York: Holt, Rinehart & Winston).

Barrera, Mario. 1979. *Race and Class in the Southwest* (Notre Dame: University of Notre Dame Press).

Bean, Frank D., Allan G. King, and Jeffrey S. Passel. 1983. "The Number of Illegal Migrants of Mexican Origin in the United States: Sex Ratio-Based Estimates for 1980," *Demography*, 20 (February): 99–109.

Bogardus, Emory S. 1930. "The Mexican Immigrant and Segregation," *American Journal of Sociology*, 13 (July):74–80.

Bradshaw, Benjamin S., and Frank D. Bean. 1970. "Intermarriage between Persons of Spanish and Non-Spanish Surname: Changes from the Mid-Nineteenth Century to the Mid-Twentieth Century," *Social Science Quarterly*, 51 (September):389–95.

Bryan, Samuel. 1971. "Mexican Immigrants on the Labor Market," in Wayne Moquin and Charles Van Doren, eds., *A Documentary History of the Mexican Americans* (New York: Bantam): pp. 255–59.

Camarillo, Albert. 1979. *Chicanos in a Changing Society* (Cambridge: Harvard University Press).

Cardoso, Lawrence A. 1980. *Mexican Emigration to the United States, 1897–1931* (Tucson: University of Arizona Press).

Castro, Tony. 1974. *Chicano Power: The Emergence of Mexican America* (New York: Saturday Review Press).

Coatsworth, John. 1982. "Railroads, Landholding, and Agrarian Protest," in W. Dirk Raat, ed., *Mexico: From Independence to Revolution, 1810–1910* (Lincoln: University of Nebraska Press): pp. 260–72.

Cornelius, Wayne A. 1978. *Mexican Migration to the United States: Causes, Consequences, and U.S. Responses* (Cambridge: Massachusetts Institute of Technology, Center for International Studies).

Cortes, Carlos E. 1980. "Mexicans," in Stephen Thernstrom, Ann Orlov, and Oscar Handlin, eds., *Harvard Encyclopedia of American Ethnic Groups* (Cambridge, Mass.: Belknap): pp. 697–719.

Cross, Harry E., and James Sandos. 1981. *Across the Border: Rural Development in Mexico and Recent Migration to the United States* (Berkeley: Institute of Government Studies).

Cuellar, Alfredo. 1970. "Perspectives on Politics," in Joan W. Moore, *Mexican Americans*, 1st ed. (Englewood Cliffs, N.J.: Prentice-Hall): pp. 137–56.

de la Garza, Rodolfo, and Robert Brischetto, with the assistance of David Vaughn. 1983. *The Mexican American Electorate: Information Sources and Policy Orientations*. Occasional Paper No. 2 (San Antonio: Southwest Voter Registration Education Project and the University of Texas Center for Mexican American Studies).

del Castillo, Richard Griswold. 1979. *The Los Angeles Barrio, 1850–1890: A Social History* (Berkeley and Los Angeles: University of California Press).

De Leon, Arnoldo. 1982. *The Tejano Community, 1836–1900* (Albuquerque: University of New Mexico Press).

———. 1983. *They Called Them Greasers* (Austin: University of Texas Press).

Dinnerstein, Leonard, and David M. Reimers. 1982. *Ethnic Americans*. 2d ed. (New York: Harper & Row).

Dunne, John Gregory. 1967. *Delano* (New York: Farrar, Straus & Giroux).

Fogel, Walter. 1983. "Research on the Chicano Workers," in Armando Valdez, Albert Camarillo, and Tomas Almaguer, eds., *The State of Chicano Research in Family, Labor, and Migration Studies* (Stanford: Stanford Center for Chicano Research): pp. 33–50.

Foley, Douglas, and Clarice Mota, Donald Post, Ignacio Lozano. 1977. *From Peones to Politicos: Ethnic Relations in a South Texas Town, 1900–1977* (Austin: Center for Mexican American Studies, Monograph no. 3).

Garcia, F. Chris, and Rodolfo de la Garza. 1977. *The Chicano Political Experience: Three Perspectives* (North Scituate, Mass.: Duxbury Press).

Garcia, John A. 1981. "Yo Soy Mexicano ...: Self-Identity and Sociodemographic Correlates," *Social Science Quarterly*, 62 (March):88–98.

Garcia, Mario T. 1981. *Desert Immigrants: The Mexicans of El Paso* (New Haven: Yale University Press).

Gomez-Quinones, Juan. 1974. "The First Steps: Chicano Labor, Conflict and Organizing, 1900–20," in Manuel P. Servin, ed., *An Awakening Minority: The Mexican-Americans*, 2d ed. (Beverly Hills: Glencoe Press): pp. 79–112.

Grebler, Leo, Joan W. Moore, and Ralph C. Guzman. 1970. *The Mexican-American People* (New York: Free Press).

Hernandez-Chavez, Eduardo, Andrew D. Cohen, and Anthony F. Beltramo. 1975. *En Lenguaje de los Chicanos: Regional and Social Characteristics of Language Used by Mexican Americans* (Arlington, Va.: Center for Applied Linguistics).

Hinojosa, Gilberto Miguel. 1983. *A Borderlands Town in Transition: Laredo, 1755–1870* (College Station: Texas A&M University Press).

Hoffman, Abraham. 1974. *Unwanted Mexican Americans in the Great Depression: Repatriation Pressures 1929–1939* (Tucson: University of Arizona Press).

Horowitz, Ruth. 1983. *Honor and the American Dream: Culture and Identity in a Chicano Community* (New Brunswick, N.J.: Rutgers University Press).

Huerta, Jorge A. 1982. *Chicano Theater: Themes and Forms* (Ypsilanti, Mich.: Bilingual Press).

Johansen, Bruce, and Roberto Maestas. 1983. *El Pueblo: The Gallegos Family's American Journey, 1503–1980* (New York: Monthly Review Press).

Jordan, Terry G. 1982. "The 1887 Census of Texas' Hispanic Population," *Aztlan*, 12 (2): 271–77.

Kerr, Louise Ano Nuevo. 1977. "Mexican Chicago: Chicano Assimilation Aborted, 1939–52," in Melvin G. Holli and Peter d'A. Jones, eds., *The Ethnic Frontier: Group Survival in Chicago and the Midwest* (Grand Rapids, Mich.: Eerdmans): pp. 293–330.

Lamar, Howard Roberts, 1970. *The Far Southwest, 1846–1912: A Territorial History* (New Haven: Yale University Press).

Levenstein, Harvey A. 1968. "The AFL and Mexican Immigration in the 1920's: An Experiment in Labor Diplomacy," *Hispanic American Historical Review*, 48 (May):206–19.

McLemore, S. Dale. 1983. *Racial and Ethnic Relations in America*. 2d ed. (Boston: Allyn & Bacon).

Mazon, Mauricio. Forthcoming. *The Zoot Suit Riots: The Psychology of Symbolic Annihilation* (Austin: University of Texas Press).

McWilliams, Carey. 1973. *North from Mexico* (New York: Greenwood).

Meyer, Lorenzo, and Josefina Zoraida Vazquez. 1982. *Mexico Frente a Estados Unidos: Un Ensayo Historico, 1776–1980* (Mexico: El Colegio de Mexico).

Montejano, David. 1979. "Frustrated Apartheid: Race, Repression, and Capitalist Agriculture in South Texas, 1920–1930," in Walter Goldfrank, ed., *The World-System of Capitalism: Past and Present* (Beverly Hills: Sage): pp. 131–68.

Moore, Joan W. 1976. *Mexican Americans*. 2d ed. (New York: Prentice-Hall).

Moquin, Wayne, and Charles Van Doren, eds. 1971. *A Documentary History of the Mexican Americans* (New York: Bantam).

Murguia, Edward. 1982. *Chicano Intermarriage* (San Antonio: Trinity University Press).

Murguia, Edward, and W. Parker Frisbie. 1977. "Trends in Mexican American Intermarriage: Recent Findings in Perspective," *Social Science Quarterly*, 58 (December): 374–89.

Nava, Julian, and Bob Barger. 1976. *California: Five Centuries of Cultural Contrasts* (Beverly Hills: Glencoe Press).

Nostrand, Richard L. 1973. "'Mexican American' and 'Chicano': Emerging Terms for a People Coming of Age," *Pacific Historical Review*, 62 (August):389–406.

Pachon, Harry P., and Joan W. Moore. 1981. "Mexican Americans," *Annals of the AAPSS*, 454 (March):111–124.

Paredes, Americo. 1958. *"With His Pistol in His Hand": A Border Ballad and Its Hero* (Austin: University of Texas Press).

Paredes, Raymund. 1978. "The Origins of Anti-Mexican Sentiment in the United States," in Ricardo Romo and Raymund Paredes, eds., *New Directions in Chicano Scholarship* (La Jolla: Chicano Studies Program, University of California, San Diego): pp. 139–66.

Penalosa, Fernando. 1970. "The Changing Mexican-American in Southern California," in John H. Burma, ed., *Mexican-Americans in the United States* (Cambridge, Mass.: Schenkman): pp. 41–54.

———. 1980. *Chicano Sociolinguistics: A Brief Introduction* (Rowley, Mass.: Newbury).

Poston, Dudley L., Jr., David Alvirez, and Marta Tienda. 1976. "Earnings Differences between Anglo and Mexican American Male Workers in 1969 and 1970: Changes in the 'Cost' of Being Mexican American," *Social Science Quarterly*, 57 (December):618–31.

Price, Glenn W. 1967. *Origins of the War with Mexico: The Polk-Stockton Intrigue* (Austin: University of Texas Press).

Reisler, Mark. 1976. *By the Sweat of Their Brow: Mexican Immigrant Labor in the United States, 1900–1940* (Westport, Conn.: Greenwood).

Romo, Ricardo, 1982. "Mexican Americans in the Southwest: Patterns of Immigration and Integration." Paper presented at the International Conference on Regionalism in American Society and Culture, Amerika Haus, Berlin, 9 June 1982.

———. 1983. *East Los Angeles: History of a Barrio* (Austin: University of Texas Press).

Rosenbaum, Robert J. 1981. *Mexican Resistance in the Southwest: "The Sacred Right of Self-Preservation"* (Austin: University of Texas Press).

Ruiz, Ramon Eduardo. 1980. *The Great Rebellion: Mexico 1905–1924* (New York: Norton).

Samora, Julian, Jose Bernal, and Albert Pena. 1974. *Gunpowder Justice: A Reassessment of the Texas Rangers* (Notre Dame: University of Notre Dame Press).

Sanchez, George I. 1943. "Pachucos in the Making," *Common Ground* 4 (Autumn):13–20.

———. 1961–62. "The American of Mexican Descent," *Chicago Jewish Forum* 20 (Winter):120–24.

Sanchez, Rosaura. 1983. *Chicano Discourse: Socio-historic Perspectives* (Rowley, Mass.: Newbury).

Schoen, Robert, Verne E. Nelson, and Marion Collins. 1978. "Intermarriage among Spanish Surnamed Californians, 1962–1974," *International Migration Review*, 12:359–69.

Scott, Robin Fitzgerald. 1974. "Wartime Labor Problems and Mexican-Americans in the War," in Manuel P. Servin, ed., *An Awakening Minority: The Mexican-Americans*, 2d ed. (Beverly Hills: Glencoe Press): pp. 134–41.

Servin, Manuel P. 1974. *An Awakening Minority: The Mexican-Americans*. 2d ed. (Beverly Hills: Glencoe Press).

Stephens, Richard C., George T. Oser, and Zena Smith Blau. 1980. "To Be Aged, Hispanic, and Female," in Margarita B. Melville, ed., *Twice A Minority: Mexican American Women* (St. Louis: Mosby): pp. 249–58.

Stoddard, Ellwyn R. 1973. *Mexican Americans*. (New York: Random House).

Swadesh, Frances Leon. 1974. *Los Primeros Pobladores: Hispanic Americans of the Ute Frontier* (Notre Dame: University of Notre Dame Press).

Taylor, Ronald B. 1975. *Chavez and the Farm Workers* (Boston: Beacon).

Tirado, Miguel David. 1970. "Mexican American Community Political Organizations: The Key to Chicano Political Power," *Aztlan*, 1 (Spring):64–66.

U.S. Bureau of the Census. 1960. *Historical Statistics of the United States, Colonial Times to 1957* (Washington, D.C.: U.S. Government Printing Office).

Valdez, Luis. 1982. "The Tale of the Raza," in Renato Rosaldo, Robert A. Calvert, and Gustav L. Seligmann, Jr., eds., *Chicano: The Evolution of a People* (Malabar, Fla.: Krieger): pp. 269–72.

Weber, David J. 1982. *The Mexican Frontier, 1821–1846: The American Southwest under Mexico* (Albuquerque: University of New Mexico Press).

2. THE PSYCHO-HISTORICAL AND SOCIOECONOMIC DEVELOPMENT OF THE CHICANO COMMUNITY IN THE UNITED STATES[1]

Rodolfo ALVAREZ, *University of California, Los Angeles*

The psychohistorical and socioeconomic development of the Mexican origin people in the United States is traced through four generations. The "Creation Generation," characterized by economic subjugation and being the object of race and ethnic prejudice, appeared in 1848 when the Mexican American people were created as a people by the signing of the Treaty of Guadalupe Hidalgo. By 1900 the majority of Mexican Americans were members of the "Migrant Generation" who left a lower-class status in Mexico to enter a lower-caste status in the United States. Around the time of World War II, there developed another state of collective consciousness termed here the "Mexican American Generation." This generation moved to the cities, experienced some upward mobility, and managed to establish their claims as bonafide citizens of the United States in the eyes of only one of the social psychologically relevant populations—themselves. Finally, in the late 1960s, a new consciousness began to make itself felt among the Mexican Americans with the emergence of the "Chicano Generation."

The closest approximation to objective knowledge can be gained from the conformation of honestly different perspectives that subsume the same or related sets of facts. What is presented in this paper is a marshaling of historical fact from a perspective not traditionally taken into account in scholarly discourse on Mexican Americans. The objective is to confront the reality of Mexican American society as it has been experienced and from that basis to generate hypotheses for future multidisciplinary research in this area. For this purpose, four historical periods are identified here, and the climate of opinion within the generation of Mexican Americans that numerically dominates the period is described. What I mean by a "generation" is that a critical number of persons, in a broad but delim-

[1]Reprinted by permission of the author and the publisher from *Social Science Quarterly*, 53 (March):920–42 (1973).

ited age group, had more or less the same socialization experiences because they lived at a particular time under more or less the same constraints imposed by a dominant United States society. Each generation
reflects a different state of collective consciousness concerning its relationship to the larger society; psycho-historical differences related to, if
not induced by, the economic system.

I begin my analysis with the assertion that, as a people, Mexican Americans are a creation of the imperial conquest of one nation by another
through military force. Our people were thrown into a new set of circumstances, and began to evolve new modes of thought and action in order
to survive, making Mexican American culture different from the culture
of Mexicans in Mexico. Because we live in different circumstances, we
have evolved different cultural modes; just as we are neither identical
to "Anglos" in the United States nor to Mexicans in Mexico, we, nevertheless, incorporated into our own ethos much from both societies. This
is because we respond to problems of existence that confront us in
unique ways, distinct from the way in which Anglos and Mexicans experience them.

How, then, did we pass from being a sovereign people into a state of
being compatriots with the newly arrived Anglo settlers, coming mostly
from the southern United States, and, finally, into the condition of becoming a conquered people—a charter minority on our own land?

The coming of the Spaniards to Mexico began the development of a
mestizo people which has come to be the largest category of Mexican
society. The mestizo is the embodiment of biological, cultural, and social
heterogeneity. This sector of Mexican society was already numerically as-
cendant by the time Mexico gained its independence from Spain. Sovereign Mexico continued more or less the identical colonization patterns
that had been developed by Spain by sending a cadre of soldiers, mis-
sionaries, and settlers to establish a mission and presidio where Indians were brought in and "Christianized" (Moquin and Van Doren, 1972).
Once the Indians were socialized to the peculiar mixture of Indian and
Hispanic-Western cultural patterns which constituted the mestizo adaptation to the locale, they were granted tracts of land, which they cultivated
to support themselves in trade with the central settlement, and through
that, with the larger society with its center in Mexico City (Rives, 1913). As
the settlement grew and prospered, new outposts were developed further and further out into the provinces. Thus, Mexican society, like the
Spanish society before it, was after *land* and *souls* in its development of
the territories over which it held sovereignty (Rives, 1913). The Indian
quickly was subjugated into the lowest stratum of society to do the heavi-
est and most undesirable work at the least cost possible—although biologically "pure" but fully acculturated Indians frequently entered into the
dominant mestizo society. They also tended to marry settlers coming
north from central Mexico to seek their fortunes (Priestly, 1929). Light- and
dark-skinned alike were "Mexican."

What is of historic significance here is that in the early 1800s, particularly on the land now called Texas, this imperialistic system came into direct conflict with another (Lowrie, 1967), that sponsored by England which resulted in the creation of the United States of America. Both systems set out aggressively to induce the economic development of the area. However, while the Hispanic system sought economic development through the acquisition of *land* and *souls*, the Anglo system that had been established on the northern Atlantic seaboard was one of acquiring *land, but not souls* (Barker, 1928; Spicer, 1962). An Indian could not have been elected president of the United States as Don Benito Juarez was in Mexico. Rather, the Indian was "pushed back" as the European settlement progressed (Priestly, 1929). He had to either be manifestly cooperative in getting out of the way (and later into reservations) or be exterminated. The new society in the United States was, therefore, a great deal more homogeneous than in Mexico since it was fundamentally a European adaptation to the new land and not in any way a mixture of Indian and European elements.

It should be said here, without wanting to overemphasize, that there is some evidence from correspondence between Thomas Jefferson and James Monroe that these and other key figures in the United States had intended to take the Southwest long before U.S. settlers started moving into Texas (Rives, 1913). Insofar as the stage was not yet set for this final move, the coming of United States citizens into Texas was a case study in peaceful cooperation between peoples with fundamentally different ideological perspectives. The Anglo settlers initially and publicly made the minimal necessary assertions of loyalty to Mexico—despite the fact that they did not live up to the letter of the settlement contracts (Lowrie, 1967) which called for them to become Mexican citizens and Roman Catholic (de Santa Ana et al., 1928).

This cooperative experience lasted until approximately 1830–35. During this time Texas was being rapidly settled by Mexicans moving north ("rapidly," considering their form of colonization). Also, some Europeans, a few of them Roman Catholic, arrived in Galveston and settled throughout the territory (Conclin, 1847). Others, in a stream that was ultimately to become the majority, came from the southern region of the United States (Barker, 1928). I call this the cooperative experience because there is historical evidence that all of these people, regardless of their point of origin, cooperated relatively well with each other. The frontier was sufficiently rugged that all needed each other's help and ideas in order to survive. Because everyone was given title to generous amounts of land, there was no struggle over land, which was the capital that they all sought. This period may be characterized as one in which every group could, apparently, optimize accomplishment of its objectives. The Mexican government needed to settle the area to secure its claim over the land and to reap the economic gain from its productivity; the settlers, whatever their origin (Indian, mestizo, European, or Anglo) came to develop their own personal economic assets. Because the country was so biologically and culturally heterogeneous, the question of how to develop a stable functioning society was crucial, once the break with Spain had been accomplished. During this period, some Anglo filibustering (insurrectionist activity in a foreign country) did take place. However, there is evidence that other Anglo groups were instrumental in helping to put these activities down. The *general* tone of the times was that of intercultural cooperation. Each group learned from the others as they applied their resources to the economic development of the area.

Somewhere around 1835 began what I call the "revolutionary experience." This was a revolutionary experience, in the usual sense of the term, only toward the end of this phase, as was perhaps inevitable given widespread territorial ambitions in the United States (subsequently labeled "manifest destiny" by historians of the period). The conflict was exacerbated by an ideological struggle within Mexican society between federalists and centralists. These political philosophies, while based to a considerable degree on economic self-interest of the partisans of either faction, also embodied widely divergent views on the nature of man himself.

The centralists were for administrative control over all Mexican territory by the governing elite in Mexico City. The federalists, on the other hand, were idealists trying to implement in Mexico the noble political principles of the rights of man as enunciated by the United States Constitution (after which the federalists' constitution of 1824 was modeled) and by French political theorists of the Enlightenment. They were for egalitarianism in practice within a culturally and racially heterogeneous society, and not only in principle within a relatively racially and culturally homogeneous society, as in the United States. The centralists were skeptical of the possibility of self-government by a heterogeneous population, the major proportion of whom they considered inferior culturally, especially so because a poor country, such as Mexico, could not invest sufficient resources to educate the masses, who were mostly Indian (Keen, 1967).

It appeared to the majority of settlers in Texas—Mexicans, as well as others—that federalism would provide the best economic outcome for them. The province of Texas became a stronghold of federalism (Nance, 1963), and the majority decided to remain loyal to the federalist Mexican constitution of 1824. Santa Ana by this time had switched his ideological stance from federalism to centralism and had taken control of the central government in Mexico City. His reaction to events in Texas was to send troops to discipline the dissident province. However, the poorly professionalized army acted badly in Texas and alienated much of the populace by the unnecessary spilling of blood. The fact that many of these settlers came from the slaveholding South probably did not make relations with Mexicans, whom they considered inferior, easier. Heightened sentiment led to hostile actions, and a revolution was started. The upshot was that

Santa Ana personally came to command the army that was to put down the revolution and was himself defeated. Once the chief executive and the army of the sovereign country of Mexico were defeated, there was no real pressure for the dissident province to remain a loyal entity within the mother country—even though many of the settlers had set out originally simply to attain a federalist rather than a centralist government in Mexico. Furthermore, when the fighting broke out, adventurers and fortune seekers poured from the United States into Texas to participate in the fight. Evidence that these people, as well as their friends and relatives who remained behind, had a great sense of their "manifest destiny" to acquire more land for the United States (Ruiz, 1963) is abundant and is illustrated by the fact that from as far away as Cincinnati, Ohio, came contributions of cannons and supplies as soon as it appeared that separating Texas from Mexico was a possibility (Connor, 1971). Once hostilities began and these people began to pour in, the federalists loyal to Mexico were outnumbered, and full-blown independence from Mexico was declared. When Santa Ana was ultimately defeated, it was still not clear that Mexico would be incapable of reassembling an army and returning to discipline the dissident province. The extreme biological and cultural heterogeneity which characterized Mexico then (as it does today) was one of the bases of Mexico's difficulty in self-government (Zea, 1963; Villegas, 1964). The depth of Mexico's internal disarray became apparent soon enough. Texas was absorbed into the United States, provoking armed conflict with Mexico. If Mexico had not been able to discipline Texas, it certainly was no match for the well-trained and well-equipped U.S. Army backed by a *relatively* homogeneous society. By 1848, Mexico had lost approximately 50 percent of its territory. It appears that perhaps Santa Ana may have personally profited by Mexico's disarray (de Santa Ana et al., 1928). With the signing of the Treaty of Guadalupe Hidalgo, the Mexican American people were created *as a people*: Mexican by birth, language, and culture; United States citizens by the might of arms.

The Creation Generation

Following incorporation of the Southwest into the United States in the mid-1800s, there developed the experience of economic subjugation, followed by race and ethnic prejudice (Hale, 1845).

> Mexico ———— simply had to accept the best deal possible under the circumstances of military defeat; that deal meant that Mexico lost any respect it might have had in the eyes of the Mexicans living on the lands annexed by the United States. This rapid change must, certainly, have given them a different social-psychological view of self than they had prior to the break. The break and annexation meant that they were now citizens of the United States, but surely they could not have changed their language and culture overnight merely because their lands were now the sovereign property of the United

States; thus they maintained their "Mexicanness." Because their cultural ties were to Mexico, they were, in effect, "Mexicans" in the United States. As the number of "Americans" in the region increased, "Mexicans" became an ever smaller proportion of the population. They were . . . a minority. They thought, spoke, dressed, acted and had all of the anatomical characteristics of the defeated Mexicans. In fact, were they not still "Mexicans" from the point of view of "Americans" even though they were United States citizens by virtue of the military defeat and treaties that gave sovereignty to the United States? For all of these reasons and more, the "Mexican" minority could be viewed as the deviants onto whom all manner of aggressions could be displaced whenever the Calvinistic desire for material acquisitions was in the least frustrated. (Alvarez, 1971:19–20)

It is the psycho-historical experience of a rapid and clear break with the culture of the parent country, and subsequent subjugation against the will of the particular population under analysis—all of this taking place on what the indigenous population considered to be its "own" land—that makes the experience of Mexican Americans different from all other ethnic populations that migrated to this country in the nineteenth and twentieth centuries.

All of the factors necessary for the development of race prejudice against Mexicans, now Mexican Americans, were present after 1836 in Texas. Any bloody war will engender very deeply felt animosity between contending factions. Furthermore, in order to kill, without feelings of remorse, it may be necessary to define the enemy as being subhuman and worthy of being killed. In the case of the fight between centralist and federalist forces in Texas it should be noted that the centralist army was almost exclusively Mexican, having been recruited deep in Mexico and brought north by Santa Ana (Garrison, 1903). The federalist forces in the province of Texas, on the other hand, were a mixture of Mexican, European, and U.S. settlers (Garrison, 1903). However, once the centralist forces were defeated, the hatred toward them, that had now become a hatred of Mexico and Mexicans, could easily be displaced onto settlers who in every respect could be said to be Mexicans, even though they had been federalists and had fought for Texas independence.

Second, since most of the settlers in Texas who came from the United States were from the slave-holding South, the idea of racial inferiority was not unknown to them and could easily be used to explain the hostile emotions they held toward the Mexicans, against whom they had just fought a winning fight.

A third factor making for the development of intense race prejudice against Mexican Americans was economic. Once Texas became independent it left the door wide open for massive migration from the United States. Title to the land had already been parceled out under Mexican sovereignty. Through legal and extralegal means, the land was taken away from those provincial Mexicans, who as Texans had cooperated to try to give the province a measure of autonomy. These were the betrayed people, betrayed by their fellow Texans once Texas became fully autonomous. By 1900 even those provincial Mexicans who had owned large tracts of land and who had held commanding social positions in Texas and throughout southwestern society had been reduced to a landless, subservient wage-earner class—with the advent of a new English-language legal system, masses of English-speaking, land-hungry migrants, and strong anti-Mexican feelings—both by force of arms and through legal transactions backed up by force of arms (Knowlton, 1972). Furthermore, it was the importation of race prejudice that created an impenetrable caste boundary between the dominant provincials of northern European background and the provincial Mexicans. Once race prejudice was imported and accepted on a broad scale as an adequate explanation and justification for the lower-caste condition of local "Mexicans," these attitudes could spread rapidly into the rest of the Southwest, when the United States acquired a large proportion of northern Mexico. The experience of socioeconomic and political subjugation was repeated throughout the Southwest, with some variations for peculiar circumstances in specific areas, New Mexico in particular. Many of the distinctly Mexican American attitudes throughout the country today stem from the subjugation experience of this period.

The Migrant Generation

By 1900 the socioeconomic as well as political subservience of the Mexican American throughout the Southwest was well established. At the same time, the United States population was slowly becoming urbanized and was increasing *very rapidly* in size (Moquin and Van Doren, 1972). Instead of small farms and ranches that provided income for one family, agriculture was increasingly conducted on very large farms in order to grow massive quantities of food profitably. Despite the growing mechanization during the period (after 1900 and before World War II), the large farms and ranches of the Southwest required massive manual labor at certain periods in the growing season. Cheap Mexican labor was inexpensive and required much less care than the machines that were only then coming on the farms.

To provide the massive agricultural labor needed, recruiters were sent deep into Mexico to spread the word of higher wages on the large farms in the United States. Coincidentally with this "pull," political upheavals in Mexico created a population "push." The resulting huge waves of migrants (Moquin and Van Doren, 1972) coming north to work the fields give the name "Migrant Generation" to this period. Until the 1920s the migrant stream flowed north predominantly through Texas (where racial attitudes were imposed) and then beyond Texas to spread out over the agricultural region of the Great Lakes and western United States. It was not until after

World War II that the migrant flow began to come predominantly through California. These people have been called "immigrants" by social scientists and by policymakers because they moved from one sovereign country to another. However true their "immigrant" status might have been *legally*, they were not immigrants either *sociologically* or *culturally* because of the peculiar psycho-historical experience of Mexican Americans in the Southwest prior to 1900. Even those who eventually settled around the Great Lakes and later in the Northwest usually lived for a period of time in the Southwest where they were socialized into the cultural mode of the period.

There are at least four reasons why Mexicans arriving after 1900 but before World War II should be sociologically viewed as "migrants" who simply expanded the number of people who had more or less the same consciousness of lower-caste status as those Mexican Americans who were here prior to 1900. First, the post-1900 waves of Mexican nationals coming into the United States did not come into a fresh social situation where they were meeting the host society for the first time. They did not arrive with the "freedom" to define themselves in the new society in accordance with their own wishes and aspirations. Not only were they denied the social-psychological process of "role taking" among the established higher-status occupations, but demands and impositions of the dominant society were such that neither could they experiment with the process of "role making," i.e., the creation of alternative but equal-status occupations (Turner, 1962). They did not arrive with "freedom" that comes from having one's self-image and self-esteem determined almost exclusively from one's presentation-of-self to strangers, where these strangers have no prior experience with which to question or invalidate the social claims being made by the performance (Goffman, 1959). Immigrants from other lands arrived in the United States, and their place in the social hierarchy was, in a sense, freshly negotiated according to what the group as a whole could do here (Garfinkel, 1967). The social situation that the post-1900 waves of Mexicans entering the United States encountered was very different from that of immigrants from other lands. Their experience upon entering the United States was predefined by the well-established social position of the pre-1900 Mexican Americans as a conquered people (politically, socially, culturally, economically, and in every other respect.) They came to occupy the category closest to simple beasts of burden in the expanding regional economy.

The people coming from Mexico, in very large numbers after 1900, viewed themselves and were viewed by the dominant host society as the "same" as those Mexican Americans who had been living on the land long before (Moquin and Van Doren, 1972), during, and after the psycho-historical experience described above as resulting in the "Creation Generation." Before they came they knew they would find, and when they arrived they did find, a large, indigenous population with whom they had language, kinship, customs, and all manner of other genetic, social, cultural, and psychological aspects in common. The very interesting and highly peculiar circumstances in the case of the post-1900 migrant from Mexico is that he left a lower-class status in Mexico to enter a lower-caste status in the United States without being aware of it. The reasons he was unaware of it are multiple, reflecting the great network of characteristics in common with the people already here. The fact is that the vast majority of Mexican Americans never realized they were in a caste, as opposed to a class, category because they never tried to escape in any substantial numbers. The permeability of normative boundaries need never be an issue so long as no one attempts to traverse them. Until World War II there existed a state of pluralistic ignorance between those few individuals and groups of Mexican Americans who tried to escape the caste and the majority of relatively unaware members of the Mexican American population. The state of development of mass communications probably prevented widespread knowledge across the Southwest of the many isolated incidents that took place during this period. When a critical proportion of Mexican Americans began to earn enough money to pay fo their children's education and began to expect services that they saw non— Mexican American members of the society enjoying, they found out that they were not viewed just simply as members of a less affluent class, but, rather, as members of a despised caste. This was the critical test. If they had achieved skills and affluence with Mexico, race and ethnicity would have been no barrier to personal mobility into a higher socioeconomic class. It was the attempt to permeate through the normative boundaries and the subsequent reaction by the larger society that brought out in the open the way they were perceived by the dominant host society. During the period designated as the "Migrant Generation," there were many isolated instances of great conflict between groups of Mexican Americans trying to alter their lower-caste status, but they were locally overpowered, and a general state of acquiescence became the state of collective consciousness.

A second factor that characterized post-1900 incoming Mexicans as migrants rather than immigrants is that the land they came to was virtually identical to the land they left (Moquin and Van Doren, 1972). Today there is a sharp contrast between the terrain north and south of the border because of mechanization and irrigation for large-scale industrialized farming on the United States side, and the same old water-starved flatland on the Mexican side. However, in the early period when the great waves of migrants came, the land was sufficiently similar to what they had left behind that it did not require a cognitive reorientation for them.

The fact that the land they came to was very similar, physically, to the land they left behind is very important because it had been part of Mexico. Thus, the post-1900 migrant from Mexico to the United States was not leaving land to which he had a deep identity-giving psychological relationship and going off to another, very different "foreign" land, to which he needed to develop another sort of identity-giving relationship. The Irish immigrant, for example, experienced a great discontinuity between the land of origin and the land of destination. Furthermore, the nation-state and the culture identified with the land to which he was going had never been part of the nation-state and culture he was leaving behind. When the Irish immigrant left "Ireland" to go to "America," there surely must have been a very clear psychic understanding that he was leaving behind a land to which he had a very special relationship that made him an "Irishman." The post-1900 migrant from Mexico need not have noticed any change. He was simply moving from one part of his identity-giving land to another. The work that he was to perform on the land of destination was identical to the work he performed on the land of origin.

A third set of factors that distinguished the Migrant Generation from immigrants from other countries involves the physical nature of the border that they had to cross to come into the United States. Over large distances the border between the United States and Mexico was never more than an imaginary line. Even in that part of Texas separated from Mexico by the Rio Grande, the natural obstacles are minimal. During much of the year people could simply walk across, and certainly at other times they could cross the river as any other river might be crossed. The amount of *time* that it takes to cross the border also affects the degree of anticipatory socialization that a person can engage in prior to arrival at his point of destination. The Irish immigrant spent the better part of *two weeks* crossing an enormous physical obstacle, the Atlantic Ocean. The great physical boundary separating his land of origin from his land of destination could not escape his notice. The time it took to traverse that boundary afforded the immigrant the opportunity gradually, but profoundly, to engage in serious contemplation that allowed him to significantly "disassociate" his identity from nation-state and its culture and to engage in more or less effective anticipatory socialization for his new identity and new life in another nation-state and its culture. The point here is that the nature of the physical border (its overpowering size) and the time it took to traverse it made it virtually impossible for the immigrant not to be deeply conscious of the fact that he was entering a new society and, therefore, a new place within the structure of that society. This was not the case with the Mexican migrant.

A fourth set of factors distinguishing Mexicans of the Migrant Generation from immigrants from other countries is the nature of their activity in coming to this country. There is undoubtedly a significant psychic impact deriving from the degree to which the individual is a free and autonomous agent in determining the course of his own behavior. The greater the degree to which the individual perceives himself as self-determining, the less his behavior will precipitate a change of his already established identity. Conversely, the more the individual perceives (and his perceptions are validated) that his behavior is significantly determined by others, the greater will be the impact of that realization on his identity. The Irish immigrant, for example, had significant others affecting his behavior in such a way that he could not avoid considering the identity that he was rejecting and the one he was assuming. He had to ask for official permission to leave his country of origin, be physically conveyed across an ocean to enter a country he had had to obtain official permission to enter. Those actions forced him to consider his purpose in making the crossing, and whether he was prepared to abandon one identity for the other; whether he was prepared to pay the psychic price. The Mexican migrants, on the other hand, were "active agents," more or less in control of their own movement. They did not, in the early 1900s, have to ask anyone for permission to leave one country to enter the other. If they made their own personal decision to go, they simply went. There was no official transaction that in any way impinged on their collective self-identity. It took seven minutes to cross a river. The significance of the decision to swim or use the bridge is analogous to the modern-day decision either to walk downtown or to pay for a taxi—hardly an identity-making decision. It was not until the mid-1930s that the border was "closed," that is, when an official transaction was required to cross the border. By this time, however, such an enormous number of people had already crossed, and the Mexican American population, within the lower caste existing in the southwestern United States, was so large that it did not matter in terms of the conceptual argument. The later migrant waves simply inflated the lower caste and took on its psychic orientation (i.e., its collective state of consciousness), despite the fact that by the official transaction they were made conscious that they were now in the sovereign territory of another nation-state. This was so because all other factors still applied, and, in addition, the impact of the large population into which they moved was overwhelming.

The post-1900 migrants came mainly to Texas and California. There they assumed the already established lower-caste position we have described, as a consequence of the prior established social structure. Social-psychologically, the migrants, too, were a conquered people, both because their land of origin had been conquered by the United States and because the Mexican Americans, with whom they were completely commingled, had been treated as a lower caste of conquered people inside the now expanded version of the United States. As such, they were powerless appendages of the regional economy. Their manual labor was essential to the agricultural development of the area. But whenever the business cycle took a turn for the worse, they were easily forced to go back to Mexico (Moquin and Van Doren, 1972); they were forcibly deported. Their United States-born children were deported right along with the parents. The deportation of Mexican Americans—United States citizens—was not uncommon, since to the U.S. Border Patrol, U.S. Immigration Service ("Migra"), and the Texas Rangers there frequently seemed little or no difference between Mexican Americans and Mexican nationals; they were all simply "Mexican" (McWilliams, 1968).

There is for Mexican Americans a very bitter irony in all of this. The irony is that the post-1900 migrants and the pre-1900 lower-caste citizens of Mexican descent learned to live more or less comfortably with all of this largely because of their frame of reference. Both constantly compared themselves to Mexican citizens in Mexico. That they should have Mexico as their cultural frame of reference is understandable. The irony is, however, that they never compared themselves to other minority groups in this country, possibly because of geographic isolation. The price the Mexican American had to pay in exchange for higher wages received for stoop labor in the fields and for lower-status work in the cities was a pervasive, universal subjugation into a lower caste that came about silently and engulfed him, long before he became aware of it. He became aware of his lower-caste, economically powerless position only when he (or his children) tried to break out of the caste and was forced to remain in it. By that time it was too late. He had learned to enjoy a higher wage than he would have had in Mexico and to accept a degrading lower-caste position. His lower socioeconomic position in the United States was never salient in his mind.

The Mexican American Generation

Starting somewhere around the time of the Second World War, and increasing in importance up to the war in Vietnam, there has developed another state of collective consciousness which I call the "Mexican American Generation." This generation increasingly has turned its sense of cultural loyalty to the United States. As members of this generation were achieving maturity, they began to ask their parents:

> What did Mexico ever do for you? You were poor and unwanted there. Your exodus reduced the unemployment rate and welfare problems that powerful economic elements in Mexico would have had to contend with, so they were happy to see you leave. You remained culturally loyal to the memory of Mexico, and you had dreams of returning to spend your dollars there. You sent money back to your family relations who remained in Mexico. Both of these acts of cultural loyalty on your part simply improved Mexico's dollar balance of payment. And what did Mexico do for you except help labor contractors and unscrupulous southwestern officials to further exploit you? I am an "American" who happens to be of Mexican descent. I am going to participate fully in this society because, like descendants of people from so many other lands, I was born here, and my country will guarantee me all the rights and protections of a free and loyal citizen. (Alvarez, 1971:24–25)

What the members of the Mexican American generation did not realize was that, relative to the larger society, they were still just as economically dependent and powerless to affect the course of their own progress as the members of the older Migrant Generation. If the Migrant Generation had Mexicans in Mexico as their socioeconomic reference, the Mexican American Generation, in similar fashion, did not effectively compare its own achievements to those of the larger society, but to the achievements of the Migrant Generation. This comparison was a happy one for the Mexican American Generation. They could see that they were economically better off than their parents had ever been. They could see that they had achieved a few years of schooling while their parents had achieved virtually none.

What the Mexican American Generation did not realize was that their slight improvement in education, income, political efficacy, and social acceptance was an accomplishment only by virtue of comparison to the Migrant Generation, which started with nothing. The Mexican American Generation was far behind the black population as the black population was behind the Anglo on every measure of social achievement, i.e., years of education achieved, political efficacy, annual income per family, etc. But these comparisons were rarely made during this period when Mexican Americans changed from being a predominantly rural population employed in agricultural stoop labor to an urban population employed predominantly in unskilled service occupations. Today, for example, approximately 83 percent of the Mexican American population lives in cities, even though in most instances the mass media still portray Mexican Americans as rural stoop laborers. This was the period when the first relatively effective community protective organizations began to be formed. The organizing documents are so painfully patriotic as to demonstrate the conceptualized ambitions of the membership rather than their actual living experience.

The change of Mexican Americans from a rural to an urban population was precipitated by the rapid industrialization of agriculture that was brought about initially by the production requirements of World War II (and the simultaneous manpower drain required for the military) and was subsequently sustained and enhanced by the scientific and technological revolution that followed the war. Agriculture had increasingly been organized around big farms since 1900 in order to meet the demands of an expanding population. The massive production required by World War II in the absence of Mexican American labor—since the Mexican American population participated disproportionately in the war—led to the increasingly rapid conversion of agriculture to resemble the industrialized factory. During the initial phases of the war, much stoop labor was imported from Mexico (McWilliams, 1964), but later this became less necessary because machines increasingly were filling the need for all but the most delicate agricultural picking jobs. The entire economic system reached the highest development of the ideals of industrialized society. Perhaps more money and somewhat better working conditions were to be found in cities, but that was not because of any gains on the part of Mexican

Americans; it was rather because of the nature of urban living and industrial production in the post–World War II era of United States capitalism. Compared to the majority, the Mexican American still had no determinative input into the economic system. Lack of unions and lack of political effectiveness meant that the Mexican American was earning less than any other group for comparable work. Lack of education meant that the Mexican American did not have sufficient understanding of the nature of the society in which he lived and its economic system to even know that he was being treated unfairly. To the extent that he became conscious of his economically disadvantaged position, he was powerless to do anything about it.

At this point it is fair to ask: If the Mexican American Generation was so poorly educated, how did it ever get the training, skills, and general awareness of things to be able to move in large numbers from the fields to the cities and survive? Here, we have to introduce another statement about socioeconomic dependency. About the time of World War II when industrialization was beginning to be felt out in the fields, a substantial proportion of the Migrant Generation was nearing old age. Older people began to move to the cities to do the lighter work that was available there. At the same time, the young people were being moved into the war effort, young men to the military and young women to work in the war production industries, and the skills and technical competency that young Mexican Americans acquired in the military were directly transferable to employment in the cities after the war ended (Meier and Rivera, 1972).

Finally, the fact that they fought and saw their military friends and neighbors die in defense of the United States led Mexican Americans generally not to question their relative status in the economy and their lack of control over it. Little did they realize that everyone else was also experiencing both a real and an inflationary increase in economic standing; that other groups were experiencing a faster rate of economic increase because of their more effective direct participation in bringing it about. The Mexican American was only experiencing a kind of upward coasting with the general economy and was not directly influencing his own economic betterment. As a group, Mexican Americans remained at the bottom of the socioeconomic ladder.

Many Mexican Americans attempted to escape their caste-like status by leaving the Southwest to seek employment in the industrial centers of the midwestern Great Lakes region and in the cities of the Northwest (Moquin and Van Doren, 1972). Others went to California. A high degree of industrialization and a very heterogeneous population (religiously, ethnically, and politically) have always been the factors that attenuated discrimination against Mexican Americans in California. In fact, it is in California (and of course in the Midwest to a smaller extent) that the Mexican American first began to have the characteristics of a lower-*class* population on a massive scale, as opposed to the lower-*caste* experience. Of course, among the southwestern states on a smaller but widespread scale, the state of New Mexico seems to have come to a condition of class as compared to caste emphasis in a prolonged, gradual manner. This was perhaps due to the fact that the experience of the Migrant Generation never took place as intensely in New Mexico. The post-1900 immigrants came in large numbers to Texas early in the period and to California later (circa World War II) (Grebler, 1966; Gamio, 1930). However, New Mexico was essentially bypassed by the Migrant Generation. Furthermore, in New Mexico the experience of the Creation Generation was neither as severe nor as complete as it was in Texas and California. In New Mexico the Creation Generation experience did take place, but so-called Hispanos managed to retain some degree of political and economic control since they represented such a large percentage of the population—even with, or in spite of, all the extensive land swindles by invading Anglos (Knowlton, 1972). Interestingly, the fact that the Mexicans in middle and northern New Mexico were never fully subjugated into a lower-caste position is reflected in the linguistic labels they use to identify themselves. It may be argued that in order to differentiate themselves from those who had been subjugated into a lower caste (Moquin and Van Doren, 1972) the so-called Hispanos in New Mexico started calling themselves Spanish Americans some time around the First World War, despite the fact that their anatomical features were those of Mexican *mestizaje* and did not resemble Spaniards. At that time, their previous geographic isolation began to be ended by large numbers of Anglos from Texas who came to settle in the southeastern part of the state of New Mexico. The Texans brought with them their generalized hatred of Mexicans and their view of them as lower-caste untouchables. Thus, out of self-protection, New Mexicans started to call themselves Spanish Americans and to insist that they could trace their racial and ethnic origins to the original Spanish settlements in the area. The linguistic ruse worked so well that Mexican Americans in New Mexico came to believe their own rhetoric. The point to be made here is that this linguistic device was used by a large and isolated population that had not been fully subjugated into a lower caste to maintain in New Mexico the semblance of a class position. It is in New Mexico more than in any of the other southwestern states that Mexican Americans have participated in the society as people who have had the freedom and possibility of social mobility to become members of various social classes. They did this, however, at the price of altering their identity to make themselves acceptable to stronger economic, if not political, interests in the state. Today, however, the younger members of the post–World War II period are developing a new consciousness even in New Mexico. It is the current high school and college-age offspring of the so-called Spanish Americans who are using the term Chicano and who are demanding documentation for the presumed historic culture links to Spain (Meier and Rivera, 1972). What they are finding—the greater links to Mexican and to Indian culture—is beginning to have an effect on their parents, many of whom are beginning to view themselves as Mexican Americans with some measure of pride.

Some of the tensions within the Mexican American community during this period of time could be explained in terms of the generalized attempt to be more like "Anglo" citizens. Those people who were themselves born in the United States had greater legitimation for their claims of loyalty to the United States and for their psychic sense of security on the land. They, in fact, would, in various disingenuous ways, disassociate themselves from those whose claim to belonging could not be as well established; even parents of family elders who were born in Mexico and came over during the period described as the Migrant Generation would be viewed as somehow less legitimate. In the cities a slight distinction was made between the older Mexican Americans who now held stable working-class and small entrepreneurial positions as compared to newly arrived migrants from Mexico who entered the urban unskilled labor pool. This, of course, increased the insecurity and decreased the willingness to engage in collective action among the members of the Migrant Generation. They were in a particularly insecure position psychically, economically, and in almost every other regard. They were rejected and mistreated by the dominant Anglo population and rebuffed (as somehow deserving of the mistreatment) by their offspring.

The Mexican American Generation purchased a sense of psychic "security" at a very heavy price. They managed to establish their claims as bona fide citizens of the United States in the eyes of only *one* of the social psychologically relevant populations: *themselves*. The dominant Anglo population never ceased to view them as part of the "inferior" general population of Mexican Americans. The Migrant Generation never fully believed that their offspring would be able to become "Anglos" in any but the most foolhardy dreams of aspiring youth. They had a very apt concept for what they saw in the younger person wanting to become an Anglo facsimile: "Mosca en leche!" The Mexican American who so vehemently proclaimed his United States citizenship and his equality with all citizens never realized that all of the comparisons by which he evaluated progress were faulty. Because of his psychic identification with the superordinate Anglo, he abandoned his own language and culture and considered himself personally superior to the economically subordinate Migrant Generation. The fact that he could see that he was somewhat better off educationally and economically than the Migrant Generation led the Mexican American of this period to believe himself assimilated and accepted into the larger society. He did not fully realize that his self-perceived affluence and privileges existed only in comparison to the vast majority of Mexican Americans. He did not realize that for the same amount of native ability, education, personal motivation, and actual performance, his Anglo counterpart was much more highly rewarded than he. He never made the observation that even when he achieved a higher education, he still remained at the bottom of the ladder in whatever area of economic endeavor he might be employed. Individuals, sometimes with the help of protective organizations, did bring some legal action against personal cases of discrimination. But despite a growing psychic security as citizens of the United States, they did not make effective collective comparisons. The greater security that the Mexican American Generation achieved was a falsely based sense of self-worth. To be sure, because a sizable proportion of the population managed to exist for several decades with a sense of self-worth, they could give birth to what will be called the Chicano Generation in the next section of this paper. However much the Mexican American Generation may have been discriminated against educationally and especially economically, they did achieve enough leisure and economic surplus so that their offspring did not begin from a hopeless disadvantage at birth. This extra measure of protection was perhaps the greatest indicator that the Mexican American Generation was now part of a class and not a caste system.

The Chicano Generation

In the late 1960s a new consciousness began to make itself felt among Mexican Americans. By this time the population was solidly urban and well entrenched as an indisputable part of the country's working underclass. Migration from Mexico had slowed and was predominantly to urban centers in the United States. Theories of racial inferiority were dying, not without some sophisticated revivals, to be sure, but in general the country was beginning to accept the capacity of human populations given equal opportunities and resources. Moreover, despite the ups and downs of the marketplace, it was becoming clear to all that both technological sophistication and economic potential existed in sufficient abundance to eradicate abject poverty in the United States. These conditions had not existed in the Southwest with regard to the Mexican American population since that historical period immediately preceding the Creation Generation.

The Chicano Generation is now comparing its fortunes with those of the dominant majority as well as with the fortunes of other minorities within the United States. This represents an awareness of our citizenship in a pluralistic society. It is perhaps early to be writing the history of the Chicano Generation, but already it is clear that we have gone through an initial phase and are now in a second phase. The first phase consisted of the realization that citizenship bestows upon those who can claim it many rights and protections traditionally denied to Mexican Americans. The second phase, only now achieving widespread penetration into the population's consciousness, is that citizenship also entails obligations and duties, which we have traditionally not been in a position to perform. These two perspectives are rapidly colliding with each other. The general mental health of the Chicano community is being severely buffeted by the change in comparative focus and the relative current inability to achieve measurable success according to the new standards.

The parameters of the Mexican American population had been slowly changing, until by the mid-1960s the bulk of the post–World War II baby boom had reached draftable age and now faced the prospect of military service in the war in Vietnam. As a cohort, these young Mexican Americans were the most affluent and sociopolitically liberated ever. The bulk were the sons and daughters of urban working-class parents. However, a small proportion were the offspring of small businessmen; and an even smaller proportion were the offspring of minor bureaucratic officials, semi-professionals, and professionals. Especially in these latter types of families a strong sense of the benefits of educational certification and of the rights of citizenship had been developed. When the bulk of this cohort of young people reached draftable age, which is also the age when young people generally enter college, they made some extremely interesting and shocking discoveries, on which they were able to act because they had the leisure and resources to permit self-analysis and self-determining action.

Despite the fact that the Mexican American population has the highest school dropout rate of any ethnic population in the country, by the mid-1960s a larger proportion than ever before were finishing high school. These young people then faced three major alternative courses of action, all of them unsatisfactory. One course was to enter an urban-industrial labor force for which they were ill-prepared because a high school education is no longer as useful as in previous generations. And even for those positions for which a high school education is sufficient, they were ill-prepared because the high schools located in their neighborhoods were so inadequate compared to those in Anglo neighborhoods (Manuel, 1930; Clark, 1970). Moreover, persistent racial discrimination made it difficult to aspire to any but lower working-class positions. Another course of action, which a disproportionate number of young men took, was to go into military service as a way to travel, gain salable skills, and assert one's citizenship, as so many Mexican Americans had done in the previous generation. But unlike the Mexican American going into the military of World War II, the young Chicano of the mid-1960s went into a highly professionalized military, the technical skills for which he found difficult to acquire because of his inadequate high school preparation. So instead of acquiring skills for the modern technical society into which he would eventually be released, he disproportionately joined the ranks of the foot soldier and was disproportionately on their war casualty list. A third course of action open to the young Mexican American leaving high school in the mid-1960s was to make application for and enter college. This alternative was unsatisfactory because colleges and universities were not prepared to accept more than the occasional few—and then only those who would be willing to abandon their ethnicity. Refusal to admit was, of course, based on assertions of incapacity or lack of preparation. The former has racist underpinnings, while the latter is class biased since poverty and the inferior schools in which Chicano youth were concentrated did not permit adequate preparation for college and eventual middle-class certification.

No matter which course of action the bulk of the young people took, they disproportionately faced dismal futures. The larger society in which this ethnic minority exists had become so technical, bureaucratized, and professionalized—in short, so *middle-class*—that the strictly lower working-class potential of the bulk of the Mexican American population was irrelevant to it. Faced with the prospect of almost total economic marginality, the Chicano Generation was the first generation since the Creation Generation to confront the prospect of large-scale failure—of, in effect, losing ground, of psychically accomplishing less than the Mexican American Generation. The low-skill, labor-intensive society into which the Migrant Generation broke from its caste-like condition and within which the Mexican American Generation had established a firm, but strictly lower working-class status was disappearing. The United States was now predominantly professionalized and middle-class, with increasingly fewer labor-intensive requirements. It is in this relatively more limited context that the Chicano Generation came to have relatively higher aspirations.

With higher aspirations than any previous generation, with the prospect of a severe psychic decline compared to its parent generation, and now, because of its greater affluence and exposure, it had to compare itself to its youth counterpart in the dominant society. The broader exposure comes from many sources, including television and greater schooling in schools that, however inferior, were better than those to which prior generations were even minimally exposed. The Chicano Generation very painfully began to ask of what value its United States citizenship was going to be. At this time a significantly large proportion of the black population of this country "revolted." That may well have been the spark that ignited the Chicano movement. The Mexican American Generation had asserted its United States citizenship with great pride, asserting a relationship between economic success and their complete "Angloization" which was now shown to be false. The Chicano Generation came to realize that it was even more acculturated than the previous generation, yet it did not have any realistic prospects of escaping its virtually complete lower and working-class status. Its new consciousness came into being at a time when the Chicano Generation could hardly find any older role models with certified middle-class status. Comparatively, for example, out of a population of 24 million there are 2,200 black persons who have earned Ph.D. degrees in all disciplines combined (author's records, unpublished research). Among the 8 million (approximately) Mexican Americans there are only 60 who have earned Ph.D. degrees, when a similar level of disadvantage would lead us to expect approximately 730. The number of Ph.D.'s in a population is used here as a sort of barometric indicator of the level and quality of technically trained and certified leadership available to a population within a predominantly middle-class society. This is so because one can guess at the ratio of lawyers and doctors as well as master's and bachelor's degrees for each Ph.D. Thus the Mexican American population which began to enter colleges and universities in noticeable numbers only as late as the mid-1960s is almost completely lacking in certification for middle-class status.

Another indication of the lack of certified leadership that is self-consciously concerned with the welfare of the community is the lack of institutions of higher learning of, for, and by Chicanos. There are over 100 black institutions of higher learning (both privately and publicly supported, including colleges, universities, law schools, and medical schools). As recently as five years ago there were no such institutions for Chicanos. Now there are a handful of schools that either have been created ad hoc or where a significant number of Chicanos have moved into administrative positions due to pressures from large Chicano student enrollments. The point here is that however inadequate the black schools may have been, compared to "white" schools, they provided the institutional foci within which a broad sector of the black population has been trained and certified for middle-class status since prior to 1900. Mexican Americans neither could get into institutions of the dominant society, nor did we have our own alternate institutions. Thus, the difficulty of acquiring broad-scale consciousness of the condition of our people is apparent, as is the insecure ethnic identification of the early few who entered "white" institutions.

The Chicano Generation has experienced the pain of social rejection in essentially the same fashion (in the abstract) that the Creation Generation experienced it. That is, having been ideologically prepared to expect egalitarian co-participation in the society in which it exists, it had instead been confronted with the practical fact of exclusion from the benefits of the society. Because it can no longer compare itself to its immediate predecessors (no matter what the quantity or quality of accomplishments of the Mexican American Generation), it has to compare itself to other groups in the larger society. Relative to them it is more disadvantaged than any other ethnic group, except the American Indian with whom it has much in common both culturally and biologically. Every new demographic analysis gives the Chicano Generation more evidence of relative deprivation (Grebler, Moore, and Guzman, 1970), which leads to the rise of a psychic sense of betrayal by the egalitarian ideology of the United States not unlike that experienced by the Creation Generation. Members of the Chicano Generation are therefore saying to the previous generation:

So you are a loyal "American," willing to die for your country in the last three or four wars; what did your country ever do for you? If you are such an American, how come your country gives you less education even than other disadvantaged minorities, permits you only low status occupations, allows you to become a disproportionately large part of casualties in war, and socially rejects you from the most prestigious circles? As for me, I am a Chicano, I am rooted in this land, I am the creation of a unique psycho-historical experience. I trace part of my identity to Mexican culture and part to United States culture, but most importantly my identity is tied up with those contested lands called Aztlan! My most valid claim to existential reality is not the false pride and unrequited loyalty of either the Migrant Generation or the Mexican American Generation. Rather, I trace my beginnings to the original contest over the lands of Aztlan, to the more valid psycho-historical experience of the Creation Generation. I have a right to inter-marriage if it suits me, to economic achievement at all societal levels, and to my own measure of political self-determination within this society. I have a unique psycho-historical experience that I have a right to know about and to cultivate as part of my distinctive cultural heritage. (Alvarez, 1971:25)

The concerns of the Chicano Generation are those which predominantly plague the middle class: sufficient leisure and affluence to contemplate the individual's origin and potential future, sufficient education and affluence to make it at least possible for the individual to have a noticeable impact on the course of his life's achievements, but not so rich an inheritance that the individual's prominence in society is virtually assured (Homans, 1961). The Chicano Generation is the first sizable cohort in our history to come to the widespread realization that it can have a considerable measure of self-determination within the confines of this pluralistic society. Yet, we are only at the threshold of this era and have hardly begun to legitimate our claims to effective self-determination, i.e., acquisition of professional-technical certification as well as establishment of relatively independent wealth. Our capacity to secure middle-class entry for a sizable proportion of its population is threatened on two major fronts.

First, we are threatened by our redundancy or obsolescence at the bottom of the social structure. This has two dimensions: we cannot earn enough money to support a United States standard of living on laborer's wages; even if we were willing to do the few remaining back-breaking jobs, there would not be enough work to go around because these are being automated, and the few that are around will be taken over by cheap Mexican labor from Mexico, unless factory and farm workers can be organized effectively (Craig, 1971). Thus, in a sense, the economic bottom of our community is falling away.

Second, we are threatened because just as the middle-class sector of the larger society is getting ready to acknowledge our capacities and our right to full participation, we find that the major proportion of our population does not have the necessary credentials for entry—i.e., college, graduate, and professional degrees. When large corporate organizations attempt to comply with federal equal employment regulations concerning the Spanish-speaking population, they do not care whether the person they hire comes from a family that has been in the United States since 1828 or whether the person arrived yesterday from Mexico or some other Latin American country. The irony is that as discrimination disappears or is minimized, those who have historically suffered the most from it continue to suffer its after effects. This is so because as multinational corporations have begun their training programs throughout Latin America, and especially in Mexico, a new technically skilled and educated middle class has been greatly expanded in those countries. Many of these persons begin to question why they should perform jobs in their home country at the going depressed salaries when they could come to the United States and receive higher salaries for the same work and participate in a generally higher standard of living. This, in effect, is part of the brain drain experienced by these countries from the point of view of their economy. From the point of view of the Chicano community, however, we experience it as being cut off at the pass. That is, just as the decline of prejudice and the increase in demand for middle-class type positions might pull the Chicano community up into the secure middle class, a new influx of people from another country comes into the United States economy above it. Because it would cost corporations more to develop Chicanos for these positions, and because there is not a sufficiently aware and sufficiently powerful Chicano middle class to fight for the selection of Chicanos, and because of federal regulations which only call for Spanish surname people to fill jobs, without regard to place of origin, it is conceivable that the bulk of the Chicano population might become relegated into relatively unskilled working-class positions. Thus, the plight of the urban Chicano in the 1970s is not only technically complicated (how do you acquire middle-class expertise with working-class resources), but psychically complex (how do you relate to urban middle-class immigrants from Spanish-speaking countries and to rapidly organizing rural Mexican Americans) at a time when the general economy of the United States appears to be in a state of contraction, making competition for positions severe. Unless we can deal creatively with these trends, we will remain at the bottom of the social structure. This, in spite of outmoded social theories that postulated that each wave of new immigrants would push the previous wave up in the socioeconomic structure.

The introspectiveness of the Chicano Generation is leading to new insights. The psycho-historical links of the Chicano Generation with the Creation Generation are primarily those of collective support against a common diffuse and everywhere present danger. The threat of cultural extinction has led the Chicano to keep introspection as to what distinguishes him both from Mexicans in Mexico and from "Anglos" in the United States. This introspection has led to a deep appreciation for the positive aspects of each culture and a creative use of our inheritance in facing the future. The fight for self-definition is leading to a reanalysis of culture. For example, Anglo research has defined "machismo" as unidimensional male dominance, whereas, its multidimensional original meaning placed heavier emphasis on personal dignity and personal sacrifice on behalf of the collectivity—i.e., family or community. This concern for the collectivity comes through again in the emphasis placed on "la familia" in activities within a Chicano movement perspective. The fight for professional and middle-class certification is the fight for our collectivity to be heard. The objective is to produce enough certified professionals who can articulate and defend the peculiarly distinct culture of the Chicano community in such a manner that educational and other institutions of the dominant society will have to be modified. Until we have our own certified savants, we will continue to be defined out of existence by outsiders insensitive to the internal dynamic of our own collectivity. The willingness to fight may be what will get us there. YA MERO!

REFERENCES

Alvarez, Rodolfo. 1971. "The Unique Psycho-Historical Experience of the Mexican American People," *Social Science Quarterly*, 52 (June):15–29.

Barker, Eugene C. 1928. *Mexico and Texas, 1821–1835* (Dallas: P. L. Turner).

Clark, Thomas P. 1970. *Mexican Americans in School: A History of Educational Neglect* (New York: College Entrance Examination Board).

Conclin, George. 1847. *A New History of Texas; and a History of the Mexican War* (Cincinnati: District Court of Ohio).

Connor, Seymour V. 1971. *Texas: A History* (New York: Crowell).

Craig, Richard B. 1971. *The Bracero Program* (Austin: University of Texas Press).

de Santa Ana, Antonio Lopez, et al. 1928. *The Mexican Side of the Texas Revolution, 1836* (Dallas: P. L. Turner).

Gamio, Manuel. 1930. *Mexican Immigration to the United States* (Chicago: University of Chicago Press).

Garfinkel, Harold. 1967. *Studies in Ethnomethodology* (Englewood Cliffs, N.J.: Prentice-Hall).

Garrison, George P. 1903. *Texas: A Contest of Civilization* (Boston and New York: Houghton Mifflin).

Goffman, Erving. 1959. *Presentation of Self in Everyday Life* (New York: Anchor Books).

Grebler, Leo. 1966. "Mexican Immigration to the United States: The Record and Its Implications." Mexican American Study Project, Advance Report no. 2. Graduate School of Business Administration, University of California, Los Angeles.

Grebler, Leo, Joan W. Moore, and Ralph C. Guzman. 1970. *The Mexican American People* (New York: Free Press).

Hale, Edward E. 1845. *How to Conquer Texas before They Conquer Us* (Boston: Redding and Co., 17 March 1845).

Homans, George C. 1961. *Social Behavior: Its Elementary Forms* (New York: Harcourt, Brace & World).

Keen, Benjamin. 1967. *Readings in Latin American Civilization: 1492 to Present*. 2d ed. (Boston: Houghton Mifflin).

Knowlton, Clark S. 1972. "Culture Conflict and Natural Resources," in William Burch et al., *Social Behavior, Natural Resources, and the Environment* (New York: Harper): pp. 109–45.

Lowrie, Samuel Harmon. 1967. *Culture Conflict in Texas, 1821–1835* (New York: AMS Press, Inc.).

McWilliams, Carey. 1968. *North from Mexico* (New York: Greenwood).

————. 1964. *Brothers under the Skin*. Rev. ed. (Boston: Little, Brown).

Manuel, Herschel T. 1930. *The Education of Mexican and Spanish Speaking Children in Texas* (Austin: University of Texas Press).

Meier, Matt S., and Feliciano Rivera. 1972. *The Chicanos: A History of Mexican Americans* (New York: American Century Series, Hill and Wang).

Moquin, Wayne, and Charles Van Doren, eds. 1972. *A Documentary History of the Mexican American* (New York: Bantam).

Nance, Joseph M. 1963. *After San Jacinto: The Texas-Mexican Frontier, 1836–42* (Austin: University of Texas Press).

Priestly, Herbert L. 1929. *The Coming of the White Man, 1492–1848* (New York: Macmillan).

Rives, George L. 1913. *The United States and Mexico, 1821–1848*. Vol. 2 (New York: Scribner).

Ruiz, Ramon Eduardo. 1963. *The Mexican War: Was It Manifest Destiny?* (New York: Holt, Rinehart & Winston).

Spicer, Edward H. 1962. *Cycles of Conquest: The Impact of Spain, Mexico, and the United States on the Indians of the Southwest, 1533–1960* (Tucson: University of Arizona Press).

Turner, Ralph. 1962. "Role Taking: Process versus Conformity," in Arnold Rose, ed., *Human Behavior and Social Process* (Boston: Houghton Mifflin).

Villegas, Daniel Cosio. 1964. *American Extremes* (Austin: University of Texas Press).

Zea, Leopoldo. 1963. *The Latin American Mind* (Norman: University of Oklahoma Press).

3. THE MEXICAN ORIGIN POPULATION IN THE UNITED STATES: A DEMOGRAPHIC OVERVIEW [1]

Frank D. BEAN, *The University of Texas at Austin*

Elizabeth H. STEPHEN, *The University of Texas at Austin*

Wolfgang OPITZ, *The University of Texas at Austin*

Based on 1980 census data, this chapter presents a brief, descriptive overview of the demographic characteristics of the Mexican origin population in the United States. This population was characterized by an extremely rapid rate of growth during the 1970s, nearly doubling in size during the decade. Also, the fertility, mortality, occupation, and income patterns reflect the generally disadvantaged socioeconomic position of members of the Mexican origin population in American society.

The purposes of this chapter are to define and to describe in demographic terms a population that we will refer to as the Mexican origin population in the United States. This is not as easy a task as it might seem. Take, for example, the question of what to call this population. As the first chapter in this volume points out, members of this population have been variously designated "Mexican Americans," "Chicanos," "Mexicanos," "Hispanos," and "Spanish Americans." The term "Mexican American" has perhaps most frequently been applied, and research has shown that this is the term most widely adopted by members of this population when referring to themselves (Garcia, 1981). However, this designation involves a classificatory ambiguity, one that serves to illustrate the difficulties besetting any single designation. This is that the term "Mexican American" may be an inappropriate label when talking about undocumented immigrants from Mexico who, though residing in the United States, are citizens of another country.

Should such persons be classified as Mexican Americans? The answer

[1] Written especially for this volume. This research was supported in part by a grant from the Russell Sage Foundation.

may depend in part upon whether they are permanently or temporarily in the United States. Those who have been here for years, have lived in the same place and worked in the same job for a long period of time, have borne children in this country, and have contributed to this country's welfare through the payment of Social Security and income taxes are indistinguishable in their behavior from law-abiding citizens. It is partly for this reason that many persons refer to this group as "undocumenteds" rather than as "illegal aliens." Because undocumented immigrants are not citizens, however, some observers might argue that they should not be included in any delimitation of the Mexican American population. Others would not be so sure, reasoning that many undocumenteds have become permanent residents of this country on a *de facto*, if not on a *de jure*, basis. In either event, one thing is certain—many undocumenteds were enumerated in the 1980 United States Census (Warren and Passel, 1984), and thus have become a part of official statistics on the Mexican origin population (Bean, Browning, and Frisbie, 1984). And if the immigration legislation recently considered by the U.S. Congress granting amnesty to the most permanent members of the undocumented group is ever enacted into law, many undocumenteds would eventually qualify for citizenship in the United States, thus making them "Americans" in the fullest sense of the term.

Because of the ambiguities involved in applying the term Mexican American to undocumenteds, and because so many of them were counted in the 1980 Census, we think it is most accurate to speak of the Mexican origin population when talking about persons living in the United States whose ancestry could be traced back to Mexico. What does this mean in concrete terms? In both 1970 and 1980 the United States Bureau of the Census, in recognition of the possibility that the most relevant criterion for establishing a person's ethnicity may be the way they define themselves, included a question in the census schedule that allowed persons to indicate whether they were of Mexican origin or of various other Spanish origins. It is this criterion that we use to define the Mexican origin population. Hence, we include as members of this population all persons who "self-identify" themselves as being of Mexican origin in the 1980 Census. Viewed in this way, the population of Mexican origin in the United States increased during the 1970s from 4.5 to 8.7 million persons, or from 2.2 to 3.9 percent of the total population. As we shall see below, the figure of 8.7 million persons includes an estimated 1.1 million undocumented migrants from Mexico. This has implications both for interpreting demographic data on the Mexican origin population and for conclusions that are drawn about public policy questions (Bean and Sullivan, forthcoming [1985]).

Population Size and Distribution

The increase in the Mexican origin population from 4.5 million persons in 1970 to 8.7 million in 1980 represented a near doubling (a 93 percent

TABLE 1

1970 and 1980 Population by Ethnic Groups, and Mexican Origin Population for States with More Than 50,000 Mexican Origin Persons (in thousands)

	1970	1980	Percent Gain
United States	203,212	226,546	11.5
Black	22,539	26,488	17.5
Total Mexican origin	4,532	8,740	93.0
Southwestern states			
California	1,857	3,637	96.0
Texas	1,619	2,752	70.0
Arizona	240	396	65.0
New Mexico	119	234	98.0
Colorado	104	207	100.0
Nonsouthwestern states			
Illinois	160	408	155.0
Washington	33	81	142.0
Florida	21	79	280.0
Ohio	27	53	99.0

SOURCE: U.S. Bureau of the Census (1982: Table 7).

gain) of population size. This increase came about for three reasons. The first derives from the fact that the 1980 Census counted substantial numbers of undocumented migrants for the first time. This was the result of improved census coverage of Hispanic groups in the 1980 Census and, in all likelihood, of an increase in the flow of undocumented persons from Mexico to the United States during the 1970s. Warren and Passel (1984) have estimated that about 1.1 million such undocumented migrants were counted in the 1980 Census. A second source of increase in the size of the Mexican origin population was the continued flow of legal migrants into the United States. During the 1970s legal immigration from Mexico averaged almost 65,000 persons per year (U.S. Department of Justice, 1981). Although a substantial fraction of such persons, perhaps as many as a third, will eventually return to Mexico, legal immigrants make up a nontrivial portion of the increase in the size of the Mexican origin population from 1970 to 1980. The third major source of increase in the size of the Mexican origin population came from what demographers call natural increase, or that portion of population growth which results from an excess of births over deaths. Women in the Mexican origin population exhibit an unusually high birth rate, a factor that has contributed appreciably to the overall growth of this population since 1970. We will discuss some of the features of this high fertility in more detail below.

Where do the members of the Mexican origin population live? The vast majority reside in five southwestern states (Arizona, California, Colorado, New Mexico, and Texas), which contain 83 percent of the members of this

FIGURE 1

States with the Largest Absolute and Percentage Increases in the Size of the
Mexican Origin Population from 1970 to 1980, among States with 50,000 or more
Mexican Origin Persons in 1980

Legend: ▨▨▨ Largest Absolute Increase   ▧▧▧ Largest Percentage Increase
          ▩▩▩ Both

population. Excluding states with less than 50,000 or more Mexican origin
persons by 1980, however, the largest percentage increases in the size of
this population from 1970 to 1980 occurred outside the southwestern
states. As Table 1 and Figure 1 reveal, four of the five states with the
largest percentage increase in the size of the Mexican origin population
from 1970 to 1980 were outside the southwest (Florida, Illinois, Ohio, and
Washington). Although the greatest population increases measured in
terms of absolute numbers took place in the southwestern states, the
greatest relative increases occurred elsewhere, indicating that the Mexican origin population increasingly distributed itself outside the southwestern region during the 1970s.

Age and Sex Distribution

The Mexican American population is a young population, as can be
seen in Table 2. In 1980, 34.5 percent of the Mexican American population was under the age of 15. For comparison, 32.0 percent of the total

TABLE 2

Age and Sex Distributions of the U.S. Mexican Origin Population and the Mexican Population: 1980

Age Group	Total	Male		Female		Sex Ratio (males/ 100 females)
		Number	Percent	Number	Percent	
A. United States, Mexican Origin Population						
0–4	1,095,801	557,995	12.6	537,806	12.5	103.8
5–9	998,765	508,027	11.4	490,738	11.4	103.5
10–14	918,149	464,553	10.5	453,596	10.6	102.4
15–19	982,479	511,215	11.5	471,264	11.0	108.5
20–24	981,982	519,356	11.7	462,626	10.8	112.3
25–29	842,505	440,880	9.9	401,625	9.3	109.8
30–34	659,519	338,371	7.6	321,148	7.5	105.4
35–39	472,936	238,899	5.4	234,037	5.4	102.1
40–44	377,256	188,177	4.2	189,079	4.4	99.5
45–49	329,877	163,236	3.7	166,641	3.9	98.0
50–54	303,676	148,077	3.3	155,599	3.6	95.2
55–59	245,675	121,028	2.7	124,647	2.9	97.1
60–64	164,343	78,045	1.8	86,298	2.0	90.4
65–69	134,569	61,410	1.4	73,159	1.7	83.9
70–74	100,360	45,857	1.0	54,503	1.3	84.1
75+	132,547	57,515	1.3	75,032	1.7	76.7
Total	8,740,439	4,442,641	100.0	4,297,798	100.0	103.4
B. Mexico						
0–4	9,311,066	4,673,603	14.0	4,637,483	13.6	100.8
5–9	10,305,821	5,212,479	15.7	5,093,375	14.9	102.3
10–14	9,326,496	4,704,694	14.1	4,621,829	13.6	101.8
15–19	7,712,236	3,777,446	11.3	3,934,780	11.5	96.0
20–24	6,202,135	3,015,193	9.1	3,186,929	9.3	94.6
25–29	4,712,907	2,281,830	6.9	2,431,064	7.1	93.9
30–34	3,847,271	1,872,561	5.6	1,974,706	5.8	94.8
35–39	3,399,287	1,637,782	4.9	1,761,493	5.2	93.0
40–44	2,833,726	1,408,460	4.2	1,425,267	4.2	98.8
45–49	2,370,841	1,160,799	3.5	1,210,039	3.5	95.9
50–54	1,916,865	938,763	2.8	978,099	2.9	96.0
55–59	1,490,552	739,039	2.2	751,514	2.2	98.3
60–64	1,126,543	543,066	1.6	583,473	1.7	93.1
65+	2,826,835	1,329,547	4.0	1,497,270	4.4	88.8
Total	67,382,581	33,295,262	100.0	34,087,321	100.0	97.7

SOURCES: U.S. Bureau of the Census (1983a: Table 48); Mexico Instituto Nacional de Estadística, Geografía e Informática (1983).

FIGURE 2

Percent Distribution by Age and Sex for the Total U.S., U.S. Mexican Origin, Total U.S. Hispanic, and Mexican Populations: 1980

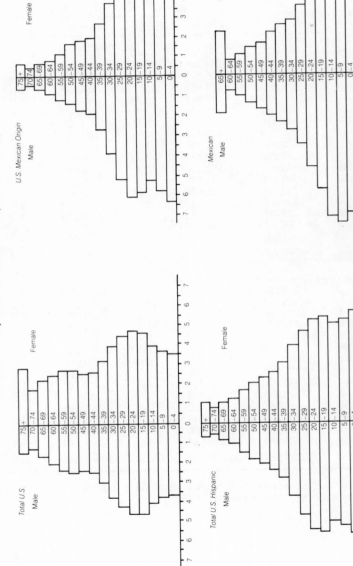

Sources: U.S. Bureau of the Census (1983a: Table 48); Mexico Instituto Nacional de Estadística, Geografía e Informática (1983).

Spanish origin population and 22.6 percent of the total U.S. population were under the age of 15. Another way to measure the youthfulness of a population is to look at its median age, or the age at which half the population is older and half is younger. The median age in the Mexican origin population was 21.9 years in 1980, compared to 23.2 years for the total Spanish origin population and 30.0 years for the total U.S. population.

The two primary factors contributing to the Mexican origin population being so young are high levels of fertility and a large number of young adults immigrating to the United States from Mexico. Evidence of immigration is most apparent in the 20−29 age group and favors males, as reflected in the sex ratio (the last column in Table 1), which shows the number of males per 100 females in the population. The greater preponderance of males until age 40 and the youthfulness of the Mexican origin population can also be seen in the population pyramid in Figure 2. The pattern of male preponderance and a young age structure is more accentuated in the Mexican American population than in the total Spanish origin population, both of whose pyramids differ greatly from the more beehived shape of the population pyramid for the total U.S. population.

It is perhaps more illuminating to compare the age and sex structure of the Mexican American population to that of Mexico. As seen in Table 2, Mexico exhibits an even younger population, with 42.9 percent of its population under age 15 in 1980. Perhaps even more interesting is that the Mexican sex ratios drop below unity (100.0) in the 15−19 age group and remain lower than would be expected through the 20−29 and 30−39 year age groups. The bulges in the male Mexican American population are neatly matched with indentations in the male population in Mexico. In both Mexico and the United States, the females show a much more graduated pattern by age group, reflecting the tendency for males to be more likely than females to immigrate to the United States (Bean, King, and Passel, 1983).

Fertility Patterns

Because the Mexican origin population constitutes a relatively small proportion of the total population and has historically been geographically concentrated in the Southwest, the only large-scale and thus the most reliable source of information on the fertility of this population comes from decennial censuses. Data on Mexican origin fertility prior to 1930 are largely restricted to Mexican-born women and their immediate offspring. Since 1930, however, a variety of operational definitions of the Mexican origin population have been applied that yield fertility data for the native as well as foreign-born populations. These include "race" ("Mexican") in the 1930 Census, Spanish mother tongue in the 1940 Census, Spanish surname (in the five southwestern states in the 1950 and 1960 Censuses), and questions on origin or descent in the November 1969 Current Population Survey (CPS) and in the 1970 and 1980 Censuses (Bradshaw and Bean, 1973). As noted above, each of these criteria define different but overlapping universes. While acknowledging the tenuous nature of the evidence for earlier periods and the problem of comparability across time periods, we would note that Mexican origin fertility has substantially exceeded that of the other white population for at least a century and a quarter. Bradshaw and Bean's (1972) study of records from the 1850 Census for Bexar County, Texas, showed that Spanish surname women had 32 percent more children under age 5 than did non-Spanish surname white women (2,040 versus 1,543 per 1,000 women).

A century later the differences were even more pronounced. For roughly the same geographical area in 1950 as that examined in 1850, 1950 Census data indicated child-woman ratios for Spanish surname women that were 63 percent higher than those for non-Spanish surname white women (Bradshaw and Bean, 1972). By 1960 this gap had diminished, but remained large at 42 percent. Such substantial ethnic differences were also characteristic of the entire Southwest in 1950 and 1960. For example, Spanish surname women aged 15–44 in the five southwestern states had 54 percent more children than did non-Spanish surname women in 1950 and 35 percent more in 1960 (Bradshaw and Bean, 1973). In 1970 substantial differences from other white fertility were still apparent. Mexican origin women aged 35–44 reported 46 percent more children ever born than did other white women (4.2 versus 2.9) (U.S. Bureau of the Census, 1973). By 1980 these numbers had dropped for both groups of women (to 3.6 children ever born for Mexican origin women aged 35–44 and to 2.5 children for other white women of the same ages), but the percentage difference remained high with Mexican origin surpassing other white fertility by 44 percent.

The continuing higher fertility of the Mexican origin population is thus readily apparent. It is of interest to ask under what circumstances the fertility of the Mexican origin population comes closest to that of the other white population. Stated differently, we might wonder whether Mexican origin women born in the United States with high levels of education are much different from other white women in their fertility levels. This question is relevant because women with higher education generally have lower fertility, and because Mexican origin women have less education than other white women. Also, women born in the United States might be expected to be more inclined to have smaller families than women born in Mexico, a country with much higher fertility than the United States. Table 3 presents data compiled by Bean and Swicegood (forthcoming [1985]) that are relevant to this question. Although computed for women aged 20–34 who thus had not yet finished their childbearing, it shows that in 1980 native-born Mexican origin women with 16+ years of education averaged about three-tenths of a child more than comparable other white women (1.21 versus 0.91 children). In other words, among both the Mexi-

TABLE 3

Mean Number of Children Ever Born by Education, Ethnic Group, and Nativity,
Ever-Married Women Ages 20–34, United States: 1980

| | Education (in years) | | | | | |
	0–8	9–11	12	13–15	16+	Total
Ethnic subgroups						
Other whites	2.41	2.09	1.54	1.27	0.91	1.45
Mexican origin	2.69	2.25	1.85	1.57	1.36	2.19
Nativity of Mexican origin women						
Foreign-born	2.58	2.05	1.81	1.67	1.74	2.31
Native-born	3.11	2.37	1.85	1.53	1.21	2.08

SOURCE: Bean and Swicegood (forthcoming [1985]).

can origin and the other white group, fertility is lower at higher levels of education. Despite the fact that it is also lower than it was at earlier periods, the fertility of highly educated native-born Mexican origin women exceeds that of highly educated other white women by 30 to 40 percent, although it falls below the level of other white women of all educational levels combined.

Family and Marital Status

As seen in Table 4, Mexican origin families and households are larger than those of both the total Spanish origin and the total U.S. population, reflecting again the higher fertility of Mexican origin families. In 1980 persons of Mexican origin were more likely to live in a married couple family (77.7 percent) than were persons of Spanish origin as a whole (74.5 percent), but less likely than persons in the total U.S. population (82.1 per-

TABLE 4

Persons Per Household and Per Family and Percent in Married Couple Families
and Female-Headed Households for Total, Mexican Origin, and
Spanish Origin Populations, United States: 1980

Persons	Total Population	Spanish Origin	Mexican Origin
Persons per household	2.75	3.48	3.74
Persons per family	3.27	3.92	4.14
Percent in married couple family	82.1	74.5	77.7
Percent female-headed household	14.3	19.9	16.4

SOURCE: U.S. Bureau of the Census (1983a: Table 48).

cent). The percent of Mexican origin families headed by a female with no husband present was also intermediate between that of the total U.S. population and that of the Spanish origin population, as shown in Table 4.

Marital status for the Mexican origin, total Spanish, and total U.S. population are shown in Table 5. Both the Mexican and the Spanish origin groups exhibit a higher percentage of single males and females than in the total U.S. population, because of the youthfulness of the population. In general, however, the marital status patterns are similar across the three groups. One exception is the high percentage of female widows in the total United States population, which is not evident in either the Spanish or Mexican origin population. It should also be noted that divorce is slightly less prevalent in the Mexican origin population, although separation is more prevalent than in the total United States (but not the total Spanish origin) population. Perhaps because many of them are Catholic and be-

TABLE 5

Marital Status for Total, Spanish Origin, and Mexican Origin Populations, United States: 1980

Marital Status	Total		Male		Female	
	Number	Percent	Number	Percent	Number	Percent
Total						
Single	46,159,302	26.3	25,132,125	30.0	21,027,177	23.0
Married	100,426,606	57.3	50,354,476	60.1	50,072,130	54.8
Separated	4,079,553	2.3	1,654,630	2.0	2,424,923	2.7
Widowed	13,473,592	7.7	2,155,696	2.6	11,317,896	12.4
Divorced	11,116,413	6.3	4,538,924	5.4	6,577,489	7.2
Total	175,255,466	100.0	83,835,851	100.0	91,419,615	100.0
Spanish Origin						
Single	3,133,397	31.5	1,747,330	35.6	1,386,067	27.5
Married	5,361,653	54.0	2,707,244	55.2	2,654,409	52.8
Separated	385,531	3.9	132,837	2.7	252,694	5.0
Widowed	443,975	4.5	80,896	1.7	363,079	7.2
Divorced	608,765	6.1	233,551	4.8	375,214	7.5
Total	9,933,321	100.0	4,901,858	100.0	5,031,463	100.0
Mexican Origin						
Single	1,804,023	31.5	1,036,075	35.6	767,948	27.3
Married	3,198,420	55.8	1,633,565	56.1	1,564,855	55.6
Separated	173,989	3.0	65,728	2.3	108,261	3.8
Widowed	239,850	4.2	47,953	1.6	191,897	6.8
Divorced	311,442	5.4	128,745	4.4	182,697	6.5
Total	5,727,724	100.0	2,912,066	100.0	2,815,658	100.0

SOURCE: U.S. Bureau of the Census (1983a: Table 48).

cause of their relatively lesser ability to afford the economic cost of divorce, members of the Mexican origin population may be more reluctant to seek divorce, being more likely instead to remain in a separated state.

Mortality

Comparative death rates provide critical indicators of the overall health status and general well-being of populations. The lower the mortality and the longer the life expectancy of a population, the greater the health status and general well-being of that population. Demographic research has for years documented the generally higher mortality and shorter life expectancy of the Mexican origin population (e.g., Roberts, 1977), differences that some observers have found to be diminishing over the past 15 years or so (Bradshaw and Fonner, 1978; Schoen and Nelson, 1981). The most recent information on this subject, based in part on 1980 Census data, tends to support this idea, namely that convergence in mortality patterns between the two populations has occurred. For example, life expectancy at birth for the Spanish surname and Spanish origin populations in Texas in 1980 have been computed by Sullivan et al. (1984), who estimated a life expectancy for Spanish surname males of 69.6 years and for Spanish origin males of 71.0 years (Table 6), either of which comes very close to the life expectancy of Anglo males, which is 70.2 years. A similar pattern obtains among females. It is of some interest that life expectancies obtained using a Spanish surname identifier are slightly lower than the Anglo life expectancies, whereas the ones obtained using the Spanish origin identifier are slightly higher. This demonstrates that the use of different identifiers can sometimes give different results, although the present differences are very small, particularly relative to the much longer life expectancies for both the Mexican origin and Anglo populations compared to the black population.

Consideration of mortality patterns classified by cause of death provides further insight into the relative health status of the Mexican origin and Anglo populations. Researchers have often observed that younger (under age 45) males exhibit higher death rates due to violent causes

TABLE 6

Life Expectancy at Birth for Mexican American, Anglo, and Black Males and Females: Texas, 1980

Sex	Spanish Surname	Spanish Origin	Anglo	Black
Male	69.6	71.0	70.2	64.4
Female	77.1	78.7	78.1	73.6

Source: Sullivan et al. (1984: Table 2).

(motor vehicle accidents, other accidents, homicide, etc.) than do Anglo males (Robinson, 1980). Less frequently emphasized is that younger Mexican origin males reveal higher mortality rates due to other causes as well. Gillespie and Sullivan (1983) have recently analyzed death rates by cause and ethnicity for New Mexico. Their results showed mortality rates for younger Mexican origin males that are higher than those for young Anglo males not only for violent but also for all other causes of death (Table 7). When the "all other causes" category is broken down, the rates are found to be higher among Mexican origin males mostly because of higher death rates due to cirrhosis of the liver and to alcoholism. In short, the fact that the life expectancies of Spanish surname or of Spanish origin males are nearly equivalent to that of Anglo males is a somewhat misleading indicator of the "well-being" of the Mexican origin population. While members of this population over age 45 enjoy a mortality advantage compared to Anglo males, younger Mexican origin males are more likely than Anglos to die of accidents and alcohol-related diseases, a pattern that seems unlikely to suggest greater well-being.

We also note that the pattern of mortality based on data from New Mexico indicates high mortality for Hispanic infants, as seen in the top row of Table 7. Studies by Powell-Griner and Streck (1982) and Roberts (1977) indicated that neonatal mortality rates among the Spanish surname population may be artificially low owing to the nonreporting of a child's death by some Mexican origin women. To the extent that this occurs, then the infant mortality ratios shown in Table 7 (in the first row) could be even higher.

TABLE 7

Ratio of Mortality for Spanish Surname Males to That of Other White Males by Age and Cause: New Mexico, 1976–78

Age	All Causes	All Violent Causes	All Other Causes
1	1.38	1.44	1.33
5	1.00	0.95	1.07
15	1.01	1.01	1.00
25	1.35	1.31	1.45
35	1.61	1.81	1.46
45	1.04	1.18	1.00
55	0.58	0.76	0.56
65	0.63	1.04	0.61
75	0.79	0.72	0.80
85	0.55	0.42	1.06

SOURCE: Gillespie and Sullivan (1983: Table 10).

Labor Force Participation, Occupational Structure, and Income Patterns

More direct evidence of the relative socioeconomic standing of different ethnic groups may be seen in their patterns of labor force participation, occupational structure, and income attainment. For example, among
all Hispanic males in 1980, Mexican origin males showed the highest labor force participation rates, exceeding even the rates for whites, as can
be seen in Table 8. In the case of females, the labor force participation
rate for Mexican origin women, while slightly lower than that of Cuban and
of other Hispanic women in 1980, has increased markedly throughout the
1970s, from 40 percent of Mexican origin women in the labor force in 1974
to 49 percent in 1980 (National Commission for Employment Policy, 1982;
U.S. Bureau of the Census, 1983b).

Employment rates do not provide as sensitive measures of the relative
socioeconomic standing of ethnic groups as do unemployment rates,
which are defined as the percentage of those who do not have a job,

TABLE 8

Labor Force Participation and Unemployment Rates by Race/Ethnicity and Sex: 1980

Race or Ethnicity by Sex	Labor Force Participation		Unemployment	
	Number	Percent	Number	Percent
Total Hispanic origin				
Male	3,686,475	78.0	304,850	8.5
Female	2,407,769	49.3	231,016	9.6
Mexican origin				
Male	2,217,766	79.7	188,560	8.7
Female	1,323,513	49.0	130,459	9.9
Puerto Rican				
Male	434,260	71.4	45,531	11.1
Female	270,693	40.1	34,029	12.7
Cuban				
Male	242,601	78.0	12,260	5.1
Female	195,361	55.4	14,005	7.2
Other Hispanic origin				
Male	791,848	77.2	58,519	5.8
Female	618,202	53.4	52,503	8.5
White				
Male	50,901,992	76.0	2,883,477	5.7
Female	35,978,867	49.4	2,001,237	5.6
Black				
Male	5,502,593	66.7	646,401	12.3
Female	5,213,796	53.3	583,837	11.3

Source: U.S. Bureau of the Census (1983b: Table 168).

TABLE 9

Occupational Distribution of Employed Men by Race and Ethnicity, 1980

Occupation	Total Hispanic	Mexican Origin	Puerto Rican	Cuban	Other Hispanic	White	Black
White-collar	26.9	21.1	30.0	45.4	35.6	45.0	26.8
Professional, technical, and kindred workers	7.4	5.5	7.0	12.3	11.3	14.8	7.9
Managers and administrators, excluding farm	6.6	5.1	6.3	12.9	9.1	13.7	5.7
Sales	5.8	4.7	5.7	10.7	7.1	9.9	3.9
Clerical and kindred workers	7.1	5.8	11.0	9.5	8.1	6.6	9.3
Blue-collar	73.1	78.9	70.0	54.6	64.4	55.0	73.2
Craft and kindred workers	20.7	21.9	16.1	18.7	20.1	21.4	15.5
Operatives and Laborers, excluding farm	32.5	35.5	34.3	22.1	26.8	21.2	37.3
Farmers and farm managers	0.5	0.6	0.1	0.2	0.5	2.4	0.5
Farm laborers and supervisors	6.0	8.6	2.1	1.2	2.3	1.9	2.9
Service workers	13.3	12.2	17.4	12.4	14.5	8.1	16.9

SOURCE: U.S. Bureau of the Census (1983b: Table 169).

among those who are employed or looking for work. When we turn to these indicators in Table 8, we find that the Mexican origin population ranks next-to-last among the Hispanic groups, exhibiting unemployment rates for men and women in 1980 that were exceeded only by those among Puerto Ricans. To obtain some perspective on these numbers, it is useful to note that they are over 50 percent higher than the unemployment rates for all whites. Hence, although the Mexican origin population is characterized by high rates of employment, it is also characterized by relatively high rates of unemployment. Taken together, these figures underscore the tendency for the members of this population to seek employment, a pattern that has been reinforced over the years by labor migration streams from Mexico.

Further evidence concerning patterns of ethnic stratification is revealed in occupational patterns (see Table 9). Only 21.1 percent of Mexican origin men held white-collar jobs in 1980, as compared to 45.0 percent of all white men. The greatest concentration of Mexican origin men occurred in the operative and laborer category (35.5 percent). Also, the tendency of this population to work in manual occupations is further evident in Mexican origin males, showing the highest percentage in the farm laborer cat-

TABLE 10

Occupational Distribution of Employed Women by Race and Ethnicity, 1980

Occupation	Total Hispanic	Mexican Origin	Puerto Rican	Cuban	Other Hispanic	White	Black
White-collar	51.5	48.3	55.4	58.6	54.2	70.3	51.8
Professional, technical, and kindred workers	9.7	8.4	10.9	11.5	11.4	18.0	15.2
Managers and administrators, excluding farm	4.9	4.2	4.6	6.5	5.8	7.9	4.7
Sales	9.4	9.5	8.0	10.1	9.6	12.1	6.1
Clerical and kindred workers	27.5	26.2	31.9	30.5	27.4	32.3	25.8
Blue-collar	48.5	51.7	44.6	41.4	45.8	29.7	48.2
Craft and kindred workers	3.9	4.0	3.5	4.4	3.7	2.2	2.3
Operatives and Laborers, excluding farm	22.0	22.0	25.5	24.3	19.9	10.4	16.1
Farmers and farm managers	0.1	0.1	0.0	0.1	0.1	0.4	0.1
Farm laborers and supervisors	1.8	2.8	0.4	0.3	0.5	0.6	0.5
Service workers	20.8	22.8	15.2	12.4	21.5	16.1	29.2

SOURCE: U.S. Bureau of the Census (1983b: Table 169).

egory. Also, among Hispanic females (Table 10), Mexican origin women exhibited the smallest percentage of white-collar workers in clerical and kindred occupations. Within the Mexican origin group, women were largely concentrated in two other broad occupational groupings—operatives and laborers and service workers.

The relatively poor occupational position of the Mexican origin population is further reflected in wages and incomes. A comparison of the racial and ethnic groups in Table 11 reveals that Mexican origin males and females received by far the lowest wages of any group shown. The median annual income of white males was over $4,000 higher than that of Mexican origin males. The median annual incomes for females were uniformly much lower than those for males, but again Mexican origin women received the next-to-lowest yearly income of any race or ethnic group. The low median annual income for 1979 was ameliorated only by the high labor force participation rates and hours worked by the Mexican origin population. The question of whether these differences in earnings owe more to such factors as low education or to patterns of discrimination is addressed elsewhere in this volume by McLemore and Romo and Reimers, although researchers do not always agree on this matter. Without

TABLE 11

Average Hourly Wage and Median Annual Income by Race/Ethnicity and Sex

Race or Ethnicity by Sex	Average Hourly Wage, 1975[a]	Median Annual Income, 1979[b]
Total Hispanic		
Male	$4.58	$9,078
Female	3.03	4,733
Mexican American		
Male	4.31	8,858
Female	2.88	4,556
Puerto Rican		
Male	4.52	8,519
Female	3.36	4,473
Cuban		
Male	5.33	10,249
Female	3.47	5,307
Other Spanish		
Male	5.20	9,855
Female	3.04	5,186
White		
Male	5.97	13,029
Female	3.67	5,378
Black		
Male	4.65	7,835
Female	3.46	4,676

SOURCES: National Commission for Employment Policy (1982: Table 8); U.S. Bureau of the Census (1983b: Table 170).

[a] Persons 14 years of age or older, working for a wage or salary.

[b] Persons 15 years of age or older with income.

question, however, there is consensus that improved education would significantly increase earnings in the Mexican origin population.

Summary and Conclusions

The purpose of this chapter has been to present a brief, descriptive overview of the demographic characteristics of the Mexican origin population in the United States. As assessed by the data from the 1980 Census, perhaps the most distinguishing feature of this population has been its extremely rapid rate of growth during the 1970s. While most of this increase could be attributed to the high fertility generally characteristic of Mexican origin women, a substantial part of it was also due to the influx and the counting in the 1980 Census of undocumented migrants from Mexico. Over a million such persons have been estimated to have been residing in the United States in 1980. It is impossible to know whether this group represents a small or large fraction of the total number of undocumented immigrants from Mexico in the country. The research of Bean, King, and Passel (1983) suggested that the total number ranges from 1.5 to 3.8 million persons. Based on their figures, the 1980 Census could have counted anywhere from 30 to more than 75 percent of the Mexican undocumented immigrants. What is most significant about all of these statistics is that they point to a number of undocumented Mexican immigrants in the United States in 1980 that is substantially below the number many observers had previously thought were in this country. Whatever the impact of such immigrants on the economy of the United States, this impact can only be diminished if the total number is substantially less than previously believed (Bean and Sullivan, forthcoming [1985]).

Second, an overriding demographic feature of the Mexican origin population is its generally disadvantaged socioeconomic status. This shows up when measured directly, as indicated by higher rates of unemployment, by a greater concentration of both males and females in lower-level white-collar occupations and manual blue-collar occupations, and by lower wages and income in the case of Mexican origin men and women, especially when compared to the earnings level of all whites. The disadvantaged position of the Mexican origin population in American society is also revealed in other demographic indicators. The fertility of Mexican origin women remains considerably higher than does that of Anglo women, although the differences are substantially reduced among native-born Mexican origin women with high levels of education. However, because only a small fraction of Mexican origin women have achieved such levels of education, the overall fertility level for the population remains high. Also, levels of infant mortality within the Mexican origin population remain considerably higher than they do in the Anglo population. This suggests that the overall health status and general well-being of the Mexican origin population falls below that of the other white population. The seemingly similar life expectancies at birth for Mexican origin males and females compared to Anglos tend to obscure a pattern of death rates among Mexican origin males that is high among younger males and higher than that of Anglo males. When these are examined by cause of death, the higher death rates due to violent causes, cirrhosis of the liver, and alcohol-related diseases suggest a mortality pattern resulting from a position of socioeconomic disadvantage in the society.

In general, the sociodemographic characteristics of the Mexican origin population imply a socioeconomic position intermediate to those of blacks and Anglos. This is consistent with the research of Massey and his associates (Massey, 1983; Massey and Mullan, 1984), which indicated that blacks are much more residentially segregated from Anglos than are members of the Mexican origin population. The research by Massey and associates has shown that racial and ethnic patterns of residential segregation imply that less discrimination has been imposed on the Mexican origin population than on the black population in this country. While the results of the present overview are consistent with this interpretation, they also indicate that a considerable amount of progress will still have to occur before the socioeconomic and demographic behavior of both groups may be said to reflect complete assimilation into American society.

REFERENCES

Bean, Frank D., Harley L. Browning, and W. Parker Frisbie. 1984. *What the 1980 Census Tells Us about the Characteristics of Illegal and Legal Mexican Immigrants*. Texas Population Research Center Papers, no. 6.010 (Austin: The University of Texas at Austin, Population Research Center).

Bean, Frank D., Allan G. King, and Jeffrey S. Passel. 1983. "The Number of Illegal Migrants of Mexican Origin in the United States: Sex Ratio-based Estimates for 1980," *Demography*, 20 (February):99–109.

Bean, Frank D., and Teresa A. Sullivan. Forthcoming, 1985. "Immigration as a Social Problem: The Simpson-Mazzoli Bill," *Society*.

Bean, Frank D., and Gray Swicegood. Forthcoming, 1985. *Mexican American Fertility Patterns*. Center for Mexican American Studies Monograph Series (Austin: University of Texas Press).

Bradshaw, Benjamin S., and Frank D. Bean. 1972. "Some Aspects of the Fertility of Mexican Americans," in *Demographic and Social Aspects of Population Growth, The Commission on Population Growth and the American Future Research Papers*, vol. 1 (Washington, D.C.: U.S. Government Printing Office): pp. 139–68.

————. 1973. "Trends in the Fertility of Mexican Americans: 1950–1970," *Social Science Quarterly*, 53 (March):688–96.

Bradshaw, Benjamin S., and Edward Fonner, Jr. 1978. "The Mortality of Spanish-Surnamed Persons in Texas: 1969–1971," in Frank D. Bean and W. Parker Frisbie, eds., *The Demography of Racial and Ethnic Groups* (New York: Academic Press): pp. 261–82.

Garcia, John. 1981. "Yo Soy Mexicano . . . : Self-Identity and Sociodemographic Correlates," *Social Science Quarterly*, 62 (March):88–98.

Gillespie, Francis P., and Teresa A. Sullivan. 1983. *What Do Current Estimates of Hispanic Mortality Really Tell Us?* Texas Population Research Center Papers, no. 5.010 (Austin: The University of Texas at Austin, Population Research Center).

Massey, Douglas S. 1983. "A Research Note on Residential Succession: The Hispanic Case," *Social Forces*, 61 (March):825–33.

Massey, Douglas S., and Brendan P. Mullan. 1984. "Processes of Hispanic and Black Spatial Assimilation," *American Journal of Sociology*, 89 (January):836–73.

Mexico Instituto Nacional de Estadística, Geografía e Informática. 1983. *X Censo General de Población y Vivienda: 1980. Resultados Preliminares a Nivel Nacional y por Entidad Federativa* (Mexico, D.F.: INEGI).

National Commission for Employment Policy. 1982. *Hispanics and Jobs: Barriers to Progress* (Washington, D.C.: National Commission for Employment Policy).

Powell-Griner, Eve, and D. Streck. 1982. "A Closer Examination of Neonatal Mortality Rates among the Texas Spanish Surname Population," *American Journal of Public Health*, 72 (September):993–99.

Roberts, R. E. 1977. "The Study of Mortality in the Mexican American Population," in C. Teller et al., *Cuantos Somos: A Demographic Study of the Mexican American Population* (Austin: Center for Mexican American Studies, Monograph no. 2): pp. 131–55.

Robinson, J. Gregory. 1980. "Estimating the Approximate Size of the Illegal Alien Population in the United States by the Comparative Trend Analysis of Age-Specific Death Rates," *Demography*, 17 (May):159–76.

Schoen, Robert, and Verne E. Nelson. 1981. "Mortality by Cause among Spanish Surnamed Californians, 1969–71," *Social Science Quarterly*, 62 (June):259–74.

Sullivan, Teresa A., Francis P. Gillespie, Michael Hout, and Richard G. Rogers. 1984. "Alternative Estimates of Mexican American Mortality in Texas, 1980," *Social Science Quarterly*, 65 (June):609–17.

U.S. Bureau of the Census. 1972. *1970 Census of Population and Housing. General Social and Economic Characteristics. Final Report.* PC(1)-C1, U.S. Summary (Washington, D.C.: U.S. Government Printing Office).

———. 1973. *1970 Census of Population and Housing. Women by Number of Children Ever Born.* PC(2)-3A (Washington, D.C.: U.S. Government Printing Office).

———. 1982. *1980 Census of Population and Housing. Persons of Spanish Origin by State: 1980. Supplementary Report.* PC80-S1-7 (Washington, D.C.: U.S. Government Printing Office).

———. 1983a. *1980 Census of Population and Housing. General Population Characteristics.* PC80-1-B1, U.S. Summary (Washington, D.C.: U.S. Government Printing Office).

———. 1983b. *1980 Census of Population and Housing. General Social and Economic Characteristics.* PC80-1-C1, U.S. Summary (Washington, D.C.: U.S. Government Printing Office).

U.S. Department of Justice. 1981. *1981 Statistical Yearbook of the Immigration and Naturalization Service* (Washington, D.C.: U.S. Government Printing Office).

Warren, Robert, and Jeffrey S. Passel. 1984. "A Count of the Uncountable: Estimates of Undocumented Aliens Counted in the 1980 Census." U.S. Bureau of the Census. Photocopy.

II. LABOR MARKET EXPERIENCES IN THE MEXICAN ORIGIN POPULATION

4. AN INTRODUCTORY OVERVIEW

Frank D. BEAN, *The University of Texas at Austin*

Ruth M. CULLEN, *The University of Texas at Austin*

Elizabeth H. STEPHEN, *The University of Texas at Austin*

The recent wave of Mexican immigration to the United States has had an important feature in common with previous immigration streams. The flow of Mexicans has largely consisted of persons migrating for labor-related reasons (Portes, 1983; Bean and Sullivan, 1985). Therefore, the impact of these new migrants—both legal and undocumented—is most likely to have occurred in the labor market. The question of the labor market experiences of the Mexican origin population is thus in part a question of the labor market implications of immigration from Mexico. It is also in part a question of the labor market experiences of the native-born Mexican origin population. In the review that follows, we devote somewhat greater attention to the former than to the latter. This is appropriate not only because excellent treatments of the labor market experiences of the native-born Mexican origin population (as well as other Hispanic populations) already exist (Tienda, 1981; Borjas and Tienda, forthcoming [1985]), but also because most of the papers in this section of this book also focus more on native-born than on immigrant groups.

The importance of immigration as a national policy issue is attested to by the attention given it by the past four presidents of this country, each of whom appointed a cabinet committee or task force to study it (Keely, 1982). One of the most recent of these, the Select Commission on Immigration and Refugee Policy (1981), singled out "as most pressing . . . the problem of undocumented/illegal immigration" (p. 35). In response, Congress proposed changes in immigration law in the form of the so-called "Simpson-Mazzoli" bill, different versions of which were passed by the United States Senate and by the House of Representatives during 1983 and 1984. Although the bill ultimately faltered in a conference committee whose purpose was to reconcile differences between the two, the possibility of future immigration reform makes it worth giving further consideration to two questions that arose repeatedly in the debate over the legislation: (1) How many undocumented persons reside in the United States? and (2) What is their impact on the earnings and employment of legal residents of the United States? Answers to these are critical in evaluating the two most controversial features of the Simpson-Mazzoli bill: (1) the granting of amnesty to undocumented persons and (2) the provision of employer sanctions for knowingly employing undocumented workers.

The Number of Undocumented Mexicans

The assessment of the labor market consequences of undocumented immigration depends upon knowing as precisely as possible the number of undocumented immigrants. Exaggerations have unfortunately been common, running sometimes as high as 12 million persons (Lesko Associates, 1975; Chapman, 1976). More careful and measured treatments have suggested 3–6 million illegals in the country (Siegel, Passel, and Robinson, 1981), of which as many as 4 million might be from Mexico. Two estimates based on analyses of 1980 data have recently appeared in the literature—one a study conducted by Bean, King, and Passel (1983) utilizing 1980 Mexican Census data, and the other a study conducted by Warren and Passel (1984) using 1980 United States Census data and extended by Passel and Woodrow (1984)—that imply even lower levels.

The approach taken in the research conducted by Bean, King, and Passel (1983) involved comparing the hypothetical sex ratio one would expect to find in Mexico in the absence of emigration to the United States with the sex ratio that was in fact reported in preliminary results from the 1980 Mexican Census. Given various assumed values for the sex ratio at birth in Mexico, they estimated the size of the illegal migrant population of Mexican origin in the United States to range from about 1.5 to 3.8 million persons. The research conducted by Warren and Passel (1984) involved the development of procedures to estimate the number of illegal migrants included in the 1980 United States Census. Their results indicated that over 1.1 million (1,131,000) illegal Mexicans were included in the 1980 United States Census, a number very nearly equal to the number of legal aliens from Mexico in the country in 1980 (1,195,000). Of even greater significance, the counted number of illegals who entered since 1975 (559,000) exceeded the size of the legal alien population entering since 1975 (293,000) by a substantial amount. In short, 66 percent of the counted alien population from Mexico entering the United States since 1975 consisted of illegal migrants.

The implications of the results of these two studies for the question of the number of illegal Mexicans not counted in the 1980 Census have been considered by Bean, King, and Passel (forthcoming [1985]). The largest estimate from the Bean, King, and Passel (1983) study (3.8 million), together with the result that 1.1 million illegal Mexicans were counted in the 1980 Census (Warren and Passel, 1984), implies that about 70 percent of the illegal Mexicans in the United States in 1980 were not counted (2.7 divided by 3.8 = 0.69). Considering that the highest undercount rate measured in the United States in a recent census was about 20 percent for black males in their 20s, and considering that the 1980 Census is known to have missed very few housing units and to have undercounted the legal population by only about 1 percent (Passel, Siegel, and Robinson, 1982; Passel, Cowan, and Walter, 1983), Bean, King, and Passel (forthcoming [1985]) concluded that the undercount rates for the illegal Mexican male and female populations were not likely to be nearly this high. Hence, they assumed the undercount rates were in fact lower. When 60 percent of illegal Mexican males and 50 percent of illegal Mexican females were assumed to be missed, the implied size of the illegal Mexican population in 1980 was estimated to be about 2.6 million persons. Undercount rates of lesser magnitude would, of course, imply a total illegal Mexican population of even smaller size. Interestingly, based upon an examination of school enrollment data, Muller (1984) concluded that the Census probably counted most illegals in Los Angeles County in 1980. All of this, of course, points to a number of undocumented Mexicans in the country in 1980 that is much closer to 2 than to 4 million persons, and possibly even considerably below 2 million.

Labor Market Impacts of Immigration

Even if the number of undocumented Mexicans in the United States is much less than previously thought, the number is nonetheless substantial, and the labor market consequences of immigration, both legal and undocumented, are still of interest. Unfortunately, existing research is limited and inconclusive. The literature that bears on this question reflects each of two possible compromises that have been struck with the fact that we do not have direct information on undocumented workers. One approach addresses this issue by studying groups that are presumed to be like the undocumented labor force (Smith and Newman, 1977; Orton, 1976; Cardenas, 1978; King, 1979, 1982) or by appealing to a priori notions of how the undocumented population is distributed geographically or has grown over time (Smith and Newman, 1977; Orton, 1976; King, 1979). Rather crude comparisons are then made among places or periods where undocumented persons are presumed to be more or less prevalent. Another approach seeks to learn more generally about whether one labor force group takes jobs and wages away from another (Hamermesh and Grant, 1979; Borjas, 1982; Grossman, 1982, 1984). This latter type of study is generally less constrained by data availability than the former, with the result that we now have a fairly reliable set of studies concerning the effects of various labor market groups on each other, e.g., younger and older workers (Freeman, 1979), blue- and white-collar workers (Berndt and Christensen, 1973), blacks, whites, and Hispanics (Borjas, 1982), and various generations of immigrants (Grossman, 1982).

In general, the results of these studies are quite mixed. Some appear to show that certain groups take jobs and wages away from other groups, while other studies do not. Given the relatively recent interest in the issue of undocumented workers, it is not surprising that only one study of this type has addressed how this labor force group interacts with other types of labor in the production process (Grossman, 1984). The major conclusion of this study was that the effect of immigrants on employment depends upon their distribution among industries. In general, the greater the concentration of illegal immigrants in the goods-producing sector of the economy, the more negative the effect of illegal immigration on domestic unskilled employment. In the case of skilled employment, the findings predicted that illegal immigration would exert a positive effect, no matter what the distribution of illegal workers between industry sectors.

While research on the labor market impacts of legal and undocumented immigration has produced inconclusive results, and thus a great deal of uncertainty about whether undocumented immigration is harmful to the economy, one thing does seem certain; illegal aliens create some new jobs. Not only is there reason to think some jobs would not exist if they could not be filled by illegals, but also other jobs are created to service the illegal aliens working in this country (Browning and Rodriguez, forthcoming [1985]; Cardenas, de la Garza, and Hansen, forthcoming [1985]; Muller, 1984). Furthermore, illegal migrants may in fact be filling jobs that American workers will not take. Given the current low levels of fertility in the United States among native-born women, within ten years there may be significant shortages of entry-level workers (Reynolds, 1979; Wachter, 1981). Entry-level jobs, which are frequently temporary, dirty, and low-paying, are often characterized as jobs that "Americans don't want"—except perhaps for American teenagers, who expect to move into more attractive jobs when they are older and more experienced. Public policies that have the effect of relegating these jobs to native-born adults from minority groups are not acceptable. To the extent that legal immigration is difficult, the "pull" of these unattractive jobs will continue to lure undocumented migrants to this country.

Other Labor Market Characteristics of Undocumenteds

While we do not know a great deal about the labor market impact of undocumented immigration, we know considerably more about other aspects of labor market experience. For example, research shows that illegal migrants typically come from the employed ranks of their home countries (Houstoun, 1983; Waldinger, 1984). In addition, a study by North and Houstoun (1976), one by Maram and Long (1981) of garment workers in Los Angeles, and research by Mines and Nuckton (1982) and Reichert and Massey (1979, 1980) also confirm that most undocumented workers came to the United States with considerable work experience, albeit in low-skilled occupations. The Government of Mexico's 1978–79 Survey of Emigration to the United States (Zazueta and Corona, 1979) also confirms research conducted in the United States showing that undocumented workers do not come from the most disadvantaged groups in their home countries. Zazueta and Corona, however, found that this is not necessarily the case among women, suggesting that lack of economic opportunity is a major precipitating factor in the illegal migration of women. Waldinger (1984) also found that a significant proportion of women in his sample had not been in the labor market prior to coming to the United States. All of these women had come to the United States to seek employment, possibly because of cultural restraints against female employment in their homelands, but also because of lack of employment opportunities (Houstoun, 1983).

Available research also suggests that, once in the United States, the labor market appears to homogenize the status of undocumented workers, whatever the nature of their labor market experience in their home countries. Waldinger (1984, Tables 1 and 2) noted that undocumented workers are concentrated in the lower tier of the labor market, although proportions vary by country of origin of the workers. Mexican undocumented workers, for example, are likely to work as nonfarm laborers, operatives, or service workers. Non-Mexican Western Hemisphere workers, although likely to be blue-collar and service workers, show somewhat higher proportions in professional, sales, and clerical occupations (Poitras, 1981). But Waldinger, as well as other studies of Mexican undocumented workers (Reichert and Massey, 1979, 1980), suggested that the patterns of Mexican undocumented workers are increasingly similar to those of non-Mexicans, i.e., increasing proportions have experience in urban labor markets in Mexico prior to immigration to the United States. Relative to American workers, immigrants both legal and illegal, are more highly concentrated in low-skilled, low-wage jobs, at least initially. As Houstoun noted, however, only a minority are paid less than the minimum wage, and in recent years the percentage receiving less than the minimum wage has declined.

The Papers on Aspects of Labor Market Experience

The papers on the labor market experiences in the Mexican origin population in this section of the book reflect concerns that are similar to the issues just discussed. They deal with a number of questions relating to immigrant Mexican labor and with a variety of wage and earnings issues. The papers do not restrict attention to the nature and consequences of undocumented migration from Mexico, but also devote attention to aspects of the labor market behavior of the native-born Mexican origin population.

In considering the labor market experiences of this population, we need to remember that the migration of Mexican workers to the United States is not a new phenomenon. A key element in the nineteenth century development of the Southwest economy was the importation of Mexican workers (Houstoun, 1983). The demand for labor was facilitated by open borders between the two countries until the 1920s, and there was only minor regulation of the border for several years following the immigration legislation passed in 1924.

McKay documents and analyzes the displacement and repatriation of the Bridgeport, Texas, coal miners in 1931. With mining having declined as a result of the Depression, efforts were made to repatriate Mexican workers who were displaced by the closing of the mines. The mine workers had been recruited and had arrived during the 1880s, so that by 1931 many of them, nearly all of whom were of Mexican descent, had been born in the United States. When some of the displaced miners left Fort Worth to seek work, fears that they would contribute to unemployment there inspired efforts to repatriate them. When efforts to repatriate the miners through official channels were unsuccessful, relief agencies such as the Red Cross began fund-raising drives to transport unemployed coal miners back to Mexico. Few were able to return to the United States until after World War II, when immigration restrictions were once again relaxed.

Much like the case of the segmented labor market where the unskilled immigrant may not affect the labor market as a whole, but may affect certain sectors, immigrants may not be injurious to the United States as a whole, but may have serious consequences for a local area. Both McKay's study and a study by Chacon (1984) indicate how local communities reacted to countrywide economic conditions, and the effect the local reaction had on Mexican workers in those areas during the 1930s. These issues regarding the impact of immigrants at the local level have been evident again in the 1980s. For instance, a lawsuit brought against the state of Texas challenged the state's contention that it has no obligation to educate the children of undocumented workers (Weintraub and Ross, 1982). The state lost the suit, with the result that the taxpayers of Texas, and in particular those in the Rio Grande Valley, ended up paying disproportionately for this education without any federal subsidization.

Jones also examines the impact of undocumented Mexican immigrants in South Texas. He utilized two sources of data for this study: (1) information from the Immigration and Naturalization Service's San Antonio district office; and (2) casework files from a refugee services agency in San Antonio. These were used to study the concept of "societal penetration." Societal penetration is constructed as a three-dimensional phenomenon consisting of spatial penetration, permanence, and occupational penetration. Indexes of penetration calculated from the INS data show only a modest change of overall societal penetration, although spatial penetration had increased substantially from the early 1970s to 1980.

Mexican labor immigration to the United States between 1946 and 1967 was primarily structured around the *bracero* program, an agreement between the United States and Mexican governments that allowed U.S. agriculture legally to import labor from Mexico. Eventually utilized on about 2 percent of U.S. farms, mostly in California and the Southwest (Weintraub and Ross, 1982), alien labor benefited both employers and workers, the former receiving labor subsidies and the latter higher wages than they would have made in Mexico. Although the bracero program ended in 1967, the flow of Mexican workers to the United States did not cease. During the years of the program, workers had drifted away from agricultural work and out of the southwestern states to jobs with higher wages. Meanwhile in Mexico, friends and neighbors of the workers received word about the job market and about wage and earnings possibilities in the United States. This raises the issue of wage and earnings patterns among Mexican origin workers.

Four papers in this anthology examine wage and earnings issues in considerable depth. The first of these papers is by Reimers and utilizes the 1976 Survey of Income and Education to analyze the way in which wages vary within various Hispanic groups according to differences in education and other characteristics. Her findings indicate that Mexican American men received just as much money for each additional year of schooling they have as did non-Hispanic white men, although this was less true for those born in Mexico, even if they had some U.S. schooling. Estimated wage loss from poor English skills was insignificant for Mexican origin men, but living in the Southwest had a negative impact on wage rates. The major policy conclusion drawn by the author is that what is most needed are programs for improving the educational level of disadvantaged minorities to parity with whites. Also, she argues that lower wages in the Southwest may be better ameliorated by the relocation of Mexican origin workers to other regions of the United States rather than by programs aimed at regional development.

Verdugo and Verdugo examine the popular belief that all ethnic/racial minorities are similarly disadvantaged and that all minorities undergo the same labor market processes. In their analysis of March 1981 Current Population Survey data, they found that poorly educated Mexican Americans earned more than similar blacks, even when they worked in the same occupation, industry, or sector of the economy. Also, results from their regression analyses indicated that industry and sector of employment help to explain earnings differentials among Mexican Americans, blacks, and Anglos, as well as differences between industries within each ethnic/racial group. The analysis demonstrates significant human capital and structural differences in earnings among blacks, Mexican Americans, and non-Hispanic whites, as well as dissimilar labor market experiences for two minority groups.

Penley, Gould, and de la Viña examine the Mexican Americans' experience in a specific education program/job sector: college graduates in business. Since previous research has shown that education is a major factor in explaining earnings differences and in accounting for the concentration of Mexican Americans in low-skill and low-paying jobs, they look at sociological and human capital variables that may condition this effect. Utilizing data from a study of alumni from 10 U.S. business colleges, they concluded that while white non-Hispanic men earn the highest incomes, followed by Mexican American men, white women, and Mexican American women, the differences owe mainly to regional variations in income patterns, the lower socioeconomic background of Mexican Americans, and academic success in college.

Miller and Valdez examine economic well-being in broader terms, asking in particular whether immigrants assess their economic status more favorably than nonimmigrants, and whether perceptions of well-being become more negative the further removed the person is from the immigrant generation. Their analysis indicated that generational differences are most pronounced for perceived income adequacy, with the first generation showing considerably less satisfaction with income than nonimmigrants. Interestingly, immigrant households also received less income than nonimmigrant households. Contrary to expectations, the authors found that assimilation was positively associated with perceived income adequacy. This analysis failed to confirm the hypothesis that dissatisfaction with economic circumstances increased with time since immigration. Rather, greater acculturation and assimilation appeared to be associated with a more positive assessment of objective status.

A number of further issues in the labor market experience of Mexican Americans are related to wage issues but revolve more centrally around the sociological concern with factors affecting entry into the labor market and movement within the labor market. Alien workers may not have the same opportunity for upward mobility as the domestic worker. But in practice, many alien workers establish themselves in this country, educate their children, and begin a pattern of upward mobility. The process of upward mobility requires an almost constantly renewable source of labor to maintain the hierarchy.

Two papers are presented in this anthology that specifically address equality and labor force participation issues among Mexican Americans from a sociological perspective. Taylor and Shields examine Mexican Americans and inequality within a particular industry—the government—rather than a specific sector. Since the federal government cannot legally discriminate on the basis of social and personal characteristics, it provides an important source of data for the analysis of inequality. This study was based on the automated personnel files of federal civilian employees maintained by the Office of Personnel Management and was limited to the five southwestern states because of its focus on Mexican Americans. The authors found that non-Hispanic whites earned more than Mexican Americans, and that non-Hispanic whites were also much more likely to be in supervisory positions, owing in part to higher educational levels and greater job experience. The authors argue that in order to ameliorate inequalities more emphasis needs to be placed on the process through which individuals are originally assigned to positions and that programs designed to assist minorities in upward mobility need to be further developed.

Ortiz and Cooney test the hypothesis that traditional sex-role attitudes regarding marriage, family, and work explain the lower labor force participation of Hispanic females. The results of their analysis indicated that when the effect of ethnicity/generational status on sex-role attitudes is examined, first generation Hispanic women seem to differ from non-Hispanics, but second and third generation Hispanics do not. The first generation women, however, were not significantly different in pattern, leading the authors to conclude that traditional sex-role attitudes do not have a stronger impact on the labor force behavior of Hispanic females compared with non-Hispanic females.

From this collection of studies, it is evident that the labor market issues pertaining to the Mexican origin population are varied and complex. The Mexican origin population itself is heterogeneous, including Mexican Americans born and raised in the United States, legal immigrants, illegal immigrants, highly skilled workers and unskilled workers. There is no one answer to the issues raised here, nor are there simple solutions to the problems. Much research lies ahead, but the authors have given us a strong foundation on which to base further studies of the labor market experiences of the Mexican origin population.

REFERENCES

Bean, Frank D., Allan G. King, and Jeffrey S. Passel. 1983. "The Number of Illegal Migrants of Mexican Origin in the United States: Sex Ratio-Based Estimates for 1980," *Demography*, 20 (February):99–109.

———. Forthcoming. "Estimates of the Size of the Illegal Migrant Population of Mexican Origin in the United States: An Assessment, Review, and Proposal," in H. Browning and R. de la Garza, eds., *Mexican Immigrants and the Mexican American People* (Austin: Center for Mexican American Studies, Monograph Series).

Bean, Frank D., and Teresa A. Sullivan. Forthcoming, 1985. "Immigration as a Social Problem: The Simpson-Mazzoli Bill," *Society*.

Berndt, E. R., and L. R. Christensen. 1973. "Testing for the Existence of an Aggregate Index of Labor Inputs," *American Economic Review*, 64 (June):391–404.

Borjas, George J. 1982. "A Methodology for Estimating the Extent of Labor Market Competition between Minority and Non-Minority Groups." Paper presented at the Rockefeller Foundation Workshop on the Labor Market Consequences of Immigration Policy, Racine, Wis., August.

Borjas, George, and Marta Tienda. Forthcoming, 1985. Hispanics in the U.S. Economy (New York: Academic Press).

Browning, Harley, and Nestor Rodriguez. Forthcoming, 1985. "The Migration of Mexican Indocumentados as a Settlement Process: Implications for Work," in George Borjas and Marta Tienda, eds., *Hispanics in the U.S. Economy* (New York: Academic Press).

Cardenas, Gilbert. 1978. "The Manpower Impact of Mexican Illegal Aliens in the San Antonio Labor Market in the Seventies." Pan American University. Mimeo.

Cardenas, G., R. de la Garza, and N. Hansen. Forthcoming. "Mexican Immigrants and the Chicano Ethnic Enterprise," in H. Browning and R. de la Garza, eds., *Mexican Immigrants and the Mexican American People* (Austin: Center for Mexican American Studies, Monograph Series).

Chacon, Ramon D. 1984. "Labor Unrest and Industrialized Agriculture in California: The Case of the 1933 San Joaquin Valley Strike," *Social Science Quarterly*, 65 (June):336–53.

Chapman, L. F. 1976. Statement before the Subcommittee on Immigration and Naturalization of the Committee of the Judiciary. United States Congress, 94th Cong., 2d Sess., Washington, D.C., 17 March.

Freeman, Richard B. 1979. "The Effect of Demographic Factors on Age Earnings Profiles," *Journal of Human Resources*, 14 (3):289–318.

Grossman, Jean Baldwin. 1982. "The Substitutability of Natives and Immigrants in Production," *Review of Economics and Statistics*, 64:596–603.

———. 1984. "Illegal Immigrants and Domestic Employment," *Industrial and Labor Relations Review*, 37 (January):240–51.

Hamermesh, D. S., and J. Grant. 1979. "Econometric Studies of Labor-Labor Substitution and Their Implications for Policy," *Journal of Human Resources*, 14 (4):518–42.

Houstoun, Marion F. 1983. "Aliens in Irregular Status in the U.S.: A Review of their Numbers, Characteristics, and Role in the U.S. Labor Market." Paper presented at the 6th Seminar on Adaption and Integration of Immigrants, 11–15 April 1983, Geneva.

Keeley, C. B. 1982. "Illegal Migration," *Scientific American*, 246 (3):41–47.

King, Allan G. 1979. "El Efecto de los Immigrantes Illegales sobre el Desempleo en Estados Unidos," *Revista Mexicana de Sociologia*, 61 (4):1233–55.

——— 1982. "The Effects of Undocumented Hispanic Workers on the Earnings of Hispanic-Americans." Paper presented at the Rockefeller Foundation Workshop on the Labor Market Consequences of Immigration Policy, Racine, Wis., August.

Lesko Associates. 1975. *Final Report: Basic Data and Guidance Required to Implement a Major Illegal Alien Study during Fiscal Year 1976*. Report prepared for the U.S. Immigration and Naturalization Service by Lesko Associates, Washington, D.C.

Maram, Sheldon, and Stewart Long. 1981. "The Labor-Market Impact of Hispanic Undocumented Workers: An Exploratory Study of the Garment Industry in Los Angeles County." California State University, Fullerton. Photocopy.

Mines, Richard, and Carole Frank Nuckton. 1982. "The Evolution of Mexican Migration to the United States: A Case Study." Giannini Foundation Information Series 82-1, Division of Agricultural Sciences, University of California, Berkeley, March. Photocopy.

Muller, T. 1984. *The Fourth Wave: California's Newest Immigrants* (Washington, D.C.: Urban Institute Press).

North, D. S., and M. F. Houstoun. 1976. *The Characteristics and Role of Illegal Aliens in the U.S. Labor Market: An Exploratory Study*. Report prepared for the U.S. Department of Labor, Employment and Training Administration (Washington, D.C.: Linton).

Orton, Eliot S. 1976. "Changes in the Skill Differential: Union Wages in Constitution, 1907–1972," *Industrial and Labor Relations Review*, 29 (4):16–24.

Passel, J. S., C. D. Cowan, and K. M. Walter. 1983. "Coverage of the 1980 Census." Paper presented at the annual meeting of the Population Association of America, Pittsburgh, 14–16 April 1983.

Passel, J. S., J. S. Siegel, and J. G. Robinson. 1982. "Coverage of the National Population by Age, Sex, and Race in the 1980 Census: Preliminary Estimates by Demographic Analysis," *Current Population Reports*, ser. P-23, no. 115 (Washington, D.C.: U.S. Government Printing Office).

Passel, Jeffrey S., and Karen A. Woodrow. 1984. "Geographic Distribution of Undocumented Immigrants: Estimates of Undocumented Aliens Counted in the 1980 Census by State." Paper presented at the annual meeting of the Population Association of America, Minneapolis, 3–5 May 1984.

Poitras, Guy. 1981. "The U.S. Experience of Return Migrants from Costa Rica and El Salvador," in Select Commission on Immigration and Refugee Policy, *U.S. Immigration Policy and the National Interest*, Appendix E, Papers on Illegal Migration to the United States (Washington, D.C.: U.S. Government Printing Office): pp. 45–196.

Portes, Alejandro. 1983. "International Labor Migration and National Development," in Mary M. Kritz, ed., *U.S. Immigration and Refugee Policy: Global and Domestic Issues* (Lexington, Mass.: Lexington Books): pp. 71–91.

Reichert, Josh, and Douglas S. Massey. 1979. "Patterns of U.S. Migration from a Mexican Sending Community: A Comparison of Legal and Illegal Immigrants," *International Migration Review*, 13 (Winter):599–623.

———. 1980. "History and Trends in U.S.-Bound Migration from a Mexican Town," *International Migration Review*, 14 (Winter):475–492.

Reynolds, Clark. 1979. "Labor Market Projections for the United States and Mexico and Their Relevance to Current Migration Controversies." Stanford University, Food Research Institute, July. Photocopy.

Select Commission on Immigration and Refugee Policy. 1981. *U.S. Immigration Policy and the National Interest* (Washington, D.C.: U.S. Government Printing Office).

Siegel, J. S., J. S. Passel, and J. G. Robinson. 1981. "Preliminary Review of Existing Studies of the Number of Illegal Residents in the United States," in Select Commission on Immigration and Refugee Policy, *U.S. Immigration Policy and the National Interest*, Appendix E, Papers on Illegal Immigration to the United States (Washington, D.C.: U.S. Government Printing Office): pp. 18–39.

Smith, B., and R. Newman. 1977. "Depressed Wages along the U.S.-Mexican Border: An Experimental Analysis," *Economic Inquiry*, 15 (1):56–66.

Tienda, Marta. 1981. *Hispanic Origin Workers in the U.S. Labor Market*. Final Report to the U.S. Department of Labor, October. University of Wisconsin–Madison. Photocopy.

Wachter, Michael L. 1981. "The Labor Market and Illegal Immigration: The Outlook for the 1980s," *Industrial and Labor Relations Review*, 33 (April):342–54.

Waldinger, Roger. 1984. "The Occupational and Economic Integration of the New Immigrants," in Richard R. Hofstetter, ed., *U.S. Immigration Policy*, (Durham, N.C.: Duke University Press): pp. 197–222.

Warren, Robert, and Jeffrey S. Passel. 1984. "A Count of the Uncountable: Estimates of the Undocumented Aliens Counted in the 1980 Census." U.S. Bureau of the Census. Photocopy.

Weintraub, S., and S. R. Ross. 1982. *"Temporary" Alien Workers in the U.S.* (Boulder, Colo.: Westview).

Zazueta, Carlos H., and Rodolfo Corona. 1979. *Los Trabajadores Mexicanos en los Estados Unidos: Primeros Resultados de la Encuesta Nacional de Emigracion* (Mexico City: Centro Nacional de Información y Estadísticas del Trabajo).

5. THE IMPACT OF THE GREAT DEPRESSION ON IMMIGRANT MEXICAN LABOR: REPATRIATION OF THE BRIDGEPORT, TEXAS, COAL MINERS

R. Reynolds MCKAY, *Texas Economic Development Commission*

Published accounts of Mexican repatriation from Texas are few. This paper focuses on the repatriation of several hundred Bridgeport, Texas, coal miners. When economic conditions deteriorated in 1931, the Bridgeport mines closed. Permanent Mexican residents and their U.S.-born children suffered severe hardships before they reluctantly returned to Mexico.

With the expansion of railroads into Texas in the late nineteenth century, coal and lignite mines were established at diverse locations. Important mining centers came into existence at Eagle Pass and Laredo in southwestern Texas and at Bridgeport, Newcastle, Strawn, Thurber, and Malakoff in North Texas (Figure 1). Although the history of these mines has been recorded, the experiences of the miners have been neglected in the published literature.

All Texas coal mines used immigrant Mexican labor, and most mines were almost exclusively dependent upon Mexican workers. When mine operations were curtailed in the early 1930s, thousands of Mexican miners lost their jobs. Virtually all of the miners suffered severe hardships, and many of these long-time Mexican residents of Texas and their U.S.-born children returned to Mexico. The purpose of this study is to document and analyze the displacement and repatriation of the Bridgeport, Texas, miners in 1931.

Although several studies have focused on Mexican repatriation from California and midwestern urban centers and on the arrival of repatriates in Mexico (McLean, 1931, 1932; McWilliams, 1933; Bogardus, 1933; Taylor, 1933; Gilbert, 1934; Humphrey, 1941; Gonzáles Navarro, 1970; Betten and Mohl, 1973; Kiser and Silverman, 1973; Hoffman, 1974; Carreras de Velasco, 1974; Dinwoodie, 1977), only a few studies have examined repatriation from Texas (Kelley, 1932; Hinojosa, 1940; McKay, 1981, 1982, 1983).

FIGURE 1

Location of Texas Coal Mines

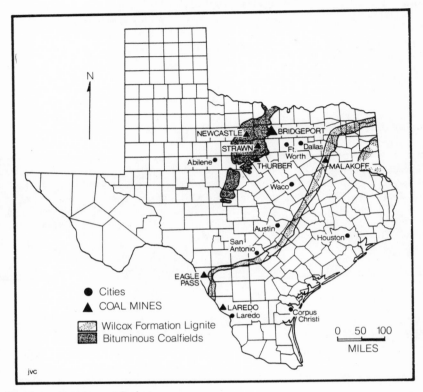

Mexican Immigrant Labor

Although coal was discovered at Bridgeport about 1860, commercial mining operations were not established there until the 1880s. By 1890 coal extracted from the mines was being hauled by wagons to Decatur and other nearby communities for domestic consumption (Cummins, 1891). The Rock Island Railroad reached Bridgeport in 1893 and became the chief purchaser of locally mined coal. Surplus coal was shipped to Oklahoma for use in industrial plants or sold locally for domestic use (Wise County Historical Survey Committee, 1975:118–19). Coal production continued to increase at Bridgeport during the first two decades of the twentieth century.

Soon after the mines were opened, immigrant laborers from Mexico were hired to extract the mineral. The number of Mexican miners employed at Bridgeport gradually increased in the 1880s and 1890s. In 1900 *Farm and Ranch* reported that about 150 miners were employed at the Bridgeport mines (Scott, 1900). Two years later a bulletin published by the University of Texas noted that about 225 miners were employed (University of Texas Mineral Survey, 1902:34–35). Most of these miners were Mexicans. By the turn of the century many of the children of the original Mexican immigrants were employed in the mines.

During the early years working conditions at the Bridgeport mines were hazardous, and a number of miners lost their lives in accidents. A visitor to the mines described conditions in 1900:

> At the bottom of the shaft we found a mule and a mining cart waiting for us into which we tumbled and rode over the rails for about a quarter of a mile, to where the tunnel became so low that the mule could not pass. Then we proceeded on our hands and knees through the tunnel to where the miners were at work, picking out the coal and brushing out the tunnel so as to leave it large enough for future entrance and exit. Brushing, in a mine, means that after the coal has been taken out they have to timber it up to prevent the earth caving in and burying the miners alive, and they also have to tunnel out the rock until the entrance is large enough to admit the mules and carts. There are a number of side galleries, which have switches leading into them over which the carts are pushed by hand to the main tunnel, where they are taken charge of by the driver of the mule and carried to the main shaft. There they are lifted to the top and dumped into the car that is waiting upon the track. I went into one of these side galleries and found the miners busy at work lying on their backs and picking away at the coal. (Scott, 1900)

The influx of miners in the early 1900s resulted in a critical housing shortage in Bridgeport. To meet the housing needs of the recent arrivals from Mexico, the mining company constructed a number of houses in an area adjacent to the mines. By 1923 the Bridgeport Coal Company provided housing for about 40 miners and their families (*La Prensa*, 3 July 1923, p. 5; Martínez, 1981), while other miners rented or purchased homes in the *colonia* near the mines.

During World War I a critical labor shortage developed in Bridgeport, as many local residents had either volunteered for military service or had been conscripted by the U.S. Army. The Bridgeport Coal Company initiated efforts to recruit additional labor from South Texas and Mexico. Advertisements for miners frequently appeared in *La Prensa*, which emphasized high wages, steady work, good schools, and churches. Although a few miners were paid a daily wage, most miners were compensated for each ton of coal extracted. Wage rates during the late 1910s and early 1920s varied from $2.23 to $2.79 per ton (*La Prensa*, 22 August 1917, p. 4; 25 April 1919, p. 7; 15 January 1920, p. 6; 21 April 1920, p. 8; 1 May 1920, p. 8). When sufficient labor could not be obtained from Laredo or San Antonio, mine owners dispatched labor recruiters to Mexico to secure additional workers (Vidal, 1981; Martínez, 1981).

The Bridgeport miners were unionized during World War I. The union negotiated higher wages, improved working conditions, and procedures to resolve worker grievances. The miners received these benefits for only a few years. During the post–World War I recession, mine owners reduced wages and refused to negotiate with union leaders. The miners went out on strike. However, within a few months most miners were destitute. Some found temporary employment as "grubbers" clearing land or as agricultural laborers on nearby farms. Eventually most of the miners returned to the mine and the union ceased to exist.

The U.S. Bureau of the Census (1922:42) reported that 354 Mexicans resided in Wise County, virtually all of whom were employed in the Bridgeport coal mines. Mexicans became an integral part of the Bridgeport community, and by the mid-1920s the town was characterized as "predominantly Latin-American" (Sipes, n.d.). During the 1920s the number of immigrant Mexicans ceased to increase, while many Mexican Americans—especially the sons of the original Mexican immigrants—found employment in the mines. By 1930 two-thirds of the miners at Bridgeport were Mexican Americans. Approximately 250 Mexican and Mexican American miners and their families, for a total of about 750 people, resided in Bridgeport in 1930.

Repatriation

With the advent of the Depression in the early 1930s, the Bridgeport Coal Company began to encounter financial difficulties. After January 1931 the mines were operated intermittently; however, most Mexican miners remained in Bridgeport, where they averaged two days work each week during 1931. By the end of July many of the miners and their families were experiencing financial difficulties. In an effort to alleviate the situation, the Mexican consul from Dallas, Juan E. Anchondo, met with the miners to discuss the possibility of their returning to Mexico. A few indicated their willingness to return if transportation was provided. Anchondo then appealed to John T. Farmer, general passenger agent for the Rock Island Railroad, to provide "charity tickets" to those who were willing to return to Mexico but lacked funds for transportation. Anchondo noted that such requests were normally made to charitable organizations, but that no relief agency existed in Bridgeport (Secretaría de Relaciones Exteriores, 1931). There is apparently no record of a response to Anchondo's request by the Rock Island Railroad. Moreover, there is no evidence that any Mexican miners departed from Bridgeport at that time.

On 23 November 1931 the Bridgeport Coal Company ceased to operate. Shortly thereafter reports began to appear in the Texas press that 250 Mexican mining families, comprised of over 750 persons, were in critical condition. They were reportedly suffering from hunger and a lack of clothing. Some families had been forced to subsist on beans for several weeks, while others had had their stoves and other household goods repossessed because they were unable to make installment payments (San Angelo Evening Standard, 7 December 1931, p. 7; Fort Worth Star-Telegram, 8 December 1931, p. 10; La Prensa, 7 December 1931, p. 1; Wise County Messenger, 10 December 1931, p. 1; Fort Worth Star-Telegram, 10 December 1931, p. 23; 11 December 1931, p. 29; La Prensa, 11 December 1931, p. 2; Eagle Pass Daily Guide, 12 December 1931, p. 2; Houston Post-Dispatch, 13 December 1931, p. 1; 14 December 1931, p. 1; San Antonio Express, 14 December 1931, p. 3; Fort Worth Star-Telegram, 15 December 1931, p. 6).

In early December a few destitute miners left Bridgeport for Fort Worth, where employment and relief opportunities appeared to be greater. Concern that all of the unemployed miners would migrate to Fort Worth resulted in efforts to repatriate them. On 7 December Rev. G. A. Walls, pastor of the Mexican Presbyterian Church and superintendent of the Mexican Mission in Fort Worth, stated that efforts should be made to prevent the Bridgeport miners from coming to Fort Worth. Walls declared, "The deprivations will be as great in the city as they are in Bridgeport and . . . their coming will put an additional burden on local [relief] agencies" (*San Angelo Evening Standard*, 7 December 1931, p. 7). Walls appealed to Mexican Consul Anchondo in Dallas to make funds available for the return of the miners to Mexico, but the Mexican consulate in Dallas lacked funds for this purpose. Anchondo then discussed the matter with the Mexican consul general in San Antonio. The consul general responded that no funds could be made available for the transportation of Mexicans in Texas; however, he stated if the miners could reach the border they would be provided transportation to their destinations in Mexico (*San Angelo Evening Standard*, 7 December 1931, p. 7; *El Continental*, 8 December 1931, p. 1; *La Prensa*, 9 December 1931, p. 1; *Wise County Messenger*, 10 December 1931, p. 1; *Fort Worth Star-Telegram*, 13 December 1931, p. 2).

Having failed to secure the support of the Mexican government to transport the miners to the Mexican border, Walls began negotiations with the Fort Worth chapter of the American Red Cross. On 8 December Walls met in Bridgeport with members of the Bridgeport Chamber of Commerce, Bridgeport town officials, a field representative of the Red Cross, the chairperson of the Wise County chapter of the Red Cross. At the meeting it was decided that a request for funds to transport the unemployed Bridgeport miners to the Mexican border should be made to the national headquarters of the American Red Cross in St. Louis. Several days later officials in St. Louis responded that no funds could be made available until all local resources had been exhausted. The Red Cross suggested that a local relief drive should be initiated. Red Cross officials in St. Louis noted that privation among Bridgeport miners was no greater than that being experienced in other American mining centers (*Laredo Tmes*, 8 December 1931, p. 2; *El Continental*, 8 December 1931, p. 1; *Fort Worth Star-Telegram*, 8 December 1931, p. 10; *Decatur News*, 10 December 1931, p. 1; *Wise County Messenger*, 10 December 1931, p. 1; *Fort Worth Star-Telegram*, 10 December 1931, p. 23; 12 December 1931, p. 1).

A local relief committee under the auspices of the Red Cross was consequently established at Bridgeport. The committee was composed exclusively of Anglo Texan community leaders; no Mexicans represented their community. From office space provided by the Bridgeport Chamber of Commerce a well-organized campaign for repatriation funds was coordinated. Red Cross field representative Cora V. Shuman served as a liaison member of the committee and was responsible for coordinating and directing the campaign in other Wise County communities. The first day of the drive to raise repatriation funds $247 was collected. Contributions diminished significantly after the first day (*Fort Worth Star-Telegram*, 9 December 1931, p. 21; 10 December 1931, p. 23; *La Prensa*, 11 December 1931, p. 2; *El Continental*, 13 December 1931, p. 1; *La Prensa*, 12 December 1931, p. 1; *Fort Worth Star-Telegram*, 12 December 1931, p. 1; *Houston Post-Dispatch*, 13 December 1931, p. 1).

The drive for Mexican repatriation funds in Bridgeport, Decatur, and other Wise County towns was intense. Community leaders were extremely concerned, since the 750 indigent miners and their families had become an immense burden to the town. Reports indicate that by early December between $25 and $40 were expended from the city treasury each day to provide them with food. In addition, the Chamber of Commerce borrowed $100 to provide other assistance to those families in greatest need (*Fort Worth Star-Telegram*, 14 December 1931, p. 1; *Decatur News*, 10 December 1931, p. 1; *Eagle Pass Daily Guide*, 12 December 1931, p. 2). Community leaders in Bridgeport knew that the town could not provide for the unemployed miners indefinitely and that there was no prospect of state or federal assistance. Their efforts to obtain the return of the miners were simply a strategy to shift responsibility for their care to Mexican authorities.

A similar campaign to raise funds was also initiated in Fort Worth. It was spearheaded by Rev. Walls, who organized and chaired the fund-raising committee. Other members of the committee included Mexican Consul Anchondo from Dallas and R. Lopez Guerra, Laureano Flores, Aurora Barron, and Vera Rogers, all of Fort Worth. During December the committee sponsored three benefits to raise funds. Funds derived from these benefits were used to aid both miners who were returning to Mexico and those who chose to remain in Texas (*Fort Worth Star-Telegram*, 13 December 1931, p. 2; *Houston Post-Dispatch*, 14 December 1931, p. 1; *San Antonio Express*, 14 December 1931, p. 3; *Fort Worth Star-Telegram*, 15 December 1931, p. 6; 19 December 1931, p. 2; 29 December 1931, p. 16).

Many of the Mexican miners had remained in Bridgeport in an effort to secure wages for work performed in November after the mines closed on 23 November 1931. The Bridgeport Coal Company owed the miners about $6,000 in back wages. Soon after the mines closed, the company announced that the proceeds from a sale of movable mining property would be distributed to the miners. An auction of the property was held on 11 December, and approximately $2,500 was raised. Funds from the local relief drive were combined with monies derived from the sale of the mining property and distributed to the unemployed miners. The miners eventually received about 60 percent of their back wages (*El Continental*, 8 December 1931, p. 1; *Fort Worth Star-Telegram*, 9 December 1931, p. 21; 10 December 1931, p. 23; 11 December 1931, p. 29; *La Prensa*, 12 December 1931, p. 1). Once it became apparent that they would receive no additional pay, the miners began to leave the town.

It is difficult to determine the number of Bridgeport miners who returned to Mexico, for they did not return en masse. They often departed in small groups. These departures were usually not covered by the press, which accorded little attention to their plight after they received partial payment of their back wages. In addition, a number of the miners and their families did not return directly to Mexico. A few migrated to South and West Texas in search of agricultural jobs. Others drifted into Dallas and Fort Worth in search of work, while one contingent migrated to the Red River Valley of Minnesota, hoping to secure employment on the sugar beet farms in the following spring (Vidal, 1981; Martínez, 1981; *Fort Worth Star-Telegram*, 29 December 1931, p. 16).

In mid-December 1931 the Missouri Pacific and Rock Island railroads offered the miners transportation to the Mexican border at reduced rates. A number of the miners returned directly to Mexico from Bridgeport after these special transportation rates were made available. The first contingent of 27 families departed from Bridgeport immediately after they received their back wages (*Houston Post-Dispatch*, 13 December 1931, p. 1; *Fort Worth Star-Telegram*, 13 December 1931, p. 2). On 11 December the Rock Island and the Missouri Pacific announced that arrangements had been made to remove 112 destitute miners, many of whom were single men, to the border free of charge (*La Prensa*, 12 December 1931, p. 1). By the end of December most of the miners had abandoned their homes in Bridgeport; one report indicated that only 50 families remained (*Fort Worth Star-Telegram*, 19 December 1931, p. 2).

By 1 January 1932 virtually all of the former miners and their families had abandoned Bridgeport. One of the few miners who remained remembered that only seven or eight Mexican families continued to reside in the town. Most of the workers had secured jobs at a local brick plant (Martínez, 1981). U.S. Bureau of the Census (1932:1079; 1943:990) data indicate that the population of Bridgeport decreased by 729 persons during the 1930s.

News reports often indicated that many of the Bridgeport miners wished to return to Mexico. It was frequently asserted that 40 percent, or about 250 of the Mexican miners, wished to return (*San Angelo Evening Standard*, 7 December 1931, p. 7; *Fort Worth Star-Telegram*, 9 December 1931, p. 21; *Wise County Messenger*, 10 December 1931, p. 1). Apparently those who organized the Bridgeport movement failed to determine whether or not the former miners really wanted to return to Mexico; two former miners—who lost their jobs when the mines were closed in 1931—asserted that virtually none of the miners or their families wished to return to Mexico (Vidal, 1981; Martínez, 1981). This is understandable when it is realized that most of the miners had been employed at the Bridgeport mines for 10, 15, or 20 years and many had children born and reared in Texas.

Initiation of the Bridgeport repatriation movement appears to have been largely the result of the efforts by Rev. G. A. Walls. Walls's efforts were strongly supported by Cora V. Shuman of the American Red Cross, Mexican Consul Juan E. Anchondo of Dallas, Anglo Texas residents of Bridgeport, members of the Bridgeport Chamber of Commerce, Bridgeport town officials, and some residents of Fort Worth. The miners and their families were not involved in the organization or implementation of the repatriation movement. Many of those individuals and organizations involved in financing and organizing the movement failed to consider the gravity of their actions. However, it does appear that Rev. Walls was aware that his efforts were not in the best interests of the Mexicans, for on 10 December 1931 he stated:

Those who go to Mexico will be no better off. Most of them have no other occupation than working in mines. They have been away from Mexico for 15 or 20 years and are completely out of touch in that country. They will actually go there as foreigners. (*Wise County Messenger*, 10 December 1931, p. 1)

Nevertheless, Walls continued to promote the repatriation of several hundred unemployed, destitute Mexican residents of Bridgeport.

Conclusions

The impact of the Great Depression on the Bridgeport coal miners was devastating. These laborers possessed few skills other than coal mining. Most were unable to obtain other employment, and many returned to Mexico. Furthermore, there were few economic opportunities for unskilled workers in Mexico in the 1930s. The economic advances achieved by these immigrant Mexican laborers and their U.S.-born children, during the early decades of the twentieth century, were probably lost, for immigration to the United States was sharply curtailed during the Depression. Few Mexican repatriates were able to reenter the United States during the 1930s. It is probable, however, that many of the Bridgeport miners returned to the United States when immigration restrictions were relaxed after the advent of World War II.

REFERENCES

Betten, Neil, and Raymond A. Mohl. 1973. "From Discrimination to Repatriation: Mexican Life in Gary, Indiana, during the Great Depression," *Pacific Historical Review,* 42 (August):370–88.

Bogardus, Emory S. 1933. "Mexican Repatriates," *Sociology and Social Research,* 18 (November/December):169–76.

Carreras de Velasco, Mercedes. 1974. *Los mexicanos que devolvió la crisis, 1929–1932* (Tlatelolco, Mexico, D.F.: Secretaría de Relaciones Exteriores).

Cummins, W. F. 1891. "Report on the Geology of Northwestern Texas," in E. T. Dumble, ed., *Second Annual Report of the Geological Survey of Texas* (Austin: State Printing Office): p. 518.

Decatur News. 10 December 1931.

Dinwoodie, David H. 1977. "Deportation: The Immigration Service and the Chicano Labor Movement in the 1930s," *New Mexico Historical Review,* 52 (July):193–206.

Eagle Pass Daily Guide. 12 December 1931.

El Continental (El Paso). 8–13 December 1931.

Fort Worth Star-Telegram, 8–29 December 1931.

Gilbert, James C. 1934. "A Field Study in Mexico of the Mexican Repatriation Movement." Master's thesis, University of Southern California.

González Navarro, Moisés. 1970. "Effectos sociales de la crisis de 1929," *Historia Mexicana,* 76 (April–June):536–58.

Hinojosa, Federico Allen. 1940. *El México de afuera* (San Antonio: Artes Gráficas).

Hoffman, Abraham. 1974. *Unwanted Mexican Americans in the Great Depression: Repatriation Pressures, 1929–1939* (Tucson: University of Arizona Press).

Houston Post-Dispatch. 13–14 December 1931.

Humphrey, Norman D. 1941. "Mexican Repatriation from Michigan: Public Assistance in Historical Perspective," *Social Services Review*, 15 (September):497–513.

Kelley, Edna E. 1932. "The Mexicans Go Home," *Southwest Review*, 17 (April):303–11.

Kiser, George, and David Silverman. 1973. "Mexican Repatriation during the Great Depression," *Journal of Mexican American History*, 3:139–64.

La Prensa (San Antonio). 22 August 1917–12 December 1931.

Laredo Times. 8 December 1931.

McKay, R. Reynolds. 1981. "The Federal Deportation Campaign in Texas: Mexican Deportation from the Lower Rio Grande Valley during the Great Depression," *Borderlands Journal*, 5 (Fall):95–120.

———. 1982. "Texas Mexican Repatriation during the Great Depression." Ph.D. dissertation, University of Oklahoma.

———. 1983. "The Texas Cotton Acreage Control Law of 1931 and Mexican Repatriation," *West Texas Historical Association Year Book*, 59 (October):143–55.

McLean, Robert N. 1931. "Goodbye, Vicente!" *Survey*, 66 (1 May):182–83.

———. 1932. "The Mexican Return," *Nation,* 135 (24 August):165–66.

McWilliams, Carey. 1933. "Getting Rid of the Mexicans," *American Mercury*, 28 (March):322–24.

Martínez, Fervin. 1981. Personal interview with author. Bridgeport, Texas, 13 January 1981.

San Angelo Evening Standard. 7 December 1931.

San Antonio Express. 14 December 1931.

Secretaría de Relaciones Exteriores. 1931. "Repatriaciones." File: IV-354-34, IV/1524.5 (73-11)/4. Tlatelolco, Mexico, D.F.

Sipes, D. E. N.d. "The Bridgeport Coal Mines." Unpublished manuscript, Wise County Historical Society Archives, Decatur, Tex.

Scott, M. C. 1900. "Down in a Coal Mine," *Farm and Ranch*, 10 March, p. 12.

Taylor, Paul S. 1933. *A Spanish-Mexican Peasant Community: Arandas in Jalisco, Mexico* (Berkeley: University of California Press).

University of Texas Mineral Survey. 1902. *Coal Lignite and Asphalt Rocks*, Bulletin No. 3 (Austin: University of Texas).

U.S. Bureau of the Census. 1922. *Fourteenth Census of the United States: 1920. Population, Composition and Characteristics of the Population, Texas* (Washington, D.C.: U.S. Government Printing Office).

———. 1932. *Fifteenth Census of the United States: 1930. Population, Composition and Characteristics*, pt. 2 (Washington, D.C.: U.S. Government Printing Office).

———. 1943. *Sixteenth Census of the United States: 1940. Population,* vol. 2, *Characteristics of the Population*, pt. 6 (Washington, D.C.: U.S. Government Printing Office).

Vidal, Manuel. 1981. Personal interview with author. Bridgeport, Texas, 13 January 1981.

Wise County Historical Survey Committee. 1975. *Wise County History: A Link with the Past*, edited by Rosalie Gregg ([Wichita Falls, Tex.]: Nortex Press).

Wise County Messenger (Decatur). 10 December 1931.

6. CHANGING PATTERNS OF UNDOCUMENTED MEXICAN MIGRATION TO SOUTH TEXAS[1]

Richard C. JONES, *The University of Texas at San Antonio*

Data from the San Antonio INS district indicate that the subpopulation of appre- hended undocumenteds has not penetrated the social institutions of South Texas to a very high degree, in that both permanence and occupational mobility remained low over the decade of the 1970s, although a substantially higher proportion of this subpopulation is choosing to live outside the immediate border region and San Antonio itself. A smaller sample of unapprehended undocumenteds from a San Antonio refugee services agency also shows little increase on societal penetration over the period, although in levels of occupational status and length of residence the refugee services sample rated much higher than the INS sample.

This paper builds upon earlier work by the author (Jones, 1982a, 1982b) at the national level. The first section is devoted to summarizing that earlier work, to provide a framework for understanding what follows. The second section describes the magnitude, characteristics, and patterns of undo- cumented migration to the San Antonio area and South Texas, as revealed in data from the files of the San Antonio INS district. The third section examines specific measures, from the INS data, which give us an idea of the degree of *societal penetration* by the undocumented population in South Texas during the decade of the 1970s. The fourth section examines the characteristics and degree of societal penetration of unapprehended Mexican undocumenteds as revealed from data from the files of a San Antonio refugee services agency. The final section summarizes the study and draws further conclusions and implications.

Undocumented Migration from Mexico to the United States

We frequently hear that immigration to the United States has gotten "out of hand"; government sources are often cited for figures such as 1–2 mil- lion new entrants per year, and a stock of 5–6 million Mexicans illegally in

[1] I would like to thank the Statistical Division of the U.S. Immigration and Naturalization Service, Washington, D.C., and the Investigative Division of the San Antonio District, INS, for providing me with information and access to their files, respectively. Without their willing help, this study would not have been possible.

this country. It is desirable to begin with the point that these figures probably are (have been shown to be) much too high. One case in point: if the
former figure were true, then one-half of all U.S. population growth would
have to be due to undocumented Mexicans, and simple observation refutes
this. Another case in point: 5–6 million undocumented Mexicans in the
United States—coming, as they are known to, from certain states in Mexico—would essentially drain the complete male labor supply from such
states; various field studies assure us that this has not happened (Cornelius, 1978; Roberts, 1980; Reichert and Massey, 1979; Jones, Harris, and
Valdez, forthcoming [1984]). A recent study by Heer (1979), employing data
from the Current Population Survey, gives a "preferred" estimate of 110
thousand additional *net* undocumented Mexicans per year. Such an estimate implies a high return rate to Mexico each year. If we accept this figure,
and there is much to warrant it, such immigration would account for about
5 percent of *total* U.S. population growth in recent years, and about one-
fourth of all immigration. It is notable that, overall, immigration in the late
1970s accounted for about 20 percent of U.S. population growth; by contrast, between 1890 and 1910, the peak of European immigration to the
United States, around 35 percent of U.S. population growth was attribut-
able to immigration.

There is little doubt, nevertheless, that undocumented migration is a phenomenon markedly on the increase, with apprehensions by the INS quad-
rupling in the decade of the 1970s (Cornelius, 1978:4–5; U.S. Immigration
and Naturalization Service, 1981). Between two-thirds and three-fourths of
Mexican immigrants enter illegally (I prefer the term "undocumented" to
"illegal," and use it from here on). From where do they come in Mexico,
and for where in the United States are they destined? Ninety-three percent
go to only six U.S. states—California, Texas, Illinois, New Mexico, Colorado,
and Arizona (Figure 1), with California receiving over half and Texas a
quarter of the totals (Zazueta and Corona, 1979). Assuming 3.5 million
undocumenteds from Mexico in this country in the late 1970s (estimated
from Heer, 1979; Corwin, 1978; Fogel, 1978), around 8 percent of California's population and 5 percent of Texas's population would be composed
of undocumenteds from Mexico. This extreme concentration in a few states
has lessened over the last decade, as migrants seek out states in the
Northeast and Northwest. In as short a time as two decades, undocumented immigration flows from Mexico could be relatively higher to areas
outside the Southwest than inside. Thus, the border zone is becoming
more of a staging area or "transshipment zone" for destinations in other
parts of the country. Regarding Mexican origins, the phenomenon of migration *al Norte* has deep historical roots and, in a spatial sense, is widespread from Mexico City northward (Figure 1). One must cumulate 16 of
the 32 Mexican states in order to reach 93 percent of the total undocumented migration (North and Houstoun, 1976). Based on the earlier assumptions, in over half the states an estimated 2 percent or more of the
population is currently residing as undocumented aliens in the United
States; these figures reach well above 10 percent for border states and
states of the western Mesa Central, and almost 30 percent for the state of

FIGURE 1

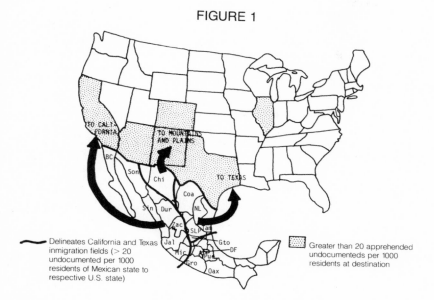

In-migration Fields for Mexican Undocumenteds to the United States, Mid-1970s state abbreviations: BC = Baja California, Chi = Chihuahua, Coa = Coahuila, DF = Distrito Federal, Dur = Durango, Gro = Guerrero, Gto = Guanajuato, Jal = Jalisco, Mic = Michoacan, NL = Nuevo Leon, Oax = Oaxaca, Pue = Puebla, Sin = Sinaloa, SLP = San Luis Potosi, Son = Sonora, Tam = Tamaulipas, Zac = Zacatecas

Zacatecas! (These figures are based on X Censo General de Poblacion, Mexico, 1980, and estimates of 3.5 million undocumenteds, cited earlier.) The migration pattern is highly channelized (Jones, 1982a), with California drawing migrants from western Mexico, and with Texas drawing from northeast Mexico. Migration-field boundaries are abrupt; Coahuila state sends thirty times as many migrants to Texas as to California, while adjacent Durango state sends three times as many to California as to Texas; and analogously for San Luis Potosi (to Texas) versus Zacatecas (to California). Chihuahua feeds its migrants northward to the Rocky Mountains and Great Plains. Very few undocumented migrants make their way from southern Mexico to the United States, although this too seems to be changing.

It is not difficult to uncover reasons for the widespread practice of U.S. migration among Mexicans. The migration streams observed today are overlain upon paths traced time and again over the past 100 years. Major migration waves into the Southwest from Mexico took place during three periods: (1) the railroad and early industrial era of the 1880s; (2) the period of southwestern agricultural development and the Mexican Revolution, 1910–30; and (3) the *bracero* epoch, 1942–64. In all of these periods, the basic family-level causes were the same: young, working-age people, chiefly male, set out to better their economic conditions in Mexico by working in the United States. They were propelled northward by episodic events in their villages—the loss of a crop to drought or a business to collapse; war; or the assumption of new family responsibilities. They were attracted by readily available jobs and the high wages in the United States, even as they were repelled by its social and physical climate. Few intended to stay permanently, and few did so. Many of the same reasons for migrating predominate today.

Undocumented Migration to South and Central Texas: INS Data

U.S. Immigration and Naturalization Service agents have for many years filled out a special form, the I-213, on each deportable alien apprehended in the country. This form includes categories on origin state and town in Mexico, place of apprehension in the United States, entry date for the most recent visit, local employer and type of work, and various other demographic data. Although methods of filling out the forms vary somewhat with the agent and year, and although apprehensions are a clearly biased sample of the total undocumented population, this is a rich, comprehensive, and neglected source of information for researchers.

The biases, nevertheless, must be noted. First, apprehensions are events rather than individuals; thus, individuals who are apprehended several times may be overrepresented and (of course) unapprehended individuals are not represented at all. Second, apprehended illegals tend to be more transient, of somewhat lower socioeconomic status, and less "savvy" than illegals as a whole. Third, undocumenteds may be less than truthful in their responses to INS agents; for example, they may give a border town as their Mexican residence even though they are from the interior of the country, in order to avoid being transported to the interior, which would entail a long return trip to the border for those intending to reenter the United States. The first two biases are not really serious, because almost everyone recognizes that apprehended undocumenteds are a transient subset of the total population, and cannot be equated to that population. The third bias is not especially serious either, because INS personnel repeatedly point out that (1) they can easily differentiate between border and interior migrants on the basis of dress, speech, decorum, etc.; and (2) given this, plus INS techniques used in querying the undocumenteds coupled with the lack of sophistication of migrants from the interior, it is unusual for an interior migrant to lie when completing the forms.

Apprehensions of Mexican undocumenteds in South Texas (combined district and border patrol figures) grew by 35 percent over the 1973–79 period (U.S. Immigration and Naturalization Service, 1981), a rate about half that of growth in apprehensions in the country as a whole. My estimate of the number of undocumenteds in South Texas (here defined as a region roughly south and east of Odessa and south and west of Waco) in the latter 1970s, utilizing previous estimates of 3.5 million nationally, 23 percent of these in Texas, and 68 percent of these in South Texas, comes out to about 550,000, which is 17.5 percent of the region's population. Many of these people are well integrated into the society and unrecognizable from resident Mexican Americans. Samples (240 cases each year) from INS district data show an interesting tendency toward spatial dispersion of undocumenteds within the 88-county district. In April 1974 approximately 25 percent of the undocumenteds were apprehended *outside* of San Antonio, the district headquarters; by April 1980 this proportion had risen to 46 percent. The urban axis between San Antonio and Waco (San Marcos, Austin, and Waco itself) has been an increasingly important target for migrants, as have the smaller outlying communities such as Kerrville, Johnson City, and Seguin. Some of this trend is due to INS policy (e.g., industrial "area control" in Austin and Waco), but most of it is due to the appearance of larger numbers of undocumenteds at these outlying sites than previously. Increased hinterland apprehensions result from larger average hauls on INS sweeps, and a greater incidence of casual pickups (mainly for drunkenness) by local county sheriffs.

Regarding origins in Mexico, South Texas reaches down into northeastern Mexico, drawing large numbers of migrants from as far south as Guanajuato state (Figure 1). Few Anglo Texans, cognizant of the fact that Texas's social and economic "sphere of influence" reaches into New Mexico and Oklahoma (Meinig, 1975:113–17), are aware of a comparable sphere of influence in northeastern Mexico. This "invisible sphere" is almost as large as Texas itself, and it binds together stem families in Mexico and branch families in the United States. INS data for the South Texas district show that in 1980 about half of the undocumenteds apprehended came from four states in the northern mesas, another third from the three border states, and the rest from areas peripheral to these two (Table 1). Guanajuato state alone, at the northern edge of the densely populated Mesa

TABLE 1

Origins of Mexican Undocumenteds Apprehended in the San Antonio
INS District, 1973–81

Regions and Selected States	Percent Distribution (three-year moving averages)		
	1974	1977	1980
Border (Coa, NL, Tam)	29.2	35.7	31.5
Coahuila	13.5	17.2	16.3
Northern Mesas			
(Gto, SLP, Zac, Dur)	45.6	49.3	46.7
Guanajuato	17.1	22.6	19.6
Periphery (Others)	25.3	15.0	21.8
Guerrero	4.0	1.0	3.6
Jalisco	2.8	2.2	3.3
Distrito Federal	1.9	2.2	3.9
Regional Totals	100.1	100.0	100.0

SOURCE: INS, S.A. District Office, Confidential files 1973–81. Appreciation is expressed to Director Richard Casillas, Deputy Director Richard Norton, and Investigators Tom Forrest and Bruce Sims for access to and help in interpreting these data.

NOTE: $N = 720$ for each year.

Central, accounted for almost one-fifth of the total, while Coahuila ac-counted for one-sixth. In Guanajuato, there are several poorer rural muni-cipios in which *ejido* lands are almost nonexistent (partly due to retaliation by the Mexican government against supporters of the church in the Cris-teros rebellion of the 1920s); most of the agricultural labor force is landless; and income is concentrated in the hands of a few *patrones*. Such towns as Dolores Hidalgo, Juventino Rosas, San Miguel de Allende, and Apaseo el Alto/el Grande are for practical purposes labor pools for South Texas agriculture, construction, and trade. In the border state of Coahuila, it is chiefly the northern towns—Piedras Negras, Ciudad Acuña, Nueva Rosita, Sabinas—which send most of the migrants. The latter are in the Sabinas Basin coalfields which, as their counterparts worldwide, suffer episodic unemployment problems. The former two cities depend heavily on U.S. tourism, also a sector sensitive to economic fluctuations.

This invisible sphere of influence for South Texas is apparently expanding southward. Up to 1977 or 1978 both the border and northern mesas were sending migrants at a faster rate than the periphery, but after 1978 migrants from the periphery have been on the uptrend and those from elsewhere on the downtrend (Table 1 and Figure 2). This is evident in the states of Gue-rrero, Jalisco, and the Distrito Federal, which although they accounted for just 10.8 percent of migrants in 1980, nevertheless showed marked gains from 1977, when they accounted for only 5.4 percent.

The INS data tell us a great deal about the mobility of undocumenteds in Mexico prior to their move to Texas. Most migrants—around 80 percent—do not move to other Mexican towns or cities prior to coming to the United States; i.e., they move directly from their places of birth to the United States. This same phenomenon has been observed in the comprehensive

FIGURE 2

Graphic Depiction of Changes in Undocumented Migrant Origins for the San Antonio INS District, 1973–81 (three-year moving averages)

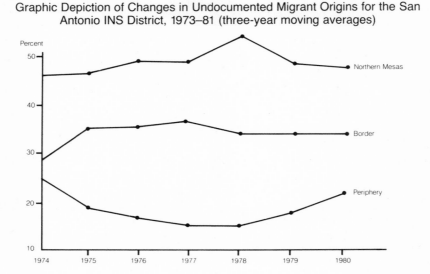

CENIET (ENEFNEU) survey by the Mexican government; one part of that survey, dealing with "absentee" migrants (migrant workers in the United States upon whom data were provided by family members in Mexico), found that in the northern mesa region only 19 percent of the U.S. migrants had prior migration experience in Mexico (calculated from Corona and Ruiz, 1979, p. 34). Furthermore, the INS data reveal that this tendency for direct migration increased over the 1970s. One might suppose that Texas is drawing an increasingly small-town migrant population, but the reverse appears to be true. There was a steady increase in the proportion of migrants from larger population centers ($\geq 50,000$) over the period; closer inspection reveals that both border cities such as Nuevo Laredo and Matamoros and interior cities such as San Luis Potosi and Mexico City were responsible for this trend. Apparently, people who previously did not consider migrating (urban dwellers able to find jobs in large cities) are now doing so.

A final bit of evidence from these data paints a picture of the migrant as nearly always male, young (average age, 27 years), single (in two-thirds of the cases), and temporary (in that only one-fifth of the migrants had been in the United States for more than three or four months prior to apprehension). In recent years, the migrant population has become younger, more migrants are single, and the average length of stay has apparently lengthened. The United States may be drawing more young, ambitious, unattached males from urban areas—a more "adventurous" population, less tied to strictly economic motives. This supposition merits further analysis, but few data exist. It should be noted that the INS data, based on apprehensions, are capturing the less established, less "savvy" migrants, who tend to be young, single, and short-term. Cardenas's interviews with unapprehended illegals in San Antonio (Cardenas, 1976, 1979), by contrast, found a population somewhat older (average age, 28 years), less single (only one-third), and more permanent (78 percent had been in San Antonio for more than six months). In the fourth section of this paper, I attempt to give a more balanced picture by analyzing the mobility and status of a sample of *unapprehended* undocumenteds in San Antonio.

Measuring the "Societal Penetration" of Undocumented Migrants

The question of impacts of undocumenteds upon their host society is exceedingly complex, both conceptually and empirically. Yet it is a question many people are answering daily, in their own particular fashions, based upon their own experiences, their own data sets, and their own latent biases. At the conceptual level, three levels of impacts may be recognized.

1. *Societal Penetration.* This involves the degree to which undocumenteds are geographically spread throughout the host population, the degree to which they hold the same jobs as the subpopulations with which they compete, and the length of time they have resided at the destination. This level of impact is relatively easily measured, but unfortunately it is the least relevant to a careful accounting of net migrant impacts. Nevertheless, INS

and other data make it possible to calculate measures of societal penetration, and to observe how they behave over time.

2. Microeconomic Impacts. These are the local, generally short-term effects of undocumenteds on the economy—for example, on local unemployment and wage rates, costs of living, social service costs, and business profitabilities. These are difficult to measure, because so many factors impinge on labor market conditions and business climate in a city, and because economic information on undocumenteds is hard to get. Nevertheless, a few case studies do exist (Cardenas, 1976; Maram, 1980).

3. *Macroeconomic Impacts*. These are nationwide, generally long-term impacts of a particular undocumented subgroup on the host society, and deal with such matters as the international balance of payments, the flight of U.S. industry abroad, and differential regional growth rates in the country, as well as the topics mentioned in item 2, at the national level. The temporal and spatial scope of these questions makes them very difficult to answer.

Societal penetration as defined here is a three-dimensional phenomenon (Figure 3, panel *A*). *Spatial penetration*, the first dimensions, represents the degree of geographical spread of the undocumented subpopulation. Higher incidence of this subpopulation in nonborder areas and in larger urban centers could place strains on local social services and employment, which previously did not have to be faced at these localities—particularly inasmuch as such services and employment were provided or located via kinship networks at the migrant's prior residence. More important, and related, is the second dimension, the *permanence* of the stay at a particular locality. The longer the stay, regardless of the area involved, the more likely for the undocumented subpopulation to bring family members from Mexico and to avail itself of local social services and job opportunities. The third dimension is *occupational penetration,* and it is the most important of the three, representing mobility from "entry" jobs such as agricultural worker, material handler, or construction worker to semiskilled and skilled jobs such as equipment operator, roofer, or bricklayer. It is probable that occupational penetration as so defined would relate to the displacement of skilled resident minorities from the latter subsectors, thus having a significant employment and welfare impact locally.

Panels *B*, *C*, and *D* of Figure 3 illustrate three scenarios over time, from a possible set of dozens. In the first scenario (panel *B*), undocumenteds spread geographically throughout a given destination region, but since they remain only temporarily and do not advance occupationally, their impacts are small. In the second scenario (panel *C*), they spread spatially and also lengthen their stay, and as a result are more prone to use local schools and medical facilities; their impact is moderate. In the third scenario (panel *D*), the undocumented subpopulation not only becomes more permanent and widespread, but it penetrates skilled job categories previously dominated by resident minorities; the impact in this scenario is considerably greater than in the other two.

The purpose of developing this schema is to discern the potential impact of the undocumented population of South Texas on the host population.

FIGURE 3

Societal Penetration of Undocumenteds: A Three-Dimensional Measure
(numbers represent sequential points in time)

A—The Three Dimensions

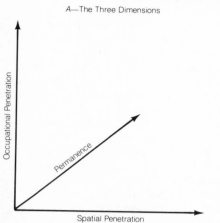

B—*Scenario 1:* Increasing Spatial Penetration (other factors constant)

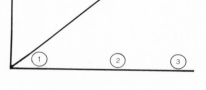

C—*Scenario 2:* Increasing Spatial Penetration and Permanence (occupational penetration constant)

D—*Scenario 3:* Increasing Spatial Penetration, Occupational Penetration, and Permanence

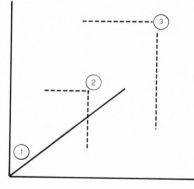

Because of the biased nature of the data, the crudeness of the indexes, and the fact that "penetration" may be a pale reflection of economic impacts, the results of this exercise have to be treated with caution.

Operational measures of the three components of societal penetration are available from the aforementioned INS data. It was previously noted that the proportion of South Texas apprehensions outside San Antonio almost doubled between 1974 and 1980. This proportion, when divided by the proportion of total resident population outside San Antonio in those years and multiplied by 100, gives an index of relative *spatial penetration*. The *permanence* measure is simply the percentage of undocumenteds who, upon apprehension, had been in the district for a work season or longer—i.e., three months or more.

The *occupational penetration* measure merits more discussion owing to its special importance. As with the other two measures, it is cross-sectional, telling us the degree of penetration for two analogous undocumented populations at two different periods in time, without revealing whether individual migrants have penetrated the host society over time. The basis for the measure is the proportion of undocumenteds engaged in skilled or semiskilled jobs—i.e., craftsmen and operatives as well as positions within the manufacturing sector. Jobs falling into these categories over the decade included mechanic, carpenter, seamstress, mason, welder, roofer, painter, baker, and worker in the lumber, meat-packing, food, and other light manufacturing industries. Table 2 shows that among the sampled undocumenteds the proportion of jobs in these categories remained almost constant over the decade. In contrast, the proportion of resident Mexican American males in these categories rose from .530 to .594 over this period. Thus, our index of occupational penetration (the ratio between the undocumented proportion and the resident Mexican American proportion at the same point in time) actually declined over the decade, as shown in the table.

All three indexes are expressed on 0–100 scales in which 0 represents no penetration and 100, complete penetration.

TABLE 2

Calculation of the Index of Occupational Penetration for San Antonio and South Texas Undocumenteds

Period	From INS Sample of 240 I-213 Forms:			From U.S. Census and Cardenas (1976): Proportion of Resident Mexican American Males in Skilled Jobs	Ratio of Proportions for Undocumented vs. Resident Mexican American Males × 100
	Number in Skilled and Semiskilled Jobs	Total Number of Jobs Identifiable by Occupation	Skilled as Proportion of Total		
1972	23	131	.176	.530	33.2
1979–80	29	181	.160	.594	26.9

Source: Calculations by author from INS and U.S. Census data, in addition to data from Cardenas (1976).

The results (Table 3) suggest that societal penetration has been moderate, undocumenteds are present in outlying parts of the district, and in skilled jobs, to around a third the level of the host population (except for spatial penetration for 1980, which had risen to two-thirds). Permanence is markedly low for both periods. The results also suggest that in 1980 societal penetration was only marginally higher than in the early 1970s. Significantly more migrants were found outside the San Antonio area and permanence did increase; but on the most significant component, occupational penetration, a decrease occurred, as noted.

These results do not necessarily imply that societal penetration by individual migrants isn't occurring. Later research by the author (Jones, Harris, and Valdez, forthcoming [1984]) indicates, in fact, that a typical migrant works on a farm or ranch in South Texas on his first job and later moves into an urban job in San Antonio, Dallas, or Houston. Thus, individual migrants may move up the job ladder and over space even though a cross-sectional profile of migrants does not show significant change over time, because there are enough new entrants at the lower job levels to offset occupational mobility of migrants to the upper levels.

It may be argued that this more recently arrived, transient subpopulation of undocumenteds which the INS data capture cannot be used to represent the established resident subpopulation of undocumenteds, just as we cannot determine an iceberg's shape and size simply by observing its tip. In a very strict sense this is correct; but this is no reason to believe that

TABLE 3

Indexes of Societal Penetration: Mexican Undocumenteds in the San Antonio INS District: Early 1970s and 1980

	Time	
Index	Early 1970s	1980
Spatial penetration: Distribution of apprehensions between San Antonio and other parts of the district (0 = no penetration [all clustered in San Antonio], 100 = apprehendees distributed as population in district)	37.0[a]	67.5
Permanence: Length of stay: percentage of undocumenteds who had been in the district for at least three months prior to apprehension (0 = no permanence [residence times all less than three months], 100 = all stayed longer than three months)	10.8[a]	18.8
Occupational penetration: Proportion of sample holding skilled jobs, relative to the proportion of resident Mexican American males holding skilled jobs (0 = no skilled jobs held; 100 = undocumenteds held skilled jobs to same degree as resident population)	33.2[b]	26.9

SOURCE: Calculations by author from INS data, and other data cited in text.

NOTE: N = 240 cases for each time period. The indexes are each on a scale of 0–100.

[a] 1974.

[b] 1970–72.

the former subpopulation cannot reflect some of the basic trends of the latter just as one *can* get an idea of an iceberg's shape and size from the visible tip. After all, the unestablished subpopulation becomes the established subpopulation through adaptational stages, and the established subpopulation becomes the legal Mexican origin subpopulation (Portes, 1977), with attrition (returnees) at various stages of the process.

Undocumented Migration to South and Central Texas: Refugee Services Data

Data made available to me from the casework files of a refugee services agency in San Antonio make it possible to calculate some of the aforementioned migrant characteristics for a group of Mexican undocumenteds who are likely to be more "established" than the INS sample. The respondents came voluntarily to the agency, generally from within 150 miles of San Antonio, to seek immigration counseling between 1973 and 1981. In all, 181 respondents constitute this sample. In the following comparisons, data for both the refugee services sample and the INS sample are grouped into two time periods, 1973–79, and 1980–81. Basically, this is done to assure adequate subsample sizes for computation of statistics on the refugee services data.

The migrants in the refugee services sample are obviously a more "established" group than the INS sample, on the criteria of permanence and age (Table 4); in 1980–81, about a third recorded a U.S. entry date of greater than 4 years ago, and the average age for these migrants was 30.5 years. They tended, in 1980–81, to come from border states, and from smaller towns, to a relatively higher degree than the other sample. The change in the origin profile between the 1970s and 1980–81 for this group is interesting. The tendency in recent years has been for the refugee services sample to come more from the border states and less from peripheral states, whereas the INS-samples have come increasingly from the periphery and less from the northern mesas. In order to understand this, first note that in the refugee services sample, a respondent was assigned to a particular period on the basis of when he or she came for immigration counseling, not when he or she entered the United States. Most of these entries were made several years ago; the median year of entry is 1977, whereas the median year of counseling is 1980. It will be noted (Figure 2) that in 1977, in the INS sample, the proportion of migrants from the border states was increasing, that from the periphery was decreasing, and that from the northern mesas was basically stable—trends which reflect those of the refugee services sample exactly. Thus, despite the greater tendency of more established migrants to come from border regions, changes in origin patterns for this group reflect those of the less-established group some 4–5 years ago; the two patterns seem to be part of the same process with a time lag.

It is difficult to make a comparison between the two groups regarding absolute levels of spatial penetration and permanence, because of the

TABLE 4

Statistics on Two Subpopulations of South Texas Undocumenteds

Category and Index	INS Data[a]		Refugee Services Data[b]	
	1973–79	1980–81	1973–79	1980–81
Mexican origins (% distributions)				
Border (Coa, NL, Tam)	32.0	32.3	45.8	49.4
Northern Mesas (Gto, SLP, Zac, Dur)	48.6	42.1	33.3	34.1
Periphery (Others)	19.3	25.6	20.8	16.5
Totals	99.9	100.0	99.9	100.0
Prior mobility				
Percent born in same town as previous town of Mexican residence	78.8[c]	81.9[d]	78.2[c]	82.7[d]
Percent whose most recent Mexican residence is city of at least 50,000 population	28.8	34.6	21.9	20.0
Average age	29.0	27.1	31.3	30.5
Societal penetration (each index on a scale of 0–100)				
Spatial: Frequency of South Texas migrants outside of San Antonio, relative to overall population in district	37.0	67.5	19.7	29.5
Permanence: Percentage of migrants who have been at least n months on this trip to the United States[e]	10.8	18.8	45.8	32.6
Occupational: Relative frequency of migrants in skilled job category— undocumented vs. resident Mexican American male labor force in district	33.2	26.9	72.3	74.7

SOURCE: Calculations by author from the two data sets.

[a] $N = 1,680$ for 1973–79 and for 1980–81.

[b] $N = 96$ for 1973–79, and 85 for 1980–81.

[c] 1978.

[d] 1980.

[e] For INS data, $n = 3$; for refugee services data, $n = 48$ (four years).

differences in the definitions of the geographic areas and the time thresholds involved. On the other hand, the level of occupational penetration is comparable; in 1980–81, the refugee services group's representation in the skilled job categories was 75 percent that of the resident male Mexican American working population—a rate three times that of the INS group. This suggests that, over time, substantial occupational gains may be made by undocumenteds who "stick it out" in South Texas.

Changes in societal penetration between the two periods under study, however, were hardly greater for the refugee services than for the INS group. Spatial penetration is quite evident, as before; but permanence actually decreased and occupational penetration increased only slightly.

FIGURE 4

Graphic Representation of Societal Penetration of Undocumenteds in the San
Antonio INS District (*1* = 1974, *2* = 1980)

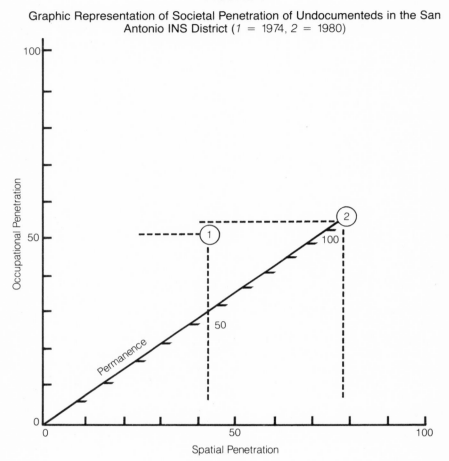

Spatial Penetration

The reason that there is little occupational progress over this period is a
function of both the length of the period and the fact that the refugee services sample had already achieved significant occupational status by the
beginning of the period.

Summary and Conclusions

Analysis of the INS sample sheds light upon a whole series of questions
concerning the characteristics and dynamics of a basically "transient" subpopulation of Mexican undocumenteds to South Texas during the 1970s.
Most migrants come from seven states in northeastern Mexico; states far-
ther south are, however, sending migrants at increasing rates relative to
the traditional migrant hearths. The migrants tend to come from small and

moderate-sized towns in Mexico, though this is also changing in favor of metropolitan areas. This subpopulation has not penetrated into the social institutions of South Texas to a very high degree, in that permanence (and as a result, social service utilization—see below) is low, and occupational mobility relative to resident Mexican Americans, negligible. However, a substantially higher proportion of this population is choosing to live outside the immediate border region and outside of San Antonio itself, which may herald impacts on the above institutions in the future.

Analysis of the smaller sample of unapprehended undocumenteds in the San Antonio area—the refugee services group—shows it to be different in significant ways. They tend to come from the Mexican border states and from smaller towns to a higher degree, and many more tend to hold skilled jobs in the area, relative to the other sample. This group holds about three-fourths as many skilled jobs, for its size, as the resident Mexican American population, even though its job mobility in the late 1970s was slight in relation to the latter population. Finally, the group is much more permanent than the INS group.

Given the trends suggested in this paper—i.e., the proliferation of younger, more adventuresome, urban origin migrants from interior Mexico—we may surmise that whole sectors of Mexican society will be participating who did not participate in U.S. migration before. Recent (spring, 1983) unprecedented INS apprehension rates along the Texas border have indeed uncovered more migrants from interior and southern Mexico, as well as more urban origin migrants. The impacts on Mexico of losing a young, skilled urban labor force may be profound; the country may find its industrial productivity stunted in years to come. Moreover, the "migrant syndrome" (Reichert, 1981) which has transformed many Mexican municipios into labor pools for southwestern business, industry, and construction is almost sure to spread and intensify. The adverse impact on the United States of this new population of undocumenteds would appear to be less than the impact on Mexico. On the negative side, migrants will be more skilled than previous undocumenteds; this will equip them for positions as middle-level craftsmen and operatives. They will displace some native workers by taking such jobs. On the other hand, they will probably remain transient, loyal to their employers, and hard-working, as interior migrants have proven to be in the past. Thus, they will help small labor-intensive firms to remain in business, generating more jobs in the long run. They may help parts of the United States maintain their high industrial productivity and/or low costs of living, without becoming burdens in those regions. Finally, their skills, gained at Mexico's expense, represent a net gain to the U.S. economy, discounting for subutilization of the skills of any U.S. workers who are displaced.

What of other types of "societal penetration" than those mentioned? Have South Texas undocumenteds placed any burden on social institutions—schools, hospitals, welfare services? In South Texas, just as in California where several studies have been carried out, the answer appears to be a resounding "no." In the school year 1980–81, following a U.S. district court ruling ordering Texas to admit children of undocumented aliens, only a miniscule 394 of an anticipated 16,000 undocumented public school children (2.5 percent) actually enrolled. With the exception of maternity services, very few public hospital services are sought by aliens in Bexar County; and welfare services are sought with even less frequency (Jones, Harris, and Valdez, forthcoming [1984]). Thus, the impact on public health, education, and welfare facilities by undocumenteds is undoubtedly much less than their impact on employment and wages.

In this paper, I have repeatedly made the point that in order to measure impacts of undocumenteds we really need to carry out detailed economic case studies of impacts on jobs, the profitability of businesses, local costs of living, and so on, at national and regional levels. The three-dimensional measure of societal penetration is only a poor man's substitute. It is quite possible that the impacts of societal penetration as defined here—spatially, temporally, occupationally—are net benefits rather than net disbenefits, in the aggregate. Hansen (1981, chap.6) has recently made this point forcefully, by arguing (1) that undocumented migrants may produce a "larger social pie" for everyone (the "positive-sum game" argument, also made by Cornelius, 1978); (2) that the present U.S. birthrate coupled with the unpopularity of "vocational" careers, may generate a shortage of blue-collar labor of all types in the near future, in the absence of immigrant labor (see Piore, 1979, for an analogous argument); and (3) that costs of living in the U.S. could well be higher without undocumented labor. These are arguments that cannot be ignored.

REFERENCES

Cardenas, Gilberto. 1976. "Manpower Impact and Problems of Mexican Illegal Aliens in an Urban Labor Market." Ph.D. dissertation, University of Illinois at Urbana-Champaign.

――――. 1979. "Mexican Illegal Aliens in the San Antonio Labor Market," *Texas Business Review*, 53 (November/December):187–91.

Cornelius, Wayne A. 1978. *Mexican Migration to the United States: Causes, Consequences, and U.S. Responses* (Cambridge: M.I.T., Center for International Studies).

Corona, Rodolfo, and Crescencio Ruiz. 1979. "Migracion Interna y Internacional." Report on a survey sponsored by the Centro Nacional de Informacion y Estadisticas del Trabajo, Mexico, D.F., presented at the Simposio Nacional Sobre Emigracion y Distribucion Espacial de la Poblacion, Guadalajara, Jalisco, 5–9 December 1979.

Corwin, Arthur F., ed. 1978. *Immigrants—and Immigrants: Perspectives on Mexican Labor Migration to the United States* (Westport, Conn.: Greenwood).

Fogel, Walter A. 1978. *Mexican Illegal Alien Workers in the United States* (Los Angeles: University of California, Institute of Industrial Relations).

Hansen, Niles M. 1981. *The Border Economy: Regional Development in the Southwest* (Austin: University of Texas Press).

Heer, David M. 1979. "What is the Annual Net Flow of Undocumented Mexican Immigrants to the United States?" *Demography,* 16 (November):417–23.

Jones, Richard C. 1982a. "Channelization of Undocumented Mexican Migrants to the U.S.," *Economic Geography,* 58 (April):156–76.

————. 1982b. "Undocumented Migration from Mexico: Some Geographical Questions," *Annals, Association of American Geographers,* 72 (March):77–87.

Jones, Richard C., Richard J. Harris, and Avelardo Valdez. Forthcoming, 1984. "Occupational and Spatial Mobility of Undocumented Migrants from Dolores Hidalgo, Guanajuato," in Richard C. Jones, ed., *Spatial Perspectives on Undocumented Migration: Mexico and the U.S.* (Totowa, N.J.: Rowman and Allanheld).

Maram, Sheldon L. 1980. *Hispanic Workers in the Garment and Restaurant Industries in Los Angeles County.* Working Papers in U.S.-Mexican Studies, no. 12 (La Jolla: University of California, San Diego, Center for U.S.-Mexican Studies, October).

Meinig, D. W. 1975. *Imperial Texas: An Interpretive Essay in Cultural Geography* (Austin: University of Texas Press).

North, David S., and Marion F. Houstoun. 1976. *The Characteristics and Role of Illegal Aliens in the U.S. Labor Market: An Exploratory Study.* Report prepared for the U.S. Department of Labor, Employment and Training Administration (Washington, D.C.: Linton).

Piore, Michael J. 1979. *Birds of Passage: Migrant Labor and Industrial Societies* (New York: Cambridge University Press).

Portes, Alejandro. 1977. "Labor Functions of Illegal Aliens," *Society,* 14 (September/October):31–37.

Reichert, Joshua S. 1981. "The Migrant Syndrome: Seasonal U.S. Wage Labor and Rural Development in Central Mexico," *Human Organization,* 40 (Spring):55–66.

Reichert, Joshua S., and Douglas S. Massey. 1979. "Patterns of U.S. Migration from a Mexican Sending Community: A Comparison of Legal and Illegal Migrants," *International Migration Review,* 13 (Winter):599–623.

Roberts, Kenneth D. 1980. *Agrarian Structure and Labor Migration in Rural Mexico: The Case of Circular Migration of Undocumented Workers in the U.S.* (Austin: The University of Texas at Austin, Institute of Latin American Studies).

U.S. Immigration and Naturalization Service. 1981. "Deportable Aliens Located by Nationality, 1974–78." Washington, D.C.: U.S. Immigration and Naturalization Service, Statistical Division. (Acknowledgment to Margaret Sullivan for providing the data.)

Zazueta, Carlos H., and Rodolfo Corona. 1979. *Los Trabajadores Mexicanos en los Estados Unidos: Primeros Resultados de la Encuesta Nacional de Emigracion a la Frontera Norte del Pais y los Estados Unidos* [ENEFNEU] (Mexico, D.F.: Centro Nacional de Informacion y Estadisticas del Trabajo [CENIET]).

7. THE WAGE STRUCTURE OF HISPANIC MEN: IMPLICATIONS FOR POLICY [1]

Cordelia W. REIMERS, *Hunter College and Graduate School of the City University of New York*

Using microdata from the 1976 Survey of Income and Education, the author estimates wage formulas for Mexican American, Puerto Rican, Cuban, Central and South American, "other Spanish," and black and white non-Hispanic men. The potential improvements in average wages for each minority group to be gained by altering specific characteristics are discussed. Increasing Hispanics' educational attainment would have the greatest impact.

Hispanic Americans are widely recognized as a disadvantaged minority. Their family incomes in 1981 averaged only 72 percent of white non-Hispanics (U.S. Bureau of the Census, 1982:9). This gap in family income is largely due to the low wage rates of Hispanic men (Reimers, 1984). Hispanic Americans suffer from a number of handicaps in the labor market that may be responsible for their low wages. Their average levels of education are lower; more of them are recent immigrants to the United States; more of them (even of those born in the United States) lack fluency in English; they are younger, on average, than white non-Hispanics; and they tend to live in low-price, low-wage parts of the country. There is also a widespread assumption that they suffer from employment discrimination; consequently, they are designated as a protected group by the government agencies charged with enforcing equal employment opportunity.

Some of these conditions are more amenable to influence by public policy than others. Command of English, educational attainment, and employment discrimination, for example, are clearly feasible targets for pol-

[1] A longer version of this paper, including more discussion of statistical issues, is in the June 1984 issue of *Social Science Quarterly*. An earlier version was presented at the annual meeting of the American Economic Association, Washington, D.C., 28–30 December 1981. This research was supported by the U.S. Department of Labor, Employment and Training Administration, Grant No. 21-34-78-60 to Princeton University. Gilles Grenier and Jesse Abraham provided excellent research assistance; Stephen Baldwin, Barry Chiswick, Mark Killingsworth, Ralph Smith, and members of the Princeton University Labor Economics/Industrial Relations Seminar made useful suggestions.

icy intervention; whereas age structure, nativity, and location cannot be directly affected. It would aid in deciding which policies would be most helpful if we knew how much impact poor English, or an additional year of school, has on a person's wage. If the returns to education are unusually low for members of an ethnic minority—due perhaps to their lack of access to highly paid crafts, managerial, or professional positions—then programs to encourage high school completion and college attendance will be less effective. Moreover, low returns to education are a "rational" reason for students' dropping out, which makes it harder to raise the group's educational level.

Such questions as these can be answered by estimating a formula for wages, which shows the impact on wages of given variables, holding other characteristics of the person constant. This study used the 1976 Survey of Income and Education to analyze the way men's wages vary within different ethnic groups according to differences in human capital and other characteristics. I estimated separate wage formulas for Mexican American, Puerto Rican, Cuban, Central and South American, and "other Spanish" males, and for black and white non-Hispanics as well, for purposes of comparison.[2] These estimated wage formulas were then used to assess the potential improvement to Hispanic males' average wages from various policy options.

Data and Methods

Despite the growing awareness of Hispanics' economic problems, relatively little research effort has been directed toward analyzing the structure of Hispanics' wages. Studies by Carliner (1976), Long (1977), Gwartney and Long (1978), Chiswick (1978), and Tienda and Niedert (1980) are notable exceptions. This neglect has been partly due to a paucity of data. Hispanics constitute only about 6 percent of the U.S. population, and most survey samples are too small to include enough Hispanics for fruitful analysis. Furthermore, until 1970 the decennial Census did not attempt to identify persons of Spanish origin outside the Southwest, beyond the second generation in the United States. The 1970 Census, for the first time, asked a sample of respondents to identify their ethnic origin, so that Hispanics of Mexican, Puerto Rican, Cuban, Central or South American, and "other Spanish" backgrounds could be studied separately.

The 1976 Survey of Income and Education, which was used in this study, is a large survey that identifies these five major Spanish origin groups and contains large enough samples for analysis of such small

[2] The seven groups in this study are mutually exclusive: the Hispanics may be of any race, the whites and blacks include non-Hispanics only, and non-Hispanics who are neither white nor black (e.g., Asians) are excluded from this study.

groups as the Cubans.[3] It also contains information on a number of wage-related characteristics that are not available in the Census, such as current language skills, years of education obtained abroad, health disability, U.S. military experience, and usual weekly hours worked last year. (The latter enables one to compute hourly wage rates more accurately, by dividing annual earnings by the product of weeks worked and usual weekly hours, all reported for the same year.) The most serious omissions are measures of accumulated work experience, job training, and ability.

The samples used to analyze wages consisted of males aged 14 or over who were employed in 1975, but who were neither self-employed nor full-time students nor in the Armed Forces. The resulting samples contain about 60 percent of all the males aged 14 or over who were surveyed. I used a statistical technique suggested by Heckman (1979) to handle the possible bias arising from the sample-selection rule.

To take account of geographical differences in prices and wages, the wage formula has as dependent variable the logarithm of the "real" wage rate, obtained by dividing the wage by a cost-of-living index.[4] Using the logarithm of the wage means that the impacts of the explanatory variables on wages are measured in percentage, rather than dollar, terms. The explanatory variables are: educational attainment, years of education obtained abroad, nativity, command of English, potential work experience in the United States (i.e., age, adjusted for age at immigration or years spent in school) and its square, potential work experience abroad and its square, U.S. military experience, health disability, government employment, race, and the fraction Hispanic in the state of residence. Educational attainment and U.S. work experience are interacted with nativity, to see whether immigrants get lower returns to these forms of human capital investment than U.S. natives.

The variables are defined in Table 1, and their average values for the male wage earners in each ethnic group are given in Table 2. They show some interesting differences among these ethnic groups. Average education levels, around 12.5 years for white non-Hispanic male wage-earners and 10.5 years for blacks, were less than 10th grade for Mexican Americans and Puerto Ricans. The other three Hispanic groups averaged between 11 and 12 grades of school. The Mexican Americans and Puerto Ricans were younger than the other groups on average, and the Cubans

---

[3] For a detailed description of this data set, which includes over 150,000 households in all 50 states and the District of Columbia, see U.S. Bureau of the Census (1978). Race was assigned by interviewer observation; ethnic origin or descent was self-identified by the respondent from a list of ethnic groups that included Mexican American, Chicano, Mexican, Mexicano, Puerto Rican, Cuban, Central or South American, and Other Spanish. The first four comprise our "Mexican American" category.

[4] The cost index used in this study was the Bureau of Labor Statistics' index of comparative cost of living based on an intermediate budget for a four-person family in autumn 1975 (U.S. Department of Labor, 1977:277). When a sample member lived in a SMSA not included in the BLS survey, the cost index for the closest comparable SMSA was used.

TABLE 1

Definitions of Variables

WAGE (*W*):	Annual earnings/(weeks × usual hours worked) in 1975.
LNWAGE (ln*W*):	Natural logarithm of WAGE.
LNCOST (ln*P*):	Natural logarithm of BLS cost index for moderate family budget in SMSA or region of residence. If SMSA of residence was not in the BLS sample, another SMSA in the same state or region was used. If residence was not identified as being in an SMSA, the BLS index for nonmetropolitan areas in the region was used.
LNRWAGE (ln(*W/P*)):	LNWAGE minus LNCOST.
ED:	Highest grade of school completed.
FORED:	Years attended school abroad (= 0 if born in United States mainland).
USEXP:	Years of potential work experience in United States: if born in mainland United States, age − highest grade attended − 5; if born outside mainland United States, estimated time in United States (using midpoint of immigration period) or age − highest grade attended − 5, whichever is smaller.
USEXPSQ:	Square of USEXP.
FOREXP:	Years of potential work experience before immigrating to United States: age − highest grade attended − 5 − USEXP.
FOREXPSQ:	Square of FOREXP.
VET	= 1 if veteran; = 0 otherwise.
FBORN	= 1 if born outside mainland United States; = 0 otherwise.
ENGNVG	= 1 if does not speak and understand English very well; = 0 otherwise.
HEALTH	= 1 if health limits ability to work; = 0 otherwise.
GOVT	= 1 if government employee; = 0 otherwise.
NONWHT	= 1 if race is nonwhite; = 0 otherwise.
PROPHIS:	Percentage Hispanic of population in state of residence.
λ:	Inverse of Mill's ratio, predicted from reduced-form probit equation for being in wage sample.

were even older than white non-Hispanics. Almost all of the Cubans and Central and South Americans were foreign-born, and the latter group had arrived in the United States even more recently than the Cubans. Eighty percent of the Puerto Ricans were born on the island. Seventy-five percent of the Mexican Americans, on the other hand, were born in the

TABLE 2

Means of Variables: Males in Wage Sample

	White Non-Hispanics	Mexican Americans	Puerto Ricans	Cubans	Central and South Americans	Other Hispanics	Black Non-Hispanics
WAGE (W)	5.97	4.31	4.52	5.33	4.94	5.20	4.65
LNWAGE (ln W)	1.607	1.303	1.389	1.515	1.397	1.466	1.374
LNCOST (ln P)	-0.025	-0.068	0.074	-0.015	0.051	-0.043	-0.028
LNRWAGE (ln(W/P))	1.632	1.371	1.316	1.530	1.346	1.509	1.402
ED	12.41	9.44	9.75	11.32	11.79	11.04	10.54
VET	.486	.304	.255	.112	.0854	.427	.374
FBORN	.0282	.269	.793	.950	.921	.119	.0149
FBORN × FORED	0.192	1.31	5.25	8.64	9.23	1.04	0.149
ED × FBORN	0.329	1.93	7.38	10.73	10.80	1.19	0.174
USEXP	20.56	16.74	15.50	12.19	9.72	20.07	22.79
USEXP × FBORN	0.574	3.64	12.02	11.04	8.20	1.51	0.125
FOREXP × FBORN	0.208	2.77	4.94	11.92	9.33	1.25	0.168
USEXPSQ	656.49	474.24	365.76	244.24	169.35	641.10	782.67
USEXPSQ × FBORN	17.79	90.80	264.10	196.42	126.95	32.50	1.63
FOREXPSQ × FBORN	4.18	60.71	91.38	293.52	191.01	27.95	3.56
PROPHIS	3.40	14.89	5.22	6.12	6.68	17.11	3.41
ENGNVG	.00756	.321	.446	.538	.482	.186	.00181
HEALTH	.101	.0917	.0764	.0562	.0549	.0900	.120
GOVT	.169	.177	.150	.0812	.104	.226	.240
NONWHT	0	.0219	.0860	.0562	.116	.0517	1
λ	.536	.416	.395	.461	.309	.454	.472

United States. The "other Hispanics" were overwhelmingly (90 percent) from the second or later generations in the United States. (This group includes persons of mixed Hispanic ancestry as well as those who did not identify with any of the listed Hispanic groups.) Not surprisingly, the percentages of each group with fluent English and with veteran status reflected the percentages born in the United States. Government employment also tended to reflect birthplace, except that Mexican Americans and Puerto Ricans were about as likely as white non-Hispanics to hold government jobs, and blacks and "other Hispanics" were much more likely to do so.

Estimates of the Wage Formulas

The estimates of the percentage effects of the explanatory variables on wages are reported in Table 3. They are not directly comparable to those found by other researchers due to differences in the data set used, the criteria for inclusion in the sample, the form of the wage formula, and the variables included in the wage formula. For instance, the present estimates are corrected for sample-selection bias, and *real* hourly earnings is used as the dependent variable to deal with regional variation in wage rates. Therefore it is not surprising that the present estimates of the returns to education and of other effects differ somewhat from those found in other studies. Nevertheless, these results are not inconsistent with those reported by DeFreitas (1982), Chiswick (1978, 1980, 1981), Tienda and Niedert (1980), Gwartney and Long (1978), and Carliner (1976).

When we examine Table 3, we find that all Hispanic groups except U.S.-born Mexicans and Central and South Americans have lower returns to education than Anglos. (The return to education is the percentage increase in the wage rate associated with an extra year of schooling.) There is no appreciable difference between U.S. and foreign schooling in enhancing earning capacity.

Except for Cubans and "other Hispanics," the foreign-born seem to have lower returns to their U.S. schooling than the native-born members of their ethnic group. For example, U.S.-born men of Mexican background have as high a return to schooling as white non-Hispanics, about 6 percent; while those born in Mexico have only a 3.6 percent return per grade of U.S. schooling. Puerto Rican men born on the mainland get the same return as U.S.-born blacks, about 5 percent; while those born in Puerto Rico have a 3.0 percent return. Foreign-born white non-Hispanics have a return of 5.2 percent per grade, and foreign-born blacks have 2.0 percent. For Central and South Americans, the return to U.S. schooling is 5 percent for those born abroad and 12 percent for the very few born in the United States. Foreign-born Cubans, on the other hand, seem to have a higher rate of return to U.S. schooling (4.1 percent) than those born in

TABLE 3

Male Wage Equations for LNRWAGE–Corrected for Selectivity Bias

(Corrected Standard Errors in Parenthesis)

	White Non-Hispanics	Mexican Americans	Puerto Ricans	Cubans	Central and South Americans	Other Hispanics	Black Non-Hispanics
INTERCEPT	0.622*	0.721*	0.619	1.320	-1.321	0.992*	0.854*
	(0.0783)	(0.0945)	(0.358)	(0.944)	(1.021)	(0.173)	(0.0908)
ED	.0611*	.0621*	.0486	-.0253	.119	.0324*	.0496*
	(.00421)	(.00599)	(.0259)	(.0731)	(.0680)	(.0104)	(.00459)
ED × FBORN	-.00940	-.0264*	-.0185	.0667	-.0685	.0152	-.0292
	(.0215)	(.00926)	(.0284)	(.0755)	(.0700)	(.0339)	(.0418)
FORED × FBORN	.00484	-.00248	-.00278	-.00876	.00826	-.0123	-.0167
	(.0140)	(.00782)	(.00810)	(.0160)	(.0162)	(.0284)	(.0411)
FBORN	.0185	.185	.298	-.548	1.639	-.297	.335
	(.343)	(.125)	(.369)	(.907)	(1.061)	(.393)	(.434)
ENGNVG	-.0578	-.0396	-.179*	-.137	-.116	-.135	.443
	(.174)	(.0391)	(.0716)	(.0958)	(.113)	(.0811)	(.277)
USEXP	.0400*	.0244*	.0474*	.0984*	.122*	.0297*	.0147*
	(.00330)	(.00412)	(.0143)	(.0453)	(.0485)	(.00762)	(.00383)
USEXP × FBORN	-.00121	.0127*	-.0185	-.0498	-.0650	.0231	.0419
	(.0179)	(.00637)	(.0160)	(.0462)	(.0512)	(.0272)	(.0563)
FOREXP × FBORN	.0156	-.00209	-.00339	.0139	-.000198	.0266	-.00142
	(.0172)	(.00553)	(.00966)	(.0109)	(.0171)	(.0194)	(.0249)

	(1)	(2)	(3)	(4)	(5)	(6)	(7)
USEXPSQ	-.000560*	-.000238*	-.000734*	-.00172*	-.00194	-.000389*	-.000182*
	(.0000664)	(.0000765)	(.000296)	(.000879)	(.00127)	(.000145)	(.0000642)
USEXPSQ × FBORN	-.0000330	-.000358*	.000303	.000744	.000706	-.000654	-.00131
	(.000388)	(.000130)	(.000356)	(.000937)	(.00135)	(.000612)	(.00215)
FOREXPSQ × FBORN	-.000447	.0000931	.0000922	-.000313	.000198	-.000485	.000239
	(.000473)	(.000119)	(.000305)	(.000273)	(.000480)	(.000437)	(.000686)
VET	-.00607	.0149	.000283	.205	-.0859	.0329	.0217
	(.0245)	(.0335)	(.0669)	(.149)	(.240)	(.0592)	(.0264)
HEALTH	-.00785	-.0201	.187	.101	.236	-.0430	.117*
	(.0389)	(.0505)	(.134)	(.197)	(.237)	(.104)	(.0452)
GOVT	-.0141	-.0316	-.0185	-.00754	.0869	.0859	.0701*
	(.0274)	(.0332)	(.0743)	(.142)	(.157)	(.0595)	(.0247)
NONWHT	—	-.104	.109	-.126	.0111	-.130	—
		(.0907)	(.0963)	(.175)	(.147)	(.113)	
PROPHIS	.00208	-.00388*	-.00790	.0156	.00320	-.00596*	-.00110
	(.00197)	(.00130)	(.00681)	(.0120)	(.00844)	(.00172)	(.00218)
λ	-.378*	-.394*	-.195	-.253	-.0637	-.194	-.432*
	(.0578)	(.0574)	(.117)	(.203)	(.215)	(.114)	(.0575)
N	2,911	1,778	314	160	164	522	2,209
R^2	.261	.236	.256	.338	.293	.216	.228
$(\sigma_{11})^{1/2}$ (corrected)	.594	.577	.447	.480	.565	.549	.577

*Significantly different from zero at .05 level.

the U.S.[5] "Other Hispanics" also seem to have a higher rate of return to U.S. schooling if they were born abroad—4.8 percent, as opposed to 3.2 percent for those who were born in the United States. The margin of error in all of these estimates is so large, however, that we cannot be sure that there is in fact a difference between the foreign-born and native-born in returns to U.S. education, except in the case of Mexican American men.[6]

Language affects the wages of Hispanics; but health, race, and sector of employment apparently do not. The estimated wage loss from a poor command of English varies across groups, from an insignificant 4 percent for Mexican origin men to 18 percent for Puerto Ricans.[7] Surprisingly, poor health does not depress the wage rate a man is offered.[8] Race has no significant impact on wages among Hispanics either; nonwhite Hispanics suffer from one handicap, not two. Black men do get 7 percent more in the public than the private sector, but government wages are not significantly different from wages in private firms for white or Hispanic men (except, possibly, "other Hispanics").[9]

In states where Hispanics constitute larger fractions of the population, white and Cuban men earn as much as elsewhere, but Mexican American and "other Hispanic" men have lower wages than in states where they are less concentrated. This may be evidence that discrimination affects Hispanics more when they are a large proportion of the labor force, as in the Southwest. If discrimination means that jobs are segregated along ethnic lines, Hispanics' wages could be depressed by crowding of the "Hispanic" industries and occupations. This effect would be greater in states where there are more Hispanics. If discrimination means that employers are unwilling to hire Hispanics except at lower pay, and if some employers are less discriminatory than others, Hispanics will try to work for the least

[5] The latter group's estimated return to education is negative, but there are only eight U.S.-born Cubans in the sample, so this may be a coincidence.

[6] Chiswick (1978) found that immigrants have a lower estimated return to education than U.S. natives, and speculated that this is due to a weaker connection among immigrants between schooling and the omitted variable, ability. Perhaps because of the smaller sample sizes, the present results only weakly support his finding.

[7] Blacks with poor English apparently earn more than other blacks, but there are so few (four) of them in the sample that this may be a coincidence.

[8] Most studies of the relationship between health and wages have found a strong negative impact of poor health on wages. However, these studies failed to take account of the bias arising from excluding nonworkers from the sample. Apparently the higher-wage men with disabilities are able to withdraw from the labor force (perhaps because they have more generous disability pensions than low-wage earners), leaving a negative relationship between disability and wage among those remaining in the observed-wage sample.

[9] Smith (1977) found that in 1975 males with similar characteristics received 14 percent higher wages in federal jobs, but 7 percent lower wages in state and local government jobs, than in private firms. She also found that in 1970 the federal-private difference was 14 percent for nonwhite men, but only 4 percent for white men. The sample sizes in the present study do not permit a separation of the levels of government, but the results appear to be broadly consistent with hers.

discriminatory employers. If Hispanics are a small minority in the population, they may be able to avoid discrimination entirely. As the fraction of Hispanics in the population grows larger, however, more and more of them will have to work for the more discriminatory employers. The wages they will have to accept to induce employers to hire all of them will consequently be lower, as the percentage of Hispanics in the population grows.

On the other hand, the geographic wage difference may arise from a preference by Mexican Americans and "other Hispanics" for living where there are many other Hispanics, or simply from the costs of migration, given the different initial locations of Mexican Americans and Anglos in the United States. Suppose all employers everywhere offered Mexican American and Anglos the same wage, on average, for the same characteristics (i.e., there were no discrimination in wage offers), but that wages varied across individuals due to chance. Suppose, moreover, that because of preferences and/or moving costs, it took a positive wage difference to induce a Mexican American to live in the North. Then the Mexican Americans who lived in the Southwest would be *observed* to have lower average wages, given their characteristics, than those in the North. The same need not be true for white non-Hispanics, if their preferences for the Southwest were weaker or were offset by the cost of moving there from the North.

Policy Implications

The estimated wage formulas and average characteristics of the various ethnic groups can give some guidance as to policies that are likely to be effective in raising the wages, and thereby the incomes, of Hispanics and blacks. In particular, the potential efficacy of massive English language training, of raising educational levels, of removing restrictions on public sector employment of noncitizens, of health improvements, of policies encouraging interregional migration or regional development, and of anti-discrimination efforts can be assessed.

To begin with the effect of health policy, we first note in Table 2 that, while disability rates are higher for black than white wage earners, they are *lower* for wage earners in every Hispanic group than for white non-Hispanics. One might be tempted to attribute this to differences in age structure; but the Cubans are the oldest group on average, yet have the next-to-lowest disability rate. There is no systematic relationship between average age and disability rate across groups. Furthermore, the effect of poor health on the wage offered to a person is either zero or *positive*. The effect of health improvements on incomes would come via increased annual hours worked, not improved wage rates.

Concerning geographic location, our results indicate that Puerto Ricans, Cubans, and Central and South Americans do not have different "real" wages in states with different proportions of Hispanics in the population. Neither do white and black non-Hispanics. However, Mexican American and "other Hispanic" men do get lower wage offers in states where Hispanics are highly concentrated. Regional underdevelopment is not the reason. These states do not have lower real wages in general, for workers with given amounts of human capital. If that were the case, the other groups' real wages would also be lower in highly Hispanic states, but they are not. Since the regional wage differential is peculiar to Mexican Americans and "other Hispanics" and does not exist for other groups, the remedy must be sought elsewhere than in industrial location or regional development policies.

Rather, the evidence suggests that the lower wage offers received by Mexican Americans and "other Hispanics" in highly Hispanic states may be due to discrimination, moving costs, and/or their own preferences as to location. One possible response to this situation would be to encourage Mexican Americans and "other Hispanics," who are now concentrated in the Southwest, to migrate to other regions. Another response would be to mount a vigorous attack on discrimination against Mexican Americans and "other Hispanics," especially in the heavily Hispanic southwestern states. However, as we saw earlier, the geographic wage differential for Mexican Americans and "other Hispanics" may be due to moving costs or to their preferences for living in Hispanic areas rather than to discrimination. If moving costs were the reason, relocation subsidies would be a possible remedy. But if the differential arose because the Hispanics prefer to live in a Hispanic area, no policy intervention would be called for.

We can now turn to the effect of public sector employment on wages. Among Cubans and Central and South Americans—the two most recent groups to arrive in the United States—the fraction of wage earners in government jobs is only 8 to 10 percent, as opposed to 15 to 18 percent for Puerto Ricans, Mexican Americans, and white non-Hispanics, and 23 to 24 percent for blacks and "other Hispanics." If, as Smith (1977) has found, the federal government paid more than private firms to employees (especially nonwhites) with similar characteristics, we would expect that limited access to federal government jobs (due to citizenship requirements, patronage, etc.) might play a role in reducing the average wages of ethnic groups with many recent immigrants. On the other hand, Smith (1977) also found an offsetting effect in the state and local government sector, which paid comparable men *less* than the private sector did. In this study we find that, when we combine all levels of government and control for all the other wage-related characteristics we are able to measure, government as a whole does *not* pay significantly more than private employment to any group of men except blacks (and, arguably, "other Hispanics"). If discrimination plays a role in setting wages, we can conclude that the public sector discriminates less than the private sector against black men, but that there is no significant difference between the two sectors in discrimination against Hispanics. Affirmative action may have aided blacks more in the public than the private sector, or governments may have been less discriminatory against blacks in the first place.

Turning to the potential effects of English language programs, we find, surprisingly, that lack of fluency in speaking and understanding English does not definitely lower wage offers in all cases. While the estimates do suggest that English difficulties lower wage offers (within groups having the same levels of education and time in the United States), the margin of error in these estimates is large. Only for Puerto Rican men is the effect clearly not zero. It indicates that a man's attaining fluency in English would raise his wage by 20 percent. The estimates for Cubans, Central and South Americans, and "other Hispanics" would suggest a wage improvement of 12 to 14 percent, but these are imprecisely estimated. For Mexican Americans and white non-Hispanics even the estimates of the effect are small: 4 to 6 percent.

When we put these estimates together with the fractions of each ethnic group who have English difficulties, we can estimate the potential gains to the average wage rates of each ethnic group from a totally effective program wherein everyone attained full command of English. For Puerto Ricans and Cubans, around half of whom have English problems, the average wage would increase by 8 percent. Nearly half of the Central and South Americans also lack fluency in English. Removing this handicap would raise their average wage by about 6 percent. For "other Hispanic" men, most of whom are already fluent in English, the potential improvement in the average wage is only 3 percent, even though they have one of the largest estimated impacts of poor English on wages. Language programs would make very little difference to Mexican American men's average wage, even though one third of them lack fluency in English. English skills per se make very little difference to wages among Mexican origin men, within age and nativity group, immigration cohort, and education level.

The final policy option we can consider is improving the education levels of the disadvantaged minorities to parity with the white non-Hispanics' average, 12.4 grades of school. On the admittedly strong assumption that unmeasured ability and motivation are unrelated to education, we can use the estimated effects to tell how much wages would improve for each extra year of school completed. The returns to education do not differ significantly between U.S. and foreign schooling, nor between the U.S.-born and the foreign-born, except in the Mexican American case.

Mexican Americans who were born in the United States have virtually the same returns to education as Anglos (6.1 percent), but none of the other minority groups have such high returns. One might be tempted to think that this explains why their educational attainments are lower than Anglos', but it cannot account for the differences among minority groups. Migrants from Puerto Rico, Mexico, and Cuba, and U.S.-born "other Hispanics" all have nearly the same returns to education (3 to 4 percent per grade), but the Puerto Ricans average 2 grades below the last two groups in level of schooling, and the foreign-born Mexican Americans average nearly 4 grades below. U.S-born blacks have over a grade less education, on average, than foreign-born Central and South Americans, though their returns are the same; and blacks have less education than Cubans and "other Hispanics," though the blacks' return to schooling is higher. Moreover, Mexican Americans who were born in the United States have the same returns to education as Anglos, yet they have the lowest education level of any U.S.-born group I studied—over two grades below the white non-Hispanics. Thus, the educational attainment of these groups cannot be entirely a "rational" response to their payoffs to schooling.

The potential gains to raising education levels are quite large, especially for Mexican Americans, Puerto Ricans, and blacks, who lag the furthest behind the white non-Hispanics. Mexican American men's average wage offer would be raised 16 percent—halfway to equality with Anglos—if their education levels could be raised the requisite three grades on average (two for U.S. natives; five for immigrants). Puerto Ricans and blacks stand to gain 9 percent in average wages—25 and 40 percent, respectively, of the way to wage-offer parity with Anglos—from attaining educational parity. This would require an average increase of 2.6 grades for the Puerto Ricans (three grades for those born on the island and one grade for those born on the mainland), and 1.9 grades for the blacks. The other ethnic groups could gain only 3 to 5 percent in average wages from closing the education gap with Anglos, because the latter is relatively small, 0.6 to 1.4 grades.

The possible effect of discrimination on wages offered to minorities can be assessed by using the estimated wage formulas to measure the effect of differences in observed characteristics on the majority-minority wage differential. The residual wage difference that cannot be explained by observed variables is often used as an "upper-bound" measure of the impact of discrimination (Oaxaca, 1973). In another paper (Reimers, 1983), I describe in detail the estimation of the possible effect of discrimination in the labor market on the average wages offered to Hispanic and black men. In that study it was found that discrimination may be responsible for as much as a 36 percent wage-offer difference between white non-Hispanics and Central and South Americans with the same measured characteristics. For Puerto Ricans, the difference is 18 percent; for blacks, 14 percent; for "other Hispanics," 12 percent. Mexican American men, however, have only a 6 percent unexplained wage-offer difference; and for Cubans the difference goes in their favor.

In summary, we can conclude that improved health care might increase labor supply but not wage offers; that removing restrictions on employment of noncitizens in government jobs would not affect the average earnings of Hispanics; and that the groups that are now concentrated in the Southwest might have slightly higher average wages if some of them were aided in migrating to other regions. The Puerto Ricans would be helped about equally by correcting their English deficiencies and by attaining the same level of education as white non-Hispanics. Mexican Americans would benefit much more from increased education than from language programs alone. Blacks, too, would benefit significantly from closing the education gap. Cubans, on the other hand, stand to gain more from language programs, as their education level is already high. The Central and South Americans and the "other Hispanics" have small potential wage improvements (less than 5 percent) from either English training or closing their small education gap with white non-Hispanics. Finally, it appears that anti-discrimination programs are needed more for the other groups than for the Mexican origin or Cuban men.

REFERENCES

Carliner, Geoffrey. 1976. "Returns to Education for Blacks, Anglos, and Five Spanish Groups," *Journal of Human Resources*, 11 (Spring):172–84.

Chiswick, Barry. 1978. "The Effect of Americanization on the Earnings of Foreign-Born Men," *Journal of Political Economy*, 86 (October):897–921.

———. 1980. *An Analysis of the Economic Progress and Impact of Immigrants*. Report submitted to the Employment and Training Administration, U.S. Department of Labor (Chicago: University of Illinois at Chicago Circle, Department of Economics and Survey Research Laboratory, June). NTIS No. PB80-200454.

———. 1981. *The Effects of Immigration on Earnings and Employment in the United States (Phase One)* (Chicago: University of Illinois at Chicago Circle, Department of Economics and Survey Research Laboratory, November).

DeFreitas, Gregory. 1982. *The Earnings and Labor Force Behavior of Immigrants*. Report submitted to the Institute of Child Health and Human Development, U.S. Department of Health and Human Services (New York: Columbia University, Barnard College, Department of Economics, July).

Gwartney, James D., and James E. Long. 1978. "The Relative Earnings of Blacks and Other Minorities," *Industrial and Labor Relations Review*, 31 (April):336–46.

Heckman, James J. 1979. "Sample Selection Bias as a Specification Error," *Econometrica*, 47 (January):153–61.

Long, James E. 1977. "Productivity, Employment Discrimination, and the Relative Economic Status of Spanish Origin Males," *Social Science Quarterly*, 58 (December):357–73.

Oaxaca, Ronald. 1973. "Male-Female Wage Differentials in Urban Labor Markets," *International Economic Review*, 14 (October):693–709.

Reimers, Cordelia. 1983. "Labor-Market Discrimination against Hispanic and Black Men," *Review of Economics and Statistics*, 65 (November):570–79.

———. 1984. "Sources of the Family Income Differential between Hispanics, Blacks, and White Non-Hispanics," *American Journal of Sociology*, 89 (January):889–903.

Smith, Sharon. 1977. *Equal Pay in the Public Sector* (Princeton, N.J.: Princeton University Press).

Tienda, Marta, and Lisa J. Niedert. 1980. "Segmented Markets and Earnings Inequality of Native and Immigrant Hispanics in the United States," *Proceedings of the American Statistical Association, Social Statistics Section*: pp. 72–81.

U.S. Bureau of the Census. 1978. *Microdata from the Survey of Income and Education*. Data Access Description No. 42 (Washington, D.C.: U.S. Government Printing Office, January).

————. 1982. "Money Income and Poverty Status of Families and Persons in the United States: 1981 (Advance Data from the March 1982 Current Population Survey)," *Current Population Reports*, ser. P-60, no. 134 (Washington, D.C.: U.S. Government Printing Office).

U.S. Department of Labor. 1977. *Handbook of Labor Statistics* (Washington, D.C.: U.S. Government Printing Office).

8. EARNINGS DIFFERENTIALS BETWEEN MEXICAN AMERICAN, BLACK, AND WHITE MALE WORKERS[1]

Naomi Turner VERDUGO, *U.S. Commission on Civil Rights*
Richard R. VERDUGO, *Library of Congress*

This research examines earnings differentials among Mexican American, black, and white male workers. The results suggest (1) that human capital and structural items are important components of earnings differentials among the three groups and account for most of the white–Mexican American and white–black earnings gap; (2) that Mexican Americans and blacks have different labor market experiences as reflected in their earnings profiles; and (3) that blacks face somewhat stiffer forms of discrimination in the labor market relative to Mexican Americans, though both groups face considerable discrimination relative to white males.

While researchers agree that ethnic/racial minorities earn considerably less than whites, the bulk of this research is concerned with analyses of black-white earnings differences; consequently, little is known about the earnings profiles of other ethnic/racial minorities. The omission of other groups from such analyses is detrimental because research—sparse as it is—indicates that there are important earnings differences among minority groups, such as Mexican Americans and blacks (Carliner, 1976; Gwartney and Long, 1978; Poston and Alvírez, 1973; Williams, Beeson, and Johnson, 1973). The failure to include other ethnic/racial groups in analyses or earnings differences results in a perpetuation of the belief that all ethnic/racial minorities are similarly disadvantaged and that all undergo the same labor market processes.

Yet we know that ethnic/racial minorities differ greatly in the human capital they bring to the labor market and the occupations they pursue or into which they are funneled. The result of these intra-minority differences might

[1] Both authors contributed equally to this paper. We wish to thank Leobardo Estrada for his comments on an earlier draft of this paper. An earlier version of this paper was presented at the annual meetings of the Eastern Sociological Society, Baltimore, March 1983. The views expressed are those of the authors and do not necessarily reflect the views of the U.S. Commission on Civil Rights or the Library of Congress.

be diverse labor market experiences, and, consequently, earnings differentials.

In this paper we examine earnings differentials among Mexican American,[2] black, and white male workers.[3] The three central concerns of this research are (1) to identify the extent of earnings differences between minorities (i.e., Mexican Americans and blacks) and whites; (2) to document the earnings differences between minorities themselves; and (3) to determine the impact of structural items, human capital, and discrimination on these earnings differentials.

This study differs from previous research in several ways. Studies of earnings differentials only rarely include Mexican Americans. In addition to comparing Mexican American–white earnings we also compare Mexican American–black earnings differences. Also, the structural variables we have included are not common to studies of earnings differentials, and are particularly rare among studies of Mexican American earnings. Earlier studies often used dissimilar samples to compare blacks, Mexican Americans, and whites. The data used in earlier studies were often less than ideally suited to the study of Hispanics. Frequently Hispanics were identified by surname only from geographically limited samples. Most importantly, the statistical technique used in this paper to estimate the economic impact of unequal opportunity and discrimination has only rarely been applied to Mexican Americans.

The Model

The Earnings Function. The model examined in the present study is:

$$Y = f(A, H, E, M, O, \Sigma I_i, S, \Sigma R_i, U)$$

where Y = year's earnings from wages and salary, A = age, H = number of hours per year worked, E = education, M = marital status, O = occupational status, ΣI_i = a series of industry dummy codes, S = sector of employment, ΣR_i = a series of dummy codes for region of residence, and U = metropolitan/nonmetropolitan residence.

Control Items. Marital status (M), hours worked per year (H), and occupational status (O) have been included as control items in this analysis. Marital status (M) was included in the model because married men tend to earn more than unmarried men. (We assume that this is the case because of the greater commitment married men have to the labor force.) Hours per year worked (H) was included since we know that hours per week and weeks per year worked have positive effects on earnings. (Hours per year worked is a combination of both hours per week and weeks per

---

[2] In reporting the results of our research, the term "Mexican American" refers to U.S.-born persons of Mexican descent, as well as Mexican-born persons. We were unable to distinguish between these two groups as the data did not provide information on respondent's place of birth.

[3] Throughout this paper the terms "black" and "white" refer to non-Hispanic blacks and non-Hispanic whites, respectively.

year worked, and thus it takes into account periods of unemployment.) Occupational status (*O*) was used as a control item because individuals in higher-status occupations tend to earn more than those in lower-status occupations.

Human Capital Items. We have included (*A*) as a proxy for experience. We expect that, in general, the greater the age, the greater the earnings, since older workers tend to have more experience in the labor force.

Perhaps the most often used human capital item is educational attainment (*E*). Education represents training, increased knowledge, and enhanced skills. It is expected that these items would increase one's earnings.

Structural Components of the Labor Market. Industry of employment (*I*), sector of employment (*S*), region of residence (*R*), and metropolitan/nonmetropolitan residence (*U*) were used to measure structural and geographical components of the labor market. Our emphasis is not on jobs, but rather on the larger characteristics of the labor market. Many social scientists, primarily economists, have used industry as an important indicator of labor market structure (Averitt, 1968). Researchers have found, for instance, that skill levels, degree of bureaucracy, rationality, monopsony, etc., not only differ by industry, but have important effects on earnings (Sapsford, 1981; Slichter, 1950; Garbarino, 1950).

We have two reasons for including sector of employment, defined as government versus private sector employment. First, Averitt (1968) has noted that the government is itself an industry, as it has an important role in the organization of production. Second, given the supposedly close surveillance of equal opportunity practices of government, we suspect that it might be less easy to discriminate against minorities in that sector.

Region of residence in 1980 (*R*) and metropolitan versus nonmetropolitan residence in 1980 (*U*) were included since there is evidence that wage scales are also likely to differ between metropolitan and nonmetropolitan areas. These variables are particularly important in analyzing minority groups, such as blacks and Hispanics, who are concentrated in particular regions of the country (Featherman and Hauser, 1978). Table 1 presents a complete listing and description of these variables.

The Data

Data for this study are from the March 1981 Current Population Survey (CPS). Only black, Mexican American, and white male civilians age 15 and over who had been employed for at least one week in 1980 as wage and salary workers were included in the analysis. (Persons living abroad in 1980 were excluded from the sample.) Males were selected for study because the bulk of previous labor force research which has focused on males could enable the comparison of our findings with these earlier studies. Certainly there is a need for similar research on females; the authors are currently working on such a study. Data were weighted in order that results might be generalized to each respective population. The final sample sizes were 3,076 blacks, 2,332 Mexican Americans; and 28,238 whites.

TABLE 1

Description of Variables Used in the Analysis

Variable	Operationalization
Y	Earnings from wages and salary in 1980.
A	Years of age as of last birthday (at time of the interview).
H	Number of hours per year worked in 1980:
	$H = HW \times WK$
	where HW = hours worked per week, and WK = weeks worked in 1980.
E	Highest grade completed as of the interview.
M	Marital status: 1 = married (including separated), 0 = unmarried (including widowed and divorced).
O	Occupational status = the Duncan socioeconomic index.
I	A series of eight dummy variables measuring the nine industrial classifications:
	I_1 = miscellaneous service (including domestic workers);
	I_2 = manufacturing;
	I_3 = wholesale and retail trade;
	I_4 = transportation, communication, public utilities;
	I_5 = construction;
	I_6 = finance, insurance, real estate;
	I_7 = mining;
	I_8 = agriculture;
	0 = public administration.
S	Sector of employment: 1 = private sector, 0 = government sector.
R	A series of three dummy variables measuring the four geographic regions of residence in 1980:
	R_1 = Northeast;
	R_2 = South;
	R_3 = West;
	0 = North Central.
U	Metropolitan versus nonmetropolitan residence in 1980: 1 = SMSA, 0 = non-SMSA.

Results and Analysis

Race/Ethnicity and Earnings Differentials. Table 2 presents means and standard deviations for all items used in this study by race/ethnicity, while Table 3 presents the regression results.

Descriptive data presented in Table 2 indicate, as expected, that whites fared better than either blacks or Mexican Americans socioeconomically. Whites earned more, had completed more years of schooling, and worked at far better jobs than either blacks or Mexican Americans. Whites also appeared to be more fully employed as they worked more hours than either blacks or Mexican Americans. Mexican American–black socioeconomic differences were also noticeable: though Mexican Americans had less education than blacks, they earned more and worked at the same sorts of jobs. Mexican Americans also worked a greater number of hours, on average, than blacks, though not as many as whites.

TABLE 2

Means and Standard Deviations of All Items in the Analysis

	Whites		Blacks		Mexican Americans	
	$\overline{X}$	SD	$\overline{X}$	SD	$\overline{X}$	SD
Y	$16,420.51	$12,376.47	$10,661.15	$8,404.06	$11,158.67	$8,081.27
A	36.88	15.49	35.66	14.42	32.50	12.75
H	1,859.46	829.24	1,639.46	804.89	1,780.72	733.97
E	12.67	3.04	11.28	3.03	9.30	4.14
M	.66	.51	.55	.51	.64	.49
O	40.12	26.08	26.96	20.37	25.15	19.31
I_1	.20	.43	.23	.42	.14	.36
I_2	.29	.49	.29	.46	.30	.47
I_3	.17	.40	.14	.35	.20	.41
I_4	.09	.30	.10	.30	.06	.24
I_5	.10	.33	.09	.29	.12	.34
I_6	.05	.22	.04	.19	.02	.15
I_7	.02	.14	.00	.07	.02	.15
I_8	.02	.17	.04	.19	.09	.29
S	.85	.39	.79	.41	.88	.33
R_1	.24	.45	.18	.39	.01	.09
R_2	.32	.50	.53	.51	.36	.49
R_3	.15	.38	.09	.30	.53	.51
U	.69	.49	.78	.42	.81	.41

Industry and sectoral differences were also apparent. Whites and blacks were more likely than Mexican Americans to be working in the service industry, while Mexican Americans were more likely to work in wholesale and retail trade. Further, while the vast majority of each group worked in the private sector, as opposed to government, a significantly greater percentage of the black sample were employed by government.

As expected, there were tremendous differences among blacks, Mexican Americans, and whites in their geographic distribution. Over 60 percent of the whites lived in the South and North Central regions, while blacks were concentrated in the South (53 percent), and 53 percent of the Mexican Americans were located in the West. Further, blacks and Mexican Americans were more likely to reside in metropolitan areas than were whites.

Table 3 shows that whites were better able to use their human capital than were minorities; the one exception was experience in the labor force—using age as a proxy. Surprisingly, Mexican Americans realized greater returns to experience than either blacks or whites. With regard to education, blacks yielded 80 percent of white returns, while Mexican Americans yielded about 60 percent of white returns. In terms of occupational status, blacks realized 61 percent of the earnings returns accruing to whites, and Mexican Americans about 92 percent. Gains resulting from hours worked were nearly identical for blacks and Mexican Americans, but significantly greater for whites. Being married yielded greater financial gains for white males (with married whites earning about $3,249 more than unmarried white men, on the average) than for blacks or Mexican Americans. Even so, married blacks earned about $2,327 more than their unmarried

TABLE 3

Regression Results of an Earnings Function among Black, Mexican American, and White Male Workers

Variable	White	Black	Mexican American
A	112.690*	70.374*	122.178*
H	5.847*	4.894*	4.798*
E	634.308*	504.109*	372.889*
M	3,248.814*	2,327.238*	948.010*
O	110.258*	66.833*	101.092*
I_1	−2,935.010*	−1,927.790*	−3,981.470*
I_2	326.582	521.653	−1,926.880*
I_3	−2,527.930*	−1,440.390*	−3,871.480*
I_4	916.023*	1,219.975*	−323.956
I_5	514.308	−564.925	−315.209
I_6	−1,286.460*	−2,741.850*	−3,631.810*
I_7	2,801.878*	3,422.421*	984.272
I_8	−2,136.810*	−1,696.200*	−3,256.780*
S	2,082.961*	−57.194	2,027.765*
R_1	−185.756	−1,674.380*	2,088.494
R_2	−992.040*	−2,258.270*	−1,960.460*
R_3	722.406*	−444.579	−607.756
U	1,912.781*	1,271.613*	702.692*
Int[a]	−15,196.900	−7,588.070	−7,023.530
R^2 [b]	.555	.552	.532

[a] Int = intercept.

[b] Adjusted $R^2 = 1 - (1 - R^2)(n - 1)/(n - p)$, where p = number of parameters.

*Coefficient is at least twice its standard error.

counterparts. Region appeared to have a significant impact on earnings, but its impact varied for each racial group. However, for whites, blacks, and Mexican Americans, working in the South appeared to have the greatest negative impact. Whites appeared to earn most in the West, followed by the North Central and Northeast regions. Blacks seemed to earn more in the North Central region, followed by the West. Mexican Americans in the Northeast appeared to earn more than Mexican Americans in other regions, but only 1 percent of the Mexican Americans resided in the Northeast, so no conclusions may be drawn. For all groups, workers in metropolitan areas earned more than those living outside such areas.

Regression results also showed that industry and sector of employment influenced earnings, and help to explain earnings differentials between the three groups. The coefficients for about half of the included industry dummy codes were negative, suggesting that earnings were greater in the omitted public administration industry; conversely, positive effects indicated greater earnings in that industry relative to the public administration industry. There seemed to be evidence of earnings differences between industries *within* each ethnic/racial group. In addition, there seemed to be some indication that important industry/race interactions were occurring.

For example, in the manufacturing industry (I_2) the sign was positive for both whites and blacks, but negative for Mexican Americans. Earnings differences within an industry across race/ethnic groups were also noted in the following: transportation, communications, and public utilities (I_4) and construction (I_5).

There were also some significant interactions between sector and race/ethnicity. Both whites and Mexican Americans earned more in the private sector than in the government sector; such was not the case, however, among blacks. Blacks earned slightly more in government, though this was not statistically significant.

Discrimination. Thus far our analysis suggests that blacks earn slightly less than Mexican Americans despite having completed more years of schooling and having more job experience, though both groups earn far less than whites. A conclusion one might draw is that blacks are more discriminated against in the labor market than are Mexican Americans. Previous research (e.g., Carliner, 1976; Gwartney and Long, 1978) presented similar results, while other studies have pointed out labor market disparities between the two minority groups in the following areas: blacks earn lower incomes within broad occupational categories than Mexican Americans (Briggs, Fogel, and Schmidt, 1979); blacks tend to be heavily concentrated in low-prestige, weakly unionized occupations relative to Mexican Americans (Romero, 1979; Grebler, Moore, and Guzman, 1970; Briggs, Fogel, and Schmidt, 1979); blacks seem to face more intense forms of cultural prejudice than do Mexican Americans (Schmidt, 1976). The expectation, then, is that blacks face greater discrimination in the labor market than do Mexican Americans. In this section we examine such a proposition.

Our aim is to place a dollar figure on discrimination in the labor force by assessing the cost of being a minority worker. Our analysis is based on a rather well-developed procedure (see, for example, Duncan, 1968; Duncan, Featherman, and Duncan, 1972; Masters, 1975), which involves estimating an equation among whites, deriving the coefficients and the intercept, and substituting the minority means into the equation to ascertain the expected black and Mexican American mean earnings. The earnings estimated for Mexican Americans and blacks using this procedure show the mean earnings these groups would receive if they had returns to education, occupation, and the other independent variables equal to white males. The difference between white mean earnings and the estimated minority earnings shows that portion of the earnings gap which is explained by the regression model. The remaining gap represents the combined effects of discrimination and other determinants of earnings not included in the model. It should be emphasized that these results are not absolutely significant and that they apply only to the model and the specific sample under analysis. The model estimates only the cost of discrimination to employed minorities, it does not examine barriers faced by minorities in gaining employment. Further, the model does not examine the difficulties minorities confront in obtaining equal education.

Results from this analysis indicated that after substituting black means into the white equation $1,399 remained unaccounted for. This suggests that if blacks had returns to education, occupation, experience, and other variables in the model equal to those of whites they would still be discriminated against to the tune of about $1,399. For Mexican Americans, similar procedures yielded a residual of $1,012, a figure about 28 percent lower than that for blacks. Thus, our initial expectation that blacks face stiffer forms of discrimination in the labor market seems to receive some support by this analysis, though the difference is not as great as expected.

Conclusion

The focus of this study has been earnings differences not only between majority whites and minorities, but earnings differentials among minority groups as well. Social scientists have attributed earnings differences to one of three competing frameworks: differences in human capital, the structure of the labor market, and to discrimination. In this study, we attempted to include items in an earnings function from the first two frameworks and address the latter, discrimination, by statistical procedures.

Three results emerge from our analysis. First, it seems clear that human capital items account for an important component of earnings differentials between the three groups. While whites, as expected, are better able to use their human capital than either blacks or Mexican Americans, Mexican Americans seem to yield returns to their human capital in excess of returns earned by blacks. The latter result is problematic because Mexican Americans have less education, yet work at the same sorts of jobs as do blacks. One would expect blacks to have greater earnings and to realize greater returns to their human capital, but such does not appear to be the case. Second, industry, sector of employment, region, and metropolitan residence, measures of labor market structure, also emerge as important determinants of earnings and of earnings differentials. Indeed, two findings bolster this conclusion: (1) substantial earnings differences by industry and region were found within each ethnic/racial group; and (2) industry, sector, region, and metropolitan residence effects differed *between* ethnic/ racial groups. Finally, we note that blacks face somewhat stiffer forms of discrimination in the labor market than do Mexican Americans; e.g., the cost of being a black worker is roughly $1,399, while the cost of being a Mexican American is $1,012. However, both Mexican American and black workers are severely penalized in several ways: lower returns for their human capital than those of whites; greater structural obstacles to achieving socioeconomic success; and ethnic/racial discrimination which "costs" each group over $1,000.

In conclusion, our analysis points out significant human capital and structural differences in earnings among blacks, Mexican Americans, and whites. Most of the white–Mexican American and white–black earnings gap is accounted for by the model, though discrimination accounts for 24 percent of the white–black gap, and 19 percent of the white–Mexican American gap. In addition, there is evidence that minorities (blacks and Mexican Americans) do not necessarily share similar labor market experiences.

REFERENCES

Averitt, Robert T. 1968. *The Dual Economy: The Dynamics of American Industry Structure* (New York: Norton).

Briggs, Vernon M., Walter Fogel, and Fred H. Schmidt. 1979. *The Chicano Worker* (Austin: University of Texas Press).

Carliner, Geoffrey. 1976. "Returns to Education for Blacks, Anglos, and Five Spanish Groups," *Journal of Human Resources,* 11 (Spring):172–84.

Duncan, Otis D. 1968. "Inheritance of Poverty or Inheritance of Race?" in Daniel P. Moynihan, ed., *On Understanding Poverty* (New York: Basic Books): pp. 85–110.

Duncan, Otis D., David L. Featherman, and Beverly Duncan. 1972. *Socioeconomic Background and Achievement* (New York: Academic Press).

Featherman, David L., and Robert M. Hauser. 1978. *Opportunity and Change* (New York: Academic Press).

Garbarino, Joseph W. 1950. "A Theory of Interindustry Wage Structure Variation," *Quarterly Journal of Economics,* 64 (May):282–305.

Grebler, Leo, Joan W. Moore, and Ralph C. Guzman. 1970. *The Mexican American People: The Nation's Second Largest Minority* (New York: Free Press).

Gwartney, James D., and James E. Long. 1978. "The Relative Earnings of Blacks and Other Minorities," *Industrial and Labor Relations Review,* 31 (April):336–46.

Masters, Stanley. 1975. *Black-White Income Differentials: Empirical Studies and Policy Implications* (New York: Academic Press).

Poston, Dudley L., and David Alvírez. 1973. "On the Cost of Being a Mexican American Worker," *Social Science Quarterly,* 53 (March):697–709.

Romero, Fred E. 1979. *Chicano Workers: Their Utilization and Development.* Monograph No. 8 (Los Angeles: UCLA, Chicano Studies Center Publication).

Sapsford, David. 1981. *Labour Market Economics* (London: George Allen & Unwin).

Schmidt. Fred H. 1976. *Spanish Surnamed Employment in the Southwest* (Washington, D.C.: U.S. Government Printing Office).

Slichter, S. H. 1950. "Notes on the Structure of Wages," *Review of Economics and Statistics,* 32 (February):80–91.

Williams, J. Allen, Peter G. Beeson, and David R. Johnson. 1973. "Some Factors Associated with Income among Mexican Americans," *Social Science Quarterly,* 53 (March):710–15.

9. THE COMPARATIVE SALARY POSITION OF MEXICAN AMERICAN COLLEGE GRADUATES IN BUSINESS[1]

Larry E. PENLEY, *The University of Texas at San Antonio*

Sam GOULD, *The University of Texas at San Antonio*

Lynda Y. DE LA VINA, *The University of Texas at San Antonio*

Mexican American graduates of colleges of business administration receive lower salaries than their white non-Hispanic counterparts. However, the differences were attributed primarily to variation in regional income, the lower socioeconomic background of Mexican Americans, and academic success in college. When these variables are controlled, income disparity disappears; Mexican Americans earn an *adjusted* income comparable to their white non-Hispanic counterparts.

Numerous studies have documented that Mexican Americans earn substantially lower incomes than white non-Hispanics (e.g., Romero, 1979; Gwartney and Long, 1978; Williams, Beeson, and Johnson, 1973). In an attempt to explain these differences, researchers have investigated a number of inter-ethnic differences which could account for this income gap. Typically, differences remaining after accounting for these factors have been attributed to labor force discrimination (e.g., Williams, Beeson, and Johnson, 1973). While this approach has merit, the unexplained variance in income is attributed to a factor, discrimination, which has not been explicitly measured or defined in the study itself. Hence, it is not clear whether residual income differences should be attributed to discrimination or whether they result from an inability to fully specify an analytical model.

Studying college of business graduates is advantageous since it controls for an important inter-ethnic difference—educational level. Education has often been cited as a basis for explaining income disparity (Blumberg, 1980; Gordon, 1977). In a recent study, Reimers (1983) concluded that the primary reason for the concentration of Mexican Americans in low skill level and low-paying jobs was due to their low educational attainment.

These assertions are consistent with studies conducted recently by Astin (1982). Based upon data from the National Longitudinal Survey, the

[1] The authors wish to express their thanks to the American Assembly of Collegiate Schools of Business, which supported this research through a grant.

National Center for Educational Statistics (NCES), and the Current Population Survey, Astin (1982:24) estimated that approximately 50 percent of Mexican American students (as compared to 17.8 percent of white non-Hispanics) drop out of school before obtaining a high school diploma. For those students who do obtain a diploma, 38 percent of Mexican American students go on to college and 40 percent of this group ultimately graduate. Forty-seven percent of white non-Hispanics by comparison go on to college, with 56 percent of this group ultimately graduating. Hence, Mexican Americans tend to have a lower level of educational attainment which may ultimately lower their earning power. However, there is evidence that even when educational attainment is statistically controlled Mexican Americans still receive lower incomes (Baca, 1978; Wilber et al., 1975). This may indicate that Mexican Americans do not receive an equitable return on their educational investment.

One problem with the research on income disparity and its relationship to education has been that education has usually been expressed as the number of years of schooling completed (e.g. Garcia, 1982; Smith and Newman, 1977; Williams, Beeson, and Johnson, 1973). There has been little effective control for quality of education (Goodman, 1979). The quality of education received may be a function of at least two factors: (1) the quality of education provided by the educational institution attended, and (2) the preparedness of the individual to receive that education.

It has been argued that Mexican Americans have frequently attended local institutions for collegiate training and typically have a lower level of preparedness for college (Astin, 1982). Furthermore, Gould and de la Viña (1983) found that Mexican Americans were likely to work more often and longer hours during college than white non-Hispanics. The result of these effects is likely to be a lower level of academic achievement during the college experience. Hence, a situation caused by a lack of financial resources common to a lower socioeconomic background may be perpetuated through the college years and into early career. In the present study the level of academic success in college and its relationship to income were investigated. Further, differences in the quality of educational institutions were controlled through a selection of subjects who have graduated from colleges accredited by the American Assembly of Collegiate Schools of Business (AACSB).

A second issue of importance, which is not independent of educational attainment, is socioeconomic background. It has been argued that educational attainment and ultimate occupational status are a function of one's family background or socioeconomic status during childhood (e.g., Duncan, 1969; Williams, Beeson, and Johnson, 1973). It has further been argued that persons from lower socioeconomic backgrounds may lack appropriate role models and mentors. This often limits their ability to develop important social skills and relationships critical to early career success (Hall, 1976).

Other factors which may impact earning levels include geographic location, occupation, industry of employment, and year since graduation. Reimers (1982) argues that the concentration of Mexican Americans in low-income regions of the United States is an important factor in the overall income level of this group. Fogel (1979) and Marshall, Levitan and Magnum (1976) further argue that this concentration results in depressed labor markets, lowering the incomes of Mexican Americans. In support of this argument, the Bureau of the Census reports that 58 percent of all Hispanics live in the southwestern United States.

Astin (1982) indicates that Mexican American high school seniors and college freshmen tend to choose occupational majors in the social sciences and humanities rather than business, engineering, and the sciences. This preference may account for some of the income differences between Mexican Americans and white non-Hispanics.

A final factor is years since graduation. Graduation from college is often a starting or turning point in a person's career. Hence, after-graduation income is generally expected to increase over time as a person progresses in job competencies. Hence, incomes should be higher for persons who have been out of college longer. Since Mexican Americans are more likely to have interruptions or delays in their pursuit of a college education (Astin, 1982), it is probable that the Mexican American will have been out of college fewer years than the white non-Hispanic and, hence, have a lower income.

This paper examines the relationship of these variables to the incomes of Mexican American and white non-Hispanic graduates of colleges of business. In particular, the education factor has been carefully modeled in order to identify more precisely the impact of this variable on income. The objective, then, is to determine the level of unexplained variance or income gap that remains in the ethnic variable after the above factors have been controlled through the application of a multivariate statistical procedure.

Method

Subjects. Subjects were respondents to a mail survey of business school graduates who graduated between 1972 and 1980. The subject pool was obtained from alumni mailing lists provided by 10 United States universities. The 10 universities were distributed geographically across the United States, and the business schools at each university were accredited by the American Assembly of Collegiate Schools of Business (AACSB), the international accrediting association of business schools. The relatively strict standards used by AACSB were considered a control on the quality of the business schools. Thus one may roughly equate the quality of the 10 universities in this study.

From the alumni lists, Hispanic graduates were identified by surname using the list of common Spanish surnames published by the U.S. Department of Commerce. All Hispanic graduates from the 10 universities were included in the subject pool. A pool of non-Hispanics, matched by year of graduation, sex, and, where possible, business major, was also chosen. Since white non-Hispanic and black surnames could not be distinguished, a larger pool of non-Hispanic subjects was chosen.

A total of 5,167 surveys were mailed. Thirty-four were returned as undeliverable. Of the 5,133 deliverable surveys, 1,245 were returned. The response rate for the Hispanics was 21.2 percent, and it was 26.6 percent for the non-Hispanics. These comparative response rates are in line with Saegert's (1983) conclusion that Hispanics are less likely to return mail surveys than are white non-Hispanics.

Self-report data from the questionnaire were used to classify subjects as Mexican American or white non-Hispanic. American natives, Asians, blacks, and Hispanics other than Mexican Americans were eliminated from the sample for this study based on their self-reports. After eliminating those who did not supply complete responses to the questionnaire and the questionnaires of Hispanics of other than Mexican descent, there remained 551 white non-Hispanics and 212 Mexican Americans.

Study Variables. Subjects reported their sex, ethnic background, current salary, year of graduation, age, college major, grade point average (GPA), and zip code (region). Subjects classified themselves into one of 12 majors that are found in colleges of business (e.g., accounting, marketing, economics). They were also asked to classify the current industry in which they worked from a list of 15 industries that included such categories as mining, construction, real estate, and education. Based on the zip codes reported, subjects were classified into 5 regional areas.

For the statistical analyses, major, industry, and region were treated as follows. A mean salary was computed for each category of the three variables. The mean salary was then employed in the analyses rather than the categorical value. This transformation of the categorical data permitted the treatment of major, industry, and region as metric covariates in the multivariate analyses.

Another variable included was the relationship of current job to educational background. Subjects indicated whether their work was directly related, indirectly related, or unrelated to their college major. Lastly, as a measure of socioeconomic background, subjects reported parents' educational level and income. Respondents classified their childhood family income as lower, lower-middle, middle, upper-middle, or upper income.

Analysis. Multiple analysis of variance (MANOVA) was used following the procedure of Hull and Nie (1981). A 2 × 2 analysis of covariance design was employed with sex and ethnicity (Mexican American, white non-Hispanics) as the two independent variables. The dependent variable was current salary, and the covariates were age of the subject, years since graduation, industry of employment, region, college major, GPA, father's education, mother's education, and childhood family income.

This 2 × 2 analysis of covariance was followed up by a 2 × 2 multiple analysis of variance in which the covariates from the previous analysis were used as multiple dependent variables. After the MANOVA procedure a discriminant analysis was undertaken in order to determine the primary areas of distinction among ethnic and sex groups (Hair et al., 1979).

Results

Current salary levels of subjects are reported in Table 1. These un-adjusted salary levels reveal that white non-Hispanic males earned the highest annual salaries with a mean salary of $31,673.68. The salary of white non-Hispanic males exceeded the Mexican American males' annual salary of $29,639.53 by $2,034.15, or 6 percent. Mexican American females and white non-Hispanic females earned lower salaries than did males of either ethnic group. Females with a mean annual salary of $23,763.03 earned $7,276.82 less than males, who had a mean salary of $31,039.85. Mexican American females earned even less, with a mean annual salary of $20,300.00.

Table 2 reports the 2 × 2 analysis of covariance with current annual salary as the dependent variable. This analysis controlled for differences in age, years since graduation, major, GPA, the extent of relationship between education and work, the industry, region, and three socioeconomic variables—family income as a child, father's education, and mother's ed-

TABLE 1

Salary Levels of Subjects

	Males	Females	Both
Mexican Americans	$\overline{X}$ = 29,639.53 σ = 12,935.21 N = 172	$\overline{X}$ = 20,300.00 σ = 7,962.09 N = 40	$\overline{X}$ = 27,877.36
White Non-Hispanics	$\overline{X}$ = 31,673.68 σ = 15,485.42 N = 380	$\overline{X}$ = 24,573.10 σ = 9,089.70 N = 171	$\overline{X}$ = 29,470.52
Both	$\overline{X}$ = 31,039.85	$\overline{X}$ = 23,763.03	

TABLE 2

The Impact of Ethnicity and Sex of the Subject on Current Salary

	F	Significance
Main effects		
Sex	26.86	.001
Ethnicity	0.24	n.s.
Sex × ethnicity	0.83	n.s.
Covariates		
Age	11.97	.001
Years since graduation	60.84	.001
Major	3.57	n.s.
GPA	15.37	.001
Education-work relationship	0.00	n.s.
Industry	30.25	.001
Region	0.46	n.s.
Family income	1.66	n.s.
Father's education	0.45	n.s.
Mother's education	0.01	n.s.

ucation. There were four significant covariates: age, years since gradua-tion, GPA, and industry.

While controlling for the variance due to covariates, there was a signifi-cant difference between the annual salaries of males and females ($F = 26.86$, $p < .001$). There was no significant difference between the salaries of Mexican Americans and white non-Hispanics in the analysis of covari-ance reported in Table 2 ($F = 0.24$, n.s.), nor was there a significant interaction ($F = 0.83$, n.s.).

Salary levels adjusted for the covariates in the 2 × 2 analysis of covari-ance are reported in Table 3. Mexican Americans' annual salary, adjusted for covariation, was $28,739.51, and the adjusted annual salary of white non-Hispanics was $27,485.28. While the difference was small between the two ethnic groups, it was much larger between males and females. Adjusted annual salary of males was $29,337.12, while it was $5,436.29 less for females, who had an adjusted mean salary of $23,900.83.

The results of the multiple analysis of variance with the ten covariates as dependent variables are reported in Table 4. There was a sex effect as well as an ethnic effect. The Wilks lambda for the sex effect was .86 ($p < .01$), and it was .63 ($p < .01$) for the ethnic effect. The significant lambdas indicate that the four cells defined by the 2 × 2 analysis differed signifi-cantly from one another on the basis of sex and ethnicity.

The structure correlations reported in Table 4 were derived from a dis-criminant analysis. They permit the researcher to consider all of the de-pendent variables simultaneously in order to determine which ones account for the variance among cells. The largest structure correlations (absolute values) for the sex factor were for GPA (−.64), years since graduation (.59), and mother's education (−.44).

Females had significantly higher college grade point averages. Non-Hispanic females possessed a mean GPA of 3.54 compared to a mean of 2.97 for non-Hispanic males, and Mexican American females had a mean GPA of 2.83 compared to a 2.49 for Mexican American males. Females had been out of college a shorter period of time than males. For example, Table 4 reports that it had been an average of 4.95 years since the Mexican American male subjects graduated, whereas it had been 4.05 years since Mexican American females graduated. Female subjects came from families whose mothers were better educated as compared to mothers of male subjects. For example, Table 4 reports that mothers of white non-Hispanic female respondents possessed a mean of 13.10 years of education while mothers of white non-Hispanic males possessed a mean of 12.26 years.

TABLE 3

Adjusted Salary Levels of Subjects

	Males	Females	Both
Mexican Americans	30,075.36	22,995.36	28,739.51
White Non-Hispanics	29,002.97	24,112.63	27,485.28
Both	29,337.12	23,900.83	

TABLE 4

Analysis of the Factors on Which Salary Was Controlled for Mexican Americans and White Non-Hispanics

Factor	Mexican American Males		Mexican American Females		Non-Hispanic Males		Non-Hispanic Females		Sex Factor F	Sex Structure Correlation	Ethnic Factor F	Ethnic Structure Correlation	Interaction Factor F
	$\bar{X}$	σ	$\bar{X}$	σ	$\bar{X}$	σ	$\bar{X}$	σ					
Age	30.82	5.78	28.60	3.99	30.30	5.69	28.92	6.32	11.71**	.31	0.53	.03	0.54
Years since graduation	4.95	3.32	4.05	2.75	5.53	3.18	3.71	2.44	41.07**	.59	2.35	-.07	2.33
Major	29.16[a]	2.99	29.48[a]	0.95	29.52[a]	3.20	29.26[a]	2.67	1.52	.11	3.44	-.09	0.53
GPA	2.49	1.02	2.83	0.87	2.97	1.05	3.54	1.04	48.79**	-.64	39.28**	-.30	1.37
Education-work relationship	1.41	0.58	1.38	0.54	1.53	0.70	1.44	0.65	1.56	.11	4.37*	-.10	0.22
Region	20.29[a]	5.45	20.25[a]	3.57	28.39[a]	13.17	27.48[a]	13.06	0.07	-.02	71.53**	-.40	0.14
Family income	2.09	0.92	2.10	0.95	2.92	0.90	3.09	0.89	10.80**	-.30	135.32**	-.56	0.84
Father's education	9.33	3.93	9.40	3.95	12.91	3.53	13.61	3.16	12.33**	-.32	163.70**	-.61	0.77
Mother's education	9.36	3.60	9.93	3.38	12.26	2.53	13.10	2.69	24.06**	-.44	158.79**	-.60	0.24
Industry	28.60[a]	2.15	27.94[a]	2.64	28.93[a]	2.26	28.52[a]	2.17	4.92*	.21	5.29*	-.11	0.01
Wilks lambda									.86**		.63**		.99[b]

[a] Values represent mean salaries (over majors, over regions, or over industries) divided by 1,000.

[b] Since the interaction effect did not differentiate the four cells, no structure correlations are shown.

*$p < .05$.

**$p < .01$.

The structure correlations for the ethnic factor indicate that variance due to ethnicity is predominantly accounted for by father's education (−.61), mother's education (−.60), family income (−.56), and region of the country (−.40). Mexican Americans' mean family income was approximately 2.0 (lower-middle income on the questionnaire) and white non-Hispanics' mean family income was approximately 3.0 (middle income level). The two ethnic groups were also significantly different in terms of the educational level of both parents. Whereas the mean educational level of the parents of Mexican American subjects was approximately 9 years, the mean educational level of parents of white non-Hispanics was more than 12 years. Regional salaries for Mexican Americans were approximately $20,000, while they were above $27,000 for white non-Hispanics.

Discussion

Mexican American graduates of colleges of business administration do receive lower salaries (other forms of compensation such as benefits were not considered) than their white non-Hispanic counterparts. However, the differences in this study were attributed primarily to variation in regional income, the lower socioeconomic background of Mexican Americans, and academic success in college. When these variables were controlled, income disparity disappeared.

The importance of these findings is essentially couched in the education variable. The education factor has been carefully modeled throughout the study. First, the subjects represented a somewhat homogeneous group since the survey only included college graduates with bachelors' degrees in business. Second, in order to account for qualitative differences in educational institutions only AACSB accredited schools were surveyed, and a matched-group sample design was utilized. Third, GPA was included as a proxy for educational success and preparedness. Fourth, college major was included in the analysis, and lastly, years since graduation was entered in the multivariate framework.

The calculated unadjusted salary differences between Mexican Americans and white non-Hispanics were limited to approximately $1,600. After adjusting salaries for age, years since the degree was granted, college major, grades, education-work relationship, region, industry, and socioeconomic background, the $1,600 disparity in income had been eliminated. In earlier studies (e.g., Williams, Beeson, and Johnson, 1973; Garcia, 1982) adjusted income still resulted in income disparity. This result led those writers (e.g., Garcia, 1982; Reimers, 1982) to conclude that the residual income disparity was due to discrimination.

The findings of this study do not support such earlier conclusions about discrimination in the workplace. The findings, however, do not imply that discrimination or other forms of discrimination are eliminated. While the advantage of this study is its carefully controlled sample, its chief limitation is the inability to generalize the results to other occupations or other educational levels.

With this sample of business graduates, Mexican Americans earned an *adjusted* income comparable to their white non-Hispanic counterparts. However *actual* salaries remained lower, primarily due to three factors: regional effect, socioeconomic effect, and the effect of average grades of Mexican Americans.

The regional effect is revealed in the southwestern concentration of Mexican Americans. Mexican Americans predominantly live in the Southwest where salaries are substantially lower than in other parts of the country. Until income levels change with the migration of industry to the region and economic development of the region, Mexican Americans who remain in the Southwest will continue to be paid less than their white non-Hispanic counterparts in other parts of the country.

In terms of the socioeconomic effect, Mexican Americans as a group come from lower socioeconomic backgrounds than do white non-Hispanics. The impact of socioeconomic background on income is well documented (e.g., Duncan, Featherman, and Duncan, 1972). With limited education and limited skills, persons from lower socioeconomic backgrounds are limited in their attainment of industrial skills (Gordon, 1971).

The Mexican American sample in this study possessed educational attainment equal to white non-Hispanics. Thus, they should have overcome a part of the limitation imposed by socioeconomic background on income. However, Thurow (1969) has argued persuasively that education alone will not erase the impact of socioeconomic background on income. Job skills and job experience must also be provided. If industry does not enhance the job skills of persons from lower socioeconomic backgrounds, education alone will not erase the disparity in income that exists.

Average grades of Mexican Americans were significantly lower as compared to grades of white non-Hispanics. Since grades were significantly associated with income, they are, therefore, an important avenue to raising income and reducing disparity. It is well documented that performance in college is dependent on the prior educational background of students. To the extent that Mexican Americans come to college with poorer educational backgrounds, their college performance will be negatively affected, and this will ultimately produce disparity in income level.

While this study does not identify a residual income disparity that is often attributed to discrimination, it does point to several areas in which discrimination may impact income. The significant impact of parents' education and family income conspicuously reveals the disparity in socioeconomic background that may have resulted from past discriminatory practices.

Educational success of Mexican Americans as measured by average grades must be increased. Mexican Americans need adequate educational opportunities in order to prepare for, have access to, and perform well in college. Mexican Americans need job opportunities that promote skill development, particularly in early career stages (Hall, 1976). To the extent that discrimination limits job opportunities and adequate early education, it limits income.

Although the purpose of this study was to investigate income disparity between white non-Hispanics and Mexican Americans, the data and formidable preliminary results direct attention to the important issue of income differences between males and females. Despite controlling for the variance in salary due to education, industry, and socioeconomic background, the female subjects in this sample possessed significantly lower adjusted annual salaries than the males (Table 3). Furthermore, Mexican American females possessed the lowest annual salaries, which were more than $7,000 less than their male counterparts and over $1,000 less than female white non-Hispanics. In unadjusted as well as adjusted salaries, the difference between male and female salaries was substantial.

Because of the nature of the sample used in this study, subjects should have been similar. Some have argued that women receive lower salaries due to interruptions in their careers (Mincer and Polachek, 1974); however, in this study the ages of the male and female subjects were similar—both were in the early stages of their careers. There was a significant difference in the number of years since graduation (Table 4), but this variable coupled with the age factor adjusts annual salary very little. As a significant corollary to the earlier conclusions, one can deduce that substantial salary differences exist for female business graduates, particularly Hispanic females. Consequently, the gravity of this result merits individual and concentrated attention beyond the scope of this paper.

REFERENCES

Astin, A. W. 1982. *Minorities in American Higher Education* (San Francisco: Jossey-Bass).

Baca, H. R. 1978. "Earnings among Arizona's Ethnic Groups." Unpublished manuscript, Arizona State University.

Blumberg, Paul. 1980. *Inequality in Age of Decline* (New York: Oxford University Press).

Duncan, O.D. 1969. "Inheritance of Poverty or Inheritance of Race?" in Daniel P. Moynihan, ed., *On Understanding Poverty* (New York: Basic Books): pp. 85–110.

Duncan, O. D., D. L. Featherman, and B. Duncan. 1972. *Socioeconomic Background and Achievement* (London: Seminar).

Fogel, W. 1979. "Research on Hispanics in the Labor Market," in *The Role of the Social Scientist in Human Resource Development Policy and Programs for Hispanics* (San Antonio: The University of Texas at San Antonio, Human Resources Management and Development Program).

Garcia, P. 1982. "Trends in Relative Income Position of Mexican-Origin Workers in the U.S.: The Early Seventies," *Sociology and Social Research,* 66 (July):467–83.

Goodman, Jerry D. 1979. "The Economic Returns of Education: An Assessment of Alternative Models," *Social Science Quarterly,* 60 (September):269–83.

Gordon, David M. 1971. *Problems in Political Economy* (Lexington, Mass.: Heath).

Gould, Sam, and Lynda Y. de la Viña. 1983. *A Study of the Educational and Career Experiences of Anglo and Hispanic College of Business Graduates* (San Antonio: The University of Texas at San Antonio, Center for Studies in Business, Economics and Human Resources).

Gwartney, James D., and James E. Long. 1978. "The Relative Earnings of Blacks and Other Minorities," *Industrial Labor Relations Review,* 32 (April):336–46.

Hair, Joseph F., Jr., Ralph E. Anderson, Ronald L. Tatham, and Bernie J. Grablowsky. 1979. *Multivariate Data Analysis* (Tulsa, Okla.: Petroleum Publishing Company).

Hall, D. T. 1976. *Careers in Organizations.* (Pacific Palisades, Calif.: Goodyear).

Hull, C. Hadlai, and Norman H. Nie. 1981. *SPSS Update 7-9* (New York: McGraw-Hill).

Marshall, R., S. Levitan, and G. Magnum. 1976. *Human Resources and Labor Market* (New York: Harper & Row).

Mincer, J., and S. W. Polachek. 1974. "Family Investments in Human Capital: Earnings of Women," *Journal of Political Economy,* 82 (March/April):S76–S108.

Reimers, C. 1982. *Why Are Hispanic Americans' Incomes So Low: An Analysis of the Family Incomes of the Major Hispanic Origin Groups in the U.S.* (Princeton, N.J.: Princeton University Press).

Romero, Fred E. 1979. *Chicano Workers: Their Utilization and Development* (Los Angeles: UCLA, Chicano Studies Center Publication).

Saegert, J. 1983. "Response Rates to Mail Questionnaires in an Ethnic Minority Population," *Proceedings of the American Psychological Association Division of Consumer Psychology* (Anaheim, Calif.: American Psychological Association).

Smith, Barton, and Robert Newman. 1977. "Depressed Wages along the U.S.-Mexico Border: An Empirical Analysis," *Economic Inquiry,* 15 (January):51–66.

Thurow, Lester C. 1969. *Poverty and Discrimination* (Washington, D.C.: Brookings Institution).

Wilber, G. L., D. E. Jaco, R. J. Hagen, and A. C. del Fierro, Jr. 1975. *Minorities in the Labor Market.* Vol. 1, *Spanish Americans and Indians in the American Labor Market* (Springfield, Va.: National Technical Information Service).

Williams, J. Allen, Peter G. Beeson, and David R. Johnson. 1973. "Some Factors Associated with Income among Mexican Americans," *Social Science Quarterly,* 53 (March):710–15.

10. IMMIGRATION AND PERCEPTIONS OF ECONOMIC DEPRIVATION AMONG WORKING-CLASS MEXICAN AMERICAN MEN[1]

Michael V. MILLER, *The University of Texas at San Antonio*

Avelardo VALDEZ, *The University of Texas at San Antonio*

Dissatisfaction with economic circumstances is commonly thought to increase with temporal or cultural distance from Mexico, if, over time, immigrants or their offspring fail to experience substantial mobility within the United States. The authors' findings do not support this argument. Immigrants and the less acculturated and assimilated did not perceive themselves as less deprived than did other Mexican Americans. Actual income was the primary factor influencing levels of reported economic well-being.

Despite the growing interest in Mexican immigration, little empirical attention has been directed to how such immigrants perceive their life situation in the United States. Data show that Mexican immigrants, both documented and otherwise, constitute an economically deprived population. However, the assumption is popular that they are not generally disturbed by their circumstances. Indeed, the conventional wisdom holds that although such people may be objectively disadvantaged, and often exploited by employers and others, they are, on the whole, a self-satisfied and contented lot.

Life-satisfaction studies typically employ a frame-of-reference orientation, positing that differences between us in terms of perceived well-being or satisfaction are based, in significant part, on our use of divergent reference groups, rather than on actual attainments or conditions alone. The feelings of inadequacy or dissatisfaction derived from comparisons with the assumed attainments of those with whom we identify are said to reflect "relative deprivation." Accordingly, objective deprivation does not necessarily produce perceptions of deprivation, since we tend to evaluate our out-

[1] Data were contributed by TAES Project H-3286 and USDA-CSRS Regional Project NC-128 "Quality of Life as Influenced by Area of Residence." We appreciate the assistance of Richard Harris, Philip Garcia, Lee Maril, and William Kuvlesky in the preparation of this manuscript.

comes against relative, rather than absolute, criteria. Inordinate dissatisfaction usually is evoked only when we perceive that others like ourselves are better off than we are, whether they actually are or not (see Merton and Kitt, 1950; Runciman, 1966; Rushing, 1968; Campbell, Converse, and Rodgers, 1976; and Coburn and Edwards, 1976, among others).

Mexican immigrant adjustment to U.S. society likewise has been viewed in terms of relative deprivation (see, e.g., Dworkin, 1965; Alvarez, 1973; Miller and Maril, 1978; and Stoddard, 1978). Although such efforts generally have been speculative, they propose that Mexican immigrants tend to be much more satisfied with their economic circumstances and place in American society than do nonimmigrants of similar condition. Immigration is thought to bring a significant rise in level of living—so much that even though the immigrant may be "poor" according to U.S. definitions, he is far better off in an objective sense now than he was previously in Mexico. Thus, the immigrant is likely to be content with his present state, given the comparison with circumstances before immigration. In a related vein, presumed satisfaction among immigrants also is believed to reflect their use of Mexican society as an evaluative frame of reference. That is, without sufficient acculturation to the host society, immigrants tend to employ standards of well-being prevailing in Mexico. Of course, this not only suggests that such standards are much lower than those within the United States, but also that immigrants are insulated from exposure to dominant consumption patterns and expectations. Furthermore, this thesis implies that immigrants are similar to those who remain in Mexico in regard to their economic aspirations. We would argue, however, that while the first point is probable, and the second, problematic, the last seems tenuous in light of the heavy social and cultural costs often incurred with immigration, and the fact that Mexican immigration is primarily motivated by an economic rationale. Thus, quite likely, immigrants hold aspirations and expectations for economic mobility that are far higher and more intense than those of their counterparts remaining in Mexico, and perhaps not altogether that different from those held by other U.S. residents.

Arguments based on assimilation logic further stipulate that with progressive acculturation, frames of reference shift from Mexico to the United States, and hence dissatisfaction grows if conditions do not substantially improve. Typically, acculturation is couched in *generational* terms. Stoddard, for example, suggests that immigrants feel positive about their economic circumstances. However, their children measure "their present conditions with the 'American dream' and the better houses in their community. Even though the second generation lives a higher quality of life than their fathers, they now feel *relatively deprived* from what they are taught every American family should enjoy" (Stoddard, 1978:56). Alvarez also employs a generational model for the evolution of Chicano militancy, arguing that acculturative differences coupled with changing social forces over the twentieth century subjected each generation to a different frame of reference. Whereas their immigrant grandparents used Mexico, and their parents used immigrants as their reference, those of the "Chicano Generation" (namely Mexican Americans with native-born parents) were forced to make a broader comparison:

> With higher aspirations than any previous generation, with the prospect of a severe psychic decline compared to its parent generation, and now, because of its greater affluence and exposure, it had to compare itself to its youth counterpart in the dominant society. . . . The Chicano Generation came to realize that it was ever more acculturated than the previous generation, yet it did not have any realistic prospects of escaping its virtually complete lower and working class status. (Alvarez, 1973:938–39)

It is relevant to note that these arguments parallel those (Piore, 1975, 1979, and others) which seek to explain the recruitment of undocumented workers into the secondary labor market in terms of the reluctance of second and third generation poor minorities to accept such jobs.

The present study attempts to test the validity of conventional understandings about relative deprivation among Mexican Americans by examining perceived well-being in relation to objective circumstances, generation of immigration from Mexico, and assimilation. In so doing, two basic questions are addressed: (1) do immigrants assess their economic status more favorably than do nonimmigrant Mexican Americans, and (2) despite similar economic conditions, do perceptions of well-being become more negative with distance from immigration, and/or with greater assimilation to U.S. society?

Methods

The Sample. Data were collected as part of a larger project conducted in 14 states to assess the influence of various objective conditions on perceived life satisfaction. The project sample was limited to intact (husband/wife) families containing at least one adolescent child. Given the dearth of information on perceptions of life quality among Mexican Americans, research collaborators in 4 southwestern states focused attention on this population exclusively. Household interviews were conducted with Mexican American men and women residing in selected metropolitan areas and small towns within Arizona, California, Colorado, and Texas, during 1978 and early 1979.

Despite such residential diversity, the present sample represents a relatively homogeneous subpopulation in comparison to the adult Mexican American populations within these communities. Respondents were living with a spouse and teenage offspring and, likewise, tended to be middle-aged. Furthermore, sampling efforts were concentrated in those neighborhoods (namely *barrios*) where sufficient numbers of respondents meeting project criteria could be located with minimal screening costs. The present sample thus includes a greater proportion of working-class respondents than would one derived from the entire Mexican American community. Although the scope of generalization is reduced, such homogeneity with respect to age, family situation, and class provides significant internal controls for adequate problem analysis with a limited sample size. For the purpose of simplification, only complete interview data for husbands are examined in this report (total N = 304: Arizona, 48; California, 77; Colorado, 60; Texas, 119).

Indicators and Measurements

Perceived Economic Well-Being. Subjective assessments of economic conditions were derived through the employment of three indicators. Level of "perceived income adequacy" was based upon five responses (ranging from 1 = "not at all adequate" to 5 = "buy what we want, and still have money to save") to the question "To what extent do you think your income is enough for you to live on?" "Income satisfaction" was determined by any of seven responses (ranging from 1 = "extremely dissatisfied" to 7 = "extremely satisfied") to the question "How satisfied or dissatisfied are you with your current total family income?" Finally, "standard of living satisfaction" was based on any of seven responses to "How satisfied or dissatisfied are you with your family's present standard of living; i.e., the goods and services consumed such as food, clothing, housing, transportation, etc.?"

Objective Economic Status. Two variables permit the measure of objective economic condition—"poverty status" and "income." "Poverty status" (poor or nonpoor), defined according to 1978 federal criteria, was determined by the respondent's specification of total household income from all sources over the previous 12 months relative to household size. "Income," providing a standardized measure of objective status, was derived by dividing the relevant poverty threshold income for a household with N members into the total reported income. Hence, a value of 1.00 placed a household exactly on the poverty line, with descending values indicating a worsening situation.

Frame of Reference. Assessments of well-being relative to objective status, as discussed, are assumed to be filtered by a frame of reference conditioned by generation of immigration, degree of assimilation, and by the length of immigrant's time in the United States. "Generation" was derived from the place of birth of respondent and the nativity of respondent's parents: "first generation" men were born in Mexico; the "second generation" were U.S.-born but had at least one Mexican-born parent; the "third generation" were U.S.-born with both parents of U.S. nativity. Assimilation was approached in both cultural and social terms. Cultural assimilation, "acculturation," was operationalized according to the time spent (ranging from 1 = "none" to 4 = "all") indicated by the respondent in listening to English-language, as opposed to Spanish-language, radio. This item was selected from a set of language-use variables given that it exhibited the greatest variability across the sample. Social assimilation, "assimilation," was determined by the respondent's report that he either had or did not have close friends of Anglo American background. For immigrants, "length of U.S. residence" was defined by the ratio of years in the United States to the respondent's age.

Results

A descriptive summary of selected variables by generation is presented in Table 1. Of the three dependent variables, generational differences were most pronounced for perceived income adequacy, with the mean for the first generation considerably lower than those for nonimmigrants. Mean values for income satisfaction and standard of living satisfaction, on the other hand, did not diverge widely across generations.

Objective economic measures revealed households headed by immigrant men were much worse off than those headed by the U.S.-born. Mean income for the former was approximately only two-thirds of that for the latter. The financial state of immigrant-headed households was further exacerbated by their larger number of members, which additionally served to produce a poverty rate considerably higher than that for the U.S.-born.

Finally, and as expected, data showed immigrant men tended to be less acculturated and assimilated with the dominant society than either of their

TABLE 1

Descriptive Summary of Selected Variables by Generation of Immigration

Variable	Generation of Immigration			Total
	First	Second	Third	
Perceived income adequacy				
$\bar{x}$	2.25	2.80	2.81	2.63
SD	1.02	1.13	.97	1.07
Income satisfaction				
$\bar{x}$	4.83	4.81	4.97	4.87
SD	2.02	1.79	1.60	1.80
Standard of living satisfaction				
$\bar{x}$	5.46	5.40	5.43	5.43
SD	1.55	1.44	1.28	1.42
Household income (dollars)				
$\bar{x}$	10,052	15,174	15,688	13,689
SD	5,800	9,345	8,517	8,460
Household size				
$\bar{x}$	6.2	5.5	5.4	5.7
SD	2.0	2.1	1.6	2.0
Poverty status				
Percent poor	42.7	23.5	20.7	28.7
Income (standardized)				
$\bar{x}$	1.26	2.17	2.18	1.88
SD	.71	1.56	1.41	1.36
Age				
$\bar{x}$	45.3	45.8	42.0	44.5
SD	10.3	8.9	9.1	9.5
Acculturation				
$\bar{x}$	2.4	2.9	2.9	2.7
SD	1.0	.8	.8	.9
Assimilation				
$\bar{x}$	1.4	1.9	1.9	1.7
SD	.5	1.0	1.2	1.0
N	97	115	92	304

generational counterparts. Perhaps of greater significance, however, was the virtual absence of mean acculturation and assimilation differences between second and third generation men.

Simple correlations (not presented) revealed that generation was slightly associated with perceived income adequacy ($r = .20$), but was not correlated with the two satisfaction variables. Rather, of all explanatory variables, income had the highest degree of association with each dependent variable. In fact, income was strongly correlated with perceived income adequacy ($r = .59$), the least evaluative subjective measure.

Within-Generation Analysis. In terms of perceived income adequacy, regression analyses indicated that income had the most significant effect on level of assessment for each generation (see Table 2). The influence of either acculturation or assimilation, on the other hand, not only was negligible but, contrary to theoretical speculation, was positively related (with the exception of assimilation for the third generation) to perceived income adequacy. Cumulatively, the three variables accounted for over 30 percent of the variance for each generation.

Income also was the best predictor of income satisfaction within each generation. However, the effect of income was neither as great nor as consistent on income satisfaction as it was on perceived income adequacy. The relative importance of acculturation among first and second generation groups was greater for income satisfaction than for perceived adequacy. Yet, the role of acculturation opposed the theoretical argument, as did that of assimilation despite its low predictive value. Together, the three variables explained little variance within each generation.

Finally, regression analyses showed that income had less bearing on standard of living satisfaction than on income satisfaction. Income only remained the best predictive variable among the second generation, while acculturation was the major contributing factor (again in a contrary direction to theory) among the first generation. The absence of explained variance among the third generation precluded meaningful interpretation relative to the influence of acculturation and assimilation.

Between-Generation Analysis. Estimates of the relative effect of generation on reported well-being are provided in Table 3. Generation was

TABLE 2

Relative Effects of Selected Variables on Reported Economic Well-Being within Generations (Standardized)

	Perceived Income Adequacy			Income Satisfaction			Standard of Living Satisfaction		
	First	Second	Third	First	Second	Third	First	Second	Third
Acculturation	.03	.06	.12	.13	.17	.06	.21	.19	−.16
Assimilation	.07	.10	−.06	.00	.05	.05	−.01	.02	−.11
Income	.56	.58	.54	.19	.33	.12	.10	.27	.00
(Constant)	(1.53)	(2.19)	(2.22)	(5.35)	(4.84)	(5.09)	(5.99)	(5.50)	(5.33)
R^2	.36	.36	.32	.09	.16	.02	.06	.14	.003

measured by two dummy variables (1 = first generation, and 1 = third generation) to compensate for the low linear associations between generation and reported well-being (see Harris, 1980, for the application of this technique to generational variables). The stepwise regressions also provided a clearer picture of the contribution of acculturation, assimilation, and income to the explained variance of each dependent variable.

In terms of perceived income adequacy, the initial effect of generation was reduced with the inclusion of acculturation and assimilation. Given the negative value for the first generation and the positive values for the latter variables, analysis suggested that immigrants and the less acculturated and assimilated tended to report their income as less adequate than did others. Nonetheless, it is important to note that perception of income adequacy was most strongly influenced by actual income, and that with the addition of income the contributions of generation, acculturation, and assimilation to the explained variance of 36 percent were minor.

Relative to income satisfaction and standard of living satisfaction, the effects of generation increased slightly with the inclusion of acculturation, assimilation, and income. However, and in light of the low level of total explained variance for both satisfaction measures, the influence of generation was minimal.

TABLE 3

Stepwise Regressions of Selected Variables on Reported Economic Well-Being between Generations (Standardized)

		Regression Coefficients of Independent Variables on Reported Well-Being					
		X_1	X_2	X_3	X_4	X_5	R^2
Perceived income adequacy							
Generation							
First	(X_1)						
Third	(X_2)	−.25	−.01				.06
Acculturation	(X_3)	−.20	−.01	.19			.10
Assimilation	(X_4)	−.18	.00	.18	.09		.10
Income	(X_5)	−.05	.00	.09	−.01	.55	.36
Income satisfaction							
Generation							
First	(X_1)						
Third	(X_2)	.00	.02				.00
Acculturation	(X_3)	.06	.02	.19			.04
Assimilation	(X_4)	.08	.03	.18	.09		.04
Income	(X_5)	.13	.03	.14	.04	.22	.08
Standard of living satisfaction							
Generation							
First	(X_1)						
Third	(X_2)	.05	.03				.00
Acculturation	(X_3)	.10	.03	.17			.03
Assimilation	(X_4)	.10	.03	.17	.02		.03
Income	(X_5)	.14	.03	.15	−.01	.14	.05

Immigrant Analysis. Data for first-generation men were further examined (see Table 4) under the proposition that those who have lived longer in the United States are more likely than recent immigrants to report dissatisfaction with economic circumstances. Analysis indicated that U.S. tenure alone, and in combination with acculturation and assimilation, was positvely associated with level of perceived adequacy. However, with the inclusion of income, the effects of residence, acculturation, and assimilation were small. With income definitely the most important factor, these variables accounted for 36 percent of the variance in perceived income adequacy.

Analyses performed for income and standard of living satisfaction provided somewhat curious findings. Length of U.S. residence was negatively associated with both satisfaction measures, while acculturation was positively related to satisfaction—suggesting that the less acculturated of longer U.S. tenure tended to be more dissatisfied than others with income and standard of living. In addition, the inclusion of the final variable, income, tended to elevate the predictive value of U.S. tenure for both satisfaction variables—indicating that dissatisfaction rose slightly with longer residence in the United States. Nonetheless, such interpretations remain tentative given the low level of explained variance for either satisfaction measure.

Conclusions

The present findings failed to confirm conventional assumptions about relative deprivation within the Mexican American community. Although frame-of-reference arguments are intuitively appealing, they have little in-

TABLE 4

Stepwise Regression of Selected Variables on Reported Economic Well-Being among Immigrant Men (Standardized)

| | | Regression Coefficients of Independent Variables on Reported Well-Being | | | | |
		X_1	X_2	X_3	X_4	R^2
Perceived income adequacy						
Length of U.S. residence	(X_1)	.19				.04
Acculturation	(X_2)	.16	.16			.06
Assimilation	(X_3)	.13	.12	.23		.11
Income	(X_4)	−.05	.03	.07	.58	.36
Income satisfaction						
Length of U.S. residence	(X_1)	.02				.00
Acculturation	(X_2)	−.02	.19			.04
Assimilation	(X_3)	−.04	.17	.16		.06
Income	(X_4)	−.11	.13	.09	.23	.10
Standard of living satisfaction						
Length of U.S. residence	(X_1)	−.01				.00
Acculturation	(X_2)	−.06	.23			.05
Assimilation	(X_3)	−.06	.23	.04		.05
Income	(X_4)	−.11	.21	.00	.14	.07

terpretive relevance for the patterns observed among the present sample of working-class men. Indeed, many of our findings appear to contradict such arguments.

Immigrants, on the whole, did not define their economic status more favorably than did nonimmigrants. While there were few differences between immigrants and others relative to reported satisfaction with income and standard of living, the former generally perceived their income to be less adequate than did the U.S.-born. This, of course, was due primarily to the fact that income returns for immigrant-headed households were so drastically lower than those for others. Between-generation analyses did find immigrants very slightly more satisfied than the second and third generation relative to income and standard of living (with income held constant).

Nor did we find among the first generation that length of residence in the United States had significant bearing on their evaluation of economic condition. Immigrants with longer U.S. tenure tended to define their income as more adequate than did those who had lived here a shorter time, but this was seen to be a function of the greater actual income of the former. With income controlled, longer-term residents tended to be very slightly less satisfied with income and standard of living than were other immigrants. A paradoxical finding, and one that sharply challenges frame-of-reference arguments, is that related to the influence of acculturation and assimilation. Such arguments hold that greater cultural and social integration with the dominant society should raise normative conceptions of economic well-being, and hence should generate discontent with low attainment. Nonetheless, we found that not only did greater acculturation and assimilation fail to promote unfavorable definitions of economic condition, they contributed, albeit in a minor way, to a more positive assessment of objective status.

In light of the seemingly high rates of satisfaction with income and standard of living reported by the present sample, one may be tempted to infer that Mexican Americans, at least on the surface, are exceptionally content within the context of American society. However, our findings are remarkably similar to those derived from the 1978 NORC survey (Davis, 1982) of household heads: among the nationwide poor, 53 percent expressed satisfaction with present income while 75 percent of the nonpoor NORC respondents reported satisfaction. Among poor men in our sample, 51 percent stated they were satisfied with current income, as were 51 percent of poor immigrants. Among nonpoor men, 74 percent of both immigrants and others reported satisfaction. Thus, economically deprived immigrants appear no less dissatisfied than other poor Mexican Americans with their objective financial condition, and furthermore they do not differ substantially from the U.S. poor in general. Rather than generational status, assimilation, or ethnicity, the present findings indicate that objective economic circumstances tend to be the most crucial determinants of perceived economic well-being.

In the face of our findings, it appears invalid to maintain that poverty among Mexican immigrants is less objectionable since they do not perceive themselves as deprived. Poor immigrants differ little from the poor of other generations in evaluating their economic plight. Consequently, we submit that if immigrants are less apt than others to engage in individual or collective protest over work and living conditions, it is not because they are more content with such conditions. Instead, the findings imply that research could fruitfully address structural factors which generate immigrant vulnerability, marginality, and hence apparent passivity within American society.

REFERENCES

Alvarez, Rodolfo. 1973. "The Psycho-Historical and Socioeconomic Development of the Chicano Community in the United States," *Social Science Quarterly,* 53 (March):920–42.

Campbell, Angus, Philip Converse, and Willard Rodgers. 1976. *The Quality of American Life* (New York: Sage).

Coburn, David, and Virginia Edwards. 1976. "Objective and Subjective Socioeconomic Status: Intercorrelations and Consequences," *Canadian Review of Sociology and Anthropology,* 13 (2):178–88.

Davis, James A. 1982. *General Social Surveys, 1972–1982* (machine-readable data file) (Chicago: National Opinion Research Center).

Dworkin, Anthony G. 1965. "Stereotypes and Self-Images Held by Native-Born and Foreign-Born Mexican Americans," *Sociology and Social Research,* 49 (January):214–23.

Harris, Richard J. 1980. "An Examination of the Effects of Ethnicity, Socioeconomic Status, and Generation on Familism and Sex Role Orientations," *Journal of Comparative Family Studies,* 9 (Spring):173–93.

Miller, Michael V., and Robert Lee Maril. 1978. *Poverty in the Lower Rio Grande Valley of Texas: Historical and Contemporary Dimensions* (College Station: Texas Agricultural Experiment Station).

Merton, Robert, and A. Kitt. 1950. "Contributions to the Theory of Reference Group Behavior," in R. Merton and P. Lazarsfeld, eds., *Studies in the Scope and Method of the American Soldier* (Glencoe, Ill.: Free Press).

Piore, Michael J. 1975. "The 'New Immigration' and the Presumptions of Social Policy," *Industrial Relations Research Association Series, Proceedings,* 1975:350–64.

––––––. 1979. *Birds of Passage* (New York: Cambridge University Press).

Runciman, W. G. 1966. *Relative Deprivation and Social Justice* (Berkeley, University of California Press).

Rushing, William A. 1968. "Objective and Subjective Aspects of Deprivation in a Rural Poverty Class," *Rural Sociology,* 33 (March):269–84.

Stoddard, Ellwyn R. 1978. *Patterns of Poverty along the U.S.-Mexico Border* (El Paso: The University of Texas at El Paso, Center for Inter-American Studies).

11. MEXICAN AMERICANS AND EMPLOYMENT INEQUALITY IN THE FEDERAL CIVIL SERVICE [1]

Patricia A. TAYLOR, *University of Virginia*

Susan Walker SHIELDS, *Boston, England*

Mexican Americans have lower average salaries than Anglos in virtually all employment settings, even in the federal Civil Service. This paper presents analyses of salary inequality between Mexican Americans and Anglos and examines the possible reasons for such inequality. We find that organizational as well as individual characteristics affect salary, but that the effects are different for Anglos as compared to Mexican Americans.

All other things being equal, women and minorities have typically earned half to two-thirds the income of white males, even in labor markets as avowedly egalitarian as the federal Civil Service (Farley, 1977; Taylor, 1979). Indeed, a growing literature on income determination and discrimination in internal labor markets, especially the federal government, suggests that even where the rules of promotion are well specified, women and minorities do not fare as well as white males (Borjas, 1980; Grandjean, 1981; South et al., 1982).

However, not all minorities have the same organizational or social history, and there is a growing recognition that studies of income inequality should specify particular minority groups in an effort to reflect diverse cultural backgrounds. Several studies have shown for example that the earnings of Mexican Americans differ not only from Anglos, but also from blacks (Mindiola, 1979; see also Poston and Alvírez, 1973). The growing research on the federal government as a labor market generally combines all minorities into one group (Grandjean, 1981; Taylor, 1979). Yet as Taylor and Kim (1980) have shown for Asian Americans, such an approach may obscure group-specific determinants of success in federal employment. One study has examined the experience of Hispanics in the govern-

[1] These analyses were undertaken while the senior author was receiving support from the National Institute of Education (DHEW), grant number NIE-G-78-0005, and from the Employment and Training Administration (DOL), grant number A20-11-79-32. The opinions and analyses presented here are those of the authors and do not necessarily reflect the opinions of any federal agency or employee. Our thanks to Alice-Lynn Rysmann for assistance with the data analysis and to Lynn Hamilton for clerical assistance. An earlier version of this paper was presented at the Southwestern Social Science Association Meetings, March 1983.

ment (Carmel and Taylor, 1977), but Mexican Americans, Puerto Ricans, Cubans, and other Hispanics may show as much intergroup variation as a comparison of the broad Hispanic category to non-Hispanics.

This study is a partial redress to the inadequate social science attention to Mexican Americans. As a minority population, Mexican Americans are second in number only to blacks, but they have not received even proportional research attention. It is also worth noting that, after native Americans, theirs is the longest history on the continent, extending beyond the landings of the English at Jamestown and Plymouth. A study of their economic success in the national government seems long overdue. This paper provides an analysis of salary determination for Mexican Americans compared to Anglos, using data from the official personnel records of the federal Civil Service.

Mexican Americans in the Federal Civil Service

The U.S. Civil Service has a long history of merit employment practices dating back to the Pendleton Act of 1883 and including Public Law 92-261 in 1972, an amendment to the 1964 Civil Rights Act. The intended effect of these laws is to eliminate discrimination in employment in the federal Civil Service, whether by race, sex, ethnicity, national origin, or religion. Each federal agency, commission, or other hiring body is responsible for the implementation of equal employment opportunity through affirmative action. Additionally, the Civil Service is a highly bureaucratized internal labor market, one in which minorities and women might expect to fare well (Grebler, Moore, and Guzman, 1970).

However, Hispanics as a group lag behind Anglos on almost every indicator of organizational success in the federal government (Carmel and Taylor, 1977). The reasons for the lack of success by Hispanics as a group, especially Mexican Americans, are not well known, but a cursory look at their employment pattern offers some possible explanations.

First, for both historical and geographical reasons, Mexican Americans in federal employment are generally concentrated in the defense agencies. These agencies (Defense Supply, Army, Navy, Air Force, etc.) have a lower-than-average grade structure. Therefore Mexican Americans are more likely to have low salaries as defense agencies in general have low salary structures.

A second possible explanation for the low average grade of Mexican Americans is that they are concentrated into the low-paying occupations of the federal Civil Service. With less education on average, Mexican Americans tend to be concentrated in lower-skilled jobs, mainly clerical, which have lower salaries than professional or administrative occupations. Federal employers are not required to eliminate disparity of qualifications of employees, only to insure equal employment policies for persons with equal qualifications.

Finally, the seeming ethnic inequality between Anglos and Mexican Americans might actually be an inequality between males and females. Considerable differences remain between Mexican Americans and Anglos in fertility rates, child spacing, age at marriage, etc., and such family concerns might act to depress the earnings of Mexican American women more than Anglo women. Hence, the average income for Anglos would be greater than the average income for all Mexican Americans. Of course, sex differences may also reflect employment practices that discriminate against women. In this case, it would be sex discrimination, but not ethnic discrimination, that helps account for the lower average salaries of Mexican Americans, and the remedies for one type of discrimination might be very different from those for the other.

Data and Method of Analysis

The data used to explore these possibilities were from a 1 percent sample of the automated personnel files of federal civilian employees maintained by the Office of Personnel Management. Included for purposes of this study were all Hispanic and Anglo (white, nonminority) full-time federal civilian employees in white-collar jobs as of June 1977. We used only white-collar employees to examine a more homogeneous group of occupations. We also limited the analysis to employees in the five southwestern states of Texas, New Mexico, Arizona, Colorado, and California. Federal personnel records do not differentiate Mexican Americans from other Hispanics, but the residential concentration of the various Hispanic groups makes region an adequate proxy for Mexican American ancestry (see Poston and Alvírez, 1973).

We began our analysis by comparing mean annual salaries and other job-related variables for Anglos and Mexican Americans. We then moved to multiple regressions predicting salary from these same variables. Although the mean differences are instructive, an important argument in studies of salary inequality is that returns on employment characteristics are the standard by which to estimate equality of opportunity. The returns to individual characteristics represent how much a worker is paid on the average for one additional year's work, one year of schooling, etc. It is preferable to use returns to estimate inequality of opportunity as returns are more likely controlled by the employer than are workers' characteristics. Hence, we need to examine the relative effects of each of the employment characteristics on earnings to determine the empirical bases of salary inequality. Furthermore, it is necessary to do so with separate regressions for Mexican Americans and Anglos, rather than a single combined regression with a dummy variable for ethnicity. The latter approach would make the unwarranted statistical assumption that all returns are identical for the two groups. Our approach, in contrast, was designed to allow the possibility that differences in returns may yield inequality even when the mean group characteristics are similar.

The independent control variables in our analysis include education, an important skills variable which was split into two continuous variables: precollege years of schooling and years of college and beyond. To capture both aging and experience effects, we entered age, the square of age, years of federal work experience, and the square of federal work experience. Supervisory status was entered to control for organizational differences in positions of authority for Anglos and Mexican Americans.

We also entered three additional variables which are particularly important in the federal bureaucratic labor market. Veterans are given preference at initial hiring and during reductions in force. We therefore entered two variables to capture effects of veterans' status: the disabled veteran (representing a greater preference given due to disability or to death of a spouse) and all other veterans (representing mostly military personnel). We also controlled for the effect of competitive or excepted service, as in the federal Civil Service the excepted service positions usually have higher incomes but lower job security. This variable, position occupied, takes on the value of one for the competitive service.

We then entered a dummy variable for defense agency. If the defense department is a poor employer for Mexican Americans, the regression coefficient for this variable would be smaller in magnitude than that for Anglos.

Like other internal labor markets, the federal Civil Service also has clusters of occupations which form job ladders and are distinguishable by the specificity of the entry requirements, the level of training, and the types of skills required. These were grouped into the broad occupational clusters of professional, administrative, technical, clerical, and other. A set of dummy variables was entered to examine the possible effects of occupational group on salary inequality.

Finally, we used a dummy variable to capture the effects of sex of employee on salary. If Mexican American women are affected more by sex discrimination or other unmeasured influences on salary than are Anglo women, there should be statistically significant differences between the effects of sex on salary between Mexican Americans and Anglos.

Findings

Presented in Table 1 are the mean values for the employment characteristics used in the analysis of Mexican American and Anglo salaries. On the average, Anglos earned $2,713 more than Mexican Americans, a statistically significant difference. This higher average salary appears due in part to the higher educational levels of Anglos, as well as their greater labor market experience as reflected in their average age and years of federal government work. Anglos were also more likely to be in supervisory positions, as only 8 percent of Mexican Americans fell into this category. Very similar proportions of Anglos and Mexican Americans had either some preference or a disabled veteran's preference.

The remaining seven variables directly concern the three organizational and demographic explanations of inequality offered earlier. As shown in Table 1, white-collar Mexican Americans in the Southwest were no more likely to be in a defense agency than were Anglo employees, as roughly 34 percent of each group were employed by the defense agencies.

The distribution of Anglos and Mexican Americans across the five white-collar occupational groups does show some significant departures from equality. Anglos were more likely to be either professional or administrative workers than were Mexican Americans, who were more likely to be employed in the clerical group. In fact, almost one-half of all Mexican Americans fell into the clerical occupational group. As career ladders are

TABLE 1

Means (and Standard Deviations) of the Employment Characteristics of Mexican
American and Anglo Federal Civil Servants, 1977 (Southwest Only)

Employment Characteristics	Anglos	Mexican Americans	*t* Test for Difference[a]
Salary	$15,830	$13,117	7.274***
	(6,859)	(4,579)	
Years of education	13.8	13.1	7.183***
	(1.7)	(1.5)	
Education beyond 12th grade	0.35	0.08	8.594***
	(0.98)	(0.40)	
Age	43.0	38.0	6.905***
	(12.2)	(11.2)	
Age squared	1,995	1,567	7.220***
	(1,054)	(910)	
Years	13.9	12.5	2.360**
	(9.8)	(9.2)	
Years squared	288	241	2.368**
	(342)	(306)	
Supervisory	0.14	0.08	3.371***
	(0.34)	(0.27)	
Position occupied	0.71	0.68	0.999
	(0.46)	(0.47)	
Veteran	0.43	0.39	1.272
	(0.50)	(0.49)	
Disabled veteran	0.06	0.06	0.000
	(0.24)	(0.24)	
Defense	0.34	0.34	0.000
	(0.47)	(0.48)	
Professional	0.19	0.07	6.791***
	(0.39)	(0.26)	
Administrative	0.21	0.18	1.226
	(0.40)	(0.38)	
Technical	0.21	0.23	0.747
	(0.40)	(0.42)	
Clerical	0.38	0.48	3.129***
	(0.49)	(0.50)	
Other	0.02	0.04	1.530[b]
	(0.14)	(0.21)	
Sex	0.65	0.64	0.325
	(0.48)	(0.48)	
N	2,422	271	

[a] The formula for computing the *t* statistic is $t = (\bar{X}_1 - \bar{X}_2)/[(S_1^2/N_1) + (S_2^2/N_2)]^{1/2}$, where $\bar{X}_1$ and $\bar{X}_2$ are the means, S_1 and S_2 are the standard deviations, and N_1 and N_2 are the sample sizes.

[b] $p \leq .10$.

**$p \leq .01$.

***$p \leq .001$.

generally shorter in this occupational group, Mexican Americans must
make substantial occupational shifts in order to be promoted at the same
rate as Anglos.

Finally, Anglo employees and Mexican American employees had nearly equal distributions of males and females, as 65 percent of all Anglo employees were male while 64 percent of the Mexican American employees were males. Of course, the sex distribution by ethnic group is only one part of the sex effect on salary determination. Another important effect stems from the salary returns by sex for each ethnic group. To assess differences in returns, we turn to the separate regressions reported in Table 2.

For both Anglos and Mexican Americans we regressed salary in 1977 onto the employment characteristics of each worker and obtained highly significant models with two-thirds of the variance in earnings explained. The regression coefficients represent the average return on a unit increase in the independent variable in estimating salary. Examining the unstandardized regression coefficients, we find that most of the variables used to estimate salary were significant predictors for both Anglos and Mexican Americans.

TABLE 2

Effects of Predictor Variables on Salary for Anglo and Mexican American Federal Civil Servants, 1977 (Unstandardized Coefficients, Southwest Only)

Employment Characteristics	Anglos	Mexican Americans	t Test for Difference[a]
Education	240***	285*	.291
Education 13+	1,369***	1,564***	.405
Age	208***	343**	.949
Age squared	−2.04***	−3.94**	−1.176
Years	495***	333***	−1.747*
Years squared	−7.90***	−4.79*	−1.214
Supervisory	2,434***	2,278***	.219
Position occupied	−341#	−870#	−1.034
Veteran	−382#	194	1.110
Disabled veteran	−1,709***	−227	1.716*
Defense	−883***	−624	.592
Administrative	−1,224***	−2,055**	−.986
Technical	−6,332***	−5,802***	.577
Clerical	−6,743***	−5,815***	1.024
Other	−7,329***	−6,878***	.353
Sex	2,555***	1,401**	−2.071*
R^2 (adjusted)	.685	.659	

NOTE: The standardized regression coefficients (betas) for each of the independent variables are as follows: for Anglos, .060, .192, .370, −.313, .619, −.394, .122, −.024, −.027, −.058, −.062, −.380, −.340, −.427, −.147, .179; for Mexican Americans, .094, .141, .840, −.783, .669, −.320, .137, −.087, .021, −.011, −.062, −.164, −.522, −.640, −.344, .140.

[a] The formula for computing the t statistic is $t = (b_1 − b_2)/(se_1^2 + se_2^2)^{1/2}$, where b_1 and b_2 are the unstandardized regression coefficients and se_1 and se_2 are the standard errors.

[b] $p \leq .10$.

*$p \leq .05$.

**$p \leq .01$.

***$p \leq .001$.

Mexican Americans received slightly higher returns from education and age than did Anglos, although the differences between the coefficients were not statistically significant. However, on most other predictors of salary, Anglos received larger returns, and indeed there were three pairs of significantly different coefficients. On the average, Anglos received higher returns to years of federal work experience and supervisory status than did Mexican Americans. Moreover, Anglos were not as likely to be negatively affected by placement into the excepted rather than the competitive Civil Service, as indicated by the coefficients for position occupied.

The coefficients for the veterans' preference variables were nonsignificant for Mexican Americans, but attained statistical significance for Anglos. That the coefficients were negative is consistent with their intended function of giving a boost or preference to armed services participants. Hence, the negative coefficients indicate that persons who did not score well on Civil Service entrance examinations were nonetheless hired into the Civil Service but remained somewhat behind the nonveteran in salary. Moreover, the greater the preference given, the larger the salary deficit. For Mexican Americans, veterans' preference apparently did not affect their salary once in the Civil Service. Possibly this is because only highly qualified Mexican Americans are hired into the Civil Service regardless of their veteran status. An explanation complementary to that above is that the armed services may provide minorities with cultural capital, and therefore assist in the minorities' preparation for careers outside the military (see Browning, Lopreato, and Poston, 1973).

Of particular interest in this study are the effects of employment in a defense agency, occupational group, and sex of employee on salary. One explanation for lower average Mexican American salaries is that as a group they are disadvantaged by employment in the defense agencies. This does not appear to be the case. In fact, Anglo salaries were reduced more by employment in a defense agency than Mexican American salaries, suggesting that the opportunities for Anglos were better in agencies other than defense, while for Mexican Americans the defense agencies were no worse than any other agency.

The dummy variables for the occupational groups were entered into the analysis to estimate whether Mexican Americans' lower salaries resulted from disproportionate representation in the low-paying occupations. Our examination of the distribution of employees presented in Table 1 partially confirmed this hypothesis. The results from the regression analyses suggested that the effects of occupation were significant for both Anglos and Mexican Americans within the same occupational group. When this analysis was run including blue-collar workers, we found that being a blue-collar worker did not diminish the earnings of Mexican Americans as much as it did for Anglos. The explanation may be similar to our interpretation of the effects of employment in the defense agencies. Lacking opportunities for the best-paying white-collar jobs outside of defense, Mexican Americans are not much disadvantaged by blue-collar work or defense employment. As regards white-collar work, however, the concentration of Mexican Americans into the technical, clerical, and other occupational groups is in part responsible for their lower salary, as these occupations are consistently lower in salary than the professional and administrative occupations. However, within those occupations they are paid, if anything, slightly higher (though not significantly so) than Anglos in the same occupational groups. What is not known is whether the placement of employees into occupational groups is achieved without ethnic bias.

Finally, the results from the regression analysis indicated that there were significant differences in the earnings of males and females for both Anglos and Mexican Americans, with Anglo males earning $2,555 more than Anglo females, all other things being equal, and Mexican American males earning $1,401 more than Mexican American females. Moreover, there was a significant difference between Anglo and Mexican Americans on the sex variable. Mexican American women were paid less than other groups, in part due to their ethnicity and sex, but also because of the unique combination of ethnic and sex effects. We have controlled some of those factors which indicate job commitment: years of work with the same employer, age, education, occupation, etc. Yet there remains a significant race by sex effect on income, suggesting that work commitment may not be the underlying reason for differences in salary. Ideally, of course, we would like direct measures of family responsibilities and a sufficient sample to run separate regression for males and females within each ethnic group. Nevertheless, our data do show that Mexican American and Anglo salary differences would be less if Mexican American women were paid at a rate no worse than Anglo women.

The method of regression decomposition provides a convenient way of summarizing the combined effects of all of the differences in returns revealed by the separate regressions. In particular, we can compute a dollar value for the difference in Anglo and Mexican American salaries that is due to different returns, holding all the other variables constant (see Mindiola, 1979; Siegel, 1965; and Taylor, 1979, for the mathematical details). The result shares the simplicity of a regression coefficient for an ethnic dummy variable in a merged regression, without the latter's assumption of equal returns. Applying this method, we calculated that even if Mexican Americans had the same average characteristics as Anglos, they would still make $915 less per year than Anglos because of different returns. This figure represents approximately one-third of the observed salary difference between the two groups, and is probably an underestimate of the true salary as there are no control variables on equality of placement.

Discussion and Conclusions

Every work organization has its own lore of successful integration into the organization. Indeed, individuals who wish to move up the career ladder must learn the lore of their organization at two levels. At the level of the individual job, new recruits must quickly learn which employee rules are observed in practice and those which are more form than substance; what staff is in charge of particular information; who knows the history of a trail of correspondence; what is the greatest annoyance of each supervisor; which secretary will offer assistance above and beyond the job description. Such knowledge can certainly facilitate a new employee's movement in an organization.

At the organizational level, however, other work lore informs the employee about the structure of work: that there are certain job combinations which facilitate a career; that there are training programs necessary to one's advancement; that an assignment in the home office enhances one's mobility among the field offices, etc. (Spilerman, 1977; Grandjean, 1981). Such information is the subject of popular books on career success, and within organizations the advancement of an individual whose career is consistent with the organizational lore is seen as evidence of the underlying reality of such lore.

No less important is the organizational wisdom regarding one's *lack* of success. An individual might fail to advance due to a lack of cultural polish, poor education, or a breakdown in the sponsor-protégé system (Kanter, 1977). Such explanations rest on perceptions of what is necessary to "get ahead" in the organization, rather than the quality of the job performance. And when such explanations become tied to distinct groups of employees due to continued use, these explanations affect the interpretations of career success (or lack of it) for all group members (Alvarez, 1979).

The implementation of outreach efforts or affirmative action is often met with, or followed by, observations on why certain groups of employees have not advanced. These observations are offered as part of the common knowledge of the organization, and as reasonable explanations for a group's failure to achieve equality of outcome rather than the organization's failure at equality of opportunity. In the case of Mexican Americans, the explanations examined shift the burden of responsibility for unequal employment outcomes from the employer to the individual.

The results presented above raise questions about explanations of inequality. While the explanations are particular to the federal Civil Service, they are analogous to explanations held to account for inequality in other organizations. The findings from this study may be summarized as follows.

First, Mexican Americans are in the lower-paying occupations, and receive less income because of that fact. However, the process which determines how individuals are assigned to occupations has not been studied here, and we cannot know whether it is unbiased. Speculation from other research on the federal government does suggest that ethnic group bias operates on decisions within the Civil Service (Carmel and Taylor, 1977; Grandjean, 1981). Although specific programs, such as Upward Mobility and Veteran's Readjustment, have been designed to move talented, but less educated, employees into higher positions, such programs have a history of stiff competition and long waiting lists. Moreover, they have traditionally been funded along with other affirmative action efforts. If the present administration's reorganization of the Commission on Civil Rights is any indication, there will be fewer rather than more positions for talented minorities.

A second major finding from this study is that Mexican Americans receive unequal returns to their employment characteristics. For example, the average Anglo earns more due to seniority than a Mexican American. Moreover, although the disabled veteran's preference should affect both groups similarly, apparently less-qualified Anglos are more likely to be hired with the preference than is true of Mexican Americans.

Third, Mexican Americans are not likely to do badly by entering a defense agency, at least in the Southwest. Although Mexican Americans seem concentrated in the defense agencies, the proportion employed in defense is similar to that of Anglos. Moreover, Mexican Americans' salaries are no worse than Anglos' for being in the defense agencies. What we need to know is which agencies are best for entry, and which agencies are best for mobility. Such agency-specific information could assist minorities in playing the rules of the organization to their own advantage.

Finally, Mexican American women earn significantly less than all other ethnic/ sex groups, even when characteristics representing job commitment are controlled. The difference reported here is greater than the difference reported between Asian Americans and Anglos (Taylor and Kim, 1980). Of course, the controls entered into this analysis are only proxies for job commitment, and do not include variables for sick leave, transfer, etc. However, a review of studies on job commitment variables such as turnover and sick leave in the federal government suggest mixed patterns by age and sex (Benokraitis and Feagin, 1978:32–33), so that there is no one general principle regarding job commitment as measured by these variables. Hence, our results indicate that Mexican American women, like Asian and black women, occupy a unique but disadvantaged position in federal employment.

How can income inequality be alleviated? We offer some other simple and straightforward ways to bring the salaries of similarly qualified Mexican Americans and Anglos into alignment. First, programs such as Upward Mobility must be pursued with greater vigor to allow Mexican Americans to rise to a level of their potential as specified in Public Law 92-261. Second, the federal government has taken few affirmative steps in recognizing the bilingual nature of the work force in the Southwest. For example, a prospective employee may do most of his or her work with a Spanish-speaking clientele in El Paso, San Antonio, etc., yet job descriptions and systems of job evaluations rarely reflect the knowledge required for bilingual speakers. Similarly, a preference could be given in supervisory positions for a bilingual speaker when a Spanish-speaking clientele or staff to be supervised reached a minimum level. This personnel requirement does not penalize any group; it is work-related, and it recognizes the bilingual nature of the Southwest. Finally, the federal government could make better use of excepted positions and presidential appointments to draw as well as to promote more Mexican Americans in the federal Civil Service. Instead, the percentage of presidential appointments, for example, who are Mexican American has declined from 1980 to 1983 (U.S. Commission on Civil Rights, 1983).

This study is but a small part of the needed information on the effect of labor markets and their operation on Mexican Americans. Much more needs to be known about a wider variety of specific agency effects and the consequences of particular personnel rules, as well as the informal practices within agencies that can promote or hinder the career prospects of any individual.

REFERENCES

Alvarez, Rudolfo. 1979. "Institutional Discrimination in Organizations and Their Environments," in R. Alvarez and B. Lutterman, eds., *Discrimination in Organizations* (San Francisco: Jossey-Bass): pp. 2–49.

Benokraitis, Nijole V., and Joe R. Feagin. 1978. *Affirmative Action and Equal Opportunity* (Boulder, Colo.: Westview).

Borjas, George. 1980. "Wage Determination in the Federal Government: The Role of Constituents and Bureaucrats," *Journal of Political Economy,* 88 (December):1110–17.

Browning, Harley L., Sally Cook Lopreato, and Dudley L. Poston, Jr. 1973. "Income and Veteran Status: Variations among Mexican-Americans, Blacks, and Anglos," *American Sociological Review,* 38 (February):74–85.

Carmel, Ann, and Patricia A. Taylor. 1977. *Hispanic Employment in the Federal Civil Service* (Washington, D.C.: U.S. Government Printing Office).

Farley, Reynolds. 1977. "Trends in Racial Inequalities: Have the Gains of the 1960s Disappeared in the 1970s?" *American Sociological Review,* 42 (April):189–208.

Grandjean, Burke D. 1981. "History and Career in a Bureaucratic Labor Market," *American Journal of Sociology,* 86 (March):1057–92.

Grebler, Leo, Joan W. Moore, and Ralph C. Guzman. 1970. *The Mexican-American People* (New York: Free Press).

Kanter, Rosabeth Moss. 1977. *Men and Women of the Corporation* (New York: Basic Books).

Mindiola, Tacho, Jr. 1979. "Age and Income Discrimination against Mexican-Americans and Blacks in Texas, 1960 and 1970," *Social Problems,* 27 (December):196–208.

Poston, Dudley L., Jr., and David Alvírez. 1973. "On the Costs of Being a Mexican American Worker," *Social Science Quarterly,* 53 (March):697–709.

Siegel, Paul. 1965. "The Cost of Being a Negro," *Sociological Inquiry,* 35 (Winter):41–57.

South, Scott J., Charles M. Bonjean, William T. Markham, and Judy Corder. 1982. "Social Structure and Intergroup Interaction: Men and Women of the Federal Bureaucracy," *American Sociological Review,* 47 (October):587–99.

Spilerman, Seymour. 1977. "Careers, Labor Market Structure, and Socioeconomic Achievement," *American Journal of Sociology,* 83 (November):551–93.

Taylor, Patricia A. 1979. "Income Inequality in the Federal Civilian Government," *American Sociological Review,* 44 (June):468–79.

Taylor, Patricia A., and Sung-Soon Kim. 1980. "Asian-Americans in the Federal Civil Service, 1977," *California Sociologist,* 3 (Winter):1–16.

U.S. Commission on Civil Rights. 1983. *Equal Opportunity in Presidential Appointment* (Washington, D.C.: U.S. Commission on Civil Rights).

Whitehead, Carlton J., and Albert S. King. 1973. "Differences in Managers' Attitudes toward Mexican and non-Mexican-Americans in Organizational Authority Relations," *Social Science Quarterly,* 53 (March):760–71.

12. SEX-ROLE ATTITUDES AND LABOR FORCE PARTICIPATION AMONG YOUNG HISPANIC FEMALES AND NON-HISPANIC WHITE FEMALES[1]

Vilma ORTIZ, *University of Wisconsin–Madison*

Rosemary Santana COONEY, *Fordham University*

The hypotheses that traditional sex-role attitudes explain lower labor force participation among Hispanic females and have an especially strong influence on the labor force participation of Hispanic females are examined using data on the youth cohort of the National Longitudinal Survey. First generation Hispanic females held significantly more traditional sex-role attitudes than second or third generation females or non-Hispanic white females, and first and second generation Hispanic females were significantly less likely to participate in the labor force than non-Hispanic white females. However, the Hispanic-white difference in labor force participation was due primarily to differences in educational attainment, not differences in traditional sex-role attitudes. Nor did sex-role attitudes have a stronger impact on labor force participation among Hispanic females.

Research has consistently shown that Hispanic females, in particular Mexican origin and Puerto Rican females, are less likely to participate in the labor force than non-Hispanic white females (Cooney, 1975; Cooney and Colon Warren, 1979; Grebler, Moore, and Guzman, 1970; Guhleman and Tienda, 1981; Jaffe, Cullen, and Boswell, 1980; Wagenheim, 1975). While research has found that socioeconomic characteristics, such as education, fertility, and headship status, explain a considerable amount of the difference in participation between Hispanic women and non-Hispanic white women, this difference has been shown to persist even after controlling for differences in socioeconomic status (Cooney, 1975).

[1] Revision of a paper presented at the annual conference of the American Sociological Association in San Francisco on 7 September 1982.

This research was supported by the Department of Labor's Employment and Training Administration Contract No. 99-1-1588-33-3 to the National Council of La Raza and by the National Institute of Mental Health Grant No. F32MH08669 to the first author. Institutional support was also provided by the Hispanic Research Center at Fordham University and the Institute for Social Research at the University of Michigan. We gratefully acknowledge comments made by Douglas Gurak, Tomas Almaguer, and anonymous reviewers at *SSQ*.

Since Hispanic females have so consistently been found less likely to participate in the labor force, it has been suggested that traditional sex-role attitudes play a role in explaining ethnic differences in participation (Grebler, Moore, and Guzman, 1970). This stems from the argument that Hispanics hold strong traditional views regarding family, marriage, and work, and that Hispanic culture is thought to place greater emphasis on the family and on having children than on personal accomplishments or work commitments. This argument has been made of the two major Hispanic national origin groups that are found in the United States and are included in this study, Mexican Americans (Grebler, Moore, and Guzman, 1970; Mirande, 1977) and Puerto Ricans (Fitzpatrick, 1971). However, the hypothesis that traditional sex-role attitudes are largely responsible for Hispanic females' lower labor force participation has not been tested empirically.

Sex-role attitudes have been found to have a direct impact on labor force participation among women in general (Dowdall, 1974; Katelman and Barnett, 1968; Kim and Murphy, 1973; one exception is Spitze and Waite, 1978). Given that sex-role attitudes influence participation among women in general, then one should expect this relationship to also be significant among Hispanic women. However, since traditional values are thought to be such an intricate aspect of Hispanic culture, it stands to reason that Hispanic females should be influenced by the presence of traditional beliefs to a greater extent than non-Hispanic females who come from cultures that place less emphasis on these beliefs. If this line of reasoning is correct, then the relationship between traditional attitudes and participation should be significantly stronger among Hispanic females than among non-Hispanic white females.

One distinction among Hispanic females that is important in terms of both behavior (e.g., fertility, Bean and Swicegood, 1982) and attitudes (e.g., Soto and Shaver, 1982) is generational status. Since first generation Hispanic females have had a greater exposure to Hispanic culture and less exposure to American customs than second or third generation Hispanic females, they should be more affected by traditional sex-role attitudes. Therefore, traditional sex-role attitudes should have an especially strong impact on the labor force participation of first generation Hispanic females in comparison to second or third generation Hispanic females or non-Hispanic white females.

Data and Methods

This analysis is based on a sample of young females from the youth cohort of the National Longitudinal Surveys (NLS) of Labor Market Experiences. The data used in this analysis are from the first-year interviews collected in 1979. This cohort of approximately 12,700 youths was sampled to be nationally representative of youths between the ages of 14 and 21. In addition, Hispanics and blacks were oversampled; disadvantaged non-Hispanic, nonblack youth were oversampled; and youth enlisted in the military were oversampled.

The focus of this paper is on Hispanic females and non-Hispanic white females; therefore, blacks and other nonwhite groups were excluded from the analysis. Race and ethnicity was obtained using a self-identification measure in which respondents could identify with more than one racial/ethnic group. Respondents who identified with a group of Hispanic origin were classified as Hispanics even if they also identified with another group. Respondents were classified as non-Hispanic white if they identified with a group of European descent or as American; did not identify with Hispanic origin groups, blacks, or other nonwhite groups; were not coded as black or other race by the interviewer; and were born in the United States.

Hispanic is a broad category composed of many national origin groups that differ along characteristics such as time period of arrival to the United States, geographic area of settlement, the political and economic circumstances surrounding their migration, and their cultural traditions. Despite these differences, we do not expect that the predicted relationships would differ for the different national origin groups. To check if this was true, the analyses that were done for all the Hispanics were done separately for those of Mexican and Puerto Rican origin (the only groups where there were sufficient numbers of respondents to allow for separate analyses). The separate analyses did not differ from the analysis of all Hispanics in any meaningful way. In other words, similar relationships were obtained for those of Mexican and Puerto Rican origin as were obtained for all the Hispanics. Therefore, the analysis presented here is based on all Hispanics.

The sample was further restricted to respondents who were 16 years old or older and who were not active in the military at the time of the interview, since these persons are usually excluded from official figures of labor force behavior. In addition, students enrolled in regular school were excluded from the analysis since their primary activity was attending school.

Sex-role attitudes is comprised of seven items tapping attitudes toward mothers and wives working outside the home. The items included in this measure were:

1. A woman's place is in the home, not in the office or shop;

2. A wife who carries out her full family responsibilities doesn't have time for outside employment;

3. A working wife feels more useful than one who doesn't hold a job;

4. The employment of wives leads to more juvenile delinquency;

5. It is much better for everyone concerned if the man is the achiever outside the home and the woman takes care of the home and family;

6. Men should share the work around the house with women, such as doing dishes, cleaning, and so forth;

7. Women are much happier if they stay at home and take care of their children.

Respondents expressed their agreement with each item on a four-point scale. The measure is an averaged composite with higher scores representing more traditional attitudes and an internal consistency of .73.[2]

Table 1 presents weighted descriptive statistics for the generational groups among Hispanic females and for the non-Hispanic white females. As expected, Hispanic females were less likely to participate in the labor force, with the lowest participation among the first generation, followed by the second generation, and then the third generation. The first generation Hispanic females were more likely to hold traditional sex-role attitudes than the second or third generation Hispanic females or the non-Hispanic white females. The Hispanics and the non-Hispanic whites were similar with respect to the percentage who have ever married and their age distribution. The percentage of Hispanic females who have had a child was greater (with little variation among the generational groups) than that of the non-Hispanic white females. The Hispanic females had completed fewer years of education in comparison to the non-Hispanic whites, with the educational attainment increasing from the first to the third generation.

Results

The regression analyses were carried out on the combined sample of Hispanic females and non-Hispanic white females with comparisons made among the first, second, and third generation Hispanic females and the non-Hispanic white females (the latter group serving as the reference group). First, the impact of ethnicity/generational status and social characteristics on traditional sex-role attitudes was examined, with only ethnicity/generational status entered in the first step of the analysis and the social characteristics added in the second step. Second, the impact of ethnicity/generational status, sex-role attitudes, and social characteristics on labor force participation was examined. The independent variables were entered into the regression equation in the following order: ethnicity/generational status was entered in the first step; traditional sex-role attitudes in the second step; sex-role attitudes were excluded and social characteristics included in the third step; sex-role attitudes were reentered in the fourth step; and finally, the interaction between ethnicity/generational status and sex-role attitudes was entered in the last step.

Table 2 presents results from the ordinary least squares regression analysis for sex-role attitudes and the logit regression analysis for labor force participation. Unstandardized regression coefficients are presented for the least squares regression and first-order partial derivatives are presented for the logit analysis. These are computed as $b_i p'(1 - p')$ where b_i is the coefficient of the relevant independent variable and p' is the proportion in the labor force. The unweighed sample proportion (.286) is chosen as a

---

[2] One item included in the questionnaire, "Employment of both parents is necessary to keep up with the high cost of living," was omitted when constructing the measure because it did not appear on substantive grounds to be tapping the same concept and did not correlate highly with the other items.

TABLE 1

Weighted Descriptive Statistics for Generational Groups among Hispanic Females and for Native Non-Hispanic White Females

	Generation 1 (N = 151)		Generation 2 (N = 90)		Generation 3 (N = 147)		White Females (N = 969)		Females (N = 1,357)	
	Mean	SD	Mean	SD	Mean	SD	Mean	SD	Mean	SD
Labor force participation	0.507	0.502	0.583	0.496	0.685	0.466	0.794	0.404	0.771	0.420
Traditional attitudes	2.465	0.571	2.114	0.448	2.103	0.531	2.107	0.470	2.121	0.472
Age	19.485	1.573	19.573	1.421	19.436	1.400	19.676	1.379	19.653	1.390
Ever married	0.409	0.493	0.406	0.494	0.438	0.498	0.394	0.489	0.397	0.489
Ever had child	0.417	0.495	0.413	0.495	0.385	0.488	0.236	0.425	0.256	0.436
Highest grade completed	9.012	3.044	10.598	2.010	11.008	1.608	11.680	1.510	11.503	1.722

TABLE 2

Regression Analysis of Traditional Attitudes and Labor Force Participation on Ethnicity/Generational Status, Traditional Attitudes,

	Traditional Attitudes		Labor Force Participation				
	Step 1	Step 2	Step 1	Step 2	Step 3	Step 4	Step 5
Generation 1	0.354**	0.199**	-0.316**	-0.234**	-0.118	-0.077	-0.451
Generation 2	0.020	-0.028	-0.180*	-0.184*	-0.093	-0.110	-0.207
Generation 3	-0.027	-0.059	-0.071	-0.082	0.014	0.004	0.121
Traditional attitudes				-0.268**		-0.202**	-0.219
Age					0.035*	0.038*	0.037*
Ever married		0.015			-0.146*	-0.140*	-0.139*
Ever had child		0.039			-0.387**	-0.394**	-0.392**
Highest grade completed		-0.057**			0.072**	0.061**	0.064**
Generation 1 × attitudes		0.008					0.155
Generation 2 × attitudes							0.046
Generation 3 × attitudes							-0.054
Constant	2.107	2.448	0.323	-0.929	-0.959	-0.478	-0.436
Proportion of variance explained	.238**	.327**	.032**	.068**	.213**	.226**	.228**

*p < .01.

**p < .001.

realistic representation of the actual overall probability of being in the labor force (the derivatives would be different if computed at other points in the logistic curve). These derivatives are interpreted as the increment to the actual probability of labor force participation associated with a one-unit increase in the independent variable.

When the effect of ethnicity/generational status on sex-role attitudes was examined without controlling for other factors, the first generation Hispanic females differed significantly from the non-Hispanic white females while the second and third generation did not differ from the non-Hispanic white females. Further comparisons revealed that the first generation females differed significantly from the second and third generation females. After controlling for social characteristics, the difference between the first generation and the non-Hispanic white females decreased by almost half the magnitude, although this difference continued to be significant. Furthermore, the only social characteristic that had a significant impact on sex-role attitudes was highest grade completed.

In the analysis of labor force participation, we found that prior to controlling for traditional sex-role attitudes and social characteristics, the Hispanic females participated considerably less in the labor force with significant differences found between the first and second generation females and the non-Hispanic white females. When traditional sex-role attitudes were entered into the equation, the first and second generation continued to differ significantly from the non-Hispanic white females, and the only change in the coefficients was a small decrease for the first generation. However, when the social characteristics were included and sex-role attitudes were excluded from the equation, the differences between the Hispanic generational groups and the non-Hispanic white females were reduced considerably and were no longer significant. Of the social characteristics included in the equation, highest grade completed was the factor most responsible for reducing the difference between the first and second generation and the non-Hispanic white females. Controlling for differences in highest grade completed explained a substantial portion of the differences in labor force participation between the Hispanic generational groups and non-Hispanic white females.

Although traditional sex-role attitudes were not important in explaining ethnic/generational differences in labor force participation, sex-role attitudes had a direct and negative impact on labor force participation. Thus females with more traditional attitudes participated significantly less in the labor force, even after controlling for social characteristics.

When the impact of the social characteristics on labor force participation was examined, all of the characteristics had a significant impact on labor force participation. The results show that older respondents and respondents with more education participated more in the labor force, and females who had married or had a child had lower participation rates.

Although sex-role attitudes did not explain much of the Hispanic-white differences in labor force participation, it is still possible that traditional attitudes have a greater impact on labor force participation among Hispanic females, and particularly among the first generation, than among non-Hispanic white females (Cohen and Cohen, 1975). This can be tested by examining the interaction between ethnicity/generational status and sex-role attitudes. As shown in Table 2, none of these interactions were significant. Not even among first generation Hispanic females who held more traditional attitudes were sex-role attitudes found to have a greater influence on labor force participation. Thus, traditional sex-role attitudes did not have a stronger impact on the labor force behavior of Hispanic females than of non-Hispanic white females.

Summary and Conclusions

The present study examined the hypotheses that traditional sex-role attitudes explain lower labor force participation among young Hispanic females and that sex-role attitudes have an especially strong influence on participation among Hispanic females, particularly among the first generation. First, we found that first generation Hispanic females were significantly more traditional in their sex-role attitudes than second and third generation females and non-Hispanic white females, and that this difference persisted even after controlling for differences in social characteristics. Second, we found that first and second generation Hispanic females were significantly less likely to participate in the labor force than non-Hispanic white females. Third, differences in sex-role attitudes did not explain the Hispanic-white difference in participation regardless of whether social characteristics were held constant or not. Instead, ethnic differences in participation resulted primarily from differences in highest grade completed. Finally, while traditional sex-role attitudes had a strong negative impact on labor force participation, this effect was similar for Hispanic females and non-Hispanic white females. Even among first generation Hispanic females who held more traditional beliefs these beliefs did not have greater consequences for their behavior.

What implications do these findings have? The results of this study and others (e.g., Farris and Glenn, 1976) suggest that Hispanic females actually are more traditional in their *beliefs*. However, they also suggest that traditional beliefs are not very important in explaining the labor force behavior of Hispanic females. Thus these findings have implications for the validity of certain popular notions regarding the role of culture in affecting *behavior*. The findings of this study, and other studies that test similar hypotheses (e.g., Bean, Curtis, and Marcum, 1977), provide little support for the argument that traditional beliefs are important for understanding the behavior of Hispanics. Thus cultural arguments need to be evaluated against empirical evidence and not simply accepted as truths.

REFERENCES

Bean, Frank, Russell Curtis, and John Marcum. 1977. "Familism and Marital Satisfaction among Mexican Americans: The Effects of Family Size, Wife's Labor Force Participation, and Conjugal Power," *Journal of Marriage and the Family,* 39 (November):759–67.

Bean, Frank, and Gray Swicegood. 1982. "Generation, Education, and Mexican American Fertility," *Social Science Quarterly,* 63 (March):131–44.

Cohen, Jacob, and Patricia Cohen. 1975. *Applied Multiple Regression/Correlation Analysis for the Behavioral Sciences* (New York: Lawrence Erlbaum Associates).

Cooney, Rosemary Santana. 1975. "Changing Labor Force Participation of Mexican American Wives: A Comparison with Anglos and Blacks," *Social Science Quarterly,* 56 (September):252–61.

Cooney, Rosemary Santana, and Alice E. Colon Warren. 1979. "Declining Female Participation among Puerto Rican New Yorkers: A Comparison with Native White Non-Spanish New Yorkers," *Ethnicity,* 6 (September):281–97.

Dowdall, Jean A. 1974. "Structural and Attitudinal Factors Associated with Female Labor Force Participation," *Social Science Quarterly,* 55 (June):121–30.

Farris, Buford, and Norval Glenn. 1976. "Fatalism and Familism among Anglos and Mexican Americans in San Antonio," *Sociology and Social Research,* 60 (July):393–402.

Fitzpatrick, Joseph. 1971. *Puerto Rican Americans: The Meaning of Migration* (Englewood Cliffs, N.J.: Prentice-Hall).

Grebler, Leo, Joan W. Moore, and Ralph C. Guzman. 1970. *The Mexican American People* (New York: Free Press).

Guhleman, Patricia, and Marta Tienda. 1981. "A Socioeconomic Profile of Hispanic-American Females Workers: Perspectives on Labor Force Participation and Earnings." Center for Demography and Ecology Working Paper 81-7 (Madison: University of Wisconsin–Madison).

Jaffe, A. J., Ruth Cullen, and Thomas Boswell. 1980. *The Changing Demography of Spanish Americans* (New York: Academic Press).

Katelman, Doris K., and Larry D. Barnett. 1968. "Work Orientation of Urban Middle Class Married Women," *Journal of Marriage and the Family,* 30 (February):80–88.

Kim, Sookon, and James A. Murphy. 1973. "Changes in Labor Force and Employment Status," in U.S. Department of Labor, *Dual Careers: A Longitudinal Study of Labor Market Experience of Women.* Manpower Research Monograph 21, vol. 2 (Washington, D.C.: U.S. Government Printing Office): pp. 21–46.

Mirande, Alfredo. 1977. "The Chicano Family: A Reanalysis of Conflicting Views," *Journal of Marriage and the Family,* 39 (November):747–56.

Soto, Elaine, and Phillip Shaver. 1982. "Sex-Role Traditionalism, Assertiveness, and Symptoms of Puerto Rican Women Living in the U.S.," *Hispanic Journal of Behavioral Sciences,* 4 (March):1–19.

Spitze, Glenna D., and Linda J. Waite. 1978. "Labor Force and Work Attitudes," *Sociology of Work and Occupations,* 7 (February):3–32.

Wagenheim, Kal. 1975. *A Survey of Puerto Ricans on the U.S. Mainland in the 1970's* (New York: Praeger).

III. POLITICAL PARTICIPATION, ORGANIZATIONAL DEVELOPMENT, AND INSTITUTIONAL RESPONSIVENESS

13. INTRODUCTION

F. Chris GARCIA, *The University of Texas at Austin*

Rodolfo O. DE LA GARZA, *The University of Texas at Austin*

Donald J. TORRES, *The University of Texas at Austin*

Historically, political scientists have manifested little interest in Mexican American political life. As of 1980, the principal political science journals in the nation had published a total of nine articles on the subject (Flood, 1980). Since the early 1970s, however, several factors including the rise of Chicano militancy, an increase in the number of Mexican origin social scientists, and the increasing size and potential political clout of the Mexican origin population have contributed to an increase in the attention researchers give to the study of Mexican American political life. Thus, the research that has been published from the early 1970s to 1984 constitutes both the core and the overwhelming majority of all social scientific research explicitly focusing on the Mexican American political experience. Our purpose in this essay is to review the literature that has been published after the 1973 *Social Science Quarterly* special issue on Mexican Americans, since studies published prior to 1973 are either referenced or reviewed in other publications (in particular Grebler, Moore, and Guzman, 1970, and the March 1973 issue of *SSQ*).

Theory Building

One major segment of this new literature utilized dual labor market theory and a political economy approach to explain Mexican American political reality. Illustrative of these efforts are the work of Barrera (1979), Santillan (1978), and Ortiz (1980). These efforts were part of a broader attempt to formulate a "Chicano political theory," an exercise that Rocco (1977) argued was handicapped by the effect that the dominant ideology of the nation has on Chicano political thinking.

The political economy and dual labor market approach enhanced our understanding of the origins of the Mexican American political experience. It soon became clear, however, that this perspective was less useful for explaining why Mexican Americans' political fortunes slowly and irreversibly began to change. Cervantes (1976) compared the merits of the traditional political science paradigm (pluralism) with the internal colonial (a variant of the political economy approach) and found both lacking. Garcia and de la Garza (1977) utilized these same two models as well as a third (elitist) model and found that the value of each varied with the time period and issues being studied. They too concluded that no existing model was adequate to explain the Chicano political experience.

Efforts to develop new conceptual and theoretical insights into Mexican American political life have had mixed results. While they have contributed to our understanding of Mexican American political foundations, they have not contributed greatly to explaining political events in more recent decades. Thus, the question of how best to conceptualize contemporary Mexican American political life remains to be answered by future researchers.

Political History

Numerous revisionist political histories preceded the recent scholarship reviewed here (see the McLemore and Romo chapter in this volume). A theme common to these was the rejection of the myth of the nonparticipant, apolitical Mexican American. Mexican American social scientists demonstrated that the Mexican origin population had indeed participated in politics but in styles that were appropriate to the tenor of the times and their position in society. The essays by Estrada et al. (1981) and Navarro (1974) offer overviews of this revisionist argument. An additional dimension of this revisionist perspective is that Mexican Americans are no longer a regional minority; instead, Parra, Rios, and Gutierrez (1976) cited the organizational activities of Mexican Americans in the Midwest to argue that Mexican Americans are a national minority and that, wherever they reside, Mexican Americans are victims of discrimination and repression.

Organizational Development

Now that it is irrefutable that Mexican Americans do indeed have a political history, researchers have examined in greater detail selected aspects of Mexican American political life. One topic that has received considerable attention has been organizational development. The importance of community organizations to Mexican American sociopolitical life was first clearly addressed by Tirado (1970). Tirado's argument is supported by the work of Hernandez (1983) and Allsup (1982) and by the studies by Mario Garcia and San Miguel included in this volume. Garcia examines in detail the efforts of one Mexican American organization to improve the conditions of the community. Located in Los Angeles during the war years, the Coordinating Council for Latin American Youth attempted to exert influence on behalf of the Mexican American people in the areas of employment and education and also participated directly in electoral activities. San Miguel (1982) documented the role that the American G.I. Forum and other groups had in advancing Mexican American educational interests. Like Allsup, however, San Miguel noted that in the efforts to advance Mexican American interests, the G.I. Forum demonstrated relatively little concern for advancing the civil rights of other oppressed groups.

Throughout the twentieth century, Mexican American organizations have struggled to improve the educational opportunities available to Mexican origin children. Since the 1960s, much of that effort has centered on the issue of bilingual education. In the article included here, San Miguel reviews the evolution of federal policy toward bilingual education and describes the various political perspectives that have influenced bilingual education policy.

Despite the activities of organizations such as those mentioned above, by the late 1970s the Mexican origin community was still being systematically denied many of its constitutional rights. Mexican American leaders realized that there was a need for an organization that had as its explicit and primary function the advancement of Mexican American civil rights. Thus was born the Mexican American Legal Defense and Educational Fund (MALDEF). The O'Connor and Epstein article included here describes the origin of MALDEF and analyzes the factors that explain its evolution and success.

Despite the role these types of organizations have played in Mexican American political life, the extent to which the Mexican American population supports them is unclear. Teske and Nelson's (1976) study of four Texas cities found very limited evidence of membership in or awareness of Mexican American political organizations; Ambrecht and Pachon (1974) found comparable low-awareness rates in Los Angeles. This lack of awareness and support is one of the reasons Mexican American organizations have not been more effective change agents. Miller (1975) argued that factors such as the economic vulnerability of the Mexican American community, the legacy of patron systems, limited opportunity structures and the lack of an ideological position that is compatible with upward mobility and being "Mexican" help explain this lack of impact at the local level.

The 1970s witnessed the development of a new type of organization, one which has overcome the problems that hampered the traditional groups and become a major political force in San Antonio and South Texas and is becoming more important in cities such as Houston and Los Angeles. The most successful of these is San Antonio's Communities Organized for Public Services (COPS). Sekul (1983) analyzed the impact that COPS has on San Antonio public policy and concluded that its efforts have contributed significantly to improving the quality of life in San Antonio's older neighborhoods i.e., the barrios. The impact that this type of organization is having on other southwestern cities has yet to be determined.

Political Participation: Voting

Prior to 1974, there was a consensus around several aspects of Mexican American electoral behavior. Researchers agreed that Mexican Americans had lower registration and turnout rates than Anglos, and that they overwhelmingly identified with and supported the Democratic party. While these patterns continue to exist, it must be noted that some of the findings of prior voting behavior studies may be of little value today because many researchers did not differentiate between citizen and noncitizen segments of the Mexican origin population when they calculated the size of the population eligible to participate in elections. Nor did they examine the age characteristics of the Mexican origin population. Their results substantially inflate the voting-eligible Mexican origin population and greatly understate Mexican American registration rates. Also, the passage of the 1975 and 1982 Voting Rights Acts significantly altered the rules of southwestern politics. Many of the factors that may have contributed to nonparticipation have been removed. Wrinkle and Miller (1984) suggested that these electoral rules changes combine with the age characteristics of the Mexican origin population to explain why there are no longer any differences between Mexican Americans and Anglos regarding turnout in primary and general elections.

Recent studies continue to find that, with few exceptions, Mexican American voter turnout continues to be lower than that of Anglos (Welch, Comer, and Steinman, 1975; Brischetto, Avina, and Doerfler, 1982). The gap between the two is narrowing, however. Numerous authors, including Lovrich and Marenin (1976), have speculated that this may be the result of culturally related factors or psychological features such as ethnic estrangement. While these undoubtedly have had an impact, demographic variables such as socioeconomic status, age, and education seem to be at least as influential. Antunes and Gaitz (1975) found, however, that Houston Mexican Americans still vote less than Anglos of similar income and age. Wolfinger and Rosenstone (1980), on the other hand, analyzed national data, and concluded that Mexican American turnout is about the same as the rest of the population when socioeconomic factors are taken into account. Buehler's (1977) Michigan-based research findings support this finding. In interpreting these results, it must be remembered that situational effects, specific to time, location, and historical traditions, have substantial bearings on such research. An analysis of national aggregate data, which subsume varying environmental contexts, may *ipso facto* produce results different from studies of closely circumscribed electoral contexts, and findings from research conducted in nonsouthwestern cities may provide little insight to southwestern political processes.

Concerning the "directions" of Mexican American voting, studies have indicated that Mexican Americans often vote in a "bloc" and that that bloc generally supports Democratic candidates (de la Garza, 1974; Freeman,

1974). Also it appears that Mexican Americans tend to vote heavily for Mexican American candidates. These tenets have been corroborated by research by Garcia (1976–77) into school board elections. It is still unclear whether this pattern holds across regions and time, and there has been little analysis of the reasons for the existence of these patterns.

The Cain and Kiewiet article included here makes an important contribution to the literature on Mexican American electoral behavior. It is the first study to analyze Mexican American voting in California and thus enables us to begin to compare patterns there with those elsewhere. It also incorporates multiple factors and determines the relative weight that each has in the electoral decision. The authors' succinct statement that "the Mexican American vote is a complex phenomenon with many indirect effects through intervening variables such as party, issue attitudes, and candidate evaluations" is a good summary statement of the complexities facing social scientists as they continue research into this area. The authors find that, as has been shown in other southwestern cities, Mexican Americans in the Los Angeles area are overwhelmingly oriented toward the Democratic party and support co-ethnics. They also find, as did de la Garza (1977) and Vigil (1978), that Anglos tend to support Anglo candidates in a race with Mexican Americans, similar to the latter's support for candidates of their own ethnic group. Their research also reminds us that Mexican Americans do not unthinkingly accept Mexican American candidates. Evaluations of particular candidates in a particular electoral situation do occur, and the outcomes of those evaluations lead to variable participation rates and differences in candidate support.

Political Socialization

Virtually no systematic research was conducted on the political socialization of Mexican Americans until the early 1960s. Guzman's (1976) pioneering work on the political experiences of the Mexican American people and the consequent effects of their political attitudes and behaviors was one of the earliest of these studies. Using sociological and psychological tools of analysis, Garcia (1973) and Gutierrez and Hirsh (1974) also broke new ground in their investigation of the politically relevant attitudes and opinions of Mexican American children. These studies provided benchmark results on the general patterns of Chicano childrens' orientations against which later research results could be measured. A more recent article by Lamare (1977) has reaffirmed that children of Mexican/Spanish ancestry, most particularly those who are most rural or Spanish-speaking, do differ in some significant ways in their orientations toward various parts of the political system. Stevens (1975) also found Mexican American children to have political orientations that differed from the expected Anglo norm.

Through the mid-1970s and early 1980s research on the political socialization of Mexican Americans diminished, partly as a reflection of the decreased interest in the subject in general among political scientists. Students of Mexican American politics continued to write about the political socialization of Mexican American political actors, but most of this material has been descriptive or anecdotal rather than analytical. There have been a few exceptions. Buzan (1980) has attempted to link Chicano attitudes supportive of political participation to political styles and degree of Chicano community control. Ambrecht and May (1976–77) analyzed how participating in the War on Poverty programs affected Mexican American political orientations. Cobas (1977) examined the effects of ethnic consciousness on "system blame" and political leftism and found that ethnic consciousness influences both of these orientations, but the relationship is clouded because of the role that class variables play in the equation.

Since the heyday of political socialization research in the 1960s, scholars have pointed to the necessity of examining the political orientations of particular segments of the population, and political elites have been at the top of the list of subjects for suggested further research. It has been asserted that while it is interesting and perhaps significant to know the orientations of children and even more so of the adult masses, it is *most* important to understand those influences which have formed the orientations of the political decision-makers themselves. The de la Garza–Vaughn study in this section is the first effort to address this question systematically on a national level. Using data from a national survey of Chicano political elites, de la Garza and Vaughn conclude that it is the shared experiences of the current generation of Chicano elites that best explains their current political attitudes. Furthermore, the overarching common feature of these experiences has been the discriminatory treatment experienced by Mexican Americans. Also, Chicano political leaders, unlike their Anglo counterparts, tend to be from the working classes. Their class characteristics, the aforementioned discriminatory treatment and their political maturation during the activist periods of the Chicano movement are seen as being distinctive and significant features of the political socialization of Chicano elites. De la Garza and Vaughn hypothesize that in combination these factors should result in distinctive attitudes, at least along several dimensions, which may in turn be reflected in distinctive attitudes on public policies, and also perhaps in recognizable styles of representing their constituencies.

The findings of Cisneros (1982) support these hypotheses. Cisneros compiled data from a mail survey of Spanish-surnamed federal executives conducted in 1979 and 1980. He found they had very diverse backgrounds and job experiences, are concerned with representing the Latino community, and are aware that Latinos expect much more from them than they are able to provide.

Mexican American Political Opinions and Attitudes

There are several reasons why little is known about Mexican American political opinions and attitudes. First, there have been relatively few surveys which have focused on the Mexican origin population. Second, while national public opinion polls and polling organizations usually are careful about including proportionate numbers of Latinos, the number of respondents in such a subsample is usually inadequate for any kind of significant generalization about Mexican American public opinion. Recently, a few additional opinion studies have been conducted, most notably the series of surveys being sponsored by the Southwest Voter Registration and Education Project and the large national sample survey conducted by the Survey Research Center at the University of Michigan. In the former both local and statewide surveys are being conducted, and some of the results have been published in the series of research monographs by Brischetto and de la Garza.[1]

A third reason is that those surveys that have been conducted have been limited to one city and sometimes to one issue. These studies usually report differences between Mexican American, Anglo, and Black attitudes. Because of differing methodologies and variation in the research sites, it is difficult to generalize from these to the overall Mexican American population. For example, MacManus and Cassell (1982) examined the opinions of Spanish-surnamed registered voters in Houston with regard to political interest, organizational awareness, party affiliation, and policy preferences. The authors suggested that it is because of their attitudes that Mexican Americans do not influence municipal political outcomes more than they do. Lovrich (1974) found similar differences. Polinard and Wrinkle (1980) surveyed Mexican Americans and Anglos in San Antonio with regard to environmental issues. They found only slight support for the hypothesis that Mexican Americans were less willing to pay for environmental quality than were Anglos.

One "opinion issue" that has received considerable attention as well as some national recognition is that of the impact of Mexican immigration into the United States. Scholars and politicians argue on both sides of the issue, that is, that undocumented workers both contribute to and detract from the American economy. Often the focus of the argument is on the impact such immigration has on working-class Americans, and most particularly on the Mexican Americans of the Southwest, who may be the population most directly affected by such an influx of workers. Depending on their ideology and interests, some spokesmen assert that Mexican Americans view the Mexican "undocumented" very sympathetically and

[1] These monographs in the Mexican American Electorate Series have been published beginning in 1983 by the Southwest Voter Registration Education Project (201 North St. Mary's, Suite 501, San Antonio) in association with the Center for Mexican American Studies at the University of Texas at Austin.

are very supportive of their plight. Others insist that it is the Mexican American who is most adversely affected by relatively free immigration across the Mexican-U.S. border, and that consequently Americans of Mexican ancestry are less favorably disposed towards the undocumented worker. The survey by Miller, Polinard, and Wrinkle included in this section demonstrates that Mexican American attitudes are quite complex and that there is a great variation of opinion on this issue among the correspondingly variegated Mexican American population. The authors find that, based on their geographically restricted sample, economic impact seems to be more influential than cultural kinship in the respondents' assessments of the undocumented worker situation. At least as important in this article are the methodological cautions which the authors have exercised and recommended to others in doing survey research among members of what is too often mistakenly assumed to be a homogeneous ethnic grouping.

The paucity of studies on Mexican American public opinion is even more glaring with reference to the political concerns of Mexican American elites. To date, only de la Garza (1982b) has systematically addressed this question. Comparing his findings to those of studies describing the views of the general Mexican American population indicates that, while there are some differences between the two particularly with regard to the undocumented worker issue, on most issues the views of the two groups are quite similar.

Political Representation

Central to the Mexican American political experience is the extent to which Mexican Americans have been represented in decision-making circles. To answer this question, it is necessary to examine representation from two perspectives. First, to what extent do Mexican Americans hold elected and appointed office; second, to what extent do officeholders, regardless of their ethnicity, respond to Mexican American interests?

The first question is relatively easy to answer. The number of Mexican Americans in all types of elected positions except U.S. senators has, in percentage terms, increased dramatically during the past decade. For example, between 1973 and 1984 the number of Mexican American congressmen will have gone from four to nine, an increase of over 100 percent. These increases reflect an expanded and more active Mexican American electorate and new electoral rules instituted as a result of the 1975 and 1982 Voting Rights Acts.

It is most likely that Mexican American bureaucratic representation has also increased at all levels, but no study has systematically measured this change over time in all jurisdictions. Where it has been measured (Welch, Karnig, and Eribes, 1983), the results revealed the expected expansion. One reason for this growth is that there were so few Mexican Americans in these positions prior to 1973. Gomez (1977), for example, found almost no Spanish-surnamed individuals holding high-level federal positions in 1973, and Cotrell (1980) found similar patterns in Texas.

The reasons for changes in the levels of Mexican American bureaucratic representation are unclear. Dye and Renick (1981) found that, as one might expect, Latino employment in high-level municipal positions did appear to be a function of political power, particularly as evidenced by Latinos. Taebel (1978) also examined the effect of minority representation on policymaking councils. Although, as in the Dye and Renick study, Latinos were but one small subset of the population Taebel studied, his results are relevant to those interested in Mexican American bureaucratic representation.

There also has been little research on the rates of Latino public employment in the literature in public administration journals. Existing studies present factual data but offer little analysis or theorizing. Moreover, attempts such as those by Davis and West (1978), Garcia, Clark, and Clark (1978) and de Krofcheck and Jackson (1974) to tie various socioeconomic and political variables to levels of Latino public employment have produced inconsistent and unclear findings.

The most recent attempt to tie together this type of research and to present findings based on its own broad-based data collection and analysis is that by Welch and Karnig (1979). These investigators examined data on municipal employment from 1973 to 1978 in more than 80 cities in the five southwestern states. They concluded that Latino employment was closer to approaching parity with population in 1978 than it had been in 1973. City characteristics other than Latino population size were not very good predictors of Latino municipal employment, nor was the economic status of the Latino community, nor was Latino political representation. Public sector employment of Latinos was near parity only in the lowest, clerical occupation.

The question regarding the extent to which political officials respond to Mexican American interests is more difficult to answer. Perhaps this is why there is so little literature on this subject. One approach is to determine the extent to which there are public policies destined to meet the specific concerns of the Mexican American people. Pachon and Moore (1981) and Martinez (1979) identified the distinctive characteristics of the Mexican origin population that should be taken into account in the development of public policy. Foremost among these are biculturalism, bilingualism, and the importance that Mexican Americans attach to the maintenance of the extended family.

Another approach is to measure how much use Mexican Americans make of existing programs and how they evaluate existing programs. In Omaha, Nebraska, Comer (1978) found that while Mexican American utilization rates were low, satisfaction was high. He indicated that these results challenge the validity of the proposition that a major reason that

Mexican Americans are not more politically active is because they are dissatisfied with the performance of governmental agencies. Because of the small sample size and the fact that the study was conducted in a city where the history of Anglo–Mexican American relations is much different than it would be in most southwestern cities, these findings must be considered as tentative and preliminary.

A third and perhaps the most effective way to determine if officials respond to Mexican American interests is to examine their behavior while in office. During the Nixon administration, de la Isla (1976) found that Mexican American political appointees had no role in policymaking; instead, they were used by the Nixon campaign to mobilize Mexican American support for Republican candidates. The behavior of those appointees may not be typical of appointees in Democratic administrations since the latter are more clearly dependent on Mexican American votes in order to be elected. The Welch and Hibbing article in this collection examines the voting behavior of Latino and non-Latino congressmen to determine the extent to which they are responsive to Latino issues. They find that Latino congressmen are more supportive of Latino issues than are non-Latinos. Furthermore, the size of the Latino population in a congressman's district influences how that congressman votes. Overall, they conclude that Latinos do have influence in Congress, but that influence is less than their numbers would warrant.

Mexican Americans and the Legal System

As evidenced by several of the studies discussed above, Mexican American political strategists have often used the court system in attempts to redress grievances when the more explicitly political branches of government have been unresponsive. Yet the relationship with the United States legal system has not always been one of protection and support. In fact, both the police and the courts have often been criticized by the Mexican American community because of the harsh and abusive way both have dealt with Mexican Americans. The articles by Welch, Gruhl, and Spohn and by Holmes and Daudistel included here examine the comparative treatment of Mexican American defendants by U.S. courts in different jurisdictions. Welch, Gruhl, and Spohn analyze 10,000 cases in Los Angeles and find that Latinos are convicted more often than Anglos or blacks and are sentenced to prison more often than Anglos. The differences in how each group is treated are not *statistically* significant, however, and they also find a slightly higher case dismissal rate for Latinos than for Anglos. Holmes and Daudistel's examination of burglary and robbery prosecutions in 1976 and 1977 finds differences in Mexican American–Anglo experiences in Texas but less so in Arizona. Together, these two articles challenge the long-held view that Mexican Americans are systematically discriminated against by the judicial process.

Books which include information on the relationships of Latinos with our system of justice include Carlos Cortez's *Mexican Americans and the Law* (1974) and Peter Sissons's *The Hispanic Experience of Criminal Justice* (1979). However, these contain very little systematic evidence on the point and either lack the sophisticated variable controls evident in the two studies included here or present mixed findings.

Mexican Americans and U.S. Foreign Policy

Scholars have recently begun to examine how Mexican Americans might influence the nation's foreign policy toward Latin America and more particularly Mexico. This concern mirrors the attention that has been given to how Eastern European, Jewish, and black ethnics affect U.S. policy toward their respective "homelands." In view of the increased salience that Central America and Mexico have for U.S. policymakers and the fact that Mexican Americans and other Latinos are becoming increasingly important domestic political actors, it is especially appropriate that researchers address this issue now.

The literature on Mexican Americans and U.S. foreign policy is of two types. The first assumes that because of cultural affinities Mexican Americans are knowledgeable and concerned about Latin America and U.S. policies in the hemisphere. Furthermore, it assumes that Mexican Americans will be more sensitive to Mexican and Latin American concerns, that they will enter into political coalitions with Latin American political actors to help redirect U.S. policies, and that they will bring a particular expertise to the conduct of U.S. policy in the region. Representative of this type are the work of Rothenberg (1978; 1980), Rendon (1981), and Zazueta (1984). The second type (de la Garza, 1980; 1982a) argues that the cultural affinities that Mexican Americans share with Mexico (and Latin America by implication) do not reflect either greater knowledge or concern about these countries and will not automatically result in the development of political coalitions supportive of Mexican or Latin American interests. Instead, various Mexican American political actors will become involved with foreign policy only when it will advance their own specific interests. The validity of each of these positions can only be tested through future case studies and public opinion surveys.

Conclusion

The activism of the Chicano movement stimulated the development of Chicano scholarship and also turned the attention of non-Chicano scholars toward a significant social phenomenon which could not be ignored. The relatively quiescent late 1970s may, however, have allowed the attention of scholars as well as policymakers to stray from Mexican American affairs. As a result, the publication of scholarly research on the Mexican American political life remains minimal.

Although all aspects of Mexican American political life are in need of additional research, three issues in particular merit increased attention. The first concerns the political role of Mexican American women. While Gonzales (1977) analyzed the relationship between Chicanas and the feminist movement, and Sosa Riddell (1974) examined the ties between Chicanas and the Chicano movement, there are no analyses of the political attitudes and behavior of Mexican American women.

There is also little information regarding the politics of coalition between Mexican Americans and other Latinos, or between Mexican Americans and blacks. The article by Padilla in this anthology is the first systematic inquiry into Latino coalitions. Two important articles that focus on black-Latino coalitions are those by Henry (1980) and by Calhoun and Arias (1980).

Finally, there is a need for additional study of the role that alternative political strategies such as the development of El Partido de la Raza Unida have and will play in Mexican American politics. Shockley's (1974) monograph continues to be the best study on La Raza Unida in Texas. Two studies, the first by Sosa Riddell and Aguallo (1978) and the second by Munoz and Barrera (1982), have examined the effect that alternative political behavior including the formation of La Raza Unida, had in California. While the former focused on a Chicano "takeover" in a small rural community, Munoz and Barrera were concerned with the role that students had in the evolution of La Raza Unida. That so little attention is now paid to third-party options may be explained in part by the demise of La Raza Unida and the changes in the electoral system that La Raza Unida's presence helped effect.

The 1980s have been termed "the decade of the Hispanics." Not only has a great deal of attention been paid by the national media to the role of Latinos in domestic affairs, i.e., electoral politics, education, and commerce, but events in Central America, as well as the continued matter of significant immigration from Mexico, have also focused attention on the nation's Latinos. These are good reasons for researchers and students in our educational and governmental institutions to once again turn their attention to the Mexican American population. Certainly both the opportunities and possibilities for a better understanding of this increasingly important and politically active segment of the U.S. population are greater than ever.

REFERENCES

Allsup, Carl. 1982. *The American G.I. Forum: Origins and Evolution* (Austin: Center for Mexican American Studies, Monograph no. 6).

Ambrecht, Biliana C. S., and Richard Fierro May. 1976–77. "Politicizing the Poor: The Legacy of the War on Poverty in a Mexican-American Community," *ATISBOS*, 1976–77 (Winter):123–24.

Ambrecht, Biliana C. S., and Harry P. Pachon. 1974. "Ethnic Political Mobilization in a Mexican American Community: An Exploratory Study of East Los Angeles 1965–1972," *Western Political Quarterly*, 27 (September):500–519.

Antunes, George, and Charles M. Gaitz. 1975. "Ethnicity and Participation: A Study of Mexican Americans, Blacks and Whites," *American Journal of Sociology*, 80 (March):1192–1211.

Barrera, Mario. 1979. *Race and Class in the Southwest: A Theory of Racial Inequality* (Notre Dame: University of Notre Dame Press).

Brischetto, Robert R., Annette A. Avina, and Yolanda Doerfler. 1982. *Mexican American Voting in the 1982 Texas General Election.* Southwest Voter Registration Education Project Research Report (San Antonio: Southwest Voter Registration Education Project).

Buehler, Marilyn. 1977. "Voter Turnout and Political Efficacy among Mexican Americans in Michigan," *Sociological Quarterly*, 18 (Autumn):504–17.

Buzan, Bert C. 1980. "Chicano Community Control, Political Cynicism and the Validity of Political Trust Measures," *Western Political Quarterly*, 33 (March):108–20.

Calhoun, Lillian, and Ron Arias. 1980. "The Coming Black/Hispanic Coalition: A Black View and a Hispanic View," *Perspective: Civil Rights Quarterly*, 12 (Spring):12–18.

Cervantes, Fred A. 1976. "Chicanos within the Political Economy: Some Questions Concerning Pluralist Ideology, Representation and the Economy," *Aztlan*, 7 (Fall):337–46.

Cisneros, Antonio. 1982. "Hispanic Executive Personnel in the Federal Service," *American Review of Public Administration*, 16 (Spring):23–25.

Cobas, Jose A. 1977. "Status Consciousness and Leftism: A Study of Mexican American Adolescents," *Social Forces*, 55 (June):1028–42.

Comer, John C. 1978. "Street Level Bureaucracy and Political Support: Some Findings on Mexican Americans," *Urban Affairs Quarterly*, 14 (December):207–28.

Cortez, Carlos. 1974. *Mexican Americans and the Law* (New York: Arnold Press).

Cotrell, Charles L. 1980. *A Report on the Participation of Mexican Americans, Blacks, and Females in the Political Institutions and Process in Texas, 1968–1978.* Texas Advisory Committee to the United States Commission on Civil Rights, San Antonio.

Davis, Charles E., and Jonathan P. West. 1978. "Analyzing Perceptions of Affirmative Action Issues: A Study of Mexican-American Supervisors in a Metropolitan Bureaucracy," *Midwest Review of Public Administration*, 12 (December):246–56.

de Krofcheck, Maria Dolores Diaz, and Carlos Jackson. 1974. "The Chicano Experience with Nativism in Public Administration," *Public Administration Review*, 34 (November/December):534–39.

de la Garza, Rodolfo O. 1974. "Voting Patterns in 'Bi-Cultural' El Paso—A Contextual Analysis of Chicano Voting Behavior," *Aztlan*, 5 (Spring/Fall):235–60.

———. 1977. "Mexican American: A Responsible Electorate," in F. Baird, ed., *Mexican Americans: Political Power, Influence on Resource* (Lubbock: Texas Tech University Press): pp. 63–76.

———. 1980. "Chicanos and American Foreign Policy: the Future of Chicano-Mexican Relations," *Western Political Quarterly*, 33 (December):571–82.

————. 1982a. "Chicano-Mexican Relations: A Framework for Research," *Social Science Quarterly*, 63 (March):115–30.

————. 1982b. *Public Policy Priorities of Chicano Political Elites*. Working paper 7, U.S.-Mexico Project Series (Washington, D.C.: Overseas Development Council).

de la Isla, Jose. 1976. "The Politics of Reelection: Se habla espanol," *Aztlan*, 7 (3):427–52.

Dye, Thomas, and James Renick. 1981. "Political Power and City Jobs," *Social Science Quarterly*, 62 (September):475–86.

Estrada, Leobardo F., F. Chris Garcia, Reynaldo Flores Macias, and Lionel Maldonado. 1981. "Chicanos in the United States: A History of Exploitation and Resistance," *Daedalus*, 110 (Spring):103–31.

Flood, Lawrence G. 1980. "Ethnic Politics and Political Science: A Survey of Leading Journals," *Ethnicity*, 7 (March):97–98.

Freeman, Donald. 1974. "Party Vote and Mexican Americans in South Tucson," in F. Chris Garcia, ed., *La Causa Politica* (Notre Dame: Notre Dame University Press): pp. 55–65.

Garcia, F. Chris. 1973. "Orientations of Mexican American and Anglo Children toward the U.S. Political Community," *Social Science Quarterly*, 53 (December):814–29.

Garcia, F. Chris, and Rudolph O. de la Garza. 1977. *Chicano Political Experience* (North Scituate, Mass.: Duxbury Press).

Garcia, John A. 1976–77. "Chicano Voting Patterns in School Board Elections: Bloc Voting and Internal Lines of Support for Chicano Candidates," *ATISBOS*, 1976–77 (Winter):1–14.

Garcia, Jose Z., Cal Clark, and Janet Clark. 1978. "Policy Impacts on Chicanos and Women: A State Case Study," *Policy Studies Journal*, 7 (2):251–57.

Gomez, Rudolph. 1977. "Mexican Americans in American Bureaucracy" in F. Baird, ed., *Mexican Americans: Political Power, Influence or Resource* (Lubbock: Texas Tech University Press): pp. 11–20.

Gonzales, Sylvia. 1977. "The White Feminist Movement: The Chicana Perspective," *Social Science Journal*, 14 (April):67–76.

Grebler, Leo, Joan W. Moore, and Ralph C. Guzman. 1970. *The Mexican American People: The Nation's Second Largest Minority*. (New York: Free Press).

Gutierrez, Armando, and Herbert Hirsch. 1974. "Political Maturation and Political Awareness: The Case of the Crystal City Chicano," *Aztlan*, 5 (Spring/Fall):295–312.

Guzman, Ralph. 1976. *The Political Socialization of the Mexican American People* (New York: Arno Press).

Henry, Charles. 1980. "Black-Chicano Coalitions: Possibilities and Problems," *Western Journal of Black Studies*, 4 (4):222–32.

Hernandez, Jose A. 1983. *Mutual Aid for Survival: The Case of the Mexican American* (Malabar, Fla.: Krieger).

Lamare, James W. 1977. "The Political World of the Rural Chicano Child," *American Politics Quarterly*, 5 (January):83–108.

Lovrich, Nicholas P., Jr. 1974. "Differing Priorities in an Urban Electorate: Service Preferences among Anglo, Black, and Mexican American Voters," *Social Science Quarterly*, 55 (December):704–17.

Lovrich, Nicholas P., Jr., and Otwin Marenin. 1976. "A Comparison of Black and Mexican American Votes in Denver: Assertive versus Acquiescent Political Orientations and Voting Behavior in an Urban Electorate," *Western Political Quarterly*, 29 (June):284–94.

MacManus, Susan A., and Carol Cassel. 1982. "Mexican Americans in City Politics: Participation, Representation, and Policy Preferences," *Urban Interest*, 4 (7):57–69.

Martinez, Maria Z. 1979. "Family Policy for Mexican Americans and Their Aged," *Urban and Social Change Review*, 12 (Summer):16–18.

Miller, Michael. 1975. "Chicano Political Control in South Texas," *Journal of Ethnic Studies*, 7 (February):70–84.

Munoz, Carlos, Jr., and Mario Barrera. 1982. "La Raza Unida Party and the Chicano Movement in California," *Social Science Journal*, 19 (April):101–19.

Navarro, Armando. 1974. "The Evolution of Chicano Politics," *Aztlan*, 5 (Spring/Fall): 57–84.

Ortiz, Isidro D. 1980. "The Political Economy of Chicano Urban Politics," *Plural Societies*, 11 (Winter):41–54.

Pachon, Harry P., and Joan W. Moore. 1981. "Mexican Americans," *Annals of the American Academy of Political and Social Science*, 454 (March):111–24.

Parra, Ricardo, Victor Rios, and Armando Gutierrez. 1976. "Chicano Organizations in the Midwest: Past, Present, and Possibilities," *Aztlan*, 7 (Summer):235–54.

Polinard, Jerry L., and Robert D. Wrinkle. 1980. "Willingness to Pay for Environmental Quality: Evidence from Survey Data," *Environmental International*, 4:325–30.

Rendon, A. B. 1981. "Latinos: Breaking a Cycle of Survival to Tackle Global Affairs," in Abul Aziz Said, ed., *Ethnicity and U.S. Foreign Policy* (New York: Praeger): pp. 183–200.

Rocco, Raymond A. 1977. "A Critical Perspective on the Study of Chicano Politics," *Western Political Quarterly*, 30 (December):558–73.

Rothenberg, Irene. 1978. "Mexican-American Views of U.S. Relations with Latin America," *Journal of Ethnic Studies*, 6 (Spring):72–86.

———. 1980. "Chicanos, the Panama Canal Issues and the Reagan Campaign: Reflections from 1976 and Projections for 1980," *Journal of Ethnic Studies*, 7 (Winter):37–50.

San Miguel, Guadalupe, Jr. 1982. "Mexican American Organizations and the Changing Politics of School Desegregation in Texas, 1945 to 1980," *Social Science Quarterly*, 63 (December):701–15.

Santillan, Richard. 1978. "Pluralism versus Political Economy: Which Direction for Chicano Political Research?" *ATISBOS*, 1978 (Summer/Fall):2–18.

Sekul, Joseph D. 1983. "Communities Organized for Public Service: Citizen Power and Public Policy in San Antonio," in David R. Johnson, John A. Booth, and Richard J. Harris, eds., *The Politics of San Antonio: Community, Progress, and Power* (Lincoln: University of Nebraska Press): pp. 175–90.

Shockley, John S. 1974. *Chicano Revolt in a Texas Town* (Notre Dame: University of Notre Dame Press).

Sisson, Peter. 1979. *The Hispanic Experience in Criminal Justice*. Hispanic Research Center Monograph no. 3 (Bronx, N.Y.: Fordham University, Hispanic Research Center).

Sosa Riddell, Adaljiza. 1974. "Chicanas and el Movimiento," *Aztlan*, 5 (Spring/Fall):155–66.

Sosa Riddell, Adaljiza, and Robert Aguallo, Jr. 1978. "A Case of Chicano Politics: Parlier, California," *Aztlan*, 9 (Spring/Summer/Fall):1–22.

Stevens, Jay A. 1975. "The Acquisition of Participatory Norms: The Case of Japanese and Mexican American Children in a Suburban Environment," *Western Political Quarterly*, 28 (June):281–95.

Taebel, Delbert. 1978. "Representation on City Councils: Blacks and Hispanics," *Social Science Quarterly*, 59 (June):142–52.

Teske, Raymond H. C., and Bardin H. Nelson. 1976. "Middle Class Mexican Americans and Political Power Potential: A Dilemma," *Journal of Political and Military Sociology*, 4 (Spring): 107–20.

Tirado, Miguel David. 1970. "Mexican American Community Political Organization, 'The Key to Chicano Political Power,'" *Aztlan*, 1 (Spring):53–78.

Vigil, Maurilio E. 1978. "Jerry Apodaca and the 1974 Gubernatorial Election in New Mexico: An Analysis," *Aztlan*, 9 (Spring/Summer/Fall):133–49.

Welch, Susan, John Comer, and Michael Steinman. 1975. "Ethnic Differences in Social and Political Participation—A Comparison of Some Anglo and Mexican Americans," *Pacific Sociological Review*, 18 (July):361–82.

Welch, Susan, and Albert K. Karnig. 1979. "Sex and Ethnic Differences in Municipal Representation," *Social Science Quarterly*, 60 (December):465–81.

Welch, Susan, Albert K. Karnig, and Richard Eribes. 1983. "Changes in Hispanic Local Public Employment in the South," *Western Political Quarterly*, 36 (December):660–73.

Wolfinger, Raymond E., and Steven J. Rosenstone. 1980. *Who Votes?* (New Haven: Yale University Press).

Wrinkle, Robert D., and Lawrence W. Miller. 1984. "A Note on Mexican American Voter Registration and Turnout," *Social Science Quarterly*, 65 (June):308–14.

Zazueta, Carlos. 1984. "Mexican Political Actors in the United States and Mexico: Historical and Political Contexts of a Dialogue Renewed," in Carlos Vasquez and Manuel Garcia y Griego, eds., *Mexican/U.S. Relations: Conflict and Convergence* (Los Angeles: UCLA Chicano Studies Research Center Publications and UCLA Latin American Center Publications): pp. 444–82.

14. AMERICANS ALL: THE MEXICAN AMERICAN GENERATION AND THE POLITICS OF WARTIME LOS ANGELES, 1941–45

Mario T. GARCIA, *University of California, Santa Barbara*

This study examines the rise of Mexican American political generational leadership in Los Angeles during World War II. It argues that the war coincided with the coming of political age of what is termed the Mexican American Generation. Representing for the most part first generation American-born Mexicans, the Mexican American Generation stressed integration into American life and pursued the politics of reform in the hope of accomplishing their goals. The war aided this reform movement through the stress on the equality and unity of all Americans. In Los Angeles, the Coordinating Council for Latin-American Youth symbolized this new breed of Americanized Mexican Americans.

World War II was a major political watershed for Mexican Americans. They fought for democracy abroad and struggled for the same goal at home. The war revealed the political coming of age of first generation American-born Mexicans, the sons and daughters of the immigrant masses who crossed the border during the early decades of the century. The war also created a more propitious climate for reform. Astute Mexican American leaders, utilizing the stated democratic goals of the conflict, promoted for the first time on a large scale the integration of Mexican Americans into the mainstream. These leaders were the vanguard of the Mexican American Generation (cf. Alvarez, 1973). This is a case study of such generational leadership.

The Mexican American Generation

A political generation can be defined by shared experiences and consciousness more so than by precise age grouping (Rintala, 1979; Mannheim, 1952; Samuels, 1977; Marias, 1970). For the Mexican American Generation, these experiences and consciousness derived from growing up during the Great Depression and maturing by World War II. Aware of and experiencing the historic racism directed at Mexicans in the Southwest, the Mexican American Generation organized community movements throughout the region in its attempt to rectify the contradictions affecting Mexican American life (Alsup, 1982; Woods, 1949; Garza, 1951; Camarillo, 1971; San Miguel, 1982). A few favored socialist alternatives, but most Mexican American leaders remained committed or at least temporarily reconciled to American capitalism. They absorbed the idealistic reform spirit of the New Deal and the vision of a new order propagandized by this country's participation in the war. They accepted reform either because it fit well with their political beliefs or because they understood that there were limits to social change at the time. United in a common front against racism, both Mexican American middle- and working-class leaders shared reformist objectives. Reform, not revolution, characterized the Mexican American Generation.

Pursuing new political initiatives, the Mexican American Generation broke with the immigrant experience in consciousness while upholding a tradition of ethnic defense. By 1940, moreover, the majority of the Mexican origin population in the United States possessed American citizenship. Politics for them meant the politics of citizenship, not the politics of Mexico, still of interest to immigrants. More Americanized than their parents and with a sense of permanently residing in the United States, Mexican Americans struggled for integration rather than separation from American society. Consequently, they demanded civil rights for all Mexican Americans. The Mexican American Generation believed in democracy and sought peaceful reforms through pressure group politics and the electoral process. Not tied to the ethnic nationalism of immigrant politics, Mexican Americans advocated alliances with Anglo American sympathizers, but recognized that ethnic politics could also be effective. Finally, the Mexican American Generation combated identity problems by promoting a pluralistic world view that stressed coexistence between the material and political rewards of the "American Dream" and the preservation of their parents' culture.

The Coordinating Council for Latin-American Youth[1]

In Los Angeles with its thousands of Mexican Americans, organizations such as the Coordinating Council for Latin-American Youth symbolized this Americanized reform-minded political generation. Founded in 1941 as a response to growing youth alienation in the barrios, the Council was one of the first significant efforts at community organizing by young Mexican American professionals. Distinctly middle-class, the Council was led by executive secretary Manuel Ruiz, Jr. A dynamic and articulate bilingual attorney, Ruiz had been among the first Mexican Americans to receive a law degree from the University of Southern California. By 1941 he headed a successful law firm specializing in international commerce. Able to function in both Mexican and Anglo circles, the Council's core of activists

[1] All correspondence and documents cited here are to be found in the Manuel Ruiz Papers (RP), Special Collections, Green Library, Stanford University. The document file numbers given in the text refer to this collection of papers.

stressed ethnic cooperation by including representatives of Anglo organizations concerned with juvenile issues (RP 295-2-14, Council Constitution, 1941). Both liberal and conservative Anglo leaders recognized the importance of endorsing middle-class Mexican American reformers to undermine the possible appeal of "radicals." As political liberals, Council members relied more on convincing the power structure of the value of reforms than on arousing mass demonstrations of civil discontent. The Council believed in elite leadership and in the responsibility of the small Mexican American middle class to uplift their poorer constituents.

Youth Work

In its reform program, the Council adopted youth work as its priority. Yet juvenile issues composed only one facet of the problems affecting the Mexican origin community. To combat delinquency, changes had to be also made in education, housing, jobs, and political participation. The Council did not see delinquency as the only issue, but it did believe the issue could be used to attack other problems (RP 295-1-26, Council Document, 26 January 1977; RP 295-1-3A, Ruiz, *Crime Prevention Digest*, December 1942; RP 295-1-14, Ruiz to Mendez, 13 April 1944). Consequently, between 1941 and 1945, the years of the Council's most active phase, it pressed forward vigorously to address some of the chief concerns of the Mexican American community.

The Council established and operated two youth clubs close to the predominantly Mexican origin section of East Los Angeles. Here, both boys and girls engaged in a variety of activities. By 1945 the Council sponsored 14 youth groups throughout Los Angeles as well as in San Fernando, Canoga Park, and Pacoima. The Council regarded athletics as a means to build character and as a deterrent to antisocial acts. Hence, the Council in conjunction with the Mexican Athletic Association of Los Angeles also supported youth teams in a variety of sports (RP 295-1-30, Minutes, 12 July 1943; RP 295-1-13, McKelvey to Ruiz, 2 July 1943; RP 295-1-25, *Aristo*, 31 July 1943 and 13 August 1941).

To complement these programs, the Council provided counseling services to youth, especially gang members. In this effort, the Council received aid from the Los Angeles County Board of Supervisors, which assigned several probation officers to work full-time in Council activities. Through conferences in East Los Angeles, the Council called attention to the problem of delinquency and offered advice to Mexican origin parents and Mexican organizations as to how best to aid in rehabilitating youth (RP 295-1-14, Ruiz to Southern Californa Council, 10 November 1943; RP 295-2-7, Ruiz to Hazan, 3 October 1945; RP 295-2-9, Minutes, 13 December 1943).

The Council strongly urged local and state agencies to improve conditions in East Los Angeles, as well as in other Mexican American communities where inadequate playground and recreation centers existed. It urged the hiring of Mexican Americans to staff these facilities. Commenting on this issue to the Los Angeles Youth Project, Ruiz insisted that work with the most culturally alienated Mexican youths, "pachucos," should be conducted by persons acquainted with the Mexican origin community. Because of their work with youth, and as a way of promoting sensitive awareness of the Mexican youth problem, Ruiz and his colleagues served on such committees as the Los Angeles Youth Project and the State Committee on Youth in Wartime (RP 295-1-24, Ruiz to Zuck, 29 August 1944; RP 295-1-24, Ruiz to Schumway, 10 March 1942; RP 295-2-7, Ruiz to Zuck, 8 February 1946).

The Council did not eradicate the social causes of juvenile delinquency, but it helped alleviate some of the symptoms. This was no small accomplishment in a period of youth dislocation and alienation in the Mexican barrios. George Gleason, executive secretary of the Los Angeles Committee for Interracial Progress in 1944, praised the Council's youth work. "May I add personally that it seems like a miracle," Gleason wrote to Ruiz, "when I remember the meager youth activities going on when I became an employee of Los Angeles County in September 1937. You and your organization have had a large share in bringing about this great advance" (RP 295-1-24, Gleason to Ruiz, 13 October 1944).

Educational Reform

Next to youth work, the Coordinating Council worked on educational reforms. It believed education to be the principal means for young people to achieve social, cultural, and economic integration. Yet it also recognized that the majority of Mexican Americans as a predominantly poor population faced obstacles in the public schools. Hence, the Council sought to create awareness among educators, superintendents, politicians, and parents about the specific language and cultural setting in which Mexican origin children lived, and about their special school problems. Council members spoke at school assemblies and at PTA meetings, and conferred with teachers and parents on how best to educate Mexican American students. The Council consistently stressed the public school's responsibility for a successful integration of Mexican American children (RP 295-1-24, Garfield High School P.T.A. Program, 12 November 1943; RP 295-1-24, Elmott to Ruiz, 23 November 1943).

Consequently, the Council struggled to desegregate the so-called "Mexican schools." Faced with the immigration of thousand of Mexicans into the American Southwest, by the turn of the century school authorities in this region had established a dual public school system. Mexican origin students attended Mexican schools. Their curriculum emphasized vocational training and Americanization, i.e., programs intended to socialize Mexican children to the norms and values of American society, but at the expense of the identity and culture they had acquired in their preschool years. The result: a public school system that limited occupational opportunities for Mexican Americans and indirectly supported an economic structure that desired cheap manual labor from the Mexican American

communities. The school system likewise caused serious cultural alienation among young Mexican Americans as they increasingly felt pulled in
two cultural directions (Garcia, 1981; Gonzalez, 1974).

Not segregated by law, the Mexican schools were in fact segregated
due to housing patterns and the lack of economic and residential mobility
among Mexican Americans. In many cases school officials citing language
differences segregated Mexican origin students until they could adequately speak and write English. Ironically, most children never left the
Mexican schools even after they had learned English. The alleged health
hazard posed by Mexican origin children was also used to justify separation. California segregated Mexican American pupils not only on these
arguments but on section 8003 of the Education Code that read:

> The governing board of any school district may establish separate schools for
> Indian children, excepting children of Indians who are wards of the United
> States government and children of all other Indians who are descendents of
> the original American Indians of the United States, and for children of Chinese,
> Japanese, or Mongolian parentage. (RP 295-1-12, Education Code)

Under this section, certain school districts separated Mexican Americans
on the ground that they were part Indian, along with language and health
rationalizations.

The Coordinating Council initiated in 1945 a campaign to repeal section
8003. In Los Angeles, it acquired the support of key officials and organizations including Mayor Fletcher Bowron. "We hold that segregation pre-
vents assimilation," Ruiz put the case to authorities, "thereby defeating the
purpose of this nation's good neighbor policy. Mexican American pupils in
many instances have been required to attend school in dilapidated structures, far from their homes. In some cases, where no facilities for segregation were available, they have been excluded from classes entirely" (RP
295-1-12, Associated Press, 30 April 1945). The Los Angeles system mixed
students more, although with increasing segregation patterns. However, in
such surrounding areas as Orange County, Carpinteria, Oxnard, Monte-
bello, and El Monte, officials widely segregated Mexican origin pupils.
Within El Monte's five elementary schools, authorities restricted Mexican
Americans to one "tumbledown building, regardless of its distance from
their homes." Mexican Americans composed 25 percent of El Monte's elementary school population, but Ruiz noted that only 38 Mexican American
students attended El Monte High School out of a total enrollment of 1,400.
"This is the extent," Ruiz concluded, "to which Latin Americans seeking
an education are discouraged during their progress through grade
schools" (RP 295-1-12, Associated Press, 1 May 1945).

To reach into Sacramento, Ruiz and the Council gained the support of
State Senator Jack B. Tenney of Los Angeles County (RP 295-1-16, Tenney
to Ruiz, 31 July 1945) and Assemblyman William H. Rosenthal of the 40th
District, Los Angeles (RP 295-1-12, Rosenthal to Ruiz, 8 June 1945). Both
agreed to sponsor the fight for the repeal of section 8003. Ruiz also obtained the backing of Governor Earl Warren, as well as other state officials
(RP 295-1-12, Ruiz to Warren, 31 October 1945). Ruiz personally led a

group of Mexican Americans to Sacramento to lobby for repeal. And in a letter to the chairman of the Education Committee of the legislature, Ruiz wrote: "Please impress the members of your committee that the attitude of the State Assembly with respect to segregation in schools, particularly as it has been practiced in our rural communities with Latin Americans, is of utmost significance at this time when the nations of earth are gathering at San Francisco . . . concerning the peace of the future" (RP 295-1-12, Ruiz to Johnson, 13 April 1945).

The Assembly repealed section 8003 in 1945, but opponents stalled it in the Senate. In the meantime, the Coordinating Council helped desegregate the El Monte School District on a local basis. Together with the Federation of Hispanic American Voters and LULAC, the Council met with Mexican origin parents of children attending El Monte schools. Persistent and effective, this Mexican American coalition pressured school officials to agree in May 1945 to integrate Mexican American children into the non-Mexican schools during the next academic year. *Aristo*, the Council's newspaper, hailed the desegregation victory and hoped that it would stimulate action where similar humiliating conditions existed (RP 295-1-12, *Aristo*, 28 April 1945). The newspaper correctly reminded its readers that only through pressure exerted by Mexican Americans themselves had desegregation in El Monte been achieved (RP 295-1-12, *Aristo*, 5 May 1945). Ruiz acknowledged and informed the Board of Trustees that it could count on the Coordinating Council for help in the process. "Of course," he added, "our principal concern is to make good Americans out of this segment of our population, and to integrate them into the community as quickly as possible" (RP 295-1-12, Ruiz to Wright, 14 May 1945).

A year later the Council supported successful legal efforts (*Mendez et al. v. Westminster School District of Orange County et al.*) by Mexican origin parents in Orange County to desegregate local schools on the basis of the Fourteenth Amendment to the Constitution of the United States, which mandates the equal protection of the laws. In the Westminster case, a U.S. district court ruled illegal the segregation of Mexican American children on the grounds of language difference. Buoyed by the victory in Orange County, the Council in 1947 achieved the repeal of section 8003. Hence, in a two-year period the Council had helped gain three significant breakthroughs in the struggle to desegregate Mexican schools in southern California. Clearly, these successes did not eliminate *de facto* segregation nor did they eradicate inferior education. Still, they constituted important political initiatives by Mexican American leaders. Mexican Americans in southern California had served notice they would no longer accept second-class status in the schools for their children (San Miguel, 1982; Wollenberg, 1976).

Job Opportunities

Job opportunities also concerned the Coordinating Council. The growth of war-related industries in Los Angeles after the attack upon Pearl Harbor moved the Council to take steps to insure that both Mexican Americans and Mexican nationals would have access to such employment. Apprehensive over equal opportunity, the Council learned that some plants discriminated against persons of Mexican origin. The Council in October 1941 publicized that it would investigate cases of job discrimination in war-related industries. Ruiz in an interview with *La Opinion*, the Spanish-language daily in Los Angeles, urged victims of such discrimination to contact the Council (RP 295-1-25, *La Opinion*, 14 October 1941). One Mexican American worker, born in Arizona, complained that state contractors had refused to hire him because he was Mexican. He had been told that not being "white" he could not be employed (RP 295-2-8, Minutes, 16 October 1941). Other housing contractors turned away Mexican nationals on projects under contract to the Los Angeles Housing Authority. Mexican nationals were likewise excluded from work on slum clearance projects under the State Housing Office (RP 295-1-18, Unsigned to President's Committee, 16 October 1941; RP 295-1-18, Fair Employment Practices, 22 June 1942).

The Council protested job discrimination against persons of Mexican origin, especially noncitizens, to both the state and federal government. Ruiz singled out contractors on public housing projects who refused to hire Mexican nationals. The contractors claimed they had no choice because of a state labor code making it a crime to contract noncitizens for public works. Ruiz countered that according to emergency provisions of the same labor code noncitizens could be hired for such jobs in time of war. He called upon the state commission to act on the matter (RP 295-1-16, Ruiz to Carrasco, 18 April 1942). Receiving no response, Ruiz took his case to the federal War Production Board and requested clarification of federal statutes to allow employment of noncitizens during war (RP 295-1-16, Ruiz to Nunn, 29 April 1942; Nunn to Ruiz, 21 May 1982). The council also issued resolutions in 1942 stressing both the importance of employing alien workers in war production and the ideological contradictions of excluding them. "The unity of the United Nations and the government's program of Pan-American solidarity," the Council stated, "are endangered by discriminatory treatment of nationals of allied countries" (RP 295-1-18, Resolution, 24 June 1942). The Council suggested that the federal government restrict only enemy aliens and allow nationals of allied countries such as Mexico to work in war production (ibid.).

In agreement, President Roosevelt in the summer of 1942 redefined policy toward the employment of alien labor. Refusal to hire aliens in war industries was discriminatory. Aliens could work both in war and non-war industries except on classified contracts. Although it could not take sole credit for this victory, the Council had assisted in bringing attention to the issue (RP 295-1-18, Newspaper Clipping, 12 July 1942).

In Los Angeles, the Council helped train persons of Mexican origin for war-related employment. With the National Youth Administration (NYA), it disseminated information on NYA job training centers in East Los Angeles. Here, Mexican origin youth could acquire free training in a variety of industrial skills while receiving approximately $25 a month (RP 295-1-23, Nunn to Ruiz, 21 June 1942).

More importantly, the Council contributed in founding the Pan American Trade School. Largely through the Council's efforts in cooperation with the Los Angeles city schools and appropriate state and federal agencies, the school opened for vocational classes in April 1943 (RP 295-1-24, "Dedication," 13 April 1943). Aimed both at youth and adults, the school offered courses in aircraft riveting, aircraft woodwork, and aircraft sheet metal. It also held classes in blueprint reading, drafting, English, and mathematics. Such a curriculum, the Council argued, would help solve the east side employment problems and provide means by which those of Mexican origin could contribute to the war effort. As an announcement for the school put it: "Our nation is at war. It is a war which demands skill of the hand in order to insure a victory. The Mexican people of East Los Angeles, by taking advantage of the War Training Program at the Pan American Trade School, can play an important part in contributing to a final victory" (RP 295-1-24, Pan American Trade School, 1943). While this type of job training maintained Mexican origin workers in blue-collar occupations, still the school aided in creating opportunities in skilled trades: jobs, for the most part, previously unavailable to this population.

Anti-Defamation

The Coordinating Council further worked to mitigate anti-Mexican sentiments in Los Angeles due to increased wartime racial tensions. It frequently sent representatives to conferences on race relations to interpret the problems of Mexican Americans (RP 295-1-18, Romero Report, 4 May 1942; RP 295-1-16, Smith to Ruiz, 1 November 1943). The Council refuted anti-Mexican statements made by individuals, organizations, and especially by the news media (RP 295-1-30, Ruiz to Scott, 3 September 1942; RP 295-1-25, Quevedo to Boddy, 18 March 1942). Fearing that any attempt to classify Mexicans as people of color might subject them to "legal" forms of discrimination and segregation, the Council rejected any implication that Mexicans were not white. The Council's insistence that Mexicans were white also appears to have stemmed from the historic ambivalence and insecurity of Mexicans on both sides of the border concerning their racial status. These feelings often led to a denial of possessing Indian blood. The Council believed that any attempt to place Mexicans in a racial category other than white to be racist and divisive. Council members did not tolerate blatant anti-Mexican expressions, but like many other Mexican Americans throughout the Southwest de-emphasized the racial issue and at times referred to themselves as Latin Americans or Spanish Americans to deflect anti-Mexican sentiment.

The Council particularly protested about the way the *Los Angeles Times* often insinuated that most Mexican origin youths belonged to delinquent gangs (RP 295-1-16, Hutchkiss to Ruiz, 1 August 1942). This practice became an explosive issue during the "Sleepy Lagoon Case" of 1942 and the "Zoot-Suit Riots" the following year when hundreds of white servicemen rampaged in downtown Los Angeles attacking Mexican origin individuals dressed in "zoot suits." Ruiz personally defended many of the riot victims. The Council blamed the news media for inciting the crisis and called upon President Roosevelt and the federal government to moderate the "attitudes of [the] local press which has openly approved these riots and is treating the news in a way that is definitely inflammatory" (RP 295-1-16, Quevedo to Davis, Cranston, and Roosevelt, June 1943).

Political Action

While the Council's activities were not overtly political, they still constituted political action. The Council as a political pressure group mediated between the Mexican origin community and the Anglo power structure. Influential Anglos recognized Council members as spokespersons for the Mexican origin community. The Council also engaged in electoral politics. It supported in 1942 the unsuccessful campaigns of two members who ran as "Roosevelt Democrats": Eduardo Quevedo for the 40th Assembly District and Fred Rubio for the 51st Assembly District (RP 295-1-25, *Aristo*, 4 July 1942). Three years later the Council again aided Quevedo's candidacy, this time for a seat on the Los Angeles city council (RP 295-2-7, Minutes, 5 March 1945). A political ad read:

> Let it be heard, for the first time in an election, the courageous voice of the Mexican colony. If you do not have the right to vote, advise those that do have it, to support Eduardo Quevedo for councilman for the ninth district of Los Angeles. It's an obligation towards our race. (RP 295-1-23, Quevedo Political Ad, 1945)

Defeated in his bid, Quevedo believed that his campaign had helped unify the Mexican origin community and urged the Council to continue raising political consciousness (RP 295-2-7, Minutes, 16 April 1945).

The Council further realized the importance of organizing a unified front among Mexican Americans in Los Angeles, or at least those of similar convictions. With this in mind and aware of postwar problems facing Mexican Americans, the Council assembled on 7 October 1945 a Postwar Congress. The Congress aimed to insure the permanent political organization of Mexican Americans following the war. "As I heretofore told you," Ruiz informed Robert Kenny, the state Attorney General, in inviting him to the Congress, "Americans of Spanish and Mexican extraction have always steered away from politics. This will be the first time that Organizations as such are uniting with the end in view of establishing a permanent political action committee" (RP 295-1-22, Ruiz to Kenny, 29 August 1945). To Ruiz the time had arrived for Mexican Americans to exercise their political power. No candidate could possibly win in a state election without Los Angeles County, and since Mexicans composed 10 percent of the county's population, the Mexican American vote could be decisive (RP 295-1-22, Ruiz to Kenny, 17 September 1945). The Congress called for a variety of reforms: the creation of an independent nonpartisan political action committee to advance the interests of Spanish-speaking people; nondiscrimination in employment and preferential hiring of war veterans; a state and federal Permanent Fair Employment Practices Commission; a federal Full Employment Bill; CIO and AFL organization of Mexican origin workers; the reintegration of returning Latin American veterans; health programs to eliminate the high rate of communicable diseases among the Mexican origin in Los Angeles; increased hiring by state and local governments of Spanish surnamed persons; social security as well as other federal labor standards for farm workers, including child labor laws; and that eligible Spanish-speaking citizens be encouraged to take the civil service examinations in law enforcement (RP 295-2-4, Postwar Congress Resolutions, 1945).

Mexican American Identity

Besides trying to meet the economic and political needs of the Mexican origin population in Los Angeles, the Council dealt with identity and the definition of what it meant to be an American of Mexican descent. Hence, Council members contributed to the making of a particular Mexican American generational world view. World War II served as a decisive watershed in this ideological process. Mexican Americans during the war repeatedly pledged their allegiance to American democratic values and to Mexican American support in the struggle against fascism. Moreover, the Council upheld the American system and looked toward integration. In their approach to integration, Council members shunned identification as a minority. For them the concept of a minority meant separation. After all, the ideology of wartime America stressed the equality of all Americans. To label someone a minority, Ruiz suggested, stigmatized them as different and made them defensive (RP 295-1-25, Newspaper Article by Ruiz, n.d.).

Desiring integration, Council members in forming their world view unfortunately drew distinctions between Mexican Americans and Afro Americans as a way of trying to avoid the stigma of racial inferiority imposed on blacks. Disregarding the fact that both groups suffered from racial discrimination, Council leaders stressed that while Afro Americans had been legally excluded from their rights Mexican Americans had not, implying that no basis for political unity existed. The Council focused on ethnic rather than racial discrimination. Ruiz, for example, refused to discuss Mexican Americans on the basis of race. He insisted that Mexicans were white and hence no different from other ethnic groups such as the Irish, Italians, or Germans (RP 295-1-30, Ruiz to Scott, 3 September 1942).

To overcome the ambiguity of identity, Council members acknowledged that Mexican Americans were first and foremost American citizens. At the same time, they called on Mexican Americans to be proud of their ethnic origin. The Council argued for a pluralistic approach to ethnicity in American life and stressed that integration could be accompanied with degrees of cultural retention.

Conclusion

The Coordinating Council by the postwar period ceased to function. Just as the war provided Mexican American reformers with greater political leverage, its conclusion and the postwar economic recession in turn weakened, yet did not eliminate, that leverage and momentum. According to Ruiz, moreover, the Mexican origin community in Los Angeles had become even more dispersed, a disadvantage for effective organizational work, and its leaders more interested in electoral politics. The Council apparently also suffered from lack of financial resources. Finally, Council leaders allowed younger returning Mexican American GIs to carry the organizational load (Ruiz, Interview, 1981).

The Council achieved modest reforms, but its importance transcends concrete accomplishments. The Council and indeed the Mexican American generation throughout the Southwest symbolized larger changes affecting the Mexican origin population in the United States. Immigrant enclaves were being transformed into Mexican American communities. More Americanized Mexicans shifted loyalties away from Mexico and to the United States. The immigrant dream of one day returning to Mexico—the "Mexican dream"—now became for Mexican Americans the dream of a good life north of the border, the "American dream." Residential stability, increased education, better employment opportunities due to a war and cold war economy, all contributed to a new Mexican American state of mind and being. Not all shared in these changes, but enough to release new political energies. In Los Angeles, the Council obtained social reforms and helped begin to alter Mexican American perceptions of themselves as a powerless group.

Yet the Council and the Mexican American Generation could only accomplish so much. Poverty continued to coexist with progress. Mexican Americans continued to face discrimination and slower rates of mobility. While the Council had hopes for a pluralistic society under capitalism, race and class discrimination together with cultural prejudice retarded the integration and assimilation of Mexicans. Mexican American middle-class leaders failed to appreciate the intransigence of race and class barriers.

Still, despite this myopic consciousness and the limits of what San Miguel (1982) calls the "politics of accommodation," the Council aided in making life slightly better for some Mexican Americans. As part of a historical process of change, the Council's reform struggles served notice that Mexican Americans would no longer accept second-class citizenship. One hundred years after the Anglo conquest of the Southwest, a political generation of Mexican Americans demanded not reannexation to Mexico, but democratic rights and full integration into the U.S. body politic. The expectations and frustrations resulting from this change in political consciousness would ignite more intense struggles in succeeding decades.

REFERENCES

Alsup, Carl. 1982. *The American G.I. Forum: A History of a Mexican-American Organization* (Austin: Center for Mexican American Studies).

Alvarez, Rodolfo. 1973. "The Psycho-Historical and Socioeconomic Development of the Chicano Community in the United States," *Social Science Quarterly,* 53 (March):920–42.

Camarillo, Albert M. 1971. "The G.I. Generation," *Aztlan,* 2 (Fall):145–50.

Garcia, Mario T. 1981. *Desert Immigrants: The Mexicans of El Paso, 1880–1920* (New Haven: Yale University Press).

Garza, Edward. 1951. "L.U.L.A.C." Master's thesis, Southwest Texas State Teachers College (San Marcos).

Gonzalez, Gilbert. 1974. "The System of Public Education and Its Function within the Chicano Communities, 1920–1930." Ph.D. dissertation, University of California, Los Angeles.

Mannheim, Karl. 1952. "The Problem of Generations," in *Essays on the Sociology of Knowledge* (New York: Oxford University Press): pp. 276–320.

Marias, Julian. 1970. *Generations: a Historical Method* (Tuscaloosa: University of Alabama Press).

Rintala, Marvin. 1979. *The Constitution of Silence: Essays on Generational Themes* (Westport, Conn.: Greenwood).

Ruiz, Manuel, Jr. 1981. Oral history interview with author, 30 January 1981.

Ruiz, Manuel, Jr. Papers. Special Collections, Green Library, Stanford University.

Samuels, Richard J., ed. 1977. *Political Generations and Political Development* (Lexington, Mass.: Lexington Books).

San Miguel, Guadalupe. 1982. "Mexican American Organizations and the Changing Politics of School Desegregation in Texas, 1945 to 1980," *Social Science Quarterly,* 63 (December):701–15.

Wollenberg, Charles. 1976. *All Deliberate Speed: Segregation and Exclusion in California Schools, 1855–1975* (Berkeley and Los Angeles: University of California Press).

Woods, Francis Jerome. 1949. *Mexican Ethnic Leadership in San Antonio, Texas* (Washington, D.C.: Catholic University Press).

15. ETHNICITY AND ELECTORAL CHOICE: MEXICAN AMERICAN VOTING BEHAVIOR IN THE CALIFORNIA 30TH CONGRESSIONAL DISTRICT[1]

Bruce E. CAIN, *California Institute of Technology*

D. Roderick KIEWIET, *California Institute of Technology*

The 1982 election in California offers a unique natural experiment in ethnic and racial bloc voting. The race in the 30th Congressional District matched a well-financed Anglo Republican, John Rousselot, against an incumbent Hispanic, Marty Martinez. On the ballot with Martinez and Rousselot were the successful Republican candidates for governor and U.S. senator George Deukmejian and Pete Wilson, and the losing Democratic candidates, Tom Bradley (who is black) and Jerry Brown. These variations in the race and ethnicity of the candidates on the ballot in 1982 were used to estimate the impact of ethnic and racial considerations in voting decisions.

The substantial growth of the Mexican American population during the last decade has created considerable interest in the Mexican American voter. Although national election surveys do not sample a sufficient number of Mexican Americans to permit adequate analysis of their attitudes and political behavior, there have been many excellent regional studies (Guzman, 1973; McCleskey and Merrill, 1973; Freeman, 1974; Levy and Kramer, 1974; Garcia and de la Garza, 1977; Baird, 1977; de la Garza and Brischetto, 1983a, 1983b; de la Garza and Weaver, 1983). Most of these surveys have focused on Texas, New Mexico, and Arizona, and many have looked at local council and gubernatorial races where Mexican Americans made their greatest gains in the seventies. However, nearly half of the Latino population in the Southwest currently resides in California, and Mexican Americans there have made great efforts to win representation in Congress. This study examines one of the congressional

[1]This chapter is an abridged and modified version of the paper which appeared in the June 1984 issue of *Social Science Quarterly*.

seats targeted by California Mexican Americans in 1982—the 30th Congressional District in Los Angeles County.

But what can be learned by looking at this one California congressional race in detail as opposed to analyzing state or national voting patterns? The answer is that it provides a nice test of Mexican American voter loyalty for several reasons. To begin with, there was a well-financed Anglo Republican candidate, John Rousselot, who ran a skillful campaign aimed in part at causing Mexican Americans to defect from the Democratic ranks. Rousselot had lost his seat in the 1981 redistricting. Rather than face a neighboring Republican incumbent in an expensive and potentially bitter primary, Rousselot chose to contest a Mexican American candidate, Marty Martinez, for the 30th Congressional District. Although the district was 65 percent Democratic in registration (a safe Democratic seat by California standards), Rousselot had reason to believe that he might succeed. Martinez had only narrowly won a July special election that was called when Danielson retired to take a position on the bench, and the bitter special election campaign had left a residue of ill feeling among the district's Anglo Democrats. Martinez was also vulnerable on certain personal issues: he had been a Republican for some years before he joined the Democratic party and, as an assemblyman, it was alleged that he had received large payments from owners of an unpopular dumpsite.

The Martinez-Rousselot race was also important because there was significant potential for Anglo backlash. The 30th Congressional District had been earmarked as a Mexican American seat in the 1981 California redistricting. The local press reported that some Anglo Democrats resented this and would not support a Mexican American candidate. In the end, Martinez's 54 percent vote share was significantly below the district's Democratic registration level. To what degree was this caused by Anglo backlash?

Thirdly, even though the seat was 50 percent Mexican American in population, the electorate was only 30 percent Mexican American, and Mexican American voters in that area had not traditionally voted in high numbers. The question was whether they would respond to this historic opportunity.

Finally, the race for the 30th was notable in a structural sense: the 1982 election offered a unique natural experiment in ethnic and racial block voting. On the ballot with Martinez and Rousselot were the successful Republican candidates for Governor and U.S. Senator, George Deukmejian and Pete Wilson, and the losing Democratic candidates, Tom Bradley (who is black) and Jerry Brown. These variations in the race and ethnicity of the candidates on the ballot in 1982 can be used to estimate the impact of ethnic and racial considerations in voting decisions.

Thus, the questions we will examine are as follows: (1) were Mexican American voters more likely to support Martinez than non–Mexican Americans? (2) was there Anglo backlash? and (3) in what other ways did ethnicity affect the vote? The data for this study were gathered in two surveys of the 30th Congressional District of California. The first was a telephone survey of 455 respondents administered during the third week of October 1982. The second was a poll of 409 voters as they left the voting booth on election day.

Evidence of Ethnic Voting

The first task is to assess the degree of ethnic and racial voting by comparing the choices among Anglo and Mexican American voters across the three races. Table 1 displays the possible combinations of choices and analyzes them by party (i.e., voter's registration) and ethnicity. The data reveal several things. First, Rousselot did succeed in winning Democratic support, including 14 percent of the Mexican American Democrats sampled. (This figure was arrived at by summing across the figures for Mexican American Democrats in the appropriate columns, i.e., columns 2, 5, 6, and 8.) Rousselot was also supported by about two-thirds of the small number of Mexican American Republicans interviewed. And, as Table 1 also shows, 7 percent of the Mexican American Democrats voted for Rousselot while simultaneously supporting both Bradley and Brown: in short, the only race they defected on was the one in which a Mexican American candidate was running.

In general, though, the predominantly Democratic Mexican American voters in this district gave strong support to all Democratic candidates. Seventy-eight percent voted a straight Democratic ballot, 2 percent split their vote on the Senate and governor's races and supported Martinez, and 6 percent voted for the Republican candidates in all the major races

TABLE 1

Pattern of Votes Cast for Congressman, Senator, and Governor by Party Registration and Ethnicity (major party registrants only)

Election	Voting Pattern								
Congress	Dem	Rep	Dem	Dem	Rep	Rep	Dem	Rep	
Governor	Dem	Dem	Rep	Dem	Rep	Dem	Rep	Rep	
U.S. Senate	Dem	Dem	Dem	Rep	Dem	Rep	Rep	Rep	*n*
Non–Mexican American Democrat	61%	10%	3%	1%	2%	4%	2%	17%	103
Mexican American Democrat	78	7	1	1	0	3	6	4	72
Non–Mexican American Republican	3	7	7	2	5	3	7	65	58
Mexican American Republican	27	0	0	0	0	0	9	64	11
Total	50	7	3	1	2	4	4	28	244

except for Congress. The finding of high Democratic loyalty among Mexican American voters is very much consistent with previous studies (Levy and Kramer, 1974; de la Garza, 1977). While the numbers are too small to permit firm conclusions, it does appear that a higher fraction of Mexican American Republicans (36 percent) than of Anglo Republicans (19 percent) defected from their party to vote for Martinez.

In sum, Mexican American voters in this district exhibited a high degree of support for Martinez and for the other Democratic candidates. Still, the 14 percent defection rate among Mexican American Democrats in the congressional race is not trivial. Combined with evidence in our poll that large numbers of Mexican American voters were undecided until very late in the campaign, this reinforces the point made in previous studies that the support of Mexican American voters for Mexican American candidates—even of the same party as themselves—is by no means automatic, and that "bloc voting" is hardly inevitable (de la Garza, 1977; Baird, 1977).

What about the behavior of Anglo voters in this district? Previous studies found that credible, salient Mexican American candidates can cause backlash among Anglo voters (Guzman, 1973; de la Garza, 1974). The question in this case is whether redistricting the seat to favor a Mexican American candidate and the ethnic emphasis of the Martinez campaign caused bloc voting against his candidacy by Anglos in his district. To begin with, the fact that 17 percent of the Anglo Democrats voted a straight Republican ticket is one of many indications that on average they were more disloyal than the Mexican American Democrats. On the other hand, the number who supported Rousselot but voted for Brown and Bradley—the clearest case of ethnic or candidate-specific backlash—was only 3 percent higher among Anglo Democrats than among Mexican American Democrats. Thus it appears that while the overall level of party disloyalty among Anglo Democrats was much higher than among Mexican American Democrats, the level of ticket splitting against Martinez specifically was not significantly higher.

It is possible, of course, to test more rigorously the proposition that Mexican American voters were more likely to support Martinez than other voters. Although the tabular data seem to suggest that this occurred, the bivariate evidence of higher Mexican American support may have been caused by random statistical error, or by the failure to control for other variables.

The complete explanation must therefore include such variables as the voter's ethnicity, party, employment status, and religion. What we want to explain is the ticket (i.e., the particular combination of senatorial, gubernatorial, and congressional candidates on the ballot) the voter chooses in 1982. Although, there are actually eight logically possible ways of voting in the three races, four of the categories are condensed to two because of their infrequency. So, for example, the first column in the table tells us

TABLE 2

Multinomial Logit Analysis of Voting for Congressman in the 30th Congressional District of California

	Voting Pattern				
	Straight Democratic vs. Straight Republican	Rousselot, Brown, and Bradley vs. Straight Republican	Martinez, Brown, or Bradley vs. Straight Republican	Rousselot, Wilson, or Deukmejian vs. Straight Republican	Martinez, Wilson, and Deukmejian vs. Straight Republican
Democrat	3.29*	1.86*	2.27*	1.15*	0.71*
	(0.41)	(0.55)	(0.75)	(0.57)	(0̄.70)
Mexican American	1.31*	0.37	1.11	0.61	1.99*
	(0.47)	(0.68)	(0.95)	(0.91)	(0.81)
Unemployed	1.21*	1.46*	−0.44	1.23*	−0.78
	(0.43)	(0.55)	(1.12)	(0.60)	(1.12)
Catholic	−0.26	−0.11	−1.85*	−2.16*	−0.49
	(0.40)	(0.56)	(0.92)	(0.87)	(0.81)
Constant	−2.11*	−2.68*	−2.84*	−1.89*	−2.59*
	(0.37)	(0.49)	(0.62)	(0.40)	(0.52)
n	147	23	11	18	11
Percent correctly predicted	66%				
Likelihood ratio index	.41				

NOTE: Cell entries are logit coefficients with *t* ratios in parentheses.

which factors seem to have caused voters to choose a straight Democratic ticket as opposed to a straight Republican one. The entries in the tables are the estimated logit coefficients, the starred ones being statistically significant. The results are displayed in Table 2.

In general, the estimates reveal several conclusions. First and foremost, Mexican Americans were more likely to vote a straight Democratic ticket—even controlling for party, religion, and employment status—than non–Mexican Americans. Secondly, when Mexican Americans split their ticket, they were more likely to vote for Martinez. The effect is statistically significant for the Martinez-Wilson-Deukmejian category, the category in which the only Democrat the voter chose was Mexican American. It would appear, then, that Mexican Americans did tend to vote more frequently for Martinez even when other factors are controlled for.

Factors Influencing the Mexican American Vote in the 30th Congressional District

Having established that Mexican Americans did vote more heavily for Martinez, their support can now be analyzed more closely. In particular, it can be broken down into three components: issues, party loyalty, and candidate-specific evaluations. To what extent did each of these components play a role in the decisions made by the voters of the 30th district?

The first component is the set of issue attitudes Mexican American voters possess. While there are many potential issues on which Anglo and Mexican American could be compared, the focus will be on those that were salient in the congressional race, such as the economy, nuclear weapons, and the various initiatives. This precludes, of course, any overall judgment as to the similarity or dissimilarity of Mexican American and Anglo Democrats; it is quite likely that there are differences between the two on issues such as bilingualism, guest workers and immigration on which we did not collect data.

To begin with, did Anglo and Mexican American voters in this district share the same perception of what the most important problems were facing the country in 1982? In the election day exit poll, voters were asked to report what they thought was the most important problem facing the nation (Table 3). As before, the sample is partitioned by ethnicity and party registration. A perusal of the data reveals that all groups believed that unemployment was the most important problem facing the nation. This is not surprising, of course, given that unemployment was running at 10.1 percent in October 1982, and that the media gave the unemployment issue a great deal of coverage. Democrats were more inclined than Republicans to cite unemployment, but the margin is surprisingly small. Intraparty differences were even weaker. Mexican American Democrats mentioned unemployment more frequently than did Anglo Democrats, and they were also somewhat less likely than Anglo Democrats to mention other sorts of economic problems (e.g., inflation, interest rates) and foreign policy, but these differences were much too small to be statistically significant. So while there were some differences, it would appear that party and ethnic factors were not strongly related to the perception of the most important problems facing the nation.

TABLE 3

Most Important Problem Facing the Nation (major party registrants only)

	Un-employ-ment	Other Economic Problems	Foreign Policy	Social Problems	Miscel-laneous Problems	n
Non–Mexican American Democrats	47%	24%	5%	8%	16	117
Mexican American Democrats	51	22	0	8	19	81
Non–Mexican American Republicans	42	27	0	20	11	59
Mexican American Republicans	40	27	0	13	20	15

TABLE 4

Voter Attitudes on Ballot Initiatives (major party registrants only)

	Favors Freeze	Favors Gun Registration	Favors Bottle Deposit	*n*
Non–Mexican American Democrats	54%	33%	38%	119
Mexican American Democrats	57	33	31	81
Non–Mexican American Republicans	39	23	37	61
Mexican American Republicans	23	27	33	13

Although differences in the salience of issues were not great in November 1982, differences in issue positions were somewhat larger (Table 4). There were, for instance, three initiatives on the ballot that drew particular attention in November 1982: Proposition 12, which called upon the United States and the Soviet Union to halt the manufacture of nuclear weapons; Proposition 15, which required the registration of handguns; and Proposition 11, which would have required a 5 cent returnable deposit with the purchase of cans and bottles. On two of these initiatives, party differences were much greater than the ethnic differences. Indeed, the nuclear freeze initiative provoked marked differences between Democrats and Republicans (Democrats being more in favor than Republicans), but no ethnic differences whatsoever. In fact, Mexican American Democrats and Republicans were more at odds on this issue than any other two groups. Party differences were less significant on the handgun registration issue, but no ethnic cleavage existed at all. Only on the bottle bill were there marked Latino-Anglo differences.

In light of the fact that the economy was acknowledged to be the most important problem in 1982, differences in opinions about economic issues are particularly meaningful. Since there was a fairly uniform pattern to the responses to these questions, it is not necessary to consider the whole battery of economic questions that were asked in both polls. Instead, we will consider a representative one that was designed to elicit a general evaluation of Reagan's economic policies, namely, whether the voter believed that Reagan's economic policies hurt the economy, helped it, or whether it was too early to tell. As one would expect, there were substantial party differences in the responses to this question; Democrats were far more likely to be critical of the President's policies than Republicans. By comparison, the intraparty differences were very small. As the figures in Table 5 indicate, Mexican American Democrats were slightly more opposed to Reagan's economic programs than Anglo Democrats,

TABLE 5

Evaluation of Reaganomics (major party registrants only)

| | Reagan Administration Economic Policies Have | | | |
	Helped	Can't Tell Yet	Hurt	n
Non–Mexican American Democrats	10%	38%	52%	120
Mexican American Democrats	5	37	58	82
Non–Mexican American Republicans	56	28	16	61
Mexican American Republicans	56	18	25	16

which is understandable given that a high percentage of them (43 percent) had either recently experienced unemployment themselves or had someone in their household who had been unemployed.

Finally, there is the issue of abortion. One conjecture that has received some attention in Republican circles recently is that Mexican Americans can be persuaded to vote Republican because they are more socially conservative than other Democrats. If this is true, then an issue like abortion should show substantial intraparty differences. Indeed, at first glance, this would appear to be the case. As Table 6 indicates, Anglo Democrats in this district were more likely than Mexican American Democrats to be pro-choice. However, these policy differences should be considered in light of the fact that 81 percent of the Mexican Americans in the sample were Catholic, as opposed to only 42 percent of the Anglos.

What happens when we control for other demographic variables? Do we find that Mexican Americans had distinctive policy positions on the issues that were central to this race? The answer appears to be no.

TABLE 6

Attitudes Concerning Abortion (major party registrants only)

| | Abortion Should Be Allowed | | | |
	Under No Circum-stances	Under Some Circum-stances	As a Matter of Personal Choice	n
Non–Mexican American Democrats	8%	24%	68%	115
Mexican American Democrats	13	40	46	82
Non-Mexican American Republicans	12	38	50	61
Mexican American Republicans	7	27	66	15

As before, the entries in Table 7 are the estimated coefficients for each variable. In general, the table shows that with the exception of the handgun initiative there is no strong association between being Mexican American and holding any of these policy attitudes, and in none of the instances is the association significant by conventional statistical standards. Even the abortion issue, which in the bivariate table showed a relation between ethnicity and attitude, displays no relationship in the presence of a control for religion. What this means is that there is no difference between Anglo and Mexican American Catholics on this issue: if the Hispanics are susceptible to the possibility of defection on this issue, so are other Catholic Democrats. By contrast, there are marked partisan differences on almost all of the issues, but especially on the economy. In sum, while there are some small ethnic differences on issues in the tabular data, these differ-

TABLE 7

Binominal Logit Analysis of Issue Positions and Support for Ballot Initiatives

	Gun Regis- tration	Bottle Deposits	Nuclear Freeze	Approve Reaga- nomics	Never Permit Abortions
Union member	−0.22	−0.28	−0.24	−0.21	−0.05
	(0.29)	(0.27)	(0.27)	(0.40)	(0.43)
Unemployed	−0.18	−0.01	0.41	−1.06*	−0.17
	(0.30)	(0.29)	(0.29)	(0.44)	(0.46)
Catholic	−0.19	0.09	0.08	−0.12	0.80*
	(0.30)	(0.28)	(0.28)	(0.42)	(0.45)
Mexican American	−0.19	0.04	−0.07	−0.06	0.01
	(0.33)	(0.32)	(0.31)	(0.49)	(0.48)
Republican	−2.22*	−1.28*	−0.99	1.85*	1.32
	(0.59)	(0.54)	(0.56)	(0.65)	(1.14)
Democrat	−1.46*	−1.07*	−0.27	−1.22*	1.21
	(0.54)	(0.49)	(0.52)	(0.64)	(1.08)
Female	0.59*	−0.01	0.53*	−0.46	0.00
	(0.28)	(0.27)	(0.27)	(0.39)	(0.42)
Constant	0.92	0.51	0.31	−0.11	−3.15
	(0.56)	(0.52)	(0.55)	(0.65)	(1.11)*
Percent correctly predicted	67%	66%	60%	57%	55%

NOTE: Cell entries are logit coefficients with *t* ratios in parentheses.

ences do not persist in the presence of control variables and are clearly less important than party and sex as explanatory variables.

While attitudes on the economy and the initiatives are one plausible explanation of the vote in the 30th, the impact of candidate evaluations is another. Was it the case that Mexican Americans, controlling for party and other demographic factors, had more favorable impressions of Martinez and less favorable impressions of Rousselot than did other voters?

Table 8 contains the results of a test of this question. Looking at the evaluations of Martinez first, it seems clear that party and ethnicity were the two major determinants of whether people had favorable or unfavorable impressions of Martinez as a candidate. That is to say, Democrats and Mexican Americans were more likely to have a favorable impression of Martinez. Conversely, they were much more likely to have an unfavorable impression of Rousselot. In fact, party and ethnicity were the only variables that affected candidate evaluations in a significant way. All the other variables, including the initiatives, did not. Clearly, even when party biases and the attitudes that are normally associated with being a Democrat in California were held constant, being a Mexican American did influence one's perceptions of the candidates.

So far we have identified two ways in which ethnicity affected the vote in this race. One was through the attitudes that voters had about issues and the other was through the evaluations they had of the candidates. The third way is through partisanship, or party loyalty. Since this is such a widely studied factor, there is no need to discuss it at great length. Registering with a party is an expression of long-standing party loyalties. Party loyalties affect positions on issues, as is evident with the initiatives. Party

TABLE 8

Multinomial Logit Analysis of Congressional Candidate Evaluations

	Favorable Impression of Martinez vs. Unfavorable	Uncertain Impression of Martinez vs. Unfavorable	Favorable Impression of Rousselot vs. Unfavorable	Uncertain Impression of Rousselot vs. Unfavorable
Democrat	0.85*	−0.00	−1.32*	−0.53
	(0.38)	(0.29)	(0.38)	(0.40)
Mexican American	1.68*	0.65	−1.02*	0.13
	(0.46)	(0.42)	(0.43)	(0.39)
Unemployed	0.41	0.35	−0.18	0.58
	(0.40)	(0.34)	(0.41)	(0.37)
Catholic	0.00	−0.04	0.17	−0.50
	(0.40)	(0.34)	(0.40)	(0.39)
Pro-freeze	0.37	0.08	−0.12	0.08
	(0.36)	(0.29)	(0.35)	(0.34)
Pro-gun registration	0.32	0.46	−0.33	0.18
	(0.36)	(0.30)	(0.35)	(0.34)
Pro-bottle deposit	0.49	0.01	−0.03	−0.55
	(0.36)	(0.29)	(0.35)	(0.34)
Constant	−1.61*	0.39	2.14*	1.40*
	(0.38)	(0.26)	(0.39)	(0.40)
Percent correctly predicted	51%		56%	
Likelihood ratio index	.13		.14	

NOTE: Cell entries are logit coefficients with *t* ratios in parentheses.

loyalties also affect candidate evaluations, as just seen. In the latter instance, being a Mexican American had an effect on candidate evaluations independent of party. But if it is also the case that Mexican Americans are more likely to be registered Democrats, then there is yet another route by which being Mexican American affects issue attitudes, candidate evaluations, and ultimately the vote; namely, the indirect effect through party loyalty.

Does such a causal connection exist? Table 9 is a test of the relation between being Mexican American and party registration, once again following the procedure of controlling for other potential effects. The variable to be explained is whether the respondent is a registered Democrat, an independent (or minor party voter), or a registered Republican (i.e., the suppressed category). The choices should be interpreted as the odds of being a Democrat versus a Republican (the first column) and of being an Independent versus a Republican (the second column).

As is evident from the table, Mexican Americans were far more likely to be registered Democrats, even when their sex, employment status, union membership, and religion were controlled for. Union members, the unemployed, and Catholics were also more likely to be registered Democrats. Gender does not seem to be related in a significant manner to party registration. Mexican Americans were also more likely to be Independents than Republicans, as were males in this district. However, no other variable seems to predict the Independent category very well. In sum, it is clear that there is an important connection between ethnicity and party

TABLE 9

Multinomial Logit Analysis of Party Registration

	Democrat vs. Republican	Independent vs. Republican
Mexican American	1.78*	1.45*
	(0.42)	(0.67)
Unemployed	0.62*	−0.04
	(0.30)	(0.61)
Union member	0.54*	0.31
	(0.29)	(0.52)
Female	0.08	−1.21*
	(0.24)	(0.51)
Catholic	0.49	−0.40
	(0.29)	(0.60)
Constant	−0.20	−1.34
	(0.22)	(0.35)*
Percent correctly predicted	61%	
Likelihood ratio index	.30	

NOTE: Cell entries are logit coefficients with *t* ratios in parentheses.

loyalty, adding yet another connection between being Mexican American and voting for Martinez.

Relating the Three Components to the Martinez Vote

Having so far identified three ways in which being Mexican American could have affected the voter's choice in the race for the 30th Congressional District, it is appropriate to ask at this point which components seemed to have been most important. The variable to be explained is the preelection indication of how the respondent would have voted if the election had been held at the time of the poll (the week before the election). The pre-election poll is used for two reasons. First, it contains all of the data necessary to test the effects of the three components, whereas the post-election poll does not. Secondly, it allows us to look at the crucial question of why so many voters—especially Democrats and Mexican Americans—were undecided so late in the campaign. The dependent variable is constructed in a manner such that the first column in Table 10 is the odds of intending to vote for Martinez versus Rousselot and the second is the odds of being undecided versus intending to vote for Rousselot.

The explanatory variables are by now familiar. Experimentation with the specification led to the final model displayed in Table 10. Earlier attempts included models that had different measures of economic performance as well as the three most salient initiatives. Since economic evaluations were highly related to party, union membership, and employment status, the presence of an economic performance variable added little to the question, and so was dropped in the final specification. Candidate evaluations were captured by variables for a favorable impression of Martinez, an unfavorable impression of Martinez, a favorable impression of Rousselot, and an unfavorable impression of Rousselot. A Mexican American variable is included in order to capture any remaining unspecified relations between ethnicity and the vote in this race.

What do we find? First, there were no residual ethnicity effects, as indicated by the fact that the coefficient on the Mexican American variable is not significant. This can be interpreted as meaning that the other variables in the model have successfully captured the various causal routes between ethnicity and vote. Of the initiatives, only the pro–gun registration initiative shows any strong association with the Martinez vote. By far the most important components of the Martinez vote were party loyalty and candidate evaluations. Of these, the largest effects were having a positive evaluation of Rousselot and party. Those who had developed a favorable impression of Rousselot were much more likely to vote for him regardless of party. By comparison, having a favorable impression of Martinez had less effect in causing defections from Rousselot. The effectiveness of Rousselot's campaign and the failure of the Martinez campaign at that point to successfully counter Rousselot's attacks are evident in these estimations.

TABLE 10

Multinomial Logit Analysis of Vote Choice for Congressman

	Martinez vs. Rousselot	Undecided vs. Rousselot
Democrat	2.05*	1.09*
	(0.54)	(0.39)
Mexican American	0.52	0.17
	(0.60)	(0.51)
Unemployed	0.67	0.22
	(0.52)	(0.43)
Catholic	0.06	0.28
	(0.55)	(0.44)
Favorable impression of Rousselot	−4.02*	−3.03*
	(0.67)	(0.41)
Unfavorable impression of Rousselot	1.45	0.40
	(0.83)	(0.77)
Favorable impression of Martinez	1.85*	0.23
	(0.60)	(0.55)
Unfavorable impression of Martinez	−1.64*	−0.78*
	(0.79)	(0.44)
Pro-freeze	0.46	0.14
	(0.48)	(0.38)
Pro−gun regulation	0.80*	0.67
	(0.48)	(0.38)
Pro−bottle deposit	−0.05	−0.44
	(0.49)	(0.39)
Constant	−1.54*	0.93*
	(0.60)	(0.42)
Percent correctly predicted	73%	
Likelihood ratio index	.41	

NOTE: Cell entries are logit coefficients with *t* ratios in parentheses.

The factors predicting the odds of being undecided versus intending to vote for Rousselot are equally plausible. Once again, Democrats appear to have been more likely to be undecided, a fact observed in the cross-tabular data. There were also no residual ethnicity effects in this equation. Third, just as in vote choice equation, those who were pro−gun control were also more likely to be undecided than intending to vote for Rousselot. What is particularly striking about this equation is how unequivocally important the negative impressions of Martinez and the positive impressions of Rousselot were to the large undecided vote at the time of the pre-election poll. Again, the impact of campaign- and candidate-specific effects in this race is underscored. Clearly, the initiatives had far less to do with the fortunes of this race than did the strategies and personalities of the candidates themselves. Also, it seems evident that the "softness" observed earlier in Mexican American support for Martinez was candidate related, suggesting that a significant segment of the Mexican American voters did not automatically throw their support to Martinez, either because they felt that they did not know enough about him or did not like what they heard.

Conclusion

The Mexican American vote is a complex phenomenon with many indirect effects through intervening variables such as party, issue attitudes, and candidate evaluations. The attractiveness of the Mexican American candidate is suggested by certain patterns of ballot splitting and the strong effect of the candidate evaluation variable. It would appear that Mexican American voters were responsive to the attempt to create representation for them in the 30th. That support, however, should not be taken for granted, for Mexican American voters will condition their vote on their information and evaluation about the quality of the candidate, Mexican American or not. At the same time, there is strong evidence that ethnicity affected voting behavior in this race. In particular, being Mexican American influenced the voter's party loyalty and candidate evaluations significantly.

REFERENCES

Baird, Frank L. 1977. "The Search for a Constituency: Political Validation of Mexican-American Candidates in the Texas Great Plains," in F. Baird, ed., Mexican-Americans: Political Power, Influence or Resource (Lubbock: Texas Tech Press): pp. 77–93.

de la Garza, Rodolfo. 1974. "Voting Patterns in 'Bi-Cultural El Paso': A Contextual Analysis of Mexican-American Voting Behavior," in F. Chris Garcia, ed., La Causa Politica: A Chicano Politics Reader (Notre Dame: Notre Dame Press): pp. 250–66.

———. 1977. "Mexican-American Voters: A Responsible Electorate," in F. Baird, ed., Mexican-Americans: Political Power, Influence or Resource (Lubbock: Texas Tech Press): pp. 63–76.

de la Garza, Rodolfo, and Robert R. Brischetto. 1982a. The Mexican-American Electorate: A Demographic Profile. Occasional Paper No. 1 (San Antonio: Southwest Voter Registration Education Project and University of Texas Center for Mexican American Studies).

———. 1982b. The Mexican-American Electorate: Information Sources and Policy Orientations. Occasional Paper No. 2 (San Antonio: Southwest Voter Registration Education Project and University of Texas Center for Mexican American Studies).

de la Garza, Rodolfo, and Janet Weaver. 1983. "Mexican Americans and Anglos in San Antonio: A City Divided." Paper presented at the American Political Science Convention, 1 September.

Freeman, Donald M. 1974. "Party, Vote and the Mexican-American in South Tucson," in F. Chris Garcia, ed., La Causa Politica: A Chicano Politics Reader (Notre Dame: Notre Dame Press): pp. 55–66.

Garcia, F. Chris, and Rudolph O. de la Garza. 1977. *The Chicano Political Experience*. (North Scituate, Mass.: Duxbury Press).

Guzman, Ralph. 1973. "The Function of Anglo-American Racism in the Political Development of Chicanos," in F. Chris Garcia, ed., *Chicano Politics: Readings* (New York: MSS Information Corporation): pp. 21–37.

Levy, Mark R., and Michael S. Kramer. 1974. "Patterns of Chicano Voting Behavior," in F. Chris Garcia, ed., *La Causa Politica: A Chicano Politics Reader* (Notre Dame: Notre Dame Press): pp. 241–49.

McCleskey, Clifton, and Bruce Merrill. 1973. "Mexican American Political Behavior in Texas," *Social Science Quarterly*, 53 (March):785–98.

16. ATTITUDES TOWARD UNDOCUMENTED WORKERS: THE MEXICAN AMERICAN PERSPECTIVE[1]

Lawrence W. MILLER, *Pan American University*

Jerry L. POLINARD, *Pan American University*

Robert D. WRINKLE, *Pan American University*

Scholars have suggested that, because of cultural and kinship ties with Mexico, Mexican Americans may be sympathetic toward Mexican immigration to the United States. At the same time Mexican Americans are more likely than Anglos to be adversely affected by the economic impact of this immigration. This study explores Mexican American attitudes toward undocumented immigration. The data suggest significant differences among Mexican Americans of different education, income, and generational levels in their attitudes toward undocumented immigration.

An impressive body of recent scholarship has contributed significantly to our knowledge about undocumented Mexican immigrants. There now is wide spread information as to their demographic characteristics, the reasons why they come to the United States, the types of employment they obtain, and their economic impact on our system (Samora, 1971; Bustamante, 1972; Stoddard, 1976; North and Houstoun, 1976; Cardenas, 1976; Johnson and Ogle, 1978; Kiser and Kiser, 1979; Weintraub and Ross, 1980; North with Wagner, 1981; de la Garza, 1982; Tarrance & Associates, 1982).

There is, however, an important dimension of this issue which has received scant attention from the academic community: the attitudes of Mexican Americans toward undocumented workers and the attendant U.S. immigration policies. The Mexican American community is neither indifferent to nor disinterested in United States immigration policy toward undocumented Mexican aliens. Mexican Americans, especially those who live along the 2,000 mile Mexico–United States border, often share common cultural and social bonds with undocumented aliens. At the same time, Mexican Americans are "political citizens" (Limon, 1982:1) of the United States with a direct stake in the impact of undocumented aliens on the marketplace. Garcia (1981:610) has described this "interface" between

[1] We acknowledge the significant contributions made by three *SSQ* reviewers. Editor's note: Reviewers were Rodolfo de la Garza, Ricardo Romo, and Ellwyn R. Stoddard.

Mexican Americans and Mexico as one which "both reinforces cultural similarities and contrasts political status."

In other words, Mexican American attitudes toward undocumented workers may be characterized by a certain play of tension between the positive feelings of ethnic and cultural kinship and ethnic identity and the negative feelings of direct and indirect economic fears, a condition which Villarreal and Gutierrez (1978:10) have described as "a dilemma of vast importance to all of the parties involved."

What is clear is that neither the relationship between United States immigration policy and Mexican American attitudes nor the consequences of this policy on the Mexican American communities are neutral. If we are to understand this relationship and these consequences, we need to identify Mexican American attitudes toward immigration policy and toward undocumented immigrants.

Some steps in this direction have been taken (Villarreal and Gutierrez, 1978; Hofstetter and Loveman, 1980; National Council of La Raza, 1980; de la Garza, 1980, 1982; de la Garza and Flores, 1983). The data reported below constitute another "step" in this important area of inquiry.

Hypotheses

The hypotheses utilized in this study are drawn from a number of sources, including the general ethnic politics literature as well as the more specific immigration literature. Predominant among our concerns is the supposition that attitudes toward undocumented immigration and support for specific immigration policies carry a strong income, educational, and generational bias. Following the general ethnic politics literature, we suspect that there might be a generational influence upon attitudes toward immigration policy and support for specific immigration policies within the Mexican American community. Another related area of concern is the economic marginality argument—that immigration in general and illegal immigration in particular either deprives lower-income Mexican Americans of job opportunities or is perceived as causing such deprivation.

Essentially, we ask to what extent are Mexican American attitudes toward undocumented workers influenced by education, income, and generation. The latter variable addresses the issue of whether attitudes among first and second generation Mexican Americans differ from Mexican Americans who are at least third generation.

We hypothesize that more highly educated and upper-income Mexican Americans will be less likely than less educated and lower-income Mexican Americans to support increased immigration rates and more likely to perceive immigration as a problem. We also hypothesize that more highly educated and upper-income Mexican Americans will be more likely than less educated and lower-income Mexican Americans to perceive illegal immigration problems in socioeconomic terms rather than employment terms, and will be less likely to support free public education for undocumented school-age children. We include job competition, employer sanctions, and the question of increased enforcement of immigration laws among the issues identified with undocumented immigration.

We believe highly educated Mexican Americans are more likely to be aware of and influenced by the large amount of editorializing against immigration found in both the print and visual media. At the same time, better educated and upper-income Mexican Americans are less likely to compete with undocumented workers for jobs and therefore less likely than less educated Mexican Americans to identify the problems of undocumented immigration in terms of employment.

We also hypothesize that first and second generation Mexican Americans will be less likely than third-generation-plus Mexican Americans to perceive illegal immigration as a problem but more likely to identify illegal immigration problems in employment terms. We suggest that first and second generation Mexican Americans will be more likely than third-generation-plus Mexican Americans to support increased immigration and free public schooling for undocumented school-age children. This hypothesis recognizes the possibility that later-generation Mexican Americans are more likely to be assimilated and less likely to be engaged in job competition with illegal immigrants.

Research Methodology

The location of our research is Hidalgo County, Texas—a county located deep in South Texas along the Mexican border. The county generally is among the poorest in the nation, with a traditional double-digit unemployment rate. The proximity to the border virtually ensures that the influences of Mexican culture and traditions will be great. There is a continuing immigration stream which ensures that immigration policies and policies relating to illegal immigrants will be highly salient to county residents. Data from the 1980 Census indicate that 81.3 percent of the population is native-born of native parents—in other words, third or later generation Mexican American (U.S. Bureau of the Census, 1981).

A sample of household telephones in the Hidalgo County telephone exchanges was obtained by a random digit production process. All obviously commercial telephones were eliminated from the sample by the use of a reverse telephone directory. The resultant sample totaled 440 households, of which 407 were contacted. Of those contacted, the refusal rate was a most acceptable 7 percent. In conducting a telephone survey in this region a major problem emerges. While more than 90 percent of all households in the nation have telephones, only approximately 83 percent of the households in the surveyed region have telephone service (Backstrom and Hursch-Cesar, 1981:21; Rush, 1983). As Hidalgo County is one of the most poverty-stricken areas in the nation, it is likely that a significant number of poor households are without telephone service. This is especially true when one considers the fact that the *colonias* (small, rural, unincorporated areas) in the area are without any telephone service. Thus, it was deemed advisable to supplement the telephone survey with 125 personal interviews conducted in those areas without access to telephone service. Of the 125 selected personal interviews, 122 were completed. The total number of completed interviews was 501 (122 personal; 379 telephone).

Interviews were conducted by a staff of trained interviewers employed by the authors. Two-thirds of the interviewers were bilingual and 277, or 45 percent, of the interviews were conducted in Spanish from an authenticated translation of the survey instrument. The instrument included both open-ended and closed questions, with the majority of the survey being open-ended. Respondents were not asked to rank immigration with other perceived problems, but respondents were asked to identify whether they perceived immigration to be a major problem. The personal interviews were conducted in 14 of the more than 40 *colonias* in Hidalgo County. Household selection in the *colonias* was done by a two-stage cluster sample, utilizing a respondent-randomizing device (Backstrom and Hursch-Cesar, 1981:94).

The sample appears to represent the population of Hidalgo County fairly well. In comparison to the 1980 Census, the sampled respondents had attained slightly more formal education and income than the residents of the county as a whole. Moreover, the college educated Spanish surnamed respondents were slightly underrepresented by our sample. All in all, the data for the sample correspond to the overall census figures for Hidalgo County.

Findings

To what degree do Mexican Americans perceive immigration to be a major problem? When asked to identify the most important problems facing the people of the Lower Rio Grande Valley, respondents overwhelmingly cited economic concerns with only one in nine (11.4 percent) specifically mentioning immigration. This corresponds with earlier findings (Peterson and Kozmetsky, 1982; de la Garza, 1982). However, when asked directly whether undocumented immigration is a problem, Mexican American respondents decidedly agreed that it was an important or very important problem. Thus, while we do not want to overstate the significance of undocumented immigration as a perceived problem, we do think it is perceived as an important issue by the Mexican American community. Our data suggest significant relationship between education, income, and gen-

TABLE 1

Comparisons between Census and Sample

	Sample	1980 Census
Median school year completed	9.7	7.2
Median family income	$12,200	$10,489
Percent Spanish surname population 25 years or older with 4 or more years of college	4.7	6.1

SOURCE: U.S. Bureau of the Census (1981).

eration and the perceptions of illegal immigration as a problem. A majority of Mexican American respondents on all three education levels perceived undocumented immigration as a problem, but, as hypothesized, respondents with elementary school education were less likely to identify this problem than those with high school or college education. And, as one moves up the education ladder, the importance of the problem increases. That is, over half of the college educated respondents cited illegal immigration as a "very important" problem compared to 46 percent of those with a high school education and just over one-third (35 percent) of those with elementary school educations.

Similarly, as we look at income levels, we find a significant relationship between amount of income and perception of the importance of the problem of illegal immigration. Over half of the Mexican American respondents with incomes in excess of $20,000 identified undocumented immigration as a "very important" problem, compared to 46 percent of the middle-income Mexican American respondents ($10,000–$20,000) and 35 percent of those with incomes less than $10,000.

Although Mexican American respondents of all generations perceived undocumented immigration as a problem, again we find significant differences in the perception of how important the problem is. Third-generation-plus Mexican Americans cited the problem as "very important" to a significantly greater degree (51 percent) than did first or second generation Mexican Americans (36 percent). This suggests, in part, that the family ties to Mexico may be stronger among first and second generation Mexican Americans than among later generations. In addition, first and second generation Mexican Americans may be more likely than later generations to share common social and economic experiences with undocumented workers and therefore less likely to blame the undocumenteds for their present social condition. Later generations of Mexican Americans may be more likely than first or second generations to adopt new perspectives toward undocumented immigration, perspectives which reduce support for and empathy with the undocumented worker.

Mexican American respondents, regardless of education level, income level, or generation, did not tend to perceive undocumented immigrants to have negative consequences on their personal lives. They distinguished the impact of undocumented immigrants as causing problems for the Rio Grande Valley, but not necessarily for their personal lives. The data did not indicate any statistical relationship between education, income, or generation and these attitudes.

Although we have no data to explain this distinction between the regional and personal impact of undocumented immigration, we suggest that part of the explanation may be found in the vast media coverage of the issue. De la Garza and Brischetto have found that more highly educated Mexican Americans are more media-attentive than less educated Mexican Americans. Constant exposure through the media to the issue might create the impression of a major problem even if the respondent had not been affected directly. And, because the problem has geographical salience, reports and

TABLE 2

Cross-Tabulation of Immigration as a Problem by Education, Income, and Generation (Percentages)

Problem	Education			Income			Generation	
	Elementary School (N = 136)	High School (N = 87)	College (N = 51)	Under $10,000 (N = 148)	$10,000–$20,000 (N = 56)	Over $20,000 (N = 46)	First and Second (N = 181)	Third-Plus (N = 96)
Very important	34.6	46.0	51.0	34.5	46.4	54.3	35.9	51.0
Important	50.0	48.3	43.1	53.4	50.0	34.8	51.9	41.7
Not important	15.4	5.7	5.9	12.2	3.6	10.9	12.2	7.3
(Totals)	(100.0)	(100.0)	(100.0)	(100.1)	(100.0)	(100.0)	(100.0)	(100.0)
Chi-square	9.50			9.51			6.27	
Degrees of freedom	4			4			2	
Significance level	.05			.05			.04	

studies of undocumented immigration are common in both the print and visual media of the area.

Media access may also explain another distinction suggested by our data. Given that undocumented immigrants are more likely to compete with less educated respondents, it is surprising to find that better educated respondents are more concerned about undocumented immigration. We speculate that this may be a function of greater attention paid by the better educated respondents to the media's coverage of the issue.

Our data suggest significant relationships between education, income, and generation variables and the identification of specific problems caused by undocumented workers. As hypothesized, elementary-school-level Mexican American respondents and high-school-level Mexican American respondents were more likely than college-level Mexican American respondents to identify job competition as the major problem caused by undocumented immigration. Mexican American respondents who had attended college were more likely than other Mexican American respondents to cite use of public schools and welfare services as significant problems.

Similarly, lower- and middle-income Mexican American respondents were more likely than upper-income Mexican American resondents to define the major problem as job competition, while upper-income Mexican American respondents were more likely to identify the use of public schools and welfare programs as problems.

First and second generation Mexican Americans were more likely (85 percent) than third-generation-plus Mexican Americans (68 percent) to name job competition as a major problem. The identification of public school use and welfare use as problems did not differ as markedly between generations as it did between education and income groups of Mexican American respondents.

Still, regardless of education, income, and generational differences, job competition was considered to be the most important problem generated by undocumented immigrants.

When asked what, if any, benefits undocumented immigrants create, there was no statistical significance to the correlations between education, income, or generation and the responses given by Mexican American respondents. The most frequently cited benefit among all Mexican American respondent groups was the "cheap labor" provided by undocumented immigrants.

We examined two other employment categories—low wages and job competition—and two important issue areas—education of undocumented children and penalties against employers of undocumented workers. These data are presented in Table 4.

We followed the bivariate analysis between the variables with a multivariate attempt to explain the attitudes of Mexican Americans toward undocumented workers. However, the combination of variables only marginally helped to explain the variance in the dependent variables. In addition to the three independent variables used in the bivariate analysis (education, income, and generation), two other variables, gender and age, were included in the multiple regression.

TABLE 3

Cross-Tabulation of Specific Problems by Education, Income, and Generation (Percentages)

Problem	Education			Income			Generation	
	Elementary School (N = 93)	High School (N = 61)	College (N = 35)	Under $10,000 (N = 104)	$10,000–$20,000 (N = 40)	Over $20,000 (N = 29)	First and Second (N = 123)	Third-Plus (N = 66)
Job competition	84.9	83.6	54.3	84.6	77.5	58.6	84.6	68.2
Crime	3.2	6.6	8.6	3.8	10.0	3.4	3.3	9.1
Use of welfare	6.5	4.9	17.1	5.8	5.0	17.2	7.3	9.1
Use of schools	5.4	4.9	20.0	5.8	7.5	20.7	4.9	13.1
(Totals)	(100.0)	(100.0)	(100.0)	(100.0)	(100.0)	(99.9)	(100.1)	(100.0)
Chi-square		17.52			14.58			8.55
Degrees of freedom		6			6			3
Significance level		.007			.02			.04

TABLE 4

Specific Attitudes about Undocumented Workers

	Percentage of Respondents Agreeing That			
	Undocumented Workers Cause Low Wages	Undocumented Workers Take Jobs from US Citizens	Employers of Undocumented Workers Should Be Penalized	Schools Should Educate Children of Undocumented Workers
Education				
Elementary	62.4*	73.1**	53.3*	48.9**
High school	64.4*	85.3**	62.7*	28.4**
College	53.7*	56.4**	63.0*	47.3**
Income				
Under $10,000	62.2**	77.4**	57.2*	43.6
$10,000–20,000	72.6**	82.5**	60.3*	39.7
Over $20,000	47.9**	58.3**	66.7*	39.6
Generation				
First and second	61.2	72.8	53.0*	47.4**
Third-plus	61.9	76.9	67.3*	31.5**

*χ^2 significant at .05 level or less.

**χ^2 significant at .01 level or less.

The dependent variable that was best explained by the five-variable combination was agreement that undocumented workers cause low wages. However, the R-square indicated that only 19 percent of the variance was explained. The dependent variable that was least explained by the variable (7 percent) was the attitude toward penalizing employers of undocumented workers, followed by agreement that undocumented workers take jobs (9 percent), agreement that schools should educate the children of undocumenteds (10 percent), agreement that illegal immigration is a problem (14 percent), and the attitudes on specific problems caused by undocumented workers (16 percent). All in all, the multiple regression added little to our analysis of Mexican American attitudes toward undocumented workers.

Of course, this lack of explanatory power of our independent variables, by itself, is significant. If income, generation, education, gender, and age do not substantially explain these attitudes, what are other relevant variables? We speculate that further research should include such variables as the source and amount of information obtained by respondents about undocumented immigration, as well as the amount of direct contact with undocumented persons and involvement in the major issues of undocumented immigration the respondents have had.

In sum, the data indicate the following:

1. A majority of Mexican Americans tended to perceive undocumented immigration as having little negative impact on their lives, but generating problems for the region in which they live.

2. Mexican American respondents tended to identify job competition as the most important problem caused by undocumented immigrants, but upper-income Mexican Americans, more highly educated Mexican Americans, and third-generation-plus Mexican Americans were more likely than other Mexican Americans to perceive the use of public schools and the welfare system as problems and less likely to view job competition as important as other Mexican Americans.

3. More Mexican American respondents opposed free schooling for children of undocumented workers than supported it. Mexican Americans with a high school education were much less supportive of free public school education for the children of undocumenteds than Mexican Americans with either elementary school or college educations.

4. First and second generation Mexican American respondents were more likely to support free schools than third-generation-plus respondents. A majority of third-generation-plus Mexican Americans opposed free schooling.

5. Upper-income Mexican Americans were more likely to support penalties for employers than lower- and middle-income respondents, although a majority of all three income groups endorsed the penalties.

6. Third-generation-plus Mexican Americans were more likely to support employer penalties than first and second generation respondents, although a majority of both groups supported the penalties.

Discussion

Public policy in the American political system does not exist in a vacuum. Rather, it is the function of the hopes and fears, likes and dislikes of the

American community. We have examined the attitudes of one segment of that community—Mexican American—toward undocumented immigration from Mexico. We have sought to learn if these attitudes are influenced by income, education, and generation.

Recent Gallup polls have indicated that Americans are opposed to any increase in immigration and seek stricter enforcement of immigration laws (Gallup Opinion Index, 1977, 1978, 1980). Our data suggest that Mexican American respondents share these concerns. We find consistent similarity in the direction, if not the strength, of attitudes toward immigration issues. Virtually all respondent groups surveyed perceive undocumented immigration to be a regional rather than personal problem, oppose free public education for undocumented school-age children, and support penalties against employers of undocumented immigrants.

Our data suggest that the traditional journalistic (and sometimes scholarly) perception of Mexican Americans as a homogeneous population is erroneous. We find significant differences among Mexican Americans of different education, income, and generational levels in the salience of their attitudes. Perhaps this is not surprising; Mexican Americans along the border live in a tricultural environment where the values of the American, Mexican, and Mexican American cultures are blended. Scholars have suggested that because of the cultural and kinship ties with Mexico, Mexican Americans may be more sympathetic toward Mexican immigration to the United States (Sommers, 1981; National Council of La Raza, 1980). At the same time Mexican Americans are more likely than Anglos to be adversely affected by the economic impact of the immigration (Gerking and Mutti, 1980; Villarreal and Gutierrez, 1978). Our data suggest that this tension between cultural kinship and economic competition is resolved in favor of the latter.

REFERENCES

Backstrom, Charles H., and Gerald Hursh-Cesar. 1981. *Survey Research*. 2d ed. (New York: Wiley).

Bustamante, Jorge A. 1972. "An Historical Context of Undocumented Mexican Immigration to the United States," *Aztlan*, 3 (Fall):257–81.

Cardenas, Gilberto. 1976. "Public Data on Mexican Immigration into the United States: A Critical Evaluation," in W. B. Littrell and C. S. Sjoberg, eds., *Current Issues in Social Policies* (Beverly Hills: Sage).

de la Garza, Rodolfo. 1980. "Chicanos and U.S. Foreign Policy: The Future of Chicano-Mexican Relations," *Western Political Quarterly*, 33 (December):571–82.

———. 1982. "Public Policy Priorities of Chicano Political Elites." U.S.-Mexico Project Series, no. 7 (Washington, D.C.: Overseas Development Council).

de la Garza, Rodolfo, and Robert R. Brischetto, with the assistance of David Vaughan. 1983. *The Mexican American Electorate: Information Sources and Policy Orientations*. Occasional Paper No. 2 (Austin: The University of Texas at Austin, The Center for Mexican American Studies).

de la Garza, Rodolfo, and Adela Flores. 1983. "The Impact of Mexican Immigrants on the Political Life of Chicanos: A Clarification of Issues and Some Hypotheses for Future Research." Paper presented at the annual meeting of the Southwest Political Science Association, Houston.

Gallup Opinion Index. 1977. Report no. 143 (June).

———. 1978. Report no. 177 (February).

———. 1980. Report no. 151 (April/May).

Garcia, John A. 1981. "The Political Integration of Mexican Immigrants: Explorations into the Naturalization Process," *International Migration Review,* 15 (Winter):608–25.

Gerking, Shelby D., and John H. Mutti. 1980. "Costs and Benefits of Illegal Immigration: Key Issues for Government Policy," *Social Science Quarterly,* 61 (June):71–85.

Hofstetter, C. Richard, and Brian Loveman. 1980. "Communication Media and Perceptions of Undocumented Immigrants: The Case of San Diego." Paper prepared for presentation at the annual meeting of the International Communication Association, Acapulco, Mexico.

Johnson, Kenneth, and Nina M. Olge. 1978. *Illegal Mexican Aliens in the United States* (Washington, D.C.: University Press of America).

Kiser, George C., and Martha W. Kiser. 1979. *Mexican Workers in the United States* (Albuquerque: University of New Mexico Press).

Limon, Jose. 1982. "Language Behavior and Undocumented Mexican Immigration: An Initial Outline for Research." Paper prepared for presentation at the Working Conference on Mexican Americans and Mexican Immigration, The University of Texas at Austin.

National Council of La Raza. 1980. *Perspectives on Undocumented Workers: Black and Hispanic Viewpoints* (Washington, D.C.: NCLR).

North, David S., and Marion F. Houstoun. 1976. *The Characteristics and Role of Illegal Aliens in the U.S. Labor Market* (Washington, D.C.: New Transcentury Foundation).

North, David S., with Jennifer R. Wagner. 1981. *Government Records: What They Tell Us about the Role of Illegal Immigrants in the Labor Market and in Income Transfer Programs* (Washington, D.C.: New Transcentury Foundation).

Peterson, Robert A., and George Kozmetsky. 1982. "Public Opinion Regarding Illegal Aliens in Texas," *Texas Business Review,* 56 (May/June):118–21.

Rush, Carl. 1983. Personal communication to the authors.

Sommers, Joseph. 1981. "The Problem of the Undocumented Worker: A View from the United States," in Rios-Bustamente, ed., *Mexican Migrant Workers in the United States* (Los Angeles: Anthology No. 2, Chicano Studies Research Center): pp. 151–60.

Samora. Julian. 1971. *Los Mojados: The Wetback Story* (Notre Dame, Ind.: University of Notre Dame Press).

Stoddard, E. R. 1976. "A Conceptual Analysis of the Illegal Alien Invasion: Institutionalized Support of Illegal Mexican Aliens in the U.S.," *International Migration Review,* 10 (Summer):157–89.

Tarrance (V. Lance) & Associates. 1982. "A Study of Undocumented Workers in the State of Texas, March–July, 1982." Report prepared for the Governor's Budget and Planning Office (Austin: Tarrance & Associates).

U.S. Bureau of the Census. 1981. *Census of Population, 1980: Texas* (Washington, D.C.: U.S. Government Printing Office).

Villarreal, Roberto E., and Richard Gutierrez. 1978. "Mexican-American Attitudes toward Mexican Migration along the United States–Mexico Border." Paper prepared for presentation at the Western Social Science Association meeting, Denver.

Weintraub, Sidney, and Stanley R. Ross. 1980. *The Illegal Alien from Mexico* (Austin: The University of Texas at Austin, Mexico–United States Border Research Program).

17. THE POLITICAL SOCIALIZATION OF CHICANO ELITES: A GENERATIONAL APPROACH[1]

Rodolfo O. DE LA GARZA, *The University of Texas at Austin*

David VAUGHAN, *McDonnell Douglas Corporation*

This study rejects traditional explanations of elite socialization in favor of a generational model to explain the development of contemporary Chicano political elites. The context within which this generation of leaders was socialized is explained and a series of hypotheses are tested to determine the validity of the approach. The analyses support the validity of the generational approach and also indicate the salience of class over region in explaining the political socialization of Chicano leaders.

Studies of elite political socialization yield a pattern of findings that may or may not adequately explain the political attitudes and motivations of Anglo American elites, but these studies surely do not explain the development of political attitudes among Chicano political elites. Our purpose is to indicate why those explanations are not applicable to Chicano elites and to suggest an alternative explanation that is more appropriate to Chicano political experiences.

This study is potentially significant for several reasons. First, it enables us to determine the relative value of competing explanations of elite socialization and recruitment. Second, it contributes to our understanding of Chicano elites, a subject about which little or nothing is known. Given the increased role that Chicanos are playing in regional and national politics, such insights should be valuable to policymakers, the Chicano community, and the public at large. Finally, understanding Chicano elite socialization should enable us to formulate hypotheses about how they will define and carry out their roles. This is ultimately the question of greatest consequence to all groups including social scientists, policymakers, and Chicano constituents who are concerned with the place of the Chicano community in American political life.

[1] We would like to thank Dr. Mario García of the University of California, Santa Barbara, for his comments on an early draft of this paper.

Elite Political Socialization: A Literature Review

Studies of American elites show that preadult socialization has a persistent and significant effect on adult attitudes and political recruitment. Although the effect of early socialization does not uniformly affect adult attitudes on all issues, overall the assumption that the consequences of those early experiences would persist and affect adult orientations "turns out to have been relatively well founded" (Sears, 1975:137).

While the content of these early experiences for elites is unknown, the context seems relatively consistent. Stated differently, these studies do not document what it is that elites learned during their youth about society and politics, but they do indicate that political elites tend disproportionately to be raised within a rather economically and racially homogeneous, narrow stratum of American society. "One of the most persistent findings in the United States, at all levels of government, is the very small proportion of politicians with a working class background"; furthermore, "there are no major differences" in terms of social background between social and political elites (Czudnowski, 1975:181–82, 183).

Nonetheless, the significance of these findings is unclear because the specific relationship between these background variables and the content of political learning is unclear. These studies, in other words, do not document that elites have "been exposed to socializing experiences which could account for their choice of political career, i.e., events or influences which the remaining 95–98% of the population experience very infrequently or not at all" (Czudnowski, 1975:186–87).

The linkage between these background variables and political socializations seems to be a function of the opportunities available to children in affluent home environments. In view of the well-established correlations between education, income, and political participation (Verba and Nie, 1972) it follows that more affluent families also tend to be more politically active. The environment in such homes, then, is likely to differ from the environment in working-class homes in at least one and often two politically relevant dimensions. First, family conversations are more likely to focus on political issues. This is supported by findings that show that preadult political or activist socialization is more frequent among families with high occupational status, while politicians from lower-status origins develop their political orientations at a later age (Eulau and Koff, 1962). Second, family members in these homes are more likely to be more involved in civic and political affairs. Children from such families thus have active and intimate role models, and this may be why politicians so frequently come from politically active families (Prewitt, 1965; Browning, 1968; Eulau et al., 1959). Indeed, politically active role models also appear to play an important role in socializing children into volunteerism. Marvick and Nixon (1961) found that almost 40 percent of campaign workers came from families in which at least one parent was politically active.

Though important, the familial environment and socioeconomic factors alone cannot explain why some individuals rather than others embark on political careers. Numerous other variables such as opportunities (and barriers), personality, and intelligence, to name a few, also influence such decisions. Nonetheless, because these types of background characteristics are the factors most commonly associated with political careers historically and perhaps even today, it seems clear that the majority of American elites were socialized into politics primarily as a consequence of the preadult experiences they had in their homes or because of social and educational opportunities beyond the home afforded them by their families' socioeconomic status.

However appropriate this model may be for Anglo elites, the argument developed in this paper is that it contributes little to our understanding of Chicano elite socialization. To understand the political socialization of Chicano political elites requires a model that is sensitive both to Chicano political culture (García and de la Garza, 1977) and the personal experiences of Chicano leaders. Such a model is developed and tested below.

Chicano Elite Socialization: A Generational Approach

Mexican American political culture reflects the history of the Mexican American people from 1848 to the present. Two aspects of that total experience are particularly relevant to the analysis presented here. First, the Chicano population has long been and continues to be among the poorest and least educated group in the nation (Grebler, Moore, Guzman, 1970; U.S. Commission on Civil Rights, 1979; Carter, 1970; Carter and Segura, 1979). Second, Chicanos have been prevented from fully and freely participating in the political process (Grebler, Moore, Guzman, 1970; Shockley, 1974; Foley et al., 1977; García and de la Garza, 1977; Cotrell, 1980). It should therefore come as no surprise that Chicanos are not well informed about the political process (Grebler, Moore, and Guzman, 1970:567), and that they have a very low voter turnout rate (García and de la Garza, 1977). These factors also help explain why Chicano youth are less positive about American leaders and institutions than are Anglo youth (Sears, 1975; García, 1973; Gutierrez and Hirsch, 1973).

Given this history, it is most unlikely that current Chicano leaders have experienced the same type of political socialization as Anglo leaders. Instead, this paper argues that the political socialization of current Chicano leaders is best explained through a generational model (Rintala, 1979; Huntington, 1977; Alvarez, 1973).

A generational approach requires us to integrate the community's political culture with the personal experiences of current leadership for two reasons. First, it demands an understanding of prior generations so that we may distinguish between them and the new generation. Second, it obliges us to make explicit what this new generation shares in common and how that manifests itself attitudinally and behaviorally.

Before developing the model, however, it is important to define what a "political generation" is. Most significantly, it is not biologically defined. Instead, it should be considered "as a group of human beings who have undergone the same basic historical experiences during their formative years" (Rintala, 1979:8). It may and often does include more than one biological generation. Because of these shared experiences, a political generation will share attitudes and behavior. Its members may consider themselves a distinctive group, and they may also interact with each other and thus further strengthen their bonds (Huntington, 1977:9–10).

It is important to emphasize, however, that membership in a generation is not voluntary, and individuals may be part of a political generation without being aware of it. As Thomas Wolfe stated: "You belong to it, too. . . . You came along at the same time. You can't get away from it. You're part of it whether you want to be or not" (Rintala, 1979:4).

In order to support the hypothesis that current Chicano leaders represent a new political generation, therefore, it is necessary to demonstrate that they differ significantly from prior generations, and that they share a series of common experiences that affect their attitudes and behavior. Through this approach, then we may integrate the community's political culture with the personal experiences of current leadership to explain the political socialization of contemporary Chicano leaders.

The model developed here has a historical and an analytical component. The first succinctly interprets the political experiences of the Mexican American community from 1848 to 1980 and highlights the differences before and after 1970. The second empirically tests a series of hypotheses regarding the background experiences and motivations of contemporary Chicano leaders.

The data analyzed in the second part are from 241 interviews conducted between June 1978 and April 1980. The respondents were interviewed in Washington, D.C., El Paso, Austin, San Antonio, Tucson, Phoenix, Denver, Santa Fe, Albuquerque, Los Angeles, and Sacramento and include 42 appointees in the Carter administration, four of the five Spanish surname Congressmen, 42 elected state officials including legislators and statewide officeholders, and four former state-level officials including a governor, a cabinet member, a state legislator, and a secretary of state. Additionally, 65 community leaders representing 13 types of professional and voluntary associations were also interviewed, as were 25 individuals identified as community leaders through reputational techniques. This last category would have been much larger except that the great majority of individuals identified through reputational inquiries had already been interviewed because they held governmental or organizational positions and are therefore included in those categories. Only three officials, all Washington-based appointees, refused to be interviewed.

At the time this research was conducted, the offices included in this study represent the highest positions held by Chicanos.[2] To insure a sample size sufficient to permit statistical analysis, every effort was made to include as many officials as could be contacted. Thus, the respondents more closely approximate the universe of top-level state and national Chicano political officials as of 1980.

[2] For analytical purposes, all respondents are considered Chicanos even though the sample included less than 3 percent non-Chicano Hispanics.

Cost and time considerations as well as the transitory nature of many Chicano organizations made it impossible to draw a random sample of organizations or community spokespeople. Nonetheless, every effort was made to include a broad range of groups and individuals, and the sample includes representatives of local and national groups and professional associations concerned with economic development, women's issues, civil rights, Mexican culture, education, partisan politics, social services, and neighborhood issues.

The sample thus is representative of Chicano elites. It includes individuals in the private sector and various types of public sector positions who "are in positions to make decisions having major consequences. Whether they do or do not make such decisions is less important than the fact that they occupy such pivotal positions" (Mills, 1956:4).

The Development of a New Generation

For a brief period following the termination of hostilities with Mexico which the Treaty of Guadalupe Hidalgo formalized in 1848, some leaders of the conquered Mexican communities shared in the decision-making process of their new society. Several factors permitted these former Mexican (as opposed to Chicano) elites temporarily to occupy similar roles in their respective new communities (Weber, 1973; Acuña, 1981). First, in Texas, California, Colorado, and New Mexico, the regional concentration and size of the Mexican origin population were such that it was more reasonable to include the population and its leadership than to exclude them from political participation. Second, these communities were so well developed that they had produced leadership of such competence that the new Anglo elites could not easily dismiss it. Third, the support given to Texas independence by some Texas Mexican elites and the guarantees of the Treaty of Guadalupe Hidalgo which applied to all Mexican communities of the Southwest assured Mexican elites throughout the region of potentially important roles in the formative political activities of their new states. Finally, in these early years, the Anglo community in the region may have been tentative in its relationship with Chicanos because it had not developed the economic, political, or legal resources necessary to impose its will on them.

That first generation of Chicano elites played an important part in the political development of the Southwest. They made substantial contributions to the founding of the Texas Republic and had a small role in drafting the state constitution in 1845. In California, they were a key group at the state's constitutional convention and succeeded in passing legislation requiring state laws to be printed in both English and Spanish. They enjoyed similar success in Colorado. In New Mexico, Chicanos greatly outnumbered Anglos throughout the nineteenth century and had enjoyed a long history of autonomous institutional development. Thus they had an even greater role in shaping that territory's political structures and serving as its early public officials.

By the mid 1870s, Chicano participation in major governmental institutions effectively disappeared except in New Mexico. There, Chicanos continued to be the majority population in the state, and that enabled them to continue to play an important role in New Mexican political life. Even there, however, their role continuously declined, and although they continued to hold key offices, they did not continue to hold their proportional share of these and their voice in state issues grew weaker as the decades passed. In the other states, with rare exceptions, Chicanos would not again hold key positions either in major municipalities, in the state legislature, or in any offices determined by statewide elections until the 1970s (García and de la Garza, 1977; Cotrell, 1980). Those few individuals who did win occasional elective positions such as state or national legislators were either from districts that were so heavily Chicano that Anglo candidates simply could not challenge them or they served for one or perhaps two terms and were soon replaced by Anglo challengers. Unable to win elective offices, Chicanos also lacked the resources to gain any major administrative appointments throughout this period (Gomez, 1977; California State Advisory Commission on Civil Rights, 1971; Grebler, Moore, and Guzman, 1970). Clearly, during these decades Chicanos had no effective representation, and their views were seldom voiced in decision-making bodies.

Chicanos struggled continuously in a variety of ways to defend themselves as a community and enjoy the rights and privileges of citizenship. They resorted to arms (Harris and Saddler, 1978; Rosenbaum, 1981), they developed civic organization explicitly advocating "Americanization," and they established explicitly political organizations designed to make the major political parties and governmental institutions more responsive (Allsup, 1982; García and de la Garza, 1977). These efforts produced occasional ad hoc victories, but overall they did not alter the politically subordinate position of the Mexican American people. Thus, analysts agreed that by the 1960s the political role of Chicanos was little different than it had been for the previous century (Acuña, 1981; García and de la Garza, 1977).

Frustrated at these conditions and directly influenced by black civil rights activities, Chicanos began their own protest movement. Although these protests did yield programmatic developments in some areas, particularly in bilingual education, university admissions and academic programs such as Chicano studies, and migrant labor services, perhaps their most significant contribution was that they changed the views Chicanos and non-Chicanos alike had of the role Chicanos should play in American society (Schockley, 1974; Foley et al., 1977). In the Southwest, these protests led political elites to accept, however grudgingly, increased Chicano involvement in all aspects of public life (de la Garza, 1979). These activities also brought Chicano issues to the attention of national elites, and for the first time officials in Washington began to recognize and address these problems (Rankin, 1971; Inter-Agency Committee, 1967).

The consequences of these changes were such that by the late 1970s the Democratic party shifted from a position of excluding Chicanos to one of having groups such as the Mexican American Democrats (in Texas) and the Chicano-initiated Hispanic American Democrats become integrated parts of state and national party structures. Moreover, the extension of the Voting Rights Act to the Southwest in 1975 prohibited many of the practices that had been used to keep Chicanos out of office, and this led to dramatic and rapid increases in the number of elected Chicano officials at local levels, and to a lesser extent at state legislative levels (Cotrell, 1980; García and de la Garza, 1977).

Equally significant changes occurred within the Chicano community. First, by challenging the behavior of Chicano incumbents, the militants set the stage for the Chicano community at large to reexamine and redefine the expectations it had of its own leadership (Santillan, 1973:38–39; Castro, 1974). Second, the movement served as a training ground for many Chicanos who quickly moved from involvement with Raza Unida and student groups to leadership positions within the Democratic party and in government as elected and appointed officials (Acuña, 1981). Third, the changes achieved in university admissions policies and curriculum enabled new generations of Chicano students to benefit from college education in unprecedented numbers, and also introduced Chicano students at all levels to radically new perspectives on Chicano history and political life (Macias, Quiñones, and Castro, 1970; Gutierrez and Hirsch, 1973).

The confluence of these alterations in societal structures and practices and in the political socialization of the Chicano community set the stage for the creation of a new generation of Chicano leadership. At the societal level, new opportunities in small but growing numbers became available to Chicanos in many sectors of public life across the Southwest. Also, for the first time since the mid-nineteenth century the sociopolitical resources of the Chicano community were sufficient to require Anglo political elites to become at least symbolically responsive, and, thanks in part to improved educational opportunities, for the first time since the 1850s (Guzman, 1976), Chicanos had produced a generation of leaders whose competence and numbers could not be denied or ignored. Finally, at the community level, the events of the 1960s had infused this generation of leaders with new motivations and ambitions.

This is the context within which this new generation of leaders developed. As is true of all such generations, these leaders should resemble their predecessors in some ways and differ from them in others. Because of the socioeconomic homogeneity of Mexican Americans, we would predict this group to be similar to the general Chicano population in terms of family backgrounds and socioeconomic status. They should, in other words, be from working-class backgrounds and thus differ significantly from their Anglo peers who tend to come from upper-middle- and upper-class families. Because of the societal environments in which they were raised, they should also have experienced the racial discrimination that has been so much a part of Chicano reality.

This group should also differ from earlier generations in fundamental ways. Unlike earlier generations, these leaders were raised in an era during which the Chicano community began mobilizing politically en masse, and they also witnessed and may have participated in the militancy of the 1960s and 1970s. They are also likely to have been influenced by the hopeful rhetoric promising civil rights and social equality voiced by national political leaders during the past two decades. Thus, unlike Chicano officials who preceded them and also witnessed and experienced racial discrimination but were unwilling or unable to challenge such practices, it is hypothesized that the discriminatory experiences of this group are the principal factor explaining their political attitudes and public behavior. The next section tests these hypotheses.

Testing the Generational Model

As Table 1 shows, the respondents are overwhelmingly from working-class backgrounds. Almost 70 percent report that their parents did not even begin high school, and only 10 percent described their fathers as professionals.

Given these working-class backgrounds, the respondents report surprisingly high levels of familial political activity. While one-third state that politics was never discussed in their home, 41 percent state that such discussions were often held. However, the sample is equally divided between those who report politically active relatives and those who have no relatives in politics. Thirty-two percent indicated that members of their nuclear family were politically active, while 17 percent reported such activity only in their extended family. These politically active relatives, as Table 2 shows, are concentrated in local-level political activities, and many include involvement in local ethnic civic groups and labor organizations. Thus, while it seems that the respondents are from families with a well-established tradition of political involvement, the types of activities in which these

TABLE 1

Parents' and Respondents' Education and Occupation in Percentages

	Father		Mother		Respondent	
Education						
0–8	69%	(161)	62%	(146)	1	(2)
9–11	7	(17)	14	(33)	4	(10)
12	10	(23)	17	(40)	17	(40)
Some college	6	(15)	4	(10)	19	(45)
College graduate	6	(13)	2	(4)	42	(99)
College +	2	(5)	1	(3)	18	(43)
Missing	—	(7)	—	(5)	—	(2)
Total	—	(241)	—	(241)	—	(241)
Occupation						
Laborer	29%	(66)	11	(26)	—	—
Skilled laborer	30	(69)	4	(9)	2	(5)
Clerk	7	(16)	5	(13)	1	(2)
Business	16	(36)	3	(8)	13	(30)
Teacher	3	(6)	5	(13)	5	(11)
Professional	7	(16)	1	(3)	79	(188)
Farmer/rancher	9	(20)	—	—	1	(2)
Housewife	—	—	70	(163)	—	—
Missing	—	(12)	2	(6)	—	(3)
Total	—	(241)	—	(241)	—	(241)

NOTE: N's are given in parentheses.

TABLE 2

Positions Held by Politically Active Relatives

Elected or appointed officials		
1. Federal	1%	(1)
2. State	12	(13)
3. Local	22	(24)
Other		
1. Local party activist	11	(12)
2. Local community activist	28	(30)
3. Labor organizer	14	(15)
Mexican official	12	(13)
None	—	(116)
Missing	—	(17)

relatives were active do not appear to be the type to orient or motivate children toward careers in public service.

Other results support this interpretation. For example, only about 25 percent of the respondents indicate either that they became interested in politics at home, or that they became involved in politics as a result of family traditions. As hypothesized, furthermore, the majority of respondents also report having been discriminated against (84 percent) and that discrimination has continued into their adult and professional lives (81 percent).

Overall, these data show that our respondents share the historical experiences of the Mexican American community and thus meet one of the minimum conditions for utilizing a generational model. Clearly, Mexican American leaders differ from Anglo elites in terms of their socioeconomic backgrounds, and they also report the types of discriminatory experiences required in the model developed here. Two questions now remain to be answered. Most important, we must determine if those experiences help explain why these individuals become politically active. First, however, it is important to explain more fully the unexpectedly high level of familial political activity (Table 1) and the lower but still impressive number of respondents who become politically motivated as a result of familial experiences.

These higher than expected activity rates may reflect regional differences in the Chicano experience (Moore, 1970; Padilla and Ramirez, 1974). As indicated previously, the New Mexican experience has differed in varying degrees from experiences elsewhere in the Southwest. It may be, therefore, that these high rates are due to differences between New Mexican and all other southwestern Chicanos. If this hypothesis is correct, it will modify but significantly add to the validity of the generational model while also contributing to the ongoing debate regarding the regional variation of the Chicano experience.

A series of analyses were done to test whether New Mexican respondents do indeed differ from other respondents.[3] These involved cross-tabulation of New Mexican vs. other respondents against other relevant variables specified below. In four of the six cross-tabulations, significant differences were found between New Mexican and other respondents.

[3] Please contact the author for more detailed information regarding these analyses.

New Mexicans were significantly more likely (χ^2 (2) = 7.41, p < .05) to have fathers whose occupations reflected higher socioeconomic status (businessmen or professional, rather than clerical or laborers), although New Mexicans are not more likely (χ^2 (2) = 4.57, p > .05) to come from families in which political discussions occur, nor did New Mexican respondents differ from other respondents concerning whether their major source of political interest was the home, rather than school, college, or adult experiences (χ^2 (4) = 5.84, p > .05).

More important, however, New Mexican respondents are much more likely to have relatives who are active in politics (χ^2 (2) = 14.34, p < .001) and to have become politically active as a result of family traditions, rather than because of personal experiences and goals, such as civil rights and political experiences (χ^2 (4) = 9.89, p < .05). Furthermore, New Mexican respondents are much less likely to report having had any discriminatory experiences (χ^2 (1) = 8.90, p < .005).

The generational model thus appears not to be applicable to Chicanos in New Mexico. Unlike other Chicano elites, New Mexican elites seem to have been raised in relatively affluent homes where they were exposed to political discussions and benefited from familial political role models. Furthermore, as a group, they have not shared in the discriminatory experiences that are the foundation of the model developed here.

The final and most important issue is whether these discriminatory experiences or family background best explains why the resondents became involved in politics. The majority of respondents (53 percent) stated that discriminatory experiences were the major reason that they became politically active, and an additional 12 percent indicated that such experiences were one of several factors motivating them. More significantly, as the model predicts, variables such as age and home political environments are unrelated to the decision to become politically active. No significant association was found between age and the degree to which effects of discrimination were a factor in political involvement (χ^2 (6) = 3.94, p > .05). Likewise, no significant association was found between amount of familial political discussion and discrimination as a political motivation (χ^2 (4) = 8.23, p > .05) or between involvement of family members in politics and discrimination as a political motivation (χ^2 (4) = .45, p > .05).

However, discriminatory experiences and respondents' birthplace have statistically significant correlations with "participatory motivations." Having personally had discriminatory experiences was significantly associated with effects of discrimination being a factor in political involvement (χ^2 (2) = 19.69, p < .0001). Also, New Mexican respondents were significantly less likely to report effects of discrimination as a political motivation than other respondents (χ^2 (2) = 11.11, p < .005). It is noteworthy, moreover, that familial socioeconomic status is also associated with discrimination as a motivation for political involvement (χ^2 (4) = 16.13, p < .005), suggesting that those Chicanos from more affluent homes may have had socialization experiences somewhat comparable to those of Anglo elites. For example, 27 percent of those whose parent(s) were professionals indicated that discrimination was a major factor in their political motivations, compared to 61 percent of respondents from working-class families and 43 percent of those whose parents are businessmen or ranchers.

These analyses thus provide strong support for the generational approach developed here. They indicate that discriminatory experiences rather than background variables and age are associated with participatory motivations. Moreover, familial socioeconomic status is inversely correlated with the significance of discrimination as a motivating factor in becoming politically active. Through the application of a log-linear model, we may now combine these results into an integrated structural model to test the existence of the relationships thus far identified. The results of log-linear analysis used in this way approximate those produced by path analysis (Goodman, 1973).

The model tested here is shown in Figure 1.

The model hypothesizes that regional variations will be reflected in familial socioeconomic status, political involvement, and discriminatory experiences, and will also have an independent effect on participatory motivation. Also, it is hypothesized that the background variables will have no direct effect on participatory motivations but that discriminatory experiences will.

Each of the five variables of major concern here—birthplace, family in politics, father's occupation, discriminatory experiences, and participatory motivation—have, as originally gathered, many categories or values. In the integrated model log-linear analysis of these variables, a five-way contingency table is constructed with the number of cells equal to the product of the numbers of categories for each of the five variables. If the variables are used in their original forms, the number of cells in this five-way table is large relative to the number of observations in the data. Thus, for statistical reasons it is desirable to reduce the number of categories for each variable. This is also desirable from the standpoint of parsimony. Thus, for each of the five variables listed above, the number of categories was reduced by combining certain categories. Table 3 lists, for each of these variables, the categories before and after collapsing categories.

Categories for the variables were combined or collapsed on a rational basis—based primarily on meanings of the categories, rather than on in-

FIGURE 1

Model of Chicano Elite Political Socialization

TABLE 3

Variable Categories before and after Collapsing for Log-Linear Analysis

	Categories	
Variable	Before Collapse	After Collapse
Birthplace		
	New Mexico	New Mexico
	Arizona	
	California	Other
	Colorado	
	Texas	
	(Missing)	(Missing)
Family in politics		
	None	None
	Brother	Immediate family
	Father or mother	
	Grandparent	Other
	(Missing)	(Missing)
Father's occupation		
	Laborer	
	Skilled laborer	Worker
	Clerk	
	Businessman	Businessman/rancher
	Farmer/rancher	
	(Missing)	(Missing)
Discrimination experiences		
	None reported	None reported
	Not recent	Some
	Recent and continuous	
	(Missing)	(Missing)
Participatory motivation		
	Not conscious of discrimination	
	One fact of several	(No collapsing done)
	Definitely	
	(Missing)	

spection of the data. Nonetheless, it is desirable to test statistically the impact of collapsing categories as was done here. Results of such an analysis are presented in Table 4. In this table, results are presented concerning association of all pairs of the five variables. The χ^2 values are likelihood ratio χ^2's obtained from log-linear model analyses. The "full" χ^2's are based on the variables before categories were collapsed, while the "collapsed" χ^2's are based on analyses after the variables were collapsed. The "difference" χ^2's are tests of the null hypothesis that no association was lost by collapsing the categories of other variable in a particular pair. Significant association loss due to collapsing was obtained in only two of the nine pairs of variables. Only one significant association became nonsignificant after collapsing. Furthermore, in no case did a nonsignificant association become significant after collapsing. Thus, in our judgment, the statistical and parsimony advantages of collapsing categories of these five variables more than outweigh the relatively small loss of information resulting from the collapsing.

TABLE 4

Tests of Pairwise Association Loss between Variables Due
to Collapsing Categories

	Likelihood Ratios[a]					
	Full		Collapsed		Difference	
	χ^2	df	χ^2	df	χ^2	df
Birthplace by						
Family in politics	20.99*	12	14.33**	2	6.66	10
Father's occupation	48.48**	24	7.15*	2	41.33**	22
Discriminatory experiences	25.29**	8	9.15**	1	16.14*	7
Participatory motivation	19.20*	8	10.79**	2	8.41	6
Family in politics by						
Father's occupation	23.06	8	6.35	4	16.71	14
Discriminatory experiences	12.72*	6	4.43	2	8.29	4
Participatory motivation	11.02	6	7.40	4	3.62	2
Father's occupation by						
Discriminatory experiences	17.24	12	1.27	2	15.97	10
Participatory motivation	25.25*	12	15.97**	4	9.28	8
Discriminatory experiences by						
Participatory motivation	20.94**	4	19.20**	2	1.74	2

[a] χ^2 values are likelihood ratio χ^2's from pairwise log-linear model analysis of associations among variables before (full) and after categories were collapsed.

*$p < .05$.

**$p < .01$.

The model of Figure 1 has three ordered stages. The log-linear analysis of this model involves testing pairwise associations of each "causal" variable (variable to the left of others in Figure 1) with each "effect" variable (to the right in Figure 1), controlling for all other variables to the left of a given "effect" variable (Goodman, 1973).

Table 5 presents results of the log-linear analysis for those "causal"-"effect" variable pairs for which significant associations ("paths") were found. Included in Table 5 are estimates of model parameters (additive form) indicating the particular categories of each variable which are associated and the direction of the association.

The results of the log-linear analysis are summarized in Figure 2. Though these results only partially support the hypotheses related to Figure 1, overall they lend strong support to the generational model as originally developed. They indicate that although regional variation in the Chicano experience accounts for differences in family background and discriminatory experiences, it has no direct effect on participatory motivations. Father's occupation and discriminatory experiences, however, have a direct effect on participatory motivations, but each affects these differently. As the model parameters in Table 5 illustrate, the effect of discrimination is as predicted, i.e., it motivated individuals to become politically active. The model parameters also show that the effects of socioeconomic factors vary

TABLE 5

Model Parameters and χ^2 Likelihood Ratios for Figure 2

Path	df	χ^2 Likelihood Ratio	Significance	Model Parameters		

1. Birthplace to father's occupation — df 2, χ^2 = 7.15, Significance <.05

| Birthplace | Father's Occupation | | |
	Laborer	Businessman/Rancher	Professional
Southwest	.268	−.178	−.091
New Mexico	−.268	.178	.091

2. Birthplace to family in politics — df 2, χ^2 = 14.33, Significance <.01

| Birthplace | Family in Politics | | |
	None	Extended	Nuclear
Southwest	.349	−.047	−.301
New Mexico	−.349	.047	.301

3. Birthplace to discriminatory experiences — df 1, χ^2 = 9.15, Significance <.01

| Birthplace | Discriminatory Experiences | |
	Yes	No
Southwest	.306	−.306
New Mexico	−.306	.306

4. Father's occupation to participatory motivations — df 4, χ^2 = 11.72, Significance <.05

| Father's Occupation | Participatory Motivation | | |
	None	One of Several Factors	Major Factor
Laborer	−.211	−.125	.336
Businessman/Rancher	.233	−.261	.028
Professional	−.023	.387	−.364

5. Discriminatory experiences to participatory motivations — df 2, χ^2 = 11.14, Significance <.01

| Discriminatory Experiences | Participatory Motivation | | |
	None	One of Several Factors	Major Factor
No	.221	.132	−.353
Yes	−.221	−.132	.353

FIGURE 2

Revised Model of Chicano Elite Socialization

by levels of affluence and status. In other words, discriminatory experiences were an important factor affecting the participatory motivations of respondents from low-status families, but these experiences were relatively unimportant motivational sources for respondents from higher-status backgrounds. Together, these results indicate that New Mexican elites are much more likely to have been raised in more affluent and politically active families, and because they were raised in such circumstances they were much less likely to have experienced discrimination. However, those New Mexicans raised in families more typical of the environments in which Chicanos from elsewhere in the Southwest were raised, i.e., lower-class homes with politically inactive parents, appear to have become politically motivated as a result of discriminatory experiences, just as the great majority of southwestern Chicanos were. Similarly, discriminatory experiences were less important to southwestern Chicanos who were raised in exceptional circumstances, i.e., in more affluent and politically active families. Finally, for Chicanos raised in this type of home environment, it may be that discriminatory experiences combined with other types of socialization to influence their participatory motivations.

Thus, discriminatory experiences rather than familial characteristics are the best predictor of the participatory motivations of this generation of Chicano elites. These experiences may have substituted for typical familial characteristics or functioned as added incentives toward political involvement. In either case, as the model predicted, not only did the majority of respondents share in these experiences, but these experiences are a primary factor in their decision to become politically active. Furthermore, although regional differences account for variations in participatory motivations, the participatory motivations of Chicanos from working-class backgrounds tend to be the same whether these Chicanos are from New Mexico or elsewhere in the Southwest. Thus, class rather than region appears to be the principal factor explaining variations in the socialization of the Chicano community. That segment of New Mexico Chicano leaders who are from the lower classes should therefore also be considered members of this new generation.

Conclusion

Our objective has been to test an alternative model of elite socialization. Because of historical circumstances and current socioeconomic conditions, it was argued that parental socioeconomic characteristics could not adequately account for why Chicano elites become politically active in the way that those variables account for Anglo elite socialization. Instead, a generational model that was sensitive to historical issues and personal experiences was suggested to best explain Chicano elite socialization. The results of that analysis support the validity of this alternative approach. Chicano elites, especially those outside of New Mexico, do indeed come from a different and lower socioeconomic stratum, and overall they have had few political role models in their families. Instead, they became oriented toward and involved in politics primarily as a result of discriminatory experiences associated with their class background.

These findings suggest that Chicano elites should differ from Anglo elites in significant ways. We would hypothesize that they will define their roles differently, that they will advocate policies directly aimed at correcting the abuses which they have experienced, and that overall they will attempt to insure that Mexican Americans will no longer be the victims of discrimination in either the public or private sector. Subsequent studies will test these hypotheses. The results presented here, however, should help persuade Chicano constituents that this new generation of leaders understands the Mexican American historical experience and became politically involved in order to change it. In time, we will know if they have achieved their objectives.

REFERENCES

Acuña, Rodolfo. 1981. *Occupied America: A History of Chicanos*. 2d ed. (New York: Harper & Row).

Allsup, Carl. 1982. *The American G. I. Forum: Origins and Evolution*. University of Texas at Austin, Center for Mexican American Studies Monograph No. 6 (Austin: University of Texas Press).

Alvarez, Rodolfo. 1973. "The Socioeconomic and Psychohistorical Development of the Chicano Community in the U.S.," *Social Science Quarterly*, 53 (March):920–42.

Browning, Rufus, P. 1968. "The Interaction of Personality and Political System in Decisions to Run for Office: Some Data and a Simulation Technique," *Journal of Social Issues*, 24:93–109.

California State Advisory Commission on Civil Rights. 1971. *Political Participation with Mexican Americans in California*. August.

Carter, Thomas P. 1970. *Mexican Americans in School: A History of Educational Neglect* (New York: College Entrance Examination Board).

Carter, Thomas P., and Roberto D. Segura. 1979. *Mexican Americans in School: A Decade of Change* (New York: College Entrance Examination Board).

Castro, Tony. 1974. *Chicano Power: The Emergence of Mexican America* (New York: Saturday Review Press, E. P. Dutton and Co., Inc.).

Cotrell, Charles. 1980. *A Report on the Participation of Mexican-Americans, Blacks and Females in the Political Institutions and Processes in Texas*. Vol. 1 (Washington, D.C.: Texas Advisory Committee to the United States Commission on Civil Rights).

Czudnowski, Moshe M. 1975. "Political Recruitment," in Fred I. Greenstein and Nelson W. Polsby, eds., *Handbook of Political Science,* vol. 2 (Reading, Mass.: Addison-Wesley): pp. 155–242.

de la Garza, Rodolfo O. 1979. "Chicano Political Power: An Increasingly Important Role," *Empire* (Magazine of the *Denver Post*), 25 November ("Colorado's Hispanic Heritage"), pp. 12–25.

Eulau, Heinz, and David Koff. 1962. "Occupational Mobility and Political Career," *Western Political Quarterly,* 15 (September):507–21.

Eulau, Heinz, William Buchanan, Leroy Ferguson, and John C. Walke. 1959. "The Political Socialization of American State Legislators," *Midwest Journal of Political Science,* 3 (May):188–206.

Foley, Douglas E., and Clarice Mota, Donald E. Post, and Ignacio Lozano. 1977. *From Peones to Políticos: Ethnic Relations in a South Texas Town, 1900–1977* (Austin: University of Texas Press).

García, F. Chris. 1973. *Political Socialization of Chicano Children* (New York: Praeger).

García, F. Chris and Rudolph O. de la Garza. 1977. *The Chicano Political Experience: Three Perspectives* (North Scituate, Mass.: Duxbury Press).

Gomez, Rudolph. 1977. "Mexican Americans in American Bureaucracy," in Frank L. Baird, ed., *Mexican Americans: Political Power, Influence or Resource.* (Lubbock: Texas Tech University, Graduate Studies, no. 14, February): pp. 11–19.

Goodman, Leo A. 1973. "The Analysis of Multidimensional Contingency Tables When Some Variables Are Posterior to Others: A Modified Path Analysis Approach," *Biometrika,* 60:179–92.

Grebler, Leo, Joan Moore, and Ralph C. Guzman. 1970. *The Mexican American People: The Nation's Second Largest Minority* (New York: Free Press).

Gutierrez, Armando, and Herbert Hirsch. 1973. "The Militant Challenge to the American Ethos: 'Chicanos' and 'Mexican Americans'," *Social Science Quarterly,* 53 (March):830–45.

Guzman, Ralph C. 1976. *The Political Socialization of the Mexican-American People* (New York: Arno Press).

Harris, Charles N., III, and Louis R. Saddler. 1978. "The Plan of San Diego and the Mexican–United States War Crisis of 1916: A Re-examination," *Hispanic American Historical Review,* 58 (August):381–408.

Huntington, Samuel P. 1977. "Generations, Cycles, and Their Role in American Political Development," in Richard J. Samuels, ed., *Political Generations and Political Development* (Lexington, Mass.: Lexington Books): pp. 9–27.

Inter-Agency Committee on Mexican American Affairs. 1967. Testimony presented at the Cabinet Committee Hearings on Mexican American Affairs, El Paso, Texas: 26–27 October.

Macias, Reynaldo, Juan Gomez Quiñones, and Raymond Castro. 1970. "Objectives of Chicano Studies." University of California, Los Angeles, Mexican American Cultural Center, June.

Marvick, Dwaine, and Charles R. Nixon. 1961. "Recruitment Contrasts in Rival Campaign Groups," in Dwaine Marvick, ed., *Political Decision-Makers* (Glencoe, Ill.: Free Press).

Mills, C. Wright. 1956. *The Power Elite* (New York: Oxford University Press).

Moore, Joan. 1970. "Colonialism: The Case of the Mexican American," *Social Problems,* 17 (Spring):463–71.

Padilla, Fernando V., and Carlos B. Ramirez. 1974. "Patterns of Chicano Representation in California, Colorado and Nuevo Mexico," *Aztlan* (Spring/Fall):210–29.

Prewitt, Kenneth. 1965. "Political Socialization and Leadership Selection," *Annals of the American Academy of Political and Social Science,* 361 (September):91–111.

Rankin, Jerry. 1971. *Mexican American and Manpower Policy.* Ph.D. dissertation, University of Arizona.

Rintala, Marvin. 1979. *The Constitution of Silence* (Westport, Conn.: Greenwood).

Rosenbaum, Robert J. 1981. *Mexicano Resistance in the Southwest: The Sacred Right of Self-Preservation* (Austin: University of Texas Press).

Santillan, Richard. 1973. *La Raza Unida* (Los Angeles: Tlaquilo Publications).

Sears, David O. 1975. "Political Socialization," in Fred Greenstein and Nelson Polsby, eds., *The Handbook of Political Science* (Reading, Mass.: Addison-Wesley): pp. 93–153.

Shockley, John. 1974. *Chicano Revolt in a Texas Town* (Notre Dame, Ind.: University of Notre Dame Press).

U.S. Commission on Civil Rights. 1979. *Social Indicators of Equality for Minorities and Women* (Washington, D.C.: U.S. Government Printing Office).

Verba, Sidney, and Norman H. Nie. 1972. *Participation in America* (New York: Harper & Row).

Weber, David, ed. 1973. *Foreigners in Their Native Land: Historical Roots of the Mexican Americans* (Albuquerque: University of New Mexico Press).

18. HISPANIC REPRESENTATION IN THE U.S. CONGRESS

Susan WELCH, *University of Nebraska–Lincoln*

John R. HIBBING, *University of Nebraska–Lincoln*

Using data on representation and voting in the U.S. Congress from 1972 to 1980, the authors examine the impact of Hispanic constituencies and Hispanic representatives on roll call voting. Findings indicate that Hispanic representatives have a more liberal voting record than their non-Hispanic counterparts, even after controlling for salient party and constituency characteristics. Representatives with substantial numbers of Hispanic constituents also vote more liberally than their counterparts. Regional differences in the impact of Hispanic populations are also explored.

While political scientists are beginning to analyze the extent, nature, and consequences of Hispanic political representation at the local level (Taebel, 1978; Dye and Renick, 1981; Karnig and Welch, 1979; Welch, Karnig, and Eribes, in press [1983]), no systematic attention has been given to their representation in Congress. This omission is both curious and unfortunate in that 1 of every 16 people in the United States is of Hispanic ancestry. Perhaps the explanation for the lack of attention to Hispanic representation in Congress is that Hispanics make up a disproportionately small percentage of the population of Congress. As of 1980, only 1 out of every 87 members of the House of Representatives (5 out of 435) was Hispanic.[1] But we believe this fact is all the more reason to study Hispanic representation.

Representation: Descriptive and Substantive

We approach this subject by using Pitkin's (1972) definitions of two types of representation.[2] The first, descriptive representation, simply refers to the

---

[1] Since 1980, some changes have occurred. One Hispanic was appointed to the House in 1980 and three more were elected in 1982. Two more Hispanics—from Puerto Rico and the Virgin Islands—serve but do not vote in the House, so they have not been included in the analysis. All but one of the Hispanics—Robert Garcia of New York—are from the Southwest.

[2] Others have drawn contrasts similar to those of Pitkin's. Alvarez (1979), for example, contrasts "representativeness" with "representation." Representation is defined as advocacy on behalf of a group, with representativeness describing the equity of location of members of the group within an organization. These terms, then, are roughly analogous to Pitkin's substantive and descriptive representation.

ability of groups to elect representatives with similar traits—in this case, being of Hispanic ancestry. John Adams, for example, hoped the Congress would become an exact miniature of the entire populace in terms of relevant demographic characteristics. While this desire has not come to fruition, it is of interest to examine the degree to which Hispanic constituents are able to elect one of their own to the U.S. House.[3]

What factors facilitate the ability of a group to achieve descriptive representation? Their numerical strength, no doubt, is a primary consideration. Assuming voters usually vote for someone of their own group if possible (Karnig and Welch, 1981), the only way for a minority group to have a chance of securing adequate representation in a single-member district system is for that minority group to be heavily concentrated in some districts. This is why district elections to city councils provide nearly equitable representation for blacks in white majority cities, but at-large elections do not (Karnig and Welch, 1981; Engstrom and McDonald, 1982). In Congress, too, black majority districts in recent years have normally sent black representatives to Congress. In the 97th Congress (1981–82), only two black majority districts had white representatives, while in only three districts where blacks were a minority were blacks elected.

The numerical strength of the Hispanic population in electing representatives is diluted by the fact that many Hispanics are not citizens. About one-fourth of the Hispanics counted in the Census were foreign-born. While many of these are citizens, many are not. This situation has implications for descriptive representation. It means that a minority of the Hispanic population have no voice in choosing their representatives. Thus the potential for equitable descriptive representation is likely to reflect not the total population but the smaller citizen population. We have not seen data on Hispanic noncitizens by congressional district. However, it is very likely that the highest proportions of noncitizens are in those districts with the largest Hispanic populations, those we might expect to be most likely to elect Hispanic representatives.

In addition to descriptive representation, one can also be represented substantively, that is by having a representative with congruent policy views (Pitkin, 1967) acting as an advocate. This means that a group can be represented without having its own members in representative roles, but rather by having its representatives act and vote in accordance with its policy preferences. If a group consensus is strong on a set of policy issues, we can say that the group is being represented in a substantive sense if representatives vote in accord with this consensus.

The problem in measuring substantive representation is that it is often difficult to determine whether or not a consensus exists on policy issues. Hispanics are not a homogenous group; unlike blacks, for example, they do not vote uniformly for Democrats. However, with the possible exception of Florida's Cuban population and some well-established groups in the

---

[3] The House of Representatives is used because of the special status it was and is accorded as a representative body. With smaller constituencies and more frequent elections, members of the House should be attuned to their constituents if anyone at the federal level is.

Southwest, we would expect Hispanics, on the whole, to be more liberal than Anglos, more likely to favor government intervention in the marketplace and in protecting individual rights.

Again, the large noncitizen component of the Hispanic population complicates our understanding. One might expect that substantive representation would refer to representation of the whole population and not just its citizen subset. Yet representatives might feel little obligation to provide substantive representation for noncitizens, especially when their interests conflict with those of constituents who are permitted to vote. In our examination of substantive representation, we explored the effect of the total Hispanic population as measured in the decennial Census.

In this analysis we examined the following questions:

1. How many of the districts with significant Hispanic populations elect Hispanic representatives?

2. Do Hispanic representatives adopt a distinctive pattern of roll call voting?

3. Do large Hispanic populations have an effect on the voting behavior of their representatives?

To conduct this analysis, we employed data on the personal traits and voting records of U.S. representatives as well as information on the nature of the various congressional districts, particularly the percentage of the district's population that is of Hispanic descent. Our study covers the period 1972–80 (the 93d through the 96th congresses).[4]

Findings

The distribution throughout the nation of the Hispanic population can help explain why Hispanics are descriptively underrepresented. Only 6 percent of the nation's congressional districts (27) have constituencies that are over one-fourth Hispanic, and only eight districts are over 50 percent Hispanic—six in the Southwest (defined as Texas, California, New Mexico, Arizona, and Colorado), and one each in the New Jersey–New York area and in Florida. Clearly, then, while the Hispanic presence is a significant one, the distribution is highly skewed with the great majority of congressional districts (308) containing Hispanic populations that are 5 percent or less of the total district population.

A majority Hispanic population in the district is no guarantee that the district will be represented by a Hispanic, although it certainly does im-

---

[4] Though it would have been useful to include the 98th Congress in our analysis, detailed information about the demographic characteristics of the newly redrawn districts is not available at this writing. (Neither are scales of roll call voting since the Congress is still in progress.) Our primary sources of data are the *Congressional Quarterly Almanac* (1972–80, various volumes) and the *Almanac of American Politics* (Barone et al., 1972–82, various editions). Since members of Congress build distinct voting records in every Congress, we have treated each representative's record in each of these two-year periods as a unique case. Thus, the total possible N for the project was 1,740 (4 × 435), even though the total number of individuals serving during these eight years was much lower. A few of these 1,740 voting records had to be removed because they were not compiled over the course of an entire Congress.

prove the odds. In 1980, for example, only four of the eight majority Hispanic districts had Hispanic representatives.[5] Some of these eight districts undoubtedly did not have a majority of Hispanics who were citizens, much less voters. Of all the districts without Hispanic majorities, only one (the 1st District of New Mexico, with 43 percent Hispanic) had a Hispanic representative. The fact that districts with 26–49 percent Hispanic populations could muster only one Hispanic representative is not surprising in light of the similar pattern for blacks noted earlier. Further, the fact that some portion of this Hispanic population was not enfranchised means that their actual political clout was even less than their sheer numbers indicated.

Descriptive representation may not mean substantive representation at all. Cynics may argue that members of minority groups who are in high positions have been coopted by the majority elites and that the value of such a representative to the minority community is symbolic only. To determine if Hispanics vote differently, we focused on the conservative coalition support scores compiled by all representatives in four recent congresses.[6] We attempted to explain variations in this score by whether or not the representative compiling the voting record was Hispanic. Since there were only a few Hispanic representatives, our findings are tentative, but our expectation was that the roll call behavior of Hispanics would be significantly different from that of non-Hispanics. If the relationship operated as expected, Hispanic representatives, other things being equal, should build more liberal voting records than their non-Hispanic counterparts. This assumption was based on the lower socioeconomic status of Hispanics and the commitment of Mexican Americans and Puerto Ricans to the Democratic party (Grebler, Moore, and Guzman, 1970; Levy and Kramer, 1973).

One could also examine Hispanic voting patterns by using votes on specific legislation as dependent variables. While this might have the advantage of allowing a focus on legislation more particularly of relevance to Hispanics (such as immigration law) rather than a wide array of legislation, the narrower approach also has limitations. What votes should be chosen? How many roll call votes deal specifically with Hispanic interests? In spite of the appeal of a case study approach, using a narrow definition of "Hispanic interest" votes might result in so few votes as to capture idiosyncratic voting patterns rather than larger underlying predispositions. Thus, while future researchers may want to fine-tune our analysis by examining individual issues, this "first pass" will be more beneficial if it provides a broad view.

We regressed conservative coalition support scores on whether or not the representative was a Hispanic. We also included in the regression the

[5] The others:
California's 30th District, 62 percent Hispanic, represented by George Danielson;
Florida's 14th District, 55 percent Hispanic, represented by Claude Pepper;
Texas's 16th District, 57 percent Hispanic, represented by Richard White;
Texas's 23d District, 53 percent Hispanic, represented by Abraham Kazen.

[6] These scores are altered by failure to vote, so we have undertaken the standard correction procedures. See Poole, 1981. The use of adjusted conservative coalition support scores as a measure of ideological voting is made attractive by Poole's finding that this measure correlates more strongly than any other with an overall conservative-liberal dimension.

party identification of the representative, as well as other variables generally believed to affect the voting behavior of representatives: the percent urban population in the district, the percent black in the district, and the percentage of the district's population with incomes ranking below the poverty line. Because these variables have known relationships with roll call voting, they are necessary in order to specify properly the equation. With them included, we were better able to isolate the true influence of being a Hispanic on roll call behavior.

Table 1 provides both the standardized and unstandardized coefficients as well as tests of significance. By concentrating on the unstandardized coefficients we see that, other things being equal, a Hispanic representative would be predicted to have a voting record that is nearly 13 points less conservative than a non-Hispanic representative. Table 1 also provides separate results for the two regions with Hispanic representatives in the 1970s—the Southwest and the New York–New Jersey area. When this division is made, we see that the strength of the overall relationship derives almost exclusively from the Southwest. For New York and New Jersey, the relationship was not significant and the size of the coefficient was quite small. For the Southwest, however, the coefficient was quite large, indicating that Hispanic representatives, on average, compiled voting records over 23 points less conservative than non-Hispanic representatives in the Southwest. This relationship easily achieved traditional levels of significance. Despite the small number of Hispanic representatives, we can say with some certainty that Hispanic representatives were more liberal than their non-Hispanic counterparts, controlling for party and constituency factors. Thus, from the perspective of the typical Hispanic constituent, residing in a district with a Hispanic representative did make a difference.

Of course, it is possible for the concerns of Hispanics to be represented by non-Hispanics. Substantive representation may occur despite the lack of descriptive representation. In fact, given the small number of Hispanic representatives, this would appear to be the major way Hispanics are currently represented in the U.S. Congress. We hypothesized that substantive representation would have taken place to the extent that the more Hispan-

TABLE 1

Hispanic Representatives and Conservative Coalition Support Scores

	Pearson's *r*	Beta	*b* (standard error)		*N*
All districts with 5 percent or more Hispanics	.04[a]	−0.07*[b]	−12.6	(6.0)	501
Southwest	.05	−0.15*	−23.2	(9.1)	304
New York–New Jersey area	−.16*	−0.02	−3.1	(10.0)	214

[a] Correlation of whether or not representative is a Hispanic with conservative coalition support scores.

[b] Relationship of conservative coalition support scores to being a Hispanic, controlling for constituency and personal characteristics described in text.

* $p \leq .05$.

ics there were in a congressional district, the more likely the representative would vote in a liberal manner.

Again using the roll call records from four recent congresses, we regressed conservative coalition voting scores on the percent Hispanic in the district. We used the same controls as in our earlier regression plus a dummy variable indicating whether or not the representative was a Hispanic. We limited the analysis to only those districts with at least a 5 percent Hispanic population. This restriction seems appropriate since there is no basis for an expectation that an extremely small Hispanic constituency will have a discernible impact on the roll call voting of representatives.[7]

As the top line of Table 2 demonstrates, the relationship was in the hypothesized direction (the more Hispanics in a district, the less conservative the roll call voting of the representative), and was significant at the .05 level. Though the R^2 was a respectable .67, meaning all the independent variables accounted for about two-thirds of the variance in the conservative coalition support scores, the size of the coefficient for percent Hispanic was not large. Since the unstandardized coefficient (b) was 0.19, an increase of about 5 percent in Hispanic population would lead to a decrease in the level of conservative voting by the pertinent representative of only about one point, *ceteris paribus*. So, while the relationship is significant and in the expected direction, it is not extremely powerful.[8]

When we performed separate analyses for the three areas of the country with major Hispanic concentrations—the Southwest, Florida, and the New York–New Jersey area, the relationship was in the predicted direction in all three regions (see Table 2). However, the coefficient fell short of significance in the Southwest even though there were more cases in this region than the others. In the New York and New Jersey area and especially in Florida the relationship was easily significant and the coefficients were much larger. In fact, in Florida every 5 percent increase in percent Hispanic

TABLE 2

Relationship of Percent Hispanic to Conservative Coalition Support Scores

	Mean Percent Hispanic	Beta[a]	b	(standard error)	R^2, All Variables	N
All districts with 5 percent or more Hispanics	18.2	−0.08*	−0.19	(0.09)	.67	501
Southwest	20.0	−0.09	−0.19	(0.12)	.52	304
New York–New Jersey area	9.6	−0.23*	−0.58	(0.16)	.75	214
Florida	9.5	−0.60*	−1.20	(0.13)	.81	60

a Controlling for percent urban, percent below poverty line, party, percent black, region (in national equations), and Hispanic representative.

[7] Even with this restriction the N is still over 500, indicating there were approximately 125 districts in each of these 4 congresses with 5 percent or more Hispanic population.

[8] Unlike the situation with the translation of black demands into roll call votes, there appears to be no curvilinearity in the relationship between number of Hispanics in a district and roll call voting (see Bullock, 1981; Black, 1978).

in a congressional district would lead to a 6 point drop in conservative voting on the part of the representative, other things being equal. This finding might seem surprising in light of accepted wisdom about Hispanics in the Southwest being more liberal than other Hispanics. However, in Florida, many districts are very conservative.[9] Thus, representatives from Florida districts with larger Hispanic populations are more liberal than those from other Florida districts, but not necessarily more liberal than non-Florida representatives with large Hispanic constituencies.

Implications

Though Hispanics are not heard in the U.S. Congress as clearly as their numbers imply they should be, their concerns and desires are not ignored completely. We have found that the number of Hispanics in a district is important in explaining the type of representation the district will receive. Not surprisingly, increased numbers of Hispanics improve the chances a district will elect a Hispanic. But given the paltry number of Hispanics in the House—an increase of only 3 Hispanics in the 98th Congress amounted to a 50 percent increase over the 97th Congress—the major implication of our research, and the most realistic immediate hope for most Hispanics, is that non-Hispanic representatives will be somewhat responsive to the needs of Hispanic constituents.

Here we find that increases in the number of Hispanics produce representatives whose voting records indicate greater support for the liberal programs favored by the majority of Hispanic voters. In two districts that were identical in number of blacks, percentage of the district's population living in central cities, race and party of the representatives, and percentage of the constituency living below the poverty line, identical in just about every way except that one district had a 5 percent Hispanic population and the other had a 50 percent Hispanic population, our findings indicate that the roll call voting of the representative of the former district would have been about 8 or 9 points more conservative than the record compiled by the representative of the heavily Hispanic district. Thus, in the U.S. House, Hispanics do not lack influence; they just lack the influence their numbers warrant.

Our research on Hispanic congressional representation has been exploratory and hence rather general. We must await the election of more Hispanic representatives to draw firm conclusions about their behavior. As more Hispanics are elected, we will need to examine their achievement of leadership positions and important relevant committee assignments. Other possible fruitful research directions include testing generalizations about conservative voting on legislation specifically concerning Hispanics, such

[9] Mean conservative coalition score for each region:

Florida	67.9
Southwest	54.9
New York–New Jersey	33.7

as policies on immigration, farm labor, bilingual education, and those directed toward low-income populations. And, of course, scholars interested in Hispanic politics will need to monitor carefully patterns of apportionment as they relate to Hispanic representation.

REFERENCES

Alvarez, Rodolfo. 1979. "Institutional Discrimination in Organizations and Their Environment," in Rodolfo Alvarez, Kenneth G. Lutterman, and Associates, eds., *Discrimination in Organizations* (San Francisco: Jossey-Bass).

Barone, Michael, et al. 1972–82. *The Almanac of American Politics.* Various editions (New York: Dutton).

Black, Merle. 1978. "Racial Composition of Congressional Districts and Support for Federal Voting Rights in the American South," *Social Science Quarterly,* 59 (December):435–50.

Bullock, Charles. 1981. "Congressional Voting and the Mobilization of a Black Electorate in the South," *Journal of Politics,* 43 (August):662–82.

Congressional Quarterly Almanac. 1972–80. Various volumes (Washington, D.C.: Congressional Quarterly, Inc.).

Dye, Thomas, and James Renick. 1981. "Political Power and City Jobs: Determinants of Minority Employment," *Social Science Quarterly,* 62 (September):475–86.

Engstrom, Richard L., and Michael D. McDonald. 1982. "The Underrepresentation of Blacks on City Councils: Comparing the Structural and Socioeconomic Explanations for South/Non-South Differences," *Journal of Politics,* 44 (November):1088–99.

Grebler, Leo, Joan W. Moore, and Ralph C. Guzman. 1970. *The Mexican-American People* (New York: Free Press).

Karnig, Albert K., and Susan Welch. 1979. "Sex and Ethnicity in Municipal Representation," *Social Science Quarterly,* 60 (December):465–81.

———. 1981. *Black Representation and Urban Policy* (Chicago: University of Chicago Press).

Levy, Mark, and Michael S. Kramer. 1973. *The Ethnic Factor* (New York: Simon & Schuster).

Pitkin, Hanna. 1967. *The Concept of Representation* (Berkeley: University of California Press).

Poole, Keith T. 1981. "Dimensions of Interest Group Evaluation of the U.S. Senate: 1969–1978," *American Journal of Political Science,* 25 (February):49–67.

Taebel, Delbert. 1978. "Minority Representation on City Councils," *Social Science Quarterly,* 59 (June):142–52.

Welch, Susan, Albert K. Karnig, and Richard Eribes. In press, 1983. "Changes in Hispanic Local Public Employment in the Southwest," *Western Political Quarterly.*

19. CONFLICT AND CONTROVERSY IN THE EVOLUTION OF BILINGUAL EDUCATION IN THE UNITED STATES—AN INTERPRETATION

Guadalupe SAN MIGUEL, Jr., *University of California, Santa Barbara*

This essay develops a historical interpretation of the political developments in bilingual education policy in the United States. It covers the period from the mid 1960s to 1982, with illustration of the manner in which several distinct political factions have struggled with each other to shape the final outcome of federal bilingual education policy.

Bilingual education enjoyed widespread support from legislators, political leaders, and special interest groups during the early 1970s, but by the end of the decade this had dwindled and in many cases turned into active educational and political opposition. Educational debates over the goals, content, effectiveness, and costs of bilingual education were reflected in the news media, scholarly journals, and government reports (Epstein, 1977; American Institute for Research, 1977; Bethel, 1979; Pifer, 1979, Stanfield, 1980; Edwards, 1980; Baker and de Kanter, 1981; Birman and Ginsburg, 1981). Political opposition to bilingual education was reflected in the efforts to modify or eliminate bilingual education policies, laws, and regulations at all levels of government (Schneider, 1976; Vega, 1983; Lyons, 1983).

What explains this high level of conflict and controversy in bilingual education? Also, what role have special interest groups played in this development? It is my contention that the basis for conflict in bilingual education lies in the different views that special interest groups have toward the role that language and culture play in the education of language minority groups. One perspective, shared largely by minority organizations and their political allies, views the native language and culture of the minority child as integral to the instructional process. Those sharing this particular philosophical perspective I call the *pluralists* since they view the plurality of languages as a necessary ingredient of American education (Andersson and Boyer, 1970, 1978; Cordasco, 1968).

The other dominant perspective, shared primarily by associations of school administrators and their political allies, views the minority native language and culture as incidental to the instructional process and to educational progress. Those sharing this perspective I refer to as the *assimilationists* since they, as a rule, do not recognize the value or utility of incorporating the language and culture of the minority child into the curriculum of the public schools (Birman and Ginsburg, 1981; Baker and de Kanter, 1981).

The involvement of special interest groups with clashing philosophical perspectives of the role minority languages and cultures play in the classroom has led to increasing conflict in bilingual education. This conflict is accentuated as political conditions change and as larger numbers of special interest groups become involved in the shaping of bilingual education policy. In this essay, federal bilingual education policy will be traced in order to illustrate the manner in which special interest groups with clashing perspectives have struggled with each other to shape the final outcome of one specific national educational program. This essay will also discuss the various judicial, administrative, executive, legislative, and political means special interest groups in bilingual education have used to accomplish their purposes.

Bilingual Education and the Ascendancy of the Pluralists

The first bilingual education bill was enacted by Congress in December 1967 and signed into law one month later by President Lyndon Baines Johnson. The purpose of the Bilingual Education Act of 1968 was twofold: (1) to encourage the recognition of the special educational needs of limited-English-speaking children and (2) to provide financial assistance to local educational agencies to develop and carry out new and imaginative public school programs designed to meet these special educational needs (U.S. Statutes at Large, 1968).

There were three important aspects to this new bill. First, congress did not specify any one single approach to instructing limited-English-speaking children. A variety of educational programs in addition to bilingual ones were eligible for funding under the new bill. Second, in keeping with federal legislative tradition, the bilingual education bill was categorical in nature and compensatory in intent. Categorical funds were provided by the federal government to local educational agencies to support services of a particular type or for a particular category of students. Under this new bill, funds were to be used to develop compensatory educational programs for those students who were limited in their ability to speak English and who came from low-income homes, i.e., those that were economically and linguistically "disadvantaged." Third, the bilingual education bill continued the principle of local control by allowing local school districts the option of participating in this federal program.

During the next several years, the proponents of bilingual education began to transform bilingual education from a minor curricular innovation aimed at teaching English only into a major reform aimed at introducing the non-English languages of low-status groups into the public schools

(Cordasco, 1968; Andersson and Boyer, 1970; Kobrick, 1972). In order to successfully transform the character of bilingual education, the proponents of this new program called upon the assistance of the federal bureaucracy. And for the next decade, the federal government became an indispensable ally to the proponents of bilingual education.

The first instance of federal involvement in promoting bilingual education occurred in 1970. On 25 May of that year, the supporters of bilingual education prompted the Office for Civil Rights to issue an important departmental policy statement which clarified the local school district's responsibility toward language minority children.

This important memo was sent to all·school districts with more than 5 percent national origin minority group children. It identified four major areas of concern related to the education of language minority children. Two of these forbade local school districts from assigning students to classes for the mentally retarded or to low-ability groups on the basis of language. One other area of concern noted that school districts had a responsibility to notify the parents of national origin minority children of regular school activities in their own language. The final one, which was given high priority by the Office for Civil Rights, stipulated that local school districts had a responsibility to "take affirmative steps to rectify the language deficiency" of these children in order to open its instructional program to them (Pottinger, 1970:2).

Although the 25 May memo was sent to several hundred school districts throughout the country, it had little impact on local educational policy. Most of these districts failed to follow the directives of this memo or to develop special educational programs aimed at providing native-language instruction for non-English-speaking children.

Two months after the 25 May memo, the Chinese American community in San Francisco asked the federal courts to force the local school district to provide special language programs and services to approximately 3,000 non-English-speaking Chinese students. After four years of litigation and with the support of other minority and legal organizations, the U.S. Supreme Court, on 14 January 1974, reached a decision in the *Lau vs. Nichols* case.[1]

In this important case the plaintiffs argued that the San Francisco Independent School District violated the constitutional rights of non-English-speaking Chinese students by failing to provide them with English language instruction or "with other adequate instructional procedures" (*Lau v. Nichols*, 1974). Defendants denied this charge and argued that the district had no legal responsibility to provide them with special language services. The Court agreed with the plaintiffs and stated that failure to provide non-English-speaking Chinese students with understandable instruction denied them their right to an equal education.

In its decision, the Court affirmed the 25 May memo and argued that federally funded school districts had to affirmatively provide to national

---

[1] The first judicially mandated bilingual education program occurred in 1971. See *United States v. State of Texas* (1972).

origin minority students with English language disabilities services which would secure to them equal access to the instructional program. The Court avoided prescribing a particular remedy and, as in all educational rights lawsuits, sent the case back to the lower court to forge an appropriate remedy (*Lau v. Nichols*, 1974).

While the Court did not mandate bilingual education, the pluralists used this particular decision to strengthen their case for demanding a more comprehensive language-based approach to instructing minority children and to shift the focus of bilingual education away from a compensatory perspective (Orfield, 1978:221). During the next several years, the pluralists won significant court decisions which judicially recognized bilingual education programs as the most appropriate method for teaching language minority children and for providing them with equal access to the instructional program.[2]

In the same year the *Lau* decision was reached, minority organizations and their political allies in Washington succeeded in amending and expanding the scope of the Bilingual Education Act of 1968. The new bilingual education bill differed in several respects from the original one of 1967.[3]

First, the coverage of the program was expanded to include all limited-English-speaking students regardless of socioeconomic status, and the experimental nature of the bilingual technique was de-emphasized. Second, the goals of bilingual education were broadened to include not only developing proficiency in English, but also providing instruction in the primary language and the cultural heritage of the student.

Most importantly, the overall objectives were expanded to include activities aimed at developing bilingual resources for present and future needs. This new aspect of the bill provided financial assistance for preparing personnel to staff bilingual programs, for providing technical assistance leading to the development of bilingual programs and for conducting and disseminating research on program effectiveness.

In order to more effectively supervise, evaluate, and monitor the implementation of this revised bill, the act also established a national bilingual education office and called for the appointment of a director to head this important program (*U.S. Statutes at Large*, 1974).

Unsatisfied with the impact of their judical and legislative successes on local school systems, the pluralists encouraged the Office for Civil Rights and the Department of Health, Education, and Welfare to engage in several actions which increased the federal role in bilingual education and which strengthened the trend of recognizing only one specific approach to instructing language minority children.

First, the Office for Civil Rights, encouraged by the *Lau* decision and pressured by minority organizations, initiated steps to outline and enforce the "affirmative steps" required of school districts to rectify the English

---

[2] For an overview of these cases see Teitelbaum and Hiller (1979).
[3] See Schneider (1976) for an analysis of the enactment of this bill and the impact the *Lau* decision had on its passage.

language "deficiencies" of language minority children. In January 1975, for instance, the Office for Civil Rights identified 333 local school districts out of compliance with the *Lau* decision and in April it announced the start of a compliance review of these 333 local school districts (Teitelbaum and Hiller, 1979:47).

Second, in an effort to provide guidelines to local school districts on complying with the *Lau* decision and to some extent with the new Bilingual Education Act of 1974, a national task force comprised largely of educators sympathetic to minorities formulated and issued the "Lau remedies" during the summer of 1975 (Office for Civil Rights, 1975). This document outlined appropriate educational approach for teaching the non-English-dominant students and for complying with the *Lau* decision. But this document actually went beyond the *Lau* decision and reinterpreted its findings. It argued for a comprehensive approach to teaching language minority students. It stipulated that in order to be in compliance with *Lau*, local educational agencies had to (a) develop elaborate procedures for identifying language minority school children, (b) assess the children's language proficiency, and (c) prescribe an appropriate bilingual educational program for non- or limited-English-speaking students. Local school districts also had to ensure that no curricular or placement practices had the effect of discriminating against language minority students, require the instructional staff to be linguistically and culturally familiar with the background of language minority students in class, and provide for adequate and periodic evaluations of the progress made in implementing the prescribed educational program (Office for Civil Rights, 1975).

Most importantly, the Lau remedies stipulated that instruction in English as a second language (ESL) by itself was not an appropriate remedy for language minority children and that the only instructional approach which would comply with the *Lau* decision was bilingual education.[4] It also put the burden on local school districts to come up with alternative educational plans that would work if they chose not to develop bilingual education. According to the document, if school districts were in violation of *Lau*, they had to develop compliance plans consistent with the Lau remedies or demonstrate affirmatively that alternative plans would be "equally effective in ensuring equal educational opportunity."[5] Although there was a careful retreat by the Office for Civil Rights as a result of the subsequent furor regarding the legality of the Lau remedies, the burden of proving the ac-

[4] Teitelbaum and Hiller (1979:30) argue that the Lau remedies did not mandate bilingual education. But in order for local schools to be in compliance with *Lau* they had to develop bilingual education programs for these children since ESL or other approaches were not allowable under the Lau remedies.

[5] Teitelbaum and Hiller (1979:48) quote Lloyd R. Henderson, Director, Elementary and Secondary Education Division, Office for Civil Rights who, in a letter to Rosa Castro Feinberg, Lau General Assistance Center B, School Education, University of Miami, on 15 March 1976 stated: "Conceivably, other methods of achieving the goals set by the 'Lau remedies' may exist, but the Office for Civil Rights will accept an alternative approach only if there is a reasonable basis to believe that it is at least as effective as the guidance set in the 'Lau remedies.' "

ceptability of an effective alternative to bilingual education rested upon the local school districts (Zirkel, 1978:50; Teitelbaum and Hiller, 1979:30).

The significance of all these documents and actions by the federal courts and agencies was quite apparent by 1976. The character of bilingual education as reflected in the 1967 bill had been transformed. As a result of federal directives and initiatives, bilingual education was not a compensatory program to be implemented on a voluntary basis; it was now a comprehensive and mandatory language-based approach to teaching all non-English-speaking minority children, regardless of socioeconomic background.

Initially, school districts wishing to develop bilingual education programs could do so at their own discretion. But by 1976 school districts having 20 or more national origin minority children of the same language group other than English had to develop bilingual education programs or be out of compliance with *Lau* and possibly lose their federal funds.[6] The possibility of losing needed funds for being out of compliance as well as the fundamental transformation of a compensatory educational program set the stage for the eventual ascendancy of those individuals and groups who believed that the program had gone too far in its intent as well as in its result.

The Emerging Criticism of and Opposition to Bilingual Education

During the next several years, largely from 1977 through 1980, the assimilationists struggled with the pluralists to gain the upper hand in education and to chip away at the tremendous growth of federal involvement in local education. Journalists, school personnel, legislators, and others worked together to challenge the need for sustained instruction in other languages besides English and to return to the original conception of bilingual education as a compensatory and voluntary program.

Criticism of bilingual education was not a new phenomenon. Congressional legislators, teacher union leaders, and others had raised questions about the goals and purposes of this program during the mid 1970s (Edwards, 1980). But these early critics were ineffective, unorganized, and limited to certain policymaking arenas such as congressional hearings. They also lacked sufficient evaluative data to challenge the need for bilingual education. By the late 1970s, a new round of reports critical of the goals and effectiveness of dual language instruction in the public schools began to appear. These reports became useful instruments in the campaign to halt the expansion of bilingual education instruction in the public schools.

For instance, in 1977 two important reports critical of bilingual education programs were published. One of these was an interim report of the first

---

[6] Teitelbaum and Hiller (1979:30) also stated that school districts with at least one limited-English-speaking-ability child were obliged to take affirmative steps, but these did not have to be as extensive and comprehensive as the educational program for those districts having 20 or more students whose language was other than English.

national evaluation of Spanish-English bilingual education programs. This evaluation was conducted by the American Institute for Research, a private educational research firm, and issued in April by the U.S. Office of Education.

The evaluation study examined 38 fourth year and fifth year projects for Hispanic American students. It found that less than 30 percent of the participating children were actually limited in their English-speaking ability and that approximately 86 percent of the projects tended to keep children in bilingual education programs long after they were able to move into regular English-language classrooms (American Institute for Research, 1977:9–10). It also found that while bilingual programs were spending, on the average, an additional $376 per student more than were regular programs, they were not having a "consistent significant" impact on student achievement in English language arts and mathematics (American Institute for Research, 1977:12, 14).

The second report critical of bilingual education was also issued in 1977. In this report, Noel Epstein, a noted *Washington Post* journalist, raised fundamental questions about the goals, effectiveness, and scope of bilingual education. For example, Epstein observed that the original Bilingual Education Act of 1968 was a small, exploratory measure aimed at poor children who were "educationally disadvantaged" because of their inability to speak English. While allowing for a multitude of special educational programs for limited-English-speaking students, transitional bilingual education came to be recognized by the federal government as the most appropriate method for these children (Epstein, 1977:10). But "after nearly nine years and more than half a billion dollars in federal funds," he concluded, "the government has not demonstrated whether such instruction makes much difference in the students' achievement, in their acquisition of English, or in their attitudes towards school" (Epstein, 1977:1).

Another question he raised related to the targeted population—the children. According to him, the definitions of eligible children in federal policies were broad enough to include many pupils who were actually proficient in English, although they also spoke another language. Since resources were limited and children who could not learn effectively in English were numerous, the federal government had to make a choice between using these resources to assist those most in need or to help fund programs aimed at providing instruction to students who were already proficient in English (Epstein, 1977:27).

The final and most important issue he raised concerned the role the federal government should play in promoting different languages and cultures through bilingual education. He argued that the proponents of bilingual education sought a policy of affirmative ethnicity, i.e., they sought federal sponsorship of language maintenance efforts while limited-English students went through the normal process of learning the common English language and the common national history (Epstein, 1977:19). Although this philosophy of affirmative ethnicity raised serious social questions concerning the assimilation of cultural groups into American society and the further segregation of language minority children in the public schools, another more fundamental issue was involved.

> The issue—and this cannot be emphasized too strongly—is not the unquestioned importance of ethnicity in individuals' lives, any more than it is the unquestioned importance of religion in individuals' lives. The issue is not the right or the desirability of groups to maintain their languages and cultures. The issue is the government role. The overriding question is whether the federal government is responsible for financing and promoting student attachments to their ethnic languages and cultures, jobs long left to families, religious groups, ethnic organizations, private schools, ethnic publications, and others. (Epstein, 1977:20)

Although proponents of bilingual education argued that these two reports were ill informed, methodologically unsound, and biased, they served to illustrate the emergence of opposition to bilingual education (Cardenas, 1977).

Within this context of an emerging criticism of bilingual education, the program was reauthorized by passage of the new Bilingual Education Act of 1978 (*U.S. Statutes at Large*, 1978). The assimilationists, largely led by Republican legislators, won several significant concessions in this reauthorization effort. For instance, they were influential in getting Congress to underscore the importance of becoming proficient in English and to deemphasize the use of the primary language or of the culture in the instructional program. Funding was also largely limited to accomplishing this goal (Pifer, 1979:13; Leibowitz, 1980:25–26).

In addition to this emphasis on achieving competency in the English language, a new provision was added stipulating that the HEW Commissioner of Education could issue an order to terminate federal funding of bilingual programs for those local school districts not having long-term needs for continued assistance under the amended act. Another provision was also added which required that applicants demonstrate that federal grants would gradually be replaced by local or state funds to help achieve a regularly funded program (*U.S. Statutes at Large*, 1978).

Despite this legislative opposition to bilingual education, the pluralists, led largely by Democratic legislators, managed to expand the scope and funding of bilingual education. The pluralists, for instance, broadened the definition of the children eligible for participation in the program from "limited-English-speaking" to "limited-English-proficient." This provision expanded the number of individuals from those who had difficulty in speaking and understanding English to include those who also had difficulty in reading and writing the same language. The amendments to the Bilingual Education Act also committed substantial funds for research, teacher preparation, and graduate fellowships and allowed up to 40 percent of the participants to be children whose first language was English (*U.S. Statutes at Large*, 1978).

After the passage of the revised bilingual education bill, the assimilationists continued to raise their voices against dual language instruction in the nation's public schools. For instance, Tom Bethel, in an extremely influential article in 1979, reiterated most of the criticisms of the goals and effectiveness of bilingual education raised by the American Institute for Research report and by Epstein. He argued that the original "transitional" character of the bilingual education bill had been transformed and many of the children were being kept in these programs long after they knew English. According to him, the bilingual program was no longer experimental in nature nor was it just for poor children or limited to those who had difficulty in understanding or speaking English (Bethel, 1979:31).

Bethel was also critical of the congressional appropriations for bilingual education which had increased from the "beggarly" $7.5 million in 1970 to $85 million in fiscal year 1975. According to him, the federal government continued to fund bilingual education "in leaps and bounds," despite the lack of evidence indicating that this technique was effective (Bethel, 1979:32).

Finally, he argued that bilingual education was now more than simply an educational program. "The bilingual education program," he stated, "is more or less the Hispanic equivalent of affirmative action, creating jobs for thousands of Spanish teachers; by which I mean teachers who speak Spanish, although not necessarily English, it has turned out." This jobs program, according to him, not only appealed to teachers of Spanish and other tongues, "but also to those who never did think that another idea, the United States of America, was a particularly good one to begin with, and that the sooner it is restored to its component 'ethnic' parts the better off we shall all be" (Bethel, 1979:28).

Bethel was not the only one critical of bilingual education. Other critics abounded. In addition to questioning the goals and effectiveness of bilingual education, these critics also argued that there was no federal legal requirement for schools to provide bilingual or bicultural education and that bilingual education potentially increased social divisions in the society (Edwards, 1980). Assimilationist opposition to the concept of providing dual language instruction for linguistically different school children was, by the end of the decade, increasingly sharp and on the increase.

The New Federalism and the Retreat of the Pluralists

In the last several years, especially since the election of Ronald Reagan as president of the United States, the assimilationists have gained the upper hand in bilingual education policy. They have quite effectively opposed the further expansion of native-language instruction in the public schools by modifying or eliminating bilingual education policies, laws, and regulations at all levels of government.

Since the 1980 elections, the executive and legislative branches under the Reagan administration have begun to redefine and reshape bilingual education to serve the limited and compensatory function it was originally meant to serve. For instance, in a very symbolic and controversial move, the Reagan administration withdrew the "proposed Lau regulations."[7] The

[7] The proposed Lau regulations were introduced into the *Federal Register* on 5 August 1980, two months before the presidential elections in which Carter overwhelmingly lost to Reagan. See "Nondiscrimination under Programs Receiving Federal Financial Assistance through the Education Department" (1980).

president, in January 1982, also unsuccessfully attempted to rescind almost $11.5 million that Congress had already appropriated for bilingual programs for fiscal year 1982 and to cut $43 million from the appropriations for fiscal year 1983 (Lyons, 1983:2).

In support of the Reagan administration's stand, the Department of Education issued two sets of reports which were extremely critical of bilingual education. The first set of reports were based on the audit of seven Texas school districts and on a review of the performance of the Texas Education Agency.[8]

Conducted by the Office of the Inspector General in the Department of Education, these audit reports questioned the effectiveness of bilingual education programs and argued that they did not permanently improve the capacity of school districts. They also found that an excessive number of non-limited-English-proficient students participated in these programs and that the Texas Education Agency did not effectively coordinate local programs with other federal and state programs serving these same students.

On the basis of these findings, the Inspector General recommended that the seven Texas districts and the Texas Education Agency refund $5.85 million to the federal government. "Such a refund would be more than the seven districts and the TEA received in 1980–1981 ($3.69 million)," reported one lobbyist, "and would equal 42 percent of their cumulative grants under Title VII" (Lyons, 1983:2).

Texas school officials contested the audit findings, challenged the validity of the "facts" cited in the audit reports, and charged that the Inspector General had utilized erronerous statutory and programmatic standards in preparing the reports. Congressional members also conducted an oversight hearing on these reports and threatened to pass legislation aimed at curtailing the power of the Inspector General unless the Education Department dropped the disputed Texas audit recommendations "mighty quick."[9] After several tumultuous weeks, the Department of Education dropped most of the claims against Texas districts for repayment of federal bilingual education funds.

But of most importance to the future of bilingual education policy at the federal level was the second set of reports issued by the Office of Planning, Budget, and Evaluation and its staff members in 1981.

The Office of Planning, Budget, and Evaluation of the U.S. Department of Education, in response to a request of the Regulatory Analysis Review Group of the Council on Wage and Price Stability, prepared a series of studies in late 1980 that provided an "empirical" basis for challenging the comprehensive approach to teaching language minority children. In October 1981 the OPBE issued a final draft of a major policy report based on the studies it had prepared.

[8] The seven Texas school districts audited were Austin, Dallas, Edgewood, Edinburg, Harlingen, Pharr–San Juan–Alamo, and San Antonio. See Lyons (1983:2).

[9] Lyons (1983:2) states that the hearings helped to dispel some of the negative publicity generated by the audit reports and to raise questions about the political motivation behind the audits.

Written by Beatrice F. Birman and Alan L. Ginsburg, the policy report, first of all, did not dispute the need for "some sort of educational assistance" to meet the needs of language minority children. But it did argue that "in the process of justifying Federal support of bilingual education, too little attention has been paid to accurately identifying which children need services, which types of services would benefit them the most, and what constraints local school districts face in providing such services" (Birman and Ginsburg, 1981:5).

In light of the new studies which provided "systematic empirical evidence from a variety of data sources," the authors of the report argued that the continued federal support for bilingual education warranted reexamination (Birman and Ginsburg, 1981:6). First, the new evidence questioned the linguistic explanation for low scholastic achievement among language minority groups. According to the evidence cited by Birman and Ginsburg, students from non-English-speaking homes did have severe educational needs, but these did not necessarily result from a dependence on a non-English language. Poverty and the children's limited proficiencies in both Spanish and English also affected their scholastic achievement. Thus if students were limited both in their native language and in English, the value of teaching them in two languages could be challenged. Likewise if children's educational needs were based on factors other than language, bilingual programs could be only partial solutions. "From the perspective of Federal government," they argued, "if students receive services that do not match their needs, Federal funds are dissipated" (Birman and Ginsburg, 1981:7).

Second, Birman and Ginsburg also questioned the government's promotion of transitional bilingual education without evidence of its effectiveness. They reached this conclusion based on an extensive review of the literature on the effectiveness of bilingual education conducted by Baker and de Kanter, two OPBE staff members. Baker and de Kanter (1981) found that little evidence existed supporting transitional bilingual education as usually more effective than other approaches.[10] Although Baker and de Kanter warned readers against broad generalizations due to the small number of acceptable studies, they, as well as Birman and Ginsburg, argued that alternative approaches such as structured immersion showed promising results (Birman and Ginsburg, 1981:8).

Third, serious financial, personnel, and assessment constraints inhibited the ability of local school districts to provide services. The high costs of establishing and maintaining bilingual education programs as well as the need for fully qualified personnel to administer these programs needed to be acknowledged by the federal government as serious problems. The lack of adequate tests to assess the children's own language proficiency increased the possibility that the educational needs of language minority children could be misdiagnosed. This in turn could lead to the delivery of ineffective services. According to the report, "Federal policy cannot require

[10] For a scathing response from the pluralists to this report see Hernandez-Chavez, Llanes, Alvarez, and Arvizu (1981).

services that presume adequate funding, teachers, and tests" (Birman and Ginsburg, 1981:11).

In conclusion, the report then made the following policy recommendations: (1) transitional bilingual education should not be the sole approach encouraged by federal policy, (2) state and school districts should have greater discretion to decide which type of special program is most appropriate for their unique settings, (3) the constraints facing states and districts in providing services to language minority children should not be ignored, and (4) improved bilingual research and program evaluations should be conducted.

Complementary to the executive actions were legislative efforts aimed at limiting the nature and scope of dual language instruction in the public schools. For instance, on 23 April and 26 April 1982 hearings were held for two bills—S. 2002 and S. 2412—which proposed fundamental changes in the Bilingual Education Act of 1978. Some of the key provisions of these bills proposed, among other things, to eliminate the use of non-English languages in instruction and to emphasize the learning of English language skills by requiring "intensive courses in English."[11] The Senate Subcommittee on Education, Arts, and Humanities, which held the hearings on the proposed bilingual education bills, did not act on them, and as a result both of them died (Lyons, 1983:1–2).

Conclusion

Although present for many years, opposition to bilingual education did not emerge until the pluralists began to change the minor piece of legislation into a major educational reform measure. Opposition tended to concentrate on expanding nature of bilingual education legislation and on the increasing role that the federal government was assuming in promoting this program. But the central issues in bilingual education have not been political or legislative in nature; rather, they have been philosophical. The issue has not been the changing character of the bill's provisions nor the federal promotion of bilingual education but rather the role that non-English languages associated with low-status minority groups should play in education.

The pluralists and the assimilationists each had a different and clashing perspective on how best to teach minorities and on the role that the students' native language would play in their education. The pluralists, through their actions, sought to introduce and incorporate the non-English languages of minority students into the curriculum. They did this by modifying the compensatory and categorical nature of the bill, by proposing bilingual education as the only appropriate instructional remedy for minority students, and by requiring local school districts to develop bilingual education programs for all of their non-English-proficient students.

The assimilationists, on the other hand, tried to limit the further introduction of non-English languages into the curriculum and to reemphasize the

---

[11] See Lyons (1983:1–2) for a discussion of these bills.

need for more English-language activities. They did this by raising questions about the goals, effectiveness, and costs of bilingual education and by cutting the funding for this program. Although unsuccessful, the assimilationists also tried to substitute new types of English-only programs for bilingual education ones.

These clashing perspectives have guided the actions of special interest groups and led to bitter struggles over how best to educate language minority students. In the years to come, no one can predict what will become of bilingual education policy. But one thing is certain: regardless of whatever group is exercising dominant influence over bilingual education, conflict and controversy will continue to accompany its development.

REFERENCES

American Institute for Research. 1977. *Interim Report, Evaluation of the Impact of ESEA Title VII, Spanish/English Bilingual Education Programs* (Palo Alto, Calif.: AIR).

Anderson, Theodore, and Mildred Boyer. 1970. *Bilingual Schooling in the U.S.* Vol. 1 (Austin: Southwest Educational Development Laboratory).

———. 1978. *Bilingual Schooling in the U.S.*, 2d ed. (Austin: National Educational Laboratory Publishers, Inc.).

Baker, Keith A., and Adriana A. de Kanter. 1981. *Effectiveness of Bilingual Education: A Review of the Literature. Final Draft Report* (Washington, D.C.: Department of Education, Office of Planning, Budget, and Evaluation).

Bethel, Tom. 1979. "Why Johnny Can't Speak English," *Harper's,* February, pp. 30–33.

Birman, Beatrice F., and Alan L. Ginsburg. 1981. *Addressing the Needs of Language-Minority Children: Issues for Federal Policy* (Washington, D.C.: Department of Education, Office of Planning, Budget, and Evaluation).

Cardenas, Jose A. 1977. "Response I," in Noel Epstein, *Language, Ethnicity, and the Schools* (Washington, D.C.: George Washington University, Institute for Educational Leadership): pp. 71–84.

Cordasco, Francesco. 1968. "The Challenge of the Non-English Speaking Child in American Schools," *School and Society,* 96 (30 March):198–201.

Edwards, John R. 1980. "Critics and Criticism of Bilingual Education," *Modern Language Journal,* 64 (Winter):409–15.

Epstein, Noel. 1977. *Language, Ethnicity, and the Schools* (Washington, D.C.: George Washington University, Institute for Educational Leadership).

Hernandez-Chavez, Eduardo, Jose Llanes, Roberto Alvarez, and Steven F. Arvizu. 1981. *The Federal Policy toward Language and Education: Pendulum or Progress?—A Response to the DeKanter/Baker Report.* Monograph No. 12 (Sacramento: California State University, Department of Anthropology).

Kobrick, Jeffrey W. 1972. "The Compelling Case for Bilingual Education," *Saturday Review,* 55 (29 April):54–58.

Lau v. Nichols. 1974. 414 U.S. 563, 94 S.Ct. 786.

Leibowitz, Arnold H. 1980. *The Bilingual Education Act: A Legislative Analysis* (Rosslyn, Va.: InterAmerica Research Associates).

Lyons, James J. 1983. "Bilingual Education: The Past and the New Year—A Report from Washington," *CABE Newsletter,* 7 (March/April):1–2, 6.

"Nondiscrimination under Programs Receiving Federal Financial Assistance through the Education Department—Proposed Rules." 1980. *Federal Register,* 45 (5 August):52052–76.

Office for Civil Rights. 1975. *Task Force Findings Specifying Remedies Available for Eliminating Past Educational Practices Ruled Unlawful under Lau v. Nichols* (Washington, D.C.: Department of Health, Education, and Welfare, Office for Civil Rights).

Orfield, Gary. 1978. *Must We Bus? Segregated Schools and National Policy* (Washington, D.C.: Brookings Institution).

Pifer, Alan. 1979. *Bilingual Education and the Hispanic Challenge, Annual Report* (New York: Carnegie Corporation).

Pottinger, J. Stanley. 1970. *Memorandum of May 25, 1970 to School Districts with More Than Five Percent National Origin–Minority Group Children* (Washington, D.C.: Department of Health, Education, and Welfare, Office for Civil Rights).

Schneider, Susan Gilbert. 1976. *Revolution, Reaction or Reform: The 1974 Bilingual Education Act* (New York: L. A. Publishing Company).

Stanfield, Rochelle L. 1980. "Are Federal Bilingual Rules a Foot in the Schoolhouse Door?" *National Journal,* 12 (18 October):1736–40.

Teitelbaum, Herbert, and Richard J. Hiller. 1979. "Bilingual Education: The Legal Mandate," in Henry T. Trueba and Carol Barnet-Mizrahi, eds., *Bilingual Multicultural Education and the Professional: From Theory to Practice* (Rowley, Mass.: Newbury House): pp. 20–53.

United Staes v. State of Texas (San Felipe–Del Rio). 1972. 342 F. Supp. 24 (E.D. Tex. 1971), aff'd per curium, 466 F. 2d 518 (5th Cir.).

U.S. Statutes at Large. 1968. Vol. 81, p. 816 (2 January 1968); 20 U.S.C.A. 880(b).

———. 1974. Vol. 88, p. 503 (21 August 1974).

———. 1978. Vol. 92, p. 2270 (1 November 1978).

Vega, Jose E. 1983. *Education, Politics, and Bilingualism in Texas* (Washington, D.C.: University Press of America).

Zirkel, Perry A. 1978. "The Legal Vicissitudes of Bilingual Education," in Hernan LaFontaine, Barry Persky, and Leonard H. Golubchick, eds., *Bilingual Education* (Wayne, N.J.: Avery Publishing Group): pp. 48–51.

20. A LEGAL VOICE FOR THE CHICANO COMMUNITY: THE ACTIVITIES OF THE MEXICAN AMERICAN LEGAL DEFENSE AND EDUCATIONAL FUND, 1968–82[1]

Karen O'CONNOR, *Emory University*

Lee EPSTEIN, *Emory University*

The authors examine the history and activities of the Mexican American Legal Defense and Educational Fund (MALDEF), which litigates on behalf of Chicanos. Previous studies of interest group litigation are drawn upon to formulate hypotheses concerning interest group success in the judicial arena. These hypotheses are then tested through an examination of the litigation activities of MALDEF between 1968 and 1982. The findings indicate that the factors considered critical to interest group litigation success are helpful in explaining the evolution of MALDEF.

Litigation long has been recognized as an important political tool of disadvantaged groups (Cortner, 1968). In this paper, we discuss the utility of litigation on behalf of the Chicano[2] community by the Mexican American Legal Defense and Educational Fund (MALDEF). More specifically, after describing the historical circumstances surrounding the creation of MALDEF, we draw on previous studies of interest group litigation to formulate hypotheses concerning interest group success in the judicial arena. We then test these hypotheses through an examination of the litigation activities of MALDEF between 1968 and 1982.

[1] We would like to thank Nancy Rossman for her research assistance. We would also like to express our appreciation to Stephen Wasby and the anonymous reviewers for their very helpful comments and criticisms of an earlier draft of this manuscript. Portions of this research were funded by the Emory University Research Fund.

[2] Although the terms Mexican American and Chicano often are used interchangeably by scholars (see Garcia and de la Garza, 1977:14; Grebler, Moore, and Guzman, 1970:385–87), we use the term Chicano because it is the term most frequently used in the briefs of the Mexican American Legal Defense and Educational Fund.

Litigation as a Political Tool

Writing in 1959, Clement E. Vose was one of the first to document the importance of group use of the courts. His examination of the National Association for the Advancement of Colored People (NAACP) and its independent Legal Defense Fund's (LDF's) use of the courts to end restrictive covenants revealed that litigation was critical; as an organization litigating on behalf of a disadvantaged group, the NAACP realized that it could not attain its goals in the legislative sphere. But, as Vose's study clearly indicated, the NAACP's recognition of the utility of litigation did not automatically lead to success. In fact, Vose's examination of the NAACP's decades-long struggle to end restrictive covenants revealed that at least three factors were critical to its ultimate success: first, after realizing that the courts were the only potentially amenable forum for the advancement of minority rights, NAACP founders recruited attorneys well schooled in the intricacies of civil rights law (Vose, 1959). According to Vose, this task was facilitated by the concentration of black attorneys in several northeastern cities and by the fact that the vast majority of these lawyers had been educated at the Howard Law School in Washington, D.C. Thus, within a relatively short period of time, the NAACP was able to recruit well-trained attorneys as well as to establish a crucial network of cooperating attorneys sympathetic to its cause.

This network, coupled with the NAACP's maintenance of a national office in Washington, D.C., facilitated the development of a direct sponsorship strategy by keeping the organization abreast of potentially good test cases, a second factor noted as critical to its success by Vose. While soon after its creation in 1909 the NAACP filed an amicus curiae brief in *Guinn v. United States* (1915), a challenge to Louisiana's grandfather clause, its leaders shortly thereafter realized that direct sponsorship would be the most effective way to achieve its goals. In fact, as Vose has noted, control over the course of litigation at the trial court level where a record could be established for later appeal was particularly critical to the NAACP's ability to obtain judicial invalidation of restrictive covenants.[3]

A third factor noted as critical to the LDF's success was its ability to garner support from other litigators. The assistance and support of the U.S. government in court, for example, lent legitimacy to the NAACP's claims and led to an almost one-sided presentation of race cases, thereby increasing the likelihood of success. Thus, according to Vose, the NAACP's simple recognition of the utility of litigation was only the first step in achieving invalidation of restrictive covenants. Additionally, expert counsel, the use of a test case strategy, and cooperation with other litigators contributed to its ultimate success in *Shelley v. Kraemer* (1948).

The importance of these factors was further substantiated in subsequent studies of the NAACP LDF's litigation activities. Both Jack Greenberg's (1974, 1977) and Richard Kluger's (1976) analyses of the LDF's role in the

[3] This recognition, in fact, partially explains why the NAACP established an independent legal defense fund in 1939 solely to litigate on behalf of black interests (Vose, 1959).

school desegregation cases that culminated in *Brown v. Board of Education* (1954) note the importance of each of these factors. For example, LDF general counsel Thurgood Marshall's decision to initiate a series of cases at the trial court level to whittle away at adverse precedent was pointed to by both authors as critical to the LDF's success. This series of cases allowed the LDF to establish itself as an expert litigator in the area of school segregation. Additionally, during the course of this litigation campaign, the LDF facilitated creation of a receptive judicial environment through securing the publication of several law review articles authored by well-respected constitutional scholars and enlisting the assistance and support of the U.S. government as amicus curiae. According to Greenberg and Kluger, these factors helped to explain the LDF's landmark victory in 1954 (see also Hahn, 1973; Barker, 1967).

Not only is there agreement among those who have studied the NAACP LDF concerning factors critical to its success, but those who have analyzed other disadvantaged groups have reached the same conclusions. For example, Manwaring's (1962) study of the Jehovah's Witnesses found that frequent participation by committed attorneys in cooperation with the American Civil Liberties Union (ACLU) facilitated its efforts to persuade the Supreme Court to invalidate compulsory flag salute requirements.

Another disadvantaged group—women—also has relied heavily on litigation to attain greater rights. However, as O'Connor (1980) has noted, women's rights organizations, unlike the LDF and the Jehovah's Witnesses, have had but mixed success because of the absence of one organization to represent their interests in court. Instead, the involvement of several groups including the National Organization for Women (NOW), the Women's Rights Project of the ACLU, and the Women's Equity Action League has made use of a test case strategy difficult. Additionally, the large number of women's rights litigators has strained foundation funds, which has reduced the ability of many of the groups to afford the often high costs incurred through direct sponsorship of litigation. Thus, women's rights groups have been unable to pursue a truly coordinated test case strategy, a factor considered critical to success.

A Formulation and Test of a Hypothesis of Interest Group Litigation: An Examination of MALDEF's Activities

As the preceding discussion suggests, studies of the litigation activities of a variety of organizations representing disadvantaged groups provide the basis for theoretical generalizations concerning interest group use of the courts to achieve rights unavailable in other forums. The findings of these and other studies (Burke, 1981; Cortner, 1975; Rubin, 1982; Shattuck and Norgren, 1979; Sorauf, 1976; Stewart and Heck, 1982; Wasby, 1981), which have thoroughly examined groups that have succeeded or obtained only limited success in court, allow us to formulate the following hypothesis: If interest groups (1) recruit expert counsel, (2) use a test case strategy, and (3) cooperate with other groups, then they will maximize their chances of success, at least at the level of the U.S. Supreme Court.

To investigate the continuing importance of the elements enumerated in this hypothesis, we examine the activities of MALDEF, the major representative of Chicano interests in court. The significance of such an examination is twofold: first, Chicanos, like blacks, the Jehovah's Witnesses, and women, can be classified as a "disadvantaged group," but litigation efforts on their behalf never have been fully examined. Second, an analysis of this sort is timely because MALDEF's victories have just begun to make a major impact on the law. Thus, a study of its activities, like those conducted of other groups that have resorted to litigation, may help to explain not only the relevance of the factors perceived as critical to litigation success, but also to provide a fuller understanding of the evolution of an interest group litigator.

The Establishment and Litigation Activities of MALDEF

Like many other disadvantaged groups, Chicanos early on recognized their inability to seek rights through traditional political avenues and thus sporadically resorted to litigation (Vigil, 1978:125). It was not until the 1960s, however, that the need for organized, sustained litigation activity on behalf of Chicanos became apparent. For example, in the course of litigating a common tort claim, Pete Tijerina, a League of United Latin American Citizens (LULAC) leader, was confronted with a jury panel of no Chicano surnamed individuals, but his client could not afford the high cost of a challenge to its discriminatory composition. Because Tijerina believed that this case symbolized the plight of Chicanos in court, he sent another LULAC member to attend a 1967 NAACP LDF conference to explore the possibility of establishing an organization to litigate on behalf of Chicanos. Tijerina's representative met with Jack Greenberg, the executive director of the NAACP LDF, who then set up a meeting between Tijerina and Ford Foundation representatives (Markham, 1983). Within a year of that meeting, MALDEF was incorporated with the assistance of a $2.2 million start-up grant from the Ford Foundation (Teltsch, 1968).

In addition to Ford's financial support, MALDEF received practical information and guidance from the NAACP LDF. In fact, LDF attorney Vilma Martinez, who later was to become the executive director of MALDEF, had not only helped prepare the initial Ford grant application but also served as a liaison between the two organizations ("San Antonio Native," 1973). Additionally, Greenberg was named to its first board of directors.

Not only was MALDEF assisted by LDF staff members, it was specifically modeled after the LDF. In fact, in announcing the Ford grant, the foundation's president McGeorge Bundy drew the following parallel: "In terms of legal enforcement of civil rights, American citizens of Mexican descent are now where the Negro community was a quarter-century ago" (Teltsch, 1968:38). Thus, at least from Ford's perspective, MALDEF was to function for Chicanos in the same way that the LDF historically had assisted blacks.

To facilitate and to direct its initial efforts, MALDEF, like the LDF, quickly acted to draw upon the expertise of prominent Mexican American attorneys to staff its headquarters in San Antonio and its Los Angeles affiliate office. Tijerina was installed as its first executive director, and Mario Obledo, a Texas assistant attorney general and former state director of LULAC, was hired as general counsel. MALDEF, however, quickly was confronted with a paucity of experienced litigators. In fact, in announcing Ford funding of MALDEF, Bundy had underscored the need for such an organization, noting that there were "not nearly enough Mexican American lawyers and most of them have neither the income or experience to do civil rights work" (Teltsch, 1968:38). To remedy this situation, the Ford grant included provisions for scholarships for 35 Mexican American law students with the goal of increasing the number of Chicano attorneys.[4] Nevertheless, this was a long-term solution to a problem that immediately confronted MALDEF. Thus, four of the nine attorneys initially "hired" by MALDEF were non-Chicano VISTA volunteers (MALDEF, n.d.). Additionally, in establishing its own network of cooperating attorneys, MALDEF was forced to rely heavily on non-Chicano lawyers.

Thus, while MALDEF was modeled after the LDF, from the start it was faced with problems unlike those experienced by the LDF. It had difficulty in recruiting experienced Chicano attorneys and in dealing with the Mexican American community at large, which from some accounts misunderstood MALDEF's objectives. For example, immediately after MALDEF established its offices in San Antonio and Los Angeles, both were inundated with claims. Many of these claims, however, involved routine "legal aid" type cases that were best settled out of court and did not necessarily present issues upon which important constitutional cases could be made.

These sorts of problems, coupled with the militancy of some of MALDEF's personnel[5] (Diehl, 1970), prompted the Ford Foundation to send in outside evaluators to examine MALDEF's day-to-day activities in 1970 ("Mexican Aid Fund," 1970:48). These evaluators made several "recommendations" that were aimed at increasing MALDEF's national presence and reputation in the LDF model. More specifically, according to Tijerina, Ford threatened to terminate MALDEF's funding if it did not move its headquarters out of Texas and relocate in a more "neutral" city such as Washington, D.C., or New York ("Ford Group," 1970). Cognizant of the importance of a presence in the West, however, MALDEF chose instead to relocate its headquarters to San Francisco while retaining its two other offices and only later opening up a D.C. office (Grover, 1970). MALDEF, however, followed other Ford suggestions; not only was Tijerina replaced as executive director as requested by Ford (Murphy, 1970), but MALDEF also combined the positions of executive director and general counsel, its board selecting Mario Obledo to fill this new position ("Mexican Aid Fund," 1970:48).

[4] This program continues to be a high-priority MALDEF project.
[5] One MALDEF staffer, for example, made widely reported "anti-gringo" statements causing the Ford Foundation to come under fire for its support of Chicano groups. Political activities on the part of employees of Ford funded operations even led the House Ways and Means Committee to hold hearings to seek ways to limit this sort of activity on the part of tax-exempt foundations (Diehl, 1970).

As executive director, Obledo immediately sought to increase MALDEF's national visibility as recommended by the Ford Foundation and to strengthen ties with other established civil rights groups. For example, during Obledo's tenure, MALDEF established a New Mexico branch office in conjunction with the New Mexico Law School, the New Mexico Legal Rights Project, and the Albuquerque Legal Aid Society. A Denver office also was opened under Obledo's leadership. Additionally, MALDEF moved to increase its national presence through association with the LDF and NOW, among others, to pressure the federal government for enforcement of fair employment practices legislation (Shanahan, 1972; Cowan, 1972).

Perhaps most important, however, aware of the problems of functioning as a quasi legal aid clinic, Obledo moved to have MALDEF bring more cases to the U.S. Supreme Court. Thus, as early as 1973, the Court handed down decisions in eight cases in which MALDEF had participated, five of which were amicus curiae briefs filed alone or in conjunction with other organizations. In the remaining three cases sponsored by MALDEF, only one, *White v. Regester* (1973), which involved the constitutionality of at-large election districts, resulted in a favorable decision. In contrast, in *Logue v. U.S.* (1973), MALDEF was unable to convince the Court that the U.S. government should be liable for the negligence of city jail employees. Far more devastating, however, was its loss in *San Antonio v. Rodriguez* (1973). In its first appearance before the Court,[6] MALDEF (1972) argued that:

> in Texas, the poor receive one type of education by every measure, while the affluent are afforded a quite different and superior educational opportunity. This Court should not allow Texas to impose upon a minority what is obviously unacceptable to the majority. (P. 56)

This argument, however, failed to convince the Court to find that education was a fundamental right protected by the Fourteenth Amendment. Instead, the justices held that Texas would not be required to subsidize poorer school districts, where there were often large concentrations of Chicanos. Thus, *San Antonio* resulted in a devastating loss, creating additional legal barriers instead of favorable precedent upon which MALDEF could build a test case strategy.

In sum, under Obledo's leadership, MALDEF attempted to implement the Ford Foundation's suggestions through a variety of different strategies. It successfully established new offices and attempted to build ties with other groups. But, as its loss in *San Antonio* revealed, MALDEF acted too quickly and did not sufficiently "prime" the Supreme Court either through frequent appearances as amicus curiae or the use of test cases. Thus, although by 1973 MALDEF had accomplished a number of its objectives, in the wake of its losses during 1973 Obledo resigned to return to private practice ("Vilma Martinez," 1973). In September 1973, Vilma Martinez was selected to replace Obledo after MALDEF's board considered several candidates

---

[6] In 1970, however, MALDEF unsuccessfully sought review from the Supreme Court in *Jiminez v. Naff*.

including Juan Rocha, who had recently been hired to head the new MALDEF D.C. office ("San Antonio Native," 1973).

Martinez immediately set into motion a series of changes: first, having always been interested in fund raising (Markham, 1983) and in fact, having played a major role in MALDEF fund raising from the beginning, Martinez restaffed the D.C. office with the objectives of improving MALDEF's government relations, funding sources, and its national visibility. Second, MALDEF began to create specialized litigation and educational projects to meet its growing needs and to afford its attorneys an opportunity to develop greater expertise. For example, in 1974 a Chicana Rights Project was created to fight sex discrimination faced by Mexican American women. Other projects established by MALDEF handled education, employment, and voting rights. A year later, it also created a legal intern/extern program to help train and later assist Chicano attorneys to set up practices in local communities. Finally, and perhaps most important, MALDEF became more selective about its involvement in cases as Ford had earlier urged. Generally, it began to limit its participation to important test cases that were considered to have "broad implications" (MALDEF, n.d.:30). This selectivity allowed MALDEF, like the LDF, not only to maximize its resources but to avoid adverse precedent such as that established in *San Antonio*.

To accomplish this goal, MALDEF began to concentrate in a number of legal issue areas but continued to be particularly interested in education. In the wake of *San Antonio*, however, MALDEF's leaders reevaluated their strategy in that area. Building upon arguments set forth in the first article about undocumented aliens ever to appear in the *American Bar Journal* and written by a MALDEF attorney (Ortega, 1972), MALDEF lawyers began to devise a strategy to create favorable precedent by which to improve the legal status of all Chicanos. Thus, under the directorship of Peter Roos, who had previously worked at the Harvard Center for Law and Education and at the Western Center of Law and Poverty, MALDEF's Education Litigation Project filed several lawsuits challenging the constitutionality of actions of many school districts that refused to enroll the children of undocumented aliens, unless tuition was paid.

After several years of litigation, one of these cases, *Plyler v. Doe* (1982), resulted in a major, landmark ruling from the U.S. Supreme Court. MALDEF attorneys including Martinez and Roos had argued that the Texas code, which allowed school districts to exclude some children, violated the Fourteenth Amendment. According to MALDEF (1981):

> When public schooling is available to all but the children of one excluded class, the members of that class are inexorably relegated to a low station in life, subject to exploitation and removed from the meaningful discourse of the day. As one is properly and regularly reminded, "A mind is a terrible thing to waste."

In adopting MALDEF's reasoning, the Supreme Court, for the first time, directly held that the children of undocumented, illegal aliens were protected by the equal protection clause. Writing for the Court, Justice Brennan noted that:

it is difficult to understand precisely what the State hopes to achieve by promoting the creation and perpetuation of a subclass of illiterates within our
boundaries, surely adding to the problems and costs of unemployment, welfare and crime. . . . If the State is to deny a discrete group of innocent children
the free public education that it offers to other children residing within its
borders, that denial must be justified by a showing that it furthers some substantial state interest. No such showing was made here. (102 S. Ct. 2382,
2402)

Thus, *Plyler* provided MALDEF's "best victory" to date (MALDEF, 1982:4)
and has presented MALDEF with a major precedent upon which to build.

Application of Hypothesis to MALDEF's Litigation Activities

Based on other studies of interest group litigation, we hypothesized that
(1) the recruitment of expert counsel, (2) the use of a test case strategy,
and (3) cooperation with other groups would maximize a group's chances
of success.

From the preceding discussion of MALDEF's activities, we can now attempt to investigate the importance of the three factors commonly assumed
to be critical to the success of interest group litigation.

Expert Attorneys. When MALDEF was established, its founders recognized the importance of recruiting highly skilled attorneys who would be
sensitive to the pervasive discrimination suffered by Chicanos. Unlike the
LDF, which could draw on a large number of black attorneys schooled in
civil rights law, there were few Chicano attorneys experienced in civil rights
litigation, which initially forced MALDEF to rely on non-Chicano attorneys
to supplement its staff. Thus, many of the first programs initiated by
MALDEF were designed to increase the number of Chicano attorneys, train
them in civil rights law, and then help establish them in practice within the
Chicano community and not necessarily toward developing legal expertise
within MALDEF.

When Martinez replaced Obledo, however, she immediately recognized
this organizational deficiency, and she actively recruited several attorneys
with strong civil rights backgrounds (Markham, 1983). For example, Morris
J. Baller, who was made head of the Developmental Litigation Project, had
formerly served, like Martinez, as an LDF staff attorney. And, Joel G. Con-
treras, who was hired to be the director of the Employment Litigation Project, had served in a similar capacity with the Lawyer's Committee for Civil
Rights Under Law (LCCRUL). He also had previously worked at the EEOC.
Both Martinez and the staff that she hired, therefore, interjected an increased level of expertise in civil rights litigation that neither Obledo nor
Tijerina possessed. Interestingly, almost all of the attorneys added to
MALDEF's staff were Chicanos,[7] and in fact, some had been trained in the
legal extern program or assisted by MALDEF scholarships.

[7] In fact, one non-Chicano attorney, George Korbel, who had litigated *White v. Regester* and
is an authority on Voting Rights Act violations ("Suit Challenges," 1972; Davidson and Korbel,
1981), was fired by Martinez and later sued to regain his position (Diehl, 1976; "MALDEF
Attorney," 1976).

Thus, unlike the LDF, MALDEF faced initial difficulties because of the absence of Chicano attorneys trained in civil rights law. This problem, which translated into major legal defeats, losses of scarce time and resources, and some internal dissension, was substantially reduced through MALDEF's programs, specialized projects, and by Martinez's recruitment efforts.

Test Case Strategy. Until the Ford Foundation report, MALDEF largely functioned as a legal aid society, albeit one that met the particular needs of the Chicano community. After 1970, however, MALDEF initiated several diverse kinds of suits that ultimately reached the Supreme Court. But, in only one of the three cases it argued during the 1972 term was it victorious. Its victory in *White* can be largely attributed to its initial emphasis on voting rights and attention to the development of a strong record at the trial court level. Conversely, its losses in *Logue v. U.S.* and *San Antonio* may be explained by its pursuit of Supreme Court resolution of issues that the Court had not yet been "primed" to address; MALDEF's 1972 term appearances were its first before the Supreme Court. Thus, unlike many other groups, which generally file amicus curiae briefs prior to bringing test cases before the Court, in 1972 MALDEF did not have any of the advantages of traditional repeat players (Galanter, 1974). And, perhaps more important, MALDEF's failure to "test the waters" in the education area produced disastrous precedent that stood as an additional legal stumbling block for litigation of other claims.

Recognizing these problems, MALDEF, under the leadership of Martinez, actively sought to increase its visibility as an amicus curiae in the Supreme Court while simultaneously developing a litigation strategy to whittle away at the adverse precedent established in *San Antonio*, in particular, and against aliens, in general. To accomplish this latter task, MALDEF closely modeled its activities after those followed by the LDF prior to *Brown*. Recognizing that the plight of children denied access to education by the state presented facts to evoke the sympathy of the Court, MALDEF initiated a series of "test cases" that culminated in *Plyler*. While *Plyler*, like the LDF's victories prior to *Brown*, is a victory standing alone, it also provided MALDEF with a major precedent upon which to build. In fact, since *Plyler*, MALDEF has initiated a number of lawsuits challenging discrimination against undocumented aliens in a variety of areas (Markham, 1983).

But, its victory in *Plyler*, perhaps, places MALDEF at a critical juncture in its history both in terms of its litigation activities and organizational viability. Believing that she had accomplished her objectives (Markham, 1983), Vilma Martinez left MALDEF shortly before the Court's announcement of the *Plyler* decision. Whether her successor and MALDEF will take full advantage of the gains won at least in part because of her insistence upon the utilization of a test case strategy is a challenge that confronts MALDEF as it moves into the 1980s.

Cooperation. Since its creation, MALDEF has cooperated with numerous civil rights organizations. For example, from the beginning, MALDEF has enjoyed strong ties with the NAACP LDF. Members of the LDF not only helped MALDEF secure Ford funding but also sat and continue to sit on its board. In fact, one of its first board members, Vilma Martinez, ultimately became its general counsel and brought several LDF staffers with her. Additionally, ties between the two groups also are evident in their support of each other's litigation efforts.

While MALDEF has regularly worked with the LDF and other like-minded groups, full cooperation has been difficult at times because MALDEF represents a class whose best interests are not always served by non-Chicano organizations. For example, in *Keyes v. Denver School District* (1973), the NAACP LDF argued that the court-ordered Denver school desegregation plan should be upheld. MALDEF, however, which was forced to participate to assure the representation of Chicano interests, urged the Court to reconsider sections of the lower court order because it did not consider minority schools to be those that contained large populations of *both* Chicano and black children.

MALDEF, to some extent, has also attempted to work with the federal and state governments. Many of its attorneys had government experience prior to coming to MALDEF; others, including Obledo, have continued to speak on behalf of MALDEF from their government positions.[8] Additionally, MALDEF's litigation efforts have been facilitated by government supported VISTA volunteers and outright grants from the U.S. government. In fact, during fiscal years 1981 and 1982, MALDEF received nearly $1.3 million dollars from the federal government (a figure derived from MALDEF, 1982:13). Thus, unlike the other factors considered critical to litigation success, MALDEF, since its establishment, has attempted to cooperate with other groups and governments. In certain types of issue areas, however, cooperation has often been difficult because of MALDEF's unique focus.

Conclusion

As the preceding analysis indicates, the factors considered critical to interest group litigation success are helpful in explaining the evolution of MALDEF. In general, our discussion indicates that until 1973 MALDEF functioned more as a legal aid society than as an interest group litigator. While the Ford Foundation tried to put MALDEF on course, it was not until under Martinez's leadership that MALDEF was reorganized and reoriented to pursue the kinds of activities for which it was originally created. *Plyler v. Doe*, which was (1) initiated by a specialized MALDEF Project, (2) begun as a test case, and (3) supported by amicus curiae briefs from several other groups, is illustrative of the potential impact MALDEF can have on the Supreme Court if litigation is properly pursued.

Thus, this analysis has not only reaffirmed the importance of all three factors to litigation success, but also of the utility of litigation for disadvan-

---

[8] For example, after Obledo became California's Secretary of Health and Welfare, he continued to file briefs on MALDEF's behalf. Similarly, Ed Idar, who formerly was associated with the San Antonio office, has participated on behalf of MALDEF since becoming an assistant attorney general in Texas.

taged groups. As MALDEF moves into the 1980s, it, as other representatives of disadvantaged groups have done in the past, can continue to build upon important precedents that it helped to create.

REFERENCES

Barker, Lucius. 1967. "Third Parties in Litigation: A Systematic View of Judicial Function," *Journal of Politics*, 29 (February):41–69.

Burke, Susan Olson. 1981. "The Political Evolution of Interest Group Litigation," in Richard A. L. Gambritta et al., eds., *Governing through Courts* (Beverly Hills, Calif.: Sage).

Cortner, Richard. 1968. "Strategies and Tactics of Litigants in Constitutional Cases," *Journal of Public Law*, 17:287–307.

———. 1975. *The Supreme Court and Civil Liberties Policy* (Palo Alto, Calif.: Mayfield).

Cowan, Edward. 1972. "FPC Urged to Bar Bias in Gas, Electric Utilities," *New York Times*, 23 June.

Davidson, Chandler, and George Korbel. 1981. "At Large Elections and Minority-Group Representation: A Re-Examination of Historical and Contemporary Evidence," *Journal of Politics*, 43 (November):982–1005.

Diehl, Kemper. 1970. "HBG Denies Role in MALD Center Move Plan," *San Antonio News*, 18 March.

———. 1976. "Fired Lawyer Sues MALDEF," *San Antonio News*, 4 March.

"Ford Group Denies Fund Cut Threat." 1970. *San Antonio News*, 19 March.

Galanter, Marc. 1974. "Why the 'Haves' Come Out Ahead: Speculation on the Limits of Legal Change," *Law and Society Review*, 9 (Fall):95–160.

Garcia, F. Chris, and Rudolph O. de la Garza. 1977. *The Chicano Political Experience: Three Perspectives* (North Scituate, Mass.: Duxbury Press).

Grebler, Leo, Joan W. Moore, and Ralph C. Guzman. 1970. *The Mexican American People* (New York: Free Press).

Greenberg, Jack. 1974. "Litigation for Social Change: Methods, Limits, and Role in Democracy," *Records of the New York City Bar Association*, 29:9–63.

———. 1977. *Judicial Process and Social Change: Constitutional Litigation* (St. Paul, Minn.: West).

Grover, Nell Fenner. 1970. "MALDEF Moving to San Francisco," *San Antonio Express*, 26 June.

Hahn, Jeanne. 1973. "The NAACP Legal Defense and Education Fund: Its Judicial Strategy and Tactics," in Stephen L. Wasby, ed., *American Government and Politics* (New York: Scribner).

Kluger, Richard. 1976. *Simple Justice: The History of Brown v. Board of Education and Black Americans Struggle for Equality* (New York: Knopf).

MALDEF. N.d. *Diez Anos*.

———. 1972. Brief for Appellees submitted in *San Antonio Independent School District v. Rodriguez*, No. 71-1332.

———. 1981. Motion to Dismiss or Affirm submitted in *Plyler v. Doe*, No. 80-1538.

————. 1982. *Annual Report.*

"MALDEF Attorney Sues to Keep His Job." 1976. *San Antonio Express,* 5 March.

Manwaring, David. 1962. *Render unto Caesar: The Flag Salute Controversy* (University of Chicago Press).

Markham, Roseanne. 1983. Interview with Lee Epstein at MALDEF Washington, D.C., office, 13 January.

"Mexican Aid Fund Getting New Look." 1970. *New York Times,* 5 April, p. 48.

Murphy, Alice. 1970. "Pete Tijerina Firing Requested by Ford," *San Antonio Express,* 21 March.

O'Connor, Karen. 1980. *Women's Organizations' Use of the Courts* (Lexington, Mass.: Lexington Books).

Ortega, Joe C. 1972. "The Plight of the Mexican American Alien," *American Bar Association Journal,* 58 (March):211.

Rubin, Eva R. 1982. *Abortion, Politics, and the Courts* (Westport, Conn.: Greenwood).

"San Antonio Native to Head MALDEF." 1973. *San Antonio Express,* 25 October.

Shanahan, Eileen. 1972. "One U.S. Agency Challenges Another on Antibias Accord," *New York Times,* 30 September.

Shattuck, Petra T., and Jill Norgren. 1979. "Political Use of the Legal Process by Blacks and American Indian Minorities," *Howard Law Journal,* 22:1.

Sorauf, Frank J. 1976. *The Wall of Separation: Constitutional Politics of Church and State* (Princeton, N.J.: Princeton University Press).

"Suit Challenges Precinct Boundaries." 1972. *San Antonio Express,* 24 August.

Stewart, Joseph, Jr., and Edward Heck. 1982. "Ensuring Access to Justice: The Role of Interest Group Lawyers in the 60s Campaign for Civil Rights," *Judicature,* 66 (August):84–95.

Teltsch, Kathleen. 1968. "Grant Aids Latins in the Southwest," *New York Times,* 2 May, p. 38.

Vigil, Maurillio. 1978. *Chicano Politics* (Washington, D.C.: University Press of America).

"Vilma Martinez Gets Top MALDEF Post." 1973. *San Antonio News,* 25 October.

Vose, Clement E. 1959. *Caucasians Only* (Berkeley, Calif.: University of California Press).

Wasby, Stephen L. 1981. "Interest Group Litigation in an Age of Complexity." Paper presented at the annual meeting of the Midwest Political Science Association, Cincinnati, Ohio.

Cases Cited

Brown v. Board of Education, 347 U.S. 483 (1954).
Guinn v. United States, 238 U.S. 347 (1915).
Jimenez v. Naff, 397 U.S. 1005 (1970).
Keyes v. Denver School District #1, 413 U.S. 189 (1973).
Logue v. U.S., 412 U.S. 521 (1973).
Plyler v. Doe, 102 S.Ct. 2382 (1982).
San Antonio Independent School District v. Rodriguez, 411 U.S. 1 (1973).
Shelley v. Kraemer, 334 U.S. 1 (1948).
White v. Regester, 412 U.S. 755 (1973).

21. DISMISSAL, CONVICTION, AND INCARCERATION OF HISPANIC DEFENDANTS: A COMPARISON WITH ANGLOS AND BLACKS[1]

Susan WELCH, *University of Nebraska–Lincoln*

John GRUHL, *University of Nebraska–Lincoln*

Cassia SPOHN, *University of Nebraska–Omaha*

This article examines the dismissal, conviction, and incarceration rates for about 10,000 male defendants in Los Angeles during the late 1970s and compares these rates for Hispanic, Anglo, and black defendants. On controlling for legal and extra-legal factors and after using multivariate analysis, little difference in the treatment of these defendants is found.

While myriad studies have examined differences in convicting and sentencing black and white defendants (for reviews see Hagan, 1974; Kleck, 1981; and Spohn, Gruhl, and Welch, 1981/1982), few studies have examined possible differences between Hispanic and other defendants. Of these, some are flawed methodologically (Lemert and Rosberg, 1948; Garza, 1973; Sissons, 1977).[2] Others are solid but limited. Unnever (1981) found that Hispanics convicted of drug offenses in Miami were more likely than Anglos to be incarcerated, but, once he controlled for pretrial detention status and attorney type, this difference disappeared. Zatz (1981) showed that Hispanics and Anglos convicted of felonies in California were sentenced for comparable lengths of time. These are useful studies but not sufficient to generalize about the treatment of Hispanic defendants. Unnever focused on only one category of offenses, and both Unnever and Zatz examined only one stage—sentencing—of the criminal justice proc-

[1] The authors would like to thank the University of Nebraska Research Council for its support of this project and the officials in Los Angeles who helped us obtain the data used herein.

[2] Lemert and Rosberg did not control for offense or prior record. Sissons did not control for race adequately, as he grouped blacks and whites together. Garza might not have controlled for relevant variables adequately, as he did not explain clearly which, if any, were used in each part of the analysis, and as he did not justify an unusual measure of prior record—two felony convictions. Further, he did not present specific findings for most of his analyses or show tests of statistical significance.

ess. Given these studies, and given the large and growing Hispanic population, which in some areas of the nation greatly outnumbers the black population, further investigation seems in order.

Our study analyzes the treatment of about 10,000 male defendants in Los Angeles. It examines the dismissal, conviction, and incarceration rates of Hispanic,[3] Anglo, and black defendants for evidence of racial disparity.

Data and Methods

We started with a complete file of felony cases heard between 1977 and 1980 in Los Angeles County Superior Court. From this file we selected those cases where only a single charge was levied against the defendant.[4] Then, because there are substantial male-female differences in convicting and sentencing which vary by race (Spohn, Welch, and Gruhl, 1982) and because our data base had relatively few Hispanic and Anglo females, we dropped cases with a female defendant. This left us with just over 20,000 cases. Because of missing data on some of the variables, we used about 10,000 cases in the multivariate analysis.[5]

[3] While people of Mexican and Spanish origin do not agree on a favored ethnic self-label (cf. Garcia, 1981), here we will use the term "Hispanic" to refer to them. In Los Angeles over 75 percent of people of Hispanic origin claim Mexican heritage (1980 Census of Population). We will use the term "Anglo" to refer to whites not of Mexican or Spanish origin. We are unsure whether black Hispanics (i.e., some Cubans) are categorized as black or Hispanic, but in Los Angeles only 1.1 percent of Hispanics are black (1980 Census of Population).

[4] Fifty-four percent of the cases in our sample had a single charge. We selected only cases where a single charge was levied against the defendant because of the nature of one of our major independent variables, the crime score, which measures the severity of the charge against the defendant. Because the score is cumulative—that is, it aggregates points for the severity of *each* charge against the defendant into one composite score—it could give a disproportionately high score to defendants charged with several less serious crimes. Thus, a defendant charged with several counts of a crime such as robbery could receive a score higher than that of a defendant charged with a single count of murder. Because prosecutors and judges tend to be guided by the most serious charge against the defendant, rather than by the number of charges, use of the crime score to measure the severity of the charge against defendants with multiple charges could produce misleading results.

[5] Because dropping cases with missing data on some of the variables significantly reduced the number of cases, in an analysis not reported here we examined the race/ethnicity-dismissal relationship without controlling for each of the three extralegal variables—attorney, employment, and injury—singly and in combination. This increased the number of cases from about 10,000 to between 12,000 and 16,000 (depending on which variable was omitted). Nevertheless, this did not substantially change the results of our analysis. This analysis showed a small though significant difference in dismissal rates between blacks and other defendants when the other variables were not controlled; blacks were more likely to have their cases dismissed than either Hispanics or Anglos. However, inspection of the bivariate correlation matrices among the dependent variables and the offense and prior record variables with each set of cases (i.e., when 10,000, 12,000, and 16,000 cases were included) revealed differences no greater than .03 in any correlation among the different sets. Thus, the slight change in findings concerning the dismissal variable is not due to the fact that our smaller number of cases is not representative of the complete file, but rather due to the fact that as controls are added, the effect of race/ethnicity changes, as would be expected. Analyses of the conviction and sentencing variables with different case bases revealed no differences from findings reported here.

Three dependent variables were used in the analysis: whether or not the charge against the defendant was dismissed, whether or not the defendant was convicted, and whether or not the defendant, once convicted, was incarcerated.[6] Use of these three variables allowed us to test for racial discrimination at three distinct stages in the processing of defendants through the criminal justice system. Most studies of racial disparity have focused on convicting and sentencing. However, this focus ignores the possible existence of discrimination at the pretrial stages. By examining the prosecutor's decision to dismiss the charge against the defendant or not, we were able to explore in part the issue of pretrial discrimination.

Six independent variables were employed: the defendant's race/ethnicity, offense score, prior record score, employment status (1 = employed, 0 = not), type of attorney (private = 1, other = 0), and whether or not the defendant injured anyone (1 = yes, 0 = no) while committing the crime.[7] Two of these variables, the offense score and the prior record score, require elaboration.

The offense score, which ranges from 1 to 99,[8] is used by the Los Angeles County district attorney's office to measure the gravity of the charge against the defendant. The score includes such items as the number of victims killed, hospitalized, or treated and released, the number of victims of forcible sexual intercourse, the number of victims threatened by a weapon or by physical force, the number of premises forcibly entered, and so on. Each item is assigned a weight,[9] and the score is calculated by multiplying the weight of the item by the number of times it occurred and then summing these. We used this score as a substitute for and, we think, an improvement upon the standard categorization of felonies. Since the score takes various facets of a criminal act into account, it enabled us to distinguish between defendants charged with more or less serious versions of the same crime.

The prior record score is used by the district attorney's office to measure the seriousness of the defendant's criminal record. Four items are included in the score: whether or not the defendant had been arrested in the last five years, the number of previous arrests, the number of arrests for crimes against persons, and whether or not the defendant ever used an alias.

---

[6] For conviction we included only defendants who were tried by a judge or jury, while for incarceration we included defendants who were convicted by a judge or jury or who pleaded guilty.

[7] Unfortunately, the defendant's pretrial detention status was not included in the data file.

[8] If the computed value of the offense score is greater than 99, it is set at 99.

[9] The 11 items included in the score and their weights are as follows: the number of victims killed (26); the number of victims of forcible sexual intercourse (10); the number of victims hospitalized (7); the number of victims treated and released (4); the number of victims threatened or intimidated by display of weapons (4); the number of victims threatened or intimidated verbally or by physical force (2); the number of victims of sex crimes intimidated by any type of weapon (2); the number of motor vehicles stolen (2); the number of premises forcibly entered (1); the dollar value of property stolen, damaged, or destroyed (less than $10 [1], $10–250 [2], $251–2,000 [3], over $2,000 [4]); and whether the defendant possessed a firearm or replica of a firearm (5) or another dangerous weapon (1) at the time of arrest.

Each item included in the score is weighted,[10] and the scores for each item are summed. This score, then, discriminates among defendants primarily on the basis of their prior arrest records.[11]

Multiple regression was used to examine the relative rates of dismissal, conviction and incarceration of Hispanics, Anglos, and blacks while controlling for the other independent variables. Since all three of our dependent variables were dichotomous, discriminant analyses were also done as a check on the validity of the regression results. With a dichotomous dependent variable, discriminant analysis yields similar coefficients to regression coefficients but more reliable tests of significance.[12] However, since our discriminant results were nearly identical with those of the regression, only the regression ones will be presented.

Findings

Table 1 presents the results of our analysis. Adjusted dismissal, conviction, and incarceration rates for Hispanic, Anglo, and black defendants were calculated controlling for the seriousness of the offense, the seriousness of the prior criminal record, employment status, type of attorney, and whether or not the defendant injured anyone while committing the crime.[13] We find few differences in the treatment of these defendants. While Hispanics are convicted more often than either Anglos or blacks, and sentenced to prison more often than Anglos but less than blacks, the differences are very small and not statistically significant. The only statistically significant difference in the regression is in the dismissal rate for Hispanics and Anglos. Even here, however, the difference is small; the rate for Hispanics is only 2 percent higher than the rate for Anglos. As such, it does not seem

[10] The weights for each item are as follows: an arrest within the last five years (10); the number of previous arrests (5); the number of arrests for crimes against persons (5); and use of an alias (2.5).

[11] Because it focuses on a defendant's arrest record, the prior record score may be an imperfect indicator of the seriousness of a defendant's prior record, at least with respect to explaining the sentence imposed. Research has shown that conviction, and especially incarceration, are better predictors of sentence than arrest (Welch, Gruhl, and Spohn, 1982). This may not be true, however, for either dismissal or conviction.

[12] To obtain accurate OLS estimates, the error terms must be normally distributed. When the dependent variable has only two values, it is impossible, or nearly so, to have such a normally distributed term. The residuals will be correlated with the independent variable, and the variance of the residuals will vary systematically with the independent variables (for general discussions of this problem, cf. Aldrich and Cnudde, 1975; Kritzer, 1978; Swofford, 1980). With large sample sizes, these problems are somewhat mitigated (Stokes, 1967), but nevertheless still remain when one has the extreme case of a truncated dependent variable, a binary dependent variable.

[13] These adjusted figures were computed in the following way. Dummy variables were created for two of the three race/ethnicity groups—Anglos and blacks. Regressions were done on each of the three dependent variables using the five independent variables as controls. See Spohn, Gruhl, and Welch (1981/1982) for an explication of the adjustment procedure. Briefly, the difference between any two categories is equal to the unstandardized regression coefficient for the relevant dummy variable. So, for example, the difference of .02 between dismissal rates for Hispanics and Anglos reflects a .02 unstandardized regression coefficient for Hispanics, when Anglos are the omitted category.

TABLE 1

Differences in Treatment of Hispanic, Anglo, and Black Defendants, Controlling for Other Factors[a]

	Charge Dismissed[b]	Convicted[c]	Sentenced to Prison[d]
Hispanic	28%	73%	62%
Anglo	26**	71	61
Black	27	70	63

[a] Controlling for offense score, prior record score, employment status, type of attorney, and whether or not the defendant injured anyone while committing the crime. For a description of the way in which the adjusted means were calculated, see note 13.

[b] N = 9,912. There were 2,552 Hispanics, 2,357 Anglos, and 5,003 blacks.

[c] Includes only defendants who were tried by a judge or jury. N = 1,440. There were 328 Hispanics, 239 Anglos, and 873 blacks.

[d] Includes defendants who were convicted by a judge or jury or who pleaded guilty. N = 6,378. There were 1,632 Hispanics, 1,619 Anglos, and 3,127 blacks.

**$p \leq .01$.

substantively significant, and in the discriminant analysis this difference was not statistically significant. Further evidence of the lack of difference among the three groups is the fact that each group is the most severely treated as measured by one indicator, the least severely treated on another, and is in the middle on a third.

Conclusions

Our findings show little difference in the dismissal, conviction, and incarceration of about 10,000 Hispanic, Anglo, and black male defendants in Los Angeles. These findings are consistent with those of Unnever (1981), who discovered little difference in incarceration, and Zatz, who discovered little difference in sentence length. Yet our findings broaden those of Unnever and Zatz, since our findings also show few differences in two additional stages of the criminal justice process—dismissal and conviction. The fact that our findings show little difference in dismissal of charges against the three groups of defendants is especially worth noting, since researchers generally have ignored this pretrial stage but at the same time have speculated that it, being less visible than the trial or sentence stages, would harbor more discrimination (Kleck, 1981:799; Radelet, 1981:926).

While our findings comparing treatment of Hispanics with other defendants are consistent with previous methodologically sophisticated research, our findings comparing treatment of blacks and whites are not entirely consistent with those of previous researchers. Several have discovered some difference in incarceration (Spohn, Gruhl, and Welch, 1981/1982; Nagel, 1969; Pope, 1975; Levin, 1977; Unnever, Frazier, and Henretta, 1980). Apparently in borderline cases, in which defendants could have been sentenced to probation or to prison, blacks were more likely to be sent to prison, while whites were more likely to be given probation (Spohn, Gruhl, and Welch, 1981/1982).

One possible explanation for our finding of no discrimination against blacks in incarceration is the western locale of our study. One can argue that the political environment of the urban West is less hostile to blacks than elsewhere. There are fewer blacks in urban areas of the West than in urban areas elsewhere, so blacks may be perceived as less of a threat in the West. At the same time blacks are more likely to be elected mayor or city council members at a rate proportional to their population in the West (Karnig and Welch, 1981). Though Pope (1975) did find evidence of discrimination against blacks in California, he found greater evidence in rural than in urban areas. Another possible explanation for our finding is our very recent data. Past research has shown diminishing levels of discrimination against blacks in sentencing over time, in accord with more general societal treatment of blacks.[14] Since most studies have employed data at least in part less recent than ours, they would be expected to uncover more evidence of discrimination.

Our findings of insignificant difference in the treatment of the three groups of defendants may come as a surprise. Theories of the criminal justice process predict that it will reflect the inequality in society (Chambliss and Seidman, 1971). Yet studies of the trial and sentence stages of the process seem to be developing a consensus that, whether there is racial discrimination or not, at least there is not as much as would be predicted (Kleck, 1981). Instead, what may appear to be racial discrimination is often the effect of legal factors, such as seriousness of offense or prior record, or extralegal factors, such as pretrial detention status, type of attorney, or employment status, which reflect wealth discrimination rather than racial discrimination.

Because we examined a large number of defendants charged with a large variety of offenses, and because we controlled for legal and some extralegal factors, we believe our findings are a contribution to the scant and fragmentary knowledge about the treatment of Hispanic defendants. Still, other cities and other stages of the process might exhibit more discrimination than we found here. For instance, past research indicated discrimination against Hispanics by law enforcement officials (Bayley and Mendelsohn, 1968; Grebler, Moore, and Guzman, 1970; U.S. Commission on Civil Rights, 1970; Morales, 1972; Cortes, 1974). So just because there may not be significant discrimination at some stages of the process does not mean that there will not be significant discrimination at other stages. On the other hand, perhaps in the more than a decade since this earlier research was done, there has been a change toward more equalitarian treatment by the police too. Clearly more research needs to be done.

REFERENCES

Aldrich, John, and Charles Cnudde. 1975. "Probing the Bounds of Conventional Wisdom: A Comparison of Regression, Probit and Discriminant Analysis," *American Journal of Political Science,* 19 (August):571–608.

[14] However, some of this may be due to methodological artifacts, especially in early studies, as well as to discrimination (Hagan, 1974).

Bayley, David H., and Harold Mendelsohn. 1968. *Minorities and the Police* (New York: Free Press).

Chambliss, William, and Robert Seidman. 1971. *Law, Order and Power* (Reading, Mass.: Addison-Wesley).

Cortes, Carolos. 1974. *The Mexican American and the Law* (New York: Arno Press).

Garcia, John. 1981. "Self Identity among the Mexican-origin Population," *Social Science Quarterly,* 62 (March):88–98.

Garza, Hisauro. 1973. "Administration of Justice: Chicanos in Monterey County," *Aztlan,* 4 (Spring):137–46.

Grebler, Leo, Joan W. Moore, and Ralph C. Guzman. 1970. *The Mexican American People* (New York: Free Press).

Hagan, John. 1974. "Extra-Legal Attributes and Criminal Sentencing: An Assessment of a Sociological Viewpoint," *Law & Society Review,* 8 (Spring):357.

Karnig, Albert K., and Susan Welch. 1981. *Black Representation and Urban Public Policy* (Chicago: University of Chicago Press).

Kleck, Gary. 1981. "Racial Discrimination in Criminal Sentencing: A Critical Evaluation of the Evidence with Additional Evidence on the Death Penalty," *American Sociological Review,* 46 (December):783–805.

Kritzer, Herbert M. 1978. "An Introduction to Multivariate Contingency Table Analysis," *American Journal of Political Science,* 22 (February):187–226.

Lemert, Edwin, and Judy Rosberg. 1948. "The Administration of Justice to Minority Groups in Los Angeles County," in R. L. Beals, Leonard Bloom, and Franklin Fearing, eds., *University of California Publications in Culture and Society,* vol. 2 (Berkeley: University of California Press).

Levin, Martin A. 1977. *Urban Politics and Criminal Courts* (Chicago: University of Chicago Press).

Morales, Armando. 1972. *Ando Sangando: A Study of Mexican American Police Conflict* (La Puente, Calif.: Perspective Publications).

Nagel, Stuart S. 1969. *The Legal Process from a Behavioral Perspective* (Homewood, Ill.: Dorsey).

Pope, Carl E. 1975. *Sentencing of California Felony Offenders* (Washington, D.C.: U.S. Department of Justice, Law Enforcement Assistance Administration, Criminal Justice Research Center).

Radelet, Michael L. 1981. "Racial Characteristics and the Imposition of the Death Penalty," *American Sociological Review,* 46 (December):918–27.

Sissons, Peter. 1977. *The Hispanic Experience of Criminal Justice* (New York: Fordham University, Hispanic Research Center).

Spohn, Cassia, John Gruhl, and Susan Welch. 1981/1982. "The Effect of Race on Sentencing: A Re-Examination of an Unsettled Question," *Law & Society Review,* 16 (Winter):71–88.

Spohn, Cassia, Susan Welch, and John Gruhl. 1982. "Women Defendants in Court: The Interaction between Sex and Race in Convicting and Sentencing." Paper presented at the annual meeting of the American Sociological Association.

Stokes, Donald. 1967. "Some Dynamic Elements of Contests for the Presidency," *American Political Science Review,* 60 (March):19–28.

Swofford, Michael. 1980. "Parametric Techniques for Contingency Table Analysis," *American Sociological Review,* 45 (August):664–90.

Unnever, James. 1981. "Institutional Racism: Direct and Structural Discrimination." Paper presented at the 76th Annual Meeting of the American Sociological Association, August, Toronto, Ontario.

Unnever, James D., Charles E. Frazier, and John C. Henretta. 1980. "Race Differences in Criminal Sentencing," *Sociological Quarterly,* 21 (Spring):197–206.

U.S. Commission on Civil Rights. 1970. *Mexican Americans and the Administration of Justice in the Southwest* (Washington, D.C.: U.S. Government Printing Office).

Welch, Susan, John Gruhl, and Cassia Spohn. 1982. "The Influence of Alternative Measures of Prior Record in Explaining Sentencing." Unpublished manuscript, University of Nebraska–Lincoln.

Zatz, Marjorie. 1981. "Differential Treatment within the Criminal Justice System by Race/Ethnicity." Paper presented at the 76th Annual Meeting of the American Sociological Association, August, Toronto, Ontario.

22. ETHNICITY AND JUSTICE IN THE SOUTHWEST: THE SENTENCING OF ANGLO, BLACK, AND MEXICAN ORIGIN DEFENDANTS[1]

Malcolm D. HOLMES, *New Mexico State University*

Howard C. DAUDISTEL, *The University of Texas at El Paso*

This study compares severity of case disposition for Anglo, black and Mexican origin burglary and robbery defendants in two metropolitan jurisdictions in the southwestern United States. Both the additive effects of the race variables and their interactions with other determinants of sentence severity were considered. Substantial evidence of discrimination in both additive and interactive models was obtained for one jurisdiction, but the evidence of discrimination was considerably weaker for the other. Jurisdictional differences which may explain this contrast are discussed.

Majority-minority sentencing differentials have been the subject of extensive social scientific and legal research. As with many studies of race and ethnic relations, the criminological literature reflects a traditional research orientation that focuses on blacks to the veritable exclusion of other minorities. Here we also examine the sentencing of black and white felons, but, more importantly, our analysis emphasizes the legal system's treatment of those of Mexican origin in the southwestern United States.

Many social scientists consider it axiomatic that racial and ethnic minorities receive harsh and unequal treatment in the American criminal justice system (e.g., Quinney, 1970; Chambliss and Seidman, 1971; Blauner, 1972). Certainly evidence of this exists with respect to blacks (National Advisory Commission on Civil Disorders, 1968) and those of Mexican origin (U.S. Commission on Civil Rights, 1970), but the data regarding sen-

[1] The data used in this study were collected under the auspices of Grant 77-NI-99-0049 awarded to H. S. Miller, W. McDonald, J. Cramer, and H. Rossman, Institute of Criminal Law and Procedure, Georgetown University Law Center, by the National Institute of Law Enforcement and Criminal Justice, Law Enforcement Assistance Administration, U.S. Department of Justice. Ronald A. Farrell and Cookie White Stephan provided very helpful comments on an earlier draft of this paper. The referees of *SSQ* also provided useful comments. The authors are solely responsible for the data analysis and points of view presented in this study.

tencing are hardly unequivocal. Two recent reviews of the substantial black-white sentencing literature (Hagan, 1974; Kleck, 1981) offer only inconclusive support for the hypothesis that otherwise similar black and white defendants receive unequal sentences. Moreover, Hagan (1974) cautions that even where *statistically* significant differences in the sentences given blacks and whites have been reported, the *substantive* significance or magnitude of the disparities has often been quite marginal (a function of the large samples commonly employed in such research). Kleck (1981) has reached an even stronger conclusion, arguing that, at least in the aggregate, *overt* discrimination in the sentencing of blacks is no longer detectable.

The relatively limited data on the sentencing of Mexican origin defendants also offer little systematic evidence of discrimination (e.g., Lemert and Rosberg, 1948; Baab and Furgeson, 1967; Garza, 1973; Sissons, 1977; Petersilia, 1983; Welch, Gruhl, and Spohn, 1984). As with many studies of black-white sentencing patterns, some of these do not adequately control relevant characteristics of the defendant or crime (Lemert and Rosberg, 1948; Garza, 1973; Sissons, 1977). However, even well-executed studies provide only mixed results (cf. Baab and Furgeson, 1967; Petersilia, 1983; Welch, Gruhl, and Spohn, 1984).

Despite the mixed data and consequent conclusions, concern about equality persists. Since it has been well documented that criminal justice agents at all stages of the system have been granted a significant amount of discretionary freedom (e.g., LaFave, 1965; Blumberg, 1967; Alschuler, 1968; Rosett and Cressey, 1976), the legal system offers relatively few real restraints to decision-makers charged with enforcing the law. Extralegal (i.e., nonstatutory) considerations may informally influence the administration of justice in ways that are formally regarded as illegitimate. Since crimes are acts which are defined as criminal by officials of the legal system who must interpret both the meaning of the law and the behavior of those alleged to have acted criminally, informal notions about the character of defendants may constitute self-fulfilling prophecies. Institutionalized within the legal system are stereotypical conceptions of criminality which affect the treatment of defendants throughout the adjudication process (e.g., Sudnow, 1965; Quinney, 1970; Swigert and Farrell, 1977). Since lower-class, minority males are more likely to fit popular images of criminality, such defendants are especially susceptible to stigmatization and, consequently, differential treatment (Simmons, 1965; Swigert and Farrell, 1977). Indeed, the "subculture of justice" (Rosett and Cressey, 1976) in a particular jurisdiction may consist of several lay theories about human behavior that disadvantage minorities.

A related consideration is whether we can expect *all* minority defendants to be sentenced differently than their majority group counterparts. The answer is unquestionably no. Characteristics of an alleged criminal act certainly affect the perceived character of the defendant. LaFree (1980), for instance, has shown that racial identities within the criminal-victim dyad strongly influence sentencing in rape cases. He concludes that "American society is characterized by a sexual stratification system which imposes more serious sanctions on men from less powerful social groups who are accused of assaulting women from more powerful social groups" (La Free, 1980:852). Thus, how the various attributes of a case affect sentence may vary because special significance can be attached to a particular combination of race and another characteristic. A number of legal (e.g., prior record, use of weapon) and extralegal (e.g., access to bail, jury trial) attributes apparently influence case disposition (e.g., Green, 1961; Ares, Rankin, and Sturz, 1963; Rankin, 1964; Sudnow, 1965; Chiricos, Jackson, and Waldo, 1972; Burke and Turk, 1975; Bernstein, Kelly, and Doyle, 1977; Uhlman and Walker, 1980), but scant attention has been paid to the possible interaction of race-ethnicity with such factors in the sentencing decision. Therefore, the research reported below not only considers whether race-ethnicity per se has an effect on sentence, net of the effects of relevant controls, but whether other predictors of sentence operate differently across subsamples of race or ethnic identity.

Finally, it is reasonable to anticipate that the relative quality of justice varies from jurisdiction to jurisdiction. Kleck (1981) suggests that not all informal notions about race-ethnicity and crime adversely affect minority defendants; rather, some actually operate to their benefit. Moreover, in cities where minorities represent a high proportion of the total population, they may be perceived as more threatening than in areas which are comprised predominantly of majority members (Blalock, 1967), thereby exacerbating the salience of negative criminality stereotypes. Since such issues could be pertinent to the present study, we conducted the analysis separately for the two metropolitan jurisdictions discussed below. The implications of jurisdictional differences are explored in our concluding remarks.

Research Setting and Data

The statistical analysis presented in this study is based on case files for "closed" (no appeal pending) burglary and robbery convictions prosecuted during the period of January 1976–August 1977 in the state district courts of El Paso, Texas, and Tucson, Arizona. Although other felonies and misdemeanors appear in these case files, the vast majority involved burglary or robbery offenses as the primary violation for which defendants were convicted.[2]

Probably one reason for the mixed results reported in sentencing studies is differences in the dependent measures used. Sentence length is commonly utilized (see Kleck, 1981:790–91), but is not without its disadvantages. Sentences of relatively indeterminate length are commonly imposed and, consequently, the actual period of incarceration (or probation) is con-

[2] Too few women, native Americans, acquittals, bench trials, and jail terms appear in these data to permit analysis of such cases. After the deletion of these cases, El Paso data only contained primary convictions for burglary or robbery offenses. Over 80 percent of the Tucson sample involved primary convictions on burglary and robbery charges. Other felonies were excluded to avoid infelicitously generalizing on the basis of a few cases (no other felony was represented by more than a handful of cases) and to maintain a high degree of comparability across the city subsamples.

tingent on factors such as inmate behavior and parole board decisions. Therefore, relatively small differences in length of imposed sentence could be essentially meaningless. A more clear-cut indicator of sentencing discrimination is variation in the likelihood of incarceration, a measure which also has been employed in previous studies. This measure corresponds well to the perceived severity of legal penalties (Erickson and Gibbs, 1979), and a great deal of the discretion available to the courts involves the decision to probate or incarcerate (Rosett and Cressey, 1976).

Although the most important distinction is probation versus incarceration, our dependent variable also included an intermediate category comprised of split sentences (e.g., prison with probation). Thus, the dependent variable was coded 0 = probation; 1 = split sentence; 2 = prison. The intermediate category represented the mode for the Tucson data (probation = 30.2%; split = 39.6%; prison = 30.2%), and it was important to separate this sentence type because maximum sentences (in years) were quite short ($\overline{X}$ = .79; SD = 1.15) compared to prison sentences ($\overline{X}$ = 9.17; SD = 7.78). Obviously this is an important distinction. In the El Paso data, only a single case was coded as a split sentence (probation = 55.2%; split = 0.6%; prison = 44.2%). Consequently, the El Paso results reported below are virtually identical to those obtained with a dichotomous dependent variable.[3]

Race-ethnicity was incorporated into the multiple regression analyses reported below as a set of dummy variables representing Anglo (non-Mexican origin white), black, and Mexican origin defendants. The use of dummy variables requires the deletion of one category (Anglo here) to avoid linear dependence, which category then serves as the baseline to interpret the regression coefficients estimated for the included categories.

As noted above, sentencing studies have been concerned with a number of other legal and extralegal predictors of sentence. An important criticism of many studies of race-ethnicity and sentencing is that they do not include such variables. Insofar as possible, we have incorporated such variables in this analysis, which helps guard against concluding that disparities in sentencing exist when the observed differences are actually a spurious indication of uncontrolled variation in other variables that may be

[3] The regression analyses reported below were also conducted with the split sentence and prison categories combined to create a dichotomous dependent variable. The regression coefficients obtained for Tucson were of the same direction, but were much weaker predictors than those reported here. The El Paso results were essentially identical, except the metric coefficients and their standard errors are approximately twice as large in the results presented here. Metric coefficients for the trichotomous dependent variable were reported because they can be compared directly to those presented for Tucson. Copies of the dichotomous regression results may be obtained from the authors upon request. It should also be noted that dependent variables such as used here technically violate the assumptions of ordinary least squares (OLS) regression, which assumes that the dependent variable is continuous. Normally, however, OLS regression is quite robust in the face of such violations (Bohrnstedt and Carter, 1971). Furthermore, an examination of the frequency distributions of the dependent variables (presented above) indicates that the distributions were not inordinately skewed, which substantially increases our confidence in the OLS regression results reported below.

correlated with race-ethnicity and sentence. Some such variables were not included in this analysis because they possessed negligible variation or too much missing data to be useful. These included factors such as type of counsel, race-ethnicity of victim, harm to victim, employment status, and citizenship.

Among the legally relevant controls is a set of dummy variables for the robbery and burglary felonies included in the data, which control for the length of sentence imposed by statute. The "felony one" category includes those offenses carrying a sentence of 5 to 99 years or life in prison in Texas, and not less than 5 years in Arizona. The felonies included in this category are aggravated robbery and major burglary offenses. The "felony two" felonies represent the necessarily deleted category for this set of dummy variables. The category includes offenses carrying a penalty of 2 to 20 years in Texas, and either 1 to 10 or 1 to 15 years in Arizona. This category is comprised of serious nonaggravated robbery and less serious burglary offenses. The "felony three" category includes crimes with sentences of 2 to 10 years in Texas, and less than 7½ years in Arizona. In the El Paso data, this category includes only burglary of an automobile, while in the Tucson data it includes several statutes concerning relatively petty burglary and robbery offenses.

Needless to say, a great deal of discretion is embodied in the essentially indeterminate sentencing codes of Texas and Arizona, particularly since these are felonies for which probation is often routinely granted. Consequently, a number of other legal factors are considered in our analysis, including prior felony convictions (0–5+), whether the conviction was for multiple charges (0 = no; 1 = yes), and whether a weapon was used in the commission of the crime (0 = no; 1 = yes).

Several extralegal attributes of the defendant or his case disposition were also included as controls. These indicated whether the defendant achieved pretrial release (0 = no; 1 = yes), whether he was convicted by a jury (0 = no; 1 = yes), and number of prior *nonconviction* arrests (0–5+).[4]

Analysis and Results

The results of our sentencing analysis appear in Table 1. For reasons mentioned above, the ordinary least squares multiple regression analyses reported here were conducted separately for El Paso and Tucson. If evidence of overt discrimination exists for only one city, combining the city subsamples could easily mitigate or inflate the strength of such evidence.

Additionally, two models were estimated for each subsample. Model 1 presents the additive statistical model that permits us to examine the main

[4] The degree of intercorrelation among the independent variables included in this analysis generally was not substantial, although the correlation of use of a weapon and the felony one dummy variable category was fairly high in Tucson (r = .67). Consequently, multicollinearity does not appear to be a significant problem in this analysis, although the Tucson coefficients for weapon use and felony one cannot be interpreted too literally. A copy of the correlation matrices and other descriptive statistics may be obtained from the authors upon request.

TABLE 1

Metric Coefficients, Standard Errors (in parentheses), and Standardized Coefficients for the OLS Regression of Sentence Severity on Legal and Extralegal Atributes

Independent Variables	El Paso (N = 163)		Tucson (N = 321)	
	Model 1	Model 2	Model 1	Model 2
Legal variables				
Felony one	−.058	−.108	.305**	.256*
	(.123)	(.115)	(.149)	(.149)
	−.029	−.053	.151	.127
Felony two[a]	—	—	—	—
Felony three	.277	.324	−.129	−.155*
	(.215)	(.201)	(.095)	(.094)
	.078	.092	−.083	−.099
Prior felony convictions				
(0–5+)	.237***	.238***	.108***	.107***
	(.044)	(.041)	(.018)	(.018)
	.344	.347	.312	.310
Multiple charge conviction (0 = no;				
1 = yes)	.535***	.448***	.044	−.036
	(.186)	(.176)	(.099)	(.115)
	.165	.138	.024	−.020
Use of a weapon				
(0 = no; 1 = yes)	.780***	.817***	.053	.052
	(.136)	(.129)	(.122)	(.122)
	.344	.360	.030	.029
Extralegal variables				
Pretrial release				
(0 = no; 1 = yes)	−.438***	−.523***	−.213**	−.211**
	(.120)	(.116)	(.084)	(.083)
	−.216	−.258	−.136	−.135
Prior nonconviction felony arrests				
(0–5+)	.122***	.108***	.090***	.089***
	(.040)	(.037)	(.028)	(.028)
	.192	.168	.166	.166
Jury trial (0 = no;				
1 = yes)	.136	−.795***	−.034	−.292
	(.149)	(.257)	(.144)	(.194)
	.054	−.315	−.012	−.108
Anglo[a]	—	—	—	—
Black	.870***	.870***	−.064	−.149
	(.218)	(.245)	(.117)	(.127)
	.246	.246	−.030	−.070
Mexican origin	.158	−.013	.013	−.084
	(.133)	(.129)	(.090)	(.100)
	.077	−.006	.008	−.050
Interaction terms				
Black × jury	—	—	—	0.548*
				(0.304)
				0.128
Mexican origin × jury	—	1.302***	—	0.757*
		(0.299)		(0.455)
		0.449		0.094

TABLE 1—continued

Independent Variables	El Paso (N = 163)		Tucson (N = 321)	
	Model 1	Model 2	Model 1	Model 2
Black × pretrial release	—	0.788* (0.404) 0.123	—	—
Mexican origin × multiple charge	—	—	—	0.292 (0.208) 0.091
Constant	0.344	0.505	0.840	0.903
R^2	.546	.611	.221	.238
Increment to R^2	—	.065***	—	.017*

a This category in each group of variables was necessarily deleted from the regression model and serves as the benchmark for interpreting this set of dummy variables.

*$p < .10$.

**$p < .05$.

***$p < .01$.

effects of the race-ethnicity variables on sentence after controlling for legal and extralegal attributes of the defendant and the crime for which he was convicted. Here an effort is made to determine if race-ethnicity affects case disposition severity independently of effects such as prior record. Model 2 permits us to assess whether the coefficients estimated in the additive model differ across race-ethnicity categories. For example, do jury trials work to the advantage or disadvantage of minority defendants? What about the use of a weapon or other facts of the case which might be perceived in a different light when the defendant is a minority member? The interaction terms added in model 2 were obtained using a forward stepwise procedure. Coefficients which achieved statistical significance ($p < .10$) were retained.

El Paso. Model 1 indicates that the use of a weapon, conviction on multiple charges, and especially prior felony convictions increased sentence severity. A felony one conviction did not increase a defendant's likelihood of being incarcerated, but those in the felony three category were actually somewhat more likely to be incarcerated than those in the deleted felony two category. We can only speculate about the latter finding, but we suspect that at least some automobile burglary dispositions involved a single offense even though the defendant may have been apprehended with a considerable amount of stolen property. Such adjudications are clearly expeditious from the standpoint of controlling court dockets.

With respect to the extralegal controls, we find that both pretrial release and prior felony arrests were related to dispositional severity. Making bail apparently reduced sentence severity, which is consistent with previous findings (Ares, Rankin, and Sturz, 1963; Rankin, 1964). Nonconviction prior arrests were associated with greater sentence severity. Although legally irrelevant, such arrests may act as a negative index of character. Although model 1 suggests that a jury trial had little effect on sentence severity, this seemingly negligible coefficient masks substantial interactions which will be analyzed with reference to model 2.

Our final observation with respect to model 1 concerns the main effects of the race-ethnicity variables on sentence severity. Here we find that the dummy variable for blacks is one of the best predictors of sentence. The metric coefficient ($b = .870$) represents nearly a full point on the severity scale. Thus, black defendants were virtually assured of incarceration, regardless of the circumstances of their personal biography and the crime for which they were convicted. Although the coefficient for Mexican origin defendants did not quite achieve statistical significance, it was again positive.

Turning to model 2, we find two interaction effects which merit attention. First and most significantly, the Mexican origin × jury interaction appears to be the best predictor of sentence among the variables contained in the regression. The metric coefficient ($b = 1.30$) approaches one-half the range of the severity scale, which attests to the virtual assurance of a prison sentence for Mexican origin defendants whose cases were heard by juries. The small coefficient for the Mexican origin category suggests that this interaction is responsible for the sentencing differential found in model 1.

In Texas, not only do juries determine guilt, they impose sentence. We cannot, however, simply attribute the Mexican origin × jury interaction to discrimination on the part of Anglo jurors. We have no systematic information about jury composition in these data, but it is general knowledge that those of Mexican origin commonly serve on El Paso juries. To the degree that they participated in these apparently discriminatory sentencing decisions, two factors may be involved. First, it has been observed that high-status jurors exert disproportionately high influence on jury decisions, while low-status jurors exert relatively little influence (Strodtbeck, James, and Hawkins, 1957). The high ethnic (and probably occupational) status of Anglo jurors might greatly influence mixed juries, even though their input may well reflect stereotypical conceptions about race-ethnicity and criminality. The other factor involves intragroup cleavages within the Mexican origin community. Some have argued that class differentiation can supersede ethnic similarity among those of Mexican origin (e.g., Stoddard, 1973). Therefore, middle-class Mexican origin jurors may perceive typically lower-class robbery and burglary defendants as threatening, not only relative to their property interests, but to their status within the middle-class community as a whole.

The substantive significance of this finding cannot be overemphasized. Thirteen percent of this subsample were Mexican origin defendants tried by juries, and the size of the interaction reported here is so great that alone it adds nearly 5 percent to the already quite substantial R^2 obtained in model 1.

The second interaction of interest is black × pretrial release. Unlike others, it would appear that blacks were not advantaged by obtaining bail. However, this interaction involved only a few cases; consequently, we must stress that great caution must be attached to any generalization from this finding.

Within the El Paso data it appears that Mexican origin defendants received harsher sentences *only* when tried by juries, while blacks consistently received more severe sentences. The El Paso state district court judges are elected officials, and the majority of El Paso's population is of Mexican origin (U.S. Bureau of the Census, 1983a). Consequently, it is likely that El Paso judges are especially sensitive to the Mexican origin community, since allegation of prejudicial sentencing could be quite damaging. Also, many courthouse actors, especially attorneys and police officers, are of Mexican origin. Blacks, on the other hand, are poorly represented both in the community and the courthouse. Thus, nothing acts to mitigate prejudicial sentencing, at least on the part of judges, who sentenced most blacks in these data.

Tucson. In this city, the legal variables which apparently affected case disposition severity are prior felony convictions and conviction for a felony one category offense. The coefficient for the felony three category was negative, although it did not achieve statistical significance. The remaining variables in the legal block appear not to have influenced the likelihood of incarceration. Use of a weapon was correlated with felony one here, which probably explains its seeming lack of influence.

Among the extralegal variables, again obtaining pretrial release worked to a defendant's advantage, while prior arrests did not. Although there appears to have been no effect of jury trial on sentence, this again is deceptive, as model 2 will demonstrate.

Insofar as race-ethnicity is concerned, the coefficients here indicate virtually no relationship to sentence. A comparison of the metric coefficients obtained here with those obtained for model 1 in El Paso indicates a marked contrast. With respect to the main effects, substantial evidence of discrimination exists in the El Paso data, while no such evidence appears in the Tucson data.

The findings of model 2 for Tucson also are not as striking as for El Paso, but an interesting parallel does exist—jury convictions affected negatively the sentences of both black and Mexican origin defendants. Juries do not sentence in Arizona, but judges appeared to punish inordinately the relatively small number of minority defendants who exercised their right to a jury trial, with 4 percent of the sample being adversely affected. This finding is consistent with evidence that justice is more punitive when defendants incur the time and cost of a jury trial (Uhlman and Walker, 1980).

Also, Mexican origin defendants convicted of multiple charges received more severe dispositions, on the average, than others (this coefficient was not quite statistically significant, but was retained because it was the first interaction entered in the stepwise regression). This is probably due to the severity of the lesser violations, which is not controlled for by the multiple charge variable.

Discussion and Conclusion

Our purpose in this study was to examine the degree to which black and Mexican origin defendants receive harsher sentences than their dominant group counterparts, *ceteris paribus*. In addition to the main effects of minority status on sentence severity, the interactions of race with other variables were considered. Within the two cities under consideration, the greatest disparities in felony sentencing were observed in El Paso. Blacks and those of Mexican origin tried before juries were considerably more likely to receive a severe sentence than otherwise similar Anglo defendants. Similarly, minority defendants in Tucson were more harshly treated when convicted by juries. On the whole, however, sentencing in Tucson appears considerably more uniform.

Perhaps the simplest explanation of this difference is that judges and juries are fairer in some areas than others. Texas, for instance, has an especially unfavorable history of mistreatment of those of Mexican origin (McWilliams, 1948/1968). Thus, our findings conceivably reflect differences in the quality of justice found in each city.

Probably more important, however, are differences in the criminal justice systems of the two cities. In one especially important aspect Tucson and El Paso were quite different during the period in which these data were collected. At that time, El Paso had instituted a policy of stringent case screening while prohibiting plea bargaining. Plea bargains were the rule in Tucson. Furthermore, minimal case screening allowed relatively unsupervised initial charge decisions by assistant prosecutors, who were also allowed a great deal of discretion in negotiating pleas (LaFree, 1983). Barriers against prejudicial charging or plea bargaining were thus quite formidable in El Paso and virtually nonexistent in Tucson. Discrimination in charging and plea negotiations could easily have occurred at an earlier stage in Tucson, with the adverse outcomes masked in the present study by focusing on evaluation at a later point in the adjudication process.

Another important factor is the sociodemographic composition of the two cities. At the end of the decade during which these data were gathered, El Paso's Spanish (primarily Mexican) origin population comprised 62 percent of the city total, while only 21 percent of Tucson's population was so classified (U.S. Bureau of the Census, 1983a, 1983b). Many have hypothesized that the larger the relative size of a minority group, the greater the perceived threat among the dominant group (e.g., Blalock, 1967). Evidence to this effect has recently been reported in the literature of race and the legal system. Jacobs (1979) has demonstrated that particularly after the urban upheaval of the 1960s, the police strength in cities is positively associated with both percent black and degree of economic inequality. Other research has demonstrated that percent black has an initially positive curvilinear relationship to police expenditures on salaries and operations (Jackson and Carroll, 1981). Plausibly, then, sentencing in high-minority areas may be more severe for minority defendants because they are perceived as threatening to the dominant community.

These arguments, while pertinent to the present research setting, are also intended to illustrate the many factors which might operate to the detriment of minority defendants convicted in particular jurisdictions. Well-executed studies also occasionally report evidence suggestive of reverse discrimination (e.g., Bernstein, Kelly, and Doyle, 1977). Kleck (1981) has argued that local conceptions about race and justice can work to the advantage of minority defendants in some jurisdictions. Ironically, the balancing equations of aggregate analyses such as Kleck's effectively ignore the possibility of direct and reverse discrimination at the jurisdiction level, even though he explicitly acknowledges that both forms of discrimination operate in at least some jurisdictions. Certainly, one important area for future research is the systematic evaluation of how community characteristics affect the sentencing of different groups.

The data presented here also emphasize the necessity of examining the interactions of race-ethnicity and other determinants of case disposition severity. If we had ignored such interactions in this study, comparatively little of importance would have appeared with respect to race-ethnicity and sentencing. We suspect that many studies reporting negative findings might have found quite different results had such interactions been considered.

Finally this analysis affirms the significance of research on race-ethnicity and sentencing. Given the paucity of data on the Southwest, the evidence presented about the sentencing of Mexican origin defendants is especially interesting. Scholars and policymakers should not facilely dismiss race as a factor in the judicial process. Increased attention to this problem from both camps is clearly warranted.

REFERENCES

Alschuler, Albert. 1968. "The Prosecutor's Role in Plea Bargaining," *University of Chicago Law Review*, 36 (Fall):50–112.

Ares, Charles E., Anne Rankin, and Herbert Sturz. 1963. "The Manhattan Bail Project: An Interim Report on the Use of Pre-Trial Parole," *New York University Law Review*, 38 (January):67–95.

Baab, George William, and William Royal Furgeson, Jr. 1967. "Texas Sentencing Patterns: A Statistical Study," *Texas Law Review*, 45 (February):471–503.

Bernstein, Ilene Nagel, William R. Kelly, and Patricia A. Doyle. 1977. "Societal Reaction to Deviants: The Case of Criminal Defendants," *American Sociological Review*, 42 (October):743–55.

Blalock, Hubert M., Jr. 1967. *Toward a Theory of Minority-Group Relations* (New York: Wiley).

Blauner, Robert. 1972. *Racial Oppression in America* (New York: Harper & Row).

Blumberg, Abraham. 1967. *Criminal Justice* (Chicago: Quadrangle).

Bohrnstedt, George W., and T. Michael Carter. 1971. "Robustness in Regression Analysis," in H. L. Costner, ed., *Sociological Methodology 1971* (San Francisco: Jossey-Bass).

Burke, Peter, and Austin Turk. 1975. "Factors Affecting Postarrest Dispositions: A Model for Analysis," *Social Problems,* 22 (February):313–32.

Chambliss, William J., and Robert B. Seidman. 1971. *Law, Order and Power* (Reading, Mass.: Addison-Wesley).

Chiricos, Theodore G., Phillip D. Jackson, and Gordon P. Waldo. 1972. "Inequality in the Imposition of a Criminal Label," *Social Problems,* 19 (Spring):553-72.

Erickson, Maynard L., and Jack P. Gibbs. 1979. "On the Perceived Severity of Legal Penalties," *Journal of Criminal Law and Criminology,* 70 (Spring):102–16.

Garza, Hisauro. 1973. "Administration of Justice: Chicanos in Monterrey County," *Aztlan,* 4 (Spring):137–46.

Green, Edward. 1961. *Judicial Attitudes in Sentencing* (London: Macmillan).

Hagan, John. 1974. "Extra-legal Attributes and Criminal Sentencing: An Assessment of a Sociological Viewpoint," *Law and Society Review,* 8 (Spring):357–83.

Jackson, Pamela Irving, and Leo Carroll. 1981. "Race and the War on Crime: The Socio-political Determinants of Municipal Police Expenditures in 90 Non-Southern U.S. Cities," *American Sociological Review,* 46 (June):290–305.

Jacobs, David. 1979. "Inequality and Police Strength: Conflict Theory and Coercive Control in Metropolitan Areas," *American Sociological Review,* 44 (December):913–25.

Kleck, Gary. 1981. "Racial Discrimination in Criminal Sentencing: A Critical Evaluation of the Evidence with Additional Evidence on the Death Penalty," *American Sociological Review,* 46 (December):783–805.

LaFave, Wayne R. 1964. *Arrest: The Decision to Take a Suspect into Custody* (Boston: Little, Brown).

LaFree, Gary D. 1980. "The Effect of Sexual Stratification by Race on Official Reactions to Rape," *American Sociological Review,* 45 (October):842–54.

———. 1983. "Adversarial and Nonadversarial Justice: A Comparison of Guilty Pleas and Trials in the United States." Unpublished manuscript, University of New Mexico, Department of Sociology.

Lemert, Edwin, and Judy Rosberg. 1948. "The Administration of Justice to Minority Groups in Los Angeles County," in R. L. Beals, L. Bloom, and F. Fearings, eds., *University of California Publications in Culture and Society,* vol. 2 (Berkeley: University of California Press).

McWilliams, Carey. 1948. *North from Mexico.* Reprint (New York: Greenwood, 1968).

National Advisory Commission on Civil Disorders. 1968. *Report of the National Advisory Commission on Civil Disorders* (New York: Bantam).

Petersilia, Joan. 1983. *Racial Disparities in the Criminal Justice System* (Santa Monica, Calif.: Rand).

Quinney, Richard. 1970. *The Social Reality of Crime* (Boston: Little, Brown).

Rankin, Anne. 1964. "The Effect of Pretrial Detention," *New York University Law Review,* 39 (June):641–55.

Rosett, Arthur, and Donald R. Cressey. 1976. *Justice by Consent: Plea Bargains in the American Courthouse* (Philadelphia: Lippincott).

Simmons, J. S. 1965. "Public Stereotypes of Deviants," *Social Problems,* 13 (Fall):223–32.

Sissons, Peter. 1977. *The Hispanic Experience of Criminal Justice* (New York: Fordham University, Hispanic Research Center).

Stoddard, Ellwyn R. 1973. *Mexican Americans* (New York: Random House).

Strodtbeck, Fred L., Rita M. James, and Charles Hawkins. 1957. "Social Status in Jury Deliberations," *American Sociological Review*, 22 (December):713–19.

Sudnow, David. 1965. "Normal Crimes: Sociological Features of the Penal Code in a Public Defender Office," *Social Problems*, 12 (Winter):255-76.

Swigert, Victoria Lynn, and Ronald A. Farrell. 1977. "Normal Homicides and the Law," *American Sociological Review*, 42 (February):16–32.

Uhlman, Thomas M., and N. Darlene Walker. 1980. "He Takes Some of My Time; I Take Some of His: An analysis of Judicial Sentencing Patterns in Jury Cases," *Law and Society Review*, 14 (Winter):323–41.

U.S. Bureau of the Census. 1983a. *Census of Population and Housing: 1980*. Census Tracts, PHC80-2-144. El Paso, TX, SMSA (Washington, D.C.: U.S. Government Printing Office).

———. 1983b. *Census of Population and Housing: 1980*. Census Tracts, PHC80-2-355. Tucson, AZ (Washington, D.C.: U.S. Government Printing Office).

U.S. Commission on Civil Rights. 1970. *Mexican Americans and the Administration of Justice in the Southwest* (Washington, D.C.: U.S. Government Printing Office).

Welch, Susan, John Gruhl, and Cassia Spohn. 1984. "Dismissal, Conviction, and Incarceration of Hispanic Defendants: A Comparison with Anglos and Blacks," *Social Science Quarterly*, 65 (June):256–63.

IV. THE SOCIAL AND CULTURAL CONTEXT OF THE MEXICAN AMERICAN EXPERIENCE IN THE UNITED STATES

23. INTRODUCTION

Ricardo ROMO, *The University of Texas at Austin*

Harriett ROMO, *The University of Texas at Austin*

To speak of Mexican origin society in contemporary times is to address an extraordinarily broad topic. The comprehensive range of issues which fall under the general area of culture and society are evident in the topics included in this section. Themes discussed here encompass religion, intermarriage, segregation, health, language, education, and ethnicity. What links these topics is the attention that the authors give to cultural factors and to aspects of assimilation.

The first Anglo American settlers to interact with the Mexicans of the present-day Southwest paid great attention to questions of cultural differences, race, and ethnicity. These frontier settlers came to the region nearly 300 years after Spaniards had established communities north of the Rio Grande, and thousands of years after the first Indians had settled the land. Those Americans who came in the 1820s, in the aftermath of Mexican independence from Spain, found the Spanish-speaking people living in Texas, California, and New Mexico grappling with the concept of identity. As Mexicans, they accepted their new citizenship, but considered themselves members of a "patria chica" (little homeland) where regionalism was of greater importance. The residents of the new states along the frontier of the Mexican Republic were affected little by nationalistic ideology and continued to identify themselves by regional terms such as *Californios* (or *Californianos*) and *Tejanos.*

Writers Josiah Royce (1887), Richard Henry Dana, Jr. (1840), and Alfred Robinson (1846), among others, introduced the Mexican origin population to an Eastern American society anxious to learn about the newly acquired region of the Southwest. These authors described the Mexicans as fatalistic, superstitious, and prone to violence. Royce (1887), for example, noted that "in politics, as in morals, and in material wealth [the California Mexican] was unprogressive" (p. 27). It took generations for others, including trained scholars, to look beyond those stereotypic characterizations.

While some areas of social science research on the Mexican origin people are relatively new, such as political science and psycho-history, such is not the case in the disciplines of sociology, history, anthropology, and education. The number of articles and books published in these fields before the 1960s are of significant magnitude. In an essay concerned with language and assimilation, educator George I. Sanchez (1966:14) noted more than 900 citations on these subjects. Furthermore, the extensive bibliography compiled by The Cabinet Committee on Opportunities for Spanish-Speaking People (1971) and the Stanford University annotated bibliography of the Mexican American (Nogales, 1969), which included 444 selected entries, demonstrate the substantial quantity of articles and books on the topics from these and related fields.

Research on the Mexican origin population has increased dramatically since the 1960s, and much of the new scholarship has represented a departure from earlier perspectives. A new generation of scholars criticized these earlier works as lacking objectivity and sensitivity to the people they sought to study. In a 1970 article, Vaca (1970) noted that in the first quarter-century of social science scholarship, 1912–35, psychological studies focused on "the question of the inherent inferiority of the Mexican immigrant" (p. 6). These early studies sought to link Mexican American racial characteristics with the group's poor performance on intelligence tests.

Sociologists had equally limited and biased perspectives of the Mexican origin population. Vaca (1970) found that sociology "concerned itself over the sources of the social ills that plagued the Mexican immigrant with one segment claiming the source to be the cultural heritage of the Mexican while another segment accused the social and economic conditions in which the Mexican found himself" (p. 6). By the 1950s the cultural determinists, those who blamed Mexican culture for the high incidence of crime, poor health, and dependence on public relief agencies, had won a prominent place in the social science literature. In his penetrating essay "Social Science, Objectivity and the Chicanos" Romano (1970:13) remarked that it was necessary "to discard classic concepts of culture," or at least to modify them. Romano's criticism of social science research focuses on its inability to consider people of Mexican origin as participants in the historical process. The articles presented in this section reflect the new scholarship concerned with the Mexican origin population in the United States. The research presented here attempts to take an objective look at some of the issues related to this ethnic group's ever-changing status in American society and their relationship to the institutions with which they are associated.

Identity

Every racial minority and ethnic group in America has encountered some confusion, if not indifference and ignorance, about its own identity. This is in part a result of the tremendous pressure in American society to assimilate, or at least to acculturate, as quickly as possible. Scholars recognize that there has been a great deal of cultural persistence among the

Mexican origin population, which can be attributed to several factors. One factor is that the Southwest was Spanish-Mexican for three centuries and, as such, native customs and values remained long after United States annexation. A second factor is that the region has been absorbing new migrants in substantial numbers over the last three generations. These new groups constantly reinforce aspects of Mexican culture which survive today in the barrios throughout the Southwest and Midwest. Third, the proximity to the homeland enables the Mexican origin population to visit Mexico frequently and inexpensively. This frequent interaction gives Mexican Americans added reason to maintain their language skills in Spanish. The Mexican origin people have far more opportunities than Irish or Italian origin Americans to stay in contact with the customs and cultures of the land of their ancestors. Today, with improved media technologies, Mexico can easily penetrate U.S. radio and television airwaves, and such communication access serves to keep cultural doors between the United States and Mexico open.

Principal terms applied to the Mexican origin people have changed over time and vary considerably even today. A comprehensive attempt to trace the source of the principal terms applied to the Mexican origin population both internally and externally is beyond the scope of this introduction. Scholars are still uncertain, for example, of the derivation of the term "Chicano" or of the new term "Hispanic," which can be traced to the age before the Spanish conquest of the New World but has taken on new meaning today. In the aftermath of the annexation of the Southwest by the United States in 1848, previously popular terms such as "Californiano" or "Tejano" began to decrease in use. It is possible that the influx of new Mexican migrants may have influenced the popularity of the term "Mexicano" by the turn of the century. "Mexicano" was most commonly used by first and second generation persons of Mexican origin during the early twentieth century (1900–1950), although other terms, such as "La Raza" or "Latino" were also used frequently. Self-referent terms such as "Chicano," "Mexican American," and "Latino" have a more recent origin.

In the late 1960s and early 1970s the term "Chicano" gained wide acceptance among social scientists, and the use of this term for the 1973 special issue of the *Social Science Quarterly*, "The Chicano Experience in the United States," reflected this trend. Even with the wide acceptance of the term "Chicano" among scholars, terms used in day-to-day interactions continued to vary significantly. In one of the earliest studies conducted on this subject, Metzgar (1974:50) found that among the New Mexicans an equal number of male respondents (38 percent) described their ethnic affiliation as "Chicano" or "Spanish American." Only 4 percent preferred the term "Mexican" or "Mexican American." In contrast, female respondents were overwhelmingly in favor of the term "Spanish American"; only 23 percent liked the term "Chicano," and 7 percent chose "Mexican" or "Mexican American." When the respondents were asked which of the terms they most disliked, 32 percent of the men and 37 percent of the women selected "Mexican" as the least appealing to them. Unfortunately, this study was limited to New Mexico, where terms such as "Spanish Americans" are unique and where there has been longtime resistance to the term "Mexican." Most social scientists saw the need at this time for a broader analysis of the identity issue.

Perhaps never before have we had as much information on self-identity as we have today as a result of the 1980 Census, which included self-referent items. There have also been efforts by government agencies and radio, television, and print media to "Hispanicize" the Mexican origin population. The complexities of ethnic identification among the Mexican origin population are apparent when we consider that in the 1980 Census, 50.4 percent of New Mexico's census respondents referred to themselves as "Other Spanish," while 49 percent marked "Mexican Origin." (The remaining 0.5 percent of the Hispanic respondents were divided between Puerto Ricans and Cubans.) "Other Spanish" counts were particularly significant in California (752,823), Texas (196,275), and Colorado (126,778). Based on the large number of these southwesterners who claimed the "Other Spanish" status, it is apparent that many whom we consider of Mexican origin identified with the "Spanish" label. These preferences reflect a cultural continuity with respect to the term "Spanish."

John Garcia (1981) using data from the 1976 Survey on Income and Education, demonstrated that a majority of the Mexican origin population in the U.S. Southwest identifies itself as "Mexican American." Of interest in this essay is the sociodemographic analysis of the respondents. We know, for example, how education, age, state of residence, income level, and language use affected the self-referent terms of this population group. While only 4.0 percent of the sample identified themselves as "Chicanos," 71 percent of this group were between the ages of 14 and 30. In Texas, where a large proportion of the population traces its roots to modern migration (post 1900), only 3.7 percent of the Mexican origin population identified as "Other Spanish" in the 1976 survey.

Because a majority of the Mexican origin population resides in the Southwest, much of the self-identity research examines terms used in the states of Arizona, California, Colorado, New Mexico, and Texas. The 1980 Census indicates, however, that the Mexican barrios of Chicago are as large as those of El Paso or Tucson. The Census also noted a new trend among Puerto Ricans and Cubans to move away from their traditional base in Atlantic coast cities to the Midwest and West. Padilla's article in this section is especially concerned with the interaction between Chicago's numerous Spanish-speaking groups. Padilla not only investigates self-identity, but looks at other factors associated with ethnicity as well. He argues that for those who are now identifying with "Latinismo" such identification is a recognition that groups must struggle together in order to resolve political and socioeconomic problems which result from racial and/or ethnic discrimination. Individuals sharing this view of Latinismo saw as their mission the changing of the existing social and political situation which controlled their destiny.

Padilla argues that those who call themselves "Latinos" form a "collective and emergent type of group" created out of the inter-ethnic relations of at least two Spanish-speaking groups during situational or historical moments. If Mexican Americans, Puerto Ricans, and Cubans unite politically in areas where they constitute a large minority group, this may have important political implications. As Padilla suggests, Latinismo signifies a bold step toward ethnic unity.

Language

The language question has concerned scholars interested in the Mexican origin community since the earliest period of social science research. Although articles and books on this topic number in the hundreds, a pioneering scholar in this field was George I. Sanchez. For more than forty years Sanchez investigated the issue of language, especially as it pertained to culture and school performance. His 1966 essay on "History, Culture, and Education" perhaps best stated his position. Sanchez (1966) wrote that "it should be clear that the retention of the Spanish language by Americans of Spanish-Mexican descent in the Southwest has been the function of default, rather than of any concerted popular or institutionalized effort" (p. 23). He argued that the attention educators and social scientists gave to the use of Spanish by Mexican Americans was not simply a linguistic concern, but rather an issue of "social policy, of school organization and administration, of educational philosophy, and of pedagogical competence." Sanchez condemned existing scholarship on the language issue and observed how segregationists employed it as pseudoscientific evidence to ideal with "language-handicapped" children and as a pretext for creating segregated Mexican and Anglo schools.

The use of Spanish in the United States has increased twofold since the time that Sanchez was writing on this issue. Indeed, Spanish is the only language other than English which has been increasing from one decennial Census to the next in number of individuals who speak it. It is apparent from census data that the rise in the number of people who speak Spanish is largely a consequence of new migration.

Grenier, who is familiar with Canadian bilingualism, examines various factors related to language shifts among the Mexican origin population including age, immigrant status, marriage, sex, neighborhood, and education. Grenier argues, in the essay included here, that the learning of English enhances the integration of the Spanish-speaking population in the United States and may well contribute to their economic mobility. Greater educational attainment and higher levels of English proficiency do help to determine employment outcomes. Stolzenberg (1982:79) suggested that English proficiency, for Hispanics, is more important and has a greater "payoff" than educational attainment.

Research by Tienda and Neidert on language and its relation to occupational status touches on economic integration. Their findings, in the essay included here, differ from those of Grenier. They argue that the retention of Spanish does not hinder the socioeconomic achievements of Hispanic origin population provided that a reasonable level of proficiency in English and Spanish is acquired. Whereas Grenier stresses "rapid Anglicization" as a means of improving economic situation, Tienda and Neidert warn that simply removing the language and schooling barriers which Hispanics face will not eliminate inequities created by discrimination in the labor market. They conclude that the groups most penalized, if they are monolingual Spanish speakers, are foreign-born Mexicans and island-born Puerto Ricans.

Schooling

Grebler, Moore, and Guzman (1970) and the reports of the U.S. Commission on Civil Rights (1971–74) showed that student-holding rates, reading achievements, and extracurricular activities were all less for Mexican origin students than for Anglos. These studies and others have consistently shown that the overall experience of Mexican origin children in U.S. schools has been one of discrimination and exclusion.

Most school studies have identified various differences between the school and classroom culture and that of Mexican origin children, and have attributed the difficulties and problems encountered by those children to such differences (Manuel, 1965; Carter, 1970). Other school studies have examined the general issue of the role of schooling in social mobility or as a means of reproducing the existing subordinate relationships in U.S. society (Bowles and Gintis, 1976; Featherman and Hauser, 1978). While these studies touched on the unique characteristic of the Mexican origin population, the researchers lacked specific data on this group. Coleman et al. (1966) made the critical distinction between equality of opportunity and equality of results, yet they concluded that family background was more important than school characteristics in explaining differences in achievement. They found that schools reinforced the inferior position of disadvantaged children with respect to educational opportunity. Overall, however, Coleman et al. had little to say about the content and process of education.

More recent studies (Carrasco, 1981; Fillmore, 1982) through micro-ethnographic investigations suggest that miscommunications and school failure are interactional accomplishments. Those studies focus on teacher-student interaction, testing practices, the curriculum, and the daily routine of school life, and attempt to describe emerging patterns. In this section, Romo uses extensive interviews, long-term observations, and discourse analysis to understand Mexican origin families' interactions in a school context.

In studying an immigrant community, the scholar, as Romo demonstrates, must take into consideration many different factors. From the studies cited earlier, we are well aware of the income and occupational differences among the various Spanish-speaking groups. We are also cognizant of the varying degree of assimilation among generations and that language skills are not uniform. One approach has been to classify these differences by social and economic class.

Another approach—the generational model—divides groups into first, second, and third generation. Romo finds differences in attitudes and behavior among recent immigrant groups, the transitional group (which included first and second generation immigrants who were longtime residents in U.S. communities), and the Chicano generation.

Studying these three Mexican origin groups in a Texas community, Romo concludes that with regard to schooling recent immigrants have lower expectations of schools than Chicanos, but Chicanos expressed more alienation and awareness of discrimination than either the foreign-born Mexicans or the transitional group.

Romo's three years of research in a Mexican origin community reveal that although Chicanos and recent immigrants lived and worked in the same areas, there was little social interaction among them. She suggests that the presence of distinctive group behavior and differing attitudes toward institutions require that we take a closer look within the Mexican origin population for distinctions that are more prevalent than many scholars perceive.

More research in other communities may enable scholars to compare levels of educational success and attitudes toward schooling within the Mexican origin population. Other comparative studies may reveal a great deal about why immigrants in certain communities appear to acculturate or assimilate at greater rates than immigrants in other communities.

Residential Segregation

In 1966 Moore and Mittelbach completed one of the first extensive investigations of residential segregation related to the Mexican origin population. The authors found a wide variation of segregation in different cities for Mexican Americans. Moore (1970) later wrote that while Mexican Americans were moving out of the barrios in increasing numbers, the "rate of change is not itself a steady even progress toward acculturation or assimilation" (p. 110).

Lopez (1981) published an important article which reported the wide degree of segregation in southwestern cities. The segregation rate ranged from a low of 22 percent in Vallejo, California, to a high 68 percent in Midland, Texas. The Mexican origin people appeared to be least segregated

from Anglos and most segregated from blacks, with black-Anglo differences being most evident. Lopez's research suggests that differences in
Mexican origin/Anglo segregation have narrowed while Mexican origin/
black segregation has become more pronounced during the last decade.

Research by Hwang and Murdock compares the levels of racial and
ethnic segregation for major Texas cities in 1980 to those for 1970. They
found significant decline in segregation from 1970 to 1980 for all groups,
but declines in segregation were small between the Anglo and Mexican
origin population. Although some might expect that the rapid growth of
the Mexican origin population in Texas over the past decade might have
led to improved social conditions for this group, the slow rate of residential integration implies that the Mexican origin people still have significant obstacles to overcome in the area of social equality. Hwang and
Murdock also concluded that segregation is unaffected by variations in
size of city, percent of population that is Spanish origin or black, or central-
city status.

The 1980 Census gives demographers much greater information on
Mexican origin residential housing patterns than previous census reports.
Social scientists are still questioning, for example, why in some cities
where the Mexican origin population is in the majority—such as Brownsville and Harlingen in Texas—the levels of segregation are not as pronounced as in other cities where the Mexican origin population is also in
the majority—such as El Paso, Texas. One apparent difference between
Brownsville and El Paso is that Brownsville is located in South Texas,
where the Mexican origin population has been a dominant ethnic group
for generations. El Paso is situated in West Texas, an area where the Mexican population has historically been the minority. Greater detail about the
ethnic makeup of large urban areas may enable scholars to better understand the processes involved in segregation. Some of those processes
are "white" and ethnic flight to the suburbs, interracial conflict over territorial boundaries, and how housing needs of undocumented Mexican families have affected the Mexican origin communities. Comparative studies
of several southwestern cities are needed before any conclusions can be
drawn about the degree of segregation in the region as a whole.

Intermarriage

Social scientists have been interested in intermarriage in part because
they view such a union as a reflection on assimilation and upward mobility. Intermarriage between Mexicans and Anglos was common in the era
when the Southwest still belonged to Mexico and Sam Houston and Davy
Crockett were seeking new lives on the Texas frontier. Jim Bowie, who
died at the Alamo, for example, married into a prominent Mexican family.
Kit Carson took a New Mexican wife in the years before he led American
soldiers against the Mexican Republic. Although there are not sufficient

data to compare Anglo/Mexican origin intermarriage rates in the periods before and after the Mexican War of 1846, one might argue that Anglos marrying Mexicans in the pre–Mexican War years may have been expressing a desire to acculturate into Mexican society. The present-day Southwest belonged to Mexico at that time.

Historical circumstance is but one reason why exogamy rates have varied over time and in different regions. Historians who discuss the high percentage of intermarriage between Spaniards and Indians in the aftermath of the conquest of Mexico in 1520 cite "availability" as a principal factor; that is, few Spanish women came to the New World and settlers and soldiers selected their brides from the available pool of candidates. Such might have been the case in the early frontier days when Anglo men far outnumbered Anglo women in the west and *Mexicanas* constituted the largest available pool of unmarried women.

Griswold del Castillo (1979) found that for Anglos in the pre–1848 era "intermarriage with the daughters of the *gente de razon* (Mexican Californians of economic means) was one route to upward mobility and social acceptance" (p. 76). In the second half of the nineteenth century, the old Mexican pueblo of Los Angeles became an Anglo-dominated town. Griswold del Castillo attributed the weakening of traditional family structure, the depressed economic situation, and the numerical increase of the Anglo male population during this period for the rise in intermarriage between the years 1856 and 1875. According to his data there was significant variation in the rate of intermarriage over the years. He speculated that economic conditions and the emergence of Anglo men as political powers in the city may have affected intermarriage rates (del Castillo, 1979:76).

Another look at the early frontier period is the study by Bean and Bradshaw (1970), who examined marriage in San Antonio, Texas, over the years 1850–60. During this period the rate of intermarriage between Anglos and Mexicans in this Texas city remained constant, with 10 percent outmarriage for both decades. Both San Antonio and Los Angeles had a predominantly Mexican origin population during the early days of statehood, although San Antonio had a larger proportion of Anglo men from the Deep South where racial antagonisms against people of color are a historical fact. Since we do not know much about the background of the individuals who intermarried in either of these cities, we can only speculate as to factors contributing to outmarriages.

In more modern times the available pool may vary according to where young people go to high school or college, where they attend church, and the types of jobs they hold. A Mexican origin woman who attends college on the East Coast will find her social environment quite different from that of a young Mexican origin woman who remains in a segregated barrio in Los Angeles or San Antonio. Research which examines the influences of family, schooling, friendship, and social interactions would help us to better understand variations of intermarriage patterns from region to region.

Panunzio (1942) looked at exogamous marriages in Los Angeles for the period 1924–33 and found outmarriage represented 17 percent of the total marriages in the Mexican origin community. What is apparent from investigations of the intermarriage phenomenon is that, like segregation, exogamous marriages vary by region and historical time period.

In California, the exogamy rate rose steadily over the period between 1920 and 1970, although it has shown a slight decrease in the 1970s. Schoen, Nelson, and Collins (1978) studied outmarriage statewide and found that in 1962 55 percent of the Mexican origin population married outside of their group. Over the years 1962 to 1974 the rate of outmarriage stabilized, dropping slightly to 51 percent in 1974. In a 1963 study of exogamy rates in Los Angeles, Mittelbach and Moore investigated income and social class of those who married out. Moore commented that in Los Angeles the foreign-born Mexicanos were the least likely of all Mexican origin individuals to marry Anglos. Children of Mexican origin parents were the next most likely, and Mexican Americans with parents born in the United States were the most likely to marry Anglos. Moore (1970:114) noted, however, that intermarriage data show that mobility may—or may not—mean assimilation, for intermarriage can also have a symbolic value.

Scholars who have contrasted the rate of outmarriage in Texas and California in the twentieth century are puzzled as to why California has historically had a higher rate of exogamous unions between Mexicans and Anglos than Texas and other regions. The discrimination factor has been the rationale most frequently offered. Further research on exogamy rates in other areas outside of these states where Mexicans live in significant proportions (e.g., Chicago, Denver, and Tucson) may yield new insights to explain why intermarriage has increased consistently in some areas and not in others.

Religion

Scholars agree that one cannot study a particular society without examining the function of religion. Individual responses to religion are equally important since the church is generally a socialization agent. In the Mexican origin communities Catholicism has been traditionally an important institution. Residents of the newly acquired territory of the Southwest were protected by the U.S. Constitution when they became American citizens. In the aftermath of the Mexican-American War of 1846, President Polk and the United States Senate chose to make specific mention of religious freedom in the Treaty of Guadalupe Hidalgo. Over the hundred and thirty years since then the western states have become integrated with the rest of the nation, and the forces of Protestantism have moved across the

Rockies as they once moved south to the Spanish Floridas and west to the French Louisiana Territory. The impact of Protestant teachings has interested social scientists, for, to an extent, the social gospel and other teachings of the Protestant religion reflect the impact of assimilation and acculturation in Mexican origin communities.

Like all institutions, the Roman Catholic church in America has changed over modern times. What remains consistent in the period of change has been strong Mexican American affiliation to Catholicism. Over the years this strong devotion by Mexican origin communities to the Catholic church has been reflected in parochial education and active participation in religious festivals. Still, the absence of sufficient parochial schools in the barrios and the decline in the practice of traditional Mexican religious events such as *Las Posadas* give evidence that the Mexican origin population's religious behavior and attitudes toward Catholic traditions are changing.

One of the first studies concerned with religious practices and attitudes of Mexican origin people was the Mexican American Study Project at the University of California, Los Angeles. Findings were published by Grebler, Moore, and Guzman (1970). Among their findings was that Mexican American Catholics in San Antonio had a higher church attendance (58 percent) than their counterparts in Los Angeles (47 percent). Their survey also showed that in Los Angeles Mexican Americans who resided in more segregated neighborhoods practiced their religion somewhat more regularly than those in mixed areas. It is likely that Mexican Americans in mixed neighborhoods did not have the benefit of a local Spanish-speaking church within their community. The researchers also found that poorer people among Los Angeles' Mexican Americans had a greater participation rate in religious activities, while income made little difference in religious participation of San Antonio's Mexican origin population (Grebler, Moore, and Guzman, 1970:474).

Using data from a three-generation study, Markides and Cole, in the article included in this section, examine change and continuity in religious affiliation and behavior among Mexican Americans in San Antonio. Findings presented here report an overwhelming majority of respondents were Catholic. According to results of the Markides and Cole survey of parents, children, and grandchildren, little change in religious affiliation took place from generation to generation. As might be expected, church attendance is highest among older women, while the percentage drops for the next two generations. The percentage of men attending church is slightly lower than that of women attending. However, the decline in church attendance is more dramatic from first to third generation men than it is for similar generations of women.

The authors suggest that among Mexican origin Catholics religious affiliation is obviously one of the dominant forces in the maintenance of ethnic identity. Markides and Cole conclude that in this relationship between religion and ethnicity Mexican Americans are closer to Italian American Catholics than to Irish and German American Catholics who have shown less continuity in religious affiliation. They are also less like Americans from Minnesota (mostly Protestants of Scandinavian origin) who showed markedly lower levels of continuity in religious affiliation from grandparents to grandchildren. If conversion to Protestantism is a vehicle for assimilation into the Anglo-Saxon core, there is little in the Markides and Cole study to suggest that Mexican Americans are assimilating in this manner.

Health

Prior to the 1970s the health of the Mexican origin population drew little research attention (Clark, 1959). Those early studies seemed to agree on only one point—that Mexican origin people approached sickness and health quite differently from their Anglo counterparts. Many of those studies focused on folk medicine practices of the Mexican origin population. No doubt *curanderos* (folk healers) and *parteras* (midwives) have commanded the respect of many among the Mexican origin population. These health practitioners were found in both rural and urban communities, although it has been assumed that their activities were part of a traditional rural culture.

Today, the Mexican origin people have no single approach to health problems. Many use public health care programs while others are attended to by private practitioners. Economics remains a major factor in the type of health care and preventive medical practices that exist in Mexican origin communities. A great number of persons of Mexican origin do not have the financial resources to enable them to have major medical problems attended to or to have access to preventive medicine.

In the essay included here, Angel concludes that the general health level of the Mexican origin population is neither better nor worse than that of other groups. What scholars should be concerned with, Angel argues, is how factors of culture, education, occupation, family structure, and medical care affect the health of particular segments of the Mexican origin population. The fact that a greater proportion of the Mexican origin population is below the poverty level than Anglos suggests that this group may have greater health problems than are reported in conventional health data.

Angel suggests that the Mexican origin poor face greater health risks than the general population, and that the disadvantages suffered by the Mexican origin population are disproportionately borne by those least fluent in English. The findings of Angel support those of Grenier and Tienda—that English proficiency can make a difference.

There are other health areas which researchers have only begun to investigate. One of these areas, Angel points out, is that which determines the relationship between occupation and health problems of Mexican origin people. Another area of research where information is sorely lacking is that of the undocumented immigrant. Immigration studies such as those of Cornelius, Chavez, and Castro (1982:86) and the article in this section by Romo suggest that immigrants have limited interactions with formal institutions. As a result, health facilities may be underutilized by undocumented immigrants.

Conclusion

Scholars interested in Mexican American society and life have long been dissatisfied with the limited data and documents to make their assessments. It is hoped that in the near future access to sources and new data will increase substantially. As revealed in several of the essays included in this section, the 1980 Census holds much more information about the Mexican origin population than previous census counts. However, because the previous censuses were so negligent about collecting data on the Mexican origin population, scholars have had limited insights into questions of intergenerational change and mobility. Different methological approaches have enabled scholars to analyze the Mexican origin people's social lives from data located in marriage, birth, and death records and other documents in the schools and churches which serve this population. What is apparent is that answers to the difficult questions pondered in the past have come under increasingly careful examination. "Right" answers are still as elusive as ever, but high interest in the Mexican origin population assures us that new approaches to the issues of assimilation, ethnicity, and interethnic relations will be tested and examined as never before.

REFERENCES

Bean, Frank D., and Benjamin S. Bradshaw. 1970. "Intermarriage between Persons of Spanish and Non-Spanish Surname: Changes from the Mid-Nineteenth to the Mid-Twentieth Century," *Social Science Quarterly*, 51 (September):388–95.

Bowles, Samuel, and Herbert Gintis. 1976. *Schooling in Capitalist America* (New York: Basic Books).

Cabinet Committee on Opportunities for Spanish-Speaking People. 1971. *The Spanish Speaking in the United States: A Guide to Materials* (Washington, D.C.: n.p.).

Carrasco, Robert L. 1981. "Expanded Awareness of Student Performance: A Case Study in Applied Ethnographic Monitoring in a Bilingual Classroom," in Henry I. Trueba, Grace Pung Guthrie, and Kathryn Hu-Pei Au, eds., *Culture and the Bilingual Classroom* (Rowley, Mass.: Newbury House).

Carter, Thomas P. 1970. *Mexican Americans in School: A History of Educational Neglect* (Princeton, N.J.: College Entrance Examination Board).

Clark, Margaret. 1959. *Health in the Mexican American Culture* (Berkeley: University of California Press).

Coleman, James S., Ernest Q. Campbell, Carol J. Hobson, James McPartland, Alexander M. Mood, Frederic D. Weinfeld, and Robert L. York. 1966. *Equality of Educational Opportunity* (Washington, D.C.: U.S. Department of Health, Education, and Welfare, U.S. Government Printing Office).

Cornelius, Wayne A., Leo R. Chavez, and Jorge G. Castro. 1982. *Mexican Immigrants and Southern California: A Summary of Current Knowledge*. Research Report Series, no. 36 (La Jolla: University of California, San Diego, Center of U.S.-Mexican Studies).

Dana, Richard Henry, Jr. 1840. *Two Years before the Mast: A Personal Narrative of Life at Sea*. 1st ed. (Boston: Bates and Lauriat).

del Castillo, Richard Griswold. 1979. *The Los Angeles Barrio. 1850–1890: A Social History* (Berkeley: University of California Press).

Featherman, David R., and Robert M. Hauser. 1978. *Opportunity and Change* (New York: Academic Press).

Fillmore, Lily Wong. 1982. "Language Minority Students and School Participation: What Kind of English Is Needed?" *Journal of Education*, 164 (Spring):142–56.

Garcia, John A. 1981. "Yo Soy Mexicano . . . : Self-Identity and Sociodemographic Correlates," *Social Science Quarterly*, 62 (March):88–98.

Grebler, Leo, Joan W. Moore, and Ralph Guzman. 1970. *The Mexican-American People* (New York: Free Press).

Hwang, Sean-Shong, and Steve H. Murdock, "Residential Segregation in Texas in 1980," *Social Science Quarterly*, 63 (December): 737–48.

Lopez, Manuel Mariano. 1981. "Patterns of Interethnic Residential Segregation in the Urban Southwest, 1960 and 1970," *Social Science Quarterly*, 62 (March):50–63.

Manuel, Herschel T. 1965. *Spanish-Speaking Children of the Southwest* (Austin: University of Texas Press).

Metzgar, Joseph V. 1974. "The Ethnic Sensitivity of Spanish New Mexicans: A Survey and Analysis," *New Mexico Historical Review*, 49:49–73.

Moore, Joan W. 1970. *Mexican Americans* (Englewood Cliffs, N.J.: Prentice-Hall).

Nogales, Luis G. 1969. *The Mexican American: A Selected and Annotated Bibliography* (Stanford: Stanford University Press).

Panunzio, Constantine. 1942. "Intermarriage in Los Angeles, 1924–33," *American Journal of Sociology*, 47 (March):690–701.

Robinson, Alfred. 1846. *Life in California during a Residence of Several Years in That Territory. . . .* 1st ed. (San Francisco: William Doxey).

Romano, Octavio Ignacio. 1970. "Social Science, Objectivity, and the Chicanos," *El Grito*, 4 (Fall):4–16.

Royce, Josiah. 1887. *California from the Conquest in 1846 to the Second Vigilance Committee in San Francisco: A Study of American Character* (New York: Knopf).

Sanchez, George I. 1966. "History, Culture, and Education," in Julian Samora, ed., *La Raza: Forgotten Americans* (Notre Dame: University of Notre Dame Press): pp. 1–27.

Schoen, Robert, Verne E. Nelson, and Marion Collins. 1978. "Intermarriage among Spanish Surnamed Californians, 1962–1974," *International Migration Review*, 12 (Fall):359–69.

Stolzenberg, Ross M. 1982. *Occupational Differences between Hispanics and non-Hispanics* (Santa Monica: Rand Corporation).

U.S. Commission on Civil Rights. 1971–74. *Mexican American Education Study*. 6 vols. (Washington, D.C.: U.S. Government Printing Office).

Vaca, Nick C. 1970. "The Mexican American in the Social Sciences: 1912–1970. Part I: 1912–1935," *El Grito*, 3 (Spring):3–24.

24. ON THE NATURE OF LATINO ETHNICITY[1]

Felix M. PADILLA, *Northern Illinois University*

In this article, an empirically based definition for the idea of Latino ethnicity in Chicago is presented. It is shown that the Latino ethnic identification is situational and political, the result of interethnic relations among various Spanish-speaking groups.

During the last two decades the Spanish-speaking groups in the United States have been a subject of interest to scholars. To date, social science research has focused exclusively on the analysis of the separate or individual ethnic experiences of Puerto Ricans, Mexican Americans, and Cubans in the United States. This approach, however, has ignored the interethnic relations between these groups and the creation and adoption of a *Latino ethnic identity,* separate and distinct from individual ethnic identifications of Mexican Americans, Puerto Ricans, and Cubans.

This paper represents an attempt toward a theoretical understanding of Latinos as an ethnic group. This requires treating "Latinos" as a collective and emergent type of group form created out of the interethnic relations of at least two Spanish-speaking groups during some situations or historical moments. As such, "Latinismo" will be analyzed as a situational type of group identity and consciousness. This conceptualization (situational Latino ethnicity) is based on the premise that particular circumstances and social conditions determine when this type of group identity and consciousness is appropriate for social action and mobilization.

In this study, the emphasis will be on the ideological or conceptual formulations used in the expression of Latino ethnic identity and consciousness by community organization leaders from the Mexican American and Puerto Rican communities in Chicago.[2] The author used a semi-structured interview schedule and spent one year of field work studying the phenomenon of Latino ethnic identity in this urban setting. Data were collected

[1] The author wishes to thank Dr. Howard Becker, Dr. Jim Pitts, and Dr. Al Hunter (Department of Sociology, Northwestern University) for their invaluable comments on this paper.
[2] This study is limited to Mexican American and Puerto Rican community organizations because there are only a handful of Cuban and Central/South American community organizations rendering services to this diverse component of the wider Spanish-speaking population in Chicago.

from a total of 34 community organization leaders—executive directors and presidents of boards of directors.

The Community Organization and Latino Identity. This study focuses on the "community organization" as the unit of analysis. The reason for this is that some groups, particularly those which lack significant political and economic leverage, have depended on the community organization and its activities for the definition and maintenance of their interests (see Alinsky, 1969). More specifically, Higham (1975) says: "In America ethnic groups have in some instances been rigidly circumscribed; but more often their boundaries are highly permeable. When boundaries weaken . . . the survival or at least the vitality of an ethnic group would seem to depend increasingly on what is happening at the foci of group activity: within the leadership. Ethnic groups, in some degree, are the creation of their leaders" (pp. 12–13). In her study of Polish immigrants, Lopata (1964) points out, for instance, that initially these immigrants "did not form a self-conscious, unified group. There were not strong bonds connecting those who came from different parts of Poland. The consciousness of bond between all persons of Polish birth or descent living in America grew up gradually as a result of the efforts of a number of different leaders [of voluntary associations]" (p. 206). In the case of Chicanos and Puerto Ricans, community organization leaders create in their respective members a consciousness of related but distinct identity, that of Latino.

In the analysis of the social construction of Latino ethnicity by community organization leaders one needs to consider the possible limitations that may be inherent in this type of group form. In other words, since Latino ethnicity is shaped primarily by the leadership of the various community organizations, one may expect resistance to Latinismo if these leaders are unable to link Chicano or Puerto Rican identity to Latino identity. How leaders recreate or expand ethnic identities is one of Smith's (1981) major concerns in his discussion of the role of elites in the making of an ethnic group. This sentiment is expressed in his analysis of the transformation of a religious group into an ethnic community:

> There are . . . difficulties in this metamorphosis. The populations of the faithful may not easily fit into this kind of historicist scheme, being either too large or too small or too scattered and divided for ethnic convenience. That has been the trouble with many "pan" nationalisms, but none more so than that of pan-Islamism, which has had to compete, not only with other linguistically based "pan" movements like pan-Arabism or pan-Turkism, but also with the nationalism of the several states into which Arabic- and Turkic-speaking peoples have been divided, many of whom possess their own specific histories apart from the general history of the Islamic umma or the "Arab nation." These complications weaken the binding power, if not the fervour, of latterday pan-Islamic crusades, and make it well-nigh impossible to organize the Muslim faithful into a politically coherent movement. (Smith, 1981:98)

One way out of this problem or conflict is to use the historicist and evolutionary framework offered by Smith (1981) in the analysis of Latinismo. The central feature of the concept of historicism "is a predilection for inter-

preting individual and social phenomena as the product of sequences of
events which unfold the identity and laws and growth of those phenomena"
(Smith, 1981:88). Smith (1981) captures the function of historicism in terms
of giving meaning to ethnicity:

> For the peoples of Asia, Africa and America, history furnished the vital clue to
> their identities, and historicism provided a framework of meaning to their dis-
> tinctive characteristics. The historical and evolutionary framework has served
> the essential purpose of endowing with meaning and coherence what might
> otherwise easily be seen as unrelated pieces of cultural information and mark-
> ers. (Pp. 89–90)

From this point of view, the leaders and supporters of Latinismo need to
conceptualize it as an identity which unfolds in a time sequence. In this
way, the role played by the Spanish language and other relevant cultural
elements in the process of the Latino group formation and consciousness
will not be confused as the defining characteristics of Latinismo. Rather,
Latino ethnic identification and consciousness will then be conceptualized
as a group generating process, dependent upon the influence or effect of
structural factors and conditions on the groups' cultural similarities. In so
doing, the leadership of different Chicano and Puerto Rican communities
will be following the overriding historicist vision of a new identity (Latinismo)
which emerges or evolves in time.

Ethnicity and Latino Ethnic Identity. For the purpose of this discussion,
at its most basic level ethnic consciousness will mean an awareness of
belonging and/or being different. In this sense, ethnicity represents a conscious sense of belonging (Patterson, 1975:309); it is a consciousness of
a kind within the group (Schermerhorn, 1970). For Chicanos and Puerto
Ricans, then, Latino ethnicity represents an intergroup identity reflecting a
consciousness of a collective uniqueness derived from shared cultural
characteristics such as language and an awareness of being different from
other social groups in the United States.

At a more general level, this study of Latino ethnicity as a collective and
emergent group form will follow the optionalist or emergent theory of ethnicity which seeks to understand the functions of ethnicity in post-industrial
societies.[3] Ethnic identity is, in this view, a strategic possibility peculiarly
suited to the requirements of political and social mobilization in the modern
state. People may shed, resurrect, or adopt ethnicity as the situation war-
rants. For example, Bell (1975) argues that ethnicity is best understood as
a "strategic choice by individuals who, in other circumstances, would
choose other group members as a means of gaining power and privilege"
(p. 397). Similarly, Patterson (1975:183) discusses how Chinese cohesion
and identity developed in Jamaica as a direct strategy aimed at maximiz-

---

[3] There are others who refer to this theory as the "ethnic competition perspective." The
basic tenet of this theory parallels the optionalist or emergent perspective: "ethnic mobilization
is a consequence of the competition between groups for roles and resources" (Ragin,
1979:622).

ing economic benefits through the development of a credit and trading network.

This approach to understanding Latinos as an ethnic group departs from the traditionalist theory of defining ethnicity. Ethnic awareness, in this sense, inhabits the primitive regions of the psyche and functions for both individual and society as an ascriptive device. For instance, Isaacs (1975:32) suggests that ethnic identity is made part of the individual even before he attains consciousness: it is an inheritance. Gordon (1975) also argues that because "society insists on its inalienable ascription from cradle to grave, a sense of ethnicity cannot be shed, like class, by social mobility" (p. 92). This traditional definition sees ethnicity as a primordial quality and focuses on the transplanted cultural heritage as the principal antecedent and defining characteristic of ethnic groups.

This paper is divided into two major sections. The first provides a definition of Latinismo as a situational type of ethnic behavior. This section will show that Latino-conscious behavior is collectively generated out of the interaction of at least two Spanish-speaking groups, which occurs during those situational contexts when the interests and concerns of the groups are the same. The second section shows the idea of Latinismo as a political phenomenon, a group identity used to gain advantages or overcome disadvantages in society. This part will also show that Latino political consciousness is further categorized in cultural-political and sociopolitical forms by the study's repsondents.

Situational Latino Ethnicity

At the outset of this kind of discussion, one is immediately confronted with the task of answering the following question: When is Latino ethnicity an operative group identity and consciousness? In other words, When does Latinismo or Hispanismo become a form of ethnic conscious behavior for Spanish-speaking groupings, distinct and separate from their individual identities as Mexican Americans or Puerto Ricans or Cubans? At a quite general level, following Pitts's (1974) discussion of black consciousness, Latinismo is viewed as a social product: "purposive action and interpretation of actions operating in social relationships" (p. 672). This means, then, that Latino ethnic identification is not the product of individual Mexican American, Puerto Rican, or Cuban groups, and it does not exist independent of their intergroup social behavior. Latino ethnic-conscious behavior, rather, is a collective generated behavior which transcends the individual national and cultural identities of the various Spanish-speaking units and emerges as a distinct and separate group identification and consciousness.

As such, the Latino ethnic identity and consciousness manifests itself when at least two Spanish-speaking groups, in this instance Puerto Ricans and Mexican Americans, interact as one during certain situational contexts. Rather than being a historically fixed or inherited type of group form and identity, Latinismo has emerged over time as part of the process of intergroup relation and communication among these groups. Further, its expression is situationally specific dependent upon the effects or impacts of some issues on the collective interests of Puerto Ricans and Mexican Americans and how well they can mobilize themselves as one unit to seek resolution collectively.

On the whole, Latino ethnic behavior represents another form of group consciousness among the Spanish-speaking population in the United States. It represents the tendency towards sentimental and ideological identification with a language group. Latinismo also signifies devotion and loyalty to the collective concerns of the Spanish-speaking expressed in some circumstances since individual Puerto Rican and Mexican American ethnic ties and sentiments continue to shape their separate group affiliations and loyalties in most other instances. In short, the Latino-conscious person sees himself as a Latino sometimes and as Puerto Rican, Mexican American, Cuban, and the like at other times.

Members of the various Spanish-speaking community organizations in Chicago gave frequent and eloquent expressions to this type of sentiment. The following is a typical expression of this feeling of a situational-collective solidarity by one of the study's respondents:

> Here [in Chicago] we have a combination of different Latino populations; however, in each community the majority takes care of its own first. . . . I try to use [Latino] as much as I can. When I talk to people in my community, I use Mexican, but I use Latino when the situation calls for issues that have city-wide implications.

The remarks of another respondent, who discussed the building of a new school in one of the city's Mexican American communities, also reflect the situational dimension of the Latino-conscious person:

> In Pilsen you have a Latino movement when they are talking or confronting the city. But in issues such as the Benito Juarez High School, you did not find a Puerto Rican being the spokesperson for the group that was putting on the pressure on the city to build the new school.

Another conceptual formulation of Latinismo as a situational type of group consciousness and identity was expressed by a community organizer from Pilsen. A strong supporter of Saul Alinsky's organizing principles, this respondent sees this form a group identity operative in those instances when the concerns and interests of both Mexican Americans and Puerto Ricans are at stake:

> When we move out of South Chicago and South Chicago is to have a relationship with the Westtown Concerned Citizens Coalition, it will have to be around issues that affect them equally. We cannot get South Chicago to get mad at Westtown if Westtown doesn't support their immigration situation [the issue of undocumented workers]. That is a Mexican problem that cannot be resolved through a Latino effort. But we can get them to come and talk to Westtown about jobs, about things that are hitting everybody.

These various examples point to the shift from a cultural and national population-group frame of reference between Puerto Ricans and Mexican Americans to a behavior-strategy frame, which views Latino ethnic consciousness generating out of intergroup social participation. Viewed differently, Latino-conscious behavior manifests itself in the interaction between two or more Spanish-speaking groups which cut across national and cultural lines. The decision of a Spanish-speaking group about when to employ its Mexican American, Puerto Rican, Cuban, or the like ethnic identification is situationally determined and based upon that group's assessment of its goals and its options to attain those goals.

Latinismo: Political Consciousness

Politics is, according to W. Lloyd Warner (Warner and Hunt, 1941:301), the process through which services and benefits are allocated among competing sectors of society. Certainly politics, as such, is central to the dynamics of Latino ethnic consciousness. Latino ethnic-conscious behavior, thus, is addressed to gaining access to American urban systems, to gaining advantages or overcoming disadvantages in society. In addition to its situational dimension, Latino ethnic consciousness is intimately related to politics.

The overwhelming majority of the study's respondents—32 out of 34—defined the idea of Latino as a political phenomenon.[4] The case of a first-generation Mexican American leader, who worked in the Westtown community for over 15 years, represents a classic expression of this sentiment.: "Latino is the only way for us to crack the political barrier; to elect our own candidates; to get better schooling for our children; and more and better jobs."

A second generation Mexican American, who is currently working for the Mexican American Legal Defense and Educational Fund (MALDEF), also sees Latinismo as a manifestation of political consciousness. He sees this group form as a political strategy that can be used to elect officials who would, in turn, serve as models for all Latinos to identify with: "Certainly, one of the biggest problems that we face in Chicago is the lack of role models in politics, academics, and all the professions." A second generation Puerto Rican community leader also indicates the political significance of Latinismo of Hispanismo. He points out that Latino implies "having one of our own deciding what portion of the pie we are entitled to."

These ideological expressions (as well as the ones that follow) show that Latino ethnic-conscious behavior is not only related to Warner's articulation of politics, but at a general level it has much in common with what other scholars call political ethnicity, i.e., a manipulative device used to gain advantages or overcome disadvantages in the society (see Hawkins and Lorinskas, 1969; Bailey and Katz, 1969; Parenti, 1967; and others). In the same way, Latinismo corresponds to Cohen's analysis of political ethnicity.

He tells us that "one need not be a Marxist in order to recognize the fact that the earning of a livelihood, the struggle for a larger share of income from the economic system, including the struggle for housing, for higher education, and for other benefits, and similar issues constitute an important variable significantly related to ethnicity" (Cohen, 1974:xv).

The several conceptual formulations of Latino ethnic behavior noted above further suggest that this kind of group consciousness be seen not only as the product of collective intergroup social relations and/or actions, a process created or initiated by the leaders of the various groups, but also as a response to structural conditions. Structural conditions in the areas of education, politics, economics, and the like (that is, those conditions that transcend the individual Mexican American and Puerto Rican community interests and thus tend to impact the Spanish-speaking population city-wide, as one respondent asserted above) trigger and intensify the need for concerted group action among Spanish-speaking groups. In short, certain structural forces create the particular situational context appropriate for the creation and expression of a politicized Latino ethnic-conscious behavior.

The structural dimension of Latinismo pertains to the disadvantaged political and economic status imposed upon the various Spanish-speaking groups by the systems of inequality of the American society. This position is similar to that assumed by Despres (1975) in a paper on ethnicity and ethnic relations in Guyana. He contends that to assert ethnic identities in interpersonal encounters advances a status claim that establishes a relationship of competitive opposition between ethnic groups, and this relationship takes into consideration the status inequalities of the group. He then concludes that situations which bring into question the differential rights and privileges associated with these status disparities between groups lead to the assertion of ethnic identities and their related claims (Despres, 1975:109).

In the same vein, it is particularly in situations involving the inequality experiences common to both Puerto Ricans and Chicanos that Latino ethnic behavior is operative. In other words, certain situational factors have increasingly come to influence interethnic relations between Mexican Americans and Puerto Ricans, often resulting in the sharing of an exclusive Latino ethnic identification. Conversely, this argument would seem to imply that individual Spanish-speaking group encounters which do not directly involve the status inequalities of this larger population do not result in the affirmation of a Latino ethnic identification. That is to say, these relationships may proceed according to the individual and/or national-cultural identities which the separate groups possess, and thus it can be seen that Latinismo or Hispanismo need not be a relevant factor in all social situations concerning structural conditions and the various groups.

In sum, the fundamental feature of a politicized Latino ethnic identity is the variable significance of this group consciousness found in the structural social relations between Chicanos and Puerto Ricans. Latino-conscious behavior may be of critical relevance in some situations, while in others it may be totally irrelevant. From this point of view, Spanish-speaking groups should not be perceived as sharing and exhibiting Latino ethnic roles in all of their social relations. In the study of Latino ethnic behavior the unit of analysis has shifted from the isolated Puerto Rican or Mexican American ethnic group defined by its national-cultural content to Latinismo as a social category, a form of structure, embedded within a larger system. Behavior that had formerly been regarded as traditional (that of the Puerto Rican and Mexican American) may now be seen as manifesting a sense toward a Latino ethnic behavior which is a response to patterns of inter-action and communication among these groups.

Not always are the ideological formulations of Latino political conscious-ness homogenous. First, some of the study's respondents use the "pre-sumable cultural aspects" of a "Hispanic tradition" in their expression of Latino identity. In this case, Mexican Americans, Puerto Ricans, Cubans, and Central and South Americans have a consciousness of kind as Latinos because they speak the same language.

Another group of community organization leaders posits its Latinismo as an entity to which they have an obligation. They see the Latino-con-scious person as a participant who directly confronts (via any method including protest) the systems of cultural discrimination and inequality of the larger society. In this case, Mexican Americans and Puerto Ricans are viewed as having or sharing a consciousness about Latinismo because they are the only groups who collectively participate in combating the in-equality of the larger American society.

The Cultural-Political Type of Latino Group Identity. To one group of leaders a Latino-conscious person is given or a priori; that is, Latino ethnic solidarity is expressed on the basis of the person's origin and cultural background. This conceptual form corresponds to the primordial interpre-tation of ethnicity discussed earlier which focused on the transplanted cultural heritage as the principal antecedent and defining characteristic of ethnic groups. In their conceptual formulation of Latino ethnicity, these leaders subsume all of the Spanish-speaking under a wider Latino category in order to enlarge the group so that it can exert more influence for social, political, and economic progress. For example, in rallying enthusiasm among the various Spanish-speaking groups in the city, a first-generation Puerto Rican community leader has occasionally viewed this group as having "all of the ingredients to become a major political force in the entire city." One of this respondent's strongest calls for a Latino perspective is reflected in the following quote:

> In Chicago we have all of these groups who can speak Spanish and the truth of the matter is that this may be the factor to bring us together. We need to look into that. There is a great deal of commonality and experience in these groups. This may very well bring us back to Spain. But this also tells us that we have more in common than in differences. In fact, I just came from Israel

and we were with this guy who had been there for 18 years—an Israeli from Peru—and his wife was an Israeli from Argentina who had lived there for 23 years. We visited their home. It was just like being back home. We eat the same food and drink the same drinks. We were just like brothers and sisters. It was something real. This was heavy, and politically here in Chicago, is the only way to go. Individually, we are not going anywhere. So respect for differences could represent a way for us to unite. The idea of Latinismo is a very good strategy, not only for me but for all Latinos.

This sentiment is also shared by first generation Mexican Americans. A respondent who has been a resident of the city of Chicago for over 20 years refers to this group consciousness as an "identity that *el pueblo* [the community] has adopted since we are experiencing that we are not only Mexicans, Puerto Ricans, Cubans, Central or South Americans—but we are also Latinos." He added:

I feel pity for those leaders who stand up in meetings and say, "we must fight and struggle for the rights of the Puerto Ricans, the Mexicans, or the Cubans." I feel pity for these leaders because they do not understand Latinismo. They do not know that we have basically the same culture and needs. And the only way to alleviate those problems and gain political respect is to work together as one group.

These remarks, and the others contained in this section, indicate how the boundaries of a Latino ethnic group are widened to include all of the Spanish-speaking groups. The singling out of language as the basic defining ingredient of Latino ethnicity by these leaders resembles "one of nationalism's abiding myths: . . . the identification of nationality with language" (Smith, 1981:45). This group of leaders had adopted a fundamentally cultural approach to Latino ethnicity; they have chosen to elevate one element of culture into the main pillar of Latino ethnic identification.

Overall, although the Spanish language is an important cultural feature of Latino ethnic consciousness (it labels the population), it still cannot be used as the primary defining characteristic of the Latino ethnic group identity and consciousness. In other words, the role played by language and other cultural elements in the process of group formation and consciousness cannot be confused with the total constitution of that group's ethnic identification. Cultural elements such as language represent a way to classify a population, and without these primordial dimensions we cannot begin to locate ethnic categories; nor would we be able to differentiate a particular ethnic group from among others. Or, as Schildkrout (1974) indicates:

Like the closely related concept descent, ethnicity minimally implies a set of social categories giving rise to communities whose members may or may not have distinct subcultures. However, in terms of the larger society of which the ethnic communities are a part, the boundaries consist of symbols, and it is perhaps even more important they be understood by outsiders than they be accepted by the members themselves. (P. 192)

Any number of criteria such as place of origin, religion, color, and the like may provide symbols for differentiating ethnic groups, and the choice of which principle of categorization and which symbols a group adopts are cultural choices. But it is maintained here that we should not regard cultural elements as defining characteristics of the ethnic unit. The groups' cultural commonality does not bring about a collective response to the needs and wants of this population, and for this reason the different groups may remain uncoordinated and atomized.

Patterson's (1975) concern about the study of ethnicity as a cultural phenomenon reflects my point:

> Most definitions of the term [ethnicity] have been descriptive and static in an attempt to isolate a set of characteristics or traits by which the term may be delineated. Herein lies much of the confusion. Such definitions emphasize culture and tradition as the critical elements, and in so doing, are so descriptive that they become analytically useless, and often so inclusive that they are not even worthwhile as heuristic devices. Cultural attributes are of no intrinsic interest from a dynamic structural perspective. . . . A theory of ethnic cultural elements and symbols is an absurdity, because these symbols are purely arbitrary and unique to each case. (P. 306)

Further, if one chooses to regard the language similarities shared by Latinos as their primary characteristics, this would entail, according to Barth's (1969) argument, a "prejudge viewpoint both on (1) the nature of continuity in time of such units, and (2) the locus of the factors which determine the form of the units" (p. 15). Instead, it is suggested that Latino ethnic identification and consciousness be theoretically understood as a group-generating process, dependent upon the influence or effect of structural factors and conditions on the groups' cultural similarities. That is to say, the fusing or the interplay between structural and cultural variables leads to the emergence of this type of group form and consciousness. It is precisely in regard to its structural significance that Latino ethnic identification reveals itself as not being primarily cultural in its determination. Thus, it would seem that if generalizations are to be established in respect to Latino ethnic identification, we need to look much more carefully into the social conditions that create the situation for the emergence or construction of this group form.

The Sociopolitical Type of Latino Group Identity. Contrary to the primordial or cultural way of defining Latino ethnic identity, another group of leaders considers Latinos to be only those actors and groups who are involved in exerting direct pressures in the form of mass demonstrations, pickets, boycotts, and the like against the system of inequality of the larger society. This sociopolitical construction of Latino ethnicity focuses on treating most Puerto Ricans and Mexican Americans as sharing a Latino consciousness because of their active participation in confronting racism and capital exploitation in urban America. For instance, a second generation Puerto Rican community leader whose organization has always been at the forefront of direct confrontation in issues concerning the Spanish-speaking said: "When we talk about a Latino group identity or coalition in Chicago, it should be built and applied to by the people who come forward and identify themselves."

The idea of a Latino ethnic group is also defined as the collective identity of Mexican Americans and Puerto Ricans by a second generation of Mexican American community organization leaders. For example, one describes it as part of a developmental process whereby Boricuas (Puerto Ricans) and Chicanos have come to grips with their own heritage: "I think that the initial points were getting involved in our own identities. What I'm saying is that before we accepted the Latino, we accepted the Chicano, we accepted the Boricua. We accepted ourselves first and Latino second." This respondent also adds:

> [H]owever, we need to be concerned with the term Latino or Hispanic because that includes everybody. It includes the Cubans, the Central and South Americans, and I have always felt that the struggle has been a Chicano-Boricua struggle. I have worked with the city in other capacities and I've always seen how they like to impose upon us a Cuban or a South American to positions of power to keep the Chicanos and Boricuas divided.

The preceding views of the Latino ethnic group defined it as the social product of Puerto Ricans and Mexican Americans. In this way, the Latino-conscious person is seen as being part of a highly self-conscious, creative process.

This conceptual form of Latino ethnic group identification can be compared to two models of ethnic change. First, there seems to be a close parallel to what Thrupp (1962) calls "relative deprivation." The basic idea here is that social groups, and their members, only compare their position and fate with a limited range of other groups or individuals, usually those a little higher in the social scale. What matters for the group's perception and action is its progress relative to that of other similar groups. In his brief discussion of this element of ethnic change, Smith (1981) attributes the development of social movements and political action as the "outcome of perceived frustrations on the part of individuals or groups, who are disadvantaged and deprived relative to others and handicapped in the race for wealth, status, services, and power" (p. 28).

The ideological sentiments attributed to Latino ethnicity in this section are also analogous to the idea of the internal colonialism model of ethnic change. In addition to Blauner (1969), who is credited with systematically developing the colonial model (Wilson, 1972:266), other scholars such as Moore (1970) and Barrera (1979) posit a perspective which considers ethnic communities as representing internal colonies of metropolitan or urban centers, with dependent, stagnant institutions and a cultural division of labor which assigns low-status roles to blacks, Mexican Americans, Puerto Ricans, and other groups. In this view, like ethnic movements, Latinismo can be explained as reactions to an exploitative system of inequality and its associated hierarchical cultural division of labor.

While assigning different ideological expressions to the political feature of Latino ethnic identity and consciousness, we can still suggest when we look at the two conceptual forms collectively that, fired by an ideology which puts a premium on language solidarity or on a perception of being victims of systems of racial inequality, the leaders of the Spanish-speaking communities are seeking to ensure that their political demands are met by the American urban political system. This is to say that the construction of Latino ethnicity as a political strategy clearly reflects on prevailing conceptions of American politics. According to one of the most sophisticated of the pluralist analyses of American politics, the "normal American process is one in which there is a high probability that an active and legitimate group in the population can make itself heard effectively at some crucial stages in the process of decision" (Dahl, 1956:145–46). Additionally, this is to be followed by what Smith (1981) has called "communalism." The aim of it is "for greater control by the ethnic community over specifically communal matters in the urban areas where [the group] predominates. There is a further claim that the [ethnic] community be recognized as a political actor on the national [or local] levels. So ethnic communities begin to act as pressure groups controlling an 'ethnic vote' and trading it for political concessions" (1981:16). In sum, the social organization of Latino ethnicity represents an attempt to alter existing social and power arrangements between the Spanish-speaking and the larger American society.

Conclusion

In the above discussion, the data point to two central features of Latino ethnicity. First and foremost, the data reflect the fact that the respondents' ideological formulations of Latino ethnic consciousness and identity are situationally specific in their expression. Latino ethnicity manifests itself in the sequences of social situations through which members of Puerto Rican and Mexican American groupings pass in the course of their urban existence and experiences. The Latino ethnic solidarity provides a particular form for intergroup relations involving more than one Spanish-speaking population; it ascribes them, according to the situation, to a relationship of incorporation, in which gains are sought for the collectivity.

Second, Latino ethnicity is viewed by the study's respondents as a political phenomenon: a strategy to attain the needs and wants of the groups. As a political type, Latino ethnicity was further defined by (1) its primordial quality or the sharing of a common language, and (2) its direct action orientation. In other words, there are some community leaders who define Latinos as a group made up of actors who speak Spanish. On the other hand, another group of leaders argues that this type of group form be assigned to those who participate collectively and apply direct action or pressures against the system of inequality of the larger society.

In sum, the politicization of a situational Latino ethnic identity and consciousness suggests the mobilization of Spanish-speaking groups into a self-conscious Latino frame of reference. It also suggests directing some of their individual group behavior toward activities in the political arena on the basis of this awareness, concern, and group consciousness. Furthermore, the politicization of a situational Latino ethnic identity and consciousness entails almost a related irony and paradox. It stresses, ideologizes, and sometimes virtually recreates the distinctive and unique national-cultural identities of the groups that it mobilizes, precisely at the historical moments when these groups are being asked to take on a Latino ethnic consciousness. Thus, the politicization of a situational Latino ethnic identification is a dialectical process that preserves individual and separate group ethnic ties and it also emphasizes a wider or global identity and consciousness by transforming them into a political conflict population.

What might be considered to be somewhat of a special case of ethnicity and ethnic relations has been described here. The fact that Latino ethnic identity is not based on one genuine cultural heritage that has been passed down from one generation to the next, and that it is situationally operative, makes the Spanish-speaking's representation of it nonetheless real. Rather than deriving from historically fixed and primordial ties, the collective representations that adhere to the Latino ethnic identity and consciousness derive from the observation of the strategic reactions of disadvantaged peoples to their assignment to underprivileged statuses offered within the context of this society's political economy.

REFERENCES

Alinsky, Saul. 1969. *Reveille for Radicals* (New York: Vintage Books).

Bailey, Barry, and Ellis Katz. 1969. *Ethnic Group Politics* (Columbus, Ohio: Merrill).

Barrera, Mario. 1979. *Race and Class in the Southwest: A Theory of Inequality* (Notre Dame, Ind.: University of Notre Dame Press).

Barth, Frederick. 1969. "Introduction," in Frederick Barth, ed., *Ethnic Groups and Boundaries: The Social Organization of Cultural Difference* (London: George Allen & Unwin): pp. 1–12.

Bell, Daniel. 1975. "Ethnicity and Social Change," in Nathan Glazer and Daniel P. Moynihan, eds., *Ethnicity: Theory and Practice* (Cambridge: Harvard University Press): pp. 141–74.

Blauner, Robert. 1969. "Internal Colonialism and Ghetto Revolt," *Social Problems,* 16 (Spring):393–408.

Cohen, Abner. 1974. "Introduction: The Lesson of Ethnicity," in Abner Cohen, ed., *Urban Ethnicity* (New York: Tavistock): pp. ix–xxiv.

Dahl, Robert. 1956. *A Preface to Democratic Theory* (Chicago: University of Chicago Press).

Despres, Leo A. 1975. "Ethnicity and Resource Competition in Guyanese Society," in Leo A. Despres, ed., *Ethnicity and Resource Competition in Plural Societies* (Chicago: Mouton): pp. 87–118.

Patterson, Orlando. 1975. "Context and Choice in Ethnic Allegiance: A Theoretical Framework and Caribbean Case Study," in Nathan Glazer and Daniel P. Moynihan, eds., op. cit.: pp. 305–49.

Pitts, James. 1974. "The Study of Race Consciousness: Comments on New Directions," *American Journal of Sociology,* 80 (November):665–87.

Parenti, Michael. 1967. "Ethnic Politics and the Persistence of Ethnic Identification," *American Political Science Review,* 61 (September):15–29.

Ragin, Charles C. 1979. "Ethnic Political Mobilization: The Welsh Case," *American Sociological Review,* 44 (August):619–35.

Schermerhorn, Richard. 1970. *Comparative Ethnic Relations* (New York: Random House).

Schildkrout, Enid. 1974. "Ethnicity and Generational Differences among Urban Immigrants in Ghana," in Abner Cohen, ed., op. cit.: pp. 187–222.

Smith, Anthony D. 1981. *The Ethnic Revival* (New York: Cambridge University Press).

Thrupp, Sylvia L. 1962. *Millennial Dreams in Action: Essays in Comparative Study* (The Hague: Mouton).

Warner, Lloyd W., and Paul S. Hunt. 1941. *The Social Life of a Modern Community* (New Haven: Yale University Press).

Wilson, William. 1972. "Race Relations Models and Explanations of Ghetto Behavior," in Peter Rose, ed., *Nation of Nations: The Ethnic Experience and Racial Crisis* (New York: Random House): pp. 259–75.

Gordon, Milton. 1975. "Toward a General Theory of Racial and Ethnic Group Relations," in Nathan Glazer and Daniel P. Moynihan, eds., op. cit.: pp. 84–110.

Hawkins, Brett, and Robert Lorinskas. 1969. *The Ethnic Factor in American Politics* (Columbus, Ohio: Merrill).

Higham, John. 1975. *Send These to Me: Jews and Other Immigrants in Urban America* (New York: Atheneum).

Isaacs, Harold. 1975. "Basic Group Identity: The Idols of the Tribe," in Nathan Glazer and Daniel P. Moynihan, eds., op. cit.: pp. 29–52.

Lopata, Helena Z. 1964. "The Function of Voluntary Associations in an Ethnic Community: 'Polonia,' " in Ernest W. Burgess and Donald T. Bogue, eds., *Contributions to Urban Sociology* (Chicago: University of Chicago Press): pp. 203–23.

Moore, Joan W. 1970. "Colonialism: The Case of Mexican Americans," *Social Problems,* 17 (Spring):463–72.

25. SHIFTS TO ENGLISH AS USUAL LANGUAGE BY AMERICANS OF SPANISH MOTHER TONGUE[1]

Gilles GRENIER, *University of Ottawa*

Using a probit regression model, the factors that determine shifts from Spanish to English are investigated in a sample of Hispanics drawn from the 1976 Survey of Income and Education. The most significant factors are age at migration, years since migration, choice of a non-Hispanic marriage partner, and education level.

In bilingual or multilingual societies where there are frequent contacts between individuals of different mother tongues, we expect the dominant or majority language to exert a power of attraction over the other language or languages. One way to measure this phenomenon is to count, from a population of a given ethnic origin or mother tongue, the number of individuals who adopt another language as the language that they predominantly use. These shifts from one language to another are an important factor to consider, along with natural population increase and migrations, in assessing the future numerical importance of a minority language group in a given geographical area.

In the United States, the most important and fastest growing linguistic minority is the group of Hispanic Americans. Although Hispanics are not a homogeneous group of people, they have some characteristics in common, the most important one being their language, Spanish, another one being their low average socioeconomic status. One of the results of the interactions of Hispanics with members of the English-speaking majority in the United States has been the gradual shift from Spanish to English as their language of communication. For instance, in 1976 more than one-fifth of the people who considered themselves as being of Hispanic origin

[1] This chapter is a slightly abridged version of the article which appeared in the June 1984 issue of *Social Science Quarterly*. I wish to thank Orley Ashenfelter, Alan Blinder, David Bloom, Doug Massey, Cordelia Reimers, the editor of *SSQ*, and anonymous referees for valuable comments and criticisms. I am, however, the only one responsible for the views expressed in this paper. Editor's note: Reviewers were Rodolfo Alvarez, Frank Bean, Rodolfo de la Garza, and Marta Tienda.

reported that English was their mother tongue. Although most of those whose mother tongue is Spanish were still using it often, about half of them used English as their main language. In the context of the situation of Hispanics in the United States, shifts from Spanish to English as usual language may have important implications. From the cultural point of view, they represent an important aspect of the anglicization process and can be seen as a threat to the conservation of the identity of the Hispanic population in the United States. One could argue that they should be stopped in order to prevent assimilation. On the other hand, one could also argue that language shifts make possible a better integration of the Hispanic population to the U.S. work force and that they should be encouraged in order to reduce socioeconomic disparities between non-Hispanics and Hispanics.

In any event, regardless of one's own feelings about the desirability of language shifts, it may be useful to study the factors that determine them. Note that several studies have been done on the subject of language shifts in different contexts. Shifts from French to English and from English to French in different regions of Canada have been studied by Castonguay (1976, 1979a, 1979b), Veltman (1978), and Lachapelle and Henripin (1980). Shifts from Swedish to Finnish in Finland have been analyzed by de Vries (1974). Shifts from Spanish to English among Hispanic Americans have also been studied recently by Veltman (1981).

The purpose of this paper is to consider further the factors that determine shifts to English among Spanish mother tongue Americans, using data from the 1976 Survey of Income and Education. While the above-mentioned studies were concerned with the factors associated with language shifts, only a small number of these factors were considered at the same time, since the typical method of analysis was to present cross-tabulations of language shift rates by different population characteristics (such as age, sex, and marital status) using aggregate data. The particular feature of this study is that microdata and multivariate analysis are used, allowing for many factors to be considered at the same time. The estimating equation is a probit in which the dependent variable is whether an individual has retained Spanish or has shifted to English as the language most often spoken at the time the survey was being taken. The independent variables are characteristics that are particular to each individual.

The Determinants of Language Shifts

Different theoretical frameworks can be used to analyze language behavior. Traditionally, sociolinguists have explained group behavior with respect to language using concepts such as ethnicity, cultural identity, nationality, etc. (e.g., Ross, 1979). In contrast, economists have tried to explain individual language behavior with the concept of human capital

(Breton, 1978; Grenier and Vaillancourt, 1983). Since this study uses data where the basic unit of observation is the individual, this latter approach seems more appropriate. Briefly, the human capital approach puts forward the hypothesis that people make investments in themselves so as to maximize the expected net return, i.e., benefits minus costs, of that investment, where these benefits and costs are to be understood as including psychic as well as financial elements. If we consider the decision to learn a language, and eventually to adopt it as one's major language, within such a framework, then one way to study that decision is to analyze its costs and benefits. Note that, by adopting this approach, we do not want to deny the importance of the factors stressed by sociolinguists. In fact, these factors can be viewed as ingredients that determine benefits and costs. On the other hand, one cannot deny either that rational economic considerations, made either consciously or unconsciously, are also very important.

Let us now consider the benefits and costs of language shifts. Three major elements seem to be important. First, there may be strong economic incentives to shift to another language. To the extent that knowledge of the dominant language and integration to the dominant economic community provides contacts which may improve someone's economic opportunities, one of the most important benefits from adopting the dominant language is probably the possibility to earn a higher income (Veltman, Boulet, and Castonguay, 1979; Grenier, forthcoming). Second, before shifting to another language, one must first learn it. Since people learn to speak languages through practice, the opportunity cost of language shifts is determined to a large extent by the environment in which someone lives. In other words, for a given desire or need to learn a language, this will be done at a lower cost if there are opportunities to speak that language with other people. Finally, a very important element to consider is the psychic cost of language shifts. Some people may resist shifting to another language because they feel that their cultural identity may be threatened. To the extent that this cost is important, we would observe fewer language shifts than purely economic considerations would indicate.

These benefits and costs cannot be measured directly from available data, but they can be related to observed individual attributes. Individuals with attributes which increase the expected net returns of an investment are more likely than others to make that investment. More precisely, drawing from earlier studies on language shifts, and given the availability of data, we will consider the following factors as determinants of language shifts:

1. Age is probably the most important factor that determines the amount of exposure to another language, since it measures the duration of that exposure. Clearly, the longer a person has been exposed to a language, the lower the opportunity cost to learn it and the higher the probability of

shifting to it. Another aspect of age, however, has to be considered. The older a person is, the shorter the period of time during which he or she receives the benefits and the lower the probability of shifting to another language.

A typical pattern of the relationship between age and language shifts was hypothesized by Castonguay (1976) and estimated with Canadian data. During the individual's childhood, we expect very few shifts to occur since the language that the person uses is determined by the language of the parents. When the individual goes to school, enters the labor market, and gets married, he or she becomes more exposed to the dominant language spoken outside the home, and is more likely to adopt it as usual language. Since these changes are usually completed by the age of thirty or thirty-five, very few language shifts are likely to occur after these ages. Empirical evidence from the 1971 Canadian census supports that hypothesis.

2. The presence of a significant number of immigrants can perturb the age pattern of language shifts postulated above. In this case, the duration of exposure to the other language is no longer measured by age, but by the period of time since migration took place. This problem was ignored by Castonguay, since immigration was almost completely absent in the group of people that he considered. This is not the case for Spanish-speaking Americans, however, since immigrants account for an important proportion of the population. Veltman (1981) found a positive relationship between anglicization and length of residence in the United States.

3. Another important variable that has to be taken into account to explain language shifts is marriage. Castonguay (1979a, 1979b) found very high levels of anglicization among French Canadians who were living in provinces other than Quebec and whose spouses were not French Canadians. Clearly, a person who is married outside his or her linguistic community faces lower costs of language shifts, since that person lives in an environment which is favorable to speaking the other language. The psychic cost of losing one's cultural identity is also lower if one is attached to a person from another culture. Note, however, that marriage may be an effect as well as a cause of anglicization, since persons who are already anglicized are more likely to choose an English-speaking spouse than persons who are not. Consequently, some caution should be used in interpreting the correlation between marriage and language shifts.

4. We may also expect language shifts to differ by sex. Men usually spend more time outside the home than women, and are therefore more exposed to the dominant language. In other words, they face lower costs of language shifts. The potential benefits are also higher because they are more attached to the labor market. On the other hand, the psychic aspects may be more important for women to the extent that mothers, in order to transmit their language and their culture to their young children, would be inclined to retain their mother tongue as usual language longer

than they would have otherwise. These factors suggest that more language shifts should occur among men and among women without children than among women with children.

5. The linguistic composition of the neighborhood in which a person lives should influence language shifts. Clearly, the larger the proportion of persons who speak a given language in a geographical area happens to be, the lower the opportunity cost to learn that language, and the more shifts to that language by individuals of other mother tongues will take place. Such a relationship was found by Veltman (1978) in a study of language shifts in different census tracts in the Montreal metropolitan area.

6. Finally, we may expect an association between language shifts and education. The more educated members of the minority language group are likely to have more economic opportunities with the majority group than the less educated ones, and we expect more language shifts among them. In his study of census tracts in the Montreal metropolitan area, Veltman (1978) found more language shifts in districts with a higher average level of education.

The Data

The determinants of language shifts among Hispanic Americans are now analyzed in relation with the available data. The data set used is the 1976 Survey of Income and Education (SIE). The sample consists of all Hispanic origin males and females, aged 14 and over, who reported that Spanish was usually spoken in the home when they were children. For the purpose of this study, these people are defined as being of Spanish mother tongue. The variable to be explained is retention of Spanish as usual language, i.e., whether the individuals in the sample reported that Spanish, as opposed to English, was the language most often spoken at the time of the survey.[2] The sample had to be restricted to individuals aged 14 and over because the two questions used to construct the dependent variables were not asked of children under 14. There are 7,366 observations in the sample.

Table 1 presents the mean values of some variables of interest for individuals in the sample for each of the Hispanic ethnic groups and by sex. Out of all Hispanic Americans in our sample whose mother tongue is Spanish, only half were still using Spanish as their main language of communication at the time of the survey, while the other half had shifted to English. Women retained Spanish as their usual language in a slightly higher proportion than men. There are also important differences in the

2 In this study, we are interested only in shifts to English as the major means of communication. The SIE questionnaire also asked respondents whether another language was also often spoken. Although this question is not used in this study, it may be worth noticing that many of the persons who reported having shifted to English were still using Spanish as a second language.

proportion who have retained Spanish among the Hispanic groups. These differences reflect the various backgrounds of these groups, mainly with regard to migration patterns and the region of the United States in which they settled. Table 1 also contains the sample means of the variables which represent the major determinants of language shifts. Since many Hispanics are immigrants, age alone is not an appropriate measure of duration of exposure to English. Two different variables were constructed to account for this fact: "age at migration" and "years since migration." Age at migration indicates the moment in the individual's life at which he or she started to be exposed to the English language, assuming no or little exposure before the time of migration.[3] Note that this variable was defined to take the value zero for individuals born in the United States, expressing by that the fact that they started to be exposed to English at age zero.[4] From the discussion above on the effects of age on language shifts, we expect age at migration to have a positive impact on Spanish retention. The other variable which accounts for duration of exposure to the English language is the number of years since migration. Note again that, for individuals born in the United States, who are assumed to have migrated at age zero, this variable is equal to the person's age. We expect this variable to have a negative impact on Spanish retention. However, the impact of one more year of exposure to the English language should become less important as the number of years since migration increases. To account for that, the square of the number of years since migration is included in the regression analysis reported below.

We can see from Table 1 that the differences in Spanish retention among the Hispanic ethnic groups are related partly to differences in age at migration and number of years since migration. These reflect to a large extent the relative composition of immigrants and U.S.-born individuals. Mexican Americans and "other Hispanics" have a low mean age at migration and a high mean number of years since migration. This is because a larger proportion of them are U.S.-born than for the other groups. It is interesting to note that these two groups are also those with the lowest Spanish retention. On the other hand, Cubans, the group with the highest

[3]Some Hispanics may have some knowledge of English before entering the U.S. mainland. For example, Puerto Ricans may have had some contact with English-speaking Americans in Puerto Rico. Similarly, many Central and South Americans are of high socioeconomic origin and may have had some language instruction prior to their entry to the United States. However, this amount of exposure to English is probably very small relative to the exposure received after entering the United States.

[4]The variables "age at migration" and "years since migration" were constructed using a question in the SIE asking the year during which the individual migrated. For recent migrants the exact year was reported, while for older migrants only an interval of years was reported. When only an interval of years is available, the midpoint of the interval was used to estimate the year of migration. However, when the migrant's age indicated that he or she was born *during* the interval, the midpoint between year of birth and the end of the interval was used to estimate the year of migration.

TABLE 1

Mean Characteristics of the Sample of Hispanics Who Spoke Spanish as a Child, by Ethnic Group and by Sex, 1976

	Mexican	Puerto Rican	Cuban	Central and South American	Other Hispanic	Total All Groups	Male	Female
Spanish retention	.476	.569	.676	.564	.440	.503	.483	.522
Age at migration (in years, = 0 if born in U.S.)	6.8	16.7	30.1	26.2	6.2	10.9	10.7	11.1
Years since migration (= age if born in U.S.)	29.7	17.9	11.6	9.8	37.9	26.9	27.1	26.6
Sex								
Male	.490	.444	.465	.398	.466	.473	1	0
Female	.510	.556	.535	.602	.534	.527	0	1
Years of education	8.86	9.09	10.61	11.45	9.85	9.32	9.52	9.14
Region								
North East	.004	.732	.351	.476	.124	.176	.159	.194
South East	.007	.052	.456	.164	.072	.066	.062	.071
North Central	.087	.130	.051	.061	.025	.079	.085	.070
West South Central	.295	.009	.034	.045	.022	.179	.181	.177
West	.607	.077	.108	.254	.757	.500	.513	.488
Marital Status								
Not married	.364	.442	.377	.370	.337	.372	.336	.404
Married, spouse Hispanic	.545	.478	.544	.436	.504	.523	.563	.487
Married, spouse non-Hispanic	.091	.080	.079	.194	.159	.105	.101	.109
Presence of children in family								
Age 0–5	.293	.259	.126	.320	.143	.254	.249	.258
Age 6–11	.402	.354	.265	.315	.320	.367	.353	.381
Age 12–17	.442	.401	.395	.211	.406	.414	.405	.422
Percentage of state population which is Hispanic	16.51	5.35	6.43	6.73	21.45	14.43	14.49	14.37
Sample size	4,230	1,010	555	422	1,149	7,366	3,484	3,882

Source: 1976 Survey of Income and Education.

Note: Each cell entry is a group mean or proportion.

Spanish retention, have a high mean age at migration and a low mean number of years since migration. Finally, we observe that the other two groups, Puerto Ricans and Central and South Americans, have about the same level of Spanish retention, but that they differ in the mean values of these two variables. Owing to the fact that the latter group includes many recent immigrants, it has a low mean value of number of years since migration and a high mean age at migration. We observe the opposite for Puerto Ricans.

Among the other variables which may affect language shifts, we observe that the groups which have the highest levels of education, Central and South Americans and Cubans, are also those which have the highest Spanish retention. Note that this is contrary to our hypotheses made above.[5]

Two variables are used to express the effect of geographical environment. The first one is a dummy variable for region.[6] The second one is the percentage of the state population which is Hispanic. Note that the two groups that live in states with the highest proportion of Hispanics are Mexican Americans and other Hispanics, which are also the groups with the smallest Spanish retention rate.[7]

The immediate family environment of an individual also has an important impact on the language that he or she usually speaks. Two variables are included to account for this: the ethnicity of the spouse (if there is one) and the presence of children in the family. Although the majority of Hispanics marry with other Hispanics, there is a significant number of marriages outside the Hispanic community: about one out of six in our sample. We observe that marriages outside the Hispanic community are particularly frequent for Central and South Americans and other Hispanics. It is interesting to note that these two groups are very different in their levels of Spanish retention. We also note that Hispanic women who are married tend to marry outside the Hispanic community a little bit more than men.

The presence of children in the family may also have an effect on the language usually spoken by other members of the family, especially by the parents. We expect the presence of young children to induce fewer

[5] The mean levels of education reported in Table 1 should be interpreted with some caution. Because the samples include all individuals aged 14 and more, many persons in the younger age groups have not yet completed their education. Therefore, these mean levels do not represent the average completed education.

[6] Note that the definition of the regions used for this paper corresponds to the usual four major regions of the United States, except for the South region, which is broken down into two parts: South East and West South Central. This is done in order to consider in two different regions Cubans who live mainly in Florida and Mexicans and other Hispanics who live mainly in the southwestern states.

[7] For Mexicans and other Hispanics these high percentages are due to the fact that these two groups are highly concentrated in the five southwestern states of Texas, Colorado, New Mexico, Arizona, and California. Note that a better indicator of the immediate linguistic environment would have been the proportion of Hispanics in the metropolitan area or in the community where a person lives. Unfortunately, this information was not available.

language shifts, especially for the mother, while the presence of older children should induce more shifts. In Table 1, the numbers for each age category represent the proportion of individuals in the sample who live in families where there is at least one child in the given age group. We observe that the groups with the highest percentages of individuals with young children are Central and South Americans, Mexican Americans, and Puerto Ricans.

Regression Analysis

The net effects of each of the above variables are now analyzed with the use of regression analysis. The results are presented in Table 2 where the numbers for each variable and for each group represent the impact of a unit change of that variable on the probability of Spanish retention for that group.[8] As an example of the interpretation of these numbers, observe that the number corresponding to the variable "age at migration" for Mexican Americans is .013. This indicates that if two individuals were identical in all the other characteristics, but one entered the United States one year older than the other, then the former would have a 1.3 percentage point higher probability to have Spanish as usual language than the latter.

In general, the results indicate that the variables have the expected effects, even in those cases where the relationships between the mean values of the variables were in the wrong direction. Perhaps the most important finding of Table 2 is the relative similarity across the groups in the process that determines shifts to English as usual language, in spite of the fact that these groups are, as we have seen, very different in their mean characteristics. In other words, for many of the variables in the regression, groups that are very different in their characteristics have similar coefficients. Note for example, the effect of age at migration for Mexican Americans, Cubans, and Central and South Americans, and the effect of years since migration for Mexican Americans, Cubans, and other Hispanics.

Besides these similarities among the groups, there are also some differences which are worth mentioning. In particular, we note that the effect of years since migration is important for Central and South Americans. This indicates that members of this group are shifting to English at a faster pace than the other groups after they enter the United States. This may be

[8] Given the dichotomous nature of the dependent variable, an appropriate technique of estimation is the probit model (see Theil, 1971:628–32). A probit equation where the dependent variable is equal to one if the individual usually speaks Spanish and equal to zero if he or she usually speaks English was estimated. The probit coefficients express the effect of changes in the independent variables on a monotonic transformation of the dependent variable and do not lend themselves to a straightforward interpretation. They can be transformed, however, to express the impact of a unit change in each variable, at the mean value of the other variables, on the probability that the dependent variable takes the value one.

TABLE 2

Transformed Probit Coefficients for Determinants of Spanish Retention among Hispanics Who Spoke Spanish as a Child, by Ethnic Group and by Sex, 1976

	Mexican	Puerto Rican	Cuban	Central and South American	Other Hispanic	Total All Groups	Male	Female
Constant	.588*	.265*	.085	.436	.030	.504*	.573*	.471*
Age at migration (in years, = 0 if born in U.S.)	.013*	.021*	.014*	.014*	.009*	.014*	.011*	.016*
Years since migration (= age if born in U.S.)	-.023*	-.017*	-.021*	-.044*	-.023*	-.022*	-.023*	-.021*
Years since migration squared	.0003*	.0002	.0003*	.0009*	.0003*	.0003*	.0003*	.0003*
Sex								
Male (reference)	—	—	—	—	—	—	—	—
Female	.005	.214*	.080*	.209*	-.008	.042*	—	—
Years of education	-.054*	-.041*	-.026*	-.063*	-.060	-.053*	-.053*	-.054*
Region								
North East	-.249	.076	.017	.169	.623*	.053	-.054	.139
South East	.048	-.068	.096	.076	.768*	.075	.075	.064
North Central (reference)	—	—	—	—	—	—	—	—
West South Central	.106*	-.572*	.049	.603*	.784*	.078*	.041	.103*
West	-.064	-.306*	-.036	-.281	.378	-.101*	-.137*	-.075
Marital status								
Not married (reference)	—	—	—	—	—	—	—	—
Married, spouse Hispanic	.084*	.060	.186*	.175*	.045	.091*	.093*	.103*
Married, spouse non-Hispanic	-.335*	-.519*	-.268*	-.396*	-.416*	-.409*	-.444*	-.385*
Presence of children in family								
Age 0–5	.015	.090	-.078	.142	-.003	.033	-.002	.063*
Age 6–11	-.008	-.041	-.027	.165*	.091*	.007	.020	-.007
Age 12–17	-.004	-.068	-.081	-.255*	-.023	-.021	-.031	-.008
Percentage of state population which is Hispanic	.008*	-.008	.013	.012	.015*	.011*	.012*	.009*

NOTE: The transformed probit coefficients represent the effect of a unit change in the independent variable on the probability of speaking Spanish, at the mean values of the other independent variables.

*Probit coefficient significantly different from zero at the 95 percent level.

explained by the fact that this group does not have a common ethnic origin and that immigrants do not usually settle in a community of their own ethnic origin when they enter the United States. Another possible explanation is that Central and South Americans are from high socioeconomic background and that many of them already know English before entering the United States. Note also the important effect of age at migration for Puerto Ricans, which indicates that older Puerto Rican immigrants are more likely to retain Spanish as their usual language than similar immigrants in the other groups. This may be explained by the fact that many Puerto Ricans live in their own ethnic neighborhood, mainly in the New York City area, and that many immigrants already have members of their family in these communities when they arrive.

Among the other variables which influence language shifts, we note in particular the very large impact of the ethnicity of the spouse. On average, for all the Hispanic groups, having a non-Hispanic spouse decreases by 40 percentage points the probability of Spanish retention, as opposed to not being married, while having a Hispanic spouse has the opposite effect, but with a smaller magnitude.

Finally, we observe that the presence of children in the family has the expected effect. Having young children in the family increases the probability of speaking Spanish, while having older children decreases it. Note, in particular, that the presence of young children has a significant positive impact on the probability of Spanish retention for women.

Conclusions

The results of this study indicate that Hispanic Americans are shifting to English at a relatively fast pace. Already half of the Spanish mother tongue Hispanic Americans have English as their major language. As Hispanics are staying more years in the United States, are becoming more educated, are marrying outside their community, and are raising their children in English, we would expect, in the absence of migrations, this percentage to increase considerably as time goes on. For example, using the results of the regression for the total of all groups and assuming age at migration to be zero without changing the average age distribution, we can calculate that about 70 percent of Hispanics, instead of 50 percent, would shift to English as usual language.[9] Some caution should be used, however, in interpreting the results of this analysis. First, the above calculation overstates the real situation because the inflow of new immi-

[9] More precisely, we obtain this number from the probit regression equation for the total of all groups by giving the value zero to the variable "age at migration," by assuming that the variable "years since migration" is equal to the mean age of the individuals in the sample and that the variable "years since migration squared" is equal to the mean age squared of the individuals in the sample, and by assuming the mean sample values for the other independent variables.

grants is not likely to stop. Second, many Hispanics who have shifted to English are still using Spanish as a second usual language. Finally, there is a potential selection bias which may also result in overstating the conclusions of this analysis. To the extent that immigrants who stay in the United States are more likely to be included in the survey than those who come and return to their country of origin, the results reflect the behavior of a selected subsample of the Hispanic population, which may be different from the behavior of the entire population.

Since shifts to English as usual language by Americans of Spanish mother tongue occur to a large extent because people want to improve their economic opportunities, the policy implications of these shifts have to be analyzed in that context. In principle, two kinds of policies are possible to help a group of people who are disadvantaged because their language is not the language of the labor market. One is to act on the labor market itself in order to increase the use of that language. The other is to help members of that group to learn the language of the labor market. Clearly, the attitude about the desirability of language shifts depends on the choice between these two policies. It is interesting to compare Canada and United States in that context. The case of Canada provides an example of the application of the first kind of policy, where laws were passed to promote the use of French. On the other hand, the policy of melting pot practiced in the United States toward the different ethnic groups is essentially of the second kind.

To a large extent, the choice of the policy to help the disadvantaged group is a question of rights. For example, the French in Quebec, because they were there before the British, believe that they have a right to use French, and would refuse any policy which would try to assimilate them. Another factor to consider is the size of the linguistic group in the total population. Since the French are the majority in Quebec, it is relatively easy to make French the working language there. Clearly, Hispanic Americans are in a different situation. First, since most of them migrated to the United States, they cannot claim a right for the Spanish language in the United States, except for the island of Puerto Rico and the areas where Mexicans lived before they became part of the United States. Second, although there are large concentrations of Hispanics in some areas of the United States, especially in the southwestern states, Hispanics nevertheless are a minority of the population, which means that it would be difficult to implement a policy making Spanish a working language, except in some very localized labor markets. All these factors suggest that the best way to help Hispanics improve their economic situation remains the implementation of policies aiming at facilitating their smooth integration into the English-speaking majority, mainly by having them learn English as rapidly as possible. In that regard, the rapid anglicization of Hispanics that we observe may be interpreted as an indication of success. This contrasts sharply with the case of Canada where the anglicization of the French-speaking population is usually interpreted as an indication of the failure of the federal government language policy.

REFERENCES

Breton, Albert. 1978. *Bilingualism: An Economic Approach* (Montreal: C. D. Howe Research Institute).

Castonguay, Charles. 1976. "Les transferts linguistiques au foyer," *Recherches Sociographiques*, 17 (September–December):341–51.

――――. 1979a. "Exogamie et anglicisation chez les minorités canadiennes-françaises," *Canadian Review of Sociology and Anthropology*, 16 (February):21–31.

――――. 1979b. "L'exogamie précoce et la prévision des taux de transfert linguistique," *Recherches Sociographiques*, 20 (September–December):403–8.

de Vries, John. 1974. "Net Effects of Language Shifts in Finland," *Acta Sociologica*, 17 (June):141–49.

Grenier, Gilles. Forthcoming. "The Effect of Language Characteristics on the Wages of Hispanic Americans," *Journal of Human Resources*.

Grenier, Gilles, and François Vaillancourt. 1983. "An Economic Perspective on Learning a Second Language," *Journal of Multilingual and Multicultural Development*, 4 (December): 471–83.

Lachapelle, Réjean, and Jacques Henripin. 1980. *La situation démolinguistique au Canada: Evolution passée et prospective* (Montreal: Institute for Research on Public Policy).

Ross, Jeffrey A. 1979. "Language and the Mobilization of Ethnic Identity," in H. Giles and B. Saint-Jacques, eds., *Language and Ethnic Relations* (New York: Pergamon): pp. 1–14.

Theil, Henri. 1971. *Principles of Econometrics* (New York: Wiley).

Veltman, Calvin J. 1978. "La structure résidentielle des transferts linguistiques dans la région de Montréal," *Recherches Sociographiques*, 19 (September–December):392–401.

――――. 1981. "Language Shifts in the United States." Mimeographed (Montreal).

Veltman, Calvin J., Jac-André Boulet, and Charles Castonguay. 1979. "The Economic Context of Bilingualism and Language Transfers in the Montreal Metropolitan Area," *Canadian Journal of Economics*, 12 (August):468–79.

26. LANGUAGE, EDUCATION, AND THE SOCIOECONOMIC ACHIEVEMENT OF HISPANIC ORIGIN MEN[1]

Marta TIENDA, *University of Wisconsin–Madison*

Lisa J. NEIDERT, *University of Michigan*

The influence of language-use patterns on the occupational achievements of Hispanic working-age men is examined to determine how Spanish-English bilingualism and English proficiency influence socioeconomic status. Retention of Spanish generally does not hinder the socioeconomic achievements of Hispanic origin men, provided that they acquire a minimum education (high school) and English proficiency. Foreign-born Mexicans and island-born Puerto Ricans are an exception to this pattern; they are penalized in terms of status if they speak no English. Implications for bilingual education programs are discussed.

The occupational achievement process of Hispanic men has not been well described in the stratification literature, where most studies have focused on white and black men, making only occasional reference to nationality-defined ethnic groups (for example, see Duncan, Featherman, and Duncan, 1972: chap. 4; Featherman and Hauser, 1978: chap. 8). In recent years, however, as government statistics have revealed the persistence of socioeconomic disadvantages among language minorities (National Center for Education Statistics, 1978; Newman, 1978), the need to examine the sources of this inequality has become more acute. Some researchers have attempted to address issues of occupational stratification (Tienda, 1982; Garcia, 1979; Suter, 1972; Lopez, 1976, 1978), but most studies of Hispanic workers focus on earnings inequality (Carliner, 1976; Chiswick, 1978, 1979; Grenier, 1981; Tienda and Neidert, 1980; Portes and Bach, 1980).

Studies of inequalities in earnings have contributed to our understanding of Hispanic labor market experiences by identifying language as a source of market stratification, but most research concerning occupational and income attainments implicitly assumes that maintenance of Spanish-

[1] This research was supported by a research grant (No. 21-55-79-27) from the U.S. Department of Labor. Computational work was supported by a grant to the Center for Demography and Ecology at the University of Wisconsin from the Center for Population Research of NICHD (HD-05876). The Institute for Research on Poverty, the Graduate School Research Committee, and the College of Agricultural and Life Sciences, all of the University of Wisconsin–Madison, furnished additional funding and institutional support.

language skills and practices precludes the socioeconomic integration of Hispanic origin groups (see Tienda, 1982, for a review of studies based on the experience of Chicanos). What has not been thoroughly examined is whether Spanish-English bilingualism influences Hispanic socioeconomic achievements, above and beyond the effects of English proficiency, yet this information is pertinent for determining the need for bilingual education programs. We discuss this point further in the concluding section.

While there is little doubt that English-language proficiency is essential for success in the U.S. labor market (Grenier, 1981; Garcia, 1979), and especially for gaining entry into some of the higher-status occupations, it may not be a sufficient condition for securing high-status positions (see Tienda, 1982). However, because individuals must receive formal schooling to move up the occupational ladder, mastery of English is limited to success in the U.S. labor market. Although this mastery frequently comes at the expense of Spanish (Bowman, 1981; Lopez, 1976), failure to gain command of English during adolescence may result in truncated educational experiences. Without an adequate command of the dominant language, linguistic minorities do not compete well with English-proficient majority groups (Grenier, 1981).

One unanswered question is whether continued use of Spanish in private as opposed to public domains necessarily impedes the socioeconomic integration of Hispanic origin workers. We argue that cultural differentiation between Hispanic and non-Hispanic whites, which is reflected in maintenance of Spanish (Bowman, 1981; Fishman, 1977; Ross, 1979; Williams, 1979), has little to do with socioeconomic achievement processes, provided that individuals acquire an acceptable level of competence in English. This view implies that language practices and possibly other aspects of ethnic diversity will neither enhance nor diminish the prospects for Hispanic workers to succeed in the U.S. labor market, once differences in pertinent individual characteristics are taken into account. Thus, the fact that many Hispanics are bilingual should not hinder their socioeconomic success, if they are reasonably proficient in English. Demonstrating this should eliminate cultural factors as a major explanation for the socioeconomic inequality between Hispanics and non-Hispanic whites.

Language and Achievement

Currently there exists spotty and inconclusive evidence about how language influences the socioeconomic achievements of Hispanics. One of the most problematic issues is that of establishing a causal ordering between linguistic behavior measures and the status outcome variables. For example, Skrabanek (1970) found significant statistical relationships showing that Chicanos with low levels of educational attainment, low income, and low-status occupations used Spanish more frequently, but he could not clearly establish the causal direction of the influences. The National Center for Education Statistics (1978) showed that of all school-aged minorities who usually speak languages other than English, Spanish-speakers have the lowest school completion rates, but the authors of that study cautioned readers against inferring that the predominant use of languages other than English, and Spanish in particular, directly causes educational disadvantages.

In other studies based on Chicanos in Los Angeles, Lopez (1976, 1978) detected a shift from predominantly Spanish usage to greater English usage through "mass bilingualism," and he demonstrated that the effects of language upon status outcomes are contingent upon social background characteristics. His findings, while restricted in generalizability to a sample of urban Mexican Americans, suggest that English proficiency may be a necessary condition for socioeconomic achievement, but not a sufficient one. Seeking to evaluate the influence of language spoken at home on the occupational attainments of Spanish origin men, Suter (1972) found a strong negative effect of Spanish language when he included an education-language interaction in a model predicting socioeconomic status. Although Suter's various estimates are not directly comparable with each other, he should be commended for a pioneering attempt to expand the life-cycle model of socioeconomic achievement to include language.

Garcia (1979) prepared a more comprehensive analysis of the relationship between language and status attainment using the Survey of Income and Education (SIE), the data base for this study. Because Garcia's analysis uses better language data, and his results are more robust, he is able to state more forcefully what Suter (1972) and Lopez (1976) could only suggest—that the effects of language-use patterns on occupational status and earnings operate indirectly through schooling. Yet, despite its many strengths—most notably, the national representativeness of the data base, the logical rigor of the analysis, and the improved operationalization of a language measure representing private versus public domains of Spanish-English bilingualism—Garcia's study did not resolve questions about the sufficiency of English monolingualism for ensuring labor market success, nor did it solve the causal ordering problem. There are several reasons for these limitations.

First, Garcia opted not to use a measure of proficiency in English in addition to the Spanish-English bilingualism variable. Also, because he used a causal model, he was forced to assign a temporal ordering to the language variable with respect to the key endogenous variables in the structural system. Garcia classified the bilingualism measure, operationalized as four discrete language domain categories, as an exogenous variable whose influence on occupational status is mediated through education. However, the language-domain categories reflect *current* linguistic behavior, whereas education refers to an attribute achieved prior to or concurrent with the acquisition of linguistic skills. Thus, there is a simultaneity bias of unknown magnitude in his results. Finally, Garcia restricted his study to Mexican origin individuals, thereby making comparisons with other Spanish-language groups impossible. Nevertheless, his study is important because it illustrates the promise of including indicators of cultural diversity, such as language practices, in models of ethnic stratification, and because it generates new insights about how language mediates the process of stratification for Mexicans, the largest of the Hispanic origin groups. His results show that language is important for explaining labor market outcomes of adults by enabling individuals to obtain the requisite skills for socioeconomic success during the later phases of the socioeconomic life cycle.

Given the incomplete evidence concerning the role of language in stratifying the Hispanic origin population, we analyze the influence of language-use patterns on the occupational achievements of Hispanic men, attempting to clarify the differential importance of Spanish-English bilingualism versus English proficiency as determinants of occupational status among each of four major nationality groups. This question has important policy implications, because information about how bilingualism affects socio-economic success is critical for determining future funding of programs that encourage the maintenance of non-English mother tongues. A second policy question centers on the necessity versus the sufficiency of English proficiency for ensuring labor market success, and the tendency for policy and program analysts to expect language programs to reduce labor market discrimination.

Data and Methods

We base our analyses on the 1976 Survey of Income and Education (SIE), which is a stratified, multi-stage cluster design sample survey commissioned by Congress to determine the number of school-age children living in poverty and the need for bilingual education. Because of its focus on the poor and non-English speaking populations, Spanish households were oversampled, thus permitting disaggregated analyses according to national origin.

In selecting the study population, we imposed a series of constraints so that the resulting Hispanic origin subgroups would be closely comparable in pertinent labor force characteristics. Our sample includes all Hispanic origin men aged 18–64 who were in the labor force in 1975. We excluded individuals who were enrolled in school or who were in the military service at the time of the survey (because their temporary activities misrepresent their occupational position) and persons with missing data on 1975 occupations or whose primary language was neither English nor Spanish. These restrictions produced a sample of 3,104 individuals, including 1,863 Mexicans, 328 Puerto Ricans, 359 Central/South Americans, and 554 men of other-Spanish origin. We combined persons of Cuban and Central/South American origin into a single category to avoid problems of small sample sizes, but this does not distort our conclusions about these men because the two groups are similar in a number of important respects, including average occupational status, educational attainment, linguistic diversity, and nativity composition.

We base our analysis of occupational status on an index of socio-economic status devised by Duncan (1961) and updated by Stevens and Featherman (1981) using 1970 census codes. Because we rely on census-type data for our empirical analyses, we are unable to consider directly how social background factors and language acquisition processes influence the educational attainment of Hispanic men. However, the inability to depict occupational attainment in a life-cycle framework using parental socioeconomic status as exogenous variable does not pose a serious problem because most previous research has shown that respondent's educational attainment mediates much of the effect of family background on adult achievement (Duncan, Featherman, and Duncan, 1972; Featherman and Hauser, 1978).

Our interest in the association between education, bilingualism, English proficiency, and occupational status defies a simple recursive causal scheme because the relationship between current linguistic attributes and prior educational attainment is most likely reciprocal. While a nonrecursive path model can take into account simultaneous effects, this requires quite stringent statistical assumptions which cannot be readily justified. For these reasons, we focus only on the direct effects of education, Spanish-English bilingualism, English proficiency, age, marital status, and foreign birth on the occupational attainment of Hispanic origin men. We use two measures of linguistic diversity—Spanish-English bilingualism as well as proficiency in English—to evaluate the effect of language on occupational achievements. In so doing, we expand upon Garcia's (1979) earlier analysis by more clearly differentiating the influence of bilingualism and English proficiency on occupational achievement.

Several authors have documented the importance of age and education in occupational achievement (Sewell and Hauser, 1975; Featherman and Hauser, 1978); that point therefore needs little elaboration beyond the definitions used in this study. The coding of age is relatively straightforward, but we operationalize education allowing for nonlinear relationships. This is important because Neidert and Tienda (1981) found that among Hispanic men the rates of return to education vary according to level of education. Since many high-status jobs (as compared to high-paying jobs) require greater amounts of schooling, we suspect that the differential effects of education on occupational status could be even more pronounced than such effects on earnings (Neidert and Tienda, 1981; Tienda and Neidert, 1980). We operationalize education as a categorical variable representing number of completed years of elementary school, high school, and college.

Our measure of English-language proficiency was constructed by summing the scores for two items representing English comprehension and speaking ability.[2] Both items originally were scored from 0 to 5, the low scores signifying a good command of English, the high scores poor or no English proficiency. We assigned individuals with missing values on these indicators the average score for their respective nationality and nativity group to avoid further loss of cases. We expect a positive relationship between English proficiency and occupational status because the higher-status jobs are more demanding of their incumbents, not only in terms of

[2] The assumption of equal weights for the speaking and comprehension items was verified with a factor analysis which generated equal loadings for both components.

general knowledge represented by completed schooling levels, but also in communication skills (Grenier, 1981).

Spanish-English bilingualism is operationalized using information about reported first and second language *usually* spoken in everyday activities, although there was no way to ascertain how much the world of work determined the overall extent of English-language usage. English and Spanish monolinguals are those individuals who speak only one language. We classified bilingual individuals according to their primary and secondary languages, so that English-bilingual individuals are those who use English as a primary language and Spanish in certain situations, and Spanish bilinguals use Spanish most of the time, but can and do speak English on occasion.[3]

Whether there are any net effects of bilingualism on status attainment after controlling for English proficiency is an empirical question which can only be answered by including both variables in the model. However, preliminary testing showed that these variables were highly correlated, largely because English-monolingual and English-bilingual individuals generally received higher scores on the proficiency index, whereas predominantly Spanish speakers usually received low proficiency scores. This problem was particularly serious for Puerto Rican and Central/South American men. To eliminate problems of collinearity between these two variables—essential for evaluating the influence of language on socioeconomic attainment—we dichotomized the English proficiency measure into two categories representing good or excellent versus moderate to poor proficiency. The cutoff point for creating this dichotomous variable was designated at 3, a division which proved to be an optimal breakpoint for all groups.

Our introductory discussion suggested that maintenance of Spanish need not constrain socioeconomic achievement among ethnically distinct minority groups. There are some circumstances in which bilingualism may be a desirable attribute, such as in ethnic enclaves where languages other than English are used. This is possible in small private commercial establishments as well as in public agencies whose service clientele is largely homogeneous in terms of ethnicity. Under those circumstances, bilingual workers could reap higher status benefits, but it is unclear just what combinations of Spanish and English might optimize the status reward structure in any particular labor market or occupational structure.

One departure from conventional specifications of status attainment models is the inclusion of a variable characterizing the ethnic composition of the labor market. This is important because of growing evidence that individual-level attributes do not fully explain labor market outcomes (Beck, Horan, and Tolbert, 1978; Boyd, 1979; Tienda and Neidert, 1980; Portes and Bach, 1980; Wilson and Portes, 1980). We use the proportion of working-age individuals of Hispanic origin in an SMSA or nonmetropolitan area[4] as

---

[3] In a few instances, Hispanic origin individuals reported that their primary or secondary language was neither Spanish nor English. Because these individuals are typically rare and may represent very particular situations of varied foreign experiences, they were excluded from the analyses.

[4] This measure was introduced in its logarithmic form to avoid distortion produced by a few extreme cases.

a proxy for the existence of ethnic enclaves. Although this consideration is especially relevant for Hispanic workers because of their high residential segregation, available evidence is inconclusive about whether ethnic enclaves operate to protect or hinder workers in the labor market. On the one hand, ethnic enclaves may enhance the occupational status of particular groups by facilitating their entry into high-status jobs controlled by members of the same ethnic group, or simply by creating an excess supply of ethnic workers which ensures that at least some individuals will eventually occupy high-status positions. Under such conditions education, the major screening criterion, may not operate in its customary way. Alternatively, a high concentration of ethnic workers may produce a "crowding" effect so that surplus minority workers are squeezed into lower-status positions. A third alternative is that no effects will emerge after taking into account linguistic factors which translate individual human capital into an ethnic world. Our analyses will permit us to address these issues.

We compute all analyses separately for each Hispanic nationality to illustrate the extent of differentiation among the groups, both in terms of average status outcomes and the processes by which status is achieved. However, because the groups differ notably in terms of their nativity composition (U.S.-born or foreign-born), it is necessary to consider how birthplace shapes the process of stratification for each group. This means entertaining the possibility of nonadditive nativity effects, particularly since other studies (Tienda and Neidert, 1980) have shown nativity interactions to be significant in determining Hispanic earnings. Taking nativity into account also helps avoid overestimating the effects of the language variables.

Results

Table 1 presents means and standard deviations of the variables included in the analysis for each national origin group. These data reveal considerable linguistic diversity among Hispanic workers, contrary to the popular conception of linguistic homogeneity. First, it is obvious that not all Hispanics use Spanish. Whereas approximately one-fifth of the total Hispanic male work force is English monolingual (pooled tabulation, not shown in table), the group-specific proportion varies from less than 10 percent for Central/South Americans to nearly half of other Spanish origin men. As expected, Spanish monolingualism is more prevalent among the foreign-born, particularly those of Mexican origin. Less than 20 percent of Puerto Ricans born on the island reported themselves to be Spanish-monolingual speakers, reflecting the emphasis on English instruction in their school curriculum. Forty percent of the Puerto Ricans born on the island are Spanish bilinguals, whereas 43 percent of those born on the island claimed to speak mostly or exclusively English. This is plausible for individuals who migrated to the mainland as children, and consequently were educated and reared in English-language settings. Because Central/South Americans are largely a recent immigrant population, nearly one-fifth of these workers reported themselves to be Spanish monolinguals, and an addi-

TABLE 1

Means and Standard Deviations of Variables Included in Regression Analysis
for Hispanic Men Aged 18–64, by National Origin and Nativity
(Standard Deviations in Parentheses)

	Mexican		Puerto Rican		Central/South American[a]		Other-Spanish	
	Native	Foreign	Native	Island	Native	Foreign	Native	Foreign
Occupational SEI	27.41	22.20	30.02	24.67	—[b]	31.28	30.35	30.28
	(15.74)	(12.92)	(17.40)	(14.05)		(19.97)	(17.52)	(19.07)
Education								
Years of education	10.39	7.43	11.36	9.21	—	11.36	11.22	10.79
	(3.53)	(4.21)	(2.71)	(3.44)		(3.50)	(3.02)	(3.64)
Years of elementary school	7.36	5.93	7.70	7.12	—	7.58	7.70	7.48
	(1.64)	(2.48)	(1.05)	(1.80)		(1.02)	(1.02)	(1.27)
Years of high school	2.51	1.23	3.14	1.83	—	2.74	2.85	2.48
	(1.75)	(1.75)	(1.44)	(1.74)		(1.72)	(1.62)	(1.84)
Years of college	0.52	0.27	0.52	0.27	—	1.03	0.68	0.84
	(1.15)	(0.89)	(1.04)	(0.83)		(1.58)	(1.32)	(1.47)
Language								
Proportion Spanish monolingual	.03	.38	.00	.16	—	.22	.02	.16
	(.17)	(.49)	(.00)	(.37)		(.42)	(.12)	(.37)
Proportion Spanish bilingual	.22	.36	.06	.39	—	.38	.18	.35
	(.41)	(.48)	(.24)	(.49)		(.49)	(.38)	(.48)
Proportion English bilingual	.45	.22	.39	.38	—	.33	.33	.39
	(.50)	(.42)	(.49)	(.49)		(.47)	(.47)	(.49)
Proportion English monolingual	.31	.04	.55	.07	—	.07	.48	.10
	(.46)	(.19)	(.50)	(.26)		(.26)	(.50)	(.30)
Proportion with good English ability	.89	.36	.97	.54	—	.50	.91	.55
	(.32)	(.48)	(.18)	(.50)		(.50)	(.29)	(.50)
Age	34.78	35.86	34.55	37.06	—	38.61	38.97	38.49
	(11.60)	(11.54)	(12.27)	(11.37)		(11.00)	(13.14)	(11.04)
Proportion married, with spouse present	.75	.71	.70	.81	—	.74	.77	.75
	(.43)	(.46)	(.46)	(.39)		(.44)	(.42)	(.44)
Log proportion Hispanic	−2.16	−2.21	−2.85	−3.01	—	−2.63	−2.28	−2.61
	(1.13)	(1.05)	(1.02)	(1.04)		(1.28)	(1.44)	(1.28)
(N)	(1,369)	(494)	(64)	(264)	(20)	(339)	(474)	(80)

[a] Includes Cubans.

[b] Sample size too small for reliable estimates.

tional 38 percent reported themselves Spanish bilinguals. Although some 40 percent of Central/South American adult men claimed to speak mostly English (i.e., were English bilingual), very few considered themselves English monolinguals.

Despite the crude operationalization of the English proficiency measure, there is evidence of substantial differences in the command of English among the groups. Of all the groups, foreign-born Mexicans are most handicapped in their English speaking and comprehension skills, as reflected by the proportion with good English ability and the proportion of Spanish monolinguals and bilinguals. Puerto Rican, Central/South American, and other-Spanish origin immigrants are about equally situated with respect to average English speaking and comprehension skills; approximately equal shares of all of these nationality groups claimed to have good to excellent English proficiency. Also, the proportions of English bilinguals and monolinguals are roughly comparable. Among the native-born populations, Mexicans appear to be more handicapped than either Puerto Ricans born on the mainland or other-Spanish origin men who are native-born. This is reflected in the lower proportion of Mexican natives who reported good to excellent command of English.

Hispanics are also differentiated with respect to their occupational status and school attainment. Foreign-born Mexicans and Puerto Ricans have a lower socioeconomic status than their native-born counterparts, but the native-foreign differential among the other-Spanish group is negligible. To emphasize how poorly Mexicans fare in the occupational structure, note that foreign-born men of Central/South American and other-Spanish origin actually surpass the average status levels of native-born Mexicans. Even though they are 95 percent foreign-born, Central/South Americans report the highest occupational status level, averaging just under 31 points on the revised socioeconomic index scale. Not surprisingly, this group also exhibits relatively higher education levels, with a greater share having some college education. In general, however, the educational attainments of Hispanics are low, especially when compared to those of non-Hispanic whites (Neidert and Tienda, 1981).

A preliminary descriptive tabular analysis of the language and occupational status variables (not shown) revealed a systematic relationship between language domains, English proficiency, and average status levels, but there was some variation among groups in the strength of gross associations. As expected, individuals most proficient in English had higher average status levels; so did those who reported themselves to be English monolingual and bilingual. Nevertheless, there are numerous reasons why differences in the occupational attainment of Hispanic workers with and without English handicaps should emerge. The most obvious is that occupational status differentials according to language categories largely capture the effects of education. However, individuals with deficiencies in English do not necessarily have low levels of education, as many Hispanics of Central and South American origin are relatively well educated and yet continue to use Spanish extensively after migrating to the United States. To evaluate whether the influence of language is entirely mediated by the differences in educational attainment, we computed a Multiple Classification Analysis using both the proficiency and bilingualism language variables along with education, coded in categorical form, to predict occupational status. This regression technique is practical when using categorical independent variables, such as our language measures, because effects for each category are expressed as deviations from the grand mean. Separate analyses for each national origin group help determine whether the process of socioeconomic achievement differs by nationality, and how.

Results from this analysis, reported in Table 2, clearly establish the overwhelming importance of schooling in determining the occupational achievements of Hispanic origin men. The unadjusted and adjusted effects of education show a strong college credentialing effect: a baccalaureate degree substantially increases the socioeconomic status of Hispanic men of working age, giving those with college educations a status level 23 to 45 points above the mean of the respective national origin group. The college credentialing effect is particularly marked for Mexicans and Puerto Ricans—the two groups with the lowest average completed schooling levels. This effect parallels price effects often observed for workers in short supply. Men who did not complete high school attain an occupational status which is 4 to 7 status points below average, but those with no high school training whatsoever fare worst of all. There is no evidence of higher status resulting from completion of high school, even among less well educated groups like Mexicans and Puerto Ricans. In fact, among the more highly educated groups, failure to go beyond high school results in status levels lower than the group averages.

With the inclusion of the English proficiency and bilingualism measures individually, then jointly, the effects of education are attenuated only slightly. For all except men of other-Spanish origin, the education-adjusted influence of Spanish-English bilingualism on occupational achievement is modest, as indicated by the adjusted deviations in the first net column and the magnitudes of the adjusted betas. English proficiency similarly influences the occupational attainment of all but other-Spanish origin workers, even after adjustments are made for educational attainment, but the partial betas are substantially attenuated. Men of Mexican and Central/South American origin with poor English proficiency attain a status level which is, on the average, 3.0 to 3.5 status points below that of their similarly educated counterparts. Central/South Americans with English-language handicaps achieve occupational statuses roughly 5.6 to 7.5 points below those obtained by comparably educated workers of their national origin group who are proficient in English. Among other Spanish-origin workers, schooling entirely mediates the effects of English-language proficiency. When both language variables are included in the analysis, bilingualism is insignificant in determining occupational status of Hispanic origin men. However, English proficiency continues significantly to determine the socioeconomic achievements of Mexicans and Central/South Americans, although its relative effect is considerably below that of education.

Overall, the results of the Multiple Classification Analysis indicate that prior educational achievements largely determine occupational status among Hispanic origin men, as such status has been observed for non-Hispanic white men (Featherman and Hauser, 1978; Duncan, Featherman, and Duncan, 1972). College attendance seems to be particularly influential

TABLE 2

Multiple Classification Analysis of Occupational Achievement among Hispanic Men Aged 18–64: Effects of Language and Education by National Origin

Selected Characteristics	Mexican				Puerto Rican				Central/South American[a]				Other-Spanish			
	Gross	Net (1)	Net (2)	Net (3)	Gross	Net (1)	Net (2)	Net (3)	Gross	Net (1)	Net (2)	Net (3)	Gross	Net (1)	Net (2)	Net (3)
Education																
0–6 years	-7.07	-6.51	-6.15	-5.88	-5.80	-4.69	-4.62	-4.05	-11.51	-10.25	-10.71	-9.94	-11.31	-13.00	-13.39	-12.83
7–11 years	-4.51	-4.54	-4.65	-4.64	-3.94	-3.74	-3.78	-3.73	-8.00	-6.93	-6.58	-6.46	-6.47	-6.65	-6.65	-6.51
High school graduate																
Some college	-0.68	-0.90	-0.99	-1.12	-0.06	-0.49	-0.63	-0.76	-4.89	-4.66	-4.41	-4.49	-2.07	-1.57	-1.45	-1.66
College graduate or more	8.46	8.29	8.20	8.03	11.60	10.66	10.85	10.27	1.46	0.60	0.57	0.25	3.85	4.68	4.53	4.53
[Eta and beta]	36.48 [.68]	35.77 [.67]**	35.50 [.66]**	35.37 [.65]**	45.00 [.64]	42.88 [.60]**	43.32 [.60]**	42.64 [.59]**	26.79 [.65]	24.74 [.59]**	24.31 [.58]**	23.92 [.57]**	28.85 [.62]	28.09 [.62]**	28.26 [.62]**	28.04 [.62]**
Mono- or bilingualism																
Spanish monolingual	-8.00	-3.32	—[b]	-1.02	-8.25	-4.68	—[b]	-3.51	-10.48	-5.50	—[b]	-3.04	-9.53	-1.92	—[b]	-0.01
Spanish bilingual	-3.39	-1.10	—	-0.59	-3.70	-1.75	—	-1.00	-0.57	-0.74	—	-0.14	-7.14	-2.36	—	-1.68
English bilingual	2.88	1.12	—	0.56	4.25	2.11	—	1.50	5.98	3.37	—	1.91	2.70	1.48	—	1.35
English monolingual																
[Eta and beta]	3.17 [.27]	1.10 [.10]**	—	0.26 [.04]	4.15 [.32]	2.34 [.17]**	—	1.34 [.12]	4.59 [.30]	3.20 [.17]**	—	0.71 [.09]	2.03 [.24]	0.10 [.08]	—	-0.27 [.06]
English-language ability																
Good	2.58	—[b]	1.15	0.98	3.46	—[b]	1.84	1.12	6.29	—[b]	3.63	2.73	1.46	—[b]	0.46	0.36
Poor	-7.57	—	-3.37	-2.86	-5.77	—	-3.07	-1.87	-6.77	—	-3.90	-2.94	-8.65	—	-2.73	-2.16
[Eta and beta]	[.29]	—	[.13]**	[.11]**	[.30]	—	[.16]**	[.10]	[.33]	—	[.19]**	[.14]**	[.20]	—	[.06]	[.05]
Grand mean	26.03				25.71				31.52				30.34			
R^2		.486	.490	.491		.439	.436	.444		.447	.453	.458		.424	.422	.425
(N)	(1,863)				(328)				(359)				(554)			

NOTE: Age and proportion Hispanic are introduced as controls in all models.

[a] Includes Cubans.

[b] Not entered in equation.

*$p < .05$.   **$p < .01$.

in the attainment of high socioeconomic status, especially among the groups with the lowest average schooling levels. Although English proficiency exerts an independent effect on the status achievements of two of the four Hispanic origin groups, this effect is relatively small in comparison to that of education. These results provide no evidence that retention of the minority language obstructs the socioeconomic achievements of Hispanic origin men, *provided that adequate levels of schooling are completed.*

For Hispanic origin workers as a whole group, this finding can not easily be translated into policy to improve their socioeconomic status because many of them are not trained in the United States. Immigration of Hispanic origin workers as adults implies that schooling has been acquired prior to migration. And, to the extent that Hispanic immigrants of each origin differ with respect to their socioeconomic backgrounds, then part of the observed differences in the status attainment processes and, in particular, the influence of language and education on occupational status, may capture differences in the schooling experiences of native- and foreign-born workers. To examine this possibility, we first computed another set of MCA analyses in which nativity was entered as an additive variable. In no instance did significant effects emerge. However, because of pronounced education, language, and occupational status differentials among the groups, we hypothesized that the effects of education and language on socioeconomic status might depend upon (interact with) nativity.

Although it is customary to introduce nativity as an additive term in analyses of socioeconomic achievement (Garcia, 1979; Duncan, Featherman, and Duncan, 1972), several recent studies (Boyd, 1979; Tienda and Neidert, 1980) have shown that nativity interacts with education and other independent variables in earnings functions. This implies that the foreign-born may achieve lower statuses not only because of their generally lower stocks of human capital, including language handicaps, but also because of the unequal evaluation of their education and linguistic skills in the labor market. If this is so, then estimation of a pooled equation for native- and foreign-born Hispanics, even after adjusting for the additive effect of nativity, would mask an important source of variation in the process of occupational achievement and produce biased results. To determine whether this is the case, we conducted a test for nativity interaction effects by computing nativity interaction terms with language, education, and control variables (age and marital status). Results (available from authors) confirmed that the occupational attainment process, represented by the additive specification shown in Table 2, differs according to nativity because significant nativity interactions emerged for all groups. This result holds whether one or both language variables are included in the model to test for interaction. Therefore, as a final step, we estimated separate equations for native- and foreign-born men of each nationality to complete our evaluation of the influence of language on occupational achievement.

Results of the regression analyses reveal some important similarities and differences among the national origin groups. In light of the evidence revealed in Table 2, one unsurprising finding is that college education exerts a strong positive influence on the status achievement of Hispanic men of all nationalities, and this holds for native- and foreign-born alike. The magnitude of the effect is greatest for island-born Puerto Rican men, and lowest for foreign-born men of Central/South American origin and for the native-born of other-Spanish origin, but the discrepancies are not large. Each additional year of college raises Hispanic origin men between 6.5 and 9.3 points on the revised socioeconomic status scale. With the exception of native-born Mexican origin men, completion of elementary school does not provide benefits with respect to occupational status, but once English proficiency differences are adjusted, this effect disappears for Mexicans. Similarly, high school education improves the status attainments of Hispanic men only modestly, an effect which seems confined to the native-born. Puerto Ricans born on the mainland appear to benefit somewhat more from high school education than do native-born Mexican or other-Spanish men, since each completed year improves their occupational standing by approximately four status points.

While the effect of Spanish-English bilingualism and English proficiency as revealed through the Multiple Classification Analysis appeared to be insignificant or substantively trivial once the effects of education were removed, the results of the nativity-specific analyses tell a slightly different story. Spanish monolingualism and bilingualism does appear to hinder the socioeconomic achievements of foreign-born Mexican, Puerto Rican and Central/South American men of working age, but not those native-born, or those of other-Spanish origin. The latter are likely to be sufficiently proficient in their use and comprehension of English. Some of these effects wash out when English proficiency is introduced in the model. Foreign-born Spanish monolinguals acquired positions with an average status of from 4.3 to 8.4 points below their otherwise equivalent English-bilingual counterparts. Spanish bilingualism seems to depress most the occupational status of foreign-born Mexican workers, who attain occupational statuses ranging from 5 to 8 points lower than their respective English-bilingual reference group. This result holds even after taking into account differences in the ability of individuals to speak and comprehend English. Recall that Mexican immigrants are the most likely of all the national origin and nativity groups to report low levels of English proficiency. Although this might reflect the presence of unskilled "undocumented" workers (lacking legal entry papers) in the sample, there is no way to ascertain this with any precision.

For all groups except Puerto Ricans and foreign-born other-Spanish men, English proficiency exerts a substantial positive influence on occupational status. Among Mexicans, the status advantage for good command of English is 3 to 4.5 points for native- and foreign-born men, respectively. Central/South American workers receive the highest premium for good to excellent levels of English proficiency, approximately 7 points on the revised socioeconomic status scale, and native-born other-Spanish men who are proficient in English receive a 5-point status advantage over their otherwise equivalent counterparts.

Residence in areas of high Hispanic concentration has no influence on the socioeconomic achievements of Central/South American or other-Spanish origin workers, but statistically significant effects emerge for foreign-

TABLE 3

Full Additive Model Predicting Occupational Achievement among Hispanic Men Aged 18–64, by National Origin and Nativity (Standard Errors in Parentheses)

	Mexican Native (1)	Mexican Native (2)[a]	Mexican Foreign (1)	Mexican Foreign (2)[a]	Puerto Rican Native (1)	Puerto Rican Native (2)[a]	Puerto Rican Island (1)	Puerto Rican Island (2)[a]	Central/South American Native (1)	Central/South American Native (2)[a]	Central/South American Foreign (1)	Central/South American Foreign (2)[a]	Other-Spanish Native (1)	Other-Spanish Native (2)[a]	Other-Spanish Foreign (1)	Other-Spanish Foreign (2)[a]
Education																
Years of elementary school	0.560 (0.254)	0.417 (0.260)	0.277 (0.288)	0.218 (0.226)	0.191 (2.143)	0.576 (2.199)	-0.244 (0.461)	-0.304 (0.461)	—b	—b	0.288 (1.113)	0.362 (1.100)	1.220 (0.776)	1.250 (0.774)	0.961 (1.525)	1.004 (1.534)
Years of high school	1.169 (0.243)	1.131 (0.243)	0.398 (0.362)	0.239 (0.361)	3.811 (1.704)	4.101 (1.745)	0.789 (0.498)	0.644 (0.502)	—	—	0.989 (0.733)	0.898 (0.724)	1.813 (0.529)	1.594 (0.539)	-0.036 (1.392)	-0.031 (1.399)
Years of college	8.345 (0.297)	8.323 (0.297)	7.043 (0.566)	6.988 (0.560)	8.153 (1.730)	8.031 (1.742)	9.315 (0.900)	9.299 (0.896)	—	—	6.724 (0.626)	6.448 (0.625)	6.500 (0.521)	6.500 (0.519)	8.373 (1.243)	8.408 (1.250)
Language																
Spanish monolingual	-1.969 (2.004)	-0.320 (2.102)	-8.407 (1.382)	-4.962 (1.701)	—c	—c	-6.048 (2.180)	-4.348 (2.371)	—	—	-7.007 (2.639)	-1.991 (3.085)	-1.484 (5.693)	2.204 (5.985)	-9.978 (5.897)	-11.967 (6.806)
Spanish bilingual	-0.189 (0.872)	0.227 (0.886)	-6.968 (1.253)	-4.921 (1.378)	-5.151 (7.705)	1.639 (11.318)	-2.820 (1.604)	-1.528 (1.753)	—	—	-3.045 (2.106)	-0.349 (2.262)	-3.560 (1.988)	-2.351 (2.078)	-6.429 (4.141)	-7.547 (4.566)
English bilingual[d]	*	*	*	*	*	*	*	*	*	*	*	*	*	*	*	*
English monolingual	0.063 (0.765)	-0.097 (0.766)	0.734 (2.480)	0.123 (2.460)	-3.104 (3.942)	-3.181 (3.955)	1.674 (2.734)	1.146 (2.738)	—	—	-1.197 (3.506)	-2.234 (3.479)	-0.489 (1.642)	-0.737 (1.642)	-1.252 (5.190)	-1.029 (6.230)
Good English ability	—e	3.017 (1.187)	—e	4.561 (1.341)	—e	11.993 (14.604)	—e	3.027 (1.697)	—	—	—e	7.011 (2.308)	—e	5.162 (2.657)	—e	-2.519 (4.244)
Age	0.178 (0.032)	0.177 (0.032)	0.115 (0.040)	0.107 (0.040)	0.173 (0.175)	0.221 (0.185)	0.050 (0.064)	0.054 (0.064)	—	—	0.183 (0.084)	0.215 (0.083)	0.309 (0.055)	0.309 (0.055)	-0.174 (0.161)	-0.162 (0.163)
Married spouse present = 1	0.341 (0.764)	0.412 (0.763)	0.676 (0.999)	0.638 (0.988)	1.081 (3.876)	1.194 (3.890)	2.034 (1.757)	2.112 (1.750)	—	—	2.043 (1.997)	1.703 (1.975)	3.090 (1.621)	3.122 (1.617)	2.962 (3.803)	2.864 (3.829)
Log proportion Hispanic	0.173 (0.293)	0.151 (0.293)	0.854 (0.425)	0.713 (0.422)	-4.727 (1.773)	-4.558 (1.791)	-0.395 (0.665)	-0.375 (0.662)	—	—	-0.075 (0.682)	0.166 (0.679)	0.008 (0.536)	0.021 (0.534)	1.160 (1.275)	1.070 (1.290)
Constant	10.041	8.377	21.141	18.017	-5.804	-22.896	18.693	17.941	—	—	13.498	7.539	-2.136	-6.584	27.683	28.781
R^2	.460	.463	.454	.467	.508	.514	.431	.438	—	—	.423	.439	.400	.405	.555	.557
(N)	(1,369)		(494)		(64)		(264)		(20)		(339)		(474)		(80)	

[a] Model (2) contains the English proficiency variable while model (1) only contains the bilingualism variables.

[b] Sample size too small for reliable estimate.

[c] No observations in this category.

[d] Reference category.

[e] Not included in equation.

born Mexicans and mainland-born Puerto Ricans. What is puzzling about these results is that the effects for Mexicans and Puerto Ricans go in opposite directions. Apparently foreign-born Mexicans, who are often extremely disadvantaged with respect to their stock of human resources upon arrival in the United States, are able to benefit from residing and working in areas where other Hispanics, mostly Mexicans, reside, whereas Puerto Ricans are penalized for living and working in ethnic enclaves, which in their case means primarily the New York–New Jersey SMSA.

These apparently contradictory findings are plausible if in fact Puerto Ricans experience greater crowding in the labor market and are consequently relegated to lower-status positions than they might be if they resided and worked outside of the enclaves. Given the polarized nature of the New York–New Jersey SMSA with respect to its occupational skill mix—it demands many very highly skilled technical and professional workers in banking and finance, as well as many low-skilled workers in personal service and apparel industries—the poorly educated Puerto Rican work force can hardly compete for high-status jobs. For them, the enclave shelter cannot operate because it does not exist in the sense of the Cuban enclave in Miami (Wilson and Portes, 1980). Consequently, Puerto Ricans are disproportionately allocated to the secondary labor market.

One possible reason that Mexicans may benefit, in terms of status, from residence in areas of high Hispanic concentration is that the older, more established contingents of the Mexican American population own and operate enterprises which serve to absorb greater proportions of low-skilled ethnic labor than would be true otherwise. However, these speculations cannot be verified directly with this type of census data, which lacks information about the ethnic characteristics of firms in which Mexican and Puerto Rican workers are employed. Our Hispanic concentration measure is too crude for detecting the existence of enclave sectors, but it suggests a promising avenue for future investigation. Our interpretation is, however, consistent with results of other studies.

Discussion and Conclusions

Overall, our results show that retention of Spanish does not hinder the socioeconomic achievements of Hispanic origin groups, provided that a reasonable level of proficiency in English is acquired. The only exceptions to this pattern are Mexican immigrants, for whom Spanish bilingualism and monolingualism exert independent negative effects on the occupational achievement of adult men. Island-born Puerto Ricans are also penalized by lower status if they speak no English (i.e., if they are Spanish monolinguals), but this effect is not found among the Spanish bilinguals.

Although for substantive and methodological reasons we chose not to compute path-analytic models to assess the influence of language and education on the occupational status of Hispanic workers, our findings parallel in many ways those of the Garcia (1979) study. Like his findings, our results indicate that the influence of language on adult socioeconomic status is largely mediated by schooling. This does not mean that language is unimportant in its own right, for there are pronounced differences in the occupational positions acquired by individuals with good and poor English-language skills. However, the acquisition of strong linguistic skills is not independent of the education process. To put it bluntly, adequate command of English is necessary to function effectively in the U.S. labor market, but such command does not, of course, ensure access to high-status positions. This is demonstrated by the fact that schooling does not render uniform socioeconomic rewards to all nationality and nativity groups, but the same can be said about the influence of language on occupational status.

The fact that foreign-born populations may be at a distinct disadvantage vis-à-vis those who were born, reared, and schooled in an English-speaking environment does have implications for employment and training policy. The experience of workers of Central/South American origin, who are likely to come from high-status backgrounds and to have acquired at least a high school education, should serve as a positive example of the possibilities for adapting the labor market skills of foreign-born workers. The design of programs to reduce inequities between native- and foreign-born workers by helping the latter overcome their language handicaps will also contribute to improving the aggregate socioeconomic status of the Hispanic population.

While the acquisition of English proficiency clearly facilitates the process of socioeconomic achievement among Hispanic men, there is no basis for assuming that bilingual education programs which encourage retention of Spanish among Hispanics will necessarily retard their socioeconomic success. Our results suggest that foreign-born workers could improve their occupational status by participating in bilingual education programs, although it is unclear how much emphasis must be placed on improving English language skills and how much should be devoted to teaching basic skills in reading, arithmetic, and communication in order to produce desired outcomes. We hasten to add that participation in bilingual education programs should not be geared to eliminate the use of Spanish, for among the native-born who tend to have a better command of English, Spanish bilingualism does not depress socioeconomic achievement. Thus, the persistent dilemma for policy analysts is assuring that ethnic populations acquire sufficient proficiency in English to equip them for successful labor market experiences while not forcing the loss of native languages. In other words, the ultimate challenge for bilingual education programs is one of balancing the pressures of assimilation and ethnic pluralism.

Among the native-born populations, the source of low status attainment appears to be slightly different—namely, low levels of educational attainment. For the immediate future, employment and training programs intended to enhance the labor market experiences of Hispanic workers would be well advised to focus on improving the high school retention levels of Mexican and Puerto Rican youth. In closing, we emphasize that resolving language and schooling obstacles confronted by Hispanics will not automatically resolve the inequities produced by labor market discrimination.

REFERENCES

Beck, E. M., Patrick Horan, and Charles M. Tolbert II. 1978. "Stratification in a Dual Economy: A Sectoral Model of Earnings Determination," *American Sociological Review,* 43 (October):704–20.

Bowman, Carl. 1981. "Between Cultures: Toward an Understanding of the Cultural Production of Chicanos." Master's thesis, University of Wisconsin.

Boyd, Monica. 1979. "Immigrants, Income Attainments and Labour Market in Canada." Paper presented at the annual meetings of the Population Association of America, Philadelphia.

Carliner, Geoffrey. 1976. "Returns to Education for Blacks, Anglos, and Five Spanish Groups," *Journal of Human Resources,* 11 (Spring):172–84.

Chiswick, Barry R. 1978. "The Effect of Americanization on the Earnings of Foreign-Born Men," *Journal of Political Economy,* 86 (October):897–921.

———. 1979. "The Economic Progress of Immigrants: Some Apparently Universal Patterns," in William Fellner, ed., *Contemporary Economic Problems* (Washington, D.C.: American Enterprise Institute): pp. 357–99.

Duncan, Otis D. 1961. "A Socioeconomic Index for All Occupations," in Albert J. Reiss, Jr., ed., *Occupations and Social Status* (New York: Free Press): pp. 109–38.

Duncan, Otis Dudley, David L. Featherman, and Beverly Duncan. 1972. *Socioeconomic Background and Achievement* (New York: Seminar Press).

Featherman, David L., and Robert M. Hauser. 1978. *Opportunity and Change* (New York: Academic Press).

Fishman, Joshua A. 1977. "Language and Ethnicity," in H. Giles, ed., *Language, Ethnicity and Intergroup Relations* (New York: Academic Press): pp. 15–57.

Garcia, Steve. 1979. "Language Usage and the Status Attainment of Chicano Males." Master's thesis, University of Wisconsin.

Grenier, Gilles. 1981. "An Analysis of the Effect of Language Characteristics on the Wages of Hispanic-American Males." Paper presented at the meetings of the Société Canadienne de Science Economique, Sherbrooke, Quebec, Canada, 13–14 May.

Lopez, David E. 1976. "The Social Consequences of Chicano Home/School Bilingualism," *Social Problems,* 24 (December):234–46.

———. 1978. "Chicano Language Loyalty in an Urban Setting," *Sociology and Social Research,* 62 (January):267–78.

National Center for Education Statistics. 1978. *The Educational Disadvantage of Language-Minority Persons in the United States, Spring 1976.* Bulletin no. 78, B4 (Washington, D.C.: U.S. Department of Health, Education, and Welfare, Education Division).

Neidert, Lisa J., and Marta Tienda. 1981. "Market Structure and Earnings Determination of Native and Immigrant Hispanics in the United States," in Marta Tienda, ed., *Hispanic Origin Workers in the U.S. Labor Market: Comparative Analyses of Employment Outcomes* (Springfield, Va.: National Technical Information Service): pp. 172–99.

Newman, Morris J. 1978. "A Profile of Hispanics in the U.S. Workforce," *Monthly Labor Review,* 101 (December):3–14.

Portes, Alejandro, and Robert Bach. 1980. "Immigrant Earnings: Cuban and Mexican Immigrants in the United States," *International Migration Review,* 14 (Fall):315–41.

Ross, J. A. 1979. "Language and the Mobilization of Ethnic Identity," in H. Giles and B. Saint-Jacques, eds., *Language and Ethnic Relations* (New York: Pergamon Press): pp. 1–13.

Sewell, William H., and Robert M. Hauser. 1975. *Education, Occupation and Earnings: Achievement in the Early Career* (New York: Academic Press).

Stevens, Gillian, and David L. Featherman. 1981. "A Revised Socioeconomic Index of Occupational Status," *Social Science Research,* 10 (December):364–95.

Skrabanek, Robert L. 1970. "Language Maintenance among Mexican-Americans," *International Journal of Comparative Sociology,* 11 (December):272–82.

Suter, Larry E. 1972. "Socioeconomic Achievement among Persons of Spanish Ancestry." Unpublished manuscript. Washington, D.C.: U.S. Bureau of the Census.

Tienda, Marta. 1982. "Sex, Ethnicity and Chicano Status Attainment," *International Migration Review,* 16 (2):435–72.

Tienda, Marta, and Lisa J. Neidert. 1980. "Segmented Markets and Earnings Inequality of Native and Immigrant Hispanics in the United States," *Proceedings of the American Statistical Association, Social Statistics Section,* 1980:72–81.

Williams, G. 1979. "Language Group Allegiance and Ethnic Interaction," in H. Giles and B. Saint-Jacques, eds., *Language and Ethnic Relations* (New York: Pergamon Press): pp. 57–65.

Wilson, Kenneth, and Alejandro Portes. 1980. "Immigrant Enclaves: An Analysis of the Labor Market Experiences of Cubans in Miami," *American Journal of Sociology,* 86 (July):295–319.

27. THE MEXICAN ORIGIN POPULATION'S DIFFERING PERCEPTIONS OF THEIR CHILDREN'S SCHOOLING[1]

Harriett ROMO, *The University of Texas at Austin*

Chicanos and undocumented immigrants have differing perceptions of children's school experiences. Recent immigrants value education but have low expectations of schooling. Chicanos have higher expectations for children but express more alienation and awareness of discrimination. Implications for additional research and school policies are discussed.

Researchers investigating immigration in the 1960s–1980s have left a considerable gap in the study of the settlement experiences of undocumented Mexican immigrant families and the experiences of immigrant children in the public school system. In pursuing this topic, an ethnographic study of Chicanos and undocumented recent Mexican immigrants in the context of the schools has numerous implications: it can contribute to a better understanding of problems faced by immigrant families; it can enhance our understanding of Chicano and recent immigrants' perceptions of opportunities in the U.S. host society; and it can lead to better informed policies that affect delivery of services to Mexican origin parents and children.

This paper focuses on the way Chicano and undocumented immigrant families perceive the school experiences of their children. Objectives in the paper are (1) to discuss some methodological problems of research involving recent immigrant and Chicano families, (2) to contrast the perceptions of schooling held by those families, and (3) to suggest some issues

[1] Research for this study was funded by a grant from the Hogg Foundation for Mental Health. This paper is part of a larger investigation of the ways Chicano and recent immigrant Mexican families obtain and process information from the schools regarding the educational status and progress of their children. The influence of language and power relationships in organizational interactions, perceptions of those interactions, and the effects of those relationships are an important aspect of community mental health. Recent immigrant families were identified through work with the University of Texas Population Research Center Undocumented Worker Project in 1981 by Harley Browning, Nestor Rodríguez, and Rogelio Nuñez.

that remain to be explored in understanding school experiences of recent Mexican immigrant and Chicano children.

Overall, there is little information on families migrating to the United States with children except for early studies dealing with European groups such as those of Child (1943), Warner and Srole (1945), and Handlin (1951). There are even fewer data available concerning Mexican immigrants. Bogardus (1929), one of the few social scientists to study the Mexican immigrant settlement process, was influenced by those characterizing the marginal man in the 1920s and found conflict between Mexican immigrant parents and children and problems resulting when the second generation lost faith in society. Recent work such as that of Portes, Parker, and Cobas (1980) looks at changing perceptions of Latin American immigrants to the United States and suggests growing alienation and increased ethnic identification over time. Most researchers, however, focus predominantly on male immigrants or on workers apprehended by U.S. immigration officials and derive their data from one-time surveys, census data, or the analysis of social service utilization. These studies provide few ethnographic insights into the immigrant's day-to-day life experiences.

While somewhat more research exists concerning Chicanos, there is little work that shows how Chicano families perceive school problems. Numerous studies of Chicano children have concluded that those most acculturated are the ones who derive the greatest benefit from the school system. Others (Rodríguez, 1981) argue that those who are successful in the schools are so at a great price—severing ties with family, language of birth, and the home culture. In much of the research concerning Chicanos, the reasons given for school problems have been cultural ones: the child or his background was said to be responsible for school failures. Focusing more on situational variables, Coleman et al. (1966) suggested that those who come from impoverished backgrounds gain considerably from being in positive learning environments. Brawner (1973) in the Coleman tradition suggested that migrant children in a positive environment who saw jobs, honors, skills, and material possessions being attained by people very much like themselves believed those possibilities within their range of achievement.

It is obvious that the problems facing Mexican immigrant and Chicano children as they attempt to achieve in the schools are complex. Perhaps a constructive way to approach the issue is to look at school experiences as the parents and children see the situations themselves in their day-to-day contacts with the schools. In pursuing that endeavor, three types of families emerged—the recent immigrant, the transitional, and the second-generation U.S.-born Chicano family—each of whom was found to see school experiences somewhat differently.

As an ethnographic investigation of immigrant families and the schools, the research is not constrained by the canons of inquiry that proceed on the logic of verification. Because this is so, collection and analysis of the data have not been constrained with rigorous methods of sampling design nor with the formulation of hypotheses against which to rigorously present highly systematized and classified empirical evidence. Careful tape recording of interviews and interactions, transcription of the tapes, and analysis of discourse used by the subjects, plus long-term observations and verification of observed patterns by informants in the anthropological tradition provide a solid basis for the discussion of emergent patterns. It is impossible to include the numerous dialogues and interactions that support this research in a short paper such as this. It is, however, possible to map out previously uncharted territory for future hypothesis testing and to illuminate the complexity and diversity of the Mexican origin population.

This study suggests that recent immigrants have lower expectations of schools than Chicanos. Chicanos, experienced in the United States, have higher expectations but at the same time have acquired heightened sensitivity to subordination and discrimination, which results in increased skepticism and alienation. Chicano parents report that rudimentary acculturation into U.S. society and the learning of English do not automatically provide parents or children with increased mastery in the school organizational setting. Language continues to be an issue in the schools, but the learning of English is not the basis of the problem. Inappropriate placement, inadequate programs, school jargon, lack of information, misunderstandings, and literacy become major issues.

Identifying the Group to be Studied

Undocumented recent immigrant families with school-age children were selected from a pool of 60 immigrant families in Austin, Texas, identified by the University of Texas Population Research Center Undocumented Worker Project in 1981 by Harley Browning, Nestor Rodríguez, and Rogelio Nuñez and were matched with Chicano families of similar income and occupation categories whose children attended the same schools. The Austin community, while not a traditional host community to Mexican immigrants like San Antonio, Texas, and Los Angeles, California, has a substantive (18 percent) Hispanic population, an established Mexican barrio, and an increasing number of recent immigrant Mexican families and single workers.

In the attempt to match Chicano families with the undocumented recent immigrant families, categorizing families as Chicano or recent immigrant became problematic, as mixed marriages and families with both recent immigrant and U.S.-born members were encountered. Families with children born in Mexico but completely U.S.-schooled also presented problems of classification. Language use, immigration status, differences in parents' educational background, place of birth of parents, and time in the United States became major discriminating criteria.

Thus, for analytic purposes, undocumented recent immigrant families were those families in which parents spoke only Spanish, parents and most of the children were born in Mexico, the family as a whole had been in the United States less than five years, and parents did not have legal residence or citizenship status in the United States. Transitional families had been in the United States long enough to have obtained some form of legal status (i.e., legal resident, suspended deportation, Silva registration, U.S.-born child, etc.), although transitional families might still have had undocumented family members and may not have taken steps to legalize their status. Transitional families had been in the United States more than five years and had children or other familly members who had learned English. Chicano families were identified as families of Mexican heritage with parents and usually grandparents U.S.-born, all children U.S.-born, children completely U.S.-schooled, and parents who spoke English and Spanish. Table 1 shows some of the similarities and differences among the families interviewed. While a broad comparison and summarization of data is helpful in placing the families in a larger context, it tends to lose important diversities, some of which are discussed in this article as methodological problems of comparing recent immigrants and Chicanos.

Although self-referent terms were not thoroughly investigated, all recent immigrant families referred to themselves as *Mexicano* and distinguished Chicanos by ability to speak English, time in the United States, and legalized citizenship status. Chicano families, although some would not use the term Chicano, made distinctions between themselves and aliens and *nacionales* by ability to speak English, kin or family members still in Mexico, place of birth, and legalized status.

Frequent contacts with Chicano, transitional, and recent immigrant families through home visits and telephone calls, attending appointments and school activities with them, and responding to needs and requests during a year-and-a-half period provided opportunities for observing and collecting data. Tape-recorded interviews with parents and children in each of the families covered topics such as parents' school experiences, contacts with their children's schools, problems they or their children had encountered with the schools, and issues concerning the schools.

All families interviewed signed protection of human subject forms describing the study and asking permission for tape-recorded interviews, classroom visits, frequent home visits, and informal discussions of school interactions and progress reports of children.

Methodological Problems of Comparing Chicanos and Recent Mexican Immigrant Families

While recent immigrant families were selected specifically to study families with school-age children and were not a randomly selected group, it was extremely difficult to match them with Chicano families who had elementary school-age children and similar income, occupation, and educational experiences. The matching process identified distinctions and complexities pertinent to any research dealing with Mexican immigrants and Chicanos.

Both the Mexican immigrant population and the Chicano population in the United States are extremely heterogeneous. The Mexican immigrant population in the United States can be temporary or long-term undocumented migrants, legal migrants of short- or long-term status, long-distance migrants or borderland commuter migrants, or permanent legal

TABLE 1

General Description of Sample of Recent Immigrant, Transitional, and Chicano Families

Number of Families	Family Category	Age of Parents	Place of Birth	Parent's Education	Average Number of Children	Household Income	Work	Language	Time in United States	Immigration Status
15	Recent Immigrant	24–42	Mexico	None	6.2	$500–$1,100 per month	Service, Laborers	Spanish	Less than 5 years	Undocumented
10[a]	Transitional	24–35	Both United States and Mexico	Some Primary	5.0	$600–$1,000 per month	Service, Laborers	Spanish, English	More than 5 years	Lawful Permanent Resident and Undocumented
15	Chicano	24–45	United States	Some Secondary and Graduate Equivalent Degree	2.6	$640–$1,200 per month	Service, Laborers	English, Spanish	Second Generation	Citizen

NOTE: This study is not dealing with a representative sample of families, but each interview and recorded interaction expands the parameters and meaning of parent-school interactions and problems perceived and encountered in the schools.

[a] After the category of transitional family emerged in the attempt to match Chicano families with recent immigrant families, five additional families who had been in the United States at least 10 years and had attempted to legalize their status were identified and interviewed.

residents (Cornelius, Chávez, and Castro, 1982). The families identified in this study were unskilled workers and long-term long-distance undocumented immigrants who entered the United States clandestinely. While large numbers of Chicanos in the United States are unskilled and low-income, there is a growing Chicano middle class, with Chicano professionals in many fields and a Chicano elite identified as political leaders, academicians, and owners of businesses (de la Garza, 1981; Alvarez, 1973). The Chicanos identified in this research project are unskilled, working-class Chicano families with a long history in the research community. The heterogeneity of both groups illustrates the importance of specifically identifying group characteristics before making comparisons.

Although Chicanos and recent immigrants lived and worked in the same areas, there was little social interaction among Chicano and recent immigrant families. Most of the Chicano families interviewed still lived in the main Mexican barrio of Austin. While the other families had moved to nearby newer neighborhoods, those neighborhoods continued to be predominantly Chicano. All Chicano families interviewed associated primarily with Chicanos in social relations. The recent immigrant families came from the southwest corner of the state of Mexico bordering the states of Michoacán and Guerrero, historically a sending area for Mexican immigrants to the United States (Dinerman, 1982). All of the recent immigrant families had family members or friends who had lived and worked in the community previously and who helped in the settlement and adjustment process. Although permanent residence may not have been their original intention, many became long-term residents when their children began attending U.S. schools, a trend evident in urban areas and becoming more prevalent (Baca and Bryan, 1980). Primary social interactions of recent immigrant families interviewed were with other recent immigrants, usually from the same sending community. While the majority of the recent immigrant families lived in the same barrio with the Chicano families, with the exception of children who sometimes played together, there were few social interactions among recent immigrants and Chicanos in the neighborhoods. This suggests that while recent immigrants may integrate physically into the Chicano host community, socially they do not.

Throughout the southwestern United States, the Mexican origin population has a history of being badly educated. Based on the 1960 Census, Moore (1970) found the median years of schooling for Mexican American adults in 1960 (4.8 years of school) only slightly better than functional illiteracy. In that same year the median years of school completed for Spanish-surnamed persons age 25 and over in the research community was only 4.4 years compared with 12.3 years completed by the Anglo population of the same age. Only 5.6 percent of Chicanos age 14 and over could report some college. Fitting well in this pattern of underachievement, few of the Chicanos interviewed in this study had finished high school. Of those who had, most had dropped out of regular public school before graduating and had enrolled as adults in community school programs to obtain a graduate equivalent degree. Few remembered successful public school experiences. Although Chicanos reported minimal school achievement, recent immigrants coming from rural *ranchos* in Mexico isolated from urban areas by geographical factors had even less education. Despite improving conditions, immigrant parents interviewed had had no schooling and many could not write their names. While Chicano groups lag behind other groups in the United States in number of school grades completed, it is difficult today to find Chicanos age 25–40 in urban areas with no schooling.

Another major difference between Chicano families and recent immigrant families was family size. Recently immigrated Mexican families tend to reflect fertility patterns typical of their rural home communities, which are quite high. Almost half of the recent immigrant families interviewed had seven or more children. Chicano families, immigrant families from border areas and urban areas of Mexico, and those who have lived in the United States for several years before having children, tend to have smaller families (Bradshaw and Bean, 1973). Only 1 of the low-income Chicano families identified had six children, and 4 of the 15 Chicano families had only one child.

Although low income was a controlled variable, household composition, the number of wage earners per household and the number of household members dependent upon those wages varied considerably. In the undocumented families, teenagers as young as age 14 found minimum-wage jobs and contributed to the household income. While both Chicano and recent immigrant families frequently had both parents working outside the home, number and care of preschool-age children became important considerations in whether the mother worked and in expenses related to her working. Chicano families seldom had more than one preschool child at home, while numerous recent immigrant families had two or more pre-school-age children at home. Among the Chicano families interviewed, two divorced women worked to support three children each with little financial support from the children's fathers. There were no single parents among the immigrant families interviewed. Creating another difference in household resources, some Chicano families qualified for public assistance such as food stamps, subsidized rent, and reduced child-care and medical fees not available to undocumented immigrants. Recent immigrant families took in boarders or single working relatives to augment their income. Or they doubled up with other families in single-family dwellings to share major expenses such as rent, food, child care, and utilities, creating households of four to six adults and numerous children.

Undocumented recent immigrant families had to anticipate financial setbacks if apprehended by the U.S. Immigration and Naturalization Service, setbacks that Chicano families did not have to consider. A third of the undocumented families had one or more working family members apprehended and deported during the research study. Others had been apprehended previously. These apprehensions resulted in work time lost plus the expense of crossing back to the United States.

In all households, various family members had spent extended time in the United States or had had greater opportunities to learn English than others. For example, one parent or both in a recent immigrant family may have spent considerable time working in the United States before bringing children. In Chicano families, parents spoke English and Spanish, but children frequently spoke only English. In almost half of the Chicano families interviewed, children spoke no Spanish. In transitional families, children frequently spoke English and Spanish, but parents spoke only Spanish. In recent immigrant families, parents spoke no English, but children learned English at school. These examples show language shifts over time occurring more quickly for children, especially for school-age children, than for adults or adolescents.

Despite the fact that all families held service and laborer occupations, many of the work situations held by Chicanos interviewed required English and some literacy skills. City meter readers had to fill out written reports; receptionists in low-income clinics and offices had to write telephone messages and record appointments; city maintenance workers and landscape crew supervisors had to read material orders and work assignments. Sometimes work positions held by Chicanos involved assisting recent immigrants in translations and filling out forms or supervising recent immigrant workers. Recent immigrants worked in manual labor, construction jobs, landscaping, dishwashing, hotel cleaning, and laundry work—positions demanding little English or literacy.

These complexities and differences among the families are not meant to be broad generalizations. Instead, they point to differences in background and work experiences and in household composition that make it difficult to make comparisons among families or to collectively refer to the different families as simply families of Mexican origin. They also point to the difficulties of identifying and isolating variables when investigating a particular phenomenon through survey or demographic research.

Perceptions of Schooling

Undocumented Recent Immigrant Families. Undocumented families considered education and the learning of English primary advantages for their families in the United States. Expressing a respect for education pervasive among the Mexican immigrants, an illiterate mother of six children explained:

> I want them to learn to write, to read and to learn the two languages, to continue in both English and Spanish. This is important to me because what else can one leave them? . . . I'm not rich, so what can I leave them? That is the only thing I can leave to them, the school, knowing how to study, knowing how to maintain themselves in whatever work they will do.[2]

In the short term, however, economic concerns—getting jobs, finding low-rent housing, paying utility bills, and providing food—dominated parents' time and energies. The parents' undocumented status continuously cast uncertainty on the lives of all family members. Nonetheless, while primary attention had to be directed toward day-to-day survival, recent

[2] Translation of Spanish transcript of an interview with recent immigrant parent, Antonio H. 2 April 1981.

immigrant parents had high aspirations for their children and wanted them to be able to choose professional careers and have easier lives than the parents had experienced.

Despite their own limited English language skills and educational background, the undocumented Mexican immigrant parents interviewed interacted with the schools. Perhaps influenced by the media during the court case in Texas debating the rights of undocumented children to schooling in the United States or through contact with Chicanos or other Mexican families with children enrolled in school, a number of undocumented workers viewed school opportunities for their children as a right in exchange for work and contributions to the community. An immigrant father who had worked in the United States for 10 years and had recently brought his seven children to the United States rationalized:

> Like now I work here, I go to the store, I buy $70 and $80 of food, they take out taxes. They take social security from my wife's check. They take social security from me, and they don't give a cent back. Also, the clothes. Everything I am earning here is staying here. It is not possible that they will not want to help with schooling for the children.[3]

Immigrant families interviewed had children enrolled in school even after the courts ruled undocumented children ineligible to attend public schools. While not all parents interviewed were politically astute, none considered themselves committing serious offenses by seeking work or education for their children in the United States. They believed schooling offered hope for better opportunities for future generations, willingly made the difficult sacrifices necessary to bring children from Mexico, and enrolled children in the U.S. schools despite possible exposure of their undocumented immigration status.

Recent immigrant parents who could not read or write and who had had few opportunities for schooling themselves in rural Mexico recognized the value of school opportunities for their children. For families who lived in rural *ranchos* in mountainous areas, schools when available frequently proved inaccessible. U.S. schools, in contrast, provided buses, subsidized lunch and breakfast programs which helped stretch already thin family budgets, medical assistance through school health screening programs, information and access to special assistance provided by private organizations, and modern air-conditioned and heated classrooms with well-equipped play areas. The U.S. schools' physical benefits, the possiblity of learning English, and hoped-for social and economic mobility for children represented positive aspects of the family's immigration to the United States even if only on a temporary basis. These benefits helped to mute criticisms parents had of school programs or staff.

---

[3] Translation of Spanish transcript of an interview with recent immigrant parent, Francisco P. 14 April 1982.

Interaction with the researcher might also have influenced parents' perceptions; however, parents interviewed expressed strong opinions about other work and immigration issues as well, opinions formulated through their own experiences and those of family and friends.

In comparison to the recent immigrant parents' own lack of schooling and illiteracy, even minimal academic achievements represented advancement for their children. Secure in their Spanish language, school achievement correlated with learning English. A recent immigrant mother described how pleased her husband was when their children attempted to speak English among themselves even though he could not understand what they said:

> He feels very content when he hears the children speaking in English, even though they may not be saying things correctly, we want them to say them in English, because in Spanish they know more and we want them to improve in English.[4]

Although few actual opportunities to use English existed in the immigrant's daily activities and contacts (as most worked with other recent immigrants and socialized with family and friends from the same community of origin), simply knowing it improved one's social status in the United States. Parents believed that learning to speak and read and write English would give their children an advantage in obtaining legal immigration status, would provide better job opportunities, and would give power in interactions with landlords, merchants, and others. Any level of achievement in English skills impressed parents who struggled with difficulties with the language. Parents recognized and praised as accomplishments passing to the next higher grade level in school and any concrete signs of achievement, such as copying words or sentences out of books. Their children, for the most part, behaved well in classrooms and showed respect toward teachers which earned them positive reports and good grades despite inadequate English literacy skills.

Of the groups of families, recent immigrants expressed the strongest feelings of isolation, lack of control over their lives, and embarrassment in school encounters because of lack of English fluency and literacy skills, but expressed the strongest support for school teachers and staff. Anxieties resulted from having to deal on a daily basis with schools in which the English language dominated and staff took literacy and written communications for granted. Recent immigrant parents attended school meetings when encouraged personally to do so; but because of lack of knowledge of the school system, the "way of doing things" in the schools, and their inability to read or speak English, they depended on school staff or translators to mediate for them. Chicanos acted as liaisons in some interactions but were not always available or always sympathetic. Recent immigrant parents became vulnerable to the availability, patience, goodwill, and honest intentions of those who helped them. Parents expressed uncomfortable feelings at having to share private information with translators or in having to depend on children or intermediaries to help them in interactions with other adults. Using a translator or explaining to school staff that they could not read or write placed parents in positions of little power.

[4] Translation of Spanish transcript of an interview with recent immigrant parent, Antonio H. 2 April 1981.

Cautious about critcizing or attracting attention to themselves or to their children, undocumented parents asked few questions in school interactions. Most did not understand how U.S. schools were organized, how their children were evaluated, what children were expected to learn, why special programs such as bilingual classes or migrant education existed or how they worked, even though their children frequently participated in such programs. Parents knew little about how their children compared with others academically.

While recent immigrant parents could not assist with school work, at home they listened to their children's problems—inability to communicate with English-speaking teachers, injustices, conflicts with other children, too little academic work, and inability to understand instruction. They sympathized with their difficulties and counseled the best they could based on their own experiences and the high aspirations they held for their children.

Transitional Families. Unlike recent immigrant families, transitional families identified more strongly with the United States than with Mexico, had no plans to return to Mexico to live, and felt fairly comfortable with routine interactions with U.S. organizations. Many had taken steps to legalize their status in the United States although none were U.S. citizens. Children knew little of their parents' community of origin and many spoke English well. The schools, however, glossed over the complex cultural and language relationships in the home. Problems of adjustment and of not fitting completely within the Mexican or the U.S. orientation surfaced in interactions with these parents and their children in the schools. A mother of three children, all of whom had been retained once (the oldest had been retained twice—once in kindergarten because she did not speak English and once in third grade because she achieved below grade expectation), explained:

> The teacher, each time she speaks with me, says that she (the oldest child) does not know how to read well. She says when she is reading in English she confuses it with Spanish, when she is reading in Spanish she confuses it with English. I talked with the teacher and I told her she had been in day care, and I told her that the child doesn't like Spanish. She speaks it at home because she has to. I don't speak English. I told the teacher, "I don't want them to teach her so much Spanish because the child cries at home because she says she doesn't like learning in Spanish."[5]

The problems rested not so much with the families, who seemed to mesh the two languages and cultures comfortably in varying combinations, but with the school organization which tended to simplistically categorize families as Chicano or Mexican or to consider all "bilingual." School staff and teachers frequently misjudged how much English or how much Spanish the transitional child knew and could use successfully in the classroom. Most home interactions continued in Spanish because one or both parents still did not speak English. Sometimes, however, the child proved to be stronger in English than Spanish in academic areas if he or she had had only English

[5] Translation of Spanish transcript of an interview with transitional parent, Rafaela A. 27 May 1982.

schooling or could handle more or less English than assumed by class-room observations. Sometimes, in the confusion, teachers identified a child erroneously as having no language or as a slow learner. Program place-ment and promotion became problematic decisions when children spoke English well but could not do academic work in English. No longer quali-fying for special language programs or bilingual instruction which focused primarily on non-English-speaking children, the transitional children sat in regular classrooms where teachers compared them with native English-speaking students.

Although transitional families seemed fairly integrated into school rou-tines and interactions, they lacked the knowledge of how the system worked, how to get information, and how to make things happen for their children in the schools. Their major source of information consisted of other parents, most of whom were no better informed than they. Transitional par-ents attended meetings and school activities, although inability to speak English in some cases continued to be troublesome, but hesitated to ques-tion school personnel's authority or to pursue issues. They did not know the appropriate channels of action and felt uncomfortable challenging de-cisions of professionals, especially when those professionals seemed sym-pathetic toward their children. Transitional parents remained supportive of their children but could not determine if school programs were inadequate or the children were having real difficulties in school. Frequently, parents blamed themselves for not being able to help their children more.

Chicano Families. Several Chicanos interviewed expressed resentment of recent immigrants, claiming they received benefits belonging rightfully to Chicano citizens, or that they depressed wages, or that recent immi-grants looked down on Chicanos as poor workers and inadequate speak-ers of Spanish. Despite some resentments, Chicanos could empathize with the problems and hardships faced by *Mexicanos* trying to make a better life for their families and trying to improve the educational opportunities for their children.

The educational process, however, did not prepare Chicanos for positive interactions with the school. Their own school experiences reinforced neg-ative perceptions of school interactions and sensitized them to prejudices and discriminations. Of all families interviewed, Chicano parents ex-pressed the most alienation from the schools. They did not consider mini-mal school achievement, such as learning to speak English and acquiring minimal reading and writing skills, acceptable achievement. They wanted their children at least to read, write, and compute better than they could. All desired college for their children. Looking at school experiences in relation to achievements and perceiving English language usage as an index of assimilation, a Chicana parent concluded, "English isn't as im-portant as it used to be."[6] Chicano parents had learned English. Their children had learned English so well that few spoke Spanish. Yet they con-tinued to do poorly and drop out of school. While Chicano families had

[6] Transcript of an interview with Chicana parent, Gloria B. 4 March 1982.

more material possessions, somewhat more permanent employment, and some work benefits not available to recent immigrants, they had not seen those opportunities their parents had projected with the learning of English. Many now wanted bilingualism for their children, and they wanted the school to help teach Spanish so the language would not be lost.

Chicano parents felt they should play an active role in their children's education because their own parents had not been actively involved in the schools and few of their generation had finished secondary school without problems. Yet Chicanos spoke with skepticism of school encounters. Many remembered difficulties in their own school experiences which influenced interactions in the schooling of their children. All felt that their own academic skills, especially in reading and writing, might be inadequate; and these feelings inhibited active participation in school-related situations that demanded display of academic skills such as political letter writing, speaking in front of a group, working with children in the classroom, or questioning methods of instruction. School jargon, incomplete explanations based on assumed knowledge of curriculum and school organization, and the hierarchy of staff responsibilities made official contacts with the schools almost as difficult for Chicano families as for recent immigrant and transitional families.

Most used what they thought were appropriate channels for getting information and results from the schools—becoming involved with parent groups, attending school functions, seeking out professional assistance and advice. Yet none of these channels proved completely satisfactory, as Chicano parents still lacked power to make things happen in the schools. Although some Chicanos became official chairpersons of bilingual parent advisory committees, talking to the school principal and officials about program improvements remained uncomfortable. Sometimes even routine meetings caused anxiety. A Chicana parent explained, "I don't know. I don't think I would understand. I don't know, you know, what they would talk about. I don't know. I don't like to go."[7]

Despite attending parent conferences, Chicano families knew little about their children's academic progress or the kinds of programs in which they participated. A few families had given up trying to get information about their children, as they did not understand what school staff told them and anticipated school problems and retentions. When Chicano parents did confront school personnel about problems, they seldom saw those problems resolved to their satisfaction. Frequently they did not agree with school personnel's description of their children or the children's abilities, but they did not know what recourse they had to contest decisions or policies. A Chicana mother described her interactions with school staff:

> I was really amazed with the different things that they would tell me, because, ah, I don't see my children the way they explain that he is to them.[8]

Familiarity with the schools and contacts with Chicano school staff on a friendship basis proved to be most effective assets in dealing with the

[7] Transcript of an interview with Chicana parent, Angie C. 19 June 1982.
[8] Transcript of an interview with Chicana parent, Melba S. 28 June 1982.

schools. Usually, Chicano families had to resort to liaisons only slightly more powerful than they for support and information. Determination not to let professionals shift the blame to parents or to families for their children's lack of achievement enabled some parents to deal effectively with the schools. It took, however, considerable time and uncountable contacts and confrontations to get attention and services due children not achieving their potential.

Chicano parents expressed support for their children and attempted to help them at home; but as children advanced through the school grades and as curriculum changed, parents could not help with schoolwork they themselves did not understand. Low achievement, discipline problems and policies, retentions, fighting at school, inadequate programs, and insufficient bilingual staff loomed as major problems confronting Chicano children in the schools. Yet none of the school meetings or conferences that parents attended dealt with these concerns. For all parents, busing children to schools away from their home neighborhoods made the difficult task of interacting in the schools prohibitive.

Areas for Future Research

While many researchers investigating issues concerning Hispanic persons in the United States differentiate by country of origin, most fail to consider the difference within a particular ethnic group. Out of these contrasts of recent immigrant and Chicano families emerged bold distinctions between Chicanos and undocumented recent arrivals from Mexico. The "transitional" family, different in many ways from both Chicano and recent immigrant, confronted problems sometimes more similar to the recent immigrant and sometimes more similar to the Chicano. Also, in making the comparisons, the similarities of Chicanos and recent immigrants in income suggest that there may be a greater number of "underclass" Chicano families than would be expected because of other commonalities with middle-class families in the use of English, fertility patterns, material acquisitions, etc.

Chicano parents' experiences in U.S. schools increased sensitivity to and perceptions of discrimination, resulting in increased hostility and alienation. They continued to have little understanding of how the school organization worked in areas such as authority relationships, informal channels of communication, and how decisions were made concerning their children. Although they participated in routine school activities and spoke English, they had little access to information and few contacts that would make them more influential in the schooling of their children.

This study suggests a need for closer and more technical comparisons of Mexican origin families from each of these groups. Each of the families interviewed valued education, but each type of family perceived school achievement differently. There seems to be a growing alienation over time, with Chicano families more alienated from the schools than recent immigrants. Also, there may be substantially more recent immigrant interaction with U.S. institutions than previously suspected, especially when those institutions directly affect family members. Further research would show more clearly how Chicano, recent immigrant, and transitional families interact with institutions and the consequences of those interactions.

Policies and programs in U.S. schools which serve these three groups of families usually do not differentiate by language abilities, time in the United States, previous experiences in the community of origin, or immigration status, especially since the U.S. Supreme Court ruled that recent immigrant children could not be denied public school education because of the undocumented status of their parents. Thus, it is common to find children from each of the three types of families in the same bilingual classrooms, studying the same curricula, evaluated by the same criteria, and served by the same policies and programs. Teachers and school personnel lacking training in ethnic relations tend to perceive all students of Hispanic origin alike. Given the differences suggested, we need to question how well programs and policies serve the interests and needs of each of these groups. We also need to determine to what extent educational opportunities are denied children because of their parents' lack of power in school interactions and because of inadequate programs.

Additional investigations of the school context might also challenge the perception of "slow" acculturation of recent immigrant children but question how successful they are in the schools. In these families, while recent immigrant children are found to learn oral English quickly, acquire an adequate command of English to help parents, and manage to navigate and maneuver in the classroom, academic accomplishments are not reflected in traditional achievement testing. We need to question what it takes to "make it" as an immigrant in the 1980s and compare those criteria for successful interaction into U.S. society with the experiences of immigrants in earlier periods, with the experiences of immigrants in other countries, and with the experiences of different ethnic groups in the United States.

REFERENCES

Alvarez, Rodolfo. 1973. "The Cycle-Historical and Socioeconomic Development of the Chicano Community in the U.S.," *Social Science Quarterly,* 53 (March):920–42.

Baca, Reynaldo, and Dexter Bryan. 1980. *Citizenship Aspirations and Residency Rights Preference: The Mexican Undocumented Worker in the Binational Community* (Compton, Calif.: SEPA-OPTION, Inc.).

Bogardus, Emory. 1929. "Second Generation Mexicans," *Sociology and Social Research,* 13:276–83.

Bradshaw, Benjamin S., and Frank D. Bean. 1973. "Trends in the Fertility of Mexican Americans," *Social Science Quarterly,* 53 (March):688–96.

Brawner, Marlyn R. 1973. "Migration and Educational Achievement of Mexican Americans," *Social Science Quarterly,* 53 (March):727–37.

Child, Irvin L. 1943. *Italian or American: The Second Generation in Conflict* (New Haven: Yale University Press).

The Mexican American Experience

Coleman, James S., Ernest Q. Campbell, Carol J. Hobson, James McPartland, Alexander M. Mood, Frederic D. Weinfeld, and Robert L. York. 1966. *Equality of Educational Opportunity* (Washington, D.C.: U.S. Department of Health, Education and Welfare, Office of Education).

Cornelius, Wayne, Leo R. Chavez, and Jorge G. Castro. 1982. *Mexican Immigrants and Southern California: A Summary of Current Knowledge*, Research Report Series, no. 36 (La Jolla, Calif.: University of California, San Diego, Center for U.S.-Mexican Studies).

de la Garza, Rodolfo O. 1981. *Chicano Political Elite Perceptions of the Undocumented Worker*. Working Papers in U.S.-Mexican Studies, no. 31 (La Jolla, Calif.: University of California, San Diego, Center for U.S.-Mexican Studies).

Dinerman, Ina R. 1982. *Migrants and Stay-at-Homes: A Comparative Study of Rural Migration from Michoacán, Mexico*. Monograph Series, no. 5 (La Jolla, Calif.: University of California, San Diego, Center for U.S.-Mexican Studies).

Handlin, Oscar. 1951. *The Uprooted: The Epic Story of the Great Migrations That Made the American People* (Boston: Little, Brown).

Moore, Joan W. 1970. *Mexican Americans* (Englewood Cliffs, N.J.: Prentice-Hall).

Portes, Alejandro, Robert N. Parker, and José A. Cobas. 1980. "Assimilation or Consciousness: Perceptions of U.S. Society among Recent Latin American Immigrants to the U.S.," *Social Forces,* 59 (September):200–224.

Rodríguez, Richard. 1981. *Hunger of Memory: The Education of Richard Rodríguez* (Boston: Godine).

Warner, W. Lloyd, and Leo Srole. 1945. *The Social System of American Ethnic Groups* (New Haven: Yale University Press).

28. MEXICAN AMERICAN INTERMARRIAGE IN A NONMETROPOLITAN CONTEXT

Ralph B. CAZARES, *Washington State University*

Edward MURGUIA, *Trinity University*

W. Parker FRISBIE, *The University of Texas at Austin*

Marriage records were examined in Pecos County, Texas, from 1880 to 1978. The analysis shows an overall outmarriage rate of .091 for marriages and .048 for individuals, documenting a considerable social distance which historically has existed between Mexican Americans and Anglo Americans in this region. However, intermarriage rates are significantly higher after 1970, which may indicate an important diminution of social distance separating Anglos and Mexican Americans in an area where close social contact between the two groups has heretofore been minimal.

Intermarriage has long been viewed as a measure of a group's social distance and as an indicator of the maintenance of ethnic boundaries (Bogardus, 1958, 1968). Rates of exogamy indicate the amount of a given group's assimilation into a larger and dominant group's social structure (Gordon, 1964).

Studies of Chicano intermarriage (Bradshaw, 1960; Gonzalez, 1969; Holscher, 1980; Murguia, 1982; Valdez, 1983) have all acknowledged intermarriage as an index of Chicano assimilation. Most investigations of Chicano exogamy have been conducted in highly urbanized settings for relatively narrow time periods. No research, with the exception of Holscher (1980), has addressed itself to Chicano intermarriage within a nonmetropolitan setting. In addition, no single study of Chicano outmarriage has systematically evaluated data for a very long period of time, and none, with the exception of Bean and Bradshaw (1970), has examined intermarriage patterns in the nineteenth century. The current study, by contrast, analyzes Chicano intermarriage in a nonmetropolitan area, Pecos County, Texas, over approximately a hundred-year period.

Pecos County is located in the western portion of Texas roughly equidistant between San Antonio and El Paso. Not only is Pecos a nonmetropolitan county, it is nonadjacent to any metropolitan county. The nearest metropolitan areas are Ector County (Odessa) and Midland County (Midland) to land) to the north. Pecos County's largest urban place and county seat is Fort Stockton (population 8,688 in 1980). Although it is the second largest county in the state in terms of area (approximately four times the size of Rhode Island), Pecos is sparsely settled. However, the county has shown fairly consistent growth. For example, its population which stood at 2,360 in 1900, had more than quadrupled in size by 1950, with continued growth to a population of 14,618 persons in 1980 (Texas Almanac, 1981).

As alluded to above, the primary aim of the analysis is to trace intermarriage patterns in a nonmetropolitan setting over an extended period of time. Previous studies indicate that urbanization has the effect of increasing intermarriage rates (Gonzalez, 1969; Holscher, 1980). Hence it was expected that intermarriage rates for Pecos County would be lower within equivalent time periods than rates for Bexar County (San Antonio), Texas (Bradshaw, 1960; Bean and Bradshaw, 1970; Murguia and Frisbie, 1977), Nueces County (Corpus Christi), Texas, or Hidalgo County (Edinburg), Texas (Alvirez and Bean, 1976), the other Texas regions where rates of outmarriage have been obtained.

Data

Data for this analysis derive from 100 percent of all marriage records in Pecos County for the years selected. The data were collected at 10-year intervals beginning with 1880 (Pecos County was established in 1872) and continuing through 1978, the most recent year for which complete information was available. Additional data were obtained for 1943 in order to gauge the effect that the World War II buildup of military facilities and personnel in Pecos County may have had on intermarriage. Also, information for 1975 was included to evaluate the possible impact of current Chicano civil rights activities at mid-decade.

Known Spanish surnames were the main criterion used in selecting Chicano marriages, and the United States Census Detailed List of Spanish Surnames, containing over 8,000 surnames, was employed for this purpose. However, some individuals are known to be Chicanos who do not have a Spanish surname, perhaps as a result of some previous intermarriage. Information on such individuals (very few in number as it turned out) was solicited from knowledgeable residents so that Chicanos without Spanish surnames could be included with the Spanish surnamed population.

Data were collected not only for marriages but also for individuals by sex because the exogamy rate for individuals will not be the same as that for marriages (Rodman, 1965) and because numerous studies have shown considerable differences between males and females in rate of exogamy (Mittelbach, Moore, and McDaniel, 1966; Murguia and Frisbie, 1977; Schoen, Nelson, and Collins, 1978; Murguia and Cazares, 1982).

The exogamy rate for individuals is operationally defined as the number of persons in a specific ethnic group who marry individuals outside the group divided by the total number of persons of that given ethnicity who marry. The rate of exogamy for marriages, on the other hand, "refers to the percentage of marriages that are mixed of all marriages involving individuals in a specific category" (Rodman, 1965:776).

Results

Table 1 presents the frequency and percentage distributions of exogamy and endogamy for each point in time covered by this research and gives an overview of the trends in in- and outmarriage in Pecos County. Also evident in Table 1 is a historical shift in the ethnic composition of the marrying population. In earlier time periods, there was either a rough equivalence in the number of Spanish surname (SS) and non-Spanish surname (non-SS) persons marrying or else a predominance of Spanish surname marriages. After about 1920, however, the number and proportion of non-Spanish surname persons marrying typically constitute well over half of the total. This shift may constitute part of the explanation for the increase in intermarriage rates documented below since the relative size of the Spanish surname population seems to be inversely associated with Chicano exogamy (Murguia and Frisbie, 1977). Nevertheless, one should not make overly much of this explanation since the 1950–70 decline in the proportional representation of the total Spanish surname population was only moderate in magnitude and by 1980 the trend appears to have been reversed (U.S. Bureau of the Census, 1982). Table 2 summarizes the information on the Spanish surname population presented in detail in Table 1.

Observed rates of exogamy for individuals and for marriages are shown in Table 3. Table 3 also combines the detailed information into two time periods since it is plausible that recent Chicano civil rights activities resulted in a push for increased structural assimilation (Gordon, 1964) and thus affected intermarriage rates. In addition, the improving socioeconomic status of Chicanos in Pecos County (as evidenced by local documentation of occupational upgrading, the election of a Spanish surname mayor, etc.) should positively impact on Chicano/Anglo intermarriage rates.

A review of Table 3 (along with Tables 1 and 2) reveals some not unexpected results. It was anticipated that the incidence of exogamy would be smaller in a nonmetropolitan environment than in a metropolitan setting. Small communities are generally more homogeneous as compared to urban centers, which should result in greater normative control over the behavior of individuals. Marriage prescriptions and proscriptions would therefore be expected to be more tightly enforced in a rural setting than in an urban center.

From 1880 to as recently as 1960 (Table 3) only 2 percent of the county's Chicanos were exogamous (4 percent of marriages). These percentages are considerably lower than intermarriage rates in metropolitan Bexar County (San Antonio) recorded in the mid-nineteenth and mid-twentieth centuries. They are also moderately to slightly lower than exogamy rates in Nueces County (Corpus Christi) and Hidalgo County (Edinburg) recorded in the early 1960s and 1970s (Bean and Bradshaw, 1970; Murguia and Frisbie, 1977). (A tabular summary of the latter comparisons is available upon request.)

TABLE 1

Endogamous and Exogamous Marriages by Ethnicity, Pecos County (Fort Stockton), Texas, 1880–1978

Year	All Classes		Non-SS Male, Non-SS Female		SS Male, SS Female		Non-SS Male, SS Female		SS Male, Non-SS Female	
	Number	Percent	Number	Percent	Number	Percent	Number	Percent	Number	Percent
1880	13	100	1	7.7	11	84.6	1	7.7	0	0.0
1890	15	100	2	13.3	13	86.7	0	0.0	0	0.0
1900	11	100	6	54.5	5	45.5	0	0.0	0	0.0
1910	16	100	8	50.0	7	43.8	0	0.0	1	6.3
1920	40	100	10	25.0	29	72.5	1	2.5	0	0.0
1930	53	100	31	58.5	21	39.6	1	1.9	0	0.0
1940	87	100	49	56.3	36	41.4	1	1.1	1	1.1
1943	129	100	101	78.3	26	20.2	2	1.6	0	0.0
1950	41	100	21	51.2	20	48.8	0	0.0	0	0.0
1960	85	100	54	63.2	30	35.3	1	1.2	0	0.0
1970	94	100	60	63.8	31	33.0	3	3.2	0	0.0
1975	127	100	82	64.6	37	29.1	4	3.1	4	3.1
1978	163	100	87	53.1	63	38.9	8	4.9	5	3.1
Total	874	100.0	512	58.6	329	37.6	22	2.5	11	1.3

TABLE 2

Endogamous and Exogamous Marriages for Spanish Surname Persons, Pecos County (Fort Stockton), Texas, 1880–1978

	Total	Endogamous	Exogamous	Exogamous as Percent of Total
Number of marriages involving Spanish surname persons	362	329	33	9.1
Number of individuals	691	658	33	4.8
Number of males	340	329	11	3.2
Number of females	351	329	22	6.3

TABLE 3

Observed Exogamy Rates for Individuals and Marriages for Spanish Surname Persons, Pecos County (Fort Stockton), Texas, 1880–1978

Year	Individuals	Marriages
1880	.043	.083
1890	.000	.000
1900	.000	.000
1910	.067	.125
1920	.017	.033
1930	.023	.045
1940	.027	.053
1943	.037	.071
1950	.000	.000
1960	.016	.032
1970	.046	.088
1975	.098	.178
1978	.094	.171
1880–1960	.022	.043
1970–78	.084	.155
Total	.048	.091

Bradshaw (1960) and Murguia (1979) both have noted that an increase in the number of military personnel in an area has the effect of increasing Chicano intermarriage rates. The reasons for this are that, first, during times of war, intergroup social distances decrease as attention is focused on a common enemy, and second, military personnel, many of marriageable age, are separated from their home communities and turn to the local population for dating and sometimes for marriage. It was expected that the 1943 data would reveal the effect of the World War II military buildup in Pecos County on Chicano intermarriage. The data at least partially support this assumption; intermarriage rates in 1940 and in 1943 reach new highs. One possible reason that an even larger increase was not recorded may be that military personnel moving to Fort Stockton were largely officers (training to be pilots) as opposed to being enlisted men. The social distance between the officer class of military men and the local Chicano population may have been too great to allow for as much interaction and intermarriage as might otherwise be expected.

Beginning in 1970, Pecos County exogamy rates show a significant increase when compared to pre-1970 rates (Table 3). This increase is particularly important because Texas, when compared to other southwestern states, has consistently exhibited the greatest amount of social distance between the two populations, regardless of the social indicator used. Residential dissimilarity, social class disparity as measured by income, educational and/or occupational differences and minority cultural maintenance have all been greater in Texas than in other areas of the Southwest (Grebler, Moore, and Guzman, 1970). In addition, nonurban areas exhibit greater ingroup cultural homogeneity and thus provide less support for diversity and change. A significant increase in intermarriage could signal a change in Mexican American–Anglo American relationships even in an area where social change would be expected to lag considerably behind other areas.

Sociohistorical Periods in the History of Mexican Americans. The differences in intermarriage rates before and after 1970 can be partially interpreted by Alvarez's (1973) sociohistorical concept of four significant Mexican American generations and their interactions with the majority society. By generation, Alvarez means "that a critical number of persons, in a broad but delimited age group, had more or less the same socialization experiences because they lived at a particular time under more or less the same constraints imposed by a dominant United States society" (1973:920). Each of his four generations experiences a different relationship with Anglo society.

The first generation, the "Creation Generation," was incorporated into the United States, with American citizenship, at the signing of the Treaty of Guadalupe Hidalgo in 1850. They were Mexican by birth, language, and culture and United States citizens by force of arms. The Creation Generation was considered "Mexican" by Anglo Americans and occupied a castelike position (Alvarez, 1973). We propose that the "Creation Generation" would not be likely candidates for intermarriage, and the data presented here offer support for this view.

When the "Migrant Generation" came into being around 1900, "the socioeconomic as well as political subservience of the Mexican American throughout the Southwest was well established" (Alvarez, 1973:926). This generation was largely "pushed" from Mexico due to its massive political difficulties in the early 1900s and "pulled" to the United States by the promise of expanded economic opportunity. They were recruited as a cheap labor source for a variety of unskilled jobs in agriculture and other industry. The Migrant Generation appears to have assumed the already established lower caste position of the previous generation (Alvarez, 1973). We propose that for the Migrant Generation there should also be a strong proscription against Mexican/Anglo intermarriage. Our data tend to support this view, although it should be noted that there is a slight but continuing increase in Chicano exogamy observed in both our study and others for this time period (Bean and Bradshaw, 1970; Alvirez and Bean, 1976).

The "Mexican American Generation" emerged around the time of the Second World War. This generation stressed its American citizenship, often to the point of rejecting its Mexican cultural heritage. Compared to the Migrant Generation, this group saw their sociohistorical position as a distinct improvement over that of their parents. Many of the Mexican American Generation attempted to escape their castelike status and were somewhat successful in acquiring characteristics of a working-class population on a massive scale (Alvarez, 1973). They began to have greater contact with large numbers of Anglos from whom they had largely been isolated. It is to be expected, therefore, that this generation would have increased exogamy rates. Our data from Pecos County only partially support this assumption. Intermarriage rates for marriages reached new highs of .05 in 1940 and .07 in 1943, but dropped considerably in 1950 and 1960.

Finally, the "Chicano Generation" emerged in the late 1960s. This group of Mexican Americans is the most affluent, sociopolitically liberated, and acculturated of the four Chicano generations. Although more prone to engage the Anglo majority in political conflict, they lay claim to the rights of all other Americans: "I have the right to intermarriage if it suits me, to economic achievement at all societal levels, and to my own measure of political self-determination within this society" (Alvarez, 1973:940). To the extent that social equity is a more salient concern than ethnic solidarity, it is reasonable to expect this generation to have the highest rates of intermarriage. Our data (Table 3) support this line of reasoning. In Pecos County, exogamy rates from 1970 to 1978 were four times as great as those between 1880 to 1960.

Table 4 displays observed incidences of intermarriage by sex in conjunction with expected incidences of intermarriage calculated as probabilities based on the size of the Spanish surname population marrying relative to the total population marrying (for computational details, see Bean and Bradshaw, 1970; Murguia and Frisbie, 1977; Valdez, 1983). Of special interest in this table are the ratios of actual (observed) to expected exogamy rates. These values represent the "proportion of the expected incidence

TABLE 4

Observed, Expected, and Ratio of Observed to Expected Incidence of Exogamy for Marriages and Individuals by Sex for Spanish Surname Persons, Pecos County (Fort Stockton), Texas, 1880–1978

Period	Observed Incidence of Exogamy			Expected Incidence of Exogamy			Ratio of Observed to Expected Incidence of Exogamy		
	Marriages	Females	Males	Marriages	Females	Males	Marriages	Females	Males
1880–1960	.043	.034	.010	.740	.592	.582	.058	.057	.017
1970–78	.155	.103	.064	.771	.635	.620	.201	.162	.103
Total	.091	.063	.032	.754	.611	.598	.121	.103	.054

realized by the actual incidence" (Bean and Bradshaw, 1970). An increase in this ratio, we believe, indicates a corresponding decrease in the normative proscriptions regarding intermarriage.

Table 4 shows that the ratio of observed to expected incidence of exogamy for marriages and individuals is greater for the period from 1970 to 1978 than for the period from 1880 to 1960. As anticipated from the results of other studies (for example, Murguia and Frisbie, 1977; Schoen, Nelson, and Collins, 1978) Spanish surname females have a higher exogamy rate than their male counterparts during both time periods. It is generally acknowledged that women tend to marry up in class more often than do men (Mittelbach, Moore, and McDaniel, 1966). Thus many Spanish surname women who marry out may also be "marrying up."

Statistical tests based on the data in Table 4 appear as Table 5. Essentially, Table 5 provides an answer to the question of whether exogamy rates for the four sex/ethnicity specific groups are significantly different in the earlier compared to the later time intervals. Based on a χ^2 test, differences are significant. The phi measure of strength of association is small to moderate in magnitude. Finally, the Somers d indicates that the effect is in the direction anticipated, viz., that intermarriage occurred with increased frequency in the 1970–78 interval.

Conclusion

The single most significant finding in our study of Pecos County intermarriage data is the rise in rates of intermarriage since 1970. This recent increase in exogamy suggests a notable lessening of normative proscriptions concerning majority-minority contact in at least one area of the nonmetropolitan Southwest. To the extent that this county is representative of other nonmetropolitan areas throughout the Southwest, this finding could signal the beginning of real change in Anglo/Chicano relationships in nonurban areas—regions where minority-majority social distance has historically been very great.

TABLE 5

Statistical Tests for Relationships Involving Exogamy and Time Period[a] by Sex and Ethnicity, Pecos County (Fort Stockton), Texas, 1880–1978

Sex and Ethnicity	N	Measure of Significance			Measure of Association Phi	Measure of Directionality Somers d[c]
		χ^2	df	$p \leq$[b]		
SS male	340	7.752	1	.01	.151	.096
Non-SS male	534	4.677	1	.05	.094	.064
SS female	351	6.829	1	.01	.139	.110
Non-SS female	523	5.974	1	.05	.107	.057

[a] T_1: 1880–1960; T_2: 1970–78.

[b] Two-tailed test.

[c] A positive Somers d indicates an increase in the likelihood of exogamy from T_1 to T_2; a negative value would indicate a decrease in the likelihood of exogamy.

REFERENCES

Alvarez, Rodolfo. 1973. "The Psycho-Historical and Socioeconomic Development of the Chicano Community in the United States," *Social Science Quarterly,* 53 (March):920–42.

Alvirez, David, and Frank D. Bean. 1976. "The Mexican American Family," in C. H. Mindel and R. W. Habenstein, eds., *Ethnic Families in America* (New York: Elsevier): pp. 271–92.

Bean, Frank D., and Benjamin S. Bradshaw. 1970. "Intermarriage between Persons of Spanish and Non-Spanish Surname: Changes from the Mid-19th to the Mid-20th Century," *Social Science Quarterly,* 51 (September):389–95.

Bogardus, Emory S. 1958. "Racial Distance Changes in the United States during the Past Thirty Years," *Sociology and Social Research,* 43 (November/December):127–35.

———. 1968. "Comparing Racial Distance in Ethiopia, South Africa, and the United States," *Sociology and Social Research,* 52 (January):149–56.

Bradshaw, Benjamin S. 1960. "Some Demographic Aspects of Marriage: A Comparative Study of Three Ethnic Groups." Master's thesis, The University of Texas at Austin.

Gonzalez, Nancie L. 1969. *The Spanish-Americans of New Mexico: A Heritage of Pride* (Albuquerque: University of New Mexico Press).

Gordon, Milton M. 1964. *Assimilation in American Life* (New York: Oxford University Press).

Grebler, Leo, Joan W. Moore, and Ralph C. Guzman. 1970. *The Mexican American People: The Nation's Second Largest Minority* (New York: Free Press).

Holscher, Louis. 1980. "Chicano Exogamous Marriages in New Mexico." Unpublished manuscript. Las Cruces: New Mexico State University, Department of Sociology.

Mittelbach, Frank G., Joan M. Moore, and Ronald McDaniel. 1966. "Intermarriage of Mexican-Americans, Advance Report 6." University of California, Los Angeles, Los Angeles Graduate School of Business Administration.

Murguia, Edward. 1979. "Military Status and Chicano Intermarriage." Paper presented at the annual meeting of the American Sociological Association, Boston.

———. 1982. *Chicano Intermarriage: A Theoretical and Empirical Study* (San Antonio: Trinity University Press).

Murguia, Edward, and R. B. Cazares. 1982. "Intermarriage of Mexican Americans," *Marriage and Family Review,* 5 (Spring):91–100.

Murguia, Edward, and W. Parker Frisbie. 1977. "Trends in Mexican American Intermarriage: Recent Findings in Perspective," *Social Science Quarterly,* 58 (December):74–89.

Rodman, Hyman. 1965. "Technical Note on Two Rates of Mixed Marriage," *American Sociological Review,* 30 (October):776–78.

Schoen, Robert, Verne E. Nelson, and Marion Collins. 1978. "Intermarriage among Spanish Surnamed Californians, 1962–1974," *International Migration Review,* 12 (Fall):359–69.

Texas Almanac. 1981. *Texas Almanac 1982–1983* (Dallas, Tex.: A. H. Bello).

U.S. Bureau of the Census. 1982. *Census of Population: 1980, General Population Characteristics.* PC80-1-B45. Texas Tables 46 and 51 (Washington, D.C.: U.S. Government Printing Office).

Valdez, Avelardo. 1983. "Recent Increases in Intermarriage by Mexican American Males: Bexar County, Texas, from 1971 to 1980," *Social Science Quarterly,* 64 (March):136–44.

29. CHANGE AND CONTINUITY IN MEXICAN AMERICAN RELIGIOUS BEHAVIOR: A THREE-GENERATION STUDY[1]

Kyriakos S. MARKIDES, *University of Texas Medical Branch*

Thomas COLE, *University of Texas Medical Branch*

Using data from a three-generation study of Mexican Americans in San Antonio, it was found that the overwhelming majority of respondents were Catholics and that little change in religious affiliation took place from generation to generation. The older and middle generations attended church more frequently than the younger generation, and large proportions in all generations defined themselves as religious. Church attendance and religiosity tended to be significantly correlated within families, with the correlations being higher between adjacent generations.

Although interest in the concept of generation as a tool for studying social change is not new (see, for example, Eisenstadt, 1956, and Mannheim, 1928/1952), few studies have attempted to systematically delineate and measure changes and continuities in values and behavior in the context of the family from generation to generation (see the recent review by Bengtson et al., in press [1983]). While research often compares unrelated generations or cohorts to examine intergenerational change and continuity, a more appropriate method is to trace change and continuity *within* intergenerationally linked families. This tradition owes a great deal to the pioneer work of Reuben Hill (1970a, 1970b).

Although there are limitations to the three-generation design, certain behaviors or statuses avoid some of the pitfalls of cross-sectional intergenerational research. These include studies of change and continuity of socioeconomic status attainment and fertility behavior. Here we may indeed speak of *change* and *continuity* since it is unlikely that status attainment and fertility of children influences the status attainment and fertility of their parents. Another area of research where studies of intergenerationally linked families can contribute to understanding of social change is that of

[1] Supported by grant R01 AG04170 from the National Institute on Aging. We would like to thank three anonymous reviewers for useful comments and suggestions.

religious affiliation and behavior. For one, religious affiliation shows high levels of continuity from generation to generation (Aldous and Hill, 1965), and it is unlikely that changes in children's affiliation would influence the affiliation of their parents. Similarly, religious behavior and values of children are less likely to influence the religious behavior and values of their parents than is the case in other types of behavior and values (sex-role orientations, for example; see Hagestad, 1982).

This paper reports findings on change and continuity in religious affiliation and behavior in a three-generation study of Mexican Americans recently conducted in San Antonio, an area about which little is known. It is often pointed out, for example, that 85 to 90 percent of Mexican Americans are Roman Catholics (e.g., Grebler, Moore, and Guzman, 1970), but little is known about how Mexican American Catholicism compares with "Anglo American" Catholicism. While there is some evidence that Mexican Americans attend church less frequently than other Catholics (Grebler, Moore, and Guzman, 1970), a recent study of older people in San Antonio found higher attendance (and overall religiosity) among Mexican Americans than among Anglos (Markides and Martin with Gomez, 1983). However, it is not known how religiosity is transmitted within families in the Mexican American population.

Methods

The data employed in this study are from home interviews conducted with 1,125 Mexican Americans residing in the San Antonio metropolitan area during the fall of 1981 and spring of 1982. An area probability sample involving selection of census tracts and city blocks was used to locate older Mexican Americans (aged 65 to 80) who had three-generationally linked families within a 50-mile radius of San Antonio was initially drawn. (For more details, see Markides et al., 1983.) From this representative sample of the city's older Mexican Americans with three-generation families, information was obtained about their children and adult (18 years +) married or ever-married grandchildren residing in the area. From these, three-generation lineages were selected randomly, and the members of the three-generation triads were visited for interviews. A total of 375 triads were interviewed, totalling 1,125 respondents.

San Antonio has an old, established, and fairly stable Hispanic population that constitutes over half the city's population. Approximately 40 percent of the older generation were born in Mexico with the remainder born in San Antonio or the surrounding area (mostly South Texas). Only about 4 percent of the middle and 1 percent of the younger generation were Mexican-born (62 and 85 percent respectively were born in San Antonio). Most respondents in all generations were bilingual. Around 95 percent in the older and middle generation reported speaking Spanish well. This figure dropped to 65 percent in the third generation (however, 96 percent of the younger generation spoke some Spanish).

Approximately two-thirds of the sample were females owing in large part to females' greater longevity (in the older generation) and earlier marriage.

The mean age of the older generation was 74; it was 49 for the middle and 26 for the younger generations. The three-generation design has been criticized for overrepresenting lower-SES, more fertile, and generally more traditional elderly (as well as younger-generation persons) (see Bytheway, 1977). Comparisons of older members of three-generation families with a random subsample of other elderly Mexican Americans in San Antonio suggested that members are more fertile and somewhat less educated. Mean years of education were under 3 for the older generation, while they were around 9 for the middle and 11 for the younger, which are somewhat lower than would be expected from a general sample of Mexican Americans in San Antonio. The study's generalizability is thus limited, but approximately 40 percent of San Antonio's elderly belong to three-generation families. This large percentage is due to the large size of San Antonio's Mexican American population as well as its high fertility and stability (see Markides et al., 1983).

The study collected data on a number of variables relating to intergenerational change and continuity as well as relationships between the generations. The critical variables for this analysis are religious affiliation, frequency of church attendance, and self-rated religiosity, all measured by straightforward single items. Respondents were asked about the religion of their socialization as well as about their current religious affiliation. Frequency of church attendance was ascertained by asking respondents to report how often they attend church services (ranging from never to once a week or more frequently). Finally, self-rated religiosity was based on responses to the question "How religious would you say you are?" (not at all, not very, somewhat, and very religious).

The findings will first be presented in frequency form by generation and sex to indicate broad differences between the generations. Subsequently correlation analysis will be employed to assess within-family similarities in the religion variables. It was hypothesized that the percentage of Catholics declines somewhat from the older to the middle to the younger generation. We also expected declines in church attendance and self-rated religiosity, findings that would be consistent with both lower religiosity at earlier stages of the life cycle and greater acculturation of the younger generations. While we expected change from generation to generation, we also expected that our correlation analysis would reveal significant continuities (similarities) within families and that these continuities would be greater between adjacent generations.

Findings

Table 1 presents the respondents' religious affiliation as children and presently by generation. As expected, the overwhelming majority in all three generations reported being Catholic: Catholics constituted 85.2 percent in the older, 83.3 in the middle, and 81.8 in the younger generation. The percentages of respondents who grew up as Catholics were slightly higher: 89.8 percent, 90.1 percent, and 87.7 percent, respectively. These

TABLE 1

Childhood and Current Religious Affiliation by Generation

	Catholic		Protestant		Other		Total	
	N	Percent	N	Percent	N	Percent	N	Percent
Older generation								
Childhood religion	336		34		4		374	
Current religion[a]	318	94.6	32	94.1	3	75.0	353	94.4
Converts	18	5.4	2	5.9	1	25.0	21	5.6
Total now	319		50		5		374	
Middle generation								
Childhood religion	336		35		2		373	
Current religion	309		32	91.4	1	50.0	342	91.7
Converts	27	8.0	3	8.6	1	50.0	31	8.3
Total now	311		53		9		373	
Younger generation								
Childhood religion	328		39		7		374	
Current religion	306	93.3	38	97.4	7	100.0	351	93.8
Converts	22	6.7	1	2.6	0	0.0	23	6.1
Total now	307		60		7		374	

[a] The second row of each panel (current religion) refers to persons who retained their childhood religious affiliation. It differs from the category "total now," which takes into consideration people who converted from their childhood affiliation to something else.

figures reflect considerable stability in religious affiliation from generation to generation. However, these are aggregate data, and may thus conceal individual change. Even though they are relatively minor, two kinds of changes in affiliation may be noted in Table 1: change from childhood to current affiliation within each generation and intergenerational change within families. Persons labeled "converts" were those whose current affiliation was other than their childhood affiliation. Of the 336 older persons who grew up Catholic, 318—or 94.6 percent—remained Catholic. Only 18— or 5.4 percent—converted, mostly to Protestantism. The numbers of such converts were only slightly greater in the second and third generations (27 and 22, amounting to 8.0 and 6.7 percent, respectively).

Looking at change and continuity within families, among Catholics, 91.2 percent in the second and 89.9 percent in the third generation had the same religious affiliation as their parents and grandparents (see top panel of Table 2). Lower continuity was observed among Protestants, where the percentages were 62 and 54, respectively. When continuity is measured by comparing the older generation's childhood religion to the other two generations' current religion, the percentages are slightly lower. As would be expected, continuity is greatest when the older generation's current affiliation is compared with childhood affiliation in the younger generations.

When continuity was traced in three-generation depth by type of sex linkage, no notable differences were observed. These findings differ from those of Aldous and Hill (1965) who found significantly greater continuity in the all-female lineages in the Minneapolis–St. Paul area.

TABLE 2

Intergenerational Continuity in Religious Affiliation

| | Catholic | | Protestant | | Other | |
	N	Percent	N	Percent	N	Percent
Current religious affiliation[a]						
Older generation	317	100.0	50	100.0	5	100.0
Middle generation	289	91.2	31	62.0	2	40.0
Younger generation	285	89.9	27	54.0	2	40.0
G_1 childhood with G_2 and G_3 current affiliation[b]						
Older generation	334	100.0	34	100.0	4	100.0
Middle generation	295	88.3	19	55.9	1	25.0
Younger generation	293	87.7	18	52.9	1	25.0
G_1 current with G_2 and G_3 childhood affiliation[c]						
Older generation	319	100.0	50	100.0	4	100.0
Middle generation	308	96.6	23	46.0	1	25.0
Younger generation	307	96.2	26	52.0	1	25.0

[a] Cross-tabulation of subjects' current religious affiliations.

[b] Childhood affiliation of older generation (G_1) is cross-tabulated with current affiliation of middle (G_2) and younger (G_3) generations.

[c] Current affiliation of G_1 is cross-tabulated with childhood affiliation of G_2 and G_3.

TABLE 3

Church Attendance by Generation and Sex

| | Older Generation | | Middle Generation | | Younger Generation | |
	N	Percent	N	Percent	N	Percent
Men						
Once a week or more	53	51.0	58	46.0	29	20.3
Twice or 3 times a month	15	14.4	12	9.5	15	10.5
Once a month	12	11.5	16	12.7	26	18.2
Every 2 or 3 months	6	5.8	13	10.3	32	22.4
Once or twice a year	10	9.6	13	10.3	23	16.1
Never (or almost never)	5	4.8	14	11.1	18	12.6
Total	104	100.0	126	100.0	143	100.0
Women						
Once a week or more	153	58.7	113	45.7	84	36.2
Twice or 3 times a month	40	14.9	53	21.5	47	20.3
Once a month	34	12.6	37	15.0	22	9.5
Every 2 or 3 months	12	4.5	23	9.3	25	10.8
Once or twice a year	17	6.3	20	8.1	38	16.4
Never (or almost never)	8	3.0	1	0.4	16	6.9
Total	269	100.0	247	100.0	232	100.0

Table 3 presents data on church attendance by generation and by sex. Church attendance was highest among older women and lowest among younger men. These overall attendance levels are slightly higher than those obtained from a Gallup study of a national sample of Hispanic Catholics in the late 1970s (Our Sunday Visitor, n.d.). The higher figures in our study are probably due to the disproportionate number of older people. The greater religiosity of the older generation and of females is also evident in their self-rated religiosity (Table 4).

To examine the extent to which religiosity is transmitted within families, we performed within-family correlation analysis. Both church attendance and self-rated religiosity were correlated significantly between generations. As expected, the correlations were higher for adjacent generations and highest between the second and third generations. No patterns were observed when the correlations were computed separately for same-sex and cross-sex dyads.

Conclusions

Our findings reveal a great deal of intergenerational continuity in religious affiliation among Mexican Americans in San Antonio. In this overwhelmingly Catholic ethnic group, religious affiliation is a dominant force in the maintenance of ethnic identity (Grebler, Moore, and Guzman, 1970). In this, Mexican Americans are closer to Italian American Catholics than to Irish and German American Catholics (Feagin, 1978), who have shown less continuity in religious affiliation. They are also less like Americans from Minnesota (mostly Protestants of Scandinavian origin), who showed markedly lower levels of continuity in religious affiliation from grandparents to grandchildren (Aldous and Hill, 1965). If conversion to Protestantism is a vehicle

TABLE 4

Self-rated Religiosity by Generation and Sex

	Older Generation		Middle Generation		Younger Generation	
	N	Percent	N	Percent	N	Percent
Men						
Not at all	2	1.9	7	5.6	6	4.2
Not very	16	15.2	20	16.1	26	18.2
Somewhat	49	46.7	72	58.1	94	65.7
Very	38	36.2	25	20.2	17	11.9
Total	105	100.0	124	100.0	143	100.0
Women						
Not at all	1	0.4	3	1.2	8	3.5
Not very	19	7.1	28	11.3	24	10.4
Somewhat	117	43.7	143	57.9	148	64.3
Very	131	48.9	73	29.6	50	21.7
Total	268	100.0	247	100.0	230	100.0

for assimilating into the Anglo-Saxon core, there is little evidence in our data that Mexican Americans have used this option to further their assimilation. Intergenerational change in religious affiliation is likely to take place when there is substantial intermarriage with other ethnic groups (Feagin, 1978). Our data (not shown) showed little intermarriage and were consistent with findings of other research (e.g., Murguia and Frisbie, 1977). Thus, low rates of marital and religious assimilation reinforce each other and suggest that Mexican Americans continue and are likely to continue to represent a distinct ethnic group for some time to come.

Mexican American Catholics have been compared to Italian American Catholics, another relatively traditional ethnic group with a strong familistic orientation and low rates of intermarriage, in that both groups exhibit high levels of allegiance to the Catholic church, but exhibit low levels of religious participation, particularly by men (Grebler, Moore, and Guzman, 1970). Our data show high rates of church attendance in the two older generations in both sexes. Attendance rates were markedly lower in the younger generation where sex differences were more pronounced.

Mexican Americans in San Antonio also see themselves as religious, though the older generation are more likely to consider themselves "very" religious than the younger two generations. Women, again, see themselves as more religious than men. It is important to note that the younger generation tend to define themselves as religious despite their lower rates of church attendance. Finally, we found that both church attendance and self-rated religiosity tend to be significantly correlated within families. Thus, despite extrafamilial influences, the family remains an important vehicle through which religious behavior and attitudes are transmitted from generation to generation. The correlations were higher for adjacent generations, particularly the middle and younger generations.

This study has the usual limitations of all cross-sectional studies. Thus, it is not clear whether observed differences reflect cohort or generation effects, or whether they reflect differences due to aging or life-cycle stage. In addition, this study is limited to the experience of Mexican Americans in San Antonio, which has a large and fairly stable Mexican American population, and may not be replicated elsewhere. Finally, three-generation families may be more stable and more cohesive; our findings, thus, may exaggerate the extent of religious continuity that might be expected in a general sample of Mexican Americans.

REFERENCES

Aldous, Joan W., and Reuben Hill. 1965. "Social Cohesion, Lineage Type, and Intergenerational Transmission," *Social Forces,* 43 (May):471–82.

Bengtson, Vern L., Neil E. Cutler, David J. Mangen, and Victor A. Marshall. In press, 1983. "The Three Faces of Generations: Aging, Age Groups and Social Change," in Robert H. Binstock and Ethel Shanas, eds., *Handbook of Aging and the Social Sciences* (New York: Van Nostrand Reinhold).

Bytheway, Bill. 1977. "Problems of Representation in the 'Three-Generation Family Study,' " *Journal of Marriage and the Family,* 39 (May):243–50.

Eisenstadt, S. N. 1956. *From Generation to Generation* (Glencoe: Free Press).

Feagin, Joe R. 1978. *Racial and Ethnic Relations* (Englewood Cliffs, N.J.: Prentice-Hall).

Grebler, Leo, Joan W. Moore, and Ralph C. Guzman. 1970. *The Mexican American People* (New York: Free Press).

Hagestad, Gunhild O. 1982. "Parent and Child: Generations in the Family," in T. M. Field, A. Huston, H. C. Quay, L. Troll, and G. E. Finley, eds., *Review of Human Development* (New York: Wiley): pp. 485–99.

Hill, Reuben. 1970a. *Family Development in Three Generations* (Cambridge, Mass.: Schenkman).

———. 1970b. "The Three Generation Research Design: Method for Studying Family and Social Change," in Reuben Hill and R. Konig, eds., *Families in East and West* (Paris: Mouton).

Mannheim, Karl. 1928. "The Problem of Generations," in D. Kecskemetti, ed., *Essays on the Sociology of Knowledge* (London: Routledge & Kegan Paul, 1952): pp. 276–322.

Markides, Kyriakos S., Sue K. Hoppe, Harry W. Martin, and Dianne M. Timbers. 1983. "Sample Representativeness in a Three-Generation Study of Mexican Americans," *Journal of Marriage and the Family,* 45 (November):911–16.

Markides, Kyriakos S., and Harry W. Martin with the assistance of Ernesto Gomez. 1983. *Older Mexican Americans: A Study in an Urban Barrio.* Center for Mexican American Studies, Mexican American Monographs, no. 7 (Austin: University of Texas Press).

Murguia, Edward, and W. Parker Frisbie. 1977. "Trends in Mexican American Intermarriage: Recent Findings in Perspective," *Social Science Quarterly,* 58 (December):374–89.

Our Sunday Visitor, Inc. N.d. *A Gallup Study of Religious and Social Attitudes of Hispanic Catholics* (Huntington, Ind.: Our Sunday Visitor, Inc.).

30. THE HEALTH OF THE MEXICAN ORIGIN POPULATION[1]

Ronald ANGEL, *Rutgers University*

In recent years the study of the health of the Mexican origin population has expanded rapidly. Studies of the physical and mental health of various Hispanic groups have begun to shed light on the impact of social class, minority group status, work, and culture on health. This chapter summarizes recent findings concerning the physical health of Mexican Americans. It includes a discussion of problems which arise in the study of the health of Hispanics and reviews some promising new directions in research and certain important policy issues concerning Hispanic health.

During the last three decades the study of the health of the Mexican origin population has changed dramatically. Thirty years ago knowledge of the medical care needs and practices of the Mexican origin population was based almost exclusively upon ethnographic studies. More recently, large-scale population surveys have been employed to assess the health care needs of this group. This chapter highlights recent findings concerning the physical health and medical care needs of the Mexican origin population. The discussion deals with some of the difficulties in collecting reliable health data for this group and discusses various policy issues concerning the health risks faced by members of the Mexican origin population as well as factors which influence the quality of medical care they receive.

The Changing Focus of Research

Early ethnographic studies of the health care beliefs and practices of the Mexican origin population focused primarily on folk practices in isolated rural communities and provided a picture in which folk medicine played an important role (Saunders, 1954, 1958; Rubel, 1966; Madsen, 1964; Clark, 1959). The ethnographers documented a system of diagnosis and treatment which was intimately interconnected with daily life

[1] Written especially for this volume.

and served as a reflection of the fundamental social relations between community members. In isolated rural communities the health care practices of the Mexican origin population of the Southwest were informed by very different traditions, including the folk medical lore of medieval Spain, local Indian folklore, Anglo folk medical practices, and finally, modern scientific medicine (Saunders, 1958).

The medical care practices documented in the earliest ethnographic studies were, even then, undergoing rapid transition as the influence of modern medicine was becoming more pervasive. The pace of that change has increased in recent years, and the importance of folk medicine has decreased proportionately. Traditional health care providers, such as *curanderos* (folk healers) and *parteras* (midwives), though they still exist (Kay, 1978), have been losing ground to scientific medical practitioners. The advent of Medicare and Medicaid and the introduction of public health clinics have brought modern medicine to even the most isolated individuals. Nonetheless, popular medical knowledge and customs have been kept alive and are still employed today in conjunction with modern medicine by members of the Mexican origin community (Velimirovic, 1978).

These early ethnographic studies were extremely useful in illustrating how the folk medical practices of the Mexican origin population represented a complex theory of disease causation and treatment. They were, however, based upon small local samples which, for the most part, consisted of individuals in the lower social classes. More recent epidemiological research has begun to take into account the fact that the Mexican origin population has become predominantly urban and is made up of individuals in all social classes. As is the case for non-Hispanics, the health of Mexican origin individuals depends upon their social class and the health risks they are exposed to. Affluent individuals of Mexican origin experience the disease patterns typical of other middle-class Americans while poorer and less assimilated individuals are exposed to the health risks and suffer from the diseases found more often among the lower classes.

It is difficult, therefore, to characterize the general health level of the Mexican origin population as either better or worse than that of other groups. The patterns of morbidity are simply too complex and the impact of social class too important to speak of the health of this population as a whole. Nonetheless, since a large proportion of the Mexican origin population is poor, health problems which are associated with poverty are particularly important in the study of the health of this group. It is necessary, therefore, to examine the prevalence of specific conditions for different socioeconomic strata within the Mexican origin population and to explore how they are related to culture, education, occupation, family structure, and medical care to determine what factors affect the health of particular segments of the Mexican origin population. Such a detailed understanding would allow us to identify health risk factors which might be eliminated and to provide medical care in such a way as to make it accessible to the neediest segments of the Mexican origin population.

A major contemporary focus of research, then, is determining the impact of social class and characteristics of the medical care system, as well as the effect of their interaction with culture, on the health and health-related behavior of the Mexican origin population. Clearly, acculturation plays an important role in health beliefs and practices for this group (Chesney et al., 1982; Angel and Cleary, 1984). The following discussion highlights some of the major methodological problems involved in studying health. It includes a summary of important findings concerning health risks faced by the Mexican origin population and ends with a discussion of policy issues which affect the health of this group.

Data Sources

Studies of physical health are based upon three types of data: (1) mortality data; (2) physiological measurements and diagnoses; and (3) self-reports of health status. There are different problems associated with the collection and interpretation of each of these types of data and with inferences made from them. Mortality data is perhaps the most objective, since death is an unambiguous event. However, the gathering of mortality data and its completeness for Hispanic subgroups can be troublesome. For example, there is evidence indicating a substantial underreporting of infant deaths among the Mexican origin population of Texas (Palloni, 1978; Powell-Griner and Streck, 1982).

A population's mortality experience is usually expressed as a rate, that is, as the number of deaths occurring during a particular period, usually a year, for a specified number of people alive at the beginning of the year (the population at risk), for example 10,000. Mortality rates are usually age-adjusted since mortality is very different at various ages. It is high among infants, low for children and young adults, and then increases with age. A major problem in the computation of mortality rates is that the numerator and denominator come from different sources. The numerator, or the number of deaths occurring per year, is collected from death certificates. The denominator, or the population at risk, is usually from census figures. Underregistration of deaths or undercounts of the population at risk can lead to erroneous death rates. This problem is not simply academic, since in both 1960 and 1970 there was a large undercount of young black males. The extent of underenumeration for the Mexican origin population is unknown.

Another problem with mortality is that it gives us information on the end stage of serious illness and tells us less about the prevalence of illness in various groups. An increasing number of the diseases of industrial civilization, such as diabetes, heart disease, and cancer are chronic, and individuals can live with them for some time given proper medical care. The probability of death from any particular cause is influenced by such factors as the availability of medical care and the life-style associated with one's social class. Mortality data, then, while it provides us with information on a group's general quality of life, gives us limited information on the prevalence of morbidity in various groups.

Diagnosed illnesses and physiological measures, such as blood pressure, blood glucose levels, and serum cholesterol, are objective assessments of important aspects of physical health but are unfortunately difficult and expensive to collect. While physiological measures can be gathered from representative population samples, rates of diagnosed illness are influenced by factors which determine whether one seeks medical care. Lower social class, for example, is associated with an increased incidence of diabetes and obesity, but may also reduce the probability that an individual seeks medical treatment for these conditions.

These problems as well as the relative economy and ease of collection of survey data lead to a great reliance on various forms of self-reported health in most health services research comparing the Mexican origin population to non-Hispanics (Andersen et al., 1981). Unfortunately, this sort of data is the least objective and most troublesome when comparing culturally distinct groups. Typically, in a study of this sort the respondent is asked whether his or her health is excellent, good, fair, or poor, or whether during a particular period his or her health has caused a great deal of worry or concern, or whether he or she has experienced pain. One commonly used self-reported health status measure consists of the number of days during some period the respondent had been kept in bed or away from his or her usual activities as the result of injury or illness. Another commonly used health status measure consists of lists of symptoms which the respondent is asked whether he or she has experienced. Other questions attempt to assess a person's physical ability to function normally. There are numerous variations on these questions but the main feature of them all is that they are self-reports and, therefore, subject to biases which may result from inaccurate memory and from social class and cultural factors that influence the perception and reporting of symptoms.

Major problems in epidemiological or health services research using these sorts of questions for the Mexican origin population result from inaccuracies in the translation of survey instruments; from differential response rates to different types of surveys, that is, mail, telephone, or personal interview; and as a result of bias stemming from the impact of culture on the understanding of and response to survey questions.

Unfortunately, the determination of the extent of bias in self-reports is difficult since we rarely have information on actual health status against which to compare self-reports. Recent investigations of this problem with scales designed to assess feelings of depression find little evidence of systematic bias associated with Mexican ethnicity (e.g., Vernon, Roberts, and Lee, 1982). Unfortunately, this research is based on a small sample, very few of whom took the interview in Spanish. Additionally, it deals only with mental health, and the findings cannot be assumed to apply to self-reported physical health.

Angel and Cleary (1984) found that language of interview, which is a rough indicator of level of assimilation, is an important predictor of reported health within the Mexican origin population. This research suggests that self-reports of physical health status may have different meanings for those whose main language is Spanish than for those who are fluent in English. Language of interview may tap residual Mexican cultural influences on health, especially since those who are not fluent in English are likely to be recent immigrants (de la Garza and Brischetto, 1982). This research also provides evidence that health may consist of different dimensions, each of which may be related to ethnicity in a different way. Spanish-speaking Mexican origin individuals, for example, report generally lower overall health levels than non-Hispanics, but do not report the worry or concern about health or the number of physical symptoms which are associated with poorer general health for non-Hispanics. This may reflect reference group factors. If, for example, most of the people in one's immediate reference group have backaches from working in the fields, such a symptom may not seem worth mentioning. There is also evidence that members of this group are more likely than others to give socially approved answers to survey questions (Ross and Mirowski, 1983). Clearly, such a tendency would lead to biased responses if certain conditions or illnesses were not reported because they are considered to be socially unacceptable. Because of these and other methodological problems, then, the seriousness of bias in self-reports of health for the Mexican origin population remains open, especially for less assimilated individuals who are not fluent in English.

It is impossible to know, therefore, the extent to which differences in self-reported health reflect inadequate translation of the survey instrument or other cultural factors and the extent to which they reflect actual differences in health. In addition to these, a number of other problems plague health survey research. The identification of the Mexican origin population, for example identification by Spanish surname or self-identification, is a major problem for health services research as it is for all research dealing with this group. With some of the methodological limitations in mind, then, let us turn to some of the differences between the Mexican origin population and non-Hispanics in mortality, morbidity, and physiological measures.

Mortality, Morbidity, and Physiological Measures

Though comparative morbidity and mortality data for the Mexican origin population is limited, there is evidence that they have higher death rates from cirrhosis of the liver, tuberculosis, diabetes, infectious and parasitic diseases, circulatory diseases, and accidents than non-Hispanics (Quesada and Heller, 1977; Aranda, 1971). Foreign-born women of Spanish surname in California have experienced an excess mortality from lung cancer beginning at age 45 when compared to Anglos. On the other hand, foreign-born males and native-born Mexican Americans of both sexes experienced lower cancer mortality rates (Menck et al., 1975). In Houston, Texas, in 1950 Mexican Americans experienced cancer death rates higher than those of blacks or Anglos. By 1960, however, only Mexican American women had elevated cancer mortality rates, while Mexican American men had the lowest rates for males (Roberts, 1977). These patterns differ for specific types of cancer. While Mexican origin individuals in Los Angeles in the early 1970s were at higher risk of cancer of the stomach, gallbladder, liver, and cervix than Anglos, they had lower rates of cancer of the mouth, colon, rectum, larynx, lung, bladder, prostate, testes, and breast (Menck et al., 1975). The reasons for these patterns are difficult to discern. Mexican origin individuals smoke less than Anglos, and this may account for their lower lung and mouth cancer rates. The relatively high rate of cervical cancer among Mexican origin women, particularly those born in Mexico, may be the result of early and prolonged fertility. At the same time this may protect them from breast cancer, since breast feeding appears to protect females from breast cancer. Clearly, a great deal more research must be conducted before we understand the factors which increase or decrease the risk of cancer for the Mexican origin population.

In Colorado, at least until the 1960s, the Mexican origin population had higher age-adjusted death rates than non-Hispanics at each age level below the age of 76 (Moustafa and Weiss, 1968). In addition, even with what appears to be serious underreporting of infant deaths (e.g., Palloni, 1978; Powell-Griner and Streck, 1982) the Mexican origin population suffers a substantially higher infant mortality rate than the non-Hispanic population in Texas. In Houston, Texas, in both 1950 and 1960 the Mexican origin population had overall mortality rates higher than those of non-Hispanic whites (Roberts and Askew, 1972). On the other hand, in recent years the Mexican origin population in New Mexico has experienced lower death rates from lung cancer and from chronic obstructive pulmonary disease like chronic bronchitis and emphysema than the Anglo population (Samet et al., 1982).

While overall mortality rates for the Mexican origin population have been generally higher than those for Anglos, they have, for the most part, been lower than those for blacks (Roberts and Askew, 1972). In addition, for several years differentials in mortality have been declining for all three groups. Nonetheless, though mortality rates appear to be converging, both minority groups suffer excess infant mortality and mortality from certain causes, such as diabetes.

A number of studies, many of them conducted at the University of

Texas Health Science Center at San Antonio, include various physiological measures (e.g., Stern et al., 1981; Hazuda et al., 1983). For the most part, these studies are based on fairly localized and homogeneous populations but reveal some interesting differences between Mexican origin individuals and non-Hispanics. Three fairly consistent findings are that Mexican origin individuals suffer more obesity than non-Hispanics; experience more hyperglycemia, an indication of diabetes; and have higher serum triglyceride concentrations, which is a minor coronary heart disease risk factor. These studies also reveal that Mexicans are less informed than non-Hispanics about behaviors associated with the prevention of coronary heart disease. Despite these higher risk factors, however, coronary heart disease mortality among the Mexican origin population is showing the same decrease as it has for non-Hispanics (Hazuda et al., 1983).

One intriguing explanation for elevated rates of diabetes among the Mexican origin population is the possibility of a genetic tendency toward diabetes among this group deriving from the fact that the Mexican origin population is a combination of European and Indian ancestry. American Indians have extremely high rates of diabetes, and there is evidence that this may be genetically determined. The Mexican origin population has rates of hyperglycemia intermediate between those of non-Hispanics and the Pima Indians of Arizona, which would be compatible with a genetic mixing hypothesis (Stern et al., 1981).

One must be cautious in accepting this genetic explanation, however, since social class factors alone may account for both the greater prevalence of overweight and of diabetes. In the developed nations obesity is more prevalent among the poor and is a precursor of diabetes as well as a coronary heart disease risk factor itself. The fact that Mexican origin individuals are overrepresented in the lower classes where their tendency to overweight is increased may account for their higher rates of diabetes. Unfortunately, the studies which have been reported so far do not contain sufficient socioeconomic variation to determine the relative importance of genetic and socioeconomic factors. This research, however, promises to answer many important questions concerning relative health levels within the Mexican origin population.

A study of respiratory disease in New Mexico has recently been reported (Samet et al., 1982). This research found lower rates of chronic bronchitis, emphysema, and asthma among the Mexican origin population of that state. In this study, as in many others, fewer Mexican origin individuals than non-Hispanics reported that they smoke. This seems to account for their lower rates of bronchitis and emphysema but not for their lower rates of asthma; Mexican origin rates of asthma are lower than those of non-Hispanics even after smoking is taken into account. These findings suggest the importance of environmental factors in chronic lung disease. New Mexico is an environmentally clean state, and this fact, combined with the lower rates of smoking by the Mexican origin population, may account for their lower rates of serious lung disease. This is one area in which comparisons with Puerto Ricans would be useful, since they live in a much more polluted environment and their asthma rates are higher than those of non-Hispanics (Rios, 1982).

In summary then, the majority of objective evidence which exists suggests that social class is a major determinant of the health levels of Mexican origin individuals. An individual's health depends upon a complex interaction of genetics, environment, and culture. The assessment of the relative importance of each of these factors is a challenge to a new generation of researchers.

Medical Care

As mentioned earlier, interest in the medical care utilization of the Mexican origin population has shifted from a concern with the influence of folk medicine to a desire to understand how social structural factors and medical care delivery system factors influence utilization. As a consequence, in recent years, increasing attention has been paid to the impact of such variables as income, education, occupation, social isolation, the ownership of health insurance, the availability of services, and satisfaction with medical care (Andersen et al., 1981; Chesney et al., 1982). While ethnic culture, especially in terms of the degree of acculturation and language ability, continues to draw attention (Angel and Cleary, 1984; Chesney et al., 1982; Quesada, 1976; Quesada and Heller, 1977), health services research concerning the Mexican origin population is increasingly informed by an appreciation of the interaction between culture and social class. Since the ascriptive characteristic of Mexican ethnicity increases the probability of lower-class membership, and thereby increases one's health risks and lowers one's ability to purchase adequate medical care, Mexican ethnicity has a significant indirect effect on health and medical care utilization in addition to any direct effect it may have.

In spite of the gains of recent years, certain segments of the Mexican origin population continue to suffer serious socioeconomic disadvantage and to receive inadequate medical care. Table 1, for example, presents data collected in 1975 and 1976 from a sample of Mexican Americans in the Southwest (Andersen et al., 1981). These results are for adults between 18 and 64 and, for the Mexican origin sample, are presented separately for those who took the interview in Spanish and for those who took the interview in English. As one can see, Mexican Americans who took the interview in English are very similar to Anglos, while those who took the interview in Spanish have large families and are severely handicapped in terms of income, education, and health insurance. In addition, while those Mexican Americans who took the interview in English reported an average number of visits to the doctor during the previous year similar to that

TABLE 1

Comparisons between Anglos, Blacks, and the Mexican Origin Populations

	Non-Hispanic	Black	Mexican Origin	
			English Interview	Spanish Interview
Median family income	$13,410	$8,907	$8,887	$6,853
Median age	38	36	29	37
Mean years of education	12.2	10.9	10.3	5.4
Mean family size	3.5	3.9	4.4	5.4
Percent below poverty	11.7	33.5	35.8	67.2
Percent with private health insurance	87.2	70.4	61.8	39.0
Average number of physician visits per year	3.7	4.5	4.6	2.1
(Unweighted N)	(2,941)	(607)	(276)	(201)

NOTE: These statistics are weighted to reflect actual population proportions. This table is from Angel and Cleary (1984).

of Anglos, those who took the interview in Spanish reported a much lower average number of visits.

This table illustrates the importance of examining differences within the Mexican origin population based upon level of acculturation. Studies which do not differentiate between individuals who are fluent in English and those who are not find little difference between the average number of physician visits per year between Anglos and Mexican origin individuals (e.g., Roberts and Lee, 1980). If, in our present sample, instead of dividing the Mexican origin group into those who took the interview in Spanish and those who took it in English we were to base our estimate on the combined sample of Mexican Americans, it would appear that there is no substantial difference between them and Anglos. Such a statistic would obscure a serious unmet need for medical services among the least assimilated Mexican origin individuals. Though language of interview is frequently used as an approximation of level of acculturation (e.g., Angel and Cleary, 1984) behavioral scientists have recently been developing more refined scales of acculturation (Olmedo, Martinez, and Martinez, 1978; Montgomery and Orozco, 1984). It would be useful to employ such scales in health surveys to examine the effect of this important variable on health and on access to medical care.

The data, then, indicate that the disadvantages suffered by the Mexican origin population are disproportionately borne by those least fluent in English. This group is particularly disadvantaged in its ability to deal with the medical care establishment because of a general lack of Spanish-speaking doctors and other health professionals. Addressing the health care needs of Mexican origin individuals who speak only Spanish requires increasing the number of Spanish-speaking health care providers (Quesada and Heller, 1977). The absence of a sufficient number of Mexican origin health professionals not only reduces utilization of services by members of this group, but also has a negative impact on the quality of their interaction with health care providers (Quesada, 1976). When patient and doctor are separated by a gulf which results from different cultures and languages, it is unlikely that either party will be satisfied. The doctor will see the patient as uncooperative, and the patient will see the doctor as insensitive to his or her needs.

Occupation and Health

One major set of factors affecting the health of the Mexican origin population is occupational health hazards. There is very little information on the health consequences of work for the Hispanic population in general, but we might safely assume that if they are overrepresented in hazardous occupations their health will be disproportionately harmed. The occupational distribution of members of the Mexican origin population is, therefore, an important determinant of the health risks they face. In an analysis of the occupational health hazards faced by Hispanics in the United States, Dicker and Dicker (1982) showed that in 1980 a disproportionate percentage of the Hispanic population was employed in industries with the highest risks of illness, injury, and fatality. These were construction, mining, transportation, public utilities, agriculture, and manufacturing. However, there is a tremendous diversity in occupational concentration depending upon specific Hispanic ethnicity. While 54 percent of Cubans were employed in white-collar occupations in 1980, the job category with the lowest health risks, only 39 percent of Puerto Ricans, and 29 percent of Mexicans were in white-collar positions. On the other hand, while less than 1 percent of Cubans were farm workers in 1980, 6 percent of Mexicans were farm workers. The effects of pesticides and inadequate medical care on the health of agricultural workers are a topic about which we know very little.

While broad industry classifications tell us something about the occupational health risks faced by the Mexican origin population, we need much more detailed information concerning the specific job hazards faced by individuals in this group. Within any particular industrial category, such as manufacturing, jobs differ greatly in terms of health risks. Certain manufacturing occupations expose workers to more dangerous processes and materials than others. If Mexican origin workers are disproportionately concentrated in the most hazardous occupations they may suffer specific health problems.

Another area about which very little is known is the causes and consequences of work-related disability. A great deal of evidence indicates that health problems which interfere with one's ability to work have serious consequences for the worker and his or her family. The inability to work up to one's potential decreases earnings and total family income and greatly increases a family's dependence on welfare (Angel, 1984).

In an analysis of a survey conducted in 1976 Angel (1984) reported that, as with occupational health risks, the Hispanic population differs greatly in the proportion of adult males who report a work-limiting health condition. Table 2 presents data on the percentage of males of the various national origins who report a disability, their work experience, and family incomes. While approximately 12.5 percent of Anglos and those of Mexican origin report a disability, 17 percent of Puerto Ricans report such a condition. On the other hand, only 9 percent of Central and South Americans (including Cubans) report a disability. This great diversity between groups is intriguing and, no doubt, accounted for by a number of factors. For example, the various groups are concentrated in different parts of the country, with Mexicans in the Southwest and Midwest, Cubans in Florida, and Puerto Ricans in the New York/New Jersey area. As mentioned earlier, they are also exposed to different occupational health risks. These various groups may also be different in the extent to which the family deals with the disability of one of its members outside of the formal structures of government. Groups which are familistic, cohesive, and suspicious of the agencies of the larger society, as the Mexican origin population is characterized as being, may deal with disability at home.

When the disability rates presented in Table 2 are adjusted for other socioeconomic and demographic factors which might account for differences in disability, such as age, marital status, family income, and the unemployment rate and wage rate in the area of residence, it becomes clear that the Mexican origin population disability rate is far lower than one would expect (Angel, 1984). Though their overall rate of self-reported disability is similar to that of Anglos, they are exposed to health hazards which should increase their rate considerably above that of Anglos. This study also revealed that Mexican origin individuals who are not fluent in English are most severely affected by disability. A lack of fluency in English makes it difficult for one to successfully deal with the governmental bureaucracies which formally label one disabled and thereby make one eligible for disability payments.

Clearly, then, while the Mexican origin population is exposed to the same types of health risks as other American workers, their greater concentration in the highest-risk industries exposes them to more of those hazards. As a consequence, there may be a great deal of disability among the Mexican origin population which has not been identified. This hidden disability represents an unknown amount of unmet need for social services. Again, as in other areas of health, there are large differences within the Mexican origin community depending upon occupation, education, and income. The impact of occupation on health and the consequences

TABLE 2
Characteristics of Disabled Males, Aged 20 to 64

	Anglo		Mexican		Puerto Rican		Central/South American	
	Disabled	Nondisabled	Disabled	Nondisabled	Disabled	Nondisabled	Disabled	Nondisabled
Personal characteristics								
Percent disabled	12.5		12.6		17.3		8.9	
Age	46.8	38.5	44.1	34.5	44.1	35.3	42.8	38.6
Education	13.0	10.7	7.4	9.8	7.6	10.3	10.7	11.5
Labor force characteristics								
Percent employed full-time	45	83	28	81	18	77	49	81
Wage rate	$3.92	$6.53	$1.99	$4.10	$1.85	$4.44	$2.84	$4.73
Individual income								
Annual earnings	$6,579	$12,697	$3,167	$8,086	$2,364	$8,317	$6,716	$9,571
Welfare:								
Percent receiving	4	1	12	1	27	4	14	2
Amount	$1,563	$1,012	$2,445	$1,740	$3,378	$1,905	$1,070	$1,869
Total income	$9,449	$13,746	$4,895	$8,623	$4,568	$8,945	$8,968	$10,115
Family characteristics								
Percent below poverty	12	4	29	14	51	12	18	9
Family earnings	$10,967	$17,668	$6,304	$11,371	$4,865	$11,433	$10,436	$13,504
Total family income	$14,865	$19,479	$8,606	$12,305	$7,910	$12,513	$13,395	$14,648
Unweighted *N*	2,247	15,689	273	1,891	73	357	38	367

Note: This table is an abbreviated version of one appearing in Angel (1984). The data are weighted to represent actual population proportions.

of disability represent two of the most important areas of research for this group.

Future Direction in Research

Though the situation is changing rapidly, the study of the health of the Mexican origin population continues to be plagued by a lack of appropriate data. Few states record ethnicity on death certificates, making it difficult to study mortality for this group. Until recently, most national surveys did not differentiate between Hispanic nationalities and treated all Hispanics as a single group. It is clear that the various Hispanic subgroups are quite different in their health risks, in their medical care utilization, in their health beliefs and practices, and in their responses to surveys. Very often, relevant distinctions must be made within Hispanic nationalities, such as distinguishing between Mexican origin individuals who are fluent in Spanish and those who are not (Angel, 1984; Angel and Cleary, 1984).

Progress in the study of the health of the Mexican origin population will depend upon collecting data which address the specific needs of this group and is sensitive to the sorts of problems caused by differences in social class and level of acculturation. Luckily, such data are beginning to be gathered. One major new source of data on Hispanic health which will become available in the next few years is a Hispanic supplement to the Health and Nutrition Examination Survey (HANES) conducted by the National Center for Health Statistics. This project, which began field operations in July 1982, combines physiological and psychological measures of health for a sample of 12,000 Hispanics. In this study respondents complete a general medical history questionnaire and undergo a physical examination which includes a number of dental, dermatological, opthalmological, and blood tests, as well as a number of other physiological measurements. This survey will provide data for Mexican Americans, Puerto Ricans, and Cubans and allow a comparison of self-reported health status to objective assessments of health as well as making possible the further investigation of the socioeconomic and sociocultural correlates of mental and physical health and help-seeking behavior. This study also provides information on alcohol consumption and drug use and includes an acculturation scale. This data set and the studies of coronary heart disease risk factors mentioned earlier are examples of the sort of information which will usher in a new era in the study of the health of the Mexican origin population.

Questions for Further Research

Hopefully, this chapter has illustrated some of the problems inherent in the study of health, as well as illustrating some of the more promising innovations in data collection. However, in the study of health it appears that as more research is completed more questions seem to emerge. Unfortunately, when it comes to the health of the Mexican origin population there are far more questions than answers. Let us end, then, by considering a few of the numerous policy issues which warrant further investigation.

As noted earlier, one of the major unanswered questions is how occupation affects health for Hispanics. We know that the Mexican origin population is overrepresented in low-status occupations where their exposure to environmental hazards may be great and where their medical benefits are minimal. Unfortunately, determining the impact of occupational health hazards is difficult since the health consequences of job-related hazards can take years to appear. To study the connection between work and health we need longitudinal data which trace health status over years and contain information on individuals' work histories.

Continued research into the impact of social class on health is crucial for the Mexican origin population since it is overrepresented in the lower classes. As is the case for individuals who are not fluent in Spanish, there are subgroups within the Mexican origin population whose health care needs require special attention. For example, migrant workers are a particularly medically underserved group. Agricultural workers are exposed to numerous pesticides which may have a long-term impact on their health. Unfortunately, they do not have the same job-related health care insurance protections as workers in other industries.

The presence of illegal aliens is a fact in the United States which we can hardly ignore. These individuals do not possess the legitimacy of citizenship with which to protect their basic human rights. While many people in the United States resent their presence and feel justified in denying them social services, simple human decency requires that we address their basic health care needs. Unfortunately, we know nothing of these needs. Clearly, the study of the health and social welfare of illegal immigrants presents serious problems. Illegal immigrants are wary of anyone who might be considered a representative of the government. If, however, as the result of recent changes in immigration law, a substantial number of longer-term illegal residents are granted citizenship, it may be possible to study their health and medical care needs in the coming years.

Another major issue which deserves attention is the health care needs of female-headed households. The rapid increase in such households in recent years has produced a population which is particularly economically disadvantaged. The combination of minority group status and female headship is likely to impose constraints upon a family which may influence the health of its members. Whether Medicaid provides sufficient medical services for this group remains an unanswered question.

It would be possible to mention numerous other areas of research. Let me close, however, by saying that it seems that the more important the question, the more difficult it is to study. The study of the health care needs of migrant workers and of illegal aliens poses formidable hurdles.

Research, however, is a cumulative process in which the dialogue generated by one set of findings leads to a refinement of the questions and suggests avenues for further research. Perhaps the increasing concern with health and, hopefully, an increasing commitment by health care researchers to this area will allow us to begin to address some of these crucial questions and to conceptualize them in ways in which they can be studied.

In conclusion, then, it is increasingly clear that the health and medical care needs of the Mexican origin population are diverse and depend upon specific vulnerabilities related to social class, environmental, occupational, and life-style risk factors. Since earlier in this century the health of the Mexican origin population has improved, and their access to medical care has increased. They have shared in decreases in coronary heart disease rates and infant mortality with other Americans, and their life expectancy has increased. As a consequence, overall health differentials between Anglos and the Mexican origin population have shrunk, though they as yet have not entirely disappeared. The major health problems which remain then are, by and large, concentrated among specific subgroups, such as the poor, the least assimilated, and migrant workers. Progress in understanding the health care needs of the Mexican origin population requires understanding how Mexican ethnicity interacts with these various vulnerabilities to affect health levels and to interfere with access to needed medical care.

REFERENCES

Andersen, Ronald, Sandra Zelman Lewis, Aida L. Giachello, Lu Ann Aday, and Grace Chiu. 1981. "Access to Medical Care among the Hispanic Population of the Southwestern United States," *Journal of Health and Social Behavior*, 22 (March):78–89.

Angel, Ronald. 1984. "The Costs of Disability for Hispanic Males," *Social Science Quarterly*, 65 (June):426–43.

Angel, Ronald, and Paul D. Cleary. 1984. "The Effects of Social Structure and Culture on Reported Health," *Social Science Quarterly*, 65 (September):814–28.

Aranda, Robert G. 1971. "The Mexican American Syndrome," *American Journal of Public Health*, 61 (January):104–9.

Chesney, Alan P., Juan A. Chavira, Rogers P. Hall, and Howard E. Gary. 1982. "Barriers to Medical Care of Mexican-Americans: The Role of Social Class, Acculturation, and Social Isolation," *Medical Care*, 20 (September):883–91.

Clark, Margaret. 1959. *Health in the Mexican American Culture* (Berkeley: University of California Press).

de la Garza, Rodolfo, and Robert R. Brischetto. 1982. *The Mexican American Electorate: A Demographic Profile*. Occasional Paper No. 1 (San Antonio: Southwest Voter Registration Education Project and University of Texas Center for Mexican American Studies).

Dicker, Lois, and Marvin Dicker. 1982. "Occupational Health Hazards Faced by Hispanic Workers: An Exploratory Discussion," *Journal of Latin Community Health*, 1 (Fall):101–7.

Hazuda, Helen P., Michael P. Stern, Sharon Parten Gaskill, Steven M. Haffner, and Lytt I. Gardner. 1983. "Ethnic Differences in Health Knowledge and Behaviors Related to the Prevention and Treatment of Coronary Heart Disease," *American Journal of Epidemiology*, 117 (June):717–28.

Kay, Margarita. 1978. "Parallel, Alternative, or Collaborative: *Curanderismo* in Tucson, Arizona," in Boris Velimirovic, ed., *Modern Medicine and Medical Anthropology in the United States–Mexico Border Population* (Washington, D.C.: Pan American Health Organization, World Health Organization, Scientific Publication No. 359): pp. 87–95.

Madsen, William. 1964. *The Mexican-Americans of South Texas* (New York: Holt, Rinehart & Winston).

Menck, H. R., B. E. Henderson, M. C. Pike, T. Mack, S. P. Martin, and J. SooHoo. 1975. "Cancer Incidence in the Mexican American," *Journal of the National Cancer Institute*, 55 (September):531–36.

Montgomery, Gary T., and Sergio Orozco. 1984. "Validation of a Measure of Acculturation for Mexican Americans," *Hispanic Journal of Behavioral Sciences*, 6 (March):53–63.

Moustafa, A. Taher, and Gertrud Weiss. 1968. *Health Status and Practice of Mexican Americans*. Mexican American Study Project Advance Report No. 11 (Los Angeles: UCLA Graduate School of Business Administration).

Olmedo, Esteban L., Joe L. Martinez, and Sergio R. Martinez. 1978. "Measure of Acculturation for Chicano Adolescents," *Psychological Reports*, 42 (February):159–70.

Palloni, Alberto. 1978. "Application of an Indirect Technique to Study Group Differentials in Infant Mortality," in F. D. Bean and W. P. Frisbie, eds., *The Demography of Racial and Ethnic Groups* (New York: Academic Press): pp. 283–300.

Powell-Griner, Eve, and D. Streck. 1982. "A Closer Examination of Neonatal Mortality among the Texas Spanish Surname Population," *American Journal of Public Health*, 72 (September):993–99.

Quesada, Gustavo M. 1976. "Language and Communication Barriers for Health Delivery to a Minority Group," *Social Science and Medicine*, 10 (June):323–27.

Quesada, Gustavo M., and Peter L. Heller. 1977. "Sociocultural Barriers to Medical Care among Mexican Americans in Texas: A Summary Report of Research Conducted by the Southwest Medical Sociology Ad Hoc Committee," *Medical Care*, 15 (May):93–101.

Rios, Lydia E. 1982. "Determinants of Asthma among Puerto Ricans," *Journal of Latin Community Health*, 1 (Fall):25–40.

Roberts, Robert. 1977. "The Study of Mortality in the Mexican American Population," in Charles H. Teller, Leo F. Estrada, José Hernández, and David Alvírez, eds., *Cuantos Somos: A Demographic Study of the Mexican American Population*. (Austin: Center for Mexican American Studies, Monograph No. 2): pp. 131–55.

Roberts, Robert E., and Cornelius Askew. 1972. "A Consideration of Mortality in Three Subcultures," *Health Services Reports* (formerly *Public Health Reports*), 87 (March):262–70.

Roberts, Robert E., and Eun Sul Lee. 1980. "Medical Care Use by Mexican-Americans," *Medical Care*, 18 (March):266–81.

Ross, Catherine E., and John Mirowsky. 1983. "The Worst Place and the Best Face," *Social Forces*, 62 (December):529–36.

Rubel, Arthur J. 1966. *Across the Tracks: Mexican-Americans in a Texas City* (Austin: University of Texas Press).

Samet, Jonathan M., Susan D. Schraag, Cheryl A. Howard, Charles R. Key, and Dorothy R. Pathak. 1982. "Respiratory Disease in a New Mexico Population Sample of Hispanic and Non-Hispanic Whites," *American Review of Respiratory Diseases*, 125 (February):152–57.

Saunders, Lyle. 1954. *Cultural Differences and Medical Care: The Case of the Spanish-Speaking People of the Southwest* (New York: Russell Sage Foundation).

———. 1958. "Healing Ways in the Spanish Southwest," in E. Gartley Jaco, ed., *Patients, Physicians, and Illness* (Glencoe, Ill.: Free Press): pp. 189–206.

Stern, Michael P., Sharon Parten Gaskill, Clarence R. Allen, Jr., Virginia Garza, Jose L. Gonzales, and Reuel H. Waldrop. 1981. "Cardiovascular Risk Factors in Mexican Americans in Laredo, Texas," *American Journal of Epidemiology*, 113 (May):546–55.

Velimirovic, Boris, ed. 1978. *Modern Medicine and Medical Anthropology in the United States–Mexico Border Population* (Washington, D.C.: Pan American Health Organization, World Health Organization, Scientific Publication No. 359).

Vernon, Saliy W., Robert E. Roberts, and Eun Sul Lee. 1982. "Response Tendencies, Ethnicity, and Depression Scores," *American Journal of Epidemiology*, 116 (September): 482–95.

DATE DUE

3/19/87			

PRINTED IN U.S.A.